When
Real Estate and
Home Building
become
Big Business:
Mergers, Acquisitions
and Joint Ventures

When Real Estate and Home Building become Big Business: Mergers, Acquisitions and Joint Ventures

Lewis M. Goodkin
Vice-President of Corporate Development
Leadership Housing, Inc.

Cahners Books
A Division of Cahners Publishing Company, Inc.
89 Franklin Street, Boston, Massachusetts 02110

Library of Congress Cataloging in Publication Data
Goodkin, Lewis M   1935–
    When real estate becomes big
business

        1. Real estate business—United States.
2. Joint ventures—United States. I. Title.
HD255.G66   333.3'3   73-84174
ISBN 0-8436-0118-3

Library of Congress Catalog Card Number: 73-84174
ISBN: 0-8436-0118-3
Copyright © 1974 by Cahners Publishing Company, Inc.
Printed in the United States of America

Matreiya: Ave sed non vale

Contents

Part Four
Joint Ventures

Epilogue

Acknowledgments

I want to thank the people with whose help and cooperation this book came into being. I owe a large debt of experience and training to my brother, Sanford R. Goodkin, chairman of the board of the Goodkin Group of Companies, with whom I worked for twelve years providing marketing consultation for U.S. housing development before heading my own firm. An equal debt is owed to the builders and developers who are the subject of these pages and whose viewpoints and experience have directly and indirectly contributed to my own understanding. They include Eli Broad, Milt Brock, Jr., Ben Deane, Harrison Lasky, Bob Grant, Philip Reilly, Seldon Ring, Art Rutenberg, Bob Winnerman, Ray Watt, and many others whom space precludes naming. That we have in most instances worked together or known each other does not lessen their courtesy in making time to contribute to this book in one form or another.

Other people who have been extremely helpful are Kenneth Leventhal, Stan Ross and Leonard Levy of the accounting firm Kenneth Leventhal & Company; Art Smith, the Los Angeles-based merger consultant; George Smith, vice president of Sonnenblick-Goldman of California; Lee Andre Davis, president of the Goodkin Executives; and Leon Ruderman, president of the Goodkin-Ruderman-Valdivia architecture and planning firm. I am likewise greatly indebted to two friends and well-known industry figures, Kenneth D. Campbell, president of Audit Investment Research, and Edward C. Birkner, president of the Marketing Information Network, both of New York, for the education I have gained from their published writings on the homebuilding industry and for occasional references to such materials here. Without the professional journals reporting on this industry it would be impossible for anyone to keep up with the flow of events. Accordingly, I am obligated to the magazines *Apartment Construction News, House & Home, NAHB Journal of Homebuilding,* and *Professional Builder* for their reportage. Particularly indispensable have been *Professional Builder*'s annual statistical reviews of the "Housing Giants" and the yearly analyses of the

ix

performance of publicly held building companies. These analyses are the housing industry's equivalent of the *Fortune 500* and *Forbes Yardsticks* and appear in the summer editions of *Professional Builder*.

It was James J. Shapiro who, as creative editor of *Professional Builder*, first suggested the idea for this book, after we each gave a talk on mergers and acquisitions at a major builder convention in Las Vegas. To Marsh Trimble, publisher of that magazine, as well as to David Link, the present chief editor, I am indescribably thankful for shepherding me along with such patience throughout this project. Beverly Miller, production manager at Cahners Books, has my admiration for miraculously piecing together the various versions of the manuscript and suffering with me during its extended birth.

I must reserve my most particular thanks, however, for a certain emigrant from Yale Law School who has found a congenial vocation in the field of entrepreneurial development. This is my close friend and business partner (in fact, at one time the executive vice president of my firm) Michael Baybak, without whose clear conception and untiring assistance this book would not have been possible.

These people may justly be associated with such merits as the book may have; they are of course exculpated from its deficiencies, for which I am on the hook.

Introduction

Crassus, who was the richest man in the entire Roman world some two thousand years ago (and that, for all practical purposes, *was* the entire world), and who amassed a good deal of his fortune through real estate, used to remark: "People who are fond of building need no enemies; they will ruin themselves by themselves." He, of course, took his own advice and rarely got into construction for his own account, preferring to concentrate on the area of interim and long-term loans, and picking up distressed properties on the cheap. Which illustrates that, in at least this respect, the world has changed precious little from Crassus's time to ours: as then, lenders (the mortgage trusts, the savings and loan associations and the insurance companies) abound; as then, the lure of real estate profits, and the perils of bringing off the successful project, spring eternal.

Were he around today, however, Crassus would certainly be surprised in one respect: while the risks may not have changed, the participants in real estate development certainly have. A short glance at the roster of big industrial and financial corporations now competing with the traditional builder-entrepreneur would be enough to set our rich and prudent Roman to asking whether something fundamental had changed, thus voiding his dictum, or whether the age had merely reached a new level of decadence and a lot of people with a lot of money had simultaneously decided to spare their enemies the necessity of doing them in.

It is tempting to agree with Crassus that the more things change the more they remain the same. From 1968 or thereabouts to the start of 1973, we did, in fact, witness a unique era in housing and real estate. It was as freewheeling (and perhaps as ill fated) as the Roaring Twenties. The name of the game was merger/acquisition by payment of astronomic earnings multiples, followed by terrific, often unsustainable, growth rates for the acquired companies. At what other time could we have seen a builder like Larry Weinberg get what ultimately amounted to about $200 million in stock for a company earning $4.7 million at the time of the sale and then drive it into a sixfold expansion in as many years? In the first phase of the era, industrial and other non-housing corporations leaped into the field by buying up selected major builders. In the second phase, droves of other housing firms going public also became acquirers of smaller building companies to shore up growth curves.

The era slowed rather abruptly at the start of 1973 when investors began awakening to the cognition that rapid expansion of housing profits along the lines achieved in 1970–1972 was unsustainable due to a multitude of economic, societal, and management problems. By early 1973, Wall Street sold off its housing stocks to sub-basement levels, and the resulting low price/earnings ratios then also inhibited builder acquisitions by builders. As nearly all public builders and corporately held subsidiaries faltered with declining sales rates, an uncomfortably large number of bankruptcy actions indicated the promotional underpinning to the industry's earlier successes. As if this were not enough, the Arab oil embargo, rising interest rates, severe inflation, and the traumatic Watergate political crisis later in the year combined to radically change the outlook for the industry's future. As a result of high interest rates, increased environmentalist pressures, gasoline scarcities, and continuing accounting reforms it became much harder to sell housing and to book profits. The building industry has traditionally been oriented to suburban development, and with events conspiring to push the next phase of development inward toward the cities it found itself largely unprepared for this role.

The stock market's dive by some 150 points at the close of 1973 and the start of 1974 completed the new scenario. With price/earnings ratios down across the board, real estate merger activity fell to a cyclical all-time low. While some acquisitions did continue by the large building companies, to be sure, in this third phase the primary interest was focused on a few gigantic domestic and foreign corporations that were looking over some of the big original acquirers and their initial builder acquisitions. Slater, Walker of America Ltd. (the U.S. merchant-banking arm of Slater, Walker Securities Ltd. of Great Britain) shopped Horizon Corp. of Tucson, Arizona, a land-development organization that had earlier acquired PAT Homes. And Gulf Oil looked over CNA Financial, together with its Larwin Group subsidiary. But neither venture was consummated.

Notwithstanding, the big non-housing corporations are in real estate to stay. Today, in fact, there's more interest than ever because of real estate's potential to create big profits in an inflationary climate. The interest is particularly strong on the part of the biggest financial institutions and commercial banks, which are at the same time pushing economic ties with the U.S.S.R. and the People's Republic of China and walking a very delicate line on the oil problem in the Middle East. Their involvement is an attestation to the importance and profitability of real estate, to be sure. But we must also ask ourselves whether the former and present involvement of the big organizations has not also been, in many ways, harmful or destructive to themselves as well as to the housing industry. Crassus, despite his dictum, could not resist the urge to overexpand and literally lost his head in the Middle East during a merger foray (he was killed in North Africa in a silly war of conquest on the Parthians). His latter-day counterparts may also run the risk of losing their heads in the Middle East, and they could bring us all down with them through the domestic social and economic consequences of their policies. Certainly, judging by the number of real estate ventures (mergers and otherwise) that have gone on the rocks or are cracking at the seams as this is being written, one wonders about the levels of care, commitment, or understanding involved — other than an unseeing, stimulus-response quest for profit and control. Any relationship that falls apart either through willful mismanagement or through specious accounting or at the first sign of external economic stress cannot have been well conceived. This is one of the themes of this book as, among other things, it explores the opportunities and the apparent as well as the possibly more real motives for mergers/acquisitions.

However, we cannot say that all the evidence is in. It is undoubtedly unfair to measure the quality of an entire sector's performance by the flare-outs and the present moves of the major high-rollers in a period of international economic turbulence. Numerous large subsidiaries and corporate real estate departments still continue to demonstrate that successful entrepreneurial relationships can be achieved and can be profitable. Undoubtedly, too, the merger/acquisition pace will pick up again either through an upswing in the stock market or as a defense against harsher marketing conditions, or both. It is my feeling that in this phase we will see larger organizations, as foreign currencies appreciate in the long term against the dollar. So let us pass on to examine the underlying changes in the real estate field that led to its corporate penetration in the first place, along with a foretaste of the unresolved problems that such changes posed for the company seeking access to this business.

Until recent times, real estate was regarded with a kind of curious inconsistency as an unsophisticated province and as a province of not entirely scrupulous buccaneers. In the folk myth of the business world, the buccaneering aura emanated from a blurred impression of entrepreneurial sleight of hand, Rube Goldbergian leverage deals, inordinate risk-taking, and the golden El Dorado of the big payoff. In the eyes of the nation's orthodox business establishment it was just not *comme il faut*. The profits, when they were there, were simply too grossly large to be moral. The collapses, usually played up by a gleeful press as divine retribution for an unholy aspiration, were piously viewed by corporate types as a fitting end for those who Labor Not But Promote.

It was not to remain so, however. The Sixties marked the emergence, to widespread notice, of a major change in the real estate game's participants. In a word, the Big Boys themselves got in. What happened was that some indefinable point was passed in the accelerating phenomena of urbanization and inflation, and these at last signaled to the major holders of capital that real estate as a positive business proposition could no longer be ignored. As the indispensable basis for human shelter, the need for which was shamefully outpacing production, real estate development and construction suddenly seemed to offer a lucrative and barely tapped market of immense proportions. The 1968 Housing Act brought this fact to Wall Street's attention. As the principal commodity fixed in quantity, real estate is, of course, the classic inflation hedge; and it seems that everybody on Wall Street also figured this out at about the same time. With inflation raging, financiers, awakening to the startling anomaly of a building industry actually dominated by builders, set about remedying the situation. It was too good a speculation to be left to builders.

A RAPIDLY CHANGED REAL ESTATE AND HOUSING INDUSTRY

The building industry changed radically as a result of the new forces unleashed within it, and as a response to the severe shortage of equity and mortgage funds. First, it rapidly began reorganizing itself from a construction-oriented to a marketing-oriented viewpoint. (In adverse financial conditions and in an atmosphere of fierce competition for lower profits, the builder who prospered was the one who could deliver well-planned homes and communities most responsive to buyers' desires and aspirations.) Second, in its vigorous search for capital the housing industry quickly developed an astonishingly varied and complex number of financial pipelines to tap heretofore untried sources of equity and mortgage finance. Wall Street came to housing, but housing was also knocking at Wall Street and corporate doors.

Thus the simultaneous occurrence of several extraordinary phenomena: (a) the rise of a public market for housing developers; (b) the commencement of a major merger boom in real estate as non-housing corporations and later the bigger builders began to acquire or merge with other builders; and (c) the rise of an entire new class of giant financial institutions serving the housing industry, the real estate investment trusts. At the same time, joint ventures between builder-entrepreneurs and non-housing corporations proliferated. Many new organizations sprang into existence to provide equity financing for joint ventures. With continuing financial pressures, a welter of sophisticated financing techniques gained ascendancy, supplanting the old fixed-interest long-term financing arrangements. The old forms were broken.

With Wall Street's and the corporate investor's entry into housing, and because adverse economic conditions have prompted many new and ingenious solutions to the problem of delivering a housing product, the housing industry since 1968 has undergone an intense streamlining and consolidation. Giant building companies suddenly dominated the scene where none existed formerly. Entirely new development empires mushroomed overnight by operating on the principle of builder mergers or wielding expanding networks of builder joint ventures. The visitor who surveyed the real estate business only a few short years ago would not recognize it today. Small wonder that Crassus would have blanched.

A SURVEY SHOWS BROAD CORPORATE ACTION IN REAL ESTATE

The corporate investors, as indicated, have moved into real estate in droves. It is impossible to estimate in their entirety the number of non-real-estate-related companies active in the field, but a study on real estate activities among major corporations issued by the Society of Real Estate Appraisers in 1971 is instructive. The SREA, based on a 24.6% response rate from a detailed questionnaire mailed to five hundred of the one thousand corporations listed in the June 1970 issue of *Fortune,* said that corporate acceleration into real estate has been largely sustained by the three hundred or so major corporations whose tables of organization reflect real estate departments. Among major manufacturers, real estate activity is surprisingly pronounced in the food, chemicals, machinery and electrical machinery industries. Surprising because this shows real estate activity spreading beyond the first generation of corporate entrants to real estate: the land-rich pulp, paper, petroleum companies and millowners who develop their lands because of the high profit potential in such activities.

From the actual survey sample, SREA determined that nearly a hundred and fifty major corporations actively participate in real estate. Of these, only 30% have real estate departments, while 70% control real estate assets by policies governing the corporate treasury. In addition to those already involved, another 5%, or thirty companies, planned to diversify via real estate operations in the near future. These findings suggest that real estate activity among corporations is far more widespread than might appear if judged by the presence of real estate departments among them.

The same survey found that the principal motivation underlying corporate real estate investment was (in 75.8% of the cases) concerned equity participation and/or diversification. About 7% of the programs were motivated by tax shelter considerations. Many of these corporations, said SREA, show a high degree of sophistication in their real estate operations and a never-ending quest for still more sophisticated techniques in the treatment of real estate as a profit-making corporate asset.

As to the extent of corporate real estate holdings, the survey estimated the aggregate value in excess of $25 billion for the study sample. Of this, only $9 billion of property was classified as "surplus" industrial property concerned with corporate production, and much of this is a candidate for profitable realty development of one form or another. For corporations with real estate departments, the average value of property held by those using market value was $16.8 million; the average for those using book value was $14.1 million. For corporations lacking real estate departments, the corresponding averages are $16.2 million for market value, and $13.1 million for book value.

Any representative summary of corporate real estate activity thus leaves the vivid impression that few if any pockets of real estate activity have remained unaffected by the big boys tossing around such hefty chunks of dollars. Real estate became Big Business in the 1960s and 1970s.

WHAT KIND OF INDUSTRY HAVE THE CORPORATE CATS PENETRATED?

The field of real estate in which the corporate plungers began taking such an active role is so broad and diversified that, like the elephant to the six blind men, it can mean something different to everyone. I had better define the main groups and subgroups of the real estate and housing business through which corporate and financial sources are participating. This classification will also let us isolate the primary real estate group with which this book deals. Briefly, the industry can be broken down into three main groups.

The first group comprises the leisure- and travel-oriented companies, principally the publicly held hotel companies such as Hilton, Sheraton, Holiday Inn, etc., but also includes some well-diversified building companies like Del E. Webb.

The second group comprises the construction-oriented companies, and these break down into three categories. The first of these is the homebuilders, often called the merchant builders. These are the high-volume producers of the nation's residential housing (houses, apartments, townhouses, condominiums, mobile-home parks). They include among their ranks such leading representatives as Kaufman & Broad, Levitt & Sons, Centex, Presley, McKeon, Larwin and U.S. Home. The second category is that of land development companies. These typically, though not always, build residential housing in volume, but they do this as an extension of their principal activity, which is the planning and development of large (sometimes extraordinarily large) parcels of land. Many of the corporate entrants to real estate drop into this category (e.g., Westinghouse, Chrysler, General Electric); other representatives are the Rouse Company, Deltona, General Development and McCulloch Properties. The third category within this group are the "cash flow" builders—Tishman, Uris, Monumental, Forest City, to name some—and they specialize in the construction of office buildings and other commercial, and sometimes industrial, buildings.

Sometimes it is difficult to tell which category a builder should be pigeonholed into. Many of the homebuilders engage in at least some commercial construction. Companies like Monumental Properties and Forest City Enterprises are thoroughly diversified, as was Boise Cascade. And Del E. Webb, although classifiable as a hotel company, also fits into the second group because of its development and homebuilding activities. But the broad classifications do hold true and provide us with a useful way of distinguishing between the varieties of real estate operations.

The third major group in real estate is the financial services organizations serving this industry. It includes the real estate investment trusts, both the mortgage type (which make loans for construction and development) and the equity type (which purchase and hold properties for appreciation and income). The other major members of this group are mortgage banking firms, savings and loan associations, savings banks and, at least to some extent, commercial banks. The Federal National Mortgage Association, as it operates a secondary market for mortgages, drops into the financial service bracket. And we should not fail to include realty syndication pools, now that they have become such a flexible investment vehicle, in this group.

Unless otherwise specified, the real estate industry this book broadly describes and discusses is Group Two, the construction-oriented companies, and their interactions with corporate merger-makers and joint-venturers. And, within this group, the principal focus is on the category of the homebuilders; although, as many of these are also in land development and commercial construction, these areas are also included, at least by implication, throughout the book. It is the homebuilding industry that taps the broadest market potential. Residential construction in 1972, for example, exceeded a dollar volume of $50 billion, rising by 22% over 1971. It is the industry that has undergone the rapid merger trend, taking shelter under the dollar-lined wings of corporate eagles thirsting for a flight into real estate. It is also principally from the ranks of the homebuilders that there rise up the entrepreneurs who lead the newcomer corporations by the hand in their trial commercial or residential real estate ventures on a joint-venture basis, and who hold the key positions in most of the major corporate land development and construction ventures. Indeed, with few exceptions, the homebuilding field is the plasma from which springs the archetypal entrepreneur for virtually all types of real estate activity. This entrepreneur's companies and activities today represent the dominant image of real estate to the corporate sector.

A MIX OF SOPHISTICATED CONTROLS AND OLD-FASHIONED FREEDOMS

And here our friend Crassus reenters the scene. How did these first encounters between the entrepreneur and the pin-stripe financiers fare? The key question to which Crassus addresses himself is whether these corporate newcomers to real estate via merger, acquisition and joint venture somehow succeeded in eliminating by the force of bigness itself the traditional entrepreneurial uncertainties in real estate. And here the answer must be: certainly not. We need only to look at the well-advertised failures of Boise Cascade or American-Standard as leading examples of outsiders who tossed up their hands and sold out to Crassus at ten cents on the dollar. And for each of these visible signs of disaffection with corporate-style real estate there are many others that have percolated and are percolating beneath the surface of corporate amiability elsewhere. The economic and political instability of the nation only operates to bring to the surface what were already unstable or bad deals.

The fact is, real estate in general, and the housing industry in particular, *is* unique among industries for a number of reasons: the volatility of its raw material supply and labor costs, its markets, and its financial sources; the quality of keen marketing and purchasing judgment and the number of decisions that must go into each project; the style and forms of management and incentive that are consequently necessary. Particularly important in this industry, as a requisite to survival, is *honest* accounting, and this has not been emphasized nearly as much as it should have been. The entry of corporate newcomers, to be sure, resulted in substantial sophistication and consolidation of the industry. But basically, where those corporate newcomers did succeed, it was because they understood certain basics, and perceived the wisdom of molding their real estate operations — and particularly their *housing* operations — to the basic prevailing pattern of the successful real estate entrepreneur, not vice versa. Because they did not always succeed, the merger trend strongly shifted from the conglomerate type to a "builder-congeneric" type (builder merging with builder), though acquisitions by major corporations unrelated to the building field will continue.

The successful corporate real estate operation is a delicate balance of sophisticated new styles of financial-managerial controls and old-fashioned entrepreneurial integrity. Its success depends, among other things, on the soundness of the initial motives for merger, on the establishment of viable management forms and realistic growth goals, on the understanding of profitability and risk and of real estate accounting, on allowance for economic fluctuations, on land acquisition and marketing programs that will put a salable product in the marketplace. Most of all, its success depends on the quality of the corporate and real estate *people* involved, and their desire to work together and understand one another. This is difficult, but it is not unachievable. It is in effect the successful translation of the entrepreneurial art of real estate to a higher harmonic of bigger corporate action in a radically transformed housing industry.

That is the subject of this book. Focusing on mergers and joint ventures as the instruments of change, it describes first of all how the housing and real estate business has been transformed since 1968. The main players of the game are highlighted, their changing forms of organization and ways of doing business, and the changing economic and marketing environment which dictates these changes. Along the way, the book describes the failed and successful mergers and draws some conclusions on the successful ingredients for a merger in real estate. It reports on the range and forms of joint-venture activity. Certain chapters also suggest specific approaches to prepare and guide both the corporate investor and the builder into a productive merger or joint venture. Each of the book's chapters (which are grouped by theme into four sections) is written more or less as a free-standing essay, and can be read individually by the browser or particularist without reference to the whole.

The reader should be alerted to two important reminders as he peruses this book.

First, I have not attempted to write a business-schoolese treatise on the subject of real estate and mergers. I have instead satisfied myself by saying what I think and feel, in language that is understandable to me. While concentrating on facts as I perceive them, I also offer occasional opinions on matters pertinent and impertinent to this industry and the nation on which it impinges. Those who may be outraged by this approach are hereby invited to spend their time more enjoyably in reading their favorite business school review.

Second, the reader should realize that the industry he will read about in this book is no longer the one he will find around him when he looks up. It changes too fast. What is presented here is an industry frozen in one moment of time — a period ending roughly in 1972 and 1973. An attempt to remain topical is suicidal; there is always a merger or joint venture either blowing up or forming in some revolutionary new combination just as you're ready to go to press. Likewise, the cyclical patterns of overbuilding and varying money-market conditions create long-term swings that alter the picture. The combination of high mortgage rates and rock-bottom stock market at the start of 1974 affected many mergers adversely, but the picture may change again within a two-year period.

While a book like this cannot be entirely topical, it can trace the basic dynamics of merger and joint venture and of real estate in general for the period of the early Seventies. The reader should remember that the descriptions of particular events and companies cited in support of this or that conclusion are now history. I underscore the point because virtually all of the companies referred to will be much different (in sales, earnings, geographic or product diversification) when this book is read than they were when I plucked them wriggling from the time stream for inspection. Their life histories, viewed from a longer perspective, may also look different; they may have been shaken up or buoyed further by great isolated or general events. Some may also have folded entirely or plunged into bad repute from their present golden glow; others, once in the doghouse with the investing public or the acquirers, may look like heroes.

PART ONE

Dynamics of the Business

Civilization!
The mighty tower of mankind
Sprung from conceptions past the
mind.

—L. C. Voorhies

1

Instruments of Profit in Real Estate

> Give me a lever long enough
> and I can move the Earth.
>
> —Archimedes

Real estate developers, at least the more colorful of them, occasionally enjoy the piratical image of having become millionaires by "making a real killing" on their investments. Who, after all, hasn't heard the story of the apartment developer telephoning his partner from the lobby of an insurance company: "Yes, Bill, they approved the $6 million loan, but there's a catch: they want us to put up $75 as our equity investment in the deal." The joke is funny because, by exaggerating, it throws into sharp focus the essence of the entire real estate game: the mechanics of leverage, the high return on investment often possible, the builder's traditional undercapitalization.

In no other industry can an enterprising individual with a small poke of cash and good judgment take himself so far with the help of leverage. This is why the real estate industry is full of self-made men. One need only point out R. A. Watt, Ben Deane or Jim Walter, all of whom started in the business as resourceful carpenters in the days after World War II and parlayed their entrepreneurial efforts into multimillion-dollar building companies. Another excellent example is Dallas-based Trammel Crow, who, having started in 1948 with a few thousand dollars, now presides over a building and real estate empire that includes more than 175 partnerships and 40 corporations holding property worth more than $1.5 billion.

The attractiveness of real estate depends not only on leverage, however, but also on the volume of demand for land and structures and on an accurate understanding of the distribution of profitability and risk by type of real estate venture. It is the combination of these three elements — leverage, demand, profitability/risk — that is responsible for the entry of corporations into real estate development and for the various forms of their participation in it. This combination also controls the patterns of the industry's financial organization and its entrepreneurial activities.

3

LEVERAGE AND TAX SHELTER

A number of major industrial and financial service corporations in the late Sixties suddenly figured out what the real estate entrepreneur's secret was: the use of borrowed money and tax advantages to produce a very high return on investment. Its attractiveness did not become clear, however, until corporate accountants could begin to distinguish between two yardsticks of corporate performance. The educational process of the major corporations was assisted by *Fortune* and the *Harvard Business Review,* which published articles in the late Sixties calling attention to real estate and discussing the points outlined here.

The yardstick by which major corporations traditionally measure performance is pretax cash flow on *total* invested capital (including debt and equity capital). By this measure, the performance of homebuilding and development companies is no great shakes. For all types of real estate firms, performance in 1970-71 varied from 8% to 15% (pretax), or in about the same range as return on corporate assets in the United States; homebuilding companies' performance, in particular, has run 5% to 8% as an average (after tax). An entirely different picture emerges, however, when performance is measured as return on equity capital only. An ROI (return on investment) of 20% to 40% is not uncommon, far greater than the return on equity commanded by industrial corporations.

The higher return on equity is possible because of the better leverage — the bigger borrowing power — inherent in the real estate business. A builder can borrow proportionately far more than an industrial corporation (or go into a venture with far less of his own money, which is the same thing) because the property he is acquiring and developing, rising in value through his labors, itself serves as collateral. If he goes broke, the lender has a property with a readily identifiable market value and demand, and can dispose of it to recoup the borrowed money. A manufacturer of widgets, however, cannot reasonably expect to borrow so much relative to his own equity. What in hell is a lender going to do with ten million widgets if the manufacturer's distribution and marketing organization folds?

Because of this basic difference in the nature of the collateral, a real estate company (of a certain type) may have debt equal to 90% of its entire capitalization, while a manufacturer starts breathing deeply at half that amount. Hence, because of the real estate company's ability to command a much higher debt-equity ratio, the return on its equity is very high. By the same token, its return on total invested assets (debt and equity) could be merely moderate or even low compared with that of an industrial corporation.

This is not to say that in many cases a building company's profits on total invested capital cannot in themselves be impressive. The performance of a number of publicly held building companies, notably Kaufman & Broad, demonstrates that expertly managed real estate development companies can perform well by both yardsticks. But the lesson is that it is impossible to fully appreciate real estate as a business proposition unless it is viewed in light of ROI. The name of the game is leverage, leverage, leverage, and the real profitability of a real estate company can't be accurately gauged without leverage taken into account. Some of the biggest post-merger problems I have seen stem from the corporation's insistence on jamming a round peg into a square hole: making nothing of the acquired builder by evaluating his performance primarily by return on total assets instead of return on equity.

Just how far debt can be leveraged is illustrated in a straightforward development or homebuilding operation. Let us assume this operation is affiliated with a major industrial corporation. The corporation, if it wishes, has its own good name to borrow against, to the limit of its senior debt agreements, and it can put this debt capital to work in its real estate operations. As the senior debt agreements of industrial corporations call for rather conservative debt-equity ratios, however, we can expect that the corporation won't get too much leverage by this route. Indeed, there is a better one, as *Fortune* once illustrated.

To avoid straining its own relatively limited borrowing capacity, the corporation can set up an independent subsidiary to handle real estate. It can, in fact, leverage its money much further through this permissible peculiarity of organization. The funds for the subsidiary may be debt funds borrowed by the parent corporation, but in the hands of the subsidiary — a separate entity — they become equity capital which can be leveraged still further, and without the conservative restrictions of senior debt agreements patterned to industrial, not real estate, debt-equity ratios.

The leveraging process then continues in the subsidiary. The land developer buys acreage with a small down payment, borrowing against the land itself for the balance. A portion of the land can be released after the down payment, and the developer then borrows against this land to finance improvement. The new lender appraises the land at its future value, disregarding its undeveloped state. The ability to deduct development expenses and interest on borrowed money protects much of the income. This process is repeated until the entire project is completed. For a homebuilder, the leverage is even better: the house is better collateral than land alone, so the landowner will take a fractional deposit until the houses are sold. The builder can then borrow construction money on both house and lot.

As attractive as leveraging of investment is in a homebuilding and sales company, the potential for leverage and profits is greater for a company that builds and retains ownership of income-producing properties such as apartments, commercial and industrial buildings. For here there is not only the prospect of leverage at a high ratio but also of shielding the resultant profits through the liberal tax shelter permitted to owners of income-producing property in the form of depreciation allowances, as well as other expense deductions associated with development and ownership (including interest expense on all borrowed funds).

In real estate, particularly with regard to land development and development of income-producing property, there is no distinction between cash flow and profit when determining return. Cash flow after meeting interest and amortization payments *is* the profit. Leverage is what you get when, for each dollar of investment, the project's cash flow after all expenses is greater than the mortgage cash flow requirement (called "the constant" in the industry). When the net cash flow is shielded by depreciation deductions, etc., all the better. (Of course, depreciation is anathema to the publicly held corporation looking for bookable earnings; such companies develop and sell income-producing properties.)

To maximize his leverage, the investor in income-producing property seeks not only to replace as much equity with debt as possible, but also to get a mortgage with the longest possible repayment period. The longer the term of the mortgage, the smaller is each year's amortization payment, thereby reducing the constant and increasing the net cash flow (i.e., profit). Again, the reason the real estate investor can get a higher debt-equity ratio, and for a longer term, than an industrial corporation can get when borrowing against its general credit, is twofold.

First, the cash flow from an income-producing property doesn't vary much, and therefore presents a comparatively modest risk for most of the committed debt capital. If the property is leased for twenty-five years to a leading department store, for example, the lender is assured of a relatively stable income stream for at least twenty-five years. Another example is an apartment building which can operate at break-even at, say, 70% occupancy, but which only under the most unusual circumstances falls below an occupancy of 90%–95%.

Second, the lender can take a lien on the piece of property without having to share title with other general creditors, as would be the case when a corporation borrows against its credit.

Having achieved a substantial leverage of his invesment by a high debt-equity ratio and a long-term mortgage, the investor finds his profit is then enhanced by tax shelter. If a financial package is structured "right" on properties like apartments or office buildings, the after-tax profits can work out to be the same as before-tax profits: since depreciation is deductible, but not a cash outflow item, the total deductible "expenses" can exceed taxable income from the project. The package can even be so set up that it will yield a "loss," and this loss can be applied to shield income from other projects or the parent corporation's profit against the 50% corporate tax. And when the property has been considerably depreciated and exhausts its tax-shelter benefits — while the real value of the property itself may often have appreciated — it can be sold for additional profit, subject only to a capital gains tax of 25%.

Here is an historic example from *Fortune* showing how leverage and tax shelter work together to produce profits from an office building, based on 1967 interest and construction costs:

The developer taking out a mortgage borrows against the future value, not present cost, from an insurance company or pension fund. His package may cost, say, $3.6 million, consisting of $2.8 million worth of construction on land costing $800,000. If the property produces a cash flow of $340,000 annually from rental income, however, the value of the package can be $4 million, if it is capitalized at 8.5%. A 75% mortgage based on a value of $4 million thus, happily, allows a $3 million loan, reducing the equity required of the developer or his joint venturer to only $600,000.

From the $340,000 of yearly operating income (that is, after operating expenses and real estate taxes), the developer must pay the insurance company or pension fund $225,000 interest plus $27,000 on principal (based on a 7½%, thirty-year mortage), leaving him with $88,000 in annual income before taxes. But he pays no tax on income from the property because the building depreciates in value from the time it goes up. On the double-declining basis permitted in 1967, its value depreciates by $140,000 in the first year. In effect, then, the developer has a "loss" of some $25,000 on the property, which he can offset against other taxable income. That saving is worth $12,500 if he is in the 50% tax bracket.

That tax saving, plus the $88,000 in cash flow, produces an after-tax return of 16.7% on his (or his partner's) $600,000 investment, equivalent to a 33% return on some other fully taxable investment. He keeps all this if he is in business for himself, or splits it if he is a joint-venturer.

It used to be that a smart developer could mortgage out completely (i.e., get a mortgage of a ratio high enough to the stated value of the project to cover his actual costs completely, reducing his own equity requirements to nil), but as we shall see in subsequent chapters 100% financing is dearer these days. Still, in the growing field of government-guaranteed housing high-ratio mortgages are available, calling for a modest equity requirement on the developer's part. Whether in conventional or government-guaranteed housing, the leverage remains pretty unbelievable over a period of time. And these returns are further increased by the operation of accelerated depreciation and capital gains.

THE SPECIAL STRENGTHS OF THE CORPORATE
INVESTOR IN REAL ESTATE

The major publicly held corporations and institutional investors, once they fully understood these mechanisms for expanding a developer's profit, were in a position to put them to work on a scale undreamed of by the independent entrepreneur. These companies tap the large sources of equity and debt capital with relative ease because they fit the mold with which Wall Street is most familiar. They then act as a conduit to funnel their funds into real estate projects which might otherwise find it difficult to obtain risk capital. Indeed, they are often already involved indirectly in real estate financing, so in many cases the move to a direct role in development is not a drastic step for them.

Real estate has not proven to be an unmixed blessing for a number of industrial corporations with their own intensive capital requirements, to be sure. But generally, their principal advantage over the entrepreneur is their impressive financial resources, including not only easier access to new capital but often large amounts of cash flow from their regular operations that must find profitable investment outlets. This is particularly true for financial service companies with large recurring cash inflows. With such revenue streams from other operations that can be used to cover debt service and other expenses of real estate operations in a squeeze, they are often in a position to undertake larger, longer-run projects where the payoff, while substantial, may be slow in getting started.

As one consequence of this factor, although the corporate experience in entrepreneurial homebuilding has been mixed, we *have* witnessed the steady growth of corporate and institutional investors' role in the development of extremely large, long-term projects. While the record of the earlier participants in such multi-thousand-acre developments was spotty, the overall trend to huge projects and "new towns" continues to grow. This is almost exclusively the province of the corporate or institutional investor, often in a joint venture with, or funding in other ways, a major building company like Arlen Properties or Levitt & Sons. Thinly capitalized, non-diversified independent real estate operations usually have to opt for investments with fairly rapid turnovers.

Like the individual entrepreneur, the industrial and commercial corporation enhances its profit potential in real estate because it can take full advantage of both the financial leverage possibilities in real estate and the shield over profits provided by tax laws. When a corporation enters this field, usually creating a subsidiary to carry the operation, the subsidiary can seek the same degree of leverage that would be available to an independent developer. In fact, the subsidiary might do even better than the independent in this respect, since it could use the financial strength, reputation, integrity, and contacts of the parent as a bargaining tool to obtain more debt capital.

"FALLOUT." Moreover, a substantial number of major corporations stand to gain not only from the profitability of the real estate projects themselves, but also from the "fallout" of new demand for their products. Many, if not most, of the early corporate entrants into real estate have been manufacturers of products used in construction. Thus, for example, we have seen the entry of Alcoa, U.S. Steel, American-Standard, Boise Cascade, Tappan, General Electric, Westinghouse, and numerous other housing materials producers and suppliers. The fallout of profits from increases in sales of a corporation's products can be significant, although the actual experience of such tie-ins has been highly variable. It remains a very valid point however that the profit potential in the corporate real estate investment alone is not the limit of profitability.

MANAGEMENT. Potential corporate investors also bring to real estate one talent that this industry genuinely needs — management skills. This is noted with some reservation because, as it has actually worked out, "corporate management skills" have frequently been a label camouflaging a corporation's systematic self-annihilation in a real estate venture when it imposed its own controls uncomprehendingly as a substitute for understanding the business. Decorum prohibits one from naming such miscreants but anyone who knows the industry can cite several examples.

It is also true, however, that in the earlier days of corporate-developer marriages there were also many complaints from the financial community that developers did not meet specific cost and time commitments. Modern management techniques, much further developed in the corporate sector than in the real estate sector, can be put to very profitable use in bringing construction activities and management of developed real estate under more effective control.

THE INSTITUTIONAL INVESTORS. The same reasons that apply to industrial and commercial corporations are even more true for institutional investors such as insurance companies, corporate pension funds and trust funds which are also channeling equity capital into real estate development.

The institutional investors have a large continuing access to capital markets, and their growth in the postwar period demonstrates this capability. Between 1960 and 1967 alone, for example, the annual cash inflow available for investment by life insurance companies increased from $6 billion to $9.2 billion. Annual cash inflow of corporate pension funds increased from $3.6 billion to $5.7 billion in the same period. Between 1967 and 1971, institutional investment in real estate has continued to grow dramatically.

Competition for the savings of individuals continues to grow, putting additional pressure on savings institutions to show more favorable returns on invested capital. To the extent that real estate investments offer an attractive investment outlet, savings institutions cannot afford to ignore them, and indeed they have not.

A big advantage that many institutional developers do have over corporate investors entering the real estate development field is the fund of expertise that they have acquired over the years in servicing developers' needs for mortgage money. This expertise was readily translatable into the successful operation of mortgage-type real estate investment trusts, and for this reason many financial and institutional investors established real estate investment trusts and public real estate partnerships in the period between 1969 and 1972. Such expertise also gives them the edge over corporate investors in spotting the best opportunities and knowing how to spot the best management talent in the building field.

PROFITABILITY AND RISK BY TYPE OF REAL ESTATE VENTURE

Leverage generally operates to make real estate an attractive proposition. But, given the fact of leverage, the distribution of profitability and risk varies considerably in this field, depending both on the type of venture (or investment) and on the investor's position with respect to that venture.

The crucial requirement is the application of leverage where it will produce the biggest profit with the least risk. An analysis of historic profit/risk relationships in the real estate industry, for which I am indebted to Edward C. Birkner of Marketing Information Network and Alan J. Smith of Associated Mortgage Investors, sets up the basis for understanding the various trade-offs between profit and risk that corporate entrants have opted for. This, in turn will clarify the various forms of corporate organization and activity in the field of real estate and help us to differentiate between them. Historical profit/risk relationships only serve as general guidelines, of course. Nothing can supplant individual competence; in its presence, the riskiest project might be safe; in its absence the safest project risky.

An outline of the types of real estate investment and the methods of investment will let us focus on profitability and risk.

An investor can invest in:

1. Land
    a. Raw tracts
    b. Under development or just ready for development
    c. Developed or bypassed

2. Construction before building starts
   a. Single-family dwellings
   b. Commercial
      i. Presold e.g., leased shopping center, presold commercial
      ii. Speculative, e.g., rental apartments or offices
3. Completed properties
   a. Assured income, e.g., leased to AAA tenants
   b. Semi-assured income, e.g., shopping center with some major leases
   c. Speculative, e.g., rental apartments

The investor's methods of investment are:

1. Debt — investment as a lender
   a. First mortgages
   b. Subordinated or junior mortgages
      i. Insured
      ii. Uninsured
   c. Leasebacks with repurchase option
2. Equity — investment as an owner, with:
   a. No management responsibility, e.g., REIT or net leases
   b. Some management responsibility such as taxes, insurance, maintenance
   c. Full management responsibility, e.g., rental apartments
   d. Development responsibility

The degrees of profitability in equity investment (as opposed to debt financing) are as follows:

Land. Land in a raw state or bypassed by development has tended to increase in value rather slowly, perhaps 3% (FHA figure) to 5% a year (though inflation in recent years has boosted this). Land when ready for development will normally sell as developed lots at a price 30% to 60% above its cost as raw land, and often higher. Thus, astute development of land ready for construction can show great profits.

Construction. There is usually little or no profit in the construction, per se, of a presold property, except to the general contractor. The profit to be made is in conceiving and selling the idea; this amount of profit is unpredictable. Profit from the sale of single-family homes is normally 5% to 20% above a builder's cost. The profit from the sale of successful speculative construction may frequently range up to 40% of cost, but over a longer time span than housing construction.

Completed Properties. Properties with an assured income normally produce an operating income of about 8% per annum on the purchase price; a high first mortgage would raise this price. A return of 10% to 12% on the equity might be anticipated. Decreased assurance of income would increase the anticipated return; a slum equity, for example, can yield over 20% per annum.

The degrees of profitability in debt financing (as opposed to equity financing), are as follows (interest rates cited are arbitrarily set for the 1967–68 period):

Land loans, if less than cost, were frequently made by banks at 6%. A loan equal, or almost equal, to cost, or a development loan (to finance land acquisition and development costs) normally yielded 12% to 14%, but with yields going as high as 14% to 20%, generally with a share of the equity also.

Construction loans, on presold properties, were normally made by banks at 6%. On speculative housing the rate was normally 9% to 11%, or 10% to 12%. On speculative commercial construction, rates are comparable to speculative housing, but usually with a share of the equity.

Loans on developed property. First mortgage loans ranged from 6½% to 7½%, and the ratio of the loan could range from 90% on single-family housing down to less than 60% of appraised value for a purely speculative project. Second mortgages could range from 8% with well-assured income to 20% on a purely speculative basis. Leasebacks were normally handled only with some assurance of income at rates ranging from 8% to 12%.

The trade-offs between profit and risk available to the investor can thus be set up in something like this form:

Fully developed properties offer the lowest rates of return on equity and debt because the risks are most easily measured and assessed. For maximum security and minimum management involvement the investor can obtain first mortgages on properties at good prevailing yields, with some residual values. Most of the corporate and institutional real estate investments up to the late 1960's were principally in the debt or equity of developed properties, but then a new trend began to emerge in search for greater profits.

Development of presold commercial and industrial properties offers good profits with relatively low risk. The profits are made by creating and selling viable ideas to major credits; a shopping center promotion, for example. Once the package is assembled, the profit is realized by selling it to another investor or by holding it for income. The risk here, however, is in the time and money spent on preselling the package itself with no assurance of success. The market for AAA tenants is relatively specialized.

Land development is a good equity investment or a good collateral for a development loan, provided the land is developed at the right time. The risk element occurs in the decision that the land is ripe for development, and in projecting the timing of the investment return. As these factors can be fairly estimated by market research and other means, and as value is created in excess of cost by improvement, the risk is not wildly speculative. Land undergoes a rapid rise in value when developed at the right time, protecting the equity or debt investment. Land loans other than development loans and equity in other than land under development are poor investments in general because the long-term appreciation in value is slow.

Speculative commercial construction can achieve very high profits but offers substantial risk. Such construction is typically highly leveraged, and this can lead to a heavy loss if the project fails to rent or sell either in the construction stage or as developed property. If such development gets over the first critical year without going under, however, it can be enormously profitable, taking advantage of the leverage inherent in economic growth, which rapidly pushes up the values of completed commercial structures.

A homebuilding operation can make the highest construction profits because of its ability to achieve rapid turnover; a small profit percentage per unit sold, achieved in high volume during the course of a year, results in high absolute profits. However, the homebuilder's profit as a percentage of sales is so small, and he is typically so leveraged, that a few bad models or a slow market can lead to losses, sometimes heavy losses, if he has to hold the houses for long. The same holds for speculative apartment construction. To spread his risk, the professional homebuilder takes on many smaller projects rather than a few big ones.

Construction and development loans, interestingly, offer the combination of highest debt yields (along with some equity participation) and best security, because value is created in excess of cost by the injection of entrepreneurial effort and skill. If the builder fails to sell his project in a slow market, he loses. But the lender who takes it back now commands an equity substantially in excess of his investment. His only loss is that of the interest income that could be generated by funds tied up in the project. But this risk, too, can be minimized by making many small investments instead of a few big ones. Construction and development loans thus offer the next best level of security after first mortgages and leasebacks on properties occupied by AAA tenants. But their yields are substantially higher, because the demand for such funds is usually large and because relatively few investors have known how to appraise or make such investments.

THE DEMAND FACTOR

Attractive as all the leverage and profitability potentials are in real estate, they acquire their true significance only in the perspective of the immense market demand for construction of all types, including shelter, which presently exists in the U.S. It is the extent of this vast hunger for new construction, with its potential for large annual earnings growth, that ultimately impels the major outsiders into real estate.

The two primary determinants of the need for home and commercial construction are population growth and demolition and retirement of existing facilities. Growth in population creates a need not only for housing but also for supporting real estate facilities such as shopping centers, service stations, medical clinics, schools, office buildings, and so on. The dimensions of the future need for real estate development can be readily understood from the following projections.

During the 1970's, the population of the United States will increase by about 26 million people. The increases should be about the same in the decades of the 1980's and the 1990's. Economists vary in their population forecasts, which have fallen from a rate of 25 per 1,000 in the 1940's to 17 per 1,000 in the 1960's. But the population should be somewhere between 260 million and 300 million by that time.

Such a growth in population translates into about 13 million (some economists say closer to 14 million) new household formations in the decade of the Seventies, or an average annual demand of about 1.3 million housing units. The statistical net new annual demand averages to about only 900,000 housing units. But the postwar baby boom will be hitting its peak influence during the 1970's as the proportion of the population in the twenty-to-forty age group comes to grow at a faster rate than the forty-to-sixty age group. And these young people will be forming the housing demand of 1.3 million units annually — larger than statistically indicated.

Estimates on replacement demand vary considerably. The National Association of Homebuilders estimated that for the five-year period 1966–70 annual replacement needs grew to 660,000 units. The NAHB predicted that replacement demand would rise to 720,000 units annually. Economist George Cline Smith optimistically estimates a figure of about 800,000 replacement units annually during the Seventies. In any event, the demand for replacement units adds substantially to the housing market.

Another source of expanded housing demand is family mobility, which requires a certain vacancy factor in available housing to allow for the increasingly transient nature of the U.S. population. This factor, though it doesn't add to housing demand in a very large way, does dictate the construction of about 100,000 additional units a year in the Seventies.

The second-home market, though it is not included in computations of annual housing starts, adds to the potentials for profit in the real estate and housing market. The NAHB estimates that the number of second homes grew from 1.3 million in 1957 to 1.8 million in 1966, averaging an annual increase of 50,000 units. Assuming that affluence will enlarge this market, the average annual demand for second homes could rise to 100,000 or even 150,000 units by 1980. As more people get frozen out of primary housing, the market for second homes may expand; they can afford the second home but not the first one, which they will rent.

Other key factors affecting the potential of the housing and real estate industry cannot be overlooked in any analysis:

Average family income is expected to rise to $15,000 by 1980, in terms of 1970 purchasing power. Allowing for containment of inflation, which erodes purchasing power faster in housing and real estate than in other sectors of the economy, this factor will have a good effect on the market for real estate and housing. About 40% of the population increase in the Seventies will be in the thirty-to-forty age group, and about half this increase will come in the second half of the decade, according to the NAHB. Taken together with the upward trend in the twenty-five-to-thirty age group, these statistics translate as follows: continuing strong support for the apartment market in the first half of the decade (with demand for apartments at close to 45% of starts), with a big boost to demand for single-family housing in the latter half of the Seventies. This is because as families grow older and their income rises, they tend to switch from apartment into single-family housing. With average family income rising and inflation contained, the market for single-family housing in the latter part of the Seventies should see a stronger rise than at any time since the 1950's. The concentration of population in urban areas should continue well into the Seventies, though we should pause to take the sudden booming of "new town" programs into account and the effect they may have, unmeasurable at this time, on reversing the concentration trend. From 1960 to 1970, at any rate, the percentage of urban population rose from 60% to 70% of the total. Such a concentration suggests a continuing demand for apartment-type housing and (given inflation of housing costs) a high proportion of condominium-ownership housing, which began finding large-scale acceptance in 1970 and 1971.

Real estate and housing should benefit from a strongly expanding American economy. A McGraw-Hill economic study estimates that between

1970 and 1985, the national output should rise 77% (in terms of constant 1970 dollars), going from $974 billion to $1,727 billion, with real output growing at an annual compounded rate of 3.9%. With the rise in real personal income mentioned above, households will be buying 50% more than they did in 1970.

Hence, taking the sum of these projections and expectations, the decade of the Seventies should see an enormous expansion of the homebuilding and real estate industry, greater than at any time since the boom days of construction following World War II. It is in the Seventies that the industry will really get consolidated and come into its own as a force in the economy. Those of you who expect to get a position in the field had better do it in this decade; by the 1980's it will be too late.

Indeed, construction in the Seventies got off to a flying start. With a total demand for the decade of approximately 22 million housing units, the industry can expect to produce for annual demand of 2.2 million units; but actual rates of housing produced may exceed this from year to year, rising to perhaps 2.4 and 2.5 million units. In 1971, as an example, total housing units hit something like 2.5 million (counting about two million housing and apartment units and about 485,000 mobile homes). This was up by 36% over 1970 production. And it was substantially more than the 2,050,000 units the industry produced in its previous record year, 1950. During the Sixties, production averaged about 1.5 million units yearly. (In 1950, of course, mobile homes were a negligible factor in housing.)

Housing performance for conventionally built apartments and homes alone attained 2.4 million units in 1972 and about 2.1 million in 1973. Construction in 1974 was pegged to drop to about 1.8 million units before swinging up again in 1975. With mobile home shipments considered, intense competition for the consumer's housing dollar will be the hallmark of the decade, with some slumps and further shakeouts inevitable because of overbuilding. But annual average production should still proceed at levels some 30% to 40% higher than during the decade of the Sixties.

This new housing, of course, leads to a large additional market for other construction. Each housing development needs schools, shopping centers, and recreational and service facilities of other types. According to some formulas, for each $10,000 invested in housing, another $2,500 must be pumped into necessary support facilities.

Within the perspective of such a large market for big-ticket purchases, and given the mechanisms by which the builder and developer can expand their profits through leverage and tax shelter in the most profitable segments of this market, one can begin to understand the motives impelling the corporate investors into this field in droves.

2

Some Forms of Corporate Action

He doth bestride the narrow
world like a Colossus.

—Shakespeare

Residential construction was important. But the dynamics of corporate and institutional participation in real estate in the 1966–1973 period also focused on: (1) land development and large-scale projects and (2) financing of construction and development through the newly risen real estate investment trusts. A look at these elements clarifies the position of the homebuilding industry in the overall context of the real estate business.

LAND DEVELOPMENT AND LARGE-SCALE PROJECTS

The corporate and institutional investors are really starting to hit their stride in this field. Their easier access to big chunks of debt and equity capital, and their financial ability to ride out slow start-up periods and heavy front-end development costs in expectation of an eventual high annually averaged return on investment makes them particularly able to get involved in large-scale projects. Their rewards are annual returns on equity of 20% to 25%, and often more. And much of that return is shelterable, as such projects benefit by deductible development costs and are almost always planned in conjunction with commercial and other income-producing construction.

The idea of settling in for a long-term pull with one major project, rather than making repeated, critical entrepreneurial decisions associated with numerous small projects, is perhaps also more appealing to the more conservative corporate style. In any case, the province of large-scale land development (including "new towns") is dominated by big industrial and commercial corporations and institutional investors. What's more, they're smarter now.

THE PROFIT PICTURE. In any substantial land development program, be it "new town" or not, profits are generated in several ways. The biggest

17

of these is the rapid capital appreciation that both the developed land and the buildings on it undergo. This is not only a source of profits; it may also be critical in determining the near-term financing capacity of the project. At the new town of Columbia, for example, the land was valued at three times its acquisition cost only three years after the project was started. This tidy boost not only secured the lender's initial exposure but also gave the developer, Jim Rouse, a strong refinancing position.

Moreover, since the project may be treated as a depreciable asset while it actually appreciates in value, a lot of this profit is tucked away from the bite of the IRS. The tax benefits come not only from deduction of development expenses, interest expense and depreciation of any income-producing properties. The proceeds from any land sales are taxable not at the corporate but at the capital gains rate, and the developer can keep a bigger chunk of the proceeds from operations in this way.

Corporate accounting procedures have not been an appropriate tool for explaining these sources of profitability, however, and a good deal of education has been going on in the corporate sector to close the "understanding gap." Such land development operations usually understate the project's financial potential considerably—which can be good or bad, depending on where you sit. The acquisition of property for development has to be recorded on the corporate books at cost, not at potential value, in the first place. So the real value of such property is usually far higher than the figures you see entered.

Moreover, the project's earnings reported on an annual basis are misleading. The project has to be evaluated on the basis of cash flows over its entire cycle, and since development costs in the start-up phases are very heavy, they usually lead to a misleadingly depressive picture of earnings potentials when you look at the picture strictly on an annual-earnings basis.

The corporate books also give a distorted picture of earnings through full-accrual accounting. This shows depreciation, although the real estate is usually rising in value and the tax savings don't get shown. Payments against principal also don't show up in conventional earnings statements, although they represent a substantial reduction in the overall debt of a project while its value is increasing.

Such bookkeeping treatment adds up to a substantial understatement of the project's actual value at any time, as well as its full profit potentials. This is usually just fine for the corporate investor, who's looking to shield his return and then to boost up the price of his stock when the earnings do start showing up in big reportable chunks in the later years. But to the extent that the orthodox financial boys failed to understand the technique in earlier days, it was sometimes difficult to get the front-end financing, or to get the stock analysts to sit still when the profits looked glum in the project's early years.

(It should be noted that it is also possible to *overstate* a project's value, and this is how a number of the big land-sales companies hiked up their gross sales curves and boosted their stock. On the installment-sales method, the full amount of the sale and related expenses was recorded after the first small down payment, while the actual income wasn't due to come in for anywhere from five to twenty years. At the time of this writing, however, substantial changes in the accounting practices of the land-development companies are under way, eliminating such bookkeeping, as the result of a study by the Accounting Principles Board of the American Institute of Certified Public Accountants.)

The basis of all such operations is, at any rate, land. Getting the right location is the key to rapid appreciation in value. To the extent that some of the larger-scale developments design and create a well-diversified, self-sustaining community, they create their own land values. Otherwise, the key to success in land development is the ability to anticipate the geographic trend of development and to buy land for development just in advance of that trend. If the location is right, the land (in a newly announced new town or in proximity to another developing area) rises dramatically in value.

One good example of how land prices can be affected in an area ripe for development is the story of the Dallas/Fort Worth Regional Airport's impact on land values in a ten-county area nearest this project. The airport, scheduled for opening in 1973, covers 16,400 acres and will have cost about $700 million to build. Studies by the regional Science Research Institute of Philadelphia for the North Central Texas Council of Governments show that the ten-county area directly affected by the airport will double in population in the next fifteen or twenty years, with 3.9 million of these 4.4 million people concentrated in Dallas County and Fort Worth's Tarrant County. By 1975 the airport will be serving 18 million passengers a year, handling 275,000 tons of cargo and employing 24,000 people directly. Its economic impact on the Dallas/Fort Worth area by 1975 is estimated at $636 million annually. By 1985, it will be handling 36 million passengers and a million tons of cargo and employing 40,000 to 50,000 people.

As a result of these projections, land prices soared from the time the firm airport boundaries were announced in 1968. This proved costly to the airport's own acquisition program, among other things. The site, originally planned at 18,300 acres for an estimated $21 million to $25 million, will cost more than $60 million for the scaled-down 16,400 acres. Most land within five miles of the site has also tripled in price and much of it has quadrupled and quintupled. One farmer sold a 100-acre tract for

$2,800 an acre to a speculator, who sold it eighteen months later for $10,000 an acre to a syndicate of ten investors. They waited for it to go up to $40,000 to $50,000 an acre within a year or so after the opening of the airport. While this is a price some choice tracts may reach, other land suitable for apartment development is bringing up to $20,000 an acre. And the whole area is booming: between 1969 and 1971, developers announced thirty-one major projects here, many of them big enough to qualify for the label "new towns," running into billions of dollars.

Land values in a developing area (whether a new town or not) are also affected beyond mere speculative rise in value by the population density and the mix and quality of residential, commercial and industrial uses. Thus the corporate investor can hike up land values further still by setting up the right mix of zoning and allowing both high population densities and certain nonresidential uses in well-planned iterrelationships. A combination of residential, commercial and industrial land uses attracts varied interests, each of whom is attracted by the complementary land use. Thus, an AAA credit will set up a store in the area because of the existence of a high-density, high-quality residential neighborhood; a family will move into the area attracted by the availability of shopping facilities and employment; and so on. This approach, boosting values for the overall mix, provides one rationale for the increase in master-planned developments of all sizes.

The one singular advantage of corporate financial strength is its capability to cut across the usual speculative pattern of suburban development. The entrepreneurial builder, short on bankroll and long on leverage, has to *follow* random, hedgehopping trends of surburban growth. He spots the right deal here, the fast opportunity there, as these reveal themselves to a close observer of randomly moving market forces, and he takes advantage of them. In so doing, he contributes to the unplanned pattern of urban growth and he never has a real assurance of tomorrow's market or his position in it.

But a developer with a big bankroll has enough muscle to blow the whistle on this whole process. By creating an entire planned community, he in effect brings the random-market process of development under his own control and can gather the profits from speculative rises in the cost of land into his own coffers. With good land and market planning, he can anticipate and create his own market values. By controlling the entire development process, including the financial structure (debt, equity, term, interest) and the timing of cash flows, he becomes the rational channeler and organizer of heretofore uncontrolled, speculative market forces usually responsible for a community's growth. In so doing, he also assures himself of his own position in such a market.

This is how it works, anyway, when the corporate cat knows what he is doing. Looking at the best examples of such development, you could say that such an investor awarely creates his own orderly universe in which he then operates. An entrepreneur-builder is, by contrast, the creature of a pretty chaotic universe randomly made by the sum of unaware actions, and his hallmark is that he has survived so well by second-guessing all the elements he must cope with.

Corporate involvement in large-scale development breaks down into two phases. In both phases, many of them have concentrated on land development alone — planning, grading, putting in streets, utility lines, greenbelts and golf courses — then sold the land to, or joint-ventured on development with, builders who put the housing product on it, usually within the constraints of a community concept established by the land developer.

The first phase can be characterized as a learning process, often expensive, about the nature of the marketing skills and financial planning that it takes to bring off a large project successfully. The second phase is seeing a broader participation by corporations in such projects, bolstered by the confidence gained of experience (their own and others') as well as (no small matter) the entry of the federal government into this field with welcome financial assistance and guarantees to help the big projects through their first lean years, when cash outlays of up to $60 million or more are often necessary with no prospect of immediate returns.

During the first phase, the impact of corporate giants in real estate was greatest in California, which accounted for a fifth of the U.S. population growth and homebuilding in the Sixties, and for the majority of new projects housing 20,000 or more people. Newhall Land & Farming Company started the multi-thousand-acre "new town" of Valencia. American Hawaiian Land Company broke ground on Westlake Village, another major bedroom "new town" in Southern California. Southern California Edison and Bechtel Corporation teamed up to produce a community for 15,000 residents on 3,000 acres called Calabasas Park, with a ten-year development plan costing $250 million and homes priced at an average of $75,000. The multi-thousand-acre new towns of Mission Viejo and Irvine sprang up and grew as Orange County, to the south of Los Angeles, became one of the nation's most rapidly growing counties.

Many manufacturing corporations began to develop their land in and around cities, a trend continuing to this day. One of the first major industrial factors to go this route was Chrysler. Long involved with real estate in company and dealership properties, the firm in 1967 formed a real estate subsidiary, and its realty holdings by the beginning of 1970 exceeded $310 million. One of its first major projects was a $100-million planned community for 20,000 people on a 1,687 acre tract in Troy, Michigan, originally acquired for a company headquarters building. Chrysler then quickly moved on to a 774-acre luxury housing project in the fashionable Detroit suburb of Bloomfield Hills, and with a whole string of other projects around the country, including townhouses, office buildings, student housing in California and Arizona, shopping centers, condominiums, and a ski resort in Montana headed by the late TV newsman Chet Huntley.

Edwin Homer, president of Chrysler Realty and the man responsible for its rapid growth, commenting on industrial corporations' entry into real estate, said: "We believe we are on the edge of a wave." And Chrysler, indeed, was in the lead. At the start of 1970, the parent company's non-automotive real estate investment accounted for about 30% of its business, and the percentage should grow as the realty subsidiary increases its assets to $1 billion by the end of the Seventies. Many of the company's developments are undertaken as joint ventures with other builders and developers. Ford Motor Company also ventured into the business, though with a slower start. In 1969, Ford bought 30% of a small West Coast factory housing outfit, Concept Environment, and provided it with a three-year credit line of $1.1 million, but unloaded its interest in the venture a year later in favor of concentrating on a 1,400-acre housing project in Dearborn.

Many other manufacturers were quick to learn that their industrial property can be vastly more valuable as developed real estate than corporate facilities. The lesson was not lost, for example, on the aerospace firm McDonnell-Douglas. Ailing from heavy reductions in defense contracts that plagued the California economy starting in 1969, McDonnell in the fall of 1971 announced it would build a $100-million office-hotel-convention center on 50 choice acres within the boundaries of the largest "new town" development in the country, Orange County's Irvine Ranch. The aircraft firm had leased the acreage from Irvine in 1961 for a research facility and exercised its option to buy in 1969, figuring to beef up with real estate development its fallen aircraft earnings. But the announcement of the project also brought news of a zoning fight, as Irvine's planners were none too pleased that the hotel project would sit right next to the carefully planned 4,000-acre Irvine Industrial Complex.

A number of the major utility companies have also moved into the housing field in and around the cities they service. Their goals are not just real estate profit but the preservation of their markets for services in the decaying areas of their cities. At the start of 1971, five builder-utilities had remodeled 2,800 units and built 669 homes, as well as having another 1,000 new units in the planning stages. Further extension of the utilities into this business has been a toss-up, however. The Securities and Exchange Commission ruled that such activity was not among the businesses permitted to utilities under the Public Utilities Holding Act of 1935. The 1970 ruling prompted Mississippi Power & Light to sell its housing interests, and Michigan Consolidated Gas fought to retain its ownership of six low-cost housing projects valued at $16.8 million. The major utilities — including AT&T, GT&E, Con Ed of New York, and Southern California Gas — accordingly organized a Utilities Housing Council to ease the regulatory strictures and encourage more utilities to move into housing.

The enactment of federal housing assistance legislation has inspired many corporations to sponsor low-income housing, of both the "for-profit" and "nonprofit" varieties, often working with religious and philanthropic groups. Typical of such projects is a 470-unit townhouse and apartment project in Wheaton, Illinois, an $8-million venture sponsored by the Franciscan nuns of that city. The sisters take particular pride that their project, housing both old people and a variety of moderate-income people, managed by a nonprofit corporation, will add to the community's tax base. The first units opened in 1972.

Starting with the late Sixties, corporations with large timber and mineral tracts also moved into land development and construction in a big way. Weyerhaeuser, owner of 3.5 million acres of timberlands, got into recreational land sales, bought land for a community of 30,000 people in Jacksonville, N.C., and bought three homebuilding and construction companies. Boise Cascade's parlay, even more dramatic (and eventually unhappy), will be discussed in a later chapter. Humble Oil converted 25,000 acres of oil and gas lands into plans for a new city, Clear Lake, on the outskirts of Houston, then moved on to a 50,000-acre residential-commercial-industrial complex on land it acquired near the new Houston airport. Standard Oil Company of California tested its entry into real estate with a joint venture on 800 acres of oil land in Huntington Beach, California, then set up a subsidiary, Chevron Land & Development, to work with the 250,000 acres of surplus Standard land.

The learning experience of the big land-rich corporations has often been painful, to be sure. Dazzled by dreams of vast dollars springing from land heretofore regarded only in the light of other raw-materials production, they often took extreme plunges into development without sufficient regard for market research, product planning, financial planning, or any of a dozen other critical elements that influence sales rates and cash flows. The problem of Leslie Salt Company, the nation's fourth-largest producer of salt, with its 4,500-acre Redwood Shores project on San Francisco Bay is an example.

Announced in 1963, the project was to cost $750-million and have a population of 60,000 by 1980. But by December of 1971, fewer than 400 housing units were built or started. The problems of marketing and financial planning had been compounded by the FHA and VA suspension of home loan guarantees on Redwood Shores housing in mid-1969 after a congressional subcommittee had criticized Leslie for its "inadequate" study of earthquake hazards at the project. The suspension lasted thirteen months, cutting severely into the project's marketing capability while carrying costs of the project ran to $50,000 a week.

After corporate debt ran up to $17 million (the company was also financing a new solar evaporation plant in Australia), and the company was only marginally in the black in 1971 after suffering losses of $758,000 on sales of $23 million in 1970, Leslie decided to bail out of the project. With $6 million in corporate debt due in 1973, there was no way to continue carrying the venture. Accordingly, a real estate subsidiary of Mobil Oil got into negotiations to buy not only Redwood Shores but Leslie's 38,000 acres of other salt-producing lands in the Bay area.

But many corporate real estate subsidiaries are prospering. Originally set up to sew up new markets for building products or construction materials, they often earn far higher rates of return on development than the parent corporations.The financial strength of the parent helps them to leverage their resources extremely well. It's not unusual for a major industrial company to get construction loans for its real estate sub at the prime rate, plus a modest compensating balance, and to get these sums in dramatic amounts — tens of millions of dollars — soley because of the relationship the parent corporation has with the banks. Hence, they can go for the longer term and can often work a variety of attractive land lease situations, subordinating their position to the permanent first mortgage. In second-home developments such land lease ventures can provide rates of return as high as 17% or 18%.

Railroads also got into real estate development. The Illinois Central developed a thousand acres outside New Orleans as an industrial park. The Union Pacific, with landholdings running to 900,000 acres, increased its activity promoting companies to build plants and warehouses along its tracks, then got into residential construction in Whittier, California. The Norfolk & Western went into the real estate business with three projects at once, one of them a $100 million residential and commercial development outside of Kansas City.

Here, we must acknowledge the role of the late, if dubiously great, Penn Central Railroad, in inspiring the entry of many corporations into real estate. Penn Central became one of the largest real estate and development companies in the United States and found this sphere of operations so profitable that it no doubt tried to wish away the fact that its primary business unfortunately remained railroading.

Even before the merger of the two railroads that became the Penn Central, they were involved in real estate in a big way. From 1957 to 1964 the New York Central made millions by selling surplus properties and then made history by developing the air rights to the Grand Central Terminal, with a rent income of $18.5 million yearly. The Pennsylvania Railroad had also become aware of the profit potentials in real estate, taking a quarter interest in Madison Square Garden Center, Inc., which directed development on and around Manhattan's old Pennsylvania Station. (Though the Penn Central is gone, the expertise that was responsible for packaging up the Madison Square Garden venture, as well as such projects as Century City in Los Angeles, lives on: Brooks, Harvey & Company, the New York real estate specialists who put these deals together, merged at the end of 1969 into Morgan Stanley & Company, an old-line investment banking house, to form a new realty subsidiary primed for bigger ventures by such direct access to Wall Street money.)

When Pennsy and the New York Central merged, the new company went on to develop such major properties as Chicago's Gateway Center, Philadelphia's Penn Center, Pittsburgh's Penn Central Park, and Washington's National Visitors Center. The railroad also bought three major real estate companies: Arvida in Florida, Great Southwest in Texas, and Macco in California, for a total cost of $88 million. When Penn Central's bubble burst at the beginning of the Seventies, the real estate holdings, though snarled in incredible tangles of accounting problems, were some of its most valuable assets.

A lot of big corporations also found themselves in real estate development for keeps after venturing into this area with the initial idea of expanding the market for their products. Reynolds Metals, in real estate for more than ten years, initially regarded its residential projects as a way to promote the uses of aluminum in construction. Alcoa, attracted for the same reasons, found itself engaged in some of the most ambitious real estate projects of all time. One of these, Century City, was started on a 180-acre tract in West Los Angeles formerly owned by Twentieth Century Fox. Originally conceived by William Zeckendorf, this "city within a city," when completed in the early Eighties, will include 12,000 residents, a giant shopping center, numerous high-rise office buildings, major hotels, and ABC's entertainment center with three theaters and a seven-level underground parking lot.

Westinghouse, thinking of setting up an "urban laboratory" for product and system testing, bought into real estate in 1966 with the acquisition of a Florida company, Coral Ridge Properties, which is developing the planned 10,400-acre community of Coral Springs northwest of Fort Lauderdale. Many other companies supplying goods and services to the construction industry also got into real estate as an extension of their activities. American-Standard was one. Ogden's real estate subsidiary, Ogden Development, was also formed to use the parent firm's plumbing, heating and air conditioning systems in construction.

The experience of the early large-scale developers and the "new town" builders has been, to be sure, mixed. U.S. Plywood-Champion Papers, which started with a single joint venture in 1960 and quickly mushroomed in one decade to a total of fifty-eight residential developments on the U.S. mainland and Hawaii, at one time had considerable problems showing profitability in such involvement before it brought the big Hawaiian-based builder, Lewers & Cooke, into its fold as a subsidiary in 1965. Gulf Oil's financial involvement in the new town of Reston, Virginia, stemmed from an original desire to build forty service stations and get a franchise for fuel-oil sales in a community designed for 80,000 people, but it got more than it bargained for. After an original guarantee of a $15 million loan for developer Robert Simon, Gulf had to take over the management of the project and spend many additional millions to keep the project afloat through its lean years of enormous cash drain with no inflow. Other excellently conceived new towns, like Westlake Village, found themselves with falling sales when the bottom fell out of the regional economy and the supply of high-income prospects dwindled. Westlake at one point had more than a year's production of unsold houses, about half of them in the $40,000 range and almost a fourth in the $50,000 range, plus over a two years' supply of custom-house lots. Like many other new-town communities, Westlake shifted its focus, reaching more of the market by building rental apartments, condominiums, and adding (where possible) mobile-home parks.

The first results of the staying power of capital are in, however, and the corporate cats and pundits who sold short on the movement to large-scale development are covering at a big loss. After years of red ink and some onerous cash binds, the prototype new town of Columbia, Maryland, and Reston showed profits in 1971. And they, along with such profit sweeties as Mission Viejo, have taught the industry many valuable lessons about the technology of viability in large-scale development, both in terms of financial planning and marketing skills.

Particularly aiding the corporate movement to large-scale development, however, has been the introduction of an increasingly ambitious program by the U.S. Department of Housing and Urban Development to provide financial assistance and guarantees for new-town financing to ease the early, critical years of such projects.

The federal commitment to a large program of new-town development for the nation began with the Housing and Urban Development Act of 1968. Congress recognized four types of "new towns" eligible for government aid: the freestanding town; the satellite (such as Columbia and Reston, near the Washington-Baltimore metropolitan areas); the "add-on," built on a nucleus of a small existing town; and the "new-town-in-town," a planned community built within or on the fringe of a major city. Under

Title IV of the act, HUD was authorized to issue loan guarantees to private developers of such communities. Backed by the credit of the government, developers could thus borrow long-term private capital through private debt placements or public offerings at considerably lower interest rates than would otherwise be possible. The guarantee under the 1968 act could be as much as $50 million for a single project, with a total of $250 million for all loan guarantees.

Congress expanded its new-town commitment in the Housing and Urban Development Act of 1970. Title VII of that law doubled the ceiling on loan guarantees to $500 million and extended the guarantee program to public agencies, such as New York State's Urban Development Corporation. Other assistance was also liberalized. HUD was enabled to issue loan guarantees covering all costs of acquiring and developing land for government-sponsored projects. The proceeds from guaranteed borrowings can be used for a broad range of new-town needs, such as schools and hospitals. And developers can even borrow money from the government to pay the interest on money borrowed without loan guarantees, for a period of up to fifteen years.

New communities approved by HUD, moreover, can receive priority for assistance under thirteen existing federal aid programs covering almost every kind of public facility, from waste-treatment plants and access roads to hospitals and neighborhood centers. And HUD can supplement these programs with additional grants. The maximum federal contribution to each "new town" can go as high as 80% of total costs. So, in addition to the $500 million in loan guarantees and the $240 million in loans for interest payments, hundreds of millions in other loans and grants can go into the new-town program.

With this sort of support, the decade of the Seventies may well see a boom in new-town development, as scores or even hundreds of such projects get under way. The results may surpass the recommended program of the 1969 National Commission on Urban Growth Policy, which suggested 100 new communities of 100,000 people each and 10 new communities of 1 million people each by the end of the century. At the end of 1971, HUD had approved six major new communities for development, and was expected to approve another nine to twelve by mid-1972, with the pace warming up thereafter.

Among the first projects to get HUD backing, Flower Mound New Town is right in the midst of the hotly booming Dallas/Fort Worth area, four miles away from the new regional airport, and was the brainchild of real estate pro Raymond Nasher (who also invested with Westinghouse in Fort Lincoln, a project for 16,000 people near Washington, D.C.). Other HUD guarantees are going for the new town of Maumelle, Arkansas, near

Little Rock, put together by insurance man James P. Odum. Park Forest South, near Chicago, has been assembled by Nathan Manilow, the developer of the original Park Forest (he brought Illinois Central Industries and U.S. Gypsum into the new venture, each as a 25% partner).

The new town of St. Charles, Maryland, located near both Reston and Columbia, was put together by developer James Wilson. Henry McKnight, a former state senator, has a stake in both the new town of Jonathan, Minnesota (built on the small existing town of Chaska), and the "new-town-in-town" of Cedar-Riverside, a 100-acre project near downtown Minneapolis. Jonathan also formed a separate building corporation for experimental low-cost housing, in partnership with Olin, Northern Natural Gas, Burlington Industries, and Stanford Research Institute.

At the conclusion of 1971 HUD also had under serious consideration a number of innovative approaches in new-town applications. One was from the father of America's new-town movement, Robert Simon, the original developer of Reston. Simon sought a $27 million loan guarantee to develop a new town called Riverton, located near Rochester, New York, up to 40% of whose projected 27,000 residents would be low- and moderate-income people.

HUD was also thinking of approving a $22 million loan guarantee for a freestanding new town to be developed by a black entrepreneur and whose population of 50,000 would be principally black. The project, charmingly named Soul City, is about forty miles from Durham, North Carolina. Two other groups were also talking to HUD about black-sponsored new towns for Alabama and South Carolina. And a public agency, New York's Urban Development Corporation, proposed HUD backing for two new communities in upstate New York: Amherst, near Buffalo, designed for 25,000 people; Lysander, near Syracuse, for 18,000.

Under the confidence-inspiring impetus of new-town planning, moreover, the entire corporate sector has already been pushed in the direction of larger real estate projects. Not all are "new towns"; some are smaller versions of good integrated planning, called planned unit developments (PUD's) for primary and recreational housing, apartments, condominiums, and commercial office space. But it is the larger project that is more attractive, because its profits are substantial enough to affect a corporation's earnings picture appreciably. As the front-end capital required for such projects is, to say the least, substantial, this trend puts the traditional entrepreneur-builders at a competitive disadvantage and has accelerated their "corporatization" by merger and joint venture to assure themselves a role in tomorrow's real estate picture.

Large-scale PUD projects are increasingly the norm for the increasing role of corporate money in development. Among such PUD projects is a

719-acre "apartment new town," the $120 million development in New Jersey called Twin Rivers, located halfway between New York and Philadelphia, formerly owned by American-Standard. Associated Developers of Kansas City is building a $150-million, 320-acre urban complex called Century 21 near the Dallas/Fort Worth Airport. Hunt Properties is developing a 3,950-acre apartment/commercial project called Dallas North, which will cost more than $532 million, exclusive of land, by the time it is completed in 1985.

New Century Town, a 650-acre project for 18,000 people north of Chicago, is a joint-venture effort of Sears, Roebuck; Marshall Field & Company; and Aetna Life & Casualty. Northridge Lakes, a 960-acre residential project near Milwaukee, is sponsored by Wisconsin's Kohl grocery chain. Aventura, a 785-acre, $700-million condominium project for 17,000 residents in Miami, is backed by three giants in real estate development: John Hancock Realty Development Corporation, which invested in seventy major projects between 1969 and 1971; Arlen Realty Development Corporation, which owns or controls properties worth $1 billion in thirty-three states; and Don-Mark Realty, a shopping center developer. Valley West, a 3,000-unit apartment project in San Jose, California, was partially financed by a stock offering to aid developer Hal H. Anderson's work. Metro Center, an 800-acre, $650 million urban development in Nashville, is sponsored by Aladdin Industries and R. C. Mathews Contractors.

Planned Unit Development (PUD) or new town, the basic trend is to large-scale development. Companies like Ford are now venturing in a big way: Ford started work in 1971 on a 2,360-acre project near Dearborn, Michigan. Westinghouse, an old veteran by now, has had good results with its first project, Coral Ridge Properties, and has entered into a joint venture with veteran builder Jim Deane (formerly of Deane Bros., the Occidental Oil subsidiary) to develop a third of the 20,000-acre Half Moon Bay project, south of San Francisco. What is more, the company was looking forward to an involvement in as many as eight or ten other large projects by 1975.

ITT-backed Levitt & Sons undertook a mammoth 100,000-acre (count 'em: 100,000 acres) preplanned community at the start of 1971 in Florida, situated midway between St. Augustine and Daytona, utilizing land acquired when ITT bought up Rayonier, a cellulose manufacturer with its own timber lands. The company expects $200 million in sales by 1980. Florida Gas has plans for a new town near Orlando. A consortium of thirty private companies has set up two subsidiaries to develop three "new towns" in or near Hartford, Connecticut. Even Gulf Oil, which lived through so many harrowing years nurturing Reston, thought it had learned enough about the business to announce its entry into other new-town development late in

1971. The roll of entrants into this business goes on and on, and notably includes many of the major commercial and investment banking firms, such as First National City Bank and Lazard Frères.

This extensive involvement in large-scale development does not exclude mobile-home parks. As more companies have realized that parks can command a return of 20% to 40% on equity, and with FHA financing available for such development, the parks, too, have been getting bigger, where availability of land zoning permits. One example is Tri-Palms Estates, a 400-acre park developed in Palm Springs, California by Mobilife Corporation, a subsidiary of DMH Corporation. United Utilities Corporation of Florida is developing a 983-acre park in Palm Beach County near Boca Raton. Both Deltona and General Development Corporation have gotten into mobile-home parks in a big way in Florida, along with a number of other companies. As the pressure for lower-income housing in the raft of large-scale projects floated in the Seventies increases, such mobile-home parks — and their cousins, the factory-manufactured homes — will have a substantial share in such projects.

Not that mobile-home parks are without their own marketing and management problems. They became too much of a good thing: overbuilt in areas where zoning permitted them; not permitted where needed most. They're tough to manage and keep full. Boise Cascade Building Corporation, which announced a program of 250 parks at an investment of $250 million through 1975, for example, ran into considerable problems by attempting to restrict site rentals only to purchasers of Boise Cascade-produced mobile homes. But, notwithstanding such specific difficulties, mobile home park development has proven very attractive because of the returns it makes possible and the large shelter market of moderate-income people to which it has access.

FINANCING OF CONSTRUCTION AND DEVELOPMENT

As large and various as the land development industry can be, it has been only one of the exciting areas in the real estate business. For while the major corporations were busy plotting out new subdivisions to conquer, an entire new financing industry was born to contribute its services in real estate. This is the large group of real estate investment trusts which came into being about 1969.

Financial services for the real estate industry are not the subject of this book. But the impact of the trusts on all aspects of realty development has been so profound, and their few years of existence have seen them diversify and grow so rapidly into a strong partner in much real estate activity that it would not be possible to understand real estate today without some accounting of their influence. For this reason, and because the trusts have certainly played a direct, dominant role in the forms of corporate and institutional action, as well as changing the entrepreneur-builder's universe completely, the small number of pages devoted to telling their story will repay the reader's attention. The stock price of the trusts sank to deep lows along with other housing issues in 1973 and early 1974 due to a projected decline in housing starts and accounting rules complications. But this group is with us to stay, in one form or another.

Construction and development lending can, as we have seen in Chapter 1, offer an excellent investment in periods of high interest rates: high profits and good security go hand in hand. This factor underlies the phenomenal growth of the trusts since 1968. What makes the REIT's even more attractive is the fact that, on meeting certain IRS provisions governing stock ownership and distribution of profits to shareholders, such lenders escape the corporate tax. The traditional lenders were quick to see the light and began sponsoring REIT's of their own by public underwritings. The REIT vehicle enabled them to get more capital to lend out on real estate, as well as broadening and complementing their other loan services, thus making them more flexible and more competitive.

The REIT was born in 1960, when Congress authorized flow-through tax treatment for earnings of trusts investing in real estate and mortgages. Trusts paying 90% or more of their earnings to shareholders as dividends are not taxed on these distributions. The underlying concept is exactly the same as for a mutual fund, the trusts being structured to let small investors share in the earnings of a professionally managed real estate portfolio.

Most of the early trusts became equity owners of income-producing properties. But two trusts, Continental Mortgage Investors and First Mortgage Investors, both publicly traded, took the lead in investing a major portion of their funds in construction and development loans. Still, the concept was slow to grow: by 1968 there were only about twenty trusts of all types, with total assets of only $200 million.

The real credit for starting the boom growth of REIT's belongs to the villain of 1968, tight money, which created an unbelievable demand for construction and development (C&D) loans at any price and propelled Wall Street into a recognition that the REIT vehicle was an ideal profit-making response to such a situation. The excellent performance records of Continental and First Mortgage Investors demonstrated the viability of the concept. But credit for actually starting the REIT boom must also go to a brilliant, young (then thirty-six years old) financial and real estate expert, Alan Smith, who in 1968, after months of articulately educating Wall Street in the concept of the mortgage-type REIT, sold a major underwriter on bringing out a $15 million issue establishing Smith's own REIT, Associated Mortgage Investors.

Wall Street had liked the idea but feared the REIT was a relatively complicated concept that the public markets would not understand. Until Smith did it, everyone said they believed the idea would fly, but no one wanted to be the first to take off with it. The activity of the ensuing four years speaks for itself, with Wall Street promoting practically everyone in the financial world who had enough energy to get out of bed in the morning to trundle their own REIT up the runway. The public went into REIT issues avidly because these offered an attractive combination of high dividends comparable to top bond yields (7% to 9%), plus the potential of growth and capital appreciation.

Kenneth D. Campbell, president of Audit Invesment Research, Inc., has chronicled the capital structures of the trusts,* including the C&D, the long-term mortgage and the equity trust varieties. They took off with a roar taking $1.6 billion of public capital, and accounting for 16% of all new issues, in 1970. In 1971 they were projected to absorb another $1.4 billion of public funds. In the first nine months of that year there were 31 offerings of REIT's totaling $980 million, and another $500-million worth were in registration. From 1968 to mid-1971 the industry had grown to 113 major REIT's with $4 billion in capital and $6.1 billion in assets.

Three types of REIT's sprang into existence, actually. By far the biggest group was the short-term (C&D) mortgage trusts. In addition to Continental Mortgage Investors, with $414 million in assets in 1971, and First Mortgage Investors, with $260 million in assets, it included Chase Manhattan Mortgage ($323 million in assets), Guardian Mortgage ($127 million), and Continental Illinois Realty ($114 million). The second group was the trusts specializing in long-term, or permanent mortgages, sponsored principally by the insurance companies who have been the traditional long-term lenders. The leading representatives of this group included Connecticut General ($212 million in assets), Diversified Mortgage ($158 million), Equitable Life ($146 million), MONY Mortgage ($131 million), and Northwestern Mutual ($102 million). The third group, forming the oldest stratum of realty trusts, was the equity REIT's, which buy and hold property for long-term appreciation. Among them were U.S. Realty Investments ($103 million in assets), Hubbard Real Estate Investments ($94 million), and B. F. Saul ($79 million).

The majority of REIT sponsors have been the mortgage bankers, insurance companies and one-bank holding companies. But a number of large developers, such as Lefrak, Larwin, Cousins, and U.S. Financial, have gone into one or another type of REIT. Lefrak was talking in 1971 about

---

* The Real Estate Trusts: The Newest Billionaires, 1971.

starting the biggest REIT of all — a $300 million giant. Larwin organized a trust to buy and hold income-producing properties by the parent firm. Cousins organized a trust placing the emphasis on short-term lending. A variety of other realty firms, some of them old-line, and investment banking firms, are directly in on REIT's. They include Brooks Harvey & Company (50%-owned by Morgan Stanley), Lazard Frères, and Cabot, Cabot & Forbes. Certain-Teed, an industrial company long associated with housing production and realty development as collateral ventures, was the first major industrial corporation to start its own REIT. Many major mortgage bankers like Sonneblick-Goldman have also sponsored trusts.

Such a rapid expansion of the REIT market was bound to have a setback. Spokesmen for the REIT industry began making warning noises early in 1971, to the effect that too many participants were moving in just for the ride, glutting the market and killing a good thing. The predicted setback came late in 1971 as trust issues took a beating on the stock market following reports of increased competition and lower earnings by some of the bigger REIT's, including Continental Mortgage. A period of consolidation set in, but the outlook was that although some tightening up was in order, the future remained bright for those trusts which had the ability to raise money at low rates in adverse conditions, as well as the ability to originate investments and the geographical diversity that would be necessary as competition continued to increase.

The C&D-type REIT's, in the hands of their shapers, became a brilliant mechanism to take advantage of the large construction and development market, which now amounts to more than $60 billion a year in volume (with $32 billion of this going into residential construction in 1971). By establishing a separate entity to handle the specialized C&D field, the corporate or institutional investor gets the leverage inherent in funding by public issue. The trust leverages its equity capital by borrowing and by subsequent issues of equity and debt, or commercial paper. The trust manager, or advisory entity, makes a fee of 1% to 1½% of total assets.

The sponsor staffs this entity with specialists having freedom of administrative action and entrepreneurial incentive to perform well. By making many relatively small investments, the trust can minimize its risk; the consequent rapid turnover is also the key to high profits and the easy liquidation of problems. The specialists staffing the trust advisory entity must be able to exercise excellent judgment in the selection of the builder-entrepreneurs to whom they make loans. They are the crucial element in the successful performance of the trust. But even in a tight bind, the trusts have displayed a resilience and safety. As a case in point, seven trusts had a total of $12.6 million in the ill-fated Four Seasons Nursing Centers of America operation when it went into bankruptcy. But all of the participating trusts came out OK. Having made good mortgage underwritings, they made money on the resale of the convalescent hospitals after foreclosing on them.

How has trusts' leveraging of capital worked? The REIT's did not make 8% or 8¾% thirty-year mortgages because it cost them 8% on their money to be competitive. This is roughly the rate the public expected on its money. On actual book value, the trusts actually had to pay closer to 10%. Plus, they needed about 1½% to operate. So, all in all, their cost of money was pretty high. They stayed competitive by borrowing at prime rate on credit lines and by selling commercial paper, making 3% to 4% above their own cost of money.

Now the mechanism of the public market would also kick in to leverage the equity. By some amorphous success, Wall Street or the investing public expects, as we have seen, a dividend of about 8%. A trust that has issued 10 shares at $10 each and earns $1 per share after operations thus finds that the value of each share appreciates to $12.50. The value of the 10 shares now rises to $125.00. Now the trust can float a secondary stock issue of another 10 shares at $12.50 per share. If it should again report earnings of 10%, when the public expects only 8%, the stock will go up in value again. This time, the per-share price would rise to $14.06 and the 20 shares would have a value of $281.25. The trust can now put out a third stock issue at $14.06 per share. And so it goes.

Such continued leveraging of course depends on the trust's ability to make a net return after all operating expenses that is higher than the dividend the public expects. In periods of tight credit, when the REIT's can lend at higher rates, the upward ride can be a good one. When lots of money is available and rates drop, the pyramid can fall.

On the investment side, the construction and realty market is large enough to absorb all the short-term capital the trusts can channel into it. In 1970, according to Ken Campbell, the trusts supplied $3.8 billion in C&D loans, certainly an impressive figure for so young an industry, but also showing how much room for growth remains in the market. If the trust industry is able to sustain its 15% annual growth rate through the Seventies, its capital should rise to $12.8 billion by 1980, and this means at least doubling its present market penetration.

In practical terms, however, the typical short-term trust faces an ongoing problem in placing loans at a continually expanding volume. The managements of such trusts have attacked the problem of loan production in a variety of ways. Many, as a result of their mortgage-banking background, have tried to build a network of correspondents consisting of other mortgage bankers, commercial banks and independent brokers. Those that have been sponsored by financial intermediaries (one-bank holding companies, insurance companies, etc.) look to their sponsor for direct or indirect availability of loans, though this often puts them in competition with their parent. A few trusts, such as Capital Mortgage Investments and Mortgage Investment Group, have chosen to originate loans directly with professional builder-developers, either on a regional or national level.

Most trusts tend to lend entirely or heavily in a given geographical area, for two reasons. The first is the ability to examine and evaluate projects close to the home office. The second is related to a greater ease in underwriting loans in a familiar area, thereby greatly reducing risk. Lien laws, foreclosure provisions and usury problems vary from state to state. Highly skilled professional C&D lenders possessing the experience necessary to do business successfully are uncommon.

As mentioned, many trusts have attempted to escape dependence on narrow geographical areas (to avoid volatile real estate cycles) by diversifying investments both by geography and venture type. Some work through networks of national correspondents; many others are buying "participations" in loans originated by other trusts. This can be risky, because control of management over the quality of the loan is weakened, but the advantages of broader diversification outweigh the risks. The REIT's have been learning to live together, as evidenced by their increased participation activity, instead of cutting their own and each other's throat, as in the early days, to achieve geographic diversification. It's not uncommon to see a New York trust originate an $8 million loan and sell half of it to a California institution, or as many as eleven trusts.

The initial portfolios of most of the "hot" trusts coming onto the market between 1969 and 1971 concentrated on C&D loans for the good reason that this was the only investment available with the higher-than-normal rates sufficient to attract the investing public. But with the growth of the REIT industry, we have seen a continuing evolution away from the pattern of the initial portfolio as the trusts have responded to a changing interest rate structure and increased competition by both diversification and specialization to broaden or assure their market position. Smaller trusts, devoted to one type of real estate only — such as hospitals, hotels, mobile-home parks — create a firm niche for themselves by the development of specialized multi-purpose services. These can also be viewed in the perspective of what is probably the industry's most significant trend in the long run — the evolution of the multipurpose trust.

This factor merits a closer look; to get to it, let us review briefly the present crop of trusts. An equity trust's income derives from property acquisitions and the related quality of the property income. The returns on such investment can run to 10% or slightly better (including equity build-up and return on equity). A C&D trust's performance is measured by overall yield obtained by the trust, giving consideration to the quality of the loan portfolio. In periods of high interest rates, C&D and related loans can be very profitable: in early 1970 C&D loans, usually the lowest-rate loans made by trusts, were going for $13\frac{1}{2}\%$, with "equity kickers" adding to profits. But, as we have seen, rates can drop and competition can rise. At least one insurance-sponsored trust was making construction loans in mid-1971 at a fixed yield of 9%, and 1971 and 1972 were definitely not good markets for equity kicker deals as money became more plentiful. The long-term mortgage trusts make their money on the loan yield as well as on the equity kickers they of course try to attach to such mortgages, to increase earnings down the line.

Actually, when a REIT talks about a long-term (or "permanent" in the parlance of the trade) loan it is usually not the same thing that an insurance or S&L lender means. "Long-term" loans in the trust lingo may often translate in the near future as three-year to five-year "permanent" loans with payments based on a twenty-year or twenty-five-year amortization table — in short, amortizing loans with a balloon payment. In a period of rapidly rising or unstable interest rates, combined with a chronic capital shortage, this solution permits a developer to build and then refinance or sell the project by permitting long-term capital to take on more of the characteristics of short-term capital. The permanent mortgage lender gets a piece of the developer's profits, in addition to the loan yield, as a condition of acceding to the deal. Needless to say, because of the risk such loans don't come cheap.

There is a wholly new type of trust coming to the fore. This is the hybrid trust, engaging in both short-term and long-term lending and a variety of related services. One of the problems with the establishing of hybrid trusts has been their relatively slow growth in earnings during their early years. The long-term rewards of equity-kicker loans (when these are made) don't show up in earnings immediately and the lower yields of long-term loans compare unfavorably with the higher yielding C&D loans placed by short-term trusts. Since the earnings of C&D trusts are higher in the first three years of a trust's activity, and since long-term loans as of 1971 were still often placed without kickers, the market favored the C&D-type trusts. But the hybrid trust could become the dominant factor in the REIT group by 1975.

Another way of looking at these emerging hybrid trusts is simply as development trusts. For they are barely shy of a direct role in development, controlling, as they do, the sources of interim and long-term financing for the builder and providing all the in-between financing services that become necessary. Essentially, a trust must remain a passive investor, but it will take a hefty "piece of the action" for providing such comprehensive financial services. The independent developer will thus increasingly find a strange bedfellow as his equity partner: his former lender. Looking for higher yields, these trusts will write long-term mortgages but will refinance them later. They give the developer more leverage going in, but at a heavy cost. A brief exposition of the trusts' actual latitude in real estate development will suffice.

There are four major forms of profit in real estate: (1) ordinary income from building and selling houses or apartments, or lending money; (2) cash flow; (3) capital gains; and (4) residual interests which may be reflected in refinancing at a later date. The loan-oriented trusts, following the law that says that a trust cannot hold property for sale in a trade business, stick solely to earning and reporting ordinary income. But the same trust law *does* give trustees the power to improve property for investment, and some of the newer trusts are buying and developing vacant property. In fact, it becomes observable that the equity-type trusts can be structured to take all three other kinds of profits as well as ordinary income — that is, they can do business across the board in real estate. This, as Kenneth Campbell has remarked, can be done especially through joint-venture arrangements which make it appear that the trust is a lender but is in reality the money partner providing funds in a loan format so that interest payments are deductible to the joint venture. Some trusts, like ASE-listed Kavanau have done much in this area, and this format will be increasingly common among REIT's.

Many of the trusts have already become incredibly sophisticated in the range of financial services they provide for developers, making the straightforward C&D loans look like the horseless carriage in the jet age. We encounter the jargon of high-powered finance in enumerating their lending activities: gap or standby commitments, wraparound second mortgages, subordinated land loans and sale-leasebacks, and takeout commitments on the permanent loan (definitions coming up shortly). The one common denominator in this trend is, however, the REIT's support of speculative development through many varieties of such financial packages; such assistance, of course, gives the developer more leverage, but he also pays a lot more. Rates are a function of risk and the leverage the developer tries to get. The REIT's that advance what amounts to the developer's own equity for a development venture will look for $12\frac{1}{2}\%$ or more on their money, not 8%.

Now, for example, REIT's don't qualify to do outright joint ventures with a real builder, but many of them will provide what amounts to 100% financing of a real estate venture by charging a very high rate on the "equity" portion of the loan. As an example, where a developer may need $1.5 million to handle a project, the trust could arrange a $1 million construction loan at, say, a 10% rate, and then also advance the remaining

$500,000 as a commercial loan at a so-called equity return rate that might range anywhere up to 30% or 50%. The return to the REIT is not broken out separately but is calculated as a combined weighted average return on the "mortgage" and "equity" loans. The advantage to the REIT is that it is doing this with all mortgage money; no equity money is involved. As of 1972, many banks were also starting to provide this kind of 100% financing for development.

A brief summary of a variety of basic types of REIT financing deals will lead us into a look at some of the fancier packages pushed by the flexible trusts as of 1972: (1) a standard construction loan given against a "takeout" (permanent mortgage) granted by a life insurance lender (trust interest rates are pretty much scaled upward from this type of loan); (2) subordinated land purchase leasebacks subject to a senior mortgage held by another party; (3) wraparound mortgage financing, a form of second-mortgage financing whereby the existing mortgage is assumed into the new, larger loan and where old interest rate is maintained on the unpaid portion of the original loan; (4) a "standing" loan (i.e., a non-amortizing mortgage, repayable in one lump sum, on a completed income-producing property) to a borrower who has no permanent takeout and who has no credit standing beyond the property pledged; (5) a standing loan to a borrower with a credit rating equivalent to a Moody Baa or Ba who has no permanent takeout; (6) long-term net bondable lease financing equivalent to 100% of certified property costs for Moody Baa or Ba credits (i.e., typical insurance company private placement net bondable lease financing); (7) an interim or bridge or construction loan which does not involve "warehousing and interim purchasing" as defined by the IRS; (8) standing loans on raw land; (9) junior mortgages (standing or amortizing, with or without collateral); (10) outright ownership of fee or leasehold income-producing property subject to mortgage debt held by others; (11) an investment in a partnership owning fee or leasehold income-producing property subject to mortgage debt held by others.

Now that we have ingested this tangle of lending formulas, let's take a few of the more prominent innovations in financing deals.

GAP FINANCING. Tightening up on their permanent mortgage commitments in face of economic uncertainties, the major long-term lenders have often in the past three years begun slapping the developer with a "holdback" on a loan. Where the income projection from a property to be developed is not guaranteed, the lender can "hold back" 10% to 20% of the mortgage until the income level is achieved. The loan less the holdback is a "floor loan." Enter the "gap commitment" in which a secondary lender finances the holdback. In one of several ways he provides the additional takeout so that the construction lender comes through with a loan equal to the maximum available in the takeout commitment. Some trusts will waive the holdback for an extra fee or provide a separate gap loan.

THE STANDBY COMMITMENT. Another approach, the "standby commitment," is an interim financing technique that completely bypasses permanent mortgage financing until the project is completed and can secure a long-term mortgage on favorable terms. A standby is a bankable commitment on the basis of which someone will make a loan when the project is built. It permits a project to be built without a permanent mortgage. One of many ways it is done: the trust in essence guarantees to purchase the project at the full value of the permanent loan and lease it back to the developer at the end of a term. To the construction lender such a commitment is as good as a permanent mortgage or takeout. When the builder rents up the project the trust goes into the mortgage market to arrange a permanent loan.

The mortgage banker Sonnenblick-Goldman Corporation, which acts as manager of the North American Mortgage Investors portfolio, is one of the outfits that works such standby deals. During 1971, for example, it issued a standby commitment for $1.5 million for one apartment project which, operating at a higher occupancy than projected when it was completed, enabled the developer to get a permanent mortgage of $1.6 million — or $100,000 more than the standby commitment. S-G also put together a similar standby deal for a $5.5 million office building in Beverly Hills. In both cases, the interim lender was a party other than the trust.

The standby gives the developer a means of getting his project built and establishing a stabilized rental income and operating history. He may resort to it when, say, venturing a luxury apartment project in an area with no history of such projects; the ordinary lender may refuse to make a loan based on a rent of 25 cents per square foot and will only offer an insufficient loan based on 20 cents per square foot rental. Or the builder may wish to get a standby if he expects permanent mortgage costs to drop in a year or so and has the hope of making a better deal down the line. He may also just want to leave himself flexible on his options. But all things considered, the standby is still a very risky way to go. It's a crapshoot. The developer takes the risk that he'll have to abide by very onerous terms if he is unable to arrange permanent financing and the issuer of the standby has to fund the loan. Such a standby is also costly: perhaps two points a year.

The term of the standby could run for eighteen to twenty-four months with a fee of 1% to 3% per annum payable at the time of commitment acceptance. In the twenty-fourth month of such an arrangement, the builder usually has the right to extend for an additional one or two six-month periods, with an additional fee of 1% to 1½% for each six-month extension. The amount of the standby loan is generally equal to slightly less than the expected end loan.

In the event the standby issuer has to fund the standby commitment, the issuer would discount the permanent loan amount at 95% to 98% of par. He would require an interest rate of 2% to 3% over prevailing long-term rates with the loan set at three to ten years (sometimes the amortization is based on a fifteen-year payout and the loan "balloons" at maturity). The object is to take 100% of cash flow, making the funding as unattractive as possible; and all of the project's cash flow would be applied to the payment of interest and the principal. Personal guarantees may be required if the loan is funded. Of course, the issuer of the standby must be acceptable to the construction lender or the standby is valueless. Some standby issuers require a participation in gross revenues as a condition of issuing the commitment.

Many banks and REIT's both issued standbys at 75% of the appraised valuation for a period of up to two years and funded the construction loan at an annual interest rate of 3 to 3½% over the prime, plus a front-end, one-time, nonrefundable fee of 1½ to 2 points per annum of the committed loan amount. At the end of two years, the construction loan could convert into a permanent loan for seven or eight years, with all of the project's cash flow applied to the interest and amortization of the loan. The loan can be prepaid with no penalty during the first two years; in the third year, at 104% (sometimes) of the unpaid loan principal; increasing thereafter by 1% a year to a maximum of 110% penalty.

Although the standby is risky to the developer, the trusts will make them because they're profitable. The trusts are allowed to take 10% of their income from "non-qualifying fees" (standbys), and they do so because this leverages their yield. The standby commitment puts up the trust's *credit,* not money. So it's a very profitable situation.

If the trust has to fund its commitment, there may be some problems, to be sure. But they're not problems of loss. As one mortgage banker observed: "It's a matter of gaining an extra yield for taking a prudent risk. For example, we arranged a standby for $1.5 million on a $2 million project in which the builder had $250,000 of his own capital. Our standby was for less than cost. We would have loved to get ownership. We could have made a profit at a 20% rent reduction and have made money on our $1.5 million." In another example, a trust put up a $5 million standby commitment on a luxury apartment project to which the developer had contributed $1.2 million equity. The project was successfully built and rented and a $5.5 million permanent or takeout loan was arranged for it. But if the trust had had to fund its commitment, it would have wound up owning a

$6.2 million project for $5 million — an attractive investment at that price.

WRAPAROUND FINANCING. How does the wraparound work? Assume a property worth $2 million was financed ten years ago with a first-mortgage loan of $1.5 million at an interest rate of 5% amortized over twenty years. Assume that present-day outstanding mortgage principal balance is $950,000 and that property is still worth $2 million. In this situation, a new 75% loan would come to $1.5 million and carry a new mortgage interest rate of, say, $8\frac{1}{2}$ or 9% per annum.

The wraparound lender making the property owner a loan of $1.5 million provides the owner with $550,000 of fresh capital. The new lender does not disturb the old first-mortgage loan; he takes over the payments of principal and interest on it, paying these out as he receives payments on the new mortgage from the land owner. In effect, the new lender advances $550,000 subject to the existing 5% mortgage.

Assuming the new lender charges 8% interest on the $1.5 million — or $120,000 — and pays the original mortgage (only 5% on $950,000 — or $47,500) — he retains for himself $72,500. This amounts to a return of 13.18% on his $550,000 investment. This investment is gradually reduced as the old first mortgage is amortized and the second mortgage gradually becomes the first mortgage. On or before the maturity date of the first mortgage, refinancing proceeds usually take out the wraparound lender. The benefit to the builder is $550,000 fresh cash, on better terms than available through a straight second mortgage, while retaining the advantageous terms of the old first mortgage.

SUBORDINATED LAND SALE-LEASEBACK. A wonderful device, this form of financing has the trusts buying the land under an existing or to-be-built project and then leasing it back to the owner or operator of the building against a set percentage of the tenant's gross annual revenues, generally including a provision for participating in any increases in the gross rents.

Everybody wins in such a deal, it appears. The major advantage of the leaseback to an owner/developer of an *existing* property is that it converts his nondepreciable land investment into cash. By selling the land, moreover, he can then deduct his land rental as standard business expense and improve his tax structure. For the developer who sells the land under a project still to be built, the subordinated sale-leaseback can reduce his equity requirement for the same project by as much as 66%, thus substantially increasing his leverage and improving the tax benefits on the venture. But this route also usually requires personal guarantees of the developer, and raises project breakeven. Relatively few projects will qualify, and those that do will be the larger ones. Most REIT's want a $500,000 minimum land buy.

The trusts fancy such deals, when they can get them. Although the leaseback carries some risk because it is subordinate to the first mortgage on a project, they can pick and choose really solid projects and make 10% to 12% a year net on the leaseback, avoiding all involvement in management, costs and taxes. With the built-in inflation hedge such deals have (an important consideration for the inflation-wary trusts), the growth in the return on this type of investment equals or exceeds the rate of inflation. Plus, they often get the benefit of the built-in capital gain, either through repurchase options exercisable by the developer in the future, at up to three times the trust's original cost, or by the reversion of the building to the trust.

One of the trusts dealing in subordinated sale-leaseback transactions on land under properties still to be developed, Boston-based Property Capital Trust has a most interesting approach. Its vice president, S. Douglas Weil, spelled out what such a deal could mean to a developer of a 312-unit apartment project with a first mortgage of $4 million. By capitalizing his $650,000 land cost at $950,000 and selling the land, then leasing it back at 12% per annum, plus 15% of gross rents over the initial rent roll, over a forty-year term (with three ten-year renewals), the developer lowers his overall front-end cash needs for the project from $1.4 million to $450,000. Accordingly, his computed return on investment rises from an original 15.8% to 23.8% and rises further still to 37.6% when the added tax shelter considerations are taken into account. Property Capital advises developers not to seek such leverage with them unless the project is so sound that risk seems inconceivable; the trust uses a joint-venture equity financing arrangement where it believes a greater risk exists.

Another trust, this one dealing with subordinated sale-leasebacks on existing properties, is Realty Income Trust. Realty Income was one of the REIT pioneers, opening its doors for business back in 1962. Under the presidency of Royal Little, the retired chairman of the large conglomerate Textron, it has innovated or been in the forefront with a number of trust approaches to real estate. Realty Income has, for example, bought the land under the new $25 million group of office buildings in Boston known as One, Two, and Three Center Plaza. After paying $2.5 million for the land, RIT leased it back to the owners on a twenty-five-year lease with seventy-four years of renewal options for $300,000 a year, or 12% net. In addition, the trust gets 10% of annual gross income over the initial rent roll of $4,250,000 — and in 1971 this brought RIT's overall return on investment to 14%. The owners have the option to repurchase the land in the 1980's for $7.5 million, three times the trust's initial cost.

RIT is also one of the trusts buying undeveloped land and selling it at a profit. The trust in 1971 owned a 50% interest in 1,500 acres of unimproved land in San Diego, for which it had paid $1,000 an acre. Early in 1971 it sold off, for $7,500 an acre, the first of eleven equal-sized parcels comprising the 1,500 acres. The purchaser, Amfac Properties, had options to buy the other ten parcels at the rate of one a year, and meanwhile pays rent and taxes on the rest of the 1,500 acres. Quite a deal. Although originally formed as an equity trust, RIT by 1971 was a combined equity and mortgage-type trust, with its investments almost equally divided between leaseholds or land (both developed and undeveloped) and buildings. One of its largest transactions in 1971 was a commitment to purchase and lease back $20 million worth of mobile home parks in California and Nevada.

COMBINATION LAND-INTERIM-PERMANENT LOAN PACKAGE. This very interesting approach to financing is calculated to work in favor of both the developer (by making it easy for him to build) and the trust (by hiking up its yield on loans and equity participation). There's a special sweetener in the deal to make the higher-than-market rate and the participation palatable to the developer. He pays the premium to get the package of land-interim-permanent financing — but when his project is built he has the option of converting to a lower-interest permanent mortgage loan from a third party. The "no-lock-in" feature makes the deal tempting: it becomes a good trade-off for the developer to pay a premium cost for a short time to get maximum front-money loans when he has the option to cut the premium costs short by converting to a cheaper first mortgage when his project is complete.

The trust wins either way. If the developer converts to a cheaper mortgage when the project is built, the REIT will still have made a premium on the money while it was working. The refinancing of the permanent mortgage also leverages the trust's remaining investment in the deal and frees up funds for reinvestment in another project. If the developer stays with the original package financing, the trust earns a premium on the ground rent and the project is no less attractive than it was originally.

The approach to real estate financing was announced by Mortgage Growth Investors in mid-1971. MGI, a new long-term mortgage trust turned all-purpose trust, was formed as a reorganization of Eastern Shopping Centers, Inc., with Cornelius C. Rose, Jr., as chairman and Lee Stanfield as president. Sonnenblick-Goldman Corporation, in addition to its duties as manager of North American Mortgage Investors, was also named as investment adviser to MGI.

Mr. Rose held great expectations for the structure of MGI's plan, seeing it as a means to raise and invest capital on terms which will achieve an attractive spread between the trust's cost of money and investment yields. The trust industry has, of course, been squeezed by the narrowing spread between long-term mortgage rates and the rates at which they borrow long-term funds. The spread has generally been too narrow to justify borrowing, so few long-term mortgage trusts have been able to increase earnings through debt securities. This is one reason in itself why the long-term trusts are pushing to transform themselves into the more flexible and more profitable hybrid-type trust. The trust's plan of full-range financing that allows the borrower to mortgage out and refinance a portion of the mortgage debt should be profitable enough to enable MGI to issue new equity at a premium over its book value (an indispensable condition to floating a public issue in the market successfully).

THE KANDY-KOLORED TANGERINE-FLAKE STREAMLINED BABY. Occasionally there arises a financing situation so specialized that it takes a highly flexible and knowledgeable REIT to package it up. Some of the hybrid trusts, resorting to every REIT lending/ownership device, offer as complete a financial package as possible, with the developer himself setting the circumstances. One example of such a specialized deal comes from Tom Gallagher, assistant vice president of Connecticut General Mortgage & Realty Investments. The deal isn't very complicated: it's a combination of construction and permanent financing with a permanent mortgage either in the form of a land purchase-leaseback plus leasehold mortgage or a direct investment in a partnership position plus a mortgage loan to the partnership. The particular situation arose when a developer needed to raise $2.75 million in cash for a blind bid on a choice piece of property within thirty days. Even if he could acquire the property, he did not plan to develop it for two years, since lower off-site improvement costs would be made possible in that time by the completion of adjacent developments. So, if he acquired the property, he would need $2.75 million cash and then have to carry it for two years. He got turned down by a life insurance lender and a savings institution before finding his ideal lender, the combination or hybrid trust.

The trust made him a complete deal. It gave him a land loan right away; it offered to close in ten days an amount sufficient to acquire the property for cash; it gave him a commitment for a construction loan available two years down the line. It offered a commitment to subordinate the land loan to permanent mortgage financing at completion of construction; or, under certain circumstances, to subordinate the land loan and convert it into a land purchase-leaseback, subordinated to permanent mortgage financing on the new project.

Note that the REIT works to a mutuality of interest by creating maximum equity value through leveraging the developer's position, at the same time leaving the door open for itself for a direct investment in a partnership position.

The trend to package financing among trusts was somewhat muddled by the emergence in early 1972 of the public real estate partnership as the "latest and hottest" in real estate. These flexible, large-scale realty syndication packages bypass some of the structural limitations of REIT's on direct development and dealing and may be more attractive to the investing public looking for a higher return; also, unlike REIT stock ownership, the limited partnership offers investors the advantage of direct pass-through of tax losses, providing handsome tax shelter. A great deal of attention was generated as of 1972 by the so-called "blind pool" public partnerships, which gave the syndicators the flexibility to act freely in all aspects of real estate, including development. Blind pools were sponsored by such organizations as Shareholders Capital, Carlsberg, Churchhill Fund, Grabb & Ellis, and Multi-Benefit Realty. (The blind pools have so far found their greatest application as buyers of built-for-sale apartments sold to them by builders.) But many of these were to go belly-up due to proposed changes in tax laws or to management problems. The trusts are sufficiently entrenched in the real estate industry by now, and have already evolved financing methods sophisticated enough to more than hold their own. For the late 1970s, many of the trusts (as subsidiary ventures of the banks and insurance companies) will emerge as the long-term owners of subsidized urban, high-density housing.

The stronger competition for higher earnings has been forcing the trusts into a more direct development or equity participation role. Hence the power of major financial support, assured lines of credit at lowest rates, and real estate expertise among REIT's, though balanced well between the institutional and financial investors, may tip toward commercial banks. Both the banks and the mortgage bankers have formed REIT's, but the mortgage bankers themselves have been largely bought up by the commercial banks.

The big First National City Bank, which until recently owned Advance Mortgage Company, one of the largest mortgage bankers, did not, so far as I know, sponsor a realty trust. But we do get a number of situations like that of First Union Bancorp, owner of a major Southeastern bank with offices in sixty-eight cities, which also owns Cameron-Brown, one of the larger mortgage bankers, which in turn serves as adviser to the REIT named after it. Crocker National Corporation, holding company for Crocker-Citizens National Bank with $6.2 billion assets, continued the acquisition trend late in 1971 by announcing plans to acquire Ralph C. Sutro Company, adviser to the $41 million Sutro Mortgage trust and one of the country's oldest and biggest mortgage bankers ($557 million in mortgage servicing).

Such combinations, the dual parental benefit for trusts of entry to the credit markets and significant loan-generating ability combined with extensive real estate expertise, can't help but tip the balance in favor of commercial banks in the long run. Outfits like Bank of America's trust will be major factors in specialized loan services with substantial equity participation.

HOMEBUILDING AND APARTMENT
CONSTRUCTION

The third, and perhaps the most important, area of corporate involvement in real estate is the homebuilding field. It is this activity, obviously, which puts the final housing product into place and thus supports on its thinly capitalized back both the vast financial service industries and land development projects which depend on the creation of the final housing product for their own existence.

Although thinly capitalized, these entrepreneurs control perhaps the dominant part of real estate investment opportunity in the nation by virtue of their talent. That is certainly leverage. It's a case of the entrepreneurial midget swinging the elephant of corporate cash by the tail. These fellows know that their ability makes or breaks the deals, so they put that talent to work only for a lion's share (say 50%) of the profits. No matter how hard the corporate and financial boys try to puzzle it out, they still haven't figured out a way to entirely squeeze out this vexing middleman who brings nothing but ability to the deal.

3

Inflation Shapes (Misshapes?) an Industry

In the gloom the gold gathers the
light against it.

—Ezra Pound

It is not possible to appreciate the problems and opportunities of real estate in general, and the ongoing evolution in the housing industry in particular, without taking into account the influence of inflation. Analyzing outward from this single datum of economic aberration, you find that it is responsible for virtually every significant phenomenon of the housing industry today, including, in a very basic way, the merger and acquisition trend itself.

It wouldn't be wrong to say that the industry's entire present environment can be viewed in some way as a direct consequence of the gnawing stable datum of inflation. This would include the forms of the industry's business organization, its myriad problems and solutions in the financial area, the availability and form of its markets and of products for these markets, its spectrum of opportunities, and its broad-sketch competitive characteristics. The inflationary rate for the overall economy hit a conservatively estimated 6% at the end of the Sixties — and do you remember those days just around the corner when all the pundits were predicting that it would moderate to an annual rate of 2% to 3% by 1973 or 1974? After seeing an officially acknowledged inflationary rate of 8.8%, we know better today. It appears that inflation is here to stay, barring fundamental changes in the economic system or its complete collapse. And there is always that uneasy suspicion that the figures we get on the current rate of inflation are purposely watered down. Remarked currency expert Dr. Franz Pick in 1973: "I don't trust the press because it caters to government propaganda. Do you attack the government's cost-of-living figures? The government says the cost of living went up $3\frac{1}{4}$% last year, but it was really 9%." Such comments tend to reinforce a general distrust of the validity of any economic statistics we are fed so often and have so little independent means to verify. One thing is sure, however. No matter what

47

the *average* rate of inflation in the overall economy, the inflation in housing and real estate has always been considerably more severe. Wildly climbing lumber prices, land, union labor, financing costs, etc., at the very least triple or quadruple its effects on the building industry. The impact of inflation has been disproportionately large and for this reason has been the dominant factor shaping that industry and will continue to be so.

Let's take a closer look at some of these effects. The housing industry essentially took form in the postwar period. The success of instruments developed to service that industry, including the private money market supplying funds for construction and long-term mortgages, was predicated on a low rate of inflation. Indeed, so long as the annual rate of inflation stayed at 1.5% or thereabouts, the industry was able to perform tolerably well. However, with the steady rise of inflation during the Sixties, capping in an annual rate of 6% at the end of the decade, a welter of disruptive crosscurrents was loosed, entirely ripping up and restructuring the industry. The nightmare of negative effects recurred in 1973 in a worsening spiral.

INFLATION'S EFFECT ON THE MORTGAGE MARKETS

Inflation pushed the general levels of interest rates progressively higher, with some wild spurts during the liquidity crisis of 1966–68. Housing had gone through contracyclical periods before this, heating up when the economy slowed down and interest rates fell. But the general rise in interest rates threatened to make housing an unattractive investment at any time. Limited interest ceilings of the thrift institutions, housing's main source of capital, ceased to be competitive with open-market rates, and housing faced a critical shortage of working and long-term capital as funds were sopped up by other sectors of the economy.

American Telephone & Telegraph's willingness to pay 8¾% plus warrants for additional stock to get $1.5 billion in its 1970 financing foray is representative of the corporate strength that the housing money market found itself competing with. There was no way for thrift institutions, paying interest rates of 6%, to keep up with the corporate sector. Moreover, they got into an even tighter bind. With short-term rates since 1965 frequently rising higher than long-term rates, they couldn't borrow short to lend long any more, and they were losing money on their existing long-term mortgage investments.

Despite the Administration's effort to bring the inflation to a slower pace in 1971 and 1972, the inflationary spiral's *long-term* effect has pretty much permanently disabled the private money-market structure serving housing. Although the savings-deposit flow of savings and loan associations was very large at the end of 1971 and the beginning of 1972, it sapped out again in fall 1973, indicating that funds available for mortgages from this source will be increasingly volatile in the future. Savings and loan associations may well become simply apartment lenders and consumer credit outlets in the future.

It is to the effects of inflation that we thus owe the massive governmental intervention in the private mortgage markets. Purists may differ, but the intervention amounts to a plain takeover of the housing money market function.

The federal government has done this directly and visibly by the creation and expansion of three super-institutions which act to establish a floor and a ceiling on mortgage rates and expand the availability of money for mortgage lending by establishing a broad secondary market for mortgages, pumping in subsidies to prevent mortgage interest rates from rising.

The organizations are Federal National Mortgage Association (FNMA), Government National Mortgage Association (GNMA), and Federal Home Loan Mortgage Corporation (FHLMC).

FNMA (now a private corporation traded on the New York Stock Exchange) and FHLMC were authorized by Congress in 1970 to operate a secondary market for conventional mortgages as well as for government-guaranteed FHA/VA mortgages, buying them up from lenders — the REIT's, mortgage bankers, commercial banks and thrift institutions — to facilitate the turnover of funds available for home mortgage lending. Their own capital they raise principally by selling long-term tax-exempt bond issues backed by government-guaranteed mortgages in the open-money market. FNMA is also the ultimate buyer of 60% of Sec. 235 mortgages and 95% of Sec. 236 mortgages, which are directly subsidized by the federal government. FNMA finally also entered into the market for conventional mortgages (which account for 80% of all mortgages) early in 1972, thus blanketing the spectrum, and its purchases were expected to run into billions in a short period. The bonds sold to finance such purchases may get less than a top-grade credit rating, since the "conventional" mortgages are not guaranteed by the government — but they could be, now that the government has gone so far.

GNMA's chief purpose has been to broaden the amount of money available for mortgage lending on government guaranteed middle- and low-income housing subsidy programs by overseeing the packaging of, and guaranteeing, a long-term "pass-through" security backed by bundles of government-backed mortgages. Mortgage banks, commercial banks and savings & loan associations package up the mortgages in pools of $2 million or more and sell a long-term, tax-exempt security, backed by these mortgages and guaranteed by GNMA, to large investors who previously haven't put their money into housing (principally pension and trust funds), as well as guaranteeing FNMA's bond issues and others of its own. GNMA guarantees the payment of principal and interest each month by the issuers to the holders of these securities, so there are no problems if individual mortgages in the pool backing the security are defaulted. The GNMA securities are the pass-through type in which the mortgage principal and interest payments are made into the private pool and passed through by the issuer to the holders.

GNMA has also become the government's chief home-finance support agency, buying up both subsidized and unsubsidized FHA/VA mortgages at prices favorable to the sponsors and reselling them at market prices (i.e., for less than it paid). The purchasers can be FNMA or the original sellers of the mortgages, who then package them up and sell them as a GNMA mortgage-backed security. The support program keeps the interest ceiling on FHA/VA mortgages down by providing a subsidized floor under mortgage prices.

The extent of GNMA's price support activity has had a strong impact. Some $1.15 billion was allocated for the support of government-subsidized mortgage prices in 1970, and another $685 million in 1971. GNMA's support role was dramatically expanded late in 1971, with the allocation of $2 billion by the Nixon Administration to provide price supports for the non-subsidized FHA/VA mortgage market on moderate-income homes, in order to keep the mortgage interest rate from rising beyond 7%.

The Federal Home Loan Mortgage Corporation, a creature of the Federal Home Loan Bank Board, also got off to a high-powered start in its first year of operation, authorized to buy $1 billion of federally guaranteed mortgages, and early in 1972 also extended its secondary-market operations to "conventional" mortgages. It also acts to prop up mortgage prices by the infusion of subsidies in order to keep mortgage interest rates down on FHA/VA loans.

In addition to the establishment of these agencies and their secondary-market and price-support operations, the government has increasingly acted through the Federal Home Loan Bank Board to give savings and loan associations more vigor in their mortgage lending. The programs range from granting subsidies on interest the S & L's pay in their own borrowings, to lowering of their liquidity requirements (thus freeing up more funds for mortgage lending), as well as permitting them to make loans up to 95% of a house's value.

Purists may differ, but in the broad view the federalization of housing's money market structure is already pretty complete. The future of the S&L's is to serve as little more than conduits in the long term for Home Loan

Bank advances, with the mortgage bankers acting as originators of loans for sale to FNMA-GNMA. With FNMA booming on the stock market, partly because it is permitted to leverage its equity far higher than other publicly traded companies, Wall Street also gains a strong interest in perpetuating this situation.

The federalized superstructure of the mortgage market took its final operating form in a period when the economy was sluggish and the Administration's anti-inflationary program stabilizing wages and prices went into effect. Lack of loan demand in the economy drove interest rates down: at the start of 1972 the prime rate dropped to 5%, and some banks dropped it to a historic eleven-year low of $4\frac{3}{4}$%. In such unusual conditions, the system worked fine. The S&L's became engorged with savings inflows and had plenty of money to lend for the first time in years. Other thrift institutions, the savings banks, also were in a good position.

But the test of this federalized mortgage apparatus, and the extent of its costs in subsidies, only becomes clear when the economy booms and competition for loanable funds sends interest rates shooting upward again, draining the deposits of thrift institutions as the money flees to higher yields elsewhere. The corporate sector has already demonstrated its willingness to pay whatever it has to for its capital, and when it roars back into the money markets to finance the large costs of the country's growing power needs and pollution cleanup as well as the further expansion of its industrial plant, the competition for money will be intense. The volatility of bank credit rates was again demonstrated as in 1973 most banks had heisted up their prime rate to an all-time record of 10%, surpassing U.S. Civil War rates, before dropping to $9\frac{1}{2}$% by the start of 1974.

The federalized mortgage superagencies have successfully learned how to tap the bond market for funds, thus gaining the means to compete with the corporate sector for money. The mortgage-backed securities floated by them — either the "pass-through" or bond-type obligations — are optimistically expected to eventually finance two-thirds to three-fourths of the nation's housing. But, irony of ironies, in a geared-up economy the superagencies paying competitive rates in the open-money market for their money will only create further competition for the hard-pressed thrift institutions, as savers switch from the limited interest ceilings of the S&L's to the higher-paying market instruments (or to the so-called wild-card certificates of deposit that commercial banks were authorized to issue in fall 1973). The S&Ls did experience some outflows late in 1973 but managed to maintain themselves as sources of mortgage funds into the start of 1974.

This federal super-apparatus can be regarded as very desirable because it pumps home financing to the average American and because it broadens housing production. But it is also regrettable that it institution-alizes the past and future effects of inflation, propping up with subsidies a level of finance costs no longer broadly supportable by the private market. By promoting the illusion of a satisfactory solution to the problem of hous-ing finance, such a setup also perpetuates basic economic distortions and makes them more costly for everyone in the long run. By steadily increasing its demands on the money market as the source of mortgage funds (and shifting away from the traditional source of S&L savings deposits), this apparatus also effectively raises the overall interest rate structure for the whole economy, thus only worsening inflation for everyone.

Other problems crop up too. FNMA found to its embarrassment early in 1972 that its role of upholding the mortgage market may not always be compatible with its objective of making a profit as a publicly traded com-pany. The clinker in the works is again inflation, which led to the formation of FNMA in the first place. The entity ran into trouble when the margin dwindled between the rapidly rising costs it pays for short-term money to finance mortgage purchases and the interest-rate earnings on those mort-gages. Government-assisted mortgage rates do not rise rapidly or much, as a matter of course. But short-term money rates can rise considerably in a short period of time. That's what happened along about March 1973 when it had to refuse commitments for two weeks on so-called twelve-month convertible standby mortgage commitments. The problem was only tem-porary but it gave pause for thought. Should inflation drive up rates sub-stantially across the board ahead of mortgages, Fannie May may have the choice of refusing to fulfill its function in order to protect itself on Wall Street. That's not much of a solution.

Just by the way, another development arising from all these federal mortgage market structure innovations: there are some strong signs that they may be adopted by housing's private sector. Preston Martin, leaving the Federal Home Loan Bank Board in November 1972, put his experience as reshaper of the S&L industry to good advantage. Setting up a private company, PMI Corporation of San Francisco, capitalized with an initial $25 million, he began promoting a security backed by solely conventional mortgages which would be guaranteed by his and other private companies and tradable on Wall Street. The idea is for his company to issue a security against pools of privately insured conventional mortgages, with PMI and others insuring the security over and above the insurance on loans. Such a security with private guarantees would be a new departure and may lead to a substantial secondary market in time. MGIC's Mortgage Corporation of Milwaukee has a similar concept in its collateral trust not issued against conventional mortgages. Significantly, Bill Ross, the president, is a former top FNMA man.

Table 3.1 Itemized Housing Expenditures Based on Median Housing Prices and Composite FHA Monthly Costs in Orange County, California

Item	1960	1970
Median selling price	$17,900.00	$33,800.00
10% down payment	$ 1,790.00	$ 3,380.00
30-year mortgage amount	$16,100.00	$30,420.00
Interest rate	5.0%	7.5%
Monthly mortgage payment (principal and interest)	$ 86.48	$ 212.70
Insurance	$ 2.44	$ 5.10
Real estate taxes	$ 27.50	$ 56.90
Subtotal	$ 116.42	$ 274.70
Heating and Utilities	$ 16.30	$ 21.59
Maintenance and Repairs	$ 8.82	$ 16.40
Total Monthly Expenditures	$ 141.54	$ 312.69
Minimum Necessary Monthly Income Based on FHA Requirement of Four Times Monthly Expenditure	$ 566.16	$ 1,250.00
Minimum Annual Income	$ 6,794.00	$15,010.00
Median County Income	$ 7,219.00	$10,700.00

Source: *FHA Area Trends:* Second Quarter 1970, *Fourth Quarter 1964; Tables for Investment Analysis*, Paul F. Wendt and Alan R. Cerf, published by the Center for Real Estate and Urban Economics, U.S. Berkeley 1966; Residential Research Report.

1970

New Single Family Home Price Range	No. of Units Offered For Sale	Percentage Distribution of Units	Required Income Needed For Purchase Of Units	Percentage Of Households In This Income Range
Under $15,000	–	–	$ 6,820	24.9
$15,000–17,499	–	–	$ 6,821– 7,950	6.8
$17,500–19,999	–	–	$ 7,951– 9,090	7.9
$20,000–24,999	318	2.7	$ 9,091–11,360	15.1
$25,000–29,999	3,172	26.6	$11,361–13,640	13.2
$30,000–34,999	3,245	27.3	$13,641–15,910	10.4
$35,000 & Over	5,170	43.4	$15,911+	21.7

Rising Costs of Housing in Orange County, California: Between 1960 and 1970 the median selling price of a home nearly doubled, rising from $17,900 to $33,800. In the same period, the *minimum* annual income required to purchase a home rose from $6,794 to $15,010. Note that in this time the median county income rose only to $10,700 from $7,219. Also note that with minimum annual income required to purchase the median home, only 10.4% of the county's households are qualified as purchasers, with 67.9% of households priced out of the market. Orange County has been regarded as one of the richest counties in per capita income in the nation.

INFLATION'S EFFECT ON THE CONSUMER

Inflation has steadily priced more people out of the market for new housing. Those who are able to afford it are steadily paying more and more money for less and less house. The actual effect of a 6% rate of inflation prevailing at the end of the Sixties is at least doubled in the housing and real estate field because of disproportionately high increases in the cost of land, as well as labor and financing costs, not to mention materials. Improved lot costs at the beginning of the Seventies were rising by 12% in cost per year. As a rough measure of what has been happening, the FHA figures for the average market price of new homesites went up from $1,035 in 1950 to $4,300 in 1969. Labor costs, rising at nearly two and a half times the rise in the cost of living in the last ten years, add considerably to the burden. The rise in the cost of financing, also rising steeply, went from an average monthly mortgage payment of $118 on an FHA home in 1965 to $212 in 1971 for a home of the same size.

Overall, the rise in the cost of housing has been exceeding the rise in the average American's income rather precipitously, and it looks like the answer is to increasingly shovel in large subsidies to close this gap. Between 1965 and 1970 alone, the average cost of buying and maintaining an average FHA-insured home increased by 78%, while the median income of Americans increased only 46%. The upshot is that prices keep rising and producers cut house size to keep them low. A $15,000 income once could buy a $50,000 house; in 1971 it qualified only for a $30,000 house located thirty miles out from the city on a tiny lot. (See Table 3.1.) In 1971, reported the U.S. Savings & Loan League, the median price of new homes again rose, going to $25,000 from $23,400 a year earlier. Only 3% of new homes were sold for $15,000; in 1964, the figure was 24%. Meanwhile, homes costing $35,000 or more rose to 22% of the total, up from 6% in 1964. In a twenty-year period from 1952 to 1972, the cost of a new home rose by 92%.

As a result of the cost spiral, fully half of America's population could not qualify to buy the cheapest nonsubsidized conventional home at the end of the Sixties. To provide for those who remained able to buy, builders have had to turn en masse to the production of very small units with high land density and to apartment construction. In 1971 only 56% of all housing started was composed of single-family units, but even this is a misleadingly high figure, because 30% of that 56% comprises mobile homes. Ownership housing with land is increasingly more compact, to combat rising prices. McKeon Construction Company revolutionized the industry by coming up with a "four-plex," a large structure with four living units, each sold separately as a condominium. High-density townhouses (800 to

1,400 square feet) and various other pint-size condominiums have to become the merchant builder's staple product if he is to serve the mass market. The severe acceleration of inflation as of 1973 squeezed even this market badly.

Price is king, and the marketing genius today is he who can deliver a home for $20,000 or less. And it takes genius, because such housing as of 1973 was nearly impossible to build because of rapidly rising costs. Grateful to buy at any price he can afford, the consumer gets at least one-third less house for his money than he did ten years ago. By shifting to higher land densities through the device of various departures from traditional single-family home ownership, the builders have been able to continue giving the consumer some environmental quality with their homes. But with the continuing rise in costs, this factor, along with the consumer's ownership ability, will be squeezed more.

Driving up the costs of housing dramatically, inflation has thus put the federal government on the road to an incredibly costly program of direct housing subsidies. The idea is to give with one hand what inflation has taken away with the other. But the subsidy program, although attractive to the building industry, has not met its objectives very well. Originally intended to provide housing for the nation's poor, the program increasingly finds as its beneficiaries the members of what we used to call the middle class, because housing costs have risen so fast. The problem of housing the poor remains a problem, while subsidization has already been costly for the American taxpayer.

The statistics on the federal government's support of housing through direct subsidies make interesting reading. As recently as 1965, the number of subsidized housing units ran to only about 70,000. Then, as tight money enveloped the housing industry and construction starts fell to dismal lows, the volume of directly subsidized units began mounting rapidly. They rose to 223,600 in 1969; to 467,500 in 1970; to 590,000 in 1971; and their number fell to about 350,000 in 1972 only because of tighter controls coming in the aftermath of abuses and scandals in the subsidy programs. As of 1971 housing subsidies still increased roughly tenfold over 1965. In 1971, the number of subsidized units *started* exceeded 25% of the total volume of conventional housing construction, compared with a microscopic 5% or thereabouts in 1965.

Presto, a brand new housing industry was born: the new patois is "government housing." Because this segment of housing has expanded so rapidly in such a short time, and has become institutionalized into our future, it changes the ballgame for the entire industry, becoming a highly important part of most entrepreneurial and corporate construction activity. Although the *form* of housing subsidies will probably change over time, shifting from subsidy of construction and financing to subsidy of the consumer direct, the basis large-scale approach to the subsidy of housing appears pretty much here to stay.

The most popular of the programs were those which provided mortgage-payment subsidies under FHA sections 235 and 236 for home owners and renters. These sections, written into the Housing Act of 1968 for families earning between $3,600 and $7,200 a year, subsidize up to all but 1% of the mortgage interest cost. The problem with these two programs alone, which account for about three-fourths of all government-assisted housing starts in 1972, is that they're not only expensive but inequitable.

The cost of such housing subsidies to the taxpayer was to run to $1.3 billion in 192 alone. As former HUD Secretary Romney observed in 1971, assuming the levels of subsidized starts are maintained and a total of 6 million subsidized units is completed by 1978, the government by that year will be paying at least $7.5 billion annually in subsidies. The cumulative costs of such subsidies over the life of the mortgages could thus amount to more than $200 billion.

It appears as of this writing that these programs will continue, however. The popular Sec. 235 and 236 programs were hit by the typical scandals attending subsidized construction programs, as various less than fully scrupulous entrepreneurs found ways of enlarging their profits at the expense of the families they were to house and of the taxpayer. Remodeled homes were sold at inflated prices; structural shortcuts abounded in newly constructed apartments and single-family homes. One investigation found that 25% of new subsidized houses, as well as 44% of existing homes purchased under the program, had serious structural defects.

The worst flaw of such programs, however, is that they arbitrarily subsidized some families in the purchase or rental of their housing, while others with identical incomes paid the full freight. Under the income criteria for the Sec. 235 and 236 programs, more than 23 million families are eligible for assistance. Thus, HUD officials have been the unhappy recipients of numerous letters from irate heads of household demanding to know why they should pay taxes to subsidize the family next door when their incomes are identical. When an income of $7,200 is regarded as "lower-income," it gets to be a problem to distribute the benefits equitably. All of this has led to the federal government's withdrawal from subsidized housing programs by late 1972 and early 1973. It was quite a flyer, and its effects linger on.

To avoid the scandals usually associated with "subsidized housing projects," the subsidy programs of the middle Seventies will probably be revised into the following politically more palatable format: direct subsidies of construction financing for builders who construct all housing in certain price rental ranges; cash allowances for "lower-income" people, enabling them to seek the housing of their choice in the open market. The latter aspect of this approach is opposed by organized builders because it takes the subsidy emphasis off new housing production alone, but it is supported by big-city mayors who would like to disperse their slum populations. The direct-allowance subsidy will, of course, add to real estate inflation by inflating rents charged by landlords. It appears to be the first major step, however, in reorienting the subsidy of housing from new production to the rehabilitation of city living.

What can one say about this broad five-year flyer, this abrupt, large-scale institutionalization of subsidies, whether in new production or in broadening the availability of all housing? One must, of course, be grateful for the creation of such an expanded profit opportunity. The program is indispensable to homebuilders, making possible the sale of large volumes of single-family housing. The subsidy program has also opened up lucrative opportunities for well-to-do investors in multifamily ownership and construction. Government-subsidized housing of one sort or another in the 1969–1972 period became one of Wall Street's hottest investment items via the limited partnership, offering handsome tax-shelter potentials in a variety of new construction and rehabilitation ventures. New Wall Street investment funds sprang up for long-term ownership of such projects, in order to maximize the tax benefits for their investors.

It should be noted, however, that a continuation of inflation in real estate values may well bring families with incomes higher than $7,200 into the fold of subsidized housing. We probably should not be too surprised to see this happen. The unfortunate effect of expanded housing subsidies is that they tend to institutionalize the past inflation of costs into the future, as is also the case with mortgage supports. The unfortunate aspect of this is that the consumer always loses ground in this inflationary process, since real estate is in itself an inflation hedge: even though he is subsidized he gets less for his money as costs continue to rise and outstrip his ability to pay. The only time such a trend is halted is when the rise in real income exceeds the rise in housing costs, and this probability is uncertain.

Projecting this trend over a long term, one could see subsidy programs growing to encompass all but the richest consumers. At the same time, as costs continue to rise beyond the consumer's ability to pay, the concept of private ownership of housing becomes obsolete and the dominant focus of subsidies in the long term shifts to rent supports as the ownership of increasingly costly property becomes concentrated in the hands of a relatively few large institutions who collect enormous subsidy as rent.

The only real beneficiaries in this long-term scenario, witting or unwitting, are the major financial institutions and the growing housing bureaucracy of the federal government. Inflation and its helpful handmaiden of subsidies could thus be viewed by an ungrateful churl as covert instruments for the displacement of the housing industry and its consumers from the private sector into centralized governmental control, not for any ultimate benefit to the consumer but for the safeguarding of real estate investment profits unsupportable by the private market and thus supported by the punitive taxation of the many for the benefit of the few.

In such a centralized, controlled environment only the largest companies will survive to develop real estate and construct housing. Thus, although the expanded profit opportunities made possible by subsidization of housing in the Seventies are certainly welcome, it is curious to see the nation's host of small builder-entrepreneurs abandon their concern for their long-term survival for the sake of short-term profit as they cheer on the very programs that hasten their own demise. The rise of a publicly held housing industry, working on the ferocious treadmill of continually growing annual profit goals to support its stock-market prices, will hasten the push for housing subsidies so as to broaden the housing market to be developed. Another irony of heavy housing subsidies in the short term is that they lead to overbuilding and plunge the housing industry into a recession.

INFLATION'S EFFECT ON THE COMPOSITION OF THE BUILDING INDUSTRY

Inflation, by promoting a general credit scarcity, has served to restrict the field of operations to the better-capitalized builders. By continually forcing upward the builder's equity capital requirement as a condition of getting credit, and by narrowing profit margins, inflationary forces are shaking out the small builder and propelling a wave of consolidations and mergers in the industry.

Developers Crow, Pope and Carter estimated that within twenty years the construction industry will be dominated by twenty-five giant national firms. Though this is pretty concentrated, the trend is in this direction. Some two hundred major firms will be taking the majority of the business by 1980, with the number of developers building less than one hundred units a year shrinking to perhaps ten thousand.

Inflation, by encouraging financial institutions to seek higher yields, has encouraged their entry into a more direct role in realty. The trend started and grew rapidly in the tight-money days of 1968, when equity participations (popularly known as "equity kickers" or "piece-of-the-action lending") became the vogue. The basic formula had the lender requiring the developer to fork over some part of the income from the property to be developed as a condition of making the interim or long-term loan for it. Starting with this inroad on the developer's equity return after years of living on the parched dole of fixed-interest yields, the financial institutions have increasingly sought what amounts to a direct development role, thus theoretically setting up a bypass of the builder-developer's function.

The "piece-of-the-action" phenomenon has gone through an entire history between 1968, when it first appeared, and 1972. It was pioneered by the major insurance firms making loans on apartment development, but quickly spread to REIT's, banks, and other lenders. As recently as the end of 1970, a survey of 118 life insurance lenders showed that for half to two-thirds of them participation lending had become a way of life. Yet by mid-1971 a declining demand for loanable funds began making it difficult for the leading insurance lenders to get the piece-of-the-action provision written into the apartment loan. Since most such participations were tied to rent-roll increases, moreover, peaking rental rates in a tight economy, and later the appearance of controlled rents, made the value of such kickers questionable.

Moreover, the piece-of-the-action apartment lenders found an unwelcome new competitor entering their ranks, and one which was often willing to lend without a participation clause. This is the big group of 2,063 federally chartered savings and loan associations, who have been largely uninvolved in piece-of-the-action deals on apartments and whose volume of lending on apartments is projected to nearly triple from 1970 to 1975, rising from $10.8 billion to $31.7 billion. The S&L's, aided by a raft of liberalizing regulations from the Federal Home Loan Bank Board, are not only responding to a changing market mix but appear to be actively seeking a larger share of the more profitable apartment-loan market to compensate for the dwindling profitability of single-family residential mortgage lending. Their investment in housing mortgages will have fallen from 69.58% of assets in 1970 to 46.65% by mid-decade. Whether the S&L's engage in piece-of-the-action mortgaging or not, the overall influx of more money into apartments dampens this trend.

The emergence of federal legislation to limit tax shelter benefits solely to income arising from apartment development early in 1973, of course, presented a further hazard. With the possibility that such "tax reforms" could be effected by 1974, apartment development could take entirely unexpected forms in the future. Production could be lowered, and with the attendant scarcity, the values of existing income properties could rise dramatically. The combination of greater scarcity and higher rents will put more pressure on the federal government than ever to shovel in *direct* subsidies to provide housing. Through tax "reforms," meanwhile, the individual investors will have been driven out of the field altogether, and the plum of subsidized multifamily development will go primarily to the financial institutions.

Although their popularity has cooled in apartment lending, equity participations do continue in the industry, particularly on high-ratio loans. Often, only the name has changed, as a lender drops "participation" but makes loans with deeper discounts. Participations remain prevalent in commercial construction. The slack-off (though it may not be long-term) has been welcomed by multifamily builders, who got so mad at piece-of-the-action lending, regarding it as little short of extortion in a tight economic situation, that in two successive years they backed legislation to outlaw it. Equity kickers remain widespread among REIT's on subordinated sale-leasebacks and on commercial liens. Some lenders, while abandoning the kicker, have come up with a more salable if not more palatable device. To guard against interest-rate fluctuations that might catch them losing money on a long-term loan, they are putting early due dates on their long-term loans without kickers. For instance, a typical $1 million apartment loan at $8\frac{1}{4}\%$ for thirty years might have a fifteen-year due date. This lets the lender get his money back (unpaid principal still $775,000) and reinvest it at 1987 interest rates if he made the loan in 1972. The advantage to the borrower in this situation exists only if rates are lower in the 1987 mortgage market than they were on his original mortgage. If they're down, he can pay off his loan without a penalty and get a lower-rate loan. If they're up (and who doubts they would be?) he has to refinance at a costlier rate.

The most widely used formula in piece-of-the-action lending, pioneered by Metropolitan Life, permitted the lender to take 10% of any increase over a project's initial income as a condition of making a loan. Another approach sought a fixed percentage, say 2% or 3%, of a gross rental income. Some lenders offered an option of a two-rate structure: one rate on an interest-only mortgage, or another, lower rate with a participation provision. Other lenders asked a percentage of gross rental only after a certain level of occupancy is attained, or they set up a split rate: a low rate on the initial level of gross receipts and a higher rate on receipts above that.

Piece-of-the-action lending fluctuates with the availability of credit, but it has represented a first step of financial institutions toward a more direct role in real estate profits. The savings and loans, for example, may have found a way of getting around the prohibition on their own direct investment in real estate and development by the vehicle of the so-called service companies they are permitted to establish as subsidiaries. The service companies are one of their major bids to become more flexible and viable financial institutions as a response to inflationary times, and have broader powers than the S&L's themselves.

The exploration of the possibilities of "service corporations" has been most intensive among the West Coast S&L's, and California's seventy service companies in 1971 were breaking new ground in the areas of mortgage banking and direct real estate development. One of the biggest, Alcal, lends to builders, sells blocks of government-backed mortgages and handles both interim and permanent financing for apartment projects. Another S&L-backed firm, Inner City Housing Corporation, was organized to build low- and middle-income housing in Los Angeles.

Under certain conditions, the service companies have an opened door to equity lending, with its lucrative lease-buyback and joint-venture dealing, which has been the special preserve of the insurance companies and mortgage bankers. By setting up service subsidiaries, the S&L's can (on meeting certain provisions) buy and improve land, build housing for sale or rental, and develop mobile-home sites. Given their long experience in the housing field, and their ready access to local entrepreneurs for purposes of joint venture, their competitive potential has become worrisome to builders.

The National Association of Home Builders, for one, was concerned about proposed expanded powers of the S&L's to invest directly in and develop residential property. In congressional testimony, President John A. Stastny opposed Sec. 104 of the proposed Housing Institutions Modernization Act of 1971, which would permit S&L's to get into the business of warehousing land and thus into competition with builders. "We would hope," he added, "that any expansion of the power to finance the acquisition and development of land would carry with it safeguards against S&L's favoring a service corporation in which they have an interest." Early in 1972 the Mortgage Bankers Association also leapt into the opposition to this development, as its executive vice president, Dr. Oliver H. Jones, lashed out against extensive federal restructuring of the private money and construction markets.

Aside from the S&L's, the major banks themselves also began moving into a direct equity role in development with the assistance of the one-bank holding company vehicle in the early 1970s. The One-Bank Holding Company Act opened the door for banks to set up any number of subsidiaries within given financial service areas, thus permitting them to form market-sophisticated real estate services such as syndications and to develop properties by joint venture with builders for clients. One example of a syndication organization operated by a one-bank holding company is Beverly Hills Bancorporation's Western Diversified Investors, which encountered difficulties late in 1973. Other institutions, such as the Bank of America, are in the lead with the development not only of client-oriented realty services but also "comprehensive financial services" for the builder-developer, taking a portion of the equity in every deal for the tailored provision of the builder's interim and long-term financial requirements.

This trend of financial institutions' entry into an equity role in development will grow, representing as it does the further displacement of the building and real estate industry toward the loci of economic power. This gradual collapsing of the lender's and the builder's functions is, as has been indicated, an outgrowth of the financial institutions' concern that the conventional lending practices of the old days are no longer sufficiently profitable in themselves because of inflation's toll. Impolitic but close to truth was the public comment of one major banker in real estate who told his builder audience: "We frankly don't need you."

The consolation for the entrepreneurial builder in such a situation is that his joint-venture opportunities today are more ample than ever before, as lenders, mortgage bankers and other investors now swing with real estate on an equity instead of a debt basis and search for the needed talent to handle their construction. Since such talent is always in short supply, it is the able builder's greatest source of leverage.

Inflation is also indirectly responsible for strengthening and consolidating the financial institutions' control of housing and real estate in yet another way. The mortgage banking industry itself has undergone a strong merger movement in the period 1968-71. The acquirees have been principally the major commercial banks, acting through the vehicle of the one-bank holding company.

The general rise in interest rates that has made the private housing money market basically noncompetitive with the open money market has been long-term and gradual. Within the long-term pattern, however, a boom-bust cycle has been operating. When the economy goes into a slump, interest rates come down. This enables housing to compete for financing, and the housing industry and all the institutions that serve it start to boom. When the economy, heated up by housing activity, comes out of the slump, housing caves in because interest rates rise too high again. The pundits call this contracyclical economic behavior.

The earnings of commercial banks are themselves subject to this cyclical behavior. They would slide when the economy went into the slump and banks' interest rates came down. But in such periods the mortgage banking firms, servicing a revived construction industry, would make handsome profits. So the banks went after the mortgage bankers, needing their high earnings capacity to even out their cyclical earnings patterns. The One-Bank Holding Company Act, originally envisaged as a barrier against the extension of bank control over American industry, effectively turned out to be an open door to banks' entry into virtually every type of financial service business heretofore prohibited to them. (Alas, Wright Patman!)

Approximately the top twenty mortgage banking firms by volume of mortgage servicing, representing about 25% to 35% of total industry volume, have been absorbed by the biggest commercial banks between 1968 and 1971, but savings banks have also made a number of acquisitions.

The uninvolved observer might note an interesting relationship here: since such mortgage banking firms originate and service a large proportion, if not the majority, of government-subsidized and government-guaranteed mortgages, they could be regarded as one of the funnels between the profit concerns of the major financial institutions and the levels of housing subsidies legislated by the housing bureaucracy of the federal government.

And it looks as if the commercial banks may come into a more dominating role than ever, judging by the proposed legislation that President Nixon submitted to Congress in 1973 to change the financial structure of the housing industry. Based on the 1971 Hunt Commission's report, Nixon's proposals would, among other things, eliminate the interest rate differential offered by the savings and loans associations and equalize it with the interest on time and savings deposits offered by commercial banks. Over a five and a half year period, moreover, all interest ceilings would be removed and all financial intermediaries could pay whatever rates the market dictates. The ostensible purpose of these proposed reforms is to broaden the flow of money into housing, an accommodation to the further ravages of inflation. However, an inevitable by-product will also be the effectual elimination of the savings and loans from the housing business, because, with the above proposals, they would be muscled out and their deposit structures siphoned off by the much larger commercial banks. It looks like the big boys have decided that they want the business. Indeed, other elements of Nixon's proposed reforms would largely divert the savings and loans into the consumer finance business.

Inflation has played a strong, if undeclared role in propelling the corporate sector into real estate development, for two reasons. The first is that the housing industry itself is, relatively speaking, an underdeveloped market in the U.S. economy and extraordinarily high rates of sales and earnings are possible in it. The second is that real estate, because it is a commodity fixed in quantity, tends to rise in value faster than inflation can eat away that value, and thus serves as a good hedge.

Inflation, scaring hell out of man-in-the-street investors, has herded them in droves into real estate, via participation in public real estate partnerships and stock ownership in real estate investment trusts. The REIT's were discussed in the last chapter; the impact of the partnerships can be summarized briefly. Much of this glamor had worn off in the gloomy stock market of late 1973, and because of the uncertainty about further tax "reforms." But the trend in big syndications was substantial enough up to early 1973 to be reviewed briefly.

The popularity of real estate syndications was pretty much localized to the West Coast and to a few big New York operators until 1970, when nosediving mutual funds and fancy real estate multiples brought them with a bang to Wall Street.

Certain refinements in the concept portended both a far more flexible and a far broader application of the syndication vehicle to real estate investment, along with a distribution of limited partnership interests in such ventures on perhaps as broad a scale as that of common-stock ownership. The first of the refinements was the development of the "blind pool" realty syndications which, instead of being raised for a specific real estate project, give the general partner freedom to invest in virtually any type of real estate venture on a debt or equity basis. The second was the development of freely transferable limited partnership interests for realty syndications, eliminating the traditional disadvantage of the nonliquid limited partnership interest, and perhaps foreshadowing the rise of a speculative market in syndication-type securities. With such a large interstate market for real estate and real estate securities shaping up, California Congressman Barry Goldwater, Jr., early in 1972 drafted legislation to create an interstate Real Estate Commission, as the industry's own equivalent of the Securities and Exchange Commission.

It appeared that a national market for real estate syndications was shaping up very swiftly. In April 1972 the National Association of Securities Dealers proposed a broad new set of rules for syndications that would be honored by all securities dealers. Shortly thereafter the Midwest Securities Commissioners Association proposed its own set of new rules. Then the Securities and Exchange Commission, about that time, also appointed an advisory committee on real estate securities. This group recommended that the two other groups come up with a single set of rules. By early 1973 a single set of rules had been substantially hammered out; commissioners of forty-nine states (only New York was still a holdout) were to join in adopting them. The new rules open the forty-nine states to blind pool partnerships.

The transferable partnership interests bear explanation. Normally the limited partners in a syndication are locked in with an interest that may not be transferred without the consent of the general partner under the limited partnership laws of most states. The new concept, pioneered at the end of 1969 by two old New York City real estate pros, Harry B. Helmsley and Irving Schneider, gets around the transferability barrier by designating one man as the limited partner and empowering him to make pro rata distributions of funds to holders of so-called limited partnership participation interests. The certificates for the participation interests are freely transferable, and brokerage firms can make markets in them.

For their part, blind pool partnerships as of 1972 had the potential to become both a major source of real estate financing and a major purchaser of income-producing real estate. Thus, they were in a position to strongly influence the type and quality and cost of housing constructed — in effect shaping the environment — by their lending and purchasing criteria. Their income and leverage requirements likewise had the potential to set a dominant tone for the conduct of the development business. The principal role of these partnerships to date is as purchasers of apartments constructed by the growing number of publicly held builders seeking bookable earnings. In the old days, before developers began going public or merging, they would hold income-producing properties corporately or personally for tax-shelter purposes. But with reportable earnings taking on new importance, such properties are now sold off; the blind pool partnerships, along with some real estate trusts, are filling the gap as the buyers. Their existence also has encouraged greater development of income-producing properties such as apartments, though with 1973 ushering in proposals to remove tax advantages from such development, it was unclear what direction they would take.

The partnerships have sought the greatest leverage possible to get the biggest write-off on the funds contributed by limited partners. They built this leverage into each deal through first and second mortgages and subordinated land-lease arrangements. The 1972 accounting reforms crimped their style, but here's how the deals used to work. The builder could get a high selling price, thus reporting high profits to the satisfaction of stockholders or corporate parents, but most of all his actual profit was tied up in not very liquid second mortgages, or all-inclusive trust deeds, as they're called. Providing only a trickle of a cash flow in the first few years after a project is sold, such arrangements were very profitable on paper because of the high sales price but left the expanding builder with a continuing shortage of working capital. The builders selling to syndication groups ran faster and faster to keep up, frequently seeking new working capital by debt or equity issues, and developing more and more highly leveraged apartment complexes in already saturated or marginal market areas.

The builders' obligations might not end with the sale of the complex, either. As a condition of the sale, they frequently agreed to guarantee a cash return of 5% to 8% to the limited partnership over a period of three to five years or longer, as well as managing the property for the partnership group. Sometimes the money the developer received as the cash down payment went right into a reserve fund to guarantee the project's return to the investors, leaving the developer extremely tight for working capital. Developers began reacting to this squeeze by refusing to guarantee the income flow to the buyers or by shortening the guarantee period. The Securities and Exchange Commission was partly responsible for this development. In 1972 it began moving toward a more conservative interpretation of profit reporting on sales of income-producing properties, specifying that profits may not be recorded until the actual risks of ownership have "substantially" passed to the buyer. The advent of this policy caused some developers such as Leadership Housing Systems to voluntarily restate their 1971 earnings.

As the broader syndication market was crystallizing, with a number of public pool partnerships appearing in 1971 and 1972, the majority of Wall Street investment banking firms also got extensively involved in the more conventional syndications for the development of federally subsidized apartment housing, with the well-to-do individual investor clients as limited partners.

Such ventures, principally Sec. 236 apartment construction but also some inner-city rehabilitation projects, offer the investor little actual cash flow. But they are structured as a gold mine of tax-shelter potentials because of this direct pass-through of tax losses, and they offer the further benefit of freeing the limited partners from any liability for the mortgage obligation on the project. Limited partnership interests purchased by the individual investor in a given project are structured to offer him an optional package of tax shelter, depending on his tax bracket or in the type of project he invests in. Thus, depending on the investor's tax bracket, his actual return on investment can range from 15% or 20% to as much as 55% or 60%, with the federal government holding the bag on the mortgage if the project folds.

From 1966 onward, the big investment banking firms all became aware of the profit potentials of real estate, as signified by their formulation of sophisticated real estate departments to actively pursue opportunities in this field. As of 1970 and 1971, "government housing" became an important subdepartment for many of these firms. Eastman Dillon, Union Securities & Company (now Blyth Eastman Dillon & Company) went so far as to start up a full-fledged subsidiary, Eastman Dillon Housing Services, devoted just to providing investment services for federally subsidized housing.

Whether government housing or the more open-ended syndications, the matter for concern here is that the large influx of new investment capital, hungrily searching for profits substantial enough to offset inflation, in itself contributed to inflation of real estate values. Everyone involved with real estate welcomed, of course, new sources of investment capital and broader opportunities for profit. The motive of housing the poor is noble and commendable, but no one who has seen the instant slums often created by Sec. 236 housing will say the solutions so far attempted have been broadly viable for anyone other than well-to-do investors. These have benefited from the tax incentives and various financing subsidies, but as they have already largely escaped liability for the project mortgage they have had no incentive to keep the properties from which they profit in good repair or to manage them soundly. Now, because of proposed tax reforms, even these investors would no longer find it profitable to participate in real estate, leaving it open to further domination by the big institutional finance organizations. The cure looks worse than the problem.

INFLATION'S EFFECT ON HOUSING PRODUCT

Inflation has steadily whittled down the volume builder's profits. His percentage of profit may be the same per unit but as he is selling a smaller, cheaper unit the actual profits per unit have been shrinking. This factor creates something of a frenzied operating climate. The builder has to sell larger volumes to maintain yesterday's profits; if he wishes to actually increase his profits he must run ever faster and faster. Such an atmosphere intensifies competition for the development of sound projects and raises the temptation to get into marginal, riskier projects. Overall, it makes the whole industry riskier, more intensely competitive.

No matter how scarce money is, there is always more money than good deals to put it into. Some of the corporate entrants into real estate, laden with cash but short of experience, demonstrate the undying truth of this maxim in their haste to meet profit projections. You can hear their agonized screams echoing through the halls of the New York Stock Exchange every so often, and you think it would be kindness for somebody to put them out of their misery.

A number of corporate entrants accordingly seek to avoid the millrace of the high-volume, low-profit merchant-housing business by getting into larger, long-term real estate projects where the payoff, though slower in coming, can be hefty. With the government now chipping in with loan guarantees and so forth, this looks like a better bet for many these days. But lacking realistic valuations of property, marketing skills and consumer-responsive planning, you can still wind up with a lemon as big as the Ritz. The housing product itself, meanwhile, keeps getting costlier and smaller.

Inflation has been the mainspring propelling the growth of the mobile-home industry. The 485,000 mobile homes sold in 1971 accounted for about 85% of home sales at $12,000 or under. The modular home industry, born out of the hope of cutting construction costs (or at least retarding their inexorable advance), will probably dominate the industry by the end of the Seventies. When the modulars first appeared in the news in 1968 and 1969 as "instant housing," some housing commentators regarded them as "instant nothing." By 1971, an estimated 85,000 were produced, a 250% increase over 1970 volume.

Virtually all of the major volume builders entered into the factory housing business as of 1970 to supply their own projects, seeing the handwriting on the wall. A number of non-building corporations were also in the field: U.S. Steel, Herculon, Alcoa, Jones & Laughlin Steel, Avco, and General Electric, to name some, with a variety of industrialized housing programs. Many of the manufacturers of single-family housing, like Levitt's subsidiary, Building Systems, Inc., were concentrated in Michigan. Levitt's 100,000-square-foot plant, opened in 1971, was projected to produce 1,400 townhouse units in 1972 and 2,000 in 1973. Beyond that, Levitt, like most of the major homebuilders, planned to drop plants into other key markets. It opened a second plant at Fountain Valley, California, to serve the Southern California market and planned on five or six more which, when completed, would have access to 85% of the country's housing markets.

As will be discussed in a later chapter, 1972 saw the beginning of a strong shakeout in the modular industry, with a number of prominent companies filing for bankruptcy. One casualty was Geistt's modular division. Many companies have had a problem gearing production capacity to fluctuating housing markets and on-site preparation. A modular manufacturer has to integrate his production closely with site acquisition, land development and marketing. But despite this setback, the industry will continue to grow in the long term.

No discussion of the modular industry would be complete without reference to former HUD Secretary George Romney's Operation Breakthrough, which spearheaded the campaign to introduce factory-housing production to the United States after it was announced in May 1969. The program's purpose was to identify all of the obstacles standing in the way of a large-scale factory-housing industry — financing, zoning, building codes, production, shipping, labor practices, governmental relations, consumer acceptance — and to devise coordinated programs to make gradual headway on these problems.

Mr. Romney undertook to do this by demonstrating to the nation that major housing producers could create desirable and attractive housing communities at a low cost based on a variety of industrialized housing plans. From a total of 236 proposals for prototype manufactured housing communities 22 major companies were selected. They shared in $62.7 million of contracts to produce a total of 2,796 units in communities specially designed by them for this purpose. The production of these communities was to serve as a focus for a coordinated attack on the obstacles to the broad manufacture and distribution of modular housing, and for the evolution of channels and procedures that would give modular housing production a permanent large role in the housing industry.

The concept in itself was masterly. Its grand design was the superimposition of an efficient production-line process, with many incredibly complicated interlocking control points all working coordinately on an existing chaos of national and local cross-purposes. The program's objective included bringing into integrated play within this envisioned production system all of the government subsidy programs, as well as the resources of the private mortgage and equity markets. And it involved the development of appropriate zoning, code, labor and subsidy programs and policies at state and city levels of government. It was an incredible problem of coordination.

The program did not go off without extensive criticism, principally from spokesmen for the traditional "stick builder" who found both himself and his method of operation increasingly bypassed. Mr. Romney did not conceal his open courting of major corporations at the expense of the small builder to get his program going. Nor was he helped by the fact that between 1969 and 1971 the production costs which his program was to reduce rose by another 15% to 20% nationwide, and by the fact that the average cost of the typical Operation Breakthrough prototype ran to $22,410 (certainly no dramatic saving over the conventionally built home). These things tended to reinforce the conventional builders' assertions that what they need is not highfalutin plans for mass production but a reduction in or relief from the high costs of land and financing.

Inflation in land and financing costs is a real problem. Such criticism misses the point of Operation Breakthrough, however. Whatever the bureaucrats say, its real purpose was not to cut costs immediately but to establish a coordinated industrialized *apparat* for the production of housing which can ultimately operate in high volume without major interruptions or obstacles. If such a delivery system could begin to function, it could at least serve to retard the present rate of increase in housing costs, if not actually reduce costs somewhat.

The Project Breakthrough program was discarded by 1972, and the modular industry was in a shambles. But Mr. Romney can still take credit for accelerated progress in five major areas, each of which is essential to a broadly functioning modular industry in the future: (1) speeded-up activity in state housing legislation, with about twenty-five states now having enacted or introduced legislation for statewide approval of industrialized housing without regard for local building codes; (2) the establishment of the country's first comprehensive performance guidelines aimed at a national housing system certification program; (3) the curmudgeonly cooperation of the major construction labor unions in working out an accommodation on factory-made housing; (4) action by lending institutions to come up with financing techniques appropriate to this form of housing production; (5) a closer working relationship between the professionals — city, state and federal housing officials, architects, planners, engineers, suppliers, builders and developers — toward solving housing problems. The emergence of fuel shortages and a general energy crisis toward the close of 1973 places a premium on more compact housing closer to urban areas. This factor would tend to assist the comeback of modular housing within a framework of a future program laid on the lines of Operation Breakthrough.

Projecting further progress on the obstacles of codes, zoning and labor restrictions, Mr. Romney's often-repeated assertion that at least two-thirds of all housing production will be factory-produced by the end of the Seventies still seems within the realm of probability, especially in light of the industry's pushback into the central cities. Now, if you consider attendant federalization of the secondary mortgage markets and the direct and indirect subsidy of both the mortgage markets and the housing consumer, it all adds up to a radically transformed housing industry by 1980. In view of the fact that high-volume production requires an assured availability of homesites, moreover, we shall be seeing a further push from state and federal governments to get the corporate sector even more involved in large-scale land and urban renewal projects, and even the government may get into the business of large-scale land purchase.

The scenario is thus complete for a highly centralized, efficiently operating — in short, *industrialized* — housing industry, backed up by a federally controlled and supported mortgage market providing a steady flow of financing and consumer housing subsidies large enough to house every family. And, in the unlikely event that the overall rate of inflation is brought under firm control, this scenario is not the worst of all possible worlds. However, given the use of real estate, like gold, as an inflation hedge, the efficiencies introduced by a broadly operating urban-oriented modular housing industry may at best only slow down, without stopping, the continuing rise in the cost of shelter. In this event, the entire streamlined and coordinated financing and production apparatus now evolving becomes in the long run little more than an efficient wonder wheel for the redistribution of subsidy funds from the taxpayer to the financial institutions serving housing via the controlling agency of the federal housing bureaucracy, with the housing consumer getting less for his own dollar every year.

THE MOBILE HOME INDUSTRY. This observation brings us to the mobile home industry, and to what I consider to be its true significance within the scenario just described.

Because of the overall trend of the housing industry, the mobile home producers' success has to some observers seemed temporary, even as the 1971 record of 485,000 units shipped surpassed all previous records and accounted for about 20% of all housing in 1972 and 1973. The industry could produce as many as 750,000 units by 1975. It has been said this industry is headed for an inevitable merger of function with the now-beleagured factory-housing industry. This is quite possibly true, but I think the mobile home will make a distinctive, if unexpected, contribution.

Nobody seems to like the mobile home very much except the consumer who gets livable shelter, the manufacturers who produce the unit at a good profit, the lenders who supply the high-cost consumer financing for it (treating the mobile-home loan like an automobile loan), the government housing bureaucracy which guarantees the loans, the dealers who sell it, and the developers and investors who make good money by renting or selling lots for its emplacement.

The consumer doesn't get a fantastic deal: he pays monthly rent for his lot, he pays high financing charges, his mobile home depreciates pretty fast, and it's not as nice as a single-family home on its own lot. But it is housing, and housing that he can afford. (The FHA guarantees mobile-home loans, thus permitting low down payments; GNMA guarantees and lets lenders sell security backed by such loans.)

If we really stop to think about it, the mobile home is successful in the market because it introduces two key concepts to housing: the rental of land for a single-family dwelling (thus lowering the consumer's purchasing cost considerably), and installment or chattel financing (which, because it is far more profitable than long-term mortgage loans, is always amply available). Thus, the mobile home at a stroke opens up an entire new field to investment capital seeking to develop or purchase income-producing properties — mobile-home parks. It also becomes the darling of the formidably arrayed lending institutions. So long as the consumer's total monthly price tag doesn't exceed his ability to pay, this form of housing will continue to grow. Because the housing project itself is very inexpensive, and because lower down payments still are made possible by government guarantees, the proportion of the consumer's monthly payment going to financing and rental charges can be very high without exceeding his ability to pay.

This is the real reason that the mobile home has grown so fast in an inflationary period. The consumer increasingly substitutes or trades off equity ownership for rental and financing charges to maintain the ability to get basic shelter for himself, and while his living unit is smaller, it is more economical than ever.

This, too, is the real significance of the mobile-home industry for us, as it continues to grow and gradually merge with the overall industrialized housing industry (it's already difficult to tell many of the newer mobile homes from some factory-built housing). It introduces and institutionalizes the divorce of shelter ownership from land ownership in the field of "single-family" housing. As land grows costlier through the Seventies and housing costs continue their rise, notwithstanding the economies of factory production, the already tested concepts of land rent and chattel finance may be too tempting to withstand. In an inflation-ridden climate, they could be adopted in the field of purchased housing as the answer to a further erosion of purchasing ability. Presumably if things continue to get worse, even land rents and chattel financing could be paid for by subsidy.

CONCLUSION

What are the practical consequences of all of this to all of us in the housing industry? The projection of the industry's inflationary future may seem churlishly bleak, and perhaps it is. We have the ability to make a more viable future by making some less pleasant but more salutary decisions in our economic policies. Even on the off chance, however, that inflation is entirely arrested in real estate, it has already done much to form the general patterns of the industry that will be with us for a long time to come. The industry's future will in any case be profitable: the only question is for whom.

It is not the purpose of this chapter to identify the sources and ultimate consequences of inflation, only to indicate broadly its effects in the building industry. However, no one who is interested in the subject should fail to read Harry Browne's *How You Can Profit from the Coming Devaluation* (Avon) and Peter Beter's *The Conspiracy Against the Dollar* (Braziller), both available in paperback.

Perhaps it is not feasible for every corporate and private entrepreneur to be concerned with the long-run consequences of inflation. But all of the new entrants into this field, as well as the old ones, as each one minds his own project and attempts to bring it off successfully, must be aware of the three most visible effects born of the inflationary impulse which today form the working climate of this industry:

1. Inflation drives more and more people beyond the reach of conventional housing and they are automatically displaced into the category of government-subsidized housing. The prolongation of this trend makes the federal government the nation's paymaster serving all spectra of income levels and housing types, with financial institutions as the property owners, and the builders as hired help.

2. The influx of well-heeled institutions and public corporations into the housing industry gives rise to a contagious attitude in this field: the attitude that only money talks. Money without care for and knowledge of our customer — people — doesn't get the big boys very far. You can hear them fall with a tremendous crash every once in a while when they've disregarded a piece of marketing intelligence once too often. Or when their accounting is to specious.

The attitude that only money talks tends in itself to inflate real estate values by poor or otherwise distortive purchases of property. The upward pressure on realty prices generated by just one offshore fund, USIF, with its top-dollar purchases of $850 million of income-producing property, mostly prominent structure in major urban areas, can only be speculated upon, but it was surely substantial. USIF owned 103 apartments with 23,866 units; 17 high-rise residential buildings with 4,527 units; 35 office buildings with 5 million square feet of space; 37 shopping centers with 7.5 million square feet; 6 industrial properties with 2.6 million square feet; and 18 motels with 2,457 units. USIF was, by the way, operated by GRAMCO and its creator, the perennially twenty-five-year-old Keith Barish, from 1966 to the end of 1970, when it closed its doors, swamped by fund redemptions from jittery overseas investors who wiped out its 20% liquidity reserve. In 1971 it was reorganized (into a closed-end fund to forestall redemptions) under the management of Arlen Realty & Development.

Big money can assert itself not only in inflated purchases by funds but in the cost-bloating impact of many blithely erroneous decisions by major financial powers in real estate. The arrogance of these money-laden entities doesn't bother me, but I am concerned by their contagious attitude of contempt for the concepts of hard work, care and loving perfection of every detail of a project. (Hell, we're big-time, just knock 'em out and never mind the details.) Human resources are so low on their totem pole that their turnover of executives is shocking, and their earnings performance is ultimately dismal.

3. The third effect forming the inflationary climate is related to the foregoing one: I call this one I Can Get Rich Quick, or the Earnout, Syndrome. Seeing the rich outside corporations as a panacea for their recurrent cash shorts, a lot of builders jumped into their arms via mergers and acquisitions. Not all such mergers have been bad. But in many instances, by joining a publicly held company a builder traded his right to select the timing and quality of his work and profit, subordinating it all to the drive for the quarterly profit statement.

In his haste to achieve clockwork earnings, the builder thus became a master compromiser, and expediency substituted for market wisdom. The irony is that as a result some of these companies (or their management) folded faster after becoming high corporate fliers. Anything worth doing is worth doing well, and that goes for the housing business particularly.

Pushing for rapid earnings growth, both corporate subsidiaries and publicly held companies perforce suspended conservative evaluation of economic feasibility in the production and sale of income-producing properties. Churning out and selling off loads of such economically marginal properties at inflated prices (gained as a concession for highly leveraged purchases via all-inclusive trust deeds and other forms of "second" paper), they thus contributed to inflation substantially. Such sloppiness, haste — and indeed greed — typify an inflationary climate. Inflation is only accelerated by the vicious circle of buck-passing in which the entrapped participants trade off a long-term rise in costs for short-term gains. The few ultimate beneficiaries of this dwindling spiral — the major financial institutions and their principal shareholders — don't mind: they'll wind up with all the marbles. But who else wins?

Drive, he said: housing demands the carrot, inflation the stick.
Where to, sir?

4

Enter the Builder: Options for Survival

> "True! — nervous — very, very
> dreadfully nervous I have been and
> am."
>
> —Edgar Allan Poe

Confronted by rapidly changing economic realities and by the disproportionate strength of the new corporate practitioners of the real estate game, the builder found himself in a vexatious bind. He was in a position roughly equal to that of a kid with his nose pressed against a candy store window: tall on desire but short of the cash to execute his plans. For the key element to survival in the hurly-burly of the late Sixties became access to capital. The present pattern of the industry indicates the ways in which builders have solved, or attempted to solve, this problem — or have it solved for them.

The capital the builder has been critically short of is equity funds. Equity capital is the builder's own "front" money, the ante for the game, the pump-primer, the price that it takes to start any venture. It is the money that he needs to finance land purchases, land development, models, architectural fees, marketing analyses, and the myriad of functions and details that usually have to be evaluated before the actual project gets under way. Equity capital is the lever that then provides access to the varieties of interim and long-term loans which enable the builder to swing a bigger line and put the principles of leverage to work for himself.

How did the builder manage to raise equity capital in the past? Many years ago, when construction was a relatively leisurely and unharried business, the equity cash was frequently obtained from such august reserves of institutional finance as friends, relatives and professional acquaintances. It was a pretty clubby and informal affair and the SEC didn't have to get involved. You went to your Uncle Harry who had made a killing in the grocery business and got the dough you needed, and then you split the profits down the middle. If Uncle Harry couldn't fork up all the front-end funds needed, you went to old Doctor Ben, who had delivered your first baby, or to Milt the Insurance Man, your Rotary Club buddy, for the additional equity capital and split up the profits proportionately. But then, in what was the first of several cyclical variations in the availability of working capital, housing developments became more expensive and most small builders found themselves unable to raise the money they needed.

Shortly after World War II, however, the need for equity capital practically disappeared. These were the boom years when most builders couldn't seem to make a mistake, and funds seemed to be available to them even without their asking. The federal government had in effect created a national housing industry by introducing the federally insured or guaranteed mortgage through the Veterans Administration and the Federal Housing Administration. The housing demand thus accommodated enormous profit expectations and created a gold-rush atmosphere. Equity capital was easily obtainable and the philosophy of the major lenders (banks, S&L's, insurers, etc.), changing dramatically, permitted the builder to lower his front-end equity requirements considerably. The lenders were willing to go along with rather generous value assessments on land, and were willing to accept the builder's own figures on estimates and costs. Theoretically, the builder still had to provide 20% of the project's equity capital, but lenders were so willing to provide larger amounts predicated on the builder's own estimates that a builder could readily obtain 90% or 100% or 110% of the project's cost in his financing applications. The phrase "mortgaging out" was added to the builder's working language, though it is used today mostly in moments of nostalgia.

The liberal lending philosophy prevailed up to about 1963 or 1964. Then money started to get "tight" through abnormal cost rises, inflationary land-price escalation, and various economic mismanagement and currency squeezes outside the industry itself. The remaining sources of capital for development, and the new investment sources opening up, put the emphasis on conservative analysis of valuation and risk. The lenders' own philosophy accordingly changed. They took to cross-examining the builders' own rosy project valuations, sending out their own appraisers to estimate values, and taking a harder look at the details of each project. The loans were smaller and they went only to the better-conceived projects, thus raising the builders' equity requirements for both construction and planning.

Other factors conspired to raise the builder's capital needs. Land values took a meteoric rise, with costs doubling within five years in many instances and, on the average, rising by over 30%. The effect was that the builder needed increasingly larger amounts for down payments on land he had heretofore acquired relatively cheaply. Overbuilding had also occurred in many markets and marketing programs became more expensive: in a buyer's market the builder found himself spending a lot more on merchandising his product than he had in the past. The upshot was that in a period of five years, from 1964 to 1968, a home selling for $25,000 required almost 50% more equity capital, with most of the added capital requirements stemming from the rise in the cost of land and in the ancillary professional details required to start a project.

The builder was thus caught in a two-way squeeze forcing upward his equity needs: rising costs within the industry and dwindling sources of investment capital and credit for the overall construction field. For a time many hoped that the currency situation might ease. But again, due to several external factors — the war in Vietnam, federal poverty programs, corporate borrowing demands, the deficit balance in overseas trade — it didn't. It became generally conceded that construction credit would remain tight and expensive for many years to come. It also became a fact of life that the buyer as well as the homebuilder would have to adjust themselves to the higher interest rates. With equity capital as scarce as hen's teeth, the builders of moderate size found themselves at a critical juncture.

The interesting thing about the liquidity crisis of the late Sixties was, however, that, while it drove up to a fifth of all builders out of business, it also demonstrated dramatically to the financial world at large that there were certain homebuilding companies in existence which had become sophisticated and resourceful enough to escape the strictures of tight money and operate successfully in a very negative environment. While moderate-sized companies struggled along with falling earnings or went out of business, a handful of homebuilders enjoying the advantages of proper financing lines, management and purchasing power were racking up impressive gains in sales and earnings. This widening efficiency gap between the smaller and the major builders, while teaching homebuilders that the handwriting was on the wall for the traditional mom-and-pop operation, also taught Wall Street that builders, if properly financed, could become a stable paying proposition.

The credit for this educational function must in a large share go to the Council of Housing Producers, a private trade organization founded by a handful of the largest homebuilders early in 1968 to represent the major builders' interests on Wall Street and in Washington. The admission standards were a minimum of 500 housing starts a year for the preceding three years and a $10,000 initial fee. The membership has varied somewhat, with the rise and fall of various fortunes, but the Council proved to be an effective voice.

The eleven initial members were Levitt & Sons (ITT); Kaufman & Broad; Alcan Design Homes (Alcan Aluminum); Deane Brothers (Occidental Petroleum); the Larwin Group; Lewers & Cooke (U.S. Plywood-Champion Papers); Macco Realty (Penn-Central); R. A. Watt (Boise

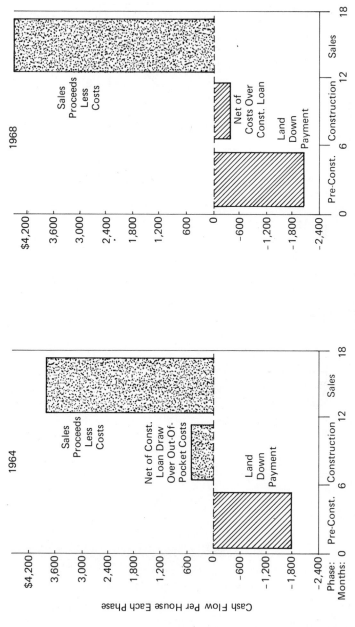

Figure 4.1. Cash Flow for Each Phase of a Typical Project of $25,000 Homes. Source: Builders Resources Corporation.

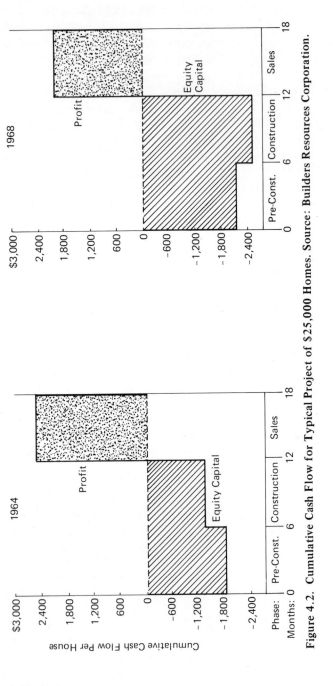

Figure 4.2. Cumulative Cash Flow for Typical Project of $25,000 Homes. Source: Builders Resources Corporation.

Cascade); Perl-Mack Companies; Bert Smokler (later Dreyfus Development); and United Homes (later ITT Levitt United). Since then, Macco and Deane Bros. have dropped out of the picture, and members entering subsequently include Centex Corporation; The Klingbeil Company (later a subsidiary of CBS); Wm. Lyon Development Company (later bought by American-Standard); National Homes Construction Corporation (a subsidiary of National Homes, Inc.); Ryan Homes, Inc.; and U.S. Home Corporation. Several of the initial and subsequent members have, as indicated, changed their name or condition by the merger route, but we will get to this in due course. At one point, Kaufman & Broad was the only publicly held firm in the group. But it has been joined by Centex and, in recent times, by the "builder congeneric" U.S. Home.

The combined staying power of such traditional homebuilding firms, as well as some new entrants like Chrysler Realty and the Kaiser-Aetna realty partnership, was well observed in 1967–69, both by smaller builders and by the corporate sector. It took some startling performance statistics. In 1969, while the housing industry was slumping, the members of the Council of Housing Producers produced 42,000 housing units, a 25% increase over their 1968 production. In 1970, their production was approximately 56,000 units, another increase of 25% over the preceding year. That this rate of growth was a sustained one was verified by the earlier performance history of the Council members. In 1960 the group (as constituted in 1969) had produced only 7,500 units. By 1965 this volume had grown to 17,400 units. In 1966, when the entire industry was in a sharp decline at the peak of the liquidity crisis, the Council members' production rose sharply to 30,000 units. The 1969 Council members produced approximately 3% of all housing starts that year. It was a small factor, indicating how widely fragmented the housing industry is. But the percentage was on a long-term rise, and its continuing growth clearly demonstrated that well-managed homebuilders had the ability to grow under the most adverse conditions.

Such firms, either publicly held themselves or subsidiaries of major publicly held corporations, enjoyed several advantages that made them immune to the fluctuations of an unstable economy. They developed secure credit lines by virtue of their own or their corporate parents' strength. (Eli Broad, chairman of Kaufman & Broad, revolutionized homebuilding in 1967 by arranging for major bank credit lines and for the financing of construction with commercial paper, bypassing the C&D loan route, and the better builders followed him.) Such builders could also develop a variety of attractive financing techniques to make their home sales the most competitive available for the retail buying public. (Some, like Bob Grant of Santa Anita Consolidated, even worked out a way for the homebuyer to charge his purchase on a credit card.) Such builders, as they can afford to buy themselves the best market research and hire the best architects and planners, also invariably come up with the superior product which, expertly marketed to a targeted audience, sells in the greatest volume. They don't have to abandon good projects because of financial instability. And, in theory, at least, because they are "multimarket" companies — i.e., diversified in both type of product and geographic location — they can keep sales going by specializing in some markets and product lines while marking time in others.

It appeared, in sum, that well-financed and well-organized builders could grow in face of a national downtrend in housing starts by taking an increasing share of the market away from the less efficient smaller builders.

THREE ROUTES TO CAPITAL

The conditions were thus ripe for a rapid large-scale consolidation of building firms with major sources of capital. The financial and corporate sector was freshly impressed with the profit potentials of well-funded development organizations; the smaller but professional builders were freshly impressed with the bleakness of their future unless they could secure a sound base of working capital. Corporation and builder ran toward each other with open arms, while Wall Street officiated as the marriage broker and in fact soon took the lead in promoting the consolidation because of the fat fees it could earn. The various approaches taken by smaller builders in an effort to survive as better-capitalized entities come down to three:

1. Going public —that is, becoming a publicly held company listed on the American or the New York Stock Exchange. This approach offers the advantages of placing the builder in a more flexible and more liquid cash position. The trade-off is that a publicly held builder is not his own man. He has to have the discipline and endurance to turn in stably increasing quarterly earnings, year in year out (if he is to be successful). And he is continuously under the scrutiny of shareholders and obstinately curious stock analysts, having to disclose many dealings which he regarded as his own affair in the past.

2. Merger. Many builders, both large and small, chose this route. The attraction has been the security of a large corporation's stock, liquidity for the builder, and the broad financial base afforded by an entity with established credit lines and ample capital of its own. But the trade-off, as we shall see subsequently, is that the builder often surrenders his own dominant position as a decision-maker. The incompatibility of corporate-style opera-

tions with the builder's has often led to tensions and frustrations and resulted in some merger breakups. The success of such mergers really depends on the quality of the management people in the acquiring and the acquired company, and on their understanding of the realities of the homebuilding business. For this reason, the focus of the merger movement in the early Seventies shifted discernibly from the corporate or conglomerate type to the "congeneric" type (builder merging with builder).

3. The third route to added financing strength, and one that has become extremely widespread in the real estate field, is the partnership or joint venture between a builder and a financial source. With the rapidly growing involvement of "outside" corporations in all aspects of development, and with the proliferation of various financial service organizations looking to share directly in the profits of development, the builder has numerous sources of capital available to fund the equity requirements of a well-conceived project. The traditional formula has the builder putting up his talents and the funding source putting up the necessary capital, and the two splitting the profits down the middle. The formula varies, of course, depending on the particular deal, as well as on the funding source and the builder's own strength and capacity to drive a good deal. But the principle is that by lowering or eliminating his own equity requirement, the joint venture leverages the builder's own position and increases the rate of return on whatever capital he might have available.

THE IMPACT OF FINANCIAL CONSOLIDATION ON THE INDUSTRY'S GROWTH. We shall return to a consideration of joint ventures and mergers elsewhere. Let us merely note at this time that in the first phase of the industry's financial consolidation, say 1966 to 1970, many of the bigger builders primarily opted for the merger route; they themselves were hotly pursued by a variety of major corporations who were eager to trade astonishingly large values of good blue-chip stock for the privilege of "owning a builder." This is always a peril for a corporation that responds to an investment opportunity not out of carefully considered commitment but out of fashion, as a number of them have learned. But if one board chairman can get the chance to score off another board chairman over lunch at the Duquesne Club by casually dropping something to the effect that his team has now joined the crusade to provide housing for America by picking up a builder — "nothing big, you know, only $60 million sales last year" — why, then, it may all have been worthwhile. At least the builders who have thus reaped secure bundles of stock in enormous ratio to their earnings will not have minded much, though for many of them the headaches of getting a decision out of a corporation that moves with all the speed of a grazing dinosaur may ultimately outweigh even the rewards of labors-capitalized-into-portfolio.

THE ROLE OF THE PUBLIC MARKET IN
MERGERS

To see the overall merger phenomenon accurately, it has to be viewed in the context of the rapidly developed market for housing issues on Wall Street and the kind of growth this market has spurred in the housing industry. It was the growth of a public market for housing issues that attracted the attention of corporate acquirers to this industry. And it is the publicly held building companies, which are held up to the most rigorous standards of achievement and whose performance is most searchingly measured by a variety of analytical tools, that provide the standards against which corporate analysts evaluate builder candidates for acquisition. The public market provides handy rules of thumb to such questions as: What is a desirable return on total assets? On equity? How often does a good builder turn over his working capital in a year's time? What is the pattern of earnings multiples (the price of all of a company's stock divided by annual earnings) and how can it serve as a guide in determining how much to pay for an acquisition? What rate of growth can be expected from a good builder?

There have always been a few building companies listed on the NYSE or the AMEX, it seems. But the public market gained its first substantial infusion of such companies back around 1960, when the first wave of builders, basking in the success of the postwar building boom, went public. Levitt & Sons was in this group (before merging with ITT in 1968). Then, as the gloom years of 1966 and 1967 hit the building industry and the builders really became concerned with survival, more and more of them succumbed like Faust, and visited the devil down on Wall Street. The Street itself, in the words of one investment banker, "went nuts for housing and real estate." The boys were beating the bushes for builders to take public: first they looked for builders with sales of as low as $10 million a year, and when these ran in short supply they started talking about builders producing as little as $5 million a year. Housing was the only bright spot in a bad bear market on the Street. In addition to these activities, they were also into development for their own account, investing in joint ventures with other building companies and offering real estate services to corporate clients.

THE GROWTH OF A PUBLIC MARKET
FOR HOUSING

The entry of building firms into the public market really warmed up in 1968, when a total of 25 companies went public. The trend turned red-hot in 1969, as another 88 housing-related firms gave up a piece of the action to the public. In 1970, though the boom was slowed by a prolonged bear mar-

Table 4.1

	New Offerings	Gross Proceeds (millions)	Average Size
1969	88	$426.13	$4.84
1970	45	148.97	3.31
Totals	133	$575.10	$4.32

Source: Professional Builder–Audit Investment Research.

ket, still another 45 housing-related firms went public (see Table 4.1). The lure of capital via the public route was so attractive that in two short years these 133 homebuilding, development, mobile home and real estate companies raised $575.1 million of equity in initial offerings. To provide some perspective, this amounted to 3.8% of the total $15 billion raised through stock sales for all types of companies in the years 1969 and 1970, according to Ken Campbell's Audit Investment Research. But this in itself was only half the story: during these years the real estate investment trusts raised another $1.8 billion, or 12% of the total, so the overall real estate industry accounted for about one-sixth of all money raised through stock sales in this period.

While the new issues were grabbing the attention, the publicly held housing companies were also showing no reluctance about financing further expansion by secondary offerings of stock and bond flotations. If this financing is counted in as housing's share of Wall Street money the impact of housing issues on the public market is greater still. In 1968, according to Campbell, new issues accounted for $147.5 million while subsequent stock offerings by publicly held firms reaped $350.1 million and preferred stock sales another $54 million. This is toted up to $497.6 million in equity raised for housing in 1968. And if you count in the $156.1 million in debentures floated in that year, housing's money in 1968 alone came to $707.8 million. This pattern continued in the subsequent boom years, as builder-corporations learned how to use Wall Street's version of "equity kicker," convertible debentures and warrants to raise money for their growing needs.*

As a result of this wave, numerous well-known building companies came into the public fold. They included such outfits as Ryan Homes, Centex Corporation, Leisure Technology, Hallcraft Homes, McKeon Construction and Presley Development. Once caught up in the high-powered Wall Street earnings game, they themselves often joined in the hunt for builder

* For an excellent analysis of housing's role in the public market, see Kenneth D. Campbell's collected columns from *Professional Builder* in the book *Money and the Builder* (Audit Investment Research, Inc., New York).

acquisitions to sustain their growth. Not all the glamorous newcomers prospered, particularly among the modular companies. Behring Company foundered and was bought by Cerro early in 1972; Sterling Homex filed for bankruptcy in July 1972. In some instances, builders also made acquisitions of mortgage bankers, finance firms and insurance companies, in their continuing moves to assure their growth by shoring up their future financial resources.

The effect of this exposure to the earnings demands of capital propelled the publicly held companies into a rapid growth curve and, forcing the rest of the industry to respond to the increased competition, is promoting a continuing streamlining, consolidation and shakeout of the building business. The majors, who set the pace for everyone, have grown incredibly fast. In 1966, Levitt was at $93 million in sales; in 1970 it was up to $228 million. Kaufman & Broad was at $8.7 million in 1960 and $34 million in 1966; in 1970 it hit $152 million. The sales of U.S. Home rose from $26.6 million to $91.6 million between 1966 and fiscal 1971. Ryan Homes, with $96 million in sales, has also grown rapidly. Although their rate of expansion declined in 1973, these large firms still dominate the U.S. housing market.

HOUSING COMPANIES OF THE FUTURE

In fact, the characteristics of the larger public companies foretell the shape of the housing industry in the later Seventies and in the Eighties. These companies are homebuilders, to be sure, but this is only their primary role. They increasingly resemble financial conglomerates. They are extensively engaged in financing of the activities of others in land acquisition and development, as well as the construction of homes, apartments and commercial properties. They underwrite insurance and insure titles and escrows. They often branch out into related businesses such as the manufacture and sale of mobile homes and factory-made housing, plus mobile-home park development. Some are in equipment leasing and other businesses not related to real estate. A number became aggressive acquirers of other building companies. The public builders' need to continue rapid growth is one of the strongest reasons why they will continue to be the dominant acquirers of smaller housing companies in the future.

The early earnings reports of the larger building companies corroborate the trend thus established toward a growing concentration of the housing and real estate business. Statistics gathered in the 1971 *Professional Builder*-Audit Investment Research survey of the performance of major publicly held building companies pointed up this factor. For the survey, homebuilding and development companies were divided into two categories — those reporting over $25 million in sales and those under that figure. The

Table 4.2 Performance of the Major Public Builders 1969–70

	Sales			Income		
	1970	1969	% Change	1970	1969	% Change
	(millions)			(millions)		
20 Firms over $25 million	$1,432.6	$1,170.6	+22.4	$52.81	$37.44	+41.1
26 Firms under $25 million	341.0	301.7	+13.0	16.20	16.11	+ 0.6
Totals	$1,773.6	$1,472.3	+20.4	$69.01	$53.55	+28.9
28 Corporate subsidiaries	$1,755.2	$1,655.7	+ 6.0			
Grand Totals	$3,528.8	$3,128.0	+12.8			

Source: Professional Builder—Audit Investment Research.

demarcation clearly showed that the big are getting bigger. Sales for the over-$25 million group were up 22.4%, vs. a gain of only 13% for the under-$25 million group. The larger builders also increased their profits dramatically by 41.1% vs. an income gain of less than 1% for the smaller companies. Excluding one major loser among the smaller companies, however, their gain in profits rose to 9.9%. (But the smaller publicly held companies did outperform the larger corporate subsidiaries engaged in construction and development.) While the earnings were not available, the latter group's sales were found to have risen only by 6.0%. (See Table 4.2.)

The smaller publicly held builders did achieve slightly better gross margins, as indicated by the survey. Their gross margins (i.e., gross profit after deduction of dollar cost of goods sold) ran to 20.2%, while the over-$25 million group could achieve 19.3%. The smaller builders operated with slightly less leverage, with equity amounting to 27.3% of total assets, vs. 24.1% of total assets for the bigger group. But the larger companies earned 21.6% on equity vs. only 14.9% for the smaller companies. They also earned more on assets available at the beginning of the year, 4.9% vs. 4.0%. Despite their larger size, they were able to turn over equity and assets at a faster rate than the smaller builders. Thus, the larger companies reported sales amounting to 5.8 times their start-of-year equity, and turned each asset dollar into $1.30 of sales. The smaller builders could turn each dollar of equity into only $3.40 of sales and each dollar of assets into only $0.90 of sales. Much of the earnings glamor had worn off the industry by 1973, to be sure, but the trend to concentration continued through the pressures of inflation.

THOSE SKY-HIGH MULTIPLES. The principal manifestation of Wall

Street's newfound infatuation with housing in general, and with the remarkable growth potential that the leading companies exhibited, was to bid up the price of many housing issues to very high price/earnings multiples (see Table 4.3), particularly from their mid-1970 lows to the first half of 1971.

The P/E multiple is the ratio of the market price of a share to per-share earnings (i.e., a stock selling for 15 times earnings has a P/E of 15). In the ideal universe, the P/E multiple is supposed to be impartially set by orderly market forces based on a combination of (1) the rate of return large enough to attract investment — the particular industry's typical cost of capital — and (2) the investor's expectations of a company's future growth. The more he can expect of a company's future earnings, based on the sum of his analyses of the firm's past history and future potential, the more willing the investor becomes to trade off the present rate of return for future earnings growth and capital appreciation.

Let's take a company selling at 10 times earnings. This P/E brings the investor a 10% return on his investment in present time. If this P/E multiple doesn't rise, in our ideal universe it is supposed to mean that the investor has rationally scouted that firm's future, doesn't see any growth potential for earnings or stock values, and so takes a high present return on his investment. A company selling at 50 times earnings (i.e., at a P/E multiple of 50) on the other hand offers the investor a present return of only 2%. His willingness to settle for such a low return in present time, bidding the stock up to such a high multiple, tells us he is buying future earnings and expecting dramatic improvement in that company's peformance in the future. If we assume purely for the sake of this oversimplified example that the investor really looks for at least a 10% return on his money, what is he really saying by taking only a 2% return in present time? He's betting, in effect, that within a foreseeable period (say, three years) the earnings will rise dramatically enough and the stock will appreciate in value sufficiently to compensate him for his low present return — and maybe then some. The high multiple shows the investor is betting on future earnings and equity appreciation. This is pretty much how the stock market discounts the future well in advance of its occurrence. If the expected earnings don't materialize, the P/E multiple drops proportionately.

In reality, which is far from our ideal universe, the orderliness of the relationship between a P/E multiple and a given company's future prospects is, shall we say, severely disturbed. The distorting factors are Wall Street promotions which, pushing this or that glamour group, drive prices up beyond earnings potential on a euphoric wind of stupidity and greed. Another distorting factor is "market psychology," which can depress the price of a stock for various silly reasons, none of which have anything to do with the company's medium-term prospects.

Table 4.3 Initial Public Stock Offerings by Selected Builder-Developers 1968–70

Company	Offering Date	Price Per Share[a]				P/E Ratio[c]	
		Offering	High[b]	Low[b]	April 30, 1971	Offering	April 30, 1971
Ryan Homes	11/68	$26	$83	$23-1/4	$82-7/8	38	41
Centex	2/69	4-3/4	27	4-3/4	26-1/2	14	53
Leisure Technol	2/69	8-3/4	34-3/4	8-3/4	24-7/8	13	28
Daniel Int'l.	3/69	17	22-1/8	10-1/2	21-1/4	26	11
Pulte Home	5/69	13	17-1/2	3-1/2	15-1/4	21	35
Newhall Land	5/69	31	54	17	32	29	30
Mid-Continental Rlty	5/69	20	22-1/4	6-1/8	9-5/8	35	15
Presley Develop.	7/69	10	43-1/2	5	43-1/2	31	41
Land Resources	7/69	12	13-3/8	2-1/8	4-1/4	43	18
Punta Gorda Isles	8/69	7-3/8	19-1/2	5-1/4	18-1/4	26	21
Shapell Industries	8/69	21	36-1/4	12-1/2	32-3/8	23	27
Turner Construc.	10/69	20	22-1/4	9-3/4	21-1/2	15	14
Leisure Living	11/69	18	22	5	13-7/8	33	10
Maui Land	12/69	21-1/2	21-1/2	8	11	–	–
3H Building	12/69	13-1/2	14-1/4	5	12-1/4	16	29
Braewood Develop.	2/70	8-1/2	10-1/4	2-1/8	9-1/8	19	–
Behring	2/70	16-1/2	24	6-1/4	15-1/8	17	26
Killearn Properties	3/70	8	15-1/4	3-3/4	14-5/8	18	21
Building Systems	7/70	7	25-1/2	5-3/8	25-1/2	15	55
Shelter of America	9/70	8-1/2	20	7-7/8	20	12	20
McKeon Construct.	11/70	16-1/2	39-5/8	16-1/2	38-3/4	17	41
Hallcraft Homes	11/70	17	40-1/4	14-1/4	40-1/4	23	54
Great Midwest	12/70	15	24-1/4	13-1/2	22	68	100

a. Adjusted for all stock splits and dividends.
b. From offering date to April 30, 1971.
c. Based on earnings for latest fiscal year reported.
Sources: Standard & Poor's; National Quotation Bureau; Audit Investment Research.

It takes an enormous effort to communicate the firm's real story to the investing public and the portfolio managers who "put away" and unload large blocks of stock. For all the expertise, there is a peculiar inability to deal beyond a generality; fixed viewpoints, once made, stick. The only thing that really assuages the market is perpetually rising earnings in clock-work quarterly segments at a predictable rate of increase. Then the fixed viewpoint is a positive one and the firm is rewarded with a sustained high P/E. But let such a firm slip, and woe. Some companies, growing so large so fast, have to keep producing increasingly larger proportions of earnings to keep up with an established growth rate of 25% or 30% per year and sustain their P/E multiple. These gather an increasingly awe-filled audience of gaping spectators who wonder what corporate strategy the company will pull out of its bag *this* year to meet its projections. Each year, the sense of marvel grows, and more and more curious bystanders gather to watch whether the high-wire walker will make it yet again.

It's no secret that the leading tightrope walker in the industry has been Eli Broad. Maintaining a 30% growth rate for Kaufman & Broad for several years, he gathered a bigger audience of spectators and admirers each year. Having set an unbroken 30% rate of growth for six years, Mr. Broad's company was one of the major supports of the market for publicly held homebuilders seeking the public's acceptance in the glow of K&B's reputation. Even K&B projected a slower growth rate for 1974, however. But it still remained an industry leader. No wonder that Roger Ladd, president of Robino-Ladd Construction, which went public in 1970, at one point said, "I pray for Eli Broad every night; I get right down on my knees and I pray for him."

Kaufman & Broad's multiple is one thing. But in the period from mid-1970 to mid-1971 housing stocks advanced to lofty P/E multiples across a broad range, boosted by Wall Street's full-bore promotion of housing and real estate. A lot of the bigger companies were trading in the range of a 40 to 50 multiple and the younger ones were getting a big boost from this activity. No question that builders could then command higher P/E's because of growth potentials, but promotion often carried them to unsupportable levels; and when the big holders sold out at the top, the stock plummeted below supportable levels and stayed there despite a builder's good performance.

The shift in portfolio investment policy of the major trust and pension-fund managers made housing issues as of 1971 subject to volatile fluctuations. The investment game they play is oriented to short-term performance, with managers looking for immediate earnings gain and capital appreciation to offset pressures of higher benefits gained by union labor contracts. These boys keep the supply of housing stocks scarce for a year or more, thus driving up the cost considerably. But fearing risk, they unload when the P/E can't get pumped much higher. The excess of supply over demand abruptly created in the market tumbles the prices.

The apprehensions arose as a result of a growing debate in 1972 as to whether builders' earnings are overstated by accounting practices generally accepted in the industry. A number of reforms concerning, among other things, discounting of receivables, joint-venture accounting, syndication sales by second wrap-around or all-inclusive mortgage, etc., were enacted. Their purpose is to clarify balance-sheet reporting and to bring earnings statements more closely in line with income actually earned in the year being reported. Though such reforms will tighten up accounting procedures and have some conservative effect on reported earnings generally, they do not severely affect the performance of most companies. Still, this kind of talk made the big investors jittery and set them to gnawing their fingernails over whether they had been running up the multiples of building stocks based on paper earnings. This contributed to the subsequent bail-outs.

While individual companies still commanded extraordinary multiples, and probably will in the future, the long-term trend among better companies thus turned downward as of late 1971, an inevitable result of expiring promotional booms plus tightened-up accounting. Prior to the market fluctuations caused by the Administration's wage/price freeze in the fall of 1971, the P/E's of the public homebuilders were declining from their 1971 highs because of adverse "market psychology." As of August 13, 1971, the more dramatic drops were Stirling Homes, whose P/E went from 99 to 48, and Behring Corp., with a decline from 65 to 32; their subsequent bankruptcies, as well as those of other modular companies, spelled the end of one round of Wall Street promotion. Newcomers to the public market subsequently found a more conservative climate.

The newcomers after 1971 did benefit from a trade-up of their multiple. But the smaller public companies were under stress to avoid being shaken out, with the promotional boom that has carried housing up since 1968 winding down. Wall Street's emphasis has turned from promotional razzle-dazzle of housing issues to a more careful evaluation of the performance of both new and existing firms. The grinding that homebuilding stocks took in the subsequent year and into 1973 bore this out. By now the Street had got used to homebuilders and the glamour aura was gone; the latter were measured by book value rather than by earnings.

For the next few years the atmosphere will be one of getting down to business. The existing public builders will dominate the show, driving hard to lift their multiples by delivering earnings in a much less hospitable economic climate. And this will intensify competition all around, further contributing to the consolidation of the building business and giving continued impetus to the merger/acquisitions and joint-venture movements.

We might mention some additional reasons why the bloom was off the

Table 4.4 Changes in Building Companies' P/E Ratios—August 13, 1971
A) Existing Builders

	Share Price				P/E Ratio	
Company	1971 High	Aug. 13, 1971	% Decline From High	Latest EPS	1971 High	Aug. 13, 1971
Kaufman & Broad	33	– 31-1/4	–5.1%	$0.66	50 –	48
Stirling Homex	26-5/8	– 13-1/4	–50.2	0.27	99 –	48
Leis. Tech.	26-1/2	– 20-3/4	–21.7	0.61	44 –	34
Uris Building	24-3/8	– 17-5/8	–28.0	0.54	45 –	33
Behring Corp.	19-3/8	– 9-3/4	–49.5	0.30	65 –	32
Hallcraft Homes	47-3/4	– 36	–24.7	1.16	41 –	31
U.S. Home	38-1/4	– 30-7/8	–21.8	1.03	37 –	30
Ryan Homes	85	– 71	–16.5	2.47	34 –	29
National Homes	37	– 30-1/8	–18.5	1.16	32 –	26
U.S. Financial	58-1/4	– 39-3/8	–32.5	1.66	35 –	24
Dev. Cp. Amer.	24-1/8	– 21-1/8	–12.4	0.87	28 –	24
Shapell Indus.	36-1/4	– 28-5/8	–21.0	1.26	29 –	23
Tishman Rlty.	29	– 23-1/2	–22.3	1.07	27 –	22
Webb (Del. E.)	13-5/8	– 8-3/8	–38.7	0.39	35 –	21
Lenner Corp.	77-1/2	– 53	–31.7	2.76	28 –	19
Key Co.	14	– 11-1/8	–20.5	0.72	19 –	15
S&P Industrials	115.84	– 105.46	–9.0			16

B) New Issues

Company	Offered 1971	Price	8/13/71 Price	% Change	Latest 12 mon. EPS	P/E Ratio
ALODEX Corp.	Mar. 31	21.50	9-1/8	–58.0	$0.32	29
Amer. Cont. Homes	July 22	10.00	8-5/8	–13.8	0.25	35
Homewood Corp.	June 16	15.00	18-3/4	+25.0	0.94	20
Hallamore Homes	July 27	10.00	9-1/4	–7.5	NO	NC
Rossmoor Corp.–unit	July 15	23.00a	14-3/4	–35.9	–	–
–shares			6-1/2		1.06	6
Woodmoor Corp.	July 22	15.88	12-1/4	–22.8	1.07	11

a. Units of two shares and one warrant. NO—No operations. NC—Not calculated.
Source: Professional Builder—Audit Investment Research.

housing stocks as a group as of 1973. First, there's the withdrawal of the government subsidized housing in the Sec. 235/Sec. 236 format, which was viewed as the removal of a major underpinning from housing. Then there was the implementation of the government's Phase Three program, which — as came to pass — was viewed as a signal of higher inflation and higher interest and thus of tough times for housing ahead. Proposed tax changes on investor participation in apartment development also prompted the departure of major builders from this field (at least for now) and spelled lower earnings. And not to be under-estimated is the investment advice of a few major brokerage houses. Figuring that housing had been promoted long enough and had peaked in potential earnings after two very fat years, a few prominent firms blow the whistle and suddenly everybody stampedes; it's a stimulus-response situation, for it overlooks the solid continuing growth potential of many major building firms. Thomas B. Stiles II, the housing specialist at Smith-Barney, called attention to this phenomenon in April 1973, pointing out the erosion of the P/E multiples of even the best-performing firms. At the conclusion of this chapter the reader will find charts and tables showing P/E ratios as of 1971 and 1972. Compare these with Stiles's tabulation of the erosion of P/E multiples in 1973:

	Price 4/6/73	Multiple on 1973 Est. Earnings	Price Erosion Since Jan 1, 1973
Ryan Homes	17	11.3X	41%
Kaufman & Broad	31	20.7X	30%
Centex	16	11.7X	41%

Wall Street began taking its bets off the housing boom as early as mid–1971 — and analysts were proven completely wrong when housing turned in its best performance ever with 2.4 million starts in 1972. They merely repeated the same forecast for 1973. With a lower level of housing starts in sight for that year, they were somewhat closer to the mark, but this still would not warrant a stimulus-response withdrawal from the housing group as a whole. With the fuel scare and a cyclical recession in housing activity brought on by a quite severe and prolonged application of monetary restraint to slow down an overheated, inflationary economy, starts in 1974 were to drop to 1.7 or 1.8 million, rebounding to about 2 million in 1975, excluding mobile homes.

For the twelve months ending May 31, 1973, the prices of forty-six homebuilders fell by 64% while their earnings rose by 41%. Their average price/earnings ratio was 7.3 based on their last twelve months earnings, but less than 6 based on their projected 1973 earnings. Many companies sold at only three to four times estimated 1973 earnings with their stock price significantly lower than their book value. This book value is worth considerably more, and is indicative of truer net worth than the book value of most industrial companies. The real net asset value is substantially greater than quoted book value because such assets consist primarily of low-cost land, which increases in value through inflation and through improvement, plus housing inventory under construction.

A PROFILE OF REAL ESTATE COMPANIES
AT THE TIME THEY WENT PUBLIC

What were the financial and other pertinent characteristics of building and real estate companies that went the public route in the late 1960s and early 1970s? Underwriters have been known to cite the following basic requirements. A company should have a five-year operating history, with a steady growth record. Its net income after taxes should run to about $500,000, and sales should be in the range of $10 million to $15 million. While providing very general criteria, such guidelines fall short of giving the builder/developer a realistic assessment of whether he qualifies for the public route.

Kenneth Leventhal & Company, the independent accounting firm which specializes in preparing builder-clients both for the public and the merger route, surveyed a sample of fifteen companies from SEC filings at the time they went public in 1970–71, in order to obtain a more detailed profile of the variety of such firms. The study provided comparative data on the characteristics of the underwritings, as well as on the characteristics of the companies, the latter often surprising in their variance from the basic guidelines set forth above.

The Leventhal analysis included the following companies:

American Home Industry Corporation
Bresler & Reiner, Inc.
CalProp Corporation
Ducor Modular Systems, Inc.
Great Midwest Corporation
Hallcraft Homes
Key Developments, Inc.
Lennar Corp.
Liberty Homes
McKeon Construction
Oriole Land & Development Corporation
Realty Industries, Inc.
Stylex Homes, Inc.
Terracor
Westchester Corporation

Of this group, six companies are involved in development of single-family or multifamily housing or commercial properties; the others are involved in the manufacturing or sale of modular homes or in the development of land for housing, shopping centers or golf courses.

The analysis produced the findings shown in Table 4.5.

Figure 4.3 shows the trend of earnings per share of four selected companies, in a group of fifteen companies studied, which in all instances hit their highest earnings in the year in which they went public.

SIZE OF ISSUANCE

The general guideline is that initial public offerings generally ranged somewhere between $1½ million and $2 million in value and were not for less than 200,000 shares, so as to attract as many shareholders as possible. The real estate companies reviewed conformed to this general guideline.

The average number of shares thus ranged from a low of 150,000 to a high of 685,000. The maximum proceeds (before costs) raised in these issues ranged from a low of $900,000 to a high of approximately $12,700,-000, and the average of proceeds raised was $5,300,000.

PRICE-EARNINGS MULTIPLES

Price-earnings multiples ranged from 8.3 to 30.8 and averaged 20.5. Figure 4.4 compares these multiples to some major independent public companies at the end of April 1971. The majors' multiples ranged from a multiple of 30 for Shapell Industries, to 37 for Ryan and 41 for Centex Corporation, up to a high of 51 for Kaufman & Broad, Inc. McKeon Construction, coming out in November 1970 at a multiple of 19, reached a multiple of 37 at the end of April 1971. Two companies showed a loss and were selling at 3.5 and 5.1 times book value, and two companies in the development stage with no operations filed S–2's (secondary stock offerings) and came out at 3.1 and 6.3 times their book value. The market price of the companies reviewed ranged from 1.7 to 8.2 times book value after issue, and averaged 3.8.

SELLING GROUP AND USE OF PROCEEDS

In 60% of the filings reviewed by Leventhal & Company, the selling shareholders received 20% to 50% of the total proceeds, and in one instance the shareholders received all of the proceeds. The magnitude of the dilution of ownership ranged from a low of 19% to a high of 31%, with an average of approximately 25%.

Table 4.5   Years of Activity Prior to Going Public

No. of Companies	Years
2	a
3	1 to 5
5	6 to 10
3	11 to 20
2	30
15	

Net Income After Taxes

No. of Companies	Low	High
5	b	$ 275,000
4	$ 400,000	$ 850,000
6	$1,100,000	$2,770,000 (high)
15		

Net Income After Tax as Percentage of Sales

No. of Companies	Low	High
7	c	2.3%
5	3.6%	7.9%
2	11.4%	14.3%
1	16.4%	d
15		

Gross Sales Volume

No. of Companies	Low	High
4	–	$ 150,000
6	$ 3,000,000	$ 8,400,000
3	$12,000,000	$28,000,000
2	$37,000,000	$47,000,000
15		

Growth Rate in Earnings per Share

Company	Year 1	Year 2	Year 3
A	80%	80%	60%
B	75%	20%	60%
C	–	175%	700%
D	–	250%	(15)%
E	45%	15%	130%
F	300%	120%	20%

a. Development stage companies with no operations.
b. Loss from operations.
c. Loss or no operations.
d. Primarily land activities.

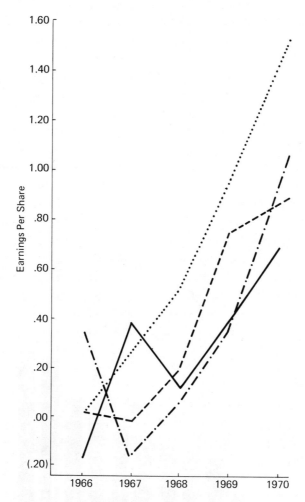

Figure 4.3. Earnings Per Share Prior to Going Public: Four Companies. Source: Kenneth Leventhal & Co.

The use of these proceeds by these companies ranged from research and development, including construction techniques, to use for specific land developments. A breakdown of the major categories in which proceeds were applied is as follows:

Use of Proceeds	Number of Companies Reporting	Weighted Average
Retirement of debt	13	50%
Working capital	13	17%
Expansion and development	13	32%

Table 4.6

Number of Companies	Initial Market Price	Shares Issued
4	$ 5–$ 6.50	150,000–330,000
4	$10–$14.00	200,000–675,000
4	$15–$16.50	300,000–600,000
3	$17–$25.00	350,000–685,000

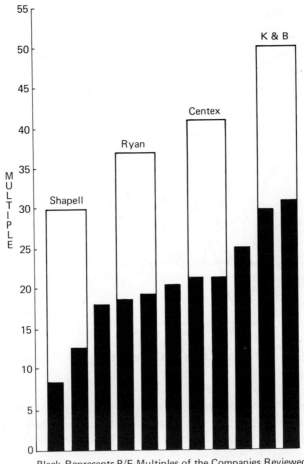

Black Represents P/E Multiples of the Companies Reviewed
White Represents Sample of Major Independent
Building Companies

Figure 4.4. Price-Earnings Multiples (as of end of April, 1971). Source: Kenneth Leventhal & Co.

COSTS OF REGISTRATION

As a general rule, the cost of a first underwriting for an average building company will range anywhere from around $80,000 to $100,000 for costs other than commissions. The total cost of issuance, as accurately as could be determined, ranged from 7.6% to 15.4%, including all expenses.

NOTE: At the end of this chapter a table is appended providing an analysis on a per-company basis of the fifteen companies surveyed in this survey sample. This table provides significant data company by company on P/E ratio and book value before and after going public, as well as information on share offerings, market value per share, and maximum proceeds before costs. In addition to the fifteen companies in this study, the table of individual companies also lists six additional firms who went public between May and September 1971. These six firms — All-American Realty; F. D. Rich Housing; Homewood; J.&S. Development; Metromodular Systems; and Wilco — have *not* been included in the foregoing grouped survey sample.

PROFILE OF A PUBLIC BUILDER

Randall Presley sits behind his desk down in California's Orange County and talks about his organization. He is a rugged, handsome man who has a natural dignity about him. Although he seems entirely unassertive, a firmness of purpose emanating from him identifies him as a person who sees clearly and rules his own future. Indeed, Randall Presley has created his own future continuously well. After service in World War II as a bombardier and pilot, he brokered real estate and subdivided lots in Bakersfield, California, until 1951 and then got directly into housing construction in a small way. In 1956 he founded Presley Development Company. In June 1969, the company went public, and on September 9, 1971, it was listed on the American Stock Exchange. By the end of its first fiscal year, in January 1971, sales had more than doubled, exceeding $25 million. Presley was not reluctant to come back to the stock market when the need for funds arose again.

In the fiscal year ending in January 1972, Presley built and delivered approximately 2,000 homes, mostly in the California market. This again more than doubled the 829 homes built and delivered in the fiscal year ending January 1971. Some idea of his growth rate is afforded by a comparison of six-month earnings: $1.38 per share ($1.28 fully diluted) in mid-1971 vs. $.43 per share ($.40 fully diluted) in mid-1970. For his third full year of production, ending January 1973, Presley planned on another 50% increase over the second year's figures. Deliveries were projected at 3,000 homes. Of these, only about 1,000 were to be built in Southern California. The rest were to come out of Northern California (500), Phoenix (750), Albuquerque (250) and Chicago (500).

By mid-1973, however, the taxing pace of heavy expansion in the face of an unstable economic situation and rising interest rates (along with poor weather in some areas) had its impact. Presley at that time projected 1973 earnings of $1.20–1.25 per share, down from the previous year's $1.46. The company's stock, along with that of nearly every other builder, was in the doghouse, and the times ahead called for hard grinding.

Presley, who had been principally a Southern California builder, built a number of projects throughout Orange County—La Palma, Fountain Valley, Irvine Ranch, Capistrano Beach—as well as in Cerritos, Riverside and Redlands. But he has moved on to Northern California markets (San Jose and Livermore) and to New Mexico, Arizona and Chicago because land for tract development in his native regions has become scarce and the game plan calls for more production.

One of the major factors he's counting on to assist the company over any rough spots in such expansion is the use of local builders, who know the markets and local housing products inside out. Although Presley will joint-venture, he appears to be going the acquisition route. One recent acquisition was Allied Home of Chicago,which joined the fold of the Presley organization in 1971. Allied will develop about 5,000 residential units in the Chicago area, benefiting by the expertise of the Presley firm: marketing surveys, model home selection, design and construction, limited commitment and subcontracting.

As with Presley's California performance, his housing product will be successful in other parts of the country. His organization has a reputation for meticulously planned products, with homes meeting high construction standards and priced from $20,000 to $40,000. Presley is a practitioner of that brand of California-born merchandising followed by the ablest builders, the "total concept" of merchant building. This involves the planned integration of every aspect of homebuilding into a rational program of site location, design, construction, pricing and marketing. One key factor is, of course, location in rapid growth areas; within such areas, projects are located with easy access to freeways and near recreation areas or parks. Presley takes pride in the fact that excellent locations and high construction standards ("they exceed FHA requirements") increase long-term values of his homes for the purchasers.

Presley's methods of profit planning and financial controls have resulted both in good profits and in extremely fine relationships with lending institutions.

The approach begins, of course, with land acquisition. The company's land acquisition department has as its prime goal a 10% pretax profit margin per home when the property is completely developed. The average cost per home lot in Southern California in late 1971 ran to $8,500, including pro rata contribution to streets, sewers, utilities and all other costs preceding the construction of a house. Presley, like many builders these days, spreads the land improvement cost over the entire development, thus bringing in uniform lot costs and certain economies for scale.

The organization minimizes its speculative exposure (the hazard of unsold inventory) by selling a project from a few model homes built on the recommendations of comprehensive market research. There is no commitment to building an entire project until homes are sold. The project is usually 85% sold out in the early phase of construction of the first homes. A typical project runs from 50 to 75 homes at a clip. Some 95% of Presley home sales are to people using FHA or VA mortgages. The default ratio in Presley developments has been so low that the company is a welcome customer for construction and mortgage funds among lenders.

Randall Presley believes in his organization, and he's backed by a youthful, well-trained staff which has incentives substantial enough to be highly motivated to do the hard work of keeping the company growing rapidly. Presley does not talk about himself; he talks about the organization and the nation's housing need.

To him, manufactured housing is not the way to meet the need for low-cost housing. "It is not the answer, especially in Southern California, where the excellent climate allows year-round work. On-site building here is less expensive than factory construction, except for single units or remote areas."

He talks about the critical need during the Seventies for zoning legislation on federal and state levels to override local ordinances so as to give builders a whack at more land and thus the opportunity to build housing at lower cost. Housing's success, he says, depends on the breaking down of traditional neighborhood zoning privilege. Housing subsidies and supports are also, obviously, important to keep the product within reach of the mass market.

Randall Presley, as you can see, is already thinking far into the future to all the obstacles he will eventually encounter in the path of his company's earnings-seeking growth curve. "We are a growing company," he says, "hoping to achieve, sometime in the future, what we consider success."

There are many Randall Presleys in the building business who have exactly the same thing on their minds. What must they do to keep growing at rates as rapid as those of 1971–72.

Table 4.7 Summary of Selected Companies and Information for S.E.C. Offerings

	Date of Filing P = Prelim. F = Final	Number of Shares	Market Value Price to Public Per Share	Maximum Proceeds Before Costs (x 1,000)	Price/Earnings Multiple		Market Value/Book Value After Issue	Book Value		Years of Operation	Product Line
					Before Issue	After Issue		Before Issue	After Issue		
American Home Industry	F 2/24/70	300,000 Company	$ 6.00	$ 1,800	Loss	Loss	5.1	$ .19	$1.18	Since 11/69	Manufacturing & sale of modular homes—minimum on-site preparation.
Bresler & Reiner, Inc.	P 12/29/70	380,000 Company	15.00	5,700	14.0	18.1	2.6	2.42	5.71	9	Single-family, operation & owner of apartments, construction for others.
Calprop Corp.	P 2/5/71	250,000 Company 75,000 S/hldrs.	15.00	3,750 1,125	16.9	21.4	3.4	3.27	4.73	9	Develops, constructs & manages garden apartments for low & moderate income.
Dukor Modular Systems	F 12/22/70	350,000 Company	10.00	3,500	N/A S-2	N/A S-2	3.1	1.17	3.19	1/1/70	Modular homes (manufactures, designs, and erects).
Great Midwest Corp.	F 12/17/70	150,000 Company 150,000 S/hldrs.	15.00	2,250 2,250	6.8	8.3	4.2	1.59	3.59	10	Land developing, mine quarry, crushed rock, asphalt paving, underground storage.
Hallcraft Homes, Inc.	F 11/19/70	450,000 Company 50,000 S/hldrs.	17.00	7,650 850	22.7	29.8	2.6	3.76	6.45	18	Single-family, apartments
Key Development, Inc.	P 7/21/70	30,000 Minimum 150,000 Maximum	5.00	150 750	N/A S-2	N/A S-2	Min. 6.3 Max. 2.5	.39	Min. .79 Max. 2.01	None	Acquires, sells, develops, owns & manages mobile parks.
Lenner Corp	F 12/8/70	175,000 Company 175,000 S/hldrs.	25.00	4,375 4,375	16.1	18.8	4.3	3.13	5.82	16	Moderate-priced single-family.
Liberty Homes (sold all by existing s/hldrs.)	F 12/8/70	684,873 S/hldrs.	18.50	12,670	30.8	30.8	8.2	2.25	2.25	30	Designs, manufactures, distributes mobile homes—wholesale to dealers.
McKeon Construction	F 11/12/70	300,000 Company 300,000 S/hldrs.	16.50	4,900 4,900	17.4	19.2	4.6	2.43	3.59	35	Quadplex residential, 2/3 interest in high-rise office building—Sacramento.
Oriole Land & Dev. Corp.	F 1/28/71	200,000 Company	11.75	2,350	15.5	20.6	2.5	2.82	-4.68	7	Single-family low-medium-priced.
Realty Industries	P 1/27/71	250,000 Company 80,000 S/hldrs.	6.00	1,500 480	19.4	25.0	1.7	2.91	3.51	20	Single-family, apartments and shopping centers for investment.
Stylex Homes, Inc.	F 12/15/70	200,000 Company	6.50	1,300	Loss	Loss	3.5	.40	1.85	1	Designs, manufactures market modular homes, principally through dealers.

Company		Date	Shares	Price								Description
Terracor	P	6/29/70	511,000 Company 164,000 S/hldrs.	13.00	6,643 2,132	9.6	12.9	2.8	2.85	4.58	2	Develops large tracts for residential homes, principally through dealers.
Westchester Corp.	F	2/19/71	270,000 Company 70,000 S/hldrs.	14.00	3,780 980	16.7	21.2	2.8	3.11	5.03	10	Single-family, multi-housing, commercial
All-American Realty Co., Inc.	F	5/25/71	15,000 bonds* 120,000 shares	100.00 per unit*	1,500	N/A	N/A	N/A	3.93	3.19	8	Recreational homesites— Low-price homes on site.
F.D. Rich Housing Corp.	P	6/28/71	380,000 Company	12.00	4,560	N/A	N/A	2.3	2.86	5.23	4/1/71	Program housing—established to low- and moderate-income housing.
Homewood Corp.	F	6/16/71	240,000 Company 144,000 S/hldrs.	15.00	3,600 2,160	18.8	23.0	2.8	3.33	5.25	6	Single-family low-medium-priced; medium to luxury apts.; land development.
J. & S. Development Corp.	P	9/22/71	200,000 Company	6.00	1,200	N/A	N/A	5.4	.13	1.11	12/7/70	Residential subsidized housing, modular construction.
Metromodular Systems, Inc.	F	6/23/71	300,000 Company	7.00	2,100	N/A	N/A	2.8	.72	2.53	2/10/70	Precast building components.
Wilco Developments, Inc.	F	7/9/71	100,000 Minimum 200,000 Maximum	10.00	1,000 2,000	N/A	N/A	3.5 2.8	1.99	2.89 3.61	11/70	Real estate land development company.

*A unit consists of one 11% $100.000 debenture plus 8 common shares.
Note: Price to public on preliminary filing was for estimate of registration fee only.
Source: Kenneth Leventhal & Co.

APPENDIX A

Comparison of Homebuilders' Price-Earnings Multiples
(December 31, 1971)

	National and Multimarket Companies: Sales $80 Million or More	Regional firms: Sales Less than $30 Million	Premium for Multimarket Companies
P/E on 1971 Earnings (est.)	27.8	16.9	65.7%
P/E When Company First Went Public	21.0*	14.9	40.9%
P/E When First Going Public For Companies With Sales of Less Than $20 Million	—	14.2	47.9%

* Based on single offering, but regarded as reasonable valuation for company of this size in 1971–73 period.

Analysis of Data

1. Multimarket builders commanded a substantial price premium over the smaller regional or single-market companies (a premium of 65.7% as of 1971–72). During this period the P/E premium for large homebuilders was rising steadily, possibly reflecting Wall Street's concern that smaller builders would run into problems with soft markets in 1972 and 1973.

2. The large homebuilders were able to raise capital during the 1971–72 period at prices more favorable than available to the small builder. Most important, however, the small builders were unable to obtain equity capital at *any* price during the 1970 bear market. In fact, the stock prices of some of these regional builders even fell below an approximate market value of the properties they owned.

3. The stock prices of the national builders rose to new highs during 1972. While the smaller companies have rebounded sharply from their lows, some of the companies on the following list did not exceed their initial offering price as of 1972.

4. The national builders had the market diversification, product mix, and capital base to increase their earnings in 1969, 1970, and 1971. Consequently, these companies were in a very favorable position to raise large sums of capital. The average offering was over $28 million. The ability to raise this capital insures that these companies will have the proper financing to plan their growth during the coming years.

5. The major banks, mutual funds, and other larger institutions are not able to buy the stock of a homebuilder until the company has a sufficient supply of shares floating in the market. When the large institutions buy these shares, they take enormous positions and, therefore, generate a further premium on the value of the national homebuilding companies. Consequently, size can be an extremely important factor in determining a price-earnings multiple. (In 1973, however, the same principle worked in reverse.)

(1)   1971 price-earnings multiples

Major Companies	Price to 1971 Earnings (Est.)	Price to 1972 Earnings (Est.)
Centex Inc.	34.3	27.5
Hallcraft	17.1	13.7
Kaufman & Broad	52.8	32.3
National Homes	22.9	18.3
Ryan Homes	30.0	24.7
U.S. Financial	18.0	15.0
U.S. Home	19.2	15.0
Average	27.8	20.9

Smaller Companies	Price to 1971 Earnings (Est.)
Bresler & Reiner, Inc.	11.2
Building Systems Inc.	27.0
Calprop	12.1
Christiana Co.	14.8
Co-Build Inc.	11.8
Development Corp. of America	21.1
Hoffman & Rosner	15.7
Homewood Corp.	15.7
Hunt Building Mart	19.0
Key Company	10.5
Leisure Technology	14.8
Lennar Corp.	21.9
McKeon Construction	13.9
National Modular	17.3
Oriole Land & Development	15.6
Perdue Housing Inc.	19.0
Prel Corp.	20.0
Presley Development	20.5
Pulte Homes	17.0
Robino-Ladd Inc.	13.1
Ryland Group	22.7
Shapell Industries	18.2
Shelter Corp. of America	19.2
Standard Pacific	22.5
3H Building Corp.	12.2
Washington Homes	16.9
Westchester Corp.	13.1
Average	16.9

(2)   Price-earnings multiple when company first went public based on latest twelve-month reported earnings at time of offering

(a)   Sales greater than $80.0 million

	P/E	Sales (millions)
Ryan Homes	20.6	$80.0

(b)   Sales between $30 million and $80 million

	P/E	Sales (millions)
Ryland Group	22.7	$31.0
Starrett Housing	20.5	32.8

Behring Corp.	17.6	46.4
Hallcraft Homes	17.0	55.2
McKeon Construction	16.8	36.0
Rossmoor Corp.	8.7	40.0
Average	17.2	

Kaufman & Broad, Ryan Homes, and U.S. Home (all with more than $80 million in sales) were able to obtain equity money from a public offering at an average price-earnings multiple of about 33.0 times twelve month earnings.

(c)   Sales less than $30 million

	P/E
Braewood Development	22.2
Bresler & Reiner	13.6
Building Systems, Inc.	15.2
Calprop	14.7
Co-Build Inc.	14.8
Hoffman & Rosner	13.3
Homewood	16.0
Leisure Technology	16.3
Lennar Corp.	16.1
Lindal Cedar Homes	13.6
McGrath Corp.	16.1
Oriole Land & Development	12.4
Perdue Housing	18.5
Presley Development	15.3
Pulte Homes	17.5
Robino-Ladd Inc.	12.4
Seligman & Assoc.	15.3
Shapell	19.6
Shelter Corp.	8.5
3 H Building Corp.	15.7
Wasington Homes	9.7
Westchester	10.3
Average	14.9

(d)   Sales less than $20 million

	P/E
Bresler & Reiner	13.6
Calprop	14.7
Co-Build	14.8
Hoffman & Rosner	13.3
Homewood	16.0
Lindal Cedar Homes	13.6
McGrath Corp.	16.1
Oriole Land & Development	12.4
Perdue Housing	18.5
Presley Development	15.3
Seligman & Assoc.	15.3
3 H Building Corp.	15.7
Washington Homes	9.7
Westchester	10.3
Average	14.2

Price History of Some Smaller Home Builders

Company	Initial Offering	1971
Braewood Development	$ 8	$ 4
Bresler & Reiner	17	13½
Calprop	14	8½
Co-Build Inc.	15	13
Hoffman & Rosner	11	11
Homewood	15	22
Lennar	25	35
McGrath Corp.	19½	8
Oriole Land & Development	11¾	25
Perdue Housing	6	9½
Prel Corp.	7	22
Pulte Homes	13½	12¾
Robino-Ladd	10	17
Shelter Corp.	8½	24
3 H Building Corp.	13½	11
Washington Homes	11	21

It is important to note that the stock market decline of 1969–70 resulted in a sharp decline in the stock prices of many of these companies. The prices of these stocks have rebounded strongly. However, even in the 1971 bullish housing atomsphere, the prices of eight of these companies (50% of the total) did not exceed their initial offering price.

APPENDIX B

STRUCTURE OF THE HOMEBUILDING INDUSTRY— MARKET SHARE ANALYSIS

The homebuilding industry in the early Seventies consisted of approximately 50,000 homebuilders who generated over $43 billion in revenues in 1972. As these figures indicate, the industry is highly fragmented. However, during the past five years two major trends have developed which are resulting in dramatic changes in the industry structure: (1) The major homebuilders have grown larger as they have consistently increased their market share and (2) the number of major homebuilders has increased.

These two trends are reducing the degree of fragmentation and resulting in a rapid consolidation in the major metropolitan markets. The following table indicates the growth and impact of those major homebuilders (and mobile home companies) with revenue over $10 million.

	Number of Major Homebuilders	Revenues (approx.) (billions)
1967	55	$ 1.4
1968	121	4.0
1969	253	8.0
1970	327	11.0
1971	372	14.7
1972	419	16.7

An analysis of 500 major homebuilders by the *Blue Book of Major Homebuilders* indicates that through 1972 this group increased its market share for the sixth consecutive year since 1967. For the fourth consecutive year, the public homebuilders increased their market share in 1972. While total housing revenues were up 22%, a group of 46 public builders increased their revenues 33% and increased their market penetration from 6.0% to 6.5%.

Market Penetration—Sales

	1972	1971	% Increase
511 major homebuilders[a]	665,000 units	430,000 units	55%
225 largest major builders[a]	520,000 units	350,000 units	60%
46 compendium builders	$2.8 billion	$2.1 billion	33%
4 national homebuilders	$1.0 billion	$0.8 billion	25%
Total housing starts (units)	2.37 million	2.08 million	14%
New residential construction value	$43.0 billion	$35.0 billion	22%

a Data are from *The Blue Book of Major Homebuilders*. The 511 homebuilders represent companies which built more than 200 units in 1972. The 225 largest builders are companies which built over 1,000 units in 1972. It should be carefully noted that the *Blue Book* data are *unaudited*.

The following tables provide further evidence of both the degree of fragmentation and the rapid consolidation which is occurring in the industry.

	% of Builders	
Number of Units Built	1969	1972
10 or less	55%	7%
11–75	37%	43%
76–250	} 8%	19%
251 or more		31%

SOURCE: Bureau of Building Marketing Research.

Census of Builder Activity

No. of Units	No. of Firms	No. of Units	No. of Firms	Single Family No. of Homes	%	Multifamily (includes rentals and condos) No. of Firms	No. of Units	%
251 or more	1,272	605,935	494	179,790	16.6	778	426,145	47.5
76–250	5,104	379,764	2,218	223,043	20.7	2,886	156,721	17.5
11–75	25,490	853,354	16,866	554,680	51.4	8,624	298,674	33.3
1–10	23,186	136,299	19,817	121,851	11.3	3,369	14,448	1.6
Total	55,052	1,975,352	39,395	1,079,364	100.0%	15,657	895,988	100.0%

SOURCE: *Professional Builder*.

In addition, many of the major metropolitan markets are now served by a number of homebuilders (delivery of 200 or more units). According to the *Blue Book*, in 1972 the average major homebuilder operated in four cities and more than 65% had projects in at least two markets.

Market	No. of Major Homebuilders	Estimated Dollar Size of Market
Los Angeles	61	$1,035 million
San Francisco	54	920
Miami	44	985
Chicago	43	1,520
San Diego	38	980
Washington, D.C.	38	1,180
Tampa/St. Petersburg	33	1,100
New Jersey	33	NA
Dallas	31	760
Houston	31	1,050
Denver	24	1,040
Phoenix	24	960
Las Vegas	23	200
Detroit/Baltimore/ Boston	20	700 Average

SOURCE: *Blue Book of Homebuilders,* NAHB.

The increase in the number of major homebuilders created significant competitive pressures in many major metropolitan markets. Chicago and Los Angeles are examples of two markets which reached a high level of competition. In this environment the mere fact that a company is national will not necessarily provide a competitive advantage on a local market basis. Kaufman & Broad, for example, experienced difficulties in both of the above markets. There is no question that the degree of competition between major builders will intensify in a number of additional metropolitan markets.

In particular, the following factors contribute to long-term success:

1. Ability to differentiate its product. The key factors in product differentiation would be housing quality, location, and cost.

2. Ability to consistently identify and penetrate the submarket segments of a broad geographic market. Each metropolitan market is actually composed of as many as thirty to forty submarkets. The importance of these submarkets places a premium on talented divisional management that can consistently identify them.

3. Ability to profitably develop large, integrated, and totally planned projects in order to meet the quality and environmental considerations of both the consumer and the community.

4. Ability to eventually develop a consumer franchise in its markets.

The trends toward larger homebuilders and an increased number of major homebuilders could continue throughout this decade because of the basic advantages of the larger builder. Some of the advantages are:

1. In-depth management.

2. Ample financial strength as a result of permanent corporate capital.

3. Access to long term mortgage financing.

4. Multimarket operations.

5. Multiproduct mix.

6. Ability to produce a lower-cost product.

7. Ability to obtain financing when money is tight.

8. Ability to obtain raw material products when housing is strong.

9. Ability to attract career management.

10. An increased ability to combine the traditional entrepreneurial skills with

the systematic approach to the business of producing, marketing and financing on-site housing.

APPENDIX C

HOW THE HOMEBUILDER MAINTAINS HIS GROWTH

There are basically two strategies a homebuilder can utilize to grow. Many companies employ both strategies.

1. The company can specialize in a particular product, such as single-family houses and expand this product into new geographical areas. The major advantage of this strategy is that it provides geographical diversification and lessens the risk of a decline in demand in one or two markets.

2. The company can develop in-depth expertise of one geographical area and diversify into a variety of products (such as single-family houses, townhouses, condos, shopping centers, office parks, etc.) within that market area. Each market area usually provides at least thirty to forty product submarkets. The major advantage of this strategy is that it provides product diversity and lessens the risk of a decline in demand for any one product. For example, demand for commercial space is usually contracyclical to demand for housing. In addition, this approach usually carries less risk and less start up cost than expanding into a new geographic area.

A homebuilder is somewhat analogous to a retailer. A retailer's growth results from additional market penetration from either increased productivity of its, current locations or the opening of new stores. A homebuilder operates and grows in a similar fashion. For example, the opening of new projects is similar to the opening of new stores. And those homebuilders which control their land usually obtain improved profit margins and therefore increased productivity as a result of their creation of additional real estate values.

The following example indicates how a homebuilder can grow. Many complicating factors have been omitted from this explanation. Some of these factors would be:

1. Companies have projects with different life cycles and different penetration sales patterns.
2. Profit margins differ depending upon the stages in the project life cycle.
3. High backlogs at certain projects can increase deliveries in sluggish housing years.
4. By-product sources of revenues and earnings.
5. Larger companies must open either larger projects or more projects to have a meaningful impact on revenues.

EXAMPLE
Assume that a homebuilder has three identical projects under development and that 100 homes were sold in each project last year at an average price of $25,000.

Project	Units Sold	Average Price	Revenue
1	100	$25,000	$2.5 million
2	100	$25,000	$2.5
3	100	$25,000	$2.5
Total	300		$7.5 million

If housing starts decline 15% in 1973, it is reasonable to expect that each of these projects would experience a similar decline in unit sales. However, because of increased costs due to inflation, it is also reasonable to assume that the average price would increase 8% to $27,000.

In addition, it is often assumed that profit margins would improve because:
1. The company's land has increased in value as a result of inflation.
2. The land has increased in value because additional real estate values have been created as a result of the proven success of the project.
3. The homebuilder acquired the land at a fixed cost.

However, in order to be conservative, this example does not consider improved profit margins. The ethics of making a profit by piggy-backing on inflation is a question, as is the long-term survival value of such an approach. With a conservative accounting, the results for 1973 would be as follows:

Project	Units Sold	Average Price	Revenue
1	85	$27,000	$2.3 million
2	85	$27,000	$2.3
3	85	$27,000	$2.3
Total	255		$6.9 million

As the above example indicates, the homebuilder would experience a decline in revenues *if* the company did not have the management and capital resources to develop additional revenues. One of the sources of additional revenues would be the opening of a new project.

As the following table indicates the opening of a fourth project results in a 25% increase in revenues for the homebuilder in 1973 even though both total national housing starts and the unit deliveries in each project declined 15% from the prior year. This explains one reason for the rapid rate of expansion that many builders strive for.

Project

	Units Sold	Average Price	Revenue
1	85	$27,000	$2.3 million
2	85	$27,000	$2.3
3	85	$27,000	$2.3
4	85	$27,000	$2.3
Total	340		$9.2 million

Kaufman & Broad's annual report provides an actual example of this concept.

Kaufman & Broad Inc.

	1972	1971	1970	1969	1968
Units sold	6,998	5,700	4,425	3,304	3,060
Communities (projects)	78	66	56	36	31
Deliveries/Project	90	86	79	92	99
Average price (est.)	$29,000	$27,000	$25,500	$24,000	$23,000
Housing revenues (mill.)	$231	$182	$126	$100	$ 70

As the above chart indicates, the slowdown in national housing starts because of tighter and more expensive money resulted in deliveries per project declining from ninety-nine units to seventy-nine units between 1968 and 1970. However, during this same period, Kaufman & Broad increased its number of projects from 31 to 56. In addition, the average price increased from $23,000 to $25,500. Therefore, total units delivered during this time period increased from 3,060 to 4,425 and housing revenues increased from approximately $70 million to $126 million. It should be noted that the above data do not include project life cycles. The company's decline in deliveries per project from 1969 to 1970 would also be the result of the substantial increase in new projects which were open for only a portion of the year.

Most homebuilders generate revenues and earnings from more sources than just single family houses. The following table provides a composite of the revenue volume of 419 giant homebuilding companies in the *Professional Builder* survey. A broad product mix could be a significant factor in producing increased revenues and earnings for the major homebuilders in future years.

Product Line	*% of Revenue*
Single family	25.1%
Townhouses, condos, quads	12.0
Low rise multifamily rentals	11.7
Low rise m.f. rentals (for own investment)	7.5
High rise	3.2
Non-residential	5.4
Rental revenue	5.0
Land sales	4.3
Miscellaneous	6.5

In order to provide a better understanding of income generation for a homebuilder, a more detailed analysis of one project is reviewed in the following example. For the sake of simplicity, many complicating details have been omitted. In addition, not all homebuilders approach a project with the same operating philosophy, and therefore this discussion would not be applicable to all companies.

EXAMPLE: After analyzing various locations, a homebuilder decides to acquire a tract of 200 acres in a well-situated suburban community. The company would usually obtain an option to acquire the land pending such approvals as zoning, environmental, sewer and water. Alternatively, the company would acquire the land with a purchase money mortgage, which is a non-recourse loan. Assume that the land cost $6,000 per acre, or a total of $1,200,000. In order to obtain all necessary approvals the company has had to prepare land planning and other designs. After approximately six to eighteen months, the approvals would be obtained and the company would then exercise its option to acquire the land. It is important to note that at this stage in the project cycle a considerable amount of corporation time and effort has been expended. Many companies expense all these associated costs. This "software" effort has resulted in a very marketable product which could easily be sold to other homebuilders. In many cases, a profit margin of 50% over the original cost could be obtained at this stage. However, since the homebuilders usually do not sell the land at this stage and since the land remains quoted at original cost on the balance sheet, it should be obvious that the company has substantial unrealized equity. Following the usual accounting procedures used by manufacturers, interest, and taxes have been capitalized and added to the cost of the project, though this inflates prices. The following table summarizes the probable costs and provides an estimate of the real value of the land at this stage of the project development cycle.

	Original Cost	Interest & Taxes	Cost on Balance Sheet	Market Value
Single-family (100 acres)	$ 600,000	$100,000	$ 700,000	$ 900,000
Multifamily rentals (30 acres)	180,000	30,000	210,000	300,000
Townhouses (30 acres)	180,000	30,000	210,000	300,000
Shopping center (40 acres)	240,000	40,000	280,000	600,000
Total	$1,200,000	$200,000	$1,400,000	$2,100,000

Most homebuilders will subcontract lot development and housing production to subcontractors who do the actual construction. The first sections to be developed would usually consist of the 130 acres for the single family homes and townhouses. The closing and delivery of these units could reasonably occur over three years and create revenues and profits as follows:

Product	Units	Average Price	Revenues	Pretax Profit
Single-family houses	300	$35,000	$10.5 mil.	$1.1 mil.
Townhouses	150	$25,000	$ 3.7 mil.	$0.4 mil.

The completion of these homes has created a viable, proven community. This has created a substantial increase in the real estate value of the remaining land in the project.

In this example, it is reasonable to expect a value of about $880,000 for the commercial land and $410,000 for the multifamily land at this stage in the project cycle. If the company decided to sell these properties, an additional $800,000 of pretax income would be realized. These land sales are by-product sales, created in the ordinary course of a homebuilder's business and, therefore, are included in ordinary income It is interesting to note that this land can usually be sold whenever the homebuilder decides to create additional income. This provides the company with an excellent management and financial ability to program earnings. Unfortunately, this approach has been abused considerably; to sustain a high rate of earnings growth, many builders float the value of such properties and trade them off between themselves, booking as "ordinary income" each such "sale." It reminds me of the story about the sardines that are not for eatin' but only for tradin'.

Some homebuilders have decided that rather than selling these land byproducts, they will continue to develop the project by building the multifamily rentals and the shopping center. Therefore, additional net income would not be recorded until the rental apartments or shopping center was sold. Some homebuilders have decided to retain ownership of these properties because of the high return on equity and consistent cash flow stream which are generated. The net income of a company which follows this strategy would be understated compared to the income of a company which immediately sold the by-product land. The company which built and retained ownership of the rental apartments and shopping center has created more value, more unrealized profit, and more net worth than the company which sold the by-product land.

APPENDIX D

DEMAND AND OUTLOOK FOR HOUSING IN THE SEVENTIES

The two most critical factors in determining the level of housing will be availability and cost of money and land availability.

1. *Availability and cost of money.* In the 23 years to 1973 the housing industry has gone through five cycles reflecting the changes in money flows and interest rates. The monetary environment and lack of clear federal housing policy in 1973–74 was generating another downward cycle.

During 1974 housing starts were projected to decline sharply as a result of a number of interrelated factors such as higher short-term interest rates, a slowdown of savings into the Savings and Loan Associations, higher mortgage rates, a freeze on federal subsidized programs, the suspension of the GNMA Tandem Plan on subsidized FHA housing, and the apparent lack of a clear-cut federal housing policy. However, over the long term ample mortgage capital will probably be available to enable consumers to purchase their own homes— though its costs will keep rising and will require expanded subsidization in one form or another. Financial mechanisms such as the Federal National Mortgage Association and the Federal Home Loan Mortgage Corporation will funnel such funds into the industry.

2. *Availability of land.* The concern for the protection of environment and natural resources has resulted in the emergence of "no growth policies" and pollution control policies (sewer and water) which sharply hindered new construction. In a number of communities the impact of these policies has been to increase processing time, hinder approval of new projects and remove a number of land tracts from the market. In other words, the availability of buildable land is becoming an increasing problem. This problem is exacerbated by the energy crisis, which promotes a higher-density use of land closer to urban and suburban areas and will be bringing out the contending parties in force.

The trend appearing as of 1972 toward construction of for-sale housing and away from rental complexes should continue to 1975, at any rate. This is the result of a number of factors including: recognition by the consumer that ownership of his own home is his best protection against inflation; the tax benefits of owning a home as consumer incomes rise; higher rents resulting from expected tax reform. Therefore, the for-sale portion of housing starts should increase even faster than the total. One recent analysis suggested that the for-sale portion could increase from an average of 900,000 units in the 1960s to an average of 1.5 million units in the 1970s. However, the energy crisis also complicates this picture, forcing development closer to work centers and away from suburban areas. A faster rate of inflation also in the longer term prices more people out of ownership housing, no matter how much they might want it. So large-scale rental (and condominium) units look like the thing for the later Seventies. The private home is on the way out.

Annual Average On-Site Housing Requirements for the 1970s
(not allowing for inflation's displacement of buyers into rental units)

1. Actual level of 1950-1970	1.4–1.5 million units
2. Average increase in family formations	0.4–0.4
3. Estimated increase in one-person and unrelated households	0.1–0.2
4. Estimated increase in second homes (leisure/recreation)	0.1–0.2
5. Estimated increase in retiree homes	0.0–0.1
6. Replacement increase	0.1–0.2
7. Demand for mobility (vacancy rates) increase	0.0–0.1
	2.1–2.6
8. Less the *net* increase in mobile home units	0.1–0.2
Total	2.0–2.4

The economics department of the National Association of Homebuilders recently completed a study indicating the housing supply which should be necessary to meet the expanding demand. The NAHB identified and quantified five major demand factors: household increase, net removals from housing inventory, net removals from mobile homes, changes in vacancy, and demand for second homes. Their study indicated that the fundamental *demand* for housing, including mobile homes, should approach 3.0 million units per year during the next ten years. How this demand would be met in light of spiralling inflation remained to be seen.

It is also important to realize that not all markets and products will reflect the higher base level of 2.0 million housing starts. Indeed, the composition of the demand is probably more important than the increase.

To be expected is a continuing trend of in-migration into the southern and southwestern markets and a continuation of the desire for the suburban form of life. During the past twelve years the South's share of housing starts has increased each year from 34% to 46% of total starts. In 1972, the 25 largest markets outside of Florida had only a 15% increase in total permits over 1971, while Florida was up approximately 70%. In addition, recent vacancy statistics indicate a sharp distinction between urban and suburban housing. The rapid entry of many major builders into this area may, however, saturate even this booming market.

A further implication of this trend is that marketwide vacancy rates have only limited meaning. The numbers must be analyzed between urban and suburban, old and new. In Detroit for example, rental vacancies are over 20% in the older in-city apartments, but under 5% in most suburban markets. On a national basis, the rental vacancies were 6.2% in the central cities and 6.3% outside the metro area, but only 4.2% in the suburbs. In addition, a significant portion of the expected increase in fundamental demand should occur in town-houses, condominiums, recreation/leisure homes, and retiree homes.

Therefore, during the next decade it will become increasingly important to analyze the ability of a homebuilder to consistently identify and enter submarket segments and to introduce new products to determine the company's potential for future growth.

The following factors provide data for the analysis of general housing demand on a short-term basis:

1. Ratio of homes for sale to homes sold.
2. Market absorption.
3. Vacancy rates.
4. Building permits.
5. Saving and loan money flows.
6. Mortgage rates.
7. Availability of mortgage money.
8. Savings rates.
9. Government housing programs and policies.
10. Consumer spending intentions.
11. NAHB quarterly metropolitan housing starts forecast.

It is important to remember that homebuilding is a local market business. Therefore, most of the above factors should be analyzed on a local as well as national basis. For example, an analysis of market absorption should include:

1. The metropolitan area.
2. The geographic submarket (e.g., northeast section or southwest area; central city or suburban).
3. The price range (e.g., higher priced homes or lower priced homes).
4. Old units or new units.
5. Rentals or single family.
6. Single family detached or townhouses.
7. Specific location (one of the most important factors affecting a particular project).

Many of the short-term factors as of 1973 were in a negative trend, result-ing in a declining rate of housing starts. In particular, the rise in mortgage rates and less availability of mortgage funds at savings and loans resulted in housing starts declining at the end of 1973. It has been estimated that a 1% increase in mortgage rates causes a drop of 150,000 housing starts.

The new mortgage market mechanisms combined with a more active fed-eral housing policy were looked to in order to prevent a severe and prolonged decline in housing starts. Projections said housing starts would return to the 2.0–2.1 million unit level by 1975.

Even though housing starts could be fluctuating sharply on a seasonally adjusted yearly figure based on monthly starts, total yearly completions could remain relatively stable, barring further economic or political reverses. Since the annual revenues of the homebuilders are based on annual completions rather than monthly, seasonally adjusted starts, an analysis of completions pro-vides further information to analyze the outlook for the companies The follow-ing table indicates possible estimates of completions for 1973–1975. It is inter-esting to note that even though starts are shown as declining in both 1973 and

1974 yearly completions are not projected to decline as much. In addition, the dollar volume of the completions could actually increase because of higher costs.

	1970	1971	1972	1973	1974	1975
Housing starts	1.5	2.1	2.4	2.1	1.8	2.0
Carry forward of unfinished units	0.9	0.9	1.3	1.7	1.7	1.5
Construction in progress	2.4	3.0	3.7	3.8	3.5	3.5
Completions	1.4	1.7	1.9	2.1	1.9	1.9
Balance	1.0	1.3	1.8	1.9	1.6	1.6
Carry forward	0.9	1.3	1.7	1.7	1.5	1.5

The supply and cost of money is one of the most important factors influencing the actual level of housing demand. During the past 20 years, housing has been a residual user of credit. Therefore, it appears to have been a highly cyclical industry dependent on the sharp changes occurring in the credit markets.

Actually, housing has been less cyclical on an annual basis than most investors realize. In fact, there was only one year during the 1961-1970 period when annual housing starts fell more than 10% from the 10 year average of 1.45 million units.

As of the Seventies, several major new mechanisms have been added to the residential mortgage market. During the Sixties there were few, if any, effective programs to insure adequate financing for housing. However, since 1970 a number of new programs have been introduced. Each of these programs is designed to provide additional credit during periods of tight money and savings disintermediation.

The major programs are:

1. *S&L's have introduced the fixed-term deposit certificate.* When short-term interest rates increased substantially above 5% in 1966 and 1969, S&L's experienced massive disintermediation of funds. In 1972, however, approximately 40-50% of S&L deposits were invested in savings certificates with a fixed term. Consumers are less likely to withdraw their savings from these fixed term deposits than from their normal passbook savings. Consequently, this program provides a stability to savings which did not exist in the Sixties.

2. *The minimum denomination of Treasury Bills has been increased* from $1,000 to $10,000. This increase prevents many consumers from withdrawing their small savings and placing the amount in high yielding Treasury Bills. Scarcely equitable, but it does prop up the mortgage market.

3. *S&L's can borrow substantial amounts from the Federal Home Loan Bank (FHLB).* The FHLB board regulates savings and loans. The FHLB can sell debt in the open market and advance the proceeds to the S&L's to support their mortgage lending

4. *A secondary mortgage market for both FHA/VA and conventional mortgages has been created.* The Federal National Mortgage Association (FNMA) and the Federal Home Loan Mortgage Corp. are the two principal organizations in the secondary mortgage market. They issue debt directly in the open credit markets to raise capital which they use to purchase mortgages. Therefore, the housing industry is not entirely dependent upon deposits to sustain its mortgage lending programs.

5. *The GNMA pooling program and Tandem Plan.*   The pooling program is actually another type of secondary mortgage market operation. The Tandem Plan was suspended on subsidized housing; this was projected to reduce housing starts by at least 100,000 units in 1974.

6. *The FHLBB 95% loan/value program.*   This program allowed the consumer to buy a house with only a 5% down payment. Housing demand in 1971–72 was definitely stimulated by this program since it enabled a significant number of additional consumers to afford the down payment. However, during the current period of less mortgage money availability, S&L's are requiring higher down payments and therefore limiting their use of the 95% loan/value ratio. In addition, many S&L's have reached the legal limit of 95% loans in their portfolios and therefore can only increase their participation in line with their total portfolio expansion.

Assuming some containment of inflation, the existence of these mechanisms combined with a subsidy-oriented federal housing policy could contribute to maintaining annual housing starts above 1.8 million units per year during 1974–1978.

The following chart details the flow of money into various savings institutions:

Flow of Funds—Selected Savings Institutions (billions)

	Mutual Savings Banks	S&L's	Commercial Banks	Life Insurance
1972	9.8	32.9	44.5	17.8
1971	9.7	28.2	40.0	14.5
1970	4.6	11.2	34.8	9.0
1969	2.5	4.2	9.3	8.8
1968	4.2	7.4	20.6	11.3
1967	5.1	10.6	23.6	10.3
1966	2.6	3.6	12.1	8.1

The following chart provides a summary breakdown of the long-term mortgage loan originations on new properties during 1972.

	Single Family (millions)	%	Multi-Family (millions)	%
Commercial banks	$ 5,843	27.9%	$ 496	7.0%
Mutual savings banks	911	4.3	654	9.2
Savings and loans	12,528	59.8	2,518	35.3
Life insurance companies	220	1.0	1,494	21.0
Private noninsured pension funds	5	—	18	0.3
Real estate investment trusts	32	0.2	193	2.7
State and local retirement funds	64	0.3	54	0.8
Federal credit agencies	1,010	4.8	1,405	19.7
State and local credit agencies	344	1.6	294	4.1
	$20,956	100.0%	$ 7,125	100.0%

SOURCE: HUD; *Professional Builder.*

Mid-1973

As of mid-1973 the outlook for new housing sales deteriorated due to two key factors:

1. *Unprecedented increases in short term interest rates.* As in 1969–1970, S&L's experienced a sharp decline in new savings inflows and, in some cases, disintermediation. This was a logical occurrence when short term interest rates (such as riskless treasury bills) exceeded 8%.

The S&L monetary situation was further aggravated when (July 5, 1973) the Federal Reserve Board reduced the interest rate differential on savings deposits to 25 basis points and permitted banks to pay an unlimited interest rate on deposits which have a minimum maturity of four years.

Yields on these time deposits immediately increased from the 6% range to 7–8% as banks and S&Ls competed for funds. As a result, residential mortgage rates increased 75–100 basis points (8½% range) and the availability of mortgage commitments (particularly for high ratio financing such as 90% and 95%) sharply declined.

In an effort to maintain mortgage availability, the Federal Home Loan Bank Board reduced the savings and loan liquidity requirement from 7% to 5½% in two separate actions. In addition, FNMA increased its level of commitment activity and GNMA was expected to increase its pass-through program of mortgage-backed securities.

2. *Lack of a clear-cut federal housing policy.* The government provided very little support for the housing market. For example, HUD suspended the Tandem Plan on unsubsidized FHA housing and there was no indication of an immediate return to subsidized programs that had been frozen.

But as additional sources of mortgage money became available, higher interest rates continued to eliminate many consumers from the market because of higher down payment requirements and higher monthly carrying charges.

In addition, inflation and higher financing "points" also eliminated consumers from the market by increasing the price of the house. For example, in 1972 the consumer could have purchased a $30,000 home with $2,000 down and a thirty-year mortgage at 7½%. In mid-1973, the same house would cost $34,000 and the interest rate would be 8¾%. The combination of a higher priced house and a higher mortgage rate resulted in increasing the monthly charge 27% from $235 to $298. Since consumer incomes have not increased at that rate, many additional consumers were not able to afford a new home unless the homebuilders could miraculously introduce a lower priced product.

Government proposals for financial reform

Later in 1973, President Nixon sent Congress a plan with dramatic new proposals to change the financial structure in the country. These proposals were developed from the Hunt Commission's study on the nation's financial structure which was issued in December, 1971. They are essentially a series of ingenious, expedient solutions to accommodate (and thus, in the nature of things, accelerate) inflation. The seven major areas covered by President Nixon's proposals included:

1. Interest ceilings on time and savings deposits to be removed over a 5¼ year period.

2. Expanded deposit service for consumers by federally chartered thrift institutions and banks to be allowed.
3. Investment and lending alternatives for federally chartered thrift institutions and banks to be expanded.
4. Federal charters for stock savings and loan institutions and mutual savings banks to be permitted.
5. Credit unions to be provided with greater access to funds.
6. FHA and VA interest ceilings to be removed.
7. The tax structure of banks and thrift institutions to be modified.

The major concern for the homebuilding industry is not whether a viable S&L system will exist, but if a viable and adequate residential mortgage market will exist.

These proposals required lengthy study and were, almost certainly, to be substantially modified before enactment.

One of the basic points of the proposed legislation, which results in greater control by the big commercial banks of this industry, was to develop a more "efficient" and "competitive" system of financial intermediaries which are all able to compete for capital in any monetary environment. Since the proposals eliminated the interest rate differential, the ability of S&Ls to compete for time deposits could only be reduced. In addition, S&Ls would probably significantly reduce the percentage of their assets which are placed in residential mortgages. However, even if this were to occur, the total availability of mortgage credit would not necessarily be adversely affected. Congress could also expand the supply of mortgage money by:

1. Creating more incentives such as a mortgage investment tax credit.
2. Requiring all deposit financial intermediaries to maintain a specified percentage of their assets in residential mortgages. For example, commercial banks could be required to increase their percentage of time deposits, which are invested in mortgages, from 32% to 50%.

PART TWO

Mergers and Acquisitions

The Passionate Shepherd to his Love
Come live with me, and be my
love;
And we will all the pleasures
prove
That valleys, groves, hills and
fields,
Woods or steepy mountain yields.

—Christopher Marlowe

The Nymph's Reply to the Passionate Shepherd
If all the world and love were
young,
And truth in every shepherd's
tongue,
These pretty pleasures might me
move
To live with thee, and be thy love.

—Sir Walter Raleigh

5

The Makings of a Merger

I saw her standing on the corner,
A yellow ribbon in her hair.

—The Coasters

I shall begin this section with a brief look at the history of mergers. Builders, being eminently practical fellows more interested in getting something done than in academic niceties, may not give a damn; but the occasional bookish soul might be glad to know how the merger phenomenon in real estate is positioned within the present economic superstructure and the economic history of the country.

There have been three major merger booms in the American economy since the 1890's. The first wave, peaking in 1899, roared through the economy over a five-year period from 1897 to 1902. The second, rising to a crest in 1929, lasted from 1924 to 1930. The third and latest period of intensive merger activity got off to a start roughly in 1965 and, hitting a high point in 1968, lasted to about mid-1970, when the combination of a despondently wallowing stock market and changes in wildly liberal merger accounting rules brought it to a close. After more than a year of quiescence, the pace of mergers again picked up in the latter half of 1971 and was trending upward in 1972 before slumping off in 1973 due to a battered economy.

The first of the big booms was responsible for the creation of national railway and communication networks (telephone and telegraph). Also leading to a consolidation of the nation's metals makers, it thus laid down the framework for the development to today's highly industrialized economy. With the connection of hundreds of regional railroad lines, and the building of many thousands of miles of track, along with the creation of national wire communication systems, the cost of transportation and communication was greatly reduced and their speed was greatly increased. Hence, national markets became a reality. Growing immensely, the opportunities for profit by combining firms into larger units and reaping the benefits of lower costs through economies of scale resulted in a rapid consolidation of industry: U.S. Steel, U.S. Rubber and American Can Company were born, among other industrial giants. The merger wave was facilitated by the development of a national money market, focused on Wall

121

Street, of course. In a growing economy, stock prices were up and their high multiples, giving them a high purchasing power in acquisition deals, gave a further boost to the merger wave. In 1899, the peak year of this boom, about 1,200 mining and manufacturing corporations with a total capitalization of $2.3 billion (about $11 billion in 1972 dollars) went the merger route.

The second merger wave, peaking in 1929, also produced enormous structural changes in the American economy and the quality of life. And it also focused on, and developed from, changes in transportation and communication. The U.S. economy was motorized after World War I with the development of reliable mass-produced automobiles and the subsequent completion of a national road network. Automobiles and trucks gave people and goods enormous mobility, enlarging markets, destroying local monopolies and creating new economies of scale. At the same time, the home radio made national advertising cheap and effective, built the value of brand names, and enhanced the advantages of national marketing. Multiple-market distribution spelled the end of the local operator as, by the mid-Twenties, businessmen generally perceived the large opportunities opened up by such changes. The booming stock market of 1921–29 also powered the merger wave by giving high purchasing power to stock. The focus was on the creation of economies of scale in marketing, but along with merchandising companies, vertical and horizontal combinations of manufacturing firms and public utilities were also prominent. In 1929, the peak year, some 1,250 mergers were reported, involving stock of much larger total value than in 1899.

The third and latest great merger boom, starting roughly in 1965, was inspired principally by the advent of high technology and a merchandising revolution in packaging. Technological advances had been accelerating at a rapid pace since World War II in both quantity and the rate of change. The merger boom was accordingly based in electronics and computers, and gave rise to many large organizations in these and related fields. Swift technological advances in other industries accelerated the rate at which new products reached the marketplace, often replacing not only the old products but the companies that produced them. The technological revolution in packaging provided the basis for the growth of new merchandising chains; the revolution in franchising transformed Main Street U.S.A. into a metropolis of temples serving chicken, pizza, hamburgers and auto parts.

The outstanding characteristic of the third merger boom was, however, the rise of the conglomerate corporation. In 1968, the peak year of the boom, more than 4,400 companies disappeared by merger, involving an estimated $43 billion of stock—an all-time record. The conglomerate companies accounted for a preponderant fraction of all the firms and assets involved, though this figure cannot be given exactly, since the definition of "conglomerate," and accordingly the number of companies involved, is variable. The Sherman and Clayton antitrust acts prohibited the agglomeration of monopoly power by consolidation of major competing businesses, but the "conglomerate" sprang into the big time by acquiring multiple businesses from noncompetitive areas. Often creating the illusion of rapid growth solely by the pace of acquisitions, the companies frequently became "go-go" issues commanding glamorous multiples. A burgeoning mutual fund industry with hordes of salesmen pumping in virginal investors added steam to the rising stock market, with investors hot for glamour issues. These factors, together with the technological revolution, gave further support to the merger boom. Many new companies and new merger combinations were formed to accommodate the market's demand.

The pattern of merger booms, insofar as can be judged by the available evidence, is that they rise through a four- or five-year curve to a peak and then drop swiftly in another year or two. This seems to have been the pattern of the latest boom. By 1970, only 1,230 major mergers were recorded, 28% below the 1969 rate (1,712 mergers) and 33% below the 1968 peak of 1,829 major corporate mergers (though some 4,400 corporations of all sizes were swallowed up that year). Merger activity fell off dramatically in mid-1970 and after a slight rise toward the end of the year slowed down even more through the first half of 1971. Depressed stock prices discouraged mergers because most acquisitions involve payment in shares of the acquiring company; management and shareholders of the other firm are reluctant to take payment in shares that are slipping in value. Also, buyers are often unwilling to make acquisitions with depressed-price shares because this lowers their buying power and control by forcing upward the number of shares that must be paid out to meet the seller's price. Thus, a couple of years into the Seventies the key word in merger activity became not acquisition but divestiture as overextended, once-acquisitive companies scrambled to unload, particularly when they could not borrow money at reasonable rates because of tight money.

The new accounting rules promulgated by the Accounting Principles Board in 1970, and pretty much enforceable by the Securities and Exchange Commission, also played an important role in dealing a death stroke to a lot of high-flying conglomerate merger activity which had been inspired by the opportunity to create instant profits by accounting gimmickry. We shall get to a discussion of these rules as they affected the real estate industry in particular in Chapter VIII, but as they severely affected all corporate merger activity they are briefly summarized here.

The most important reform applied to the popular method of accounting for mergers is known as "pooling of interests." In pooling, the acquiring company wrote the assets of another firm into its books at their original cost rather than their current value. A high-flying conglomerate using inflated stock would pay a high paper price for such assets but book them at cost instead of market value, then turn right around and sell the assets at a high price and report the difference between book value and sale price as profit. Many a conglomerate sustained its high P/E multiple in this fashion without an iota of real, (i.e., internal) growth. An astute management, having produced no real earnings for the quarter, could make a fast sale of an asset of "submerged value" from a prior acquisition just in time to make the printing deadline for the quarterly earnings report, and then look like geniuses to the gullible sheep investing to the siren call of Wall Street's "recommendations." The resulting high P/E multiples of the conglomerates gave them buying power that enabled them to repeat this process, making further acquisitions with a variety of securities predicated on high-multiple stock and selling off the acquired assets at a "profit." Needless to say, both the shareholders and the sellers of the merged companies took a bath when the inflated stock burst.

The accounting rule-makers, to discourage such situations, prohibited the use of pooling if merger plans call for disposing of acquired assets within two years, as well as deciding to require special disclosure to the public if the assets are sold at any time. Further, the new pooling rules prohibited companies from using "funny money" — preferreds, convertible preferred, warrants, convertible debentures — in acquisitions, limiting such deals to a straight common-stock-for-common-stock exchange. Such instruments made it easier to buy and sell: preferred stock, having a guaranteed future value, is immune from stock-market fluctuations that would worry a seller; convertible debentures maturing in ten to forty years pay interest which is tax-exempt.

In mergers ineligible for pooling, companies are forced to adopt "purchase accounting." The disadvantage of this system is that acquiring companies usually must enter part of the cost of acquisition on their books as "goodwill" and write it off over a forty-year period; the expenses of the merger, heretofore treated as a one-time charge against capital, now have to be charged against current earnings. Because goodwill is not tax-deductible, the write-off becomes a direct and sometimes substantial drain on profits.

The merger boom in real estate only began with the last big merger wave. No matter what the overall rate of mergers might be in the U.S. economy, several particular industries will continue to experience great activity in mergers and acquisitions throughout much of the Seventies. Real estate development and construction is one of these fields. These are greatly fragmented industries where, in many cases, growth by affiliation with a larger company is now indispensable to survival because of the combination of scarce money and the increasingly hard-driving competitive atmosphere created by the larger publicly held building firms. These factors in themselves will accelerate the industry's consolidation via mergers and then subsequent reconsolidations. I feel this is true despite the great stock market decline late in 1973.

If we look over the preconditions that set off the three big merger booms in the U.S. economy, we come up with two basics: (1) The perception of unexploited opportunities for profit arising from basic technological or social changes; and (2) the availability of large sources of capital, channeled through investment banking firms, and linked with a rising stock market, to develop and control the perceived opportunity. Wall Street stock promotions and hustling to create unsound business combinations, in order to make a fast buck by riding a trend, always add a characteristic touch of color to such merger booms, and this is why in the aftermath of every boom a number of hot new companies fold their tents by night and steal away into Chapter X or XI of the Bankruptcy Act.

The basic preconditions, as we have seen, were certainly present in the real estate industry. Once the need was declared by the 1968 Housing and Urban Development Act, which set a ten-year goal of 26 million housing units for the nation, anyone could figure out that this called for annual construction volumes nearly double what the industry was then producing. The Council of Housing Producers called attention to the fact that professional builders were really professional. The result was a merger wave that in its first phase continued even when the bottom fell out of the stock market, so eager were major corporate acquirers to get in on future housing profits as well as getting an inflation hedge. As with the earlier booms, this merger wave reflects a structural change in the economy—but this time one that consolidates the manufacture, distribution and marketing of housing.

Importantly, as the conditions basic to further consolidation in real estate will hold true for at least the next several years, we will see a continuation of mergers and acquisitions in this field, though in altered form from the first phase of this boom. The first phase saw conglomerate mergers in real estate. The second, while preserving some acquisitions by companies from unrelated industries, will emphasize the congeneric type of acquisition.

MOTIVATIONS UNDERLYING SPECIFIC MERGERS

Although the business of real estate and construction differs in many significant ways from other types of corporate enterprise, it, too, has been subject to merger and acquisition from some of the same general underlying motivations that have powered the latest merger boom in the U.S. economy. It will be useful to examine these general motivating factors as they have inspired the major corporations to turn to real estate.

TAXES. As anyone who has been in business knows, corporate income taxation has risen steeply since World War II. In 1940 the effective federal corporate income tax was 27%; in 1968 it was 53%, including the 10% surtax. The rates of state and local taxes on business incomes have risen commensurately.

The effects of heavy income taxation on corporate policies are too numerous to list here. But rising taxes have been a prime reason for mergers, as corporations of all types have formed combinations based on tax-shelter considerations. In its simplest form this type of merger has a company with profits merging with one having tax losses carried over from previous years and using the loss to offset the profits. But such combinations can get far more sophisticated. International oil and mineral companies with unused foreign tax credits acquire companies whose incomes can be sheltered by those credits. American petroleum producers with high drilling write-offs, for example, also acquire high-profit firms for the same reason.

Many railroads have found that diversification lets them use their past losses to reduce taxes of the companies they acquire. One of the main reasons behind Container Corporation's union with Montgomery Ward to form Marco was to defer payment for several years of more than $60 million a year of federal income taxes by taking fuller advantage of Ward's ability to defer taxes on profits arising from installment credit sales.

Because it has offered an unparalleled tax-shelter opportunity, as already outlined in Chapter I, real estate has been a prime candidate for mergers and acquisitions undertaken for tax considerations. This is particularly true in the instance of corporations acquiring organizations that build and retain ownership of income-producing properties, where tax "losses" resulting from development costs and depreciation schedules can be used to offset corporate taxation.

The equity securities of companies acquired by merger have often been replaced by convertible debentures of the surviving company. This was particularly true before the accounting reforms of 1970, though it is a continuing practice in some type of mergers. The net effect of such a deal is the replacement of taxable income paid out as dividends by tax-deductible interest. (The interest paid on convertible debentures is, of course, tax-exempt.) Also, debenture holders have been able to defer income taxes on their profits until the debentures are almost paid off. Prior to the accounting reforms, these factors encouraged mergers and acquisitions between companies in unrelated industries and gave impetus to real estate mergers, as well as encouraging generally the conglomerate form of combination over vertical or horizontal combinations. It illustrates the point that tax avoidance has been one of the most important motives for merger.

FINANCING. The cost of capital — the going rate of return to investors — has more than doubled since World War II. Industrial bonds yielding 3.3% in 1945 returned 7.2% in late 1968, while home mortgage loan rates went from 4% to about 8% in the same span of time. The basic reason for this increase in the cost of money was scarcity. Scarcity of money was caused by expanded investments in less developed foreign economies where a higher rate of return was possible, and by vastly expanded spending in sectors generating no investment return at all, such as the Vietnam war and domestic antipoverty and welfare programs. Inflation, joining these factors, then pushed rates up further. In Europe, where capital allocation was even more imbalanced, and inflation more pronounced, the scarcity of investment funds was greater. European investment rates thus rose higher than domestic rates and pulled investment capital out of the United States, compounding domestic difficulties. This factor contributed to a rise in U.S. interest rates in the latter half of the Sixties, to a point where the price of money became about equal in the world's major money markets.

The higher price of capital has had many consequences in the domestic economy. Cash management programs sprang up among corporations, and they tried to use their money more efficiently. Investment projects were screened more rigorously. The finance officer became the kingpin in the corporate hierarchy. The significant effect of capital costs on the merger wave has been, however, that corporate managements began to aggressively search for companies with cash or liquid assets. Finance and insurance companies were especially sought by industrial firms because of their steady inflow of premiums and loan repayments. But any company with liquifiable and low-earning assets was a target for takeover, followed by sale of assets.

Real estate and development firms, offering the potential of an inordinately high return on investment because of the leverage they employ, also became a natural prospect for acquisitions by major corporations, as the pervasive quest for financial resources became the motive for many a corporate merger.

MERGERS FOR "WRONG" REASONS

If we apply a little ethical perspective in judging the acts of corporations, we can say that a merger is "wrong" or unethical if it is engineered principally for the private gain of a few individuals at the expense of the public purse. Such mergers have been of two types — undertaken for promotional profits or reductions in taxes. In the former, the public gets burned by investing in inflated (and soon deflated) stock; in the latter, the public assumes the added tax burden avoided by the merged entity. We can narrow down the definition of "wrong" mergers to those in the two given categories which do not intend to generate internal effectiveness in the production of goods and services for the actual production of profits.

The stock-promotion merger is predicated on the observation that the market will often value the equity of the expanded, merged entity at a higher multiple of earnings. Earnings per share of the acquiring firm increase as a result of the merger and the market, applying the acquiring company's established multiplier, bids up the price of the stock. This makes further acquisitions through exchange of stock attractive, forming the foundation for further expansions in reported earnings per share and further inflation of the market price of the stock.

This type of growth, in the language of Wall Street, is an *extreme* example of "synergism," where the sum is greater than its parts. How it is achieved is briefly illustrated in the following example:

1. Company A has earnings of $100 and 100 shares. This gives it per-share earnings of $1.00. As its stock is priced at $20 in the market, this gives the stock a P/E multiple of 20 and a total market value of $2,000.

2. Company B has earnings of $50 and 50 shares. This also gives it per-share earnings of $1.00. Its stock is priced at $10 in the market, giving it a total market value of $500 on its P/E multiple of 10.

3. Company A acquires Company B in a stock-for-stock exchange. The rate of exchange (established as a ratio of market price) is 0.25 share of Company A stock for 1 share of Company B stock.

4. The enlarged Company A now has earnings of $150 and a new total of 125 shares. By the fact of acquisition alone, Company A's earnings thus rise by $0.20, to $1.20 per share. Since its established P/E multiple had been 20, the market applies this multiplier and boosts up the price of the stock to $24.00 from $20.00.

Financial synergism of this type has an important role in the tailoring of many economically sound mergers. But in those instances it is only one of several key considerations, and its importance is subordinated to the evaluation of a potential acquisition's real earnings capacity, the quality of its management and the ways in which an acquirer can genuinely contribute to the subsidiary's growth curve. In the extreme case of mergers whose principal motivation was to run up the price of the stock as rapidly as possible, such financial synergism was, however, the *only* consideration governing acquisitions. A conglomerate making multiple mergers could thus achieve the appearance of phenomenal growth in per-share earnings. But so long as such acquisitions are made without a careful eye on sustaining the company's growth long-term through real earnings production, the whole enterprise sooner or later falls apart.

This stock-promotion game continues until the public recognizes there is no growth in the operating earnings of the acquired companies. The stock price then plummets to a point where the P/E ratio reflects a realistic rather than hopeful view of future earnings. At this much lower price, further acquisitions become unattractive and cease. Meanwhile, of course, the promoters will have unloaded their shares on less sophisticated investors, and the bankers, brokers and sundry middlemen will have pocketed their commissions. The accounting reforms on pooling put a crimp into such high-flying schemes but do not eliminate the possibility of their recurrence. Public policy can't prevent such mergers, beyond enforcing SEC regulations for the full disclosure of all pertinent facts. But, as P. T. Barnum said, "There's a sucker born every minute." A few unfortunate real estate or building firms swept up in such mergers have suffered painful falls.

The other type of private gain from merger is reduction of tax load at the expense of the public. When a company bungles sufficiently to build up a heavy tax-loss carryover, it can, as things are set up, merge with a profitable company to reduce the taxable earnings of the enlarged entity. The government is thus compelled to seek heavier taxes from others to restore the level of collected revenues; the tax burden shifts from the stockholders of the merged companies to the public. Which is, you might say, inequitable. The protests from segments of the business community that get jolted with bigger tax bills because of such special treatment can and do stir legislators to introduce and pass tax reforms. The closing of tax loopholes is a constant process.

MERGERS FOR "RIGHT" REASONS — CONGLOMERATE AND CONGENERIC

A "right" reason for a merger, insofar as there is one, is that the new business combination enhances the long-term survival prospects of the acquiring and the acquired entities, producing real economic gains. Sound mergers are thus undertaken for basically the following four reasons:

1. Reduction of risks. Conglomerate-type and major congeneric-type organizations can sometimes combine operations in unrelated raw materials, technologies or markets in such a way that the annual sales or profits of the different operations average out the ups and downs of the various subsidiaries to produce a stable upward earnings curve. Overall, such a combination can produce a more stable return on investment, based on the principle of portfolio diversification. For any given risk, the expected reward will be higher. This enhances the company's survival because the reduction in the premium for risk is the same as a cut in the company's costs, and via market competition, in the prices of its products. One conglomerate corporation that exemplifies this pattern is City Investing Com-

pany, which is diversified in a half-dozen industries and has holdings in homebuilding and mobile-home and land development. The congeneric like U.S. Home similarly lowers its risk by diversification of geographic markets and products.

2. Cheaper money and the capability to wait it out. Related to gains of diversification are the advantages reaped by the larger acquirer of lower money costs and the ability to wait out adverse effects in the financial markets. A conglomerate or congeneric can raise funds on a debt or equity basis at a lower cost than the smaller firms that join it. Such organizations can also finance temporary financing losses of a component organization that would bankrupt the smaller independent. The big boys can outspend, outdare and outwait smaller and financially less secure firms in an effort to win the market.

3. Economies of scale. Acquisitions enable the congeneric and the conglomerate to apply over a wider sales base the talents of a skilled general management team in functions such as planning, organization, staffing, budgeting, finance, marketing and controlling. While the organizational structures of conglomerates differ, the central corporate management commonly delegates wide authority to each divisional management, holding the latter accountable for meeting that division's earnings projections. The central corporate officers implement a planning and controlling discipline for all divisional managers and make the major decisions on capital allocation. This holds true for the congeneric form of organization as well. But in view of the fact that a congeneric consists of companies all within the same industry, usually a far more intimate degree of cooperation and support is possible between divisional managers and the central corporate office, based on a close knowledge of each other's working realities.

4. Spreading costs of expensive services and consultants. Both the conglomerate and the congeneric, possessing greater resources, can employ specialized experts in operations analysis, marketing research, technological innovations, computer sciences, incentive systems, international business, promotion, public relations, and so on. Such services enable an organization to respond to new opportunities and increase its share of the market in an increasingly competitive business environment. The scale of operations of smaller firms is often too small to justify such costs.

BASIC MOTIVATIONS FOR MERGER/ACQUISITION (BUYER)

Given a sound economic underpinning to the concept of a merger, there are a number of specific reasons why a conglomerate or congeneric would want to go the acquisition route. Let's recapitulate these:

1. To grow more quickly than is possible through internal growth. One major building industry congeneric, projecting a 40% growth rate, expects to meet fully half of that rate on an annual basis by acquisitions.

2. To expand or diversify at lower cost through mergers/acquisitions than would be possible through internal growth. In some industries, the cost of buying a product line runs as low as 2% of what it would cost to develop such a line internally.

3. To improve earnings, yield, or book value of stocks through a bargain purchase when a company is bought at a low P/E ratio or for substantially below book value, as in our example of financial synergism.

4. To achieve greater capital and earnings strength through the combination of two companies. This often makes possible the financing of additional inventories or new plant equipment (in real estate, it can accelerate new project development) which can increase profits and better meet the competition.

5. To enter new markets which cannot be tapped with existing resources. New markets can be geographic or of product variety.

6. To recruit needed managerial skills by acquiring companies. Presumably the acquirer always searches for skilled management. Sometimes, however, an older management recognizes that it needs new leadership and has no younger men in the organization who can take over. It makes an acquisition to infuse new talent into its executive suite.

7. To acquire a listing on a national stock exchange. Many financial people feel that such a listing gives a company certain stability and respectability, as well as the prospect of making a profit from a stock with a listed market value and presumably a rising P/E. They combine two or more companies to create an entity large enough to be taken public. One such example in the building industry is the Robino-Ladd Construction Company, which in 1969 was created by merger and later went public.

8. To protect markets, products or customers when it is known that the company to be acquired is contemplating entry into the markets and product areas of the acquiring company. This is not a frequent occurrence in the building industry at this time, but will become more of a possibility as the industry consolidates further.

9. To improve the long-term sales picture through a broader or more diversified product line, or to acquire new technological skills or patents. A number of builders, for example, have acquired mobile-home manufacturers and factory-housing plants.

10. To increase sales and earnings through horizontal diversification or vertical integration. The theory is that excess facilities can be eliminated and personnel costs reduced, and facilities such as warehousing, as well as accounting and overhead costs, can be combined to cut costs. This motiva-

tion underlies industrial mergers more strongly than it does market-oriented building industry mergers, where size often can actually reduce efficiency. In its stricter sense, vertical integration implies manufacturing cost savings where the product line of one of the combining companies is used in making the products of the other company. Many of the lumber and building-supply manufacturers have moved forward into housing production.

BASIC MOTIVATIONS FOR MERGER/ACQUISITION (SELLER)

The motivations of the seller do not always coincide with the motivations of the buyer in an acquisition deal. On the other hand, the buyer is looking for a strong addition to his firm to bolster sales and earnings. But the nature of the situation is such that the seller wouldn't be selling if he didn't have a problem of some sort. The trick in evaluating acquisition candidates thus becomes one of distinguishing between "negative" and "positive" problems of the sellers. The best example of a positive problem is one of a bright, aggressive management which finds a shortage of capital impeding company growth. An acquiring corporation can both solve this problem and help itself by picking up such a company. A negative problem is a management of a failing company looking for a bailout. Acquisition situations basically resolve to these two categories of candidates, but there are refinements.

In the instance of smaller or closely held "family" companies, the motivations for selling are usually quite simple. The owners may, of course, want to unload a business which is deteriorating in terms of sales and earnings, or for which the outlook has become uncertain. But they may also wish to sell because of advanced age, ill health, or inability to cope with changes and competition. Convertibility of ownership into stockholdings can solve an impending estate-tax problem. Such owners may, of course, also be looking for greater security by joining forces with a larger and financially stronger company. Or they may be looking at merger as a way to grow more quickly by virtue of the acquirer's better financial capabilities, market position or special know-how.

In the instance of larger companies, the motivations for selling out may include all of the above, as well as certain other inducements. They may wish to avoid serious losses or even bankruptcy. They may be attracted by lavish stock options, profit sharing, retirement and other benefits dangled before them by the buyer. Or, they may have to divest certain operations in compliance with decrees of regulatory agencies, and accordingly sell a subsidiary or division.

MOTIVATIONS OF BUILDER/DEVELOPERS GOING THE MERGER ROUTE

Among all the entrepreneurs I've known who have gone the merger/ acquisition route (as well as "going public"), the overriding reason for doing so, the paramount motivation, was to get working capital. Ben Deane, who formerly headed the building subsidiary Deane Bros. at Occidental Petroleum, summarized this motive very well:

"My main problem as a builder was always 'how in hell do we finance it?' With capital, you can pick the good deals without having to rush into them, and you can ride out the bad times. The worst thing that can happen to a man in the real estate industry is that he gets into a defensive position. We've all done it. Some of us never got out of it, and suffered the consequences. The year 1966 played havoc with very responsible builders, for example; they went down the drain for circumstances beyond their control. The minute you're in a defensive position in real estate, it is very evident. The lenders and the competition will pick your feathers off one by one and you will die."

The spectrum of financial reasons for builder mergers consequently breaks out as follows:

They wanted to broaden their financial base. The builders who had achieved stability in the business by the late Sixties found themselves in the unique position of outgrowing their capacity to generate additional working capital. Operating in a situation where the cost of money and labor had been on a consistently upward curve, they were finding the leverage they had enjoyed in the past, and the productivity of each working dollar, was becoming severely limited. It became difficult to plan for orderly growth without impairing their own financial stability.

The important related motive for merger was that it afforded a builder the possibility of eliminating personal risk in his entrepreneurial activities. Most builders get their loans by signing off everything they and their friends own as collateral. By assuming responsibility for credit lines, the acquiring firm lifts a great burden from the entrepreneur's shoulders. Moreover, the builder can take advantage of decreased risk which comes from larger-scale operation and deeper financial resources, enabling him to ride out temporary reverses that could have bankrupted him as an independent.

Importantly, the builders also wanted to achieve personal equity, to translate the tangible and intangible assets of their many years of hard work into stock with a listed price that is readily marketable. Most builders start out as individual entrepreneurs with everything riding on their backs. Suddenly they look in a mirror and find they've reached an age when estate planning to safeguard acquired capital becomes an important issue.

Some builders want to just sell out. This is a phrase which most potential acquirers don't want to hear, but which some builders have in the back of their minds. The sellout can take two forms. One is an open and straightforward sale of assets. As the value of the building company resides principally in the talent it brings to future earnings potential, such sales don't bring much. On an assets basis in a reasonable merger deal, the rule of thumb is a price of two to three times assets for such a transaction. The other type of sellout is more covert and deadlier. The acquirer thinks he is buying the builder's future talents and profit projections and pays a high multiple of the builder's earnings to get the company. But the builder just wants to get the stock and then within a year or two bail out of the company to sit back and enjoy his winnings.

There are, of course, additional motivations impelling builders into mergers which have non-financial aspects. One is a need or desire to satisfy a larger ambition or make a bigger contribution to the industry, which can only be done through a larger vehicle. As a subsidiary of a major corporation, for example, the builder gets into the national economic spotlight. He can speak to effect changes for his industry. Alternatively, he can use the position as a springboard to the presidency of the acquiring corporation. The merger also appeals to the builder by letting him diversify, investing his own capital in industries other than his own business. The merger frees him from twenty-four-hour bondage to a personal business and permits him to satisfy his desires to engage in charitable, educational and political activities. Finally, no small matter, it makes it possible for him to fulfill a basically *non-financial* desire to become a millionaire. Whether this motive is questionable or not, it does drive men to work many hours a day many days a week. As one builder said: "If I were well off, I'd want to be rich. If I were rich, I would want to be wealthy. And if I were wealthy, I'd want to be *very* wealthy."

Many builder/developers looking at the merger/acquisition route are really looking for a vehicle that can fulfill all these ambitions and desires.

THE MERITS OF MERGER/ACQUISITION VS. GOING PUBLIC

For smaller builders earning less than $200,000 to $400,000 net annually, the merger route is obviously the advantageous one. Too small to enter the public market, they gain the advantages of bigness and increased growth potential by merging either with a building congeneric or with a diversified conglomerate. Because many of the larger building firms have already either gone public or been acquired, the wave of builder mergers next lapped up the large group of entrepreneurs with sales in the range of $5 million annually or less. The majority will be snapped up by publicly held congeneric building companies and some corporations unrelated to real estate will also be buying them up. But as many of these smaller privately held builders grow up, all of them sooner or later confront the question that now confronts the bigger privately held companies planning their future growth. And that question is: Should I go public, should I go the acquisition/merger route or should I just go my own way? There are advantages and disadvantages to each. The choice can be difficult, as witness the performance of some building companies who have tried first one route then the other.

Assuming a stock market anything unlike the one we experienced late in 1973, to Eli Broad the advantages of going public are clear. He summarizes them in the following way:

"Going public provides the capital base necessary to obtain financing. For example, Kaufman & Broad has the ability to raise all the funds we need at prime or below-prime rates. Being public provides the means for attracting quality management. Through stock options and broad incentive compensation plans, Kaufman & Broad's executives have a truly proprietary interest in their operations. This incentive has been more important to our management staff than base salary. For example, 1,000 shares issued in October of 1966 as an option to one of our managers is now [December of 1971] worth over a half-million dollars.

"Being a public company has been instrumental to Kaufman & Broad's growth in other ways also. We have found that many large corporations, bankers, major landowners and others would much prefer to do business with a listed company than with the average builder. Government, too, is looking to the large producer to help solve the housing problems of our nation, and on a consumer level, we find a certain percentage of homeowners who prefer to buy a Kaufman & Broad home because we are a publicly held company."

But Eli cautions that it took K&B ten years as a public company, a 30% annual growth record, and a favorable housing environment to reap all these rewards. During those ten years, the company's sales have gone from $11.7 million to about $225 million in 1971, while pretax income rose from $6 million to approximately $238 million in December of 1971, while shareholders' equity went from $2.7 million to $155 million in the ten-year period.

Following Kaufman & Broad's success formula, what elements does a building company need to make it as a publicly held builder?

1. Management depth and proven expertise — "Not a one-man band,"

says Eli Broad, "or an entrepreneur with marketing genius who has been highly successful in one market but has no professional management skills or financial controls."

2. Expertise in corporate finance.

3. Willingness to make a ten-year commitment to a 25% or 30% growth rate, year after year, quarter after quarter, and the ability to achieve it. The pressure of achieving continuous growth is unrelenting and tough to live with, and breaks up many managements.

4. "The stamina to withstand the traumas of seeing your stock sell as low as three or four times earnings," says Eli Broad. "Most of us forget that today we enjoy the best of all worlds with Wall Street's present attitude toward housing. We remember when housing wasn't glamorous. And we know the merry-go-round keeps going — and not always up."

5. The ability to work in the environment of total openness, with full disclosure of all financial aspects of the operation. "This open environment," says Eli, "is furthered by the growing number of security analysts covering the housing and shelter industry. These analysts probe into all aspects of your business and have grown increasingly sophisticated and knowledgeable about the industry in the past several years. They have been known to visit your developments, query your salesmen and customers, count unoccupied units, and then return to management with some tough questions. It is almost impossible to hide a slow development or to cover up some aspect of your business which you don't want known."

6. A builder who goes public must be prepared to spend a great deal of time in financial relations which private companies and subsidiaries are not faced with. These include public speaking dates; meetings with investment bankers, security analysts and shareholders; and preparation of annual and quarterly reports and other announcements. "The time spent on such efforts cannot be discounted," says Eli Broad. "It takes a top management team which is adept at public speaking, at walking the fine line between disclosure and insider information, at fielding tough questions from analysts in public or private meetings, at presenting the company accurately and candidly and still in the best light possible, and at buying credibility with the Street and investors. Many executives do not relish this chore or handle it badly — a fact generally known by the price of their company's stock."

When all is said and done, the choice to merge or go public must be made on the basis of the builder's own personality and his goals. By going public, he has the opportunity to control his own destiny and take his own whack at building an empire that will be a reflection of his ability in a fiercely competitive industry. He gives up his independence of action by having to assume all the problems of handling a public image on Wall Street, the problems of sophisticated relations with the financial community, the detailed inquiries of stock analysts. To report higher earnings with every quarterly income statement becomes his entire reason for being. He does gain liquidity, but his stock values are directly exposed to the vagaries of market fluctuations and subject to the quarterly-earnings grind. The liquidity is not immediate, moreover, and he usually has to wait for a period of about two years to sell some of his stock in a secondary issue. He has to be an extremely sophisticated financing man to engage in the financial planning necessary for growth and to undertake the repeated necessary trips to the public markets for capital. But all these things are bearable, and indeed they are just a part of the bigger game, for the man of iron determination to become a dominant factor in his industry.

SOME REASONS NOT TO GO TO THE PUBLIC MARKET. For most builder/ developers who do not have the temperament or financial skills to undertake the tough pace of the stock-market game, the going can be rough. The builder who wants mainly to build (or have someone else shoulder the main burden of sophisticated managerial/financial responsibility) is probably far better off going into a merger — into a conglomerate type or a building-congeneric type. In the latter, particularly, he finds himself in the company of other builders and gains many of the benefits of being a publicly held outfit without exposing himself to the risks of going it alone.

What such a builder really wants to achieve is a broader capital base. He needs enough money or borrowing power to eliminate expensive construction financing by replacing it with open lines of credit. He also wants to eliminate the necessity of personally guaranteeing such financing as he gets. He'd like to get enough money to pay off the indebtedness he has already incurred, especially those loans he's on the line for personally. Unless he is extremely dedicated to the goal of building his own empire, is a tough manager, and can play the stock market game well, he can run into severe disappointment by attempting to solve his immediate financing problems by the public route.

Take, as an example, a company with $400,000 after-tax earnings. Assume a P/E ratio on the initial issue of 15, which was well above average for new issues. This produces a total value of $6 million for the company. The best this builder can do would be to sell one-third of that value to the public, raising $2 million cash. Of that amount, the underwriter's fee and other expenses grab about $200,000. So the builder is left with a net new capital of $1,800,000. This amount is scarcely enough to achieve any of his financial aims. The money usually must go almost entirely into the company, with little left on the first issue for the builder to pocket personally. Assume that half to two-thirds would go toward the elimination of existing loans, and the builder is pretty close to being back in his original position. In several instances I am familiar with, the primary stockholders of newly public companies were still forced to sign personally for loans and their financial problems were thus left unsolved — except for the aspect of liquidity on a secondary issue. Only now, the builder is hooked on the treadmill of quarterly earnings reports and has to drive hard for profit. If he doesn't come through right away, the value of his stock plummets into the basement. This phenomenon occurred with several building companies in 1970 and 1971, though we will not name them in the hope that such a drop-off is not representative of their future performance.

A word on the liquidity of the principal shareholders of newly public building corporations. As mentioned, most of the funds from the initial issue go into the business. This leaves the builder the owner of two-thirds of his company. It may be only a middle-size or small company that is operating in one geographical area. This makes the price of his stock subject not only to his own performance but to an element he cannot control, the economic climate for construction in his area. True, he eventually plans to diversify by product and location, but in his first year when it is extremely important for him to produce profits to support his stock, he may be the victim of a regional economic slowdown. Moreover, his stock will not have broad attention and national distribution in this early period, being perhaps only locally traded. Facing these ungenerous conditions, he must work like hell for about two years before he can dispose of some of his stock in a secondary issue, this being the usual duration of the underwriter's lock-in on such issues.

And when the builder does attempt to sell, he may face a market for his stock that is so thin that he has to sell the stock through private placement to keep the stock price from coming down. After his first secondary sale, he has to spread subsequent selling over a long period and handle it carefully so as not to overload the market or appear to be bailing out. The sale of all or a large block of stock by an owner while he is still active in management often causes unfavorable market reaction and criticism.

REASONS WHY MANY BUILDER/DEVELOPERS HAVE PREFERRED THE MERGER/ACQUISITION ROUTE

Now that we have examined the risks of going public in some detail, the advantages of merger become evident by contrast. From the builder's viewpoint, the merger or acquisition route appeared to have four basic advantages:

First, he could sell out or exchange his interest in a small company for a smaller percentage interest in a larger company. He could usually do so at an attractive multiple of his own earnings (though the prices paid by industrial corporations have been luxuriously higher than those that savvy builders pay for smaller builders). Such a deal, which is usually transacted on a tax-free basis, lets him switch into the ownership of a larger company without paying tribute to Uncle Sam, and he can participate in its growth. Should he wish to sell, he has complete liquidity.

In the earlier phase of the merger boom in construction and real estate, the majority of the builder/developers going this route were wooed by major corporations from unrelated fields. The attractions of alignment with such blue-chip outfits seemed almost too good to be true. In addition to the foregoing good reasons for joining up with corporate titans, the builders were lured by the huge prices the big fellows would pay for them. But the attractions often paled when promises of financial commitment were not made good or when corporate-style bureaucratic controls slowed the builder's decision-making process to a crawl. In the building business, time is money or swiftly vanishing opportunity. The disillusionment with conglomerate-type building subsidiaries was given focus by the failed earnings of some major organizations during 1971. This development led a number of building companies with sales in the $15 million to $25 million range to prefer the risk of going public as the merger bloom wore off, thus enlarging the market of publicly held building companies. Now many such builders also embarked on a growth curve that encouraged them to seek the acquisition of other builders. As these organizations know the building business, they promised to be a more receptive parent for privately held entrepreneurs still seeking merger havens. With that, the popularity of the building congeneric was born.

6

Merger Plungers Old and New—1

> There is a tide in the affairs of
> men
> Which, taken at the flood, leads
> on to fortune.
>
> —Shakespeare
>
> Ve grow too soon oldt und too
> late schmardt.
>
> —Old German aphorism

The merger tide in real estate has ebbed and flowed in three distinct movements, each of which has left its own configuration of survivors and wrecks
on the beach. Ken Leventhal is one person who rode in on the tide each
time. A crusty and sharp-eyed CPA, Ken piloted his own accounting firm to
national prominence in the Sixties by providing sophisticated accounting
services for the big, fast-growing builders of the West Coast. When the urge
to merge came along, he became in short order the accounting specialist for
the technical aspects of more builder-industrial mergers than (as has been
claimed) anyone else in the world. Some call him the Henry Kissinger of
the housing industry.

Ken summarizes the cycle of mergers since the mid-Sixties in this way:
"The first mergers were synergistic in purpose. They were pursued by conglomerates like ITT and Boise Cascade. Then came the Housing Act of
1968, spelling out for the first time the housing needs of the country. Industrial companies became aware that housing could give repetitive income,
and this brought on the second wave of mergers. This was the period of the
high P/E multiples paid for builders. Then tight money struck again in
1970 and brought in a disenchantment. You got some breakups. But after a
pause, the merger movement resumed as industrial companies like Singer
reentered the market." Along with the newer trend of industrial-builder
combinations, of course, there was also the rise of the builder-merging-with-
builder, or congeneric merger, movement.

The merger movement in real estate did indeed start with the big conglomerates, which bought up builders not necessarily because these fitted
into their long-term schemes but, one sometimes suspects, primarily out of

140

the consideration that through the "synergism" of such combinations the acquirer's P/E multiple would rise. Along with such purely conglomerate-type acquisitions, a number of the big companies supplying raw materials and a variety of building supplies to the housing industry were also among the first to enter the development field via acquisitions. The latter, although not classifiable as purely conglomerate because of the acquirers' positions in related fields, did in fact have a conglomerate cast to them, as real estate by the late Sixties had become the hot word in the financial markets and inspired a gold-rush fever of acquisitions. Some companies could and did make enormous commitments in the housing and development field in a relatively short span of time with relatively little understanding of the long-term complexities of such diversification.

Effectively, we thus owe the overall merger/acquisition rush in real estate to about a half-dozen such gigantic corporations who were among the first to signal the attractiveness of this field by their entry into it. These widely heralded moves caught the attention of the corporate sector with the impact of a two-by-four clouted across the head of an ox. The result was that the entire corporate herd was reoriented into the direction of real estate. Hundreds of acquisitions followed. Numerous other major corporations got directly into the housing and development field not by acquisition but by establishing their own real estate departments and building divisions. Notable among the latter is Chrysler Real Estate, mentioned in Chapter II. Other prominent ones include Alcoa's formation in 1970 of a separate building division, which got into a direct construction and development role on its own. as well as by the acquisition of a San Francisco developer, Challenge Developments. U.S. Steel and Keene Corporation are also into a direct construction role, as well as fielding extensive builder supply services. Kaiser Steel and Aetna Insurance formed a $150-million realty partnership to undertake a broad variety of direct development ventures. Among other things, this partnership bought up a Southern California builder, Ponderosa Homes, which is now busily developing office buildings, apartments and single-family-home subdivisions around Los Angeles, in Orange County, and in the San Francisco Bay area.

THE TREND-SETTING GIANTS

Who exactly were these half-dozen big corporate guns to whom we owe recognition for pushing the entire corporate sector into real estate? No two analysts would agree in every instance on who did what first with the most impact, but anybody's list would include the following group.

OCCIDENTAL PETROLEUM. To the extent that any single individual can be credited with starting the merger boom in the development field, that credit must go to an intense and brilliant man who holds a doctorate and possesses the surreal name of Armand Hammer. Dr. Armand Hammer, the wizard of oil, Middle East politics, Soviet trade, and the U.S. stock market, steered an outfit called Occidental Petroleum from an obscure little company into one of the powers of the Fortune 500 in a handful of years. Acutely perceptive regarding future investment areas, Dr. Hammer was alive to the slowly germinating potentials of real estate well nigh before anybody else in the corporate sector. We might also say that he was not oblivious to the favorable jog and tickle that Wall Street would give to Occidental stock when he branched out from oil and chemicals into real estate.

Accordingly, Dr. Hammer brought off the first of the major developer acquisitions, and that was way back in homebuilding's Ice Age — July of 1964. The company he bought was the Southern California firm of S. V. Hunsaker & Sons, at that time booking about $42-million annually in sales selling homes on the installment contract plan. The price was $4.8 million — a paltry sum by comparison with the astronomic prices builders were getting from the gentleman corporations by 1969 and 1970, but a hefty one in those days. A couple of years later, the good Doctor discovered that things did not seem to be going so well with his new acquisition, as unsold homes piled up in inventory. So, in November of 1966, he bought up another big Southern California building firm, Deane Brothers, hoping to kill two birds with one stone: solve his in-house real estate problems and at the same time give a further boost to the growth of Occidental's good fortunes down on Wall Street. The Deane brothers, Ben and Jim, were a real catch. The sharpest marketeers in an awfully sophisticated and competitive market, they had revolutionized homebuilding by initially exploiting such now standard concepts as the Garden Kitchen. At the time of their merger into Occidental, they were doing $25 million a year in volume, and they got $4 million for their company.

BOISE CASCADE. Following hot on the heels of Occidental's initial entry into real estate, another company that created a spectacular early splash was Boise Cascade, the lumber producer. With a series of six major acquisitions in the homebuilding and real estate field, plus other ventures in related fields, Boise became between 1964 and 1969 the biggest, most diversified and most integrated shelter group in the country. These were the years in which its head, R. V. Hansberger, could do no wrong, and the business magazines were full of glowing write-ups on how the corporate whiz kids under Hansberger's patriarchal leadership were piloting Boise to new realms of glory. Boise had, indeed, grown to a position as one of the four major forest-product companies with a series of thirty-three acquisitions in a period of about twelve years, plus aggressive internal growth. But an entrepreneurial role in development was something new.

Boise's first venture into a direct housing role came with the acquisition of a Georgia prefabricator, Kingsberry Homes, in December of 1964. Kingsberry, operated by Al Hildebrandt, had built up a distribution network to independent builder-developers that was bringing $16 million in annual sales at the time Boise picked it up for $11 million. Boise then rested for a couple of years and scouted the real estate field more intensively. But late in 1967 it set off on another whirlwind acquisition program. In quick succession, it bought out builder Dan Schwartz in September of that year; Tom Perine's recreational land sales organization, U.S. Land, in October; and the big Southern California homebuilder, the R. A. Watt Company, in December. Watt was the heftiest acquisition, with Boise shelling out approximately $17 million for a building company with sales of $52 million annually at the time of purchase. But with the additional acquisition of Lake Arrowhead recreational development, Boise's land sales programs soon burgeoned vastly beyond the $25 million in sales that U.S. Land reported at the time of acquisition. At about the same time, Boise also got heavily involved in urban construction and picked up a minority interest in a black-owned Washington, D.C., urban renewal outfit, Winston Burnett, renaming the company Burnett-Boise. In 1969, it rounded out its housing-related acquisitions by buying up Divco-Wayne, a mobile-home producer.

ITT. Just as Boise was making its biggest impact on the Wall Street buzz line and among the real estate pros, another elephant galumphed with a tremendous splash into the real estate merger pool: Harold Geneen's vast conglomerate, International Telephone & Telegraph. ITT grabbed all the headlines by acquiring the biggest builder in the nation, Levitt & Sons, in February of 1968. Levitt, headquartered on Long Island in New York, had been publicly held since 1960. At the time of the acquisition, it was reporting annual sales of $120 million and it went to ITT for a cool $92 million in stock. (That seemed like the all-time highest price a builder could dream of, but within two years, as the dazzle of real estate increased, the Wall Street deal-makers were clucking their tongues and saying that if only Bill Levitt had held out another year or so he could have received upwards of $150 million.) Exactly one year later, in February of 1969, ITT struck again, this time buying a big Washington State homebuilder, United Homes. United's entrepreneurial founder, Herman Sarkowsky, got $11.2 million on the downstroke for a company that had reported about $600,000 in earnings on $25 million sales in the year of acquisition. The company became Levitt-United and gave ITT Levitt access to the hot West Coast market.

AMERICAN-STANDARD. Steered by William D. Eberle, American-Standard, the big plumbing and air-conditioning manufacturer supplying the housing field, also weighed into a direct role in real estate in April of 1968, shortly after ITT's acquisition of Levitt. American-Standard picked up another one of those sharp, self-taught Southern California builders, Wm. Lyon & Company, for a price of $12.2 million. The company, operated by brothers Bill and Leon Lyon, earned $1.3 million on sales of $20 million in the year of acquisition. Not long thereafter, the plumbing giant's new subsidiary expanded its housing operations to South America by picking up a Washington, D.C., housing developer International Homes, specializing in the Latin markets.

The acquisitions continued with the buy-ups of Kendall Development in New Jersey and an Alabama prefabber and scattered-lot builder, Builders Homes, in 1970, plus the acquisition of the remaining 50% interest in the big Twin Rivers apartment "new town" (originally started as a joint venture) for 249,353 American-Standard shares. During 1970, Lyon also made a deal to invest a total of $8 million in American Mobilhome Corporation, a mobile-home-park developer (also backed by R. A. Watt, the builder who sold his company out to Boise). Lyon had already picked up $4 million of American Mobilhome's convertible debentures and advanced it another $1-million. The total investment was convertible into a controlling interest (50.1%) of American Mobilhome.

CNA FINANCIAL. Shortly following the Lyon acquisition, along about May of 1969, another announcement hit the homebuilding industry like a bombshell: CNA Financial, the big insurance holding firm, declared it was buying up Lawrence and William Weinberg's Larwin Group of Companies. What was staggering was not the acquisition but the price paid in relation to earnings: $100 million in stock on the downstroke, with another $100 million to come subject to performance, for a privately-held company that had achieved $4.7 million in earnings on sales of $76 million in the year of its acquisition. Larry Weinberg had long had a reputation as the most sophisticated of the sophisticated Southern California merchant builders. Now he also got the reputation for making what was also one of the biggest and fanciest-priced deals ever made in a real estate merger.

INTERNATIONAL PAPER. Probably the only deal to acquire a privately held developer that exceeded Larry's was the astronomic price that International Paper paid to acquire still another Southern California builder, the Don L. Bren Company. IP, also announcing its acquisition in May of 1969, paid Don Bren $37 million in stock on the downstroke, with another $37 million payable subject to performance, for a company then earning $572,000 on sales of $15 million. This amounted to an initial acquisition cost at the astronomic P/E multiple of 64! Even CNA's initial acquisition cost, paying Larry Weinberg somewhat better than 20 times earnings, pales by comparison.

The years 1969 and 1970, in short, ushered in a dazzling era of sky-high earnings multiples paid by the outside corporations as they lusted to buy into the action at any cost. And Larry Weinberg's and Don Bren's were the two biggest deals of all. When the dust cleared, the reality of such phantasmagoric sums of money changing hands was enough to make any builder considering the merger route grow pallid, and perhaps to tremble as his breath came haltingly, and perhaps to sit in a feverish nimbus of rapid calculation.

INLAND STEEL. By mid-1969, the acquisition pattern for the corporate sector was pretty decidedly set by the foregoing configuration of builder mergers, and a substantial number of developers were scampering into the corporate fold. It only remained for giant Inland Steel (with revenues of $1.2 billion in 1969) to drive the point home with a rapid consummation of a builder acquisition in February of 1970. Inland made a fast deal to buy up the publicly held Toledo-based consortium of prefabrication, mobile-home and development companies headed by Donald J. Scholz. Inland paid $87 million in stock, or about 25 times earnings, for the publicly listed Scholz Homes group, which had 1969 sales of $58 million. The component companies of the group were, of course, Scholz Homes, which had earned for itself a nationwide reputation for prefabrication of extremely attractive homes and apartments and had carried on a large building program; Schult Mobile Homes; Public Facilities Associates, (partly owned by football coach Vince Lombardi), a Wisconsin builder of public housing; and Allstate Homes, a Detroit builder and developer.

DID THE TREND-SETTING ACQUIRERS KILL THE MERGER BOOM?

It was these half-dozen or so major corporations — conglomerate industrial — who played a dominant role in shaping the merger pattern in real estate for the public eye — i.e., for Wall Street. But now an interesting question arises. Readers familiar with the development industry will recognize a peculiar similarity linking these otherwise unrelated mergers. With the exception of the Larwin deal, they have all spelled failure for their acquirers, a failure that varies by degree, but which in specific cases reaches horrific proportions. And so the question that should be asked is: Did these early entrants cast such a pall of negative feeling about real estate that they queered the idea of similar mergers forever? Or have they merely paid the price that the first plungers often pay — valuable experience at the cost of failure? Let's take a look at the outcome of our trend-setters' grand strategies:

OCCIDENTAL PETROLEUM. If Dr. Hammer had expected S. V. Hunsaker to stick around after the acquisition, he was disappointed. Old S. V. retired a day after the July 1964 merger. His son, Richard, resigned two years later, about the time of the Deane Brothers acquisition. The Deanes themselves lasted only three years. Despite restrictions, they managed to build up their 1968 sales volume to about $41 million from the $25 million they were doing annually when acquired. But they couldn't do much because, during their three-year stint as a corporate subsidiary, they were permitted to start only one new project. Quitting in 1969, Ben Deane and his son Larry went into business for themselves in a modest way, building high-priced townhouses in Newport Beach. Brother Jim, meanwhile, set up Deane & Deane to undertake a joint venture with Westinghouse for development of Half Moon Bay, the big land project near San Francisco. Occidental's real estate activities were subsequently reduced to sales of inventoried land, and most or all development was eliminated.

BOISE CASCADE. Boise fared little better than Occidental in retaining the entrepreneurial talent that had been responsible for the success of the acquired companies. The departures started early. Al Hildebrandt was fired within three months after his Kingsberry Homes was bought up because he disagreed with R. V. Hansberger about Boise's projected competitive role in construction with that of Kingsberry's builder-customers. Builder Dan Schwartz retired a day after his Perma-Bilt Homes merged with Boise. Tom Perine, the creative dynamo who had shown everybody how to sell recreational land, also quit less than a year after his U.S. Land went into Boise's organization.

Perhaps the biggest loss was that of R. A. "Ray" Watt. Ray became a millionaire many times over after his company went to Boise. And somehow after that deal, the challenge of the old entrepreneurial rough-and-tumble was gone. Boise's chief, R. V. Hansberger, tried to motivate him with high pay and the challenge of steering Boise into a big construction role, but couldn't find the key. Ray hung around for about a year, then quit to take a job that seemed to revive the missing element of challenge. A proposed appointment as FHA Commissioner and Deputy HUD Secretary fell through. But Ray was appointed president of the National Corporation for Housing Partnerships, a new private, government-sponsored corporation authorized by the 1968 Housing Act. Ray's job was to raise $37.5 million in corporate seed capital for investment in low- and moderate-cost housing joint ventures, and to raise the money against a very tight deadline. He then moved on again, becoming the president of the Federal Home Loan Bank in San Francisco.

Notwithstanding such departures, Boise was exuberant and preoccupied with the chores of organizing its new empire. In the aftermath of the acquisition splurge it suddenly found itself the biggest integrated producer of shelter in the United States, and that was exciting enough. After some experimentation, the acquisitions were reorganized into a number of "groups" and "divisions." The chief administrator of the housing empire was first William M. Agee, a young and talented Boise senior vice president. When he shifted to full-time duties as chief financial officer, Charles C. Tillinghast III stepped to the helm. The new housing chief also had a reputation as one of R. V. Hansberger's bright young men; he was the son of another Mr. Tillinghast who was running the corporate show over at big Trans World Airlines. With the entrepreneurs gone, Boise's housing involvement thus came under the control and direction of financially oriented corporate managers who, although exceptionally able in their own profession, were unfamiliar with the realities of development and on-site construction. But unlike Dr. Hammer, they had no hesitations about driving for expansion as fast as the horses could run.

By 1970, Boise's involvement in housing, development, and land sales amounted to a net equity investment of no less than $142.4 million and looked like this on the corporate table of organization:

1. Residential Communities Group: 34 projects in 7 regions, including California, Illinois, New Jersey, Washington and Washington, D.C.
2. Mobile Home Parks Division: 16 projects in Arizona, California, Colorado, Nevada and Washington.
3. Industrial Parks Division: 7 projects in California.
4. Manufactured Housing Group: 10 plants in Alabama, Idaho, Iowa, Maryland, Ohio, Utah and Virginia.
5. Metal Buildings Division: 2 plants in Alabama and Ohio.
6. Mobile Housing Group: 22 plants in California, Florida, Indiana, Kansas, Michigan, Minnesota, Mississippi, North Carolina, Oregon, Pennsylvania, Texas, Alberta (British Columbia), Ontario (Quebec), and England.
7. Urban Housing Group: 17 projects in California, Florida, Idaho, Indiana, Louisiana, Maryland, New York, Ohio, Pennsylvania and Texas.
8. Recreation Communities Group: 29 land sales projects in California, Connecticut, Hawaii, Illinois, Indiana, Maryland, Nevada, Ohio, Pennsylvania and Virginia.
9. Recreation Vehicles Division: 10 plants in California, Indiana, Iowa, Michigan, Pennsylvania, Ontario, England, France, the Netherlands, and Sweden.

The initial operating results of the huge shelter group seemed to justify Boise's large commitment. In 1969, the company's combined housing and recreation activities produced $32 million in income on sales of $270 million, accounting for 28% of Boise's sales. In the same year, Boise's commitment to recreational land sales leaped from 12 projects to 26, and included in its combined shelter income were earnings of $11 million from its Recreation Group (the figures primarily reflect land sales, but also include recreation vehicle sales and earnings, as well as those from the operation of two cruise ships).

But by 1970 the picture was changing rapidly. Housing and related activities accounted for only $234 million in revenues, a decline of 14%, while earnings fell to $6 million, representing a 71% drop from the year before. Boise's commitment to land sales had meanwhile increased to 29 projects, but sales and earnings in this sector became a disaster area. The recreation group's sales dropped to $158 million from $209 million, for a decline of 24%, while earnings went completely out the bottom and the company actually showed an $11 million loss for this activity, compared with the $11 million profit in 1969. Thus, the performance of Boise's new acquisitions severely affected its overall 1970 earnings. While 1970 corporate revenues of $1.717 billion were close to the $1.739 billion reported in 1969, overall earnings fell by 54% to $37 million, from $81 million in 1970.

Boise's bad luck continued into 1971, as the company announced a write-off of $78 million ($44 million after taxes) in the second quarter. By this time, Boise had a new source of problems: Burnett-Boise. The outfit had contracted with several nonprofit groups in the Washington, D.C., area to rehabilitate old apartments. The work was contracted on a cost-

Boise Cascade Corporation

Operating Results by Major Markets	Income		Sales and Services	
	1970	1969	1970	1969
		(millions)		
Timber and building materials	$ 10	$ 38	$ 334	$ 369
Paper and Packaging	46	42	484	455
Housing	6	21	234	270
Engineering and construction	15	18	379	299
Recreation	(11)	11	158	209
Utilities and miscellaneous investments	31	40	128	137
	$ 97	$170	$1,717	$1,739
Corporate administration	(22)	(18)		
Interest expense, net of interest income	(23)	(24)		
Income taxes	(15)	(47)		
Net income	$ 37	$ 81		

plus basis, with fixed ceilings. Boise Cascade eventually discovered that most of the contract ceilings were far too low for Burnett-Boise to complete its contracted work. Although Boise's own investment in Burnett-Boise was minor, it was on the hook to finish the projects. This accounted for half the $78 million write-off.

As long as they had gone that far, Boise officials decided to pull in their belts and take the necessary write-offs in the problem-ridden areas of land sales and housing development as well. The housing development group had the capacity to perform, but its sprawling size bogged it down in corporate red tape, and it also was saddled with a lot of unmarketable and/or overpriced land that had come in with Boise's original acquisitions; mobile-home park development was also a costly operation. Recreational land sales had exposed the company not only to the vagaries of sales fluctuating with interest rates but also to the wrath of environmentalists who had somehow singled out Boise almost exclusively for their attacks and who succeeded in slowing down or stopping the sales of several projects, while also driving Boise to raise its front-end development costs considerably in an effort to stave off unfavorable criticism. So Boise allotted the remaining half of the $78 million write-off about equally to a write-down of values of several recreational projects, now blocked, and of its housing and residential land projects.

With that decision made, Boise in mid-1971 thus effectively chose to get out of the residential development field entirely, and to severely restrict its recreation land sales activities. The whole residential group went up on the block. Most of the company's mobile-home parks were sold by the end of 1971, and the multimarket building company was being sold division by division. Singer Housing Company (formerly Besco) negotiated extensively to buy two or more of Boise's housing divisions located in San Francisco, in the Midwest and on the East Coast, but these negotiations fell through early in 1972. But Boise was more successful with other buyers. Larwin bought most of the landholdings of the company's Chicago housing operation in March 1972 and was negotiating for the purchase of other divisions, including Washington, D.C. Kaufman & Broad bought Boise's land in New Jersey.

And guess who was reentering the housing picture to buy Boise's Southern California housing division? None other than Ray Watt, who had originally sold the housing company to Boise more than three years earlier. Ray in March 1972 was set to purchase the division in partnership with Al Borstein, the youthful entrepreneurial head of the division, and convert it into a significant entity joint-venturing on projects with outside financial sources and perhaps with other builders. Ray was also involved in another big deal. The venture, a $24 million, 3,200-acre resort-recreation community named San Diego County Estates, was opened to the public in July

1972. He remains chairman of the executive committee of the National Corporation for Housing Partnerships and chairman of the board of the Federal Home Loan Bank of San Francisco.

Boise's retrenchment was painful but necessary. The full extent of its debacle in real estate became apparent with the company's fourth-quarter statement for 1971. In the final three months of the year, Boise reported a net loss of $48.14 million, or $1.55 a share, on sales of $457.95 million. This performance brought the company's total loss for fiscal 1971, ended December 31, to $85.15 million on sales of $1.786 billion. (By contrast, Boise reported a profit of $34 million on sales of $1.724 billion for 1970.) The 1971 loss included an operating loss of $37.15 million plus the extraordinary charge of $48 million, representing the write-off of Boise's investment in Burnett-Boise Corp., and the additional write-down of assets primarily in the company's real estate activities.

Boise had of course been badly burned by the Nader report on the company's land sales operations and by civil class-action suits brought by the State of California against the company's recreation-community subsidiaries. According to Hansberger, a "substantial" portion of fourth-quarter losses in 1971 were attributable to the lawsuits. After deciding to get out of on-site construction and to curtail land-sales activity, Boise by the spring of 1972 had picked up about $115 million in cash and notes from the sale of development properties, housing divisions and other miscellaneous assets. "Our remaining trouble spots," Hansberger said in March 1972, "are the determination of our future course of action in our recreation community activities in California and certain of our Latin American situations." (Boise also had difficulty in collecting principal and interest payments from the Chilean government on notes outstanding in the amount of $75 million.)

Boise did undertake one successful measure to improve its cash position. One of the company's big problems had been a heavy cash drain, as front-end development and other costs mounted while much of the real estate and housing income was paper profit. Receivables, principally due over one- to seven-year periods, rose by $127.4 million to a total of $285.4 million in 1969, and increased by another $53.6 million to a total of $339 million in 1970. So, in 1970, Boise worked out a way to convert a sizable chunk of such paper profit into cash. It did so by forming Boise Cascade Credit Corporation and funding it by the issuance of $75 million of 10%, five-year debentures in a public offering. The credit corporation's function is to buy from Boise's recreational-land subsidiaries the customers' notes and contracts receivable that Boise would normally not be able to convert into cash for up to five or more years. The concept was intended to get Boise out of the finance business, and it has worked extremely well. The credit corporation's operations will thus also in all probability be extended to the purchase of accounts receivable arising from sales of Boise mobile homes and recreational vehicles. This appears to be one of Boise's most successful endeavors, and it will be an important adjunct to its remaining housing operations in the Seventies.

Where do these changes leave Boise? In a nutshell, Boise paid heavily to learn that a manufacturing corporation operated by sophisticated, financially oriented managers can't always succeed in the traditionally entrepreneurial endeavors of land development and on-site residential construction. Boise had gone into these areas expecting a 30% return on its investment, but by mid-1971 the handwriting was on the corporate wall. However, the changes do leave Boise still heavily committed to the manufacture and sale of prefabricated and panelized housing, plus mobile homes — as befits a manufacturer. The basic manufacturing and sales functions, aided by a dealer network, have been Boise's strong points all along; it was only when the company attempted to take on the developer's role as well that it got into trouble.

Retrenching, Boise began to shift its attention to the solacing rewards of the manufactured-shelter field. In mid-1971, while it was cutting back on recreational-land sales and starting to shut down on-site construction, it began expanding its modular plant capacity. It quadrupled manufacturing capacity at plants in Ohio, Alabama and Idaho and opened a fourth in Arabi, Georgia. It also opened a new 100,000-square-foot panelized housing plant in Holdenville, Oklahoma. And it geared up to promote the sale of prefabricated homes through its Vacation Housing operations. A vacation housing division opened in New England, with headquarters in Lexington, Massachusetts, at the start of 1972, and other divisions were planned for the East Coast and the Midwest. With sales of vacation homes projected at 200 for 1972, it was a small but promising beginning in this field.

ITT-LEVITT. Let us at this point keep the Levitt story brief. Suffice it to say that this subsidiary's sales had nearly doubled between the time it was acquired in 1968 and the conclusion of 1970. They went from $120 million to about $228 million. Earnings, while not publicly reported, were believed not to have kept pace with the growth in sales. As Levitt pushed harder to keep up its growth (including the expansion of overseas residential housing operations beyond France to Spain and Germany), key execs chafed under the strictures of corporate management styles. The company suffered a loss of top-notch managerial ability when Richard Wasserman and Richard Bernhard pulled out in 1971. One key reason for the defections was ITT's insistence on evaluating the Levitt group's performance on the basis of contributed earnings per share (where it wasn't doing so well) instead of on return investment (where it was doing extremely well). When the Justice Department came out with the ruling that ITT had to divest itself of some companies in order to keep others, Levitt was one of the organizations chosen for bye-bye. ITT has until sometime in 1974 to unload the subsidiary, and it appears that its flirtation with housing and development is thus ended.

AMERICAN-STANDARD. The history of this foray into real estate presents us with another instance of an acquiring corporation that leapt whole hog into the field, only to pull up extremely short at the first sign of problems faced by skittish corporate management. Bill Lyon was an expert builder of single-family homes. But when American-Standard acquired his company, it enthusiastically prodded him to expand into every aspect of real estate, and it backed the expansion by supplying Lyon Development with an additional $5.2 million in equity and $28.3 million in loans and advances between 1968 and 1970.

Soon, Bill Lyon, who had been a single-family builder in the Southern California market, also found himself running a nationally sprawling, mushrooming company which was operating a half-dozen recreational-land sales projects, knocking out built-for-sale apartments in large quantities, building housing in Latin America, and operating prefabricated housing plants — among other things. Sales accordingly zoomed from an estimated $20 million in 1968, to $58 million in 1969 and $90 million in 1970. Counting revenues from joint ventures, 1970 sales actually hit $135.2 million. But the problems of efficiently coordinating such rapid growth showed up in earnings, which failed to match the growth in sales. Earnings were $1.3 million in 1968 and rose to about $2.0 million in 1969 before falling to $1.7 million in 1970.

Moreover, such profits as were reported were paper profits, while the company actually experienced a continuing cash drain. Cash expenditures for recreational project development were convertible into receivables paper. There was likewise a cash outflow in the company's built-for-sale apartment operation. By selling apartments on the all-inclusive first-and-second-mortgage arrangement, the company books a paper profit but may retrieve a lesser amount in cash than it lays out to build the apartment. Paper profits are a fact of life for development companies, but American-Standard tolerated them only while profits were rising.

American-Standard had made its large financial commitments with eyes wide open. But as its debt load mounted and it was faced with operating problems in its manufacturing divisions, it plainly lost all heart. Midway into 1971, the big plumbing-ware company did an abrupt about-face in real estate, deciding to get out of the business entirely by selling the development company back to Bill Lyon for $44.7 million. The move would have restored the company's ailing cash position. But to vast dismay all around, Lyon was unable to arrange the financial backing and the deal, which was to have been completed October 15, 1971, fell through. Forced to continue the association, American-Standard gritted its teeth and wrote off $100 million in anticipation of extensive cutbacks and consolidation in its overall activities, including real estate. The first to go were Lyon's international housing operations and recreational-land sales programs.

Bill Lyon's story is retold in a later chapter. Let us here only note that American-Standard, retrenching its operations all around, reported a loss of $83.8 million on sales of $1.4 billion in 1971. The operating loss for Lyon was 42 cents of American-Standard's loss of $7.13 per share. Early in 1972, Bill finally quit and went out to set up another development company.

INLAND STEEL. While some acquiring corporations got themselves into trouble by expanding too fast, Inland Steel serves as an example of a company that lost its chief housing entrepreneur because it wouldn't move fast enough to suit him. Only, unlike the Deane Brothers, Don Scholz didn't wait three years. The Inland-Scholz merger closed in February of 1970. Don quit on July 15 of the same year. But, although buffeted by the abrupt departure of the key man who had assembled the empire for which it had paid $87 million in stock, Inland's venture into the housing field has been successful.

The full story of the remarkable Don Scholz, his in-and-out with Inland, and his post-merger comeback as the head of a new congeneric building company is recounted in a separate chapter. But let us note here that his rift with the acquirer provided a classic illustration of the conflicts that crop up between the entrepreneurial builder and the strictures of corporate management. Scholz was not overly happy with the merger in the first place, having been more or less forced into it by the other major stockholders of Scholz Homes — the heads of the three companies he had acquired not long before, plus (can you believe it?) his own investment banker. But after deciding to make a go of it, he was confronted with time-consuming corporate meetings and reporting process to handle what had heretofore been perfunctory matters. Moreover, he was overruled by Inland's staff on projects and other acquisitions he wanted to undertake. For its part, Inland, after having invested $87 million and being new to the business, had a not unreasonable desire to go slow so as not to ruffle its shareholders. Don understood this logic, but he also saw that it would mean an end to his own successful operating formula. His vision of the housing organization he wanted to create and the way he wanted to run it, was too compelling to be compromised. So he quit.

Inland, however, regards the merger as a success. The housing activities were organized under the umbrella of a new subsidiary, Inland Steel Urban Development Corporation, headed by Inland corporation man William E. Rothfelder. The key men of Schult Mobile Homes, Public

Facilities Associates and Allstate Homes (acquired as part of the Scholz Homes package) all stayed on, satisfied with the merger deal. Moreover, before Scholz left he arranged for Inland's acquisition of Jewel Builders of Columbus, and Jewel's president, Julie Cohen, a very able developer, stepped in to fill Scholz's own role. As Rothfelder puts it, "There were lots of goodies in the Scholz package; Don was only one." The Inland group's 1970 revenues were an estimated $67 million, and were projected to rise by about 15% in 1971.

Reviewing the merger in mid-1971, Rothfelder said Inland was "unequivocally delighted with the acquisition of these various companies. They have by and large provided us with what we were seeking; that is, entry into one of the growth areas we had targeted for diversification." He was also "generally well pleased with the nature and quality of the leadership" of the acquired companies. David Carley, the head of Inland Steel Development (renamed from Public Facilities Associates) was also pleased, as was Walter Wells, the old owner of Schult Mobile Homes. But it should be pointed out that Rothfelder reserved his particular commendation for the performance of Schult Mobile Homes and its record profits in 1970. Perhaps it's only a coincidence, but as in the case of Boise Cascade, another industrial corporation seems to have more affinity for the manufacture of housing than for the entrepreneurial perils of actual development.

INTERNATIONAL PAPER-BREN COMPANY. Nor did the merger between International Paper and the Donald L. Bren Company, based in Sherman Oaks, California, prove to be a charmed relationship.

Bren had built an exceptionally strong reputation for his company as a developer of homes of sophisticated design and planned communities. The inside word is that he was one of the few major builders who was simply not interested in selling out when the merger fever hit in 1969 and major corporations were hunting for builder-partners. But IP wanted to get into the housing field in a bad way, and it had an unquenchable desire for Bren's organization in particular. In the upshot, the IP wheeler-dealers made the offer too attractive for the Bren people to turn down. Where else can you get $37 million in stock on the downstroke for earnings of $400,-000 and another $37 million contingent on future earnings?

Don Bren thought he was also getting IP's financial strength to help him achieve the organization's growth objectives. Following the acquisition, unfortunately, the Bren organization ran into a tough year in the slumping Southern California housing market, which was severely affected by the moribund aerospace economy. This, as one insider says, brought on constricting financial controls by IP on the housing subsidiary which cut across the entrepreneurial activities of the company. As in many such situations, the contrasting impulses were for the once-zealous corporate newcomer to suddenly proceed with caution to safeguard investment capital, while the acquired builder, following his own understanding of the building game, sought expansion. Having paid so much to get into the housing business, many an acquirer is unpleasantly surprised at how much continuing financing support he is required to contribute for the subsidiary's expanding activities. In IP's case, one consequence of the go-slow signal presented the building subsidiary with practical problems in achieving the earnings volume necessary to pick up the additional $37 million payment, insiders say.

The financial controls were apparently relaxed somewhat after the first year, and one top insider said late in 1971, "We're still having lots of problems with the parent company but this is one merger that will not lead to a divorce." But by March of 1972 IP had apparently decided that it would cost too much to carry the subsidiary alone and passed the word along that it was interested in selling a substantial portion of its interest. At the Bren Company, there was, meanwhile, a cutback in the staff that had been taken on in expectation of big expansion.

When the public announcement came in May of 1972 that IP was getting out of the real estate business, it was no surprise. What was surprising, however, was the innovative and amicable — and the potentially profitable — way in which IP handled its exodus. The paper maker sold the Bren Company back to Donald L. Bren for $3.5 million in cash and received a warrant to repurchase 49% of the developer's stock within a five-year period beginning in mid-1975 at its book value at the time. IP also got $18.5 million in secured, interest-bearing notes to cover cash advances made to the Bren Company since the acquisition. Where American-Standard failed to unwind itself from its real estate activities, IP succeeded. The sale price of $3.5 million was considerably smaller than the $37 million in stock the company originally paid for the developer. But by gaining the option to buy 49% of Bren's stock at book value in the future, IP at least still stands the chance of eventually recouping its investment, particularly if Bren should go public and enjoy a high P/E multiple.

International Paper also dismantled other elements of its real estate empire in May of 1972. It sold Spacemakers, Inc., of Canton, Massachusetts, a prefabricator, for $1.2 million. The small subsidiary had sales of $2.5 million in 1970. But IP decided to keep, for the time being, American Central Corporation of Lansing, Michigan, the subsidiary specializing in recreational-land sales. Developing mostly land already owned by IP, American Central was described by IP's management as "highly profitable" and had sales of $30.1 million in 1970.

Thus, another industrial acquirer learned, after paying a spectacular entry price, that the homebuilding business requires a firm long-term commitment and a willingness to be exposed to the entrepreneurial ups and downs that so often come with it. For International Paper, it just wasn't worth it. Assessing the experience, IP's executive vice president, Arthur R. Taylor, told the *Wall Street Journal* that the flexible operating style required in the development business proved "difficult to mesh into a large corporation." Moreover, while the Bren Company had been profitable under real estate accounting methods, its earnings — described as "very, very small" because of a downturn in California homebuilding — didn't represent an adequate return on IP's investment.

"We bought [the Bren Company] not only in the heyday of the appetite of large corporations for builders, but also in the heyday of the California economy before the decline in aerospace had such an effect on the economy," Mr. Taylor said. "We make a very strong point of this return on investment. The nature of the real estate business is that it's very, very capital-intensive, even more so than the paper industry. We just didn't have an adequate return on our total investment."

Don Bren, free again, observed that the "divestiture appears to successfully resolve the basic issues that have confronted Bren Company and International Paper, and most similar mergers of real estate development companies and major capital-intensive manufacturing organizations." With restrictions on access to capital lifted, he planned to rapidly expand homebuilding operations in the reviving California market. The company had performed extremely well in 1972 up to the time of its divestiture from IP. Sales for the first four months of the year were $9.5 million, rising by 190% over the first four months of 1971. Don Bren was shooting for $48 million in sales for 1972, up from $40 million in 1971.

. . . AND SOME MERGERS BROKE DOWN AT THE ALTAR: AN ASIDE

While some builder-mergers encounter problems after the marriage, inevitably some such ventures don't get even that far, and the prospective partners change their minds at the very last minute. There's no way to estimate whether such last-minute turnabouts are a tragedy or a blessing to the would-be acquirers, but they do illustrate that the business of merger negotiation is extremely skittish.

One case in point was U.S. Plywood-Champion Paper's proposed acquisition of Carl M. Freeman Associates, an aggressive diversified apartment, shopping center and community developer, with 1970 revenues of $52.5-million, based in Silver Spring, Maryland. U.S. Plywood, prior to its own merger with Champion Papers, had acquired the major Hawaiian developer Lewers & Cooke (1970 volume: $32.3 million), back in 1965, and had cast about with a variety of joint-venture developments with other building companies. Looking to expand its homebuilding penetration, it started talks with the Freeman group in the fall of 1970, just as the deadline on the changes in pooling rules governing mergers neared. Several months of tough and thorough negotiating followed. At the end of 1970, the acquisition agreement was reached in principle. The price: 550,000 shares of U.S. Plywood-Champion Papers common (then valued at $14.9 million), with another 36,000 shares payable contingent upon 1971-73 earnings. But in early 1971, the agreement floundered at the next stage — approval by the boards of directors of both companies and the Freeman shareholders. The upshot was no deal.

Ross Cortese's Rossmoor Corporation was another bride that was left at the altar — not once but twice. Cortese had acquired an outstanding reputation in the housing industry as a specialist in the retirement and luxury housing markets. His company had built more than 25,000 homes in its Leisure World communities at Seal Beach, Laguna Hills and Walnut Creek, California, and began construction of other Leisure Worlds near Cranbury, New Jersey, and Washington, D.C., before tight money in 1966 forced some cutbacks. But Ross remained active. In the late Sixties, he expanded beyond his specialty and began planning to get into mobile-home parks, rental apartments and low-cost housing. Observers who know what a distinctive mark he made in retirement housing were expecting a similar performance in low-cost housing.

This kind of expansion called for new capital, and that spelled merger. The first of the potential acquirers was the Crane Company, the big NYSE-listed plumbing-products supplier to housing. The merger agreement in principle was announced in April of 1969. The deal was a handsome one for Cortese, the principal owner of Rossmoor Corporation, as Crane agreed to buy the company for a $40 million twenty-five-year note bearing 7% interest from twelve months after closing. But the acquisition fell through in the negotiating stage. Cortese then went after another merger deal. In February of 1970, another announcement duly appeared: Zero Manufacturing Company of Burbank, California, an electronics producer, said it would pay $25 million in stock for Rossmoor. But by May of 1970 these negotiations were also broken off, by mutual consent. The problems arose in determining operating responsibility for the organization that would have resulted from the merger, as Zero's size would have doubled and Rossmoor's stockholders would have wound up as the majority owners of the electronics firm.

Not long afterwards, to no one's surprise, Ross Cortese went public. The company's 1970 sales were $35.7 million. In addition to its building activities in Orange County and in Silver Spring, Maryland, it also entered the Arizona and Nevada markets.

7

Merger Plungers Old and New—2

> When the going gets tough, the tough get going.
>
> —Ex–U.S. Attorney General Mitchell

While the first wave of high-roller mergers broke up primarily as a result of internal management problems, the succeeding waves have found themselves battered not only by the backwash of bad publicity attending the first but also encountered such an abruptly changing social, economic, and legislative scene affecting the building industry in general that their survival was often hazardous even when they were well-managed. Probably the most important thing to be learned is just how volatile and unpredictable the real estate industry really is when so many of the rules on which future planning depends can be changed without notice. Ecological and conservationist groups rise up in one's back yard and make it a hazard to carry large pieces of land; changes in accounting principles and proposed tax changes suddenly make it unprofitable to build and sell apartments, throwing hundreds of major builders for a loop; high interest rates lop off sales curves. The issues and the battles change almost daily and one day's heroes turn out to be the next day's bankrupt high rollers.

A balanced assessment of the merger trend as of early 1973 would have shown that there were more successful mergers than not. If this seemed surprising at the time, it was only because the successful ventures don't as a rule get as much publicity as the failed ones. The rapidly changing conditions since that time put that statement more in the category of assertion than fact. We have made no claim to prescience, certainly no more so than the SEC and was *it* ever surprised. The uncomfortable thing about this industry has always been its volatility. The uncomfortable thing about its volatility is that this very chapter on what would appear to be the successful merger deals could reverse dramatically by the time you read this book. Unlike some major research organizations, we do not have the advantage of a wiretap to aid us in learning what is really going on in the boardrooms of many builders.

Still, baring the unforseen always, credit is due to those unsung heroes who have so far successfully fought a host of hostile conditions and have preserved their corporate relationships and their profitability.

Who, for example, hears much about a sharp outfit like Ring Bros. of Los Angeles after they've merged into Monogram Industries? Yet this superlative builder of apartments continued to function very well. Or, as another little-noticed example, there is Pacesetter Homes of Newport Beach, California, a subsidiary of American Pacesetter (formerly American Electronics), which turned out a volume of $14.5 million in 1970. Barclay Hollander Curci's acquisition by Castle & Cooke in 1969 has also worked out very well. And Lear Siegler's acquisition of Truesdale Construction for about $10 million plus earnout was another thriving deal.

A representative summary of the thriving mergers as of early 1973 does present something of a corrective view. Though the ones that have been affected strongly by accounting reforms and proposed tax changes on apartment development may be in difficulty, as are those few that have been so unfortunate as to get their land blocked by conservationist lobbying, the majority do continue to be viable through the first difficult days of 1974.

For the sake of convenient classification, I have broken down the acquirers of building and real estate companies according to the following categories:

1. *Conglomerate type,* which includes a number of industrial and manufacturing companies not normally classified as conglomerates but which are thus grouped because the primary activity is unrelated to housing.
2. *Building materials and products companies,* including lumber, chemical, and hardware firms supplying the housing industry, though some of them are so diversified as to deserve the name conglomerate.
3. *Financial services companies,* including casualty insurance and mutual-fund management firms.
4. *Congeneric companies,* i.e., firms already primarily engaged in housing and real estate developemnt.

THE CONGLOMERATE-TYPE ACQUISITIONS

Two of the conglomerates in the homebuilding field are Avco and City Investing. While City Investing continued to perform well in the home building business, Avco late in 1973 found itself faced with difficulties stemming from ecological issues. The question of the company's future growth depended on the resolution of ecological obstacles to development of its large property holdings which are concentrated primarily in San Diego and Orange Counties of southern California, where ecology groups wield large power.

Avco Corporation, which had large, diversified holdings in, among other things, motion pictures and financial services, bought into the field with the acquisition of Southern California's Rancho Bernardo, a large master-planned development just north of San Diego. Changing its name to Avco Community Developers, the new subsidiary expanded in 1971 by the acquisition of another large Southern California land-and-housing project, Laguna Niguel, and by the expansion of housing operations to Phoenix. In 1970, prior to the acquisition of Laguna Niguel, which nearly doubled its size, the subsidiary reported revenues of $20.5 million. (Avco's involvement in real estate started informally enough at a racetrack, where the Avco exec in charge of acquisitions and Harry Summers, head of the development company, had adjoining boxes. The two got to talking things over, and before you knew it they had themselves a deal.)

City Investing Company, for its part, also operates with great success in three major areas: Financial services, manufacturing, and housing and land development. And it has been expanding its role in the latter category. The company had already owned 53.6% of Guerdon Industries, one of the largest modular and mobile-home manufacturers, and 49% of General Development Corporation, the Florida land developer and builder. Guerdon reported sales of $160.4 million and earnings of $5 million in fiscal 1971. General Development earned $17.1 million on revenues of $120.5 million in 1970, with 1971 performance projected to increase by about 13%. With these solid performers giving it confidence, City Investing in September of 1971 acquired a traditional homebuilder, Wood Bros. Homes of Denver, which had about $40 million sales in the year of acquisition.

Food products and tobacco companies are also active in the development field, and until 1973 successfully so. This trend began with the acquisition by the Pillsbury Company of a substantial interest in Pemtom, the Minneapolis builder and developer, which reported $18.1 million in revenues for 1970. In March 1970, Pillsbury acquired 122,000 shares (approximately 23%) of the common stock of Pemtom for a cash purchase price of $1,464,000 and acquired $2.1 million of Pemtom's 8% convertible subordinated debentures which were convertible into 150,000 shares of Pemtom common stock. Pillsbury also committed itself, under a revolving credit agreement, to loan Pemtom up to $5 million until June 1975. However, Pemtom, an apartment developer, ran into tougher sledding with the changed accounting rules.

Foremost-McKesson, the big San Francisco food and drug manufacturer, put a solid bet on its future in housing by the acquisition of two

California development firms. The first of the acquisitions was Ditz-Crane of Santa Clara, a builder of high-priced single-family homes (1970 revenues: $15 million). The second, completed early in 1971, was Gentry Development of Dublin, California, a diversified builder with 1970 sales of $19 million. Leading the tobacco companies in diversification moves, Philip Morris early in 1970 acquired through outright purchase and options roughly 50.1% interest in the Mission Viejo Company, the builder of one of America's most successful "new towns." Mission Viejo had revenues of $29.8 million in 1970. Late in 1972, the tobacco-maker moved to buy complete ownership of Mission Viejo. Phil Reilly, the president of the development subsidiary, has been delighted with the relationship and the company quickly expanded operations to the Phoenix and Denver markets.

Inland was not the only steelmaker to go the acquisition route to get into housing. Another member of the steelmaking fraternity, Bethlehem Steel, early in 1970 acquired Multicon Properties, the big Columbus, Ohio, apartment developer. As of 1973, this company was experiencing serious difficulties because of the changed climate for apartment development. Multicon took in about $38 million in gross revenues from construction and sale of apartments and condominiums, plus another $17 million in rents from retained properties, in 1970. The acquisition, consummated for $13 million in securities, gave Bethlehem access to the future of industrialized housing. "It hasn't been such a good deal for Bethlehem so far," one of Multicon's top officials confided late in 1971, "because industrialized housing is still a long way off and Multicon is still primarily in conventional construction." But Multicon's officials credited the steel company, and especially Frank Rabold, Bethlehem's real estate chief, with creating a compatible management environment while the merger was first setting in.

One of the newest major manufacturing companies to enter the development field successfully in a big way has been the Singer Company, which in 1970 had revenues of $2.14 billion and earnings of $75.1 million. A diversified manufacturer, Singer drew its revenue from sales of household and industrial sewing machines, and from a variety of high-technology products—information systems, aerospace and marine systems, and educational and training products. Early in 1971 the company completed the acquisition of the Besco group of companies, a large homebuilding organization operating in Northern California. Besco, which has since changed its name to Singer Housing Company, earned about $4 million on sales of $57 million in 1970. The subsidiary continued to prosper after acquisition, as sales for the first nine months of 1971 were up 35% from the comparable period in 1970, and President John Brooks forecast a similar performance for 1972. If entrepreneurial housing development is bad business for industrial corporations, Singer certainly didn't know it. In mid-1972 it expanded its housing role by making another major acquisition, Mitchell Corporation of Mobile, Alabama (1970 sales: $23 million). The new subsidiary operates in Mississippi, Alabama, Florida and Georgia.

The terms of the Besco acquisition agreement were interesting. Singer issued to the principal owners, Wayne F. Valley and Brooks, preferred stock convertible into 954,090 shares of Singer common over a period from April 1, 1976, to April 1, 1980. Under certain circumstances, however, the preferred can be converted earlier — giving the owners an option to sell out to the public up to one-half of the common stock underlying the preferred stock. Because the dividend rate on the preferred is initially lower than the rate on the underlying common stock, Singer avoided dilution of its own earnings in 1970.

CBS, the broadcasting giant, has also taken a strong position in housing by paying $10 million in cash late in 1970 for a 49% interest in the Klingbeil Company, the big apartment developer based in Columbus, Ohio. With six operating divisions scattered from San Francisco to Washington, D.C., the company was well diversified for continuing growth but was also affected by changed accounting rules on apartments. It grossed about $37 million in 1970 from the construction and sale of apartments and condominiums, while collecting another $18 million in rents from retained properties. The acquisition agreement gave CBS the option to buy the remaining 51% of the company in 1975. Meanwhile, with operating control remaining in the hands of young (thirty-five years old) founder and president, Jim Klingbeil, there was little question that the relationship between the two companies would remain first-rate. Klingbeil shareholders themselves got only $5 million for selling the equivalent of a $24\frac{1}{2}$% interest in the company. The other $5 million, representing another $24\frac{1}{2}$% interest, went directly to the company in exchange for new and treasury shares, thus providing the developer with a strong capital base for growth through 1975. CBS also made a $2.5 million subordinated loan to the company.

For CBS, this may be only the first of several moves into the housing and real estate field. Diversification has been the keynote for this major corporation for several years, as CBS's longtime president, Dr. Frank Stanton, tried to lessen the company's dependence on the rigidly regulated broadcast business. Broadcast revenues in 1970 already accounted for only about 60% of net sales of $1.2 billion. Pursuing diversification, CBS had made such acquisitions as the New York Yankees baseball club (sold in 1972); the publishing firm Holt, Rinehart & Winston; the toymaker Creative Playthings; and other businesses in musical instruments, records and educational materials. Housing has been the most recent of its ventures.

The focus on further acquisitions was emphasized in late 1971 by the appointment of a diversification expert as the successor to Dr. Stanton. The new man, who was to become chief operating officer on Stanton's retirement in 1973, was Charles T. Ireland, Jr., who joined CBS after four years of service as a top lieutenant for arch-conglomerator Harold S. Geneen at ITT. When Mr. Ireland died unexpectedly in mid-1972, Dr. Stanton appointed thirty-seven-year-old whiz kid Arthur R. Taylor to the CBS presidency. Taylor came from International Paper, where he had served as vice president and chief financial officer for two years, revamping the company's financial management in a series of well-publicized deals. Taylor, as it happens, also knows the housing business well, having presided over IP's lately dissolved real estate empire, including the Donald L. Bren Company. With CBS looking for further diversification, will it give housing a bigger role?

BUILDING MATERIALS AND SUPPLY COMPANIES

One of the forest-products companies that pursued housing activities, primarily in the area of prefabrication, is Evans Products Company of Portland, Oregon. The company operated a separate Home Group, based in Minneapolis, which oversaw three subsidiary companies: International Homes of Minneapolis; Capp Homes of Des Moines; and Ridge Homes of Conshohocken, Pennsylvania. Revenues in 1970 were at an estimated $62 million, resulting principally from the production of prefabricated single-family homes.

Potlatch Forests, based in San Francisco, is another timber-products giant operating a growing shelter group. The company's initial venture into construction was represented by Speedspace, the big modular producer of school buildings. Speedspace, headquartered in Santa Rosa, California, also operated plants in Carlisle, Indiana, and Hometown, Pennsylvania. It later extended its prefabrication activities to include single-family housing. In April of 1970 Potlatch also acquired an 80% stake in the big San Francisco area developer Brown & Kaufmann. B&K had built $100-million worth of luxury housing in the Bay Area, including some outstanding examples of planned-unit projects. The Potlatch shelter group produced about $27 million in revenues in 1970.

But among the timber-products companies it is Weyerhaeuser that has been taking the strongest position in the actual development of housing, with all its entrepreneurial perils. Its activities are infrequently publicized, but the volume of its activities and the aggressiveness of its builder-acquisition program puts it in the same league as the biggest homebuilders — Kaufman & Broad, Levitt & Sons, U.S. Home, and Larwin, among others. The company formed a real estate subsidiary, Weyerhaeuser Real Estate Company, based in Tacoma, Washington, when it picked up the big Los Angeles-based homebuilder Pardee Construction in the late Sixties and its mortgage-banking subsidiary. By 1970, revenues from these and related land-sales activities rose to $86.2 million.

The forest-products company is widely involved in joint ventures with independent builders as a financial partner through its venture subsidiary. Moreover, during 1971 Weyerhaeuser stepped up its direct participation in housing considerably by acquiring two additional homebuilding and development firms. In January of 1971 the company completed the acquisition of the second-biggest homebuilder in Dallas, Centennial Construction, in a $13 million stock deal. Centennial, reporting $1.4 million in earnings on 1970 sales of $17 million, projected 1971 revenues at $26 million. In September of 1971, Weyerhaeuser also acquired Westminster Co., a Greensboro, North Carolina homebuilder with 1970 sales exceeding $9 million. Bolstered by the parent company's financing, both of the recent acquisitions planned to expand beyond their present markets and to diversify their construction activities. More acquisitions, and certainly more joint ventures may be in store.

Certain-Teed Product Corporation is one major housing supplier that is not new to the housing field. Back in 1961 its stock rose to towering heights as it led the field in the shell-house boom, and then collapsed when the boom busted. But it reentered the development field in a different way as of 1970, profiting by its earlier experiences. The company's 56%-owned subsidiary, Valley Forge Corporation (renamed in early 1971 from Modular Sciences Corporation) is a corporate descendant from the shell-house days, but it has become a diversified development company with conventional and factory-housing production in St. Louis, Atlanta, North Carolina and Puerto Rico. Key to Valley Forge's housing operations are two of its own 1970 acquisitions, Concord Homes, a prefabber, and Fischer & Frichtel Development Corporation, both of St. Louis. With the acquired companies Valley Forge also got their founder and chief executive, John J. Fischer, an extremely canny and successful builder-developer, who began guiding overall factory housing.

The interesting thing about Valley Forge's housing plants is that, in addition to serving independent builder-dealers and their own development activities, they could also serve the major development projects undertaken by the parent corporation. Certain-Teed's in-house development group, built around Realtec, Inc., of Fort Lauderdale, Florida, got off to a fast start with three major programs: lot sales ($4,000 to $12,000) at a 3,900-acre project in North Carolina's Blue Ridge Mountains; condominium sales ($30,000 to $55,000) at the 5,000-acre Sapphire Valley Inn and Golf Club, near Asheville, North Carolina; and master planning of a 2,800-acre residential community near Atlanta, to be developed over a ten-year period. With this kind of interaction, both the parent and the subsidiary benefited.

(Certain-Teed, moreover, is the only building-supply company to have sponsored its own real investment trust.) Valley Forge's revenues for 1970 came to $15 million. But they rose sharply in the first half of 1971, up to $12.9 million from $5 million in the comparable period a year earlier.

American Cyanamid, the huge chemical company based in Wayne, New Jersey, which counts laminated products supplier Formica among its subsidiaries and which reported $1.16 billion in sales for 1970, also took a decisive step into housing. In September of 1970 it acquired a big Charlotte, North Carolina, developer, the Ervin Company. Known on the Atlantic seaboard for its quality work as a developer of planned communities, Ervin was also diversified in apartment and nonresidential construction. The company's 1970 revenues ran to $70 million. Following the acquisition, Ervin made plans to expand both southward and northward, beyond its present markets. This resulted in a second homebuilding acquisition for American Cyanamid shortly after the first, as Sunstate Builders of Tampa, Florida, came into the fold in January of 1971 to facilitate Ervin's growth. Subsequently, American Cyanamid expanded its string of homebuilders to four by purchasing Edmund J. Bennett Associates and Croyder Irvin, Inc.

Olin is another conglomerate in the billion-dollar class (1969 revenues $1.15 billion) which is staking out a strong position in housing. The manufacturer, based in Stamford, Connecticut, produces chemicals, plastics, metals and forest products and has a heavy involvement in supply of building products for the housing industry. Between 1969 and 1971 it entered the housing field directly by the acquisition of four subsidiaries. These produced $49.2 million in 1970 revenues, or about 5% of Olin's overall sales volume. But Olin has ambitious plans. Its five-year plan targeted homebuilding revenues at $157.5 million by 1974. To achieve this, Olin President Gordon Grand kept an active eye open for further acquisitions, as well as hustling the present subsidiaries along to achieve annual growth rates of 20% to 30%. Olin recently rounded out its builder buy-ups by acquiring Robert H. Young and his Young/America Corporation of Dallas, and Young became head of all Olin real estate activities as head of Olin-America Company.

The biggest in Olin's stable of developers is Steve Yeonas's Yeonas Corporation, the Washington, D.C.-Baltimore area homebuilder, acquired in April of 1969. Grand has commented that this acquisition had problems meeting its high projections because of tough housing-market conditions in the two years following acquisition, but growth is in the eyes of the beholder. Yeonas produced $22 million in revenues in 1969, up from $15 million in the preceding year, and turned in $27 million in 1970, while projecting $34 million for 1971. The other companies in the shelter group included Baltimore's Maryland Housing Corporation, acquired in April of 1970, a $10 million modular housing manufacturer and developer of government-subsidized projects; Morrison Homes, the $10 million West Coast homebuilder based in Oakland, California, acquired late in 1970; and Chesapeake Homes, a Baltimore housing firm.

Pacific Holding Corporation of Los Angeles also entered the residential development business in August 1969 with the acquisition of an Anaheim-based builder, McCarthy Company. In June 1971 McCarthy emerged from its status as a private subsidiary and went public. Pacific Holding bought McCarthy for 137,310 shares of common valued at approximately $5.7 million at the time of the acquisition. McCarthy in that year had sales of $5.2 million and earnings just under $200,000. When the company went public, Pacific Holding distributed as a dividend to its shareholders about 20% of McCarthy stock. They received 257,400 McCarthy shares of common in all, on the basis of one share of McCarthy's common stock for each seven shares of Pacific's common stock.

FINANCIAL SERVICE COMPANIES

The builder mergers with financially oriented companies are fewer in number, but as a group they appeared to be the most stable and successful. Among such firms, for example, we find American Financial of Cincinnati, Ohio, whose housing subsidiary, American Continental Homes, raised 1970 revenues to $24 million from $12.8 million in 1969, an increase of 88%, while earnings also more than doubled, rising to $2 million from $960,000. MGIC, the Milwaukee mortgage insuring firm, also fielded two successful building organizations through its investment subsidiary: Janis Properties of Miami (1970 revenues: $14.5 million), and La Monte-Shimberg of Tampa (1970 revenues: $12.07 million). With sales rising by 40% or more over 1969, and profits shooting up by 80% (to $2.5 million), the subsidiaries were busy expanding beyond their market areas to Orlando, Clearwater and Brandon, Florida, in 1971.

Perhaps one important reason this category of mergers has worked out well, at least in the early phases, was that the financially oriented acquirers understood the builder's financial language and requirements. Unlike some earnings-oriented companies, the financial firms have also been more inclined to evaluate the builder's performance by return on investment rather than by contribution to earnings. In many cases where the acquirer's primary activities provide a large continuing cash flow, a subsidiary building organization offers an attractive funnel for the cash because of the high return obtainable on this category of investment. Some other examples of such firms:

Dreyfus Corporation, the big mutual-fund management company, surprised its financial brethren in the stock-and-bond trade in May of 1969 by taking the unusual step of moving directly into the housing field with the acquisition of a Detroit-based builder, Bert L. Smokler Company. Smokler's firm had earned about $1 million on $28 million in sales during 1969, and merged into Dreyfus for 360,000 shares of common then valued at $14 million. The acquirer subsequently organized a realty subsidiary, Dreyfus Development Corporation, with Mandel Berman (Smokler's partner and top exec in the builder organization) as president, and development activities were expanded broadly.

The Smokler organization had been closely tied to the Detroit market, and in the first year following the acquisition it was hurt by the General Motors strike which crippled the regional economy. Revenues in 1970 fell about $19.1 million from $28.2 million the year before. But in 1971 the company anticipated regaining its pre-strike level of revenues. Meanwhile, operations were also diversified beyond Michigan to Minnesota, Ohio and Florida, with twenty-five projects in all under way. (In Minnesota alone, Dreyfus was involved in four projects within the "new town" of Jonathan, plus three other condominium developments totaling 1,000 units and a 500-unit government-subsidized project.) Despite the setback in the post-acquisition year, the Dreyfus merger was remarkably free of the internal chafing that characterized some merger deals. As Bert Smokler put it: "There's a lot more reporting paperwork, but we have complete freedom of decision. We're very happy with this merger. They're good people and we relate well with them." But there was a change in April 1973. After four years in the building business Dreyfus decided it wanted out. Its real estate subsidiaries were sold to Lennar Corporation of Miami for $7 million, thus giving the acquirer, a major homebuilding firm, access to the Michigan, Minnesota and Ohio markets. Lennar's acquisition of the Dreyfus operations lent further credence to the growing popularity of the congeneric form of merger (builder buying builder).

The Monumental Corporation of Baltimore saw in the realty-acquisition route the potential to become a broader financial service organization. It had put together an insurance combine consisting of Monumental Life, a life insurance company specializing in medium-size policies, and Volunteer Life, handling larger life insurance policies. At the end of 1969, it put itself into a strong position in real estate by acquiring Harvey M. Meyerhoff's Baltimore-based Continental Properties. The realty organization, whose name has since been changed to Monumental Properties, had turned to investment building in the early Fifties after thirty years as a Baltimore-area homebuilder. At the time of the acquisition, more than 80% of its income came from rentals of commercial and apartment properties it had developed — an enviable source of recurring income.

The developer has considerably stepped up its program since the merger. As of 1971, Monumental owned 5.25 million square feet of shopping centers out of the 9.1 million square feet it completed or had under development. Plans also called for an increase in company-held apartment units from 6,000 in 1969 to 11,000 by the end of 1971. Homebuilding and general contracting also contributed to sales. With this kind of growth, the company has been expanding well beyond Baltimore to Atlanta, Tampa, St. Petersburg, Miami and Hialeah, Florida. Revenues in 1970 from combined activities climbed to $63.3 million.

Giant INA Corporation, the diversified casualty insurance holding company, also weighed into the housing field with the acquisition in September of 1969 of M. J. Brock & Sons, the Los Angeles-based homebuilder and general contractor. The relationship between this old line building firm and the acquirer has been very stable. The Brock organization's contribution to INA's per-share earnings is small in view of the acquirer's size, but the company has been regularly producing a high return on INA's invested capital. Since the acquisition, Milt Brock, Jr., has expanded the subsidiary's operations beyond Sacramento and the Los Angeles area to Colorado Springs and Florida. The company's 1970 revenues were $42 million, with $26 million of this coming from general contracting operations.

Last but not least, we have CNA Financial's mid-1969 acquisition of a big, diversified Beverly Hills-based developer, the Larwin Group. We have already observed how Larry Weinberg initially got $100 million in stock for his organization, with another $100 million to come subject to earnings performance, and we shall return to an examination of Larwin's fortunes in still another chapter. But it's worth observing here that it was not until 1973 that the company encountered problems.

Stimulated by the prospect of the additional $100 million waiting in the wings subject to earnings performance, Larwin for four years barrelled along flat-out, expanding into new markets and getting into new product and service lines. The particularly active single-family and apartment divisions operated throughout California and in the Chicago and New York markets, with further expansion under way. Larwin also got heavily into commercial development and recreational-land sales, as well as operating a $350 million mortgage-banking subsidiary and its own publicly held real estate investment trust, Larwin Mortgage Investors.

THE CONGENERIC COMPANIES

While the term "conglomerate" denotes an organization which operates many unrelated businesses under one corporate roof, "congeneric" identifies a single-business company which makes acquisitions only among companies engaged in the same business. This term provides us with a general classification for all mergers between builders. But, as we shall see, there are some important distinctions within the general category.

The growth of such builder-into-builder mergers has two underlying reasons. The first is that the emerging large building organizations must inevitably resort to acquisitions of one sort or another, whether to sustain their growth, to enter new markets, or to respond to a specific investment opportunity — or for a combination of all these reasons. The second is the attraction of joining up with a parent who already understands the business and is prepared to provide meaningful assistance without imposing the sometimes vexatious demands of corporate-style bureaucracy on the acquired builder.

To be sure, not all such mergers work out for the merged entrepreneurs either. If we can squeeze the big mobile home maker, Redman Industries of Dallas (1970 sales: $150 million), into the congeneric category, we find that its acquisition of the apartment developer Kansas Quality Construction early in 1969 for $18 million resulted in the departure of the acquired entrepreneur, young (thirty-five years old) Jack Bertoglio a year later.* Entrepreneurs who merge their smaller building companies into bigger ones also sometimes find they prefer operating on a more individual level. Hence, you get departures like that of Harlan Lee, who left Leisure Technology, the Lakewood, New Jersey, developer of planned leisure communities late in 1971, a year after merging his Sherman Oaks, California, company into the organization (it now operates as a division of the parent firm, the name changed from Harlan Lee & Associates to Leisure Technology of California).

There is ample precedent for the acquisition of smaller builders by bigger ones. Kaufman & Broad, for example, has acquired five housing and real estate organizations between 1968 and 1970 and absorbed them right into its corporate structure without even a burp. The acquired organizations, substantially smaller than the acquiring firm, were Kay Homes, Leisure Industries, Biltmore Mobile Homes, and Wayside Homes. Big U.S. Financial of San Diego, the joint-venturing giant, bought up San Jose's Due & Elliot homebuilding firm in 1969 and three more organizations during 1970: Development Creators, Shelter Corporation, and Mosser Construction. Shapell Industries, the Beverly Hills-based homebuilder (1970 sales: $39.6 million), likewise bought Sterling Home Developers in Northern California and turned it into an operating division of the parent company.

---

* Redman also entered the single-family housing market in 1971, operating primarily in Dallas. But in April 1973 it announced it was getting out of that field as well as slowing down "dramatically" its apartment construction handled by Redman Development Corporation, the old Bertoglio company. Redman's president, Lee Posey, said the halt in apartment construction was temporary, "to get a better handle on what we are doing."

I—Conglomerate Selected Mergers/Acquisitions

Acquirer	Acquired	Year	Sales & Earnings in Year Acquired (in millions)		Price Paid	Addl. Payment Contingent on Earnings After Acquisition	Comment
			Sales	Earnings			
Bethlehem Steel	Multicon, Columbus, Ohio	4/70	$38	N.A.	$13 Mil.	None	Pooling
CBS, New York	Klingbeil Company, Columbus, Ohio	4/70	$37	N.A.	$10 Mil. cash	None (at present)	Bought 49% interest, option to pick up remainder in 1975. Accounted as pooling.
Castle & Cooke, Honolulu	Barclay-Hollander-Curci, Los Angeles	1/69	$26	$1.1	425M shs. ($16.3 Mil.)	125M shs. (max. value, $4.8 Mil.)	Accounted as pooling.
Cerro Mining, New York	Leadership Housing Systems, Newport Beach, CA	9/70	Not reported separately	Not reported separately	$11 Mil. cash; $34 Mil. assumption of liabilities	$5 Mil. cash payable over 10 years	80% of company purchased from Great Southwest; option on 20% retained by management of Leadership. Accounted as pooling.
	ICX Co., Denver	8/72	$43.3 (1971)	$4.4 (1971)	N.A.	N.A. purchase	Accounted as purchase.
City Investing, New York	Wood Bros., Denver Estes Bros., Tucson	9/71	$39.4	$2.74	$10 Mil.	$10 Mil.	Accounted as purchase.
Inland Steel, Chicago	Scholz Homes, Toledo	2/70	$58	$3.5	cash & stock* ($87 Mil.)	None	*For 3.9 Mil. Scholz shares outstanding, Inland offered option of exch. each share for $22 cash or ½ share Inland 5½% preferred convert. Inland common at $44, non-*callable* 6 yrs.
	Jewel Builders, Toledo, Ohio	6/70	$10	$1	132,900 sh.	70,000 sh. pd. over 5 yrs.	Purchase
ITT, New York	Levitt & Sons, Lake Success, L.I.	2/68	$120	N.A.	1.8 Mil. sh. $92 Mil.	None	Pooling
	United Homes,	2/69	$25	$572M*	186,722 shs.	32,193 shs. (Max.	Accounted as pooling.

Acquirer	Company acquired	Date	Price	Earnings/Sales	Consideration	Other	Notes
Lear Siegler, Santa Monica, CA	Federal Way, Wash.				$11.2 Mil.	val. $1.9 Mil.)	Pooling
	Trousdale-Construction, Bel Air, CA	8/69	$866,000	–$257,000 loss	500,000 shs. $9.8 Mil.	500,000 shs. (Max. val. $10 Mil.)	Pooling
Occidental Petroleum, Los Angeles	S.V. Hunsaker, Santa Ana, CA	7/64	$43.5	$2.0 Mil.	160,938 sh. $5.1 Mil.	None	Pooling
Pacific Holding, Los Angeles	Deane Bros., Newport Beach, CA	8/66	$25	N.A.	97,561 sh. ($3.7 Mil.)	None	Pooling
	McCarthy Co., Anaheim, CA	9/69	$5.2	$184,000	137,310 sh. $5.8 Mil.	None	Pooling. Note: McCarthy went public 6/71.
Pacific Lighting, Los Angeles	Fredericks Develop, Fullerton, CA	1/70	$12	600,000	Sh. val. $7 Mil.	N.A.	N.A.
Pillsbury Mills, Minneapolis	Pemtom, Bloomington, Minn.	3/70	N.A.	N.A.	23% of co. acquired for cash $1.46 Mil.; plus, pd. $2.1 Mil. for convertible subordin. debentures conv. into 150,000 Pemtom shares. Gave Pemtom revolving credit line of $5 Mil. to 6/75.		Pooling
Philip Morris	Mission Viejo Co., Orange County, CA	1/70	$30 (1970) ($30 Mil. 1971)	($1.35 Mil. 1971)	$20 Mil. (bought $15 Mil. in conv. debs. to buy approx. 27% of co., plus pd. $5 Mil. for option to buy controlling int. (50.1%) within 3 yrs for approx. $13 Mil. more.	None	Initially bought control of 50.1% of co. In Sept. 1972, began negotiating to buy remaining 49.9%.
Santa Anita Consolidated, Arcadia, CA	Grant Co.	6/70	$35	$1.26	267,540 pref. conv. into 1,112,160 shs. comm. ($10.7 Mil.)	267,540 pref. conv. into 1,112,160 shs. comm. ($10.7 Mil.)	Accounted as pooling.
Signal Companies	Shattuck & McHone Enterprises, Santa Ana, CA	11/69	$32	$831M*	426,667 shs. ($10.8 Mil.)	414,000 shs. (Max. val. $10.6M)	Accounted as pooling.
Singer Co.	Singer Housing Co. (BESCO) San Leandro	2/71	$63	$4	Prfd. stk. conv. into 954,090 (value 2/71)	Company has option of going public in 1975.	Note: Prfd. stock conv. between 4/1/76 & 4/1/80. Accounted as purchase.
	Mitchell Corp., Mobile, Alabama	5/72	N.A.	N.A.	N.A.	N.A.	Purchase

*Stated in thousands.

II—Building Materials and Supply Companies

Acquirer	Acquired	Year	Sales & Earnings in Year Acquired (in millions)		Price Paid	Addl. Payment Contingent on Earnings After Acquisition	Comment
			Sales	Earnings			
American Cyanamid (Formica), Wayne, N.J.	Ervin Co., Charlotte	9/70	N.A.	N.A.	487,805 sh. ($15 Mil.)	487,804 sh.	Pooling
	Croyder Irvin, Inc.	11/70	N.A.	N.A.	109,091 sh.	None	Pooling
	Sunstate Builders, Tampa		N.A.	N.A.	N.A.	N.A.	Purchase
	Edmund J. Bennet Assoc.		N.A.	N.A.	64,687 sh.	None	Purchase
American-Standard, New York	Wm. Lyon & Co., Newport Beach, CA	4/69	$20	$1.3	350,000 sh. (Val. $12.2 Mil.)	50,000 sh. ($1.7 Mil.)	Accounted as pooling.
	Carmichael, Washington, D.C.	/69	N.A.	N.A.	N.A.	N.A.	
	Builders Homes, Dothan, Alabama	/69	N.A.	N.A.	N.A.	N.A.	Prefabricator
Certain-Teed (Valley Forge), Valley Forge, PA	Concord Homes, St. Louis	4/70	$4.3	$133,000	548,667 sh. common	None	Pooling Modular Housing Manufacturer
	Fisher & Frichtel, St. Charles, Mo.	4/70	$1.8	92,000	23,022 sh.	23,020 sh.	
	W.H. Miller Co.						
International Paper, New York	Donald L. Bren Co., Sherman Oaks, CA	5/69	$15	$572M*	960,000 sh. (Val. $36.2 Mil.)	960,000 sh. (Max. Val. $87 Mil.)	Pooling

*Stated in thousands.

III – Financial Services Companies

Acquirer	Acquired	Year	Sales & Earnings in Year Acquired (in millions)		Price Paid	Addl. Payment Contingent on Earnings After Acquisition	Comment
			Sales	Earnings			
CNA Financial, Chicago	Larwin Group, Beverly Hills, CA	6/69	$76	$4.7	3,745,318 sh. ($100 Mil.)	3,745,318 sh. ($100 Mil., Max. Val.)	Accounted as pooling.
Dreyfus Corp., New York	Bert L. Smokler & Co., Southfield, Michigan	5/69	$28	$1	360,000 sh. (Val. $14 Mil.)	17,000 sh. 6-mo. earnout	Accounted as pooling.
INA Corp.	M.J. Brock & Co., Los Angeles	9/69	N.A.	N.A.	N.A.	None	Accounted as pooling
MGIC Financial Corp., Milwaukee	Janis, Miami	7/70	$12.2	$717,000	125,000 sh. $5 Mil.	None	Pooling
	Lamonte-Shimberg, Tampa		N.A.	N.A.	N.A.	N.A.	Part purchase, part pooling.
Monumental Corp., Baltimore	Monumental Properties, Baltimore, Md.	12/69	N.A.	N.A.	$5 Mil. cash plus 2.7 Mil. sh. val. $78 Mil. at time of merger.	None	Pooling

IV – Building or Related Companies (CONGENERIC)

Acquirer	Acquired	Year	Sales & Earnings in Year Acquired (in millions)		Price Paid	Addl. Payment Contingent on Earnings After Acquisition	Comment
			Sales	Earnings			
Centex, Dallas	Winston Development Co., Pallatine, Illinois	2/70	$30	$1.7	358,000 sh. ($15.7 Mil.)	Contingent sh. included in 358,000	Bought from N.K. Winston Corp., NYC
	Fox & Jacobs, Dallas	1/72	$37 (1971)	(1971)	1,295,000 sh. ($38 Mil.)	None	Accounted as pooling.

IV—Building or Related Companies (CONGENERIC)

Acquirer	Acquired	Year	Sales & Earnings in Year Acquired (in millions)		Price Paid	Addl. Payment Contingent on Earnings After Acquisition	Comment
			Sales	Earnings			
Horizon Land, Tucson	P.A.T. Homes, Tucson	7/72	$15 (1971)	$700,000 (1971)	Common stock val. $6.5 Mil. at time of merger.	None	Accounted as pooling.
Kaufman & Broad, Los Angeles	Kay Homes, Burlingame, Calif.	4/68	$8.4	$328,000	159,262 sh. $2.5 M.	None	Accounted as purchase.
	Biltmore Mobile Homes	10/69	N.A.	N.A.	N.A.	N.A.	Accounted as purchase.
	Leisure Industries, Los Angeles	12/68	$4.08	$461,000	32,000 sh. ($952,000)	32,000 sh. ($952,000–12/68)	Purchase of 80% interest.
	Victoria Wood (Revenue Properties), Toronto, Ontario	2/70	$4.5	$105,000	$7.75 Mil. cash, $2.75 Mil. 6¾ capital note	None	Accounted as purchase.
	Wayside Homes, Ft. Worth, Tex.	11/70	$2.13	$221,000	Undisclosed amt. of cash.	None	Accounted as purchase.
Leisure Technology, Lakewood, N.J.	Karpay Construction, Tampa	10/69	$2.7	$34M*	37,834 sh. ($681,000)	Approx. 37,834 sh. ($681,000–10/69)	Pooling
	R.J. Brown Assoc., Chicago	11/69	$7.2	$35M*	131,674 sh. ($3.5 Mil.)	Approx. 131,674 sh. ($3.5 Mil.)	Pooling
	Fred Frankel Assoc. & Block Land Inc., Fairlen Hills, Pa.	3/70	$335M*	-74,000 (loss)	101,351 sh. ($2.4 Mil.)	Approx. 101,351 sh. ($2.4 Mil.)	Pooling & part purchase.
	Harlan Lee & Assoc., Sherman Oaks, CA	5/70	$169,692	37,000	48,031 sh. ($781,000)	Approx. 48,031 sh. or sh. with min. val. of 1 Mil.	Pooling
Redman Industries, Dallas	Kansas Quality Const., Kansas City	2/69	$13	$323,000	80,000 sh. (3.6 Mil.)	-	Pooling with one-yr. earnout.
Shapell Industries, Beverly Hills, CA	Sterling Homes, San Jose, CA	4/71	None	None	78,000 sh.	None	Pooling

Other Mergers and Acquisitions in Brief

Acquirer	*Acquired*
Conglomerate:	
American Pacesetter	Pacesetter Homes Newport Beach, Calif.
Alcoa Bldg. Industries Div.	Challenge Developments Redwood City, Calif.
Foremost-McKesson	Ditz-Crane Santa Clara, Calif.
	Gentry Development Dublin, Calif.
Medical Growth Industries	Stanley C. Swartz Co. La Jolla, Calif.
Monogram Industries	Ring Brothers Los Angeles, Calif.
Titan Group	Multiplex Cleveland, Ohio
	Farley Construction Louisville, Ky.
	Sovereign Construction Fort Lee, N.J.
Bldg. Materials & Supply Cos.:	
Evans Products	Capp Homes Des Moines, Iowa
	Ridge Homes Conshohocken, Pa.
	International Homes Minneapolis, Minn.
Olin Corporation	Yeonas Co. Vienna, Va.
	Maryland Housing Co. Baltimore
	Morrison Homes Oakland, Calif.
	Chesapeake Homes Baltimore, Md.
Potlatch Forests	Speedspace Co.
	Brown & Kaufmann (80% owned) Palo Alto, Calif.
U.S. Plywood-Champion Papers	Lewers & Cooke Honolulu, Hawaii
Weyerhaeuser	Pardee Construction Los Angeles
	Par-West Financial Los Angeles
	Centennial Construction Carolton, Texas
	Quadrant Corp. Bellevue, Washington

Acquirer	*Acquired*
	Westminster Construction Greensboro, N.C.
Financial Services Cos.:	
American Financial	American Continental Homes, Cincinnati, Ohio
Building or Related Cos.:	
Kaiser-Aetna Realty	El Dorado Homes Riverside, Calif.
	Deal Development Co. Dallas, Texas
	Artisan Development Co. Cincinnati, Ohio
	Mackay Homes Santa Clara, Calif.
	Ponderosa Homes Irvine, Calif.
U.S. Financial	Development Creators Honolulu, Hawaii
	Shelter Corporation San Diego, Calif.
	Mosser Construction Fremont, Ohio
	Duc & Elliot Builders San Jose, Calif.
	Aurora Modular Industries

Centex, the big Dallas-based builder and cement-products company (fiscal 1971 sales: $149 million; earnings: $7.6 million) has also facilitated its growth by key builder acquisitions. These aren't small acquisitions, by any means. Early in 1970, for example, Centex bought Winston Development Company of Palatine, Illinois, for $15.7 million in stock. The acquired firm, which had sales of $30 million and earnings of $1.7 million in 1969, now operates as a subsidiary, renamed in 1972 from Centex-Winston to Centex Homes Corporation. The big Dallas-based builder opened 1972 with a bang, moreover, by acquiring the biggest independent homebuilder in Dallas, the well-known Fox & Jacobs Construction Company. The transaction, on a pooling-of-interests basis, entailed the exchange of 1,295,000 Centex shares, valued at more than $38 million as of January 14, 1972. Fox & Jacobs earned $1.8 million on revenues of $37 million in 1971. The new subsidiary kept its name and absorbed Centex-Dallas Corporation, a local Centex subsidiary. Other Centex subsidiaries include Centex Construction, Centex West and Great Lakes Development Company. The company now operates in Florida, Illinois, Georgia, Nevada, Texas, California, New York, Puerto Rico, Oklahoma, Kansas, Louisiana and Hawaii.

Certainly one of the biggest factors in the development field is the

Kaiser-Aetna Realty partnership. Working with a minimum of publicity, the company not only engages in major land-development ventures but has quietly become one of the largest congeneric operations in the country. At the end of 1972 Kaiser-Aetna ran a string of no less than eight residential homebuilding companies. Three of these were developed in-house as start-up operations. (They are Rural Housing of Concord, California; Westard Builders of Richmond, California; and Whiteoak Builders of Marquette, Michigan.) The other five firms were acquired within a three-year period commencing in 1970. (They are Ponderosa Homes of Irvine, California; Mackay Homes of Santa Clara, California; Artisan Development of Cincinnati; I. C. Deal Development of Dallas; and El Dorado Homes of Riverside, California.) This group does not divulge its sales and earnings.

Another big general builder and developer that expanded rapidly through acquisitions is the Titan Group of Louisville, Kentucky (1970 revenues: $109 million). Its recent buy-ups included Multiplex, an $18 million Cleveland apartment developer; Farley Construction of Louisville, a home-builder; and Sovereign Construction, a Fort Lee, New Jersey, general contractor.

Leisure Technology Corporation is one excellent example of a specialized development firm which has resorted to acquisitions of small but talented organizations in order to facilitate its own objectives of geographic dispersal and take advantage of opportunities in new markets. Publicly held, LTC is the creation of a dynamic and innovative man, Robert J. Schmertz. The company has carved a distinctive niche for itself by concentrating on the development of the leisure, recreational and retirement-oriented housing markets. Although it produces some tract housing, its emphasis is increasingly on the development of large planned communities.

Schmertz's first venture into overall development of a large-scale planned community came in 1964 when he opened Leisure Village at Lakewood, New Jersey. The 3,900-home project was outstandingly successful, and by the end of fiscal 1971 (March 31, 1971), the company had sold about 2,800 of the planned homes. The success inspired Schmertz to plan several other major communities. In November of 1970 he opened another Leisure Village, this one planned for 5,200 homes, in Suffolk County (Long Island), New York. At the same time, a 4,000-home Leisure Towne started sales in southern New Jersey to serve the Camden-Philadelphia market, and a 1,600-home Seven Lakes community planned in Fort Myers, Florida. In January of 1971 a fifth planned development, Cambridge-on-the-Lake in Cook County, Illinois, started selling the first of its 450 homes. LTC was also planning a similar project for California, as well as engaging in the development and sale of vacation homesites in the Pocono Mountain area of Pennsylvania.

To undertake this kind of expansion, Schmertz acquired between October of 1969 and May of 1970 four experienced development organizations to operate as divisions of Leisure Tech. It is the nature of this man that his prices for the acquired builders were gauged more on the basis of their entrepreneurial talents rather than their directly visible earnings. Karpay Construction of Tampa, now developing Seven Lakes as Leisure Technology of Florida, had earnings of $34,000 on sales of $2.7 million prior to its acquisition late in 1969. George Karpay and other shareholders received 37,834 LTC shares valued at $681,000, plus another payment in the same amount contingent on future earnings. R. J. Brown Associates of Chicago, now operating as Leisure Technology of Illinois, had earnings of $35,000 on sales of $7.2 million before the merger. Richard J. Brown and other shareholders got 131,674 LTC shares valued at about $3.5 million in early 1970, plus the right to a like amount contingent on future earnings. Harlan Lee & Associates, now headed by the California pro Jerry Lawrence, had earnings of $37,000 on sales of $169,692 prior to the acquisition. The shareholders, Harlan Lee and Jerry Lawrence, got 48,031 LTC shares valued at approximately $1 million, plus the right to another $1 million subject to future earnings. The Pennsylvania organization reported a loss of $74,000 on sales of $335,000 prior to the acquisition. Fred Frankel and other shareholders got 101,351 LTC shares on merging, with the right to another like amount subject to earnings performance.

For the year ended March 31, 1971, Leisure Tech still booked $4.5 million in sales of tract homes, principally from the activities of the recently acquired subsidiaries. But the company's long-term aim is to phase out such single-family construction entirely and to concentrate entirely on the development and sale of units within its planned communities. Planned-community units, in fact, represented 69% of Leisure Tech's sales in 1971, up from 50% in 1969, while other single-family construction fell to 19% from 45% of sales in the same period. Within four of the planned communities, LTC builds and sells condominiums priced from $18,000 to $50,000. At the fifth, Leisure Towne, it is selling both single-family and townhouse units priced from $13,900 to $23,750.

Because of a generally depressed economy and its adverse effects on sales of homes and homesites, Leisure Tech finished out its fiscal year in March 1971 with sales at $24.3 million and earnings of $1.8 million, a setback from the previous year when sales ran to $30.9 million and earnings to $3 million. But with several new communities opened in time to meet the rising economy and the boom in housing sales for 1971 and 1972, the company was expecting to rapidly return to and surpass its 1969 levels of performance. The new operating divisions of Leisure Tech, established since its 1969 sales year, were projected to play an important role in establishing its future growth.

A handful of companies abroad in the land also generally fit into the congeneric category because they've been formed by the simultaneous merger of several developers and other construction-related firms, thus becoming major factors in the industry almost overnight. A better name for this group, though, might be "synergetic" — the whole becoming greater than the sum of its parts.

The publicly held firm of Robino-Ladd, for example, was formed by a merger of two private builders with the initial idea of going public after the combination. The marriage worked well: early in 1973 Robino-Ladd did some more acquiring of a congeneric type. The company bought up all the outstanding stock of Federal Construction Company of Florida. The new subsidiary brought 700 acres of prime land in the Orlando area and other properties in Gainesville and Daytona.

But the single company which most fittingly deserves the description "congeneric," and which has made the greatest impact on the homebuilding industry by the congeneric-acquisition approach, is U.S. Home. Between 1969 and the close of 1971, the company acquired seventeen entrepreneurial housing and building-related organizations. In the course of the acquisition program, U.S. Home's sales went from less than $8 million in 1968 to $91.65 million in the fiscal year ending February 1971, while earnings rose from $600,000 to $4.62 million. For the company's fiscal year ending February 1972, sales were close to $200 million and income shot to approximately $11 million while per-share earnings rose by 50%. U.S. Home projected an annual growth rate of 40% through at least 1975, with expansion divided equally between internal growth and further acquisitions. At that clip, U.S. Home stood to become the biggest shelter producer (of any type) in the United States by 1975. Although the company was adversely affected by a multitude of factors in 1973 and scaled down its projections, it remains a major factor.

The structure of this organization was set up to preserve the entrepreneurial incentive of acquired builders. This was a more active philosophy prior to the acquirer's difficulties in 1973, but it still deserves telling. Other building or manufacturing companies make builder acquisitions and subordinate these to a centralized operating structure. But U.S. Home operates on the principle that each builder ought to remain almost entirely autonomous, and that in fact he makes a greater contribution to the overall organization when he is in full control of his own organization. The acquired builders thus constitute a society of independent equals. The company does have a central office, of course, but this used to operate more in a support and centralized reporting role than as a control center. Each of the acquired builders became an operating division of the parent company while retaining near-complete autonomy in his market area. He would submit an annual budget, and work against a five-year plan that he developed. He also reports his operations to the central office. But he makes all his own decisions and was pretty much on his own in controlling the penetration of his market area. While the merger doesn't guarantee the division head any new working capital, local banks have usually been willing to increase the acquired company's bank lines and make them open and unsecured as a result of U.S. Home's entering the picture. If the builder wants to get a big chunk of capital for a project otherwise beyond his own financial capabilities, he applies to the central office for a loan. But approval is dependent on his convincing his builder-peers that his project is worthy of a claim on total company resources.

Housing is still very much a business of local markets, local land-acquisition skills, local zoning ability, and local marketing strength. By its congeneric structure, U.S. Home devised an approach that combined the strength of local organization with the benefits of rapid growth and nationwide diversification. The genius of the plan was that it delegated the great multitude of key decisions governing each market area to the person most capable of making them — the builder who has been making those decisions successfully for years. This swept the corporate decks clean and freed the top U.S. Home execs for the corporate functions of budgeting, support activities, monitoring performance and corporate planning.

The entrepreneurial incentive was maintained by the constituent builders' friendly competition against one another to achieve their own projections (they meet several times a year as a "peer group" of builder barons at the corporate round table) and by their desire to make USH stock grow. At the same time, the parent corporation is safeguarded from earnings declines by its extreme diversification both in geography and product type: By the start of 1972 it was operating twenty local operations in nearly as many market areas and had perhaps fifty housing-project types in construction. The ability to change product mix rapidly in response to local changes in market demand also aids U.S. Home in this regard. As an upshot, the performance of U.S. Home stock is thus insulated to a degree from the performance of a specific division head.

By structuring itself so flexibly, and with the local entrepreneur as the kingpin, U.S. Home for a long time avoided the topheaviness of centralized management and the remoteness of decision-making that inevitably greet the rapidly expanding building organizaton. Where the major builders have succeeded, it is because they've set up a decentralized management with stock ownership and entrepreneurial prerogatives that looks very much like the U.S. Home arrangement. But there's a difference: Instead of training or hiring junior managers, U.S. Home just acquires top-rated entrepreneurs lock, stock and barrel with their existing building organizations. Thus it solves the management problems inherent in rapid growth by the very nature of its structure.

The heavy stock market shakeout of building stocks in 1972 and 1973 forced U.S. Home to tighten up this procedure. But it remains to be said that the problems are more in the nature of national economic instability than in the congeneric concept itself.

Other congeneric companies began to be formed on a principle similar to, though not identical with, U.S. Home's. One was the privately held Omega Housing Corporation, based in Clearwater, Florida, and organized by Arthur Rutenberg, the former president of U.S. Home Corporation. The organization initially comprised eight fast-growing development companies located in five states and producing approximately $50 million in sales for 1972. Six to eight additional building organizations were to join the Omega group in the near future, and Omega was to go public in the spring of 1974. But the stock market decline killed these plans, at least for the time being.

8

Was It a Funny-Money Merger Boom?

Just gimme some truth.

—John Lennon

As everybody knows, "funny money" was the cheeky name given to securities other than voting common stock, or to inflated stock, as a reflection of their occasionally spurious uses in mergers. Various types of funny money — say, convertible debentures or convertible preferred stock — were favorite instruments of the big gunslinging conglomerators hunting for mergers in the good old days of the late Sixties. Funny money wasn't the only key ingredient of the merger boom. But it gave its name to the furious era of mergers which, rising to a peak in 1969 and early 1970, was made possible by the old accounting rules for the pooling of interests. The mid-1970 bear market stopped the merger boom. But the funny money era itself officially ended on October 31, 1970, when the Accounting Principles Board of the American Institute of Public Accountants put into effect the sharply revised rules for the pooling-of-interests method of merger accounting. A lot of people were very busy that Halloween, and it wasn't trick-or-treating. They were frantically locking up last-minute merger deals.

With this change, the "prehistoric" era of dinosaur-sized builder mergers also drew to a close. The drop-off in mergers and acquisitions of real estate companies following the changes in the accounting rules on pooling and purchase transactions was perceptible. A number of mergers were, to be sure, finalized in 1971, but most of these — including the Singer-Besco, CBS-Klingbeil and Weyerhaeuser-Centennial deals — had been in the works prior to the rules change. In fact, allowing for an inevitable omission or two, only three major companies did any substantial acquiring in the first eighteen months following the rules changes: City Investing, Weyerhaeuser, and U.S. Home (though UH did a heroic volume of business as an acquirer under the new rules in 1971). Not until the close of 1971 and at the start of 1972, as the stock market turned up from its mid-1970 lows, did other acquirers begin rustling around. And their character was changed. No longer were they primarily industrial firms looking for builders; they tended to be companies already involved in some form of real estate activity or financial services. The deals made became smaller, more compactly priced. The congeneric merger boom was born.

As we further scan the tables to notice how many acquirers hustled their merger deals under the wire for the old rules, the question must inevitably arise: To what extent was the initial real estate merger boom, particularly as regards non-housing acquirers, primarily a creature of the old, now-void pooling rules? The accounting rules changes are examined in some detail in this chapter. The most significant change in the conditions under which two companies could merge by a pooling of their assets held that the transaction must be completed in one year. This made "earnouts" impractical with pooling and resulted in the acquirer's losing control over his acquisition. Without such control, companies from outside the housing field were no longer so eager to take the plunge. And it may be just as well. The illusion of control often blinded the acquirer to his own serious deficiencies in management ability. That's why so many of the mergers made under the old pooling rules failed. Most mergers going belly-up in the future will also be from this era.

The elimination of certain cushions and hedges from merger accounting exposed the acquirer to more risk or less profit. (The earnout with "purchase" accounting yields less profit; pooling with no earnout yields greater risk.) These changes suddenly imposed upon him the rude requirement that he have a good understanding of the business he was buying if he was to safeguard his investment. But while narrowing the field of would-be acquirers, the rules reforms by no means eliminated builder mergers. They *have* had a salutary effect on the real estate industry in that they've cut down the entry of the glamour operators who in former times based the hope of profits less on a serious commitment to development than on the pleasure of numbers-juggling. In their stead, a new group of smarter acquirers arose, as evidenced by the first 1971 acquisitions and by many other mergers in the works by early 1972. Even the more "reality-oriented" rules did not keep several of these from difficulties in the tougher climate of 1973.

MERGER ELEMENTS

To get a perspective on the old and new accounting rules governing mergers, and how they shape the merger game, let us first touch on some of the central elements often discussed in merger negotiations.

How much is a development company worth? Always a knotty question. Texts abound giving detailed formulae for the precise calculation of the multiple of the candidate's earnings that an acquirer can safely pay. These equations, resembling the Einsteinian complexities of nuclear physics, correlate the potential acquisition's rate of growth and profitability with the acquiring company's cost of capital (be it equity or debt) and its expected return on invested capital, calculated over 100 years, to provide the resultant P/E multiple the acquirer will fork up. But however valuable such approaches might be, they need not detain us, for we are well served by a few adequate rules of thumb.

Acquirers, after spending hundreds of hours calculating the precise price they will pay for a builder, are surprised at how often their calculations reflect Ken Leventhal's handy rule: Merging companies command a price reflecting a multiple of earnings that is roughly one-half to two-thirds the P/E multiples of a comparable publicly held builder. During the high-riding days of an expanding stock market, if a company comparable to yours on the public market had a P/E of, say, 21, on a merger deal you could get about 14 times your earnings. The particular deal is always negotiable, but an acquirer paying substantially less runs into a no-deal situation because the public market's rewards then become more attractive to the prospective acquisition. The value is essentially set by earnings capacity, with the public market thus instrumental in setting merger prices. With homebuilding industry stocks tumbling in 1973, those inflated acquisition prices were long gone. You were now lucky to get one or two times your offset value — if that. It seems incredible that in 1969, when everybody was looking for a builder, the frenzy of desire drove merger price P/E ratios as high as or higher than the high P/E multiples of the booming housing issues in the stock market. Even as late as 1972, a company like Centex was going counter to the more conservative trend of paying 22 or 23 times earnings for builder Fox & Jacobs. As a rule, a builder acquiring another builder drives the toughest bargain, evaluating the acquisition on assets and demonstrable talent, while outside corporations buying into the field pay the biggest premium. But the change in merger rules had the general effect of lowering acquisition prices, for reasons we shall explore, even before the stock market shakeout.

Another controlling factor works to put a ceiling on merger price in a stock-for-stock deal. No matter how gorgeous an acquisition looks, few if any acquirers will pay a higher P/E multiple for it than the P/E multiple of their own stock. During the early 1970s, a builder selling himself to a company whose stock was priced at 17 times earnings could be pretty certain that the very most he'd be able to get was 17 times his own firm's earnings. Why? If the acquirer paid a higher P/E multiple for an acquisition than that which he obtains on his own stock, his reported earnings are diluted. This is a no-no insofar as the parent company's stockholders are concerned. So, since most industrial companies acquiring builders have fairly conservative P/E ratios, say in the 14 to 18 range, this is about the best that a builder could get on the downstroke as a multiple of his own earnings. One reason that Centex could pay 22 times earnings for Fox & Jacobs is that its own P/E multiple was just about twice as high. Ken Leventhal says the only dilutive merger he's seen is the Bren-IP deal, in which the acquirer paid stock valued at 64 times the acquisitions earnings. This "ceiling" factor also explains why acquisitions prices fell off so sharply in 1973. With their own P/E ratios in the sub-basement, the active acquirers couldn't pay much.

THE JOYS OF SYNERGISM. One of the important elements that entered merger considerations, particularly in the early 1970s, was the question of how much the acquired company's earnings contribute to annual earnings per share of the parent company. A company with, say, 5 million shares outstanding that bought a builder earning $1.5 million bought itself 30 cents earnings per share. If this is a satisfactory addition to current earnings, fine. And if the builder was a good one, came in for about 14 times his earnings, and had a 20% to 30% annual growth potential, then the deal looked good. But here, with the question of earnings, the concept of synergism also enters the picture to leverage the acquirer's gains from a merger.

The stock of an acquiring company earning $1 per share and selling for $20 has a P/E multiple of 20. In acquiring a builder who shows earnings of $1 million, the most the acquirer can pay in stock while remaining non-dilutive is $20 million. But such a deal has no synergism; that is, when both parties combine at the same multiple, the merger mechanics do not in themselves influence the movement of the surviving entity's stock price. The trick that many of the old acquirers, and some of the new ones, try to achieve is to pick up the builder for a lower P/E than their own — following our example, to buy him at a P/E of, say, 10 if theirs is 20. Then the deal has immediate implications for the acquirer's stock price, in addition to the longer-term rewards of an acquisition (presumably) soundly based on management and marketing strengths.

Here's how such a deal might work. The acquiring company's stock, earning $1 and selling at a P/E of 20, has a market price of $20; the company earns $10 million on its 10 million shares outstanding. This company buys a builder earning $2 million for 10 times earnings, paying him $20 million (or 1 million shares) in stock. The surviving entity now has 11 million shares outstanding and earnings of $12 million. This means the acquirer's earnings per share are now up from $1.00 to $1.09. Since the stock market is likely to apply the acquirer's old multiple of 20 to the stock, the stock price purely as a result of acquiring the builder at the lower multiple now rises to $21.80. This may seem like a conservative example of synergism, but consider that a gain of $1.80 multiplied by 11 million shares results in an immediate paper profit of $19.8 million. With that kind of action, you almost forget that you're still in the development business. There is an excellent reason, of course, why a publicly held firm would pay a lower P/E multiple for a private company — and it goes beyond the rationale of synergism. From the acquiring company's viewpoint, the risk of buying a private company is significant because the latter's performance capacity is not fully known; therefore, a lower P/E than the acquirer's is fair. The publicly held acquirer's history and operations are more fully disclosed; it deserves the multiple it has.

ENTER THE EARNOUT. The earnout, or contingent payment agreement, has been common with most acquisitions. Essentially, it is a clause in the acquisition contract which entitles the selling builder to receive additional shares of stock or other compensation beyond the initial payment if his earnings over an agreed period (usually over five years) achieve the projections he submits at the time he's acquired. Earnout agreements in real estate actually vary considerably. Some are based on achieving a growth rate of anywhere between 15% and 30% annually, while others are based on larger earnings in the first year or two following the acquisition and lower multiples thereafter. A typical earnout agreement provides that any earnings in excess of a specified base are to be compensated with a specified multiple of stock, either in yearly increments or at the end of a specified number of years, with each year of increased earnings then becoming the new base. The formulas for the payment of the contingent shares also vary, but the stock is usually valued on averaged prices during the period of the earnout. The most important characteristic of the earnout is that the acquired builder has to achieve increased earnings in order to pocket the additional payment dangled before his nose.

In real estate mergers, especially prior to the changes in the accounting rules, the earnout became a wondrously useful tool with many apparent benefits. Most importantly, perhaps, it gave the acquirer the appearance of control over the building company's future and its earnings prospects for the first several years, protecting much if not all of his investment by harnessing the builder's incentive to perform like hell. Secondly, the earnout enabled the acquirer to get around the problem of diluting earnings and still pick up some high-priced builders selling themselves at the fancy stock market multiples of publicly held building firms. By paying the builder, say, 20 times earnings initially while letting him have a crack at a contingent payment of another 20 times multiple, the acquirer could escape dilution because the added earnings would offset the additional shares outstanding against earnings. The high multiples paid for builders have receded, but along about 1969 some pretty fancy prices were thus paid. Parenthetically, it was this early crop of mergers at very rich prices that were so highly publicized. Typically, they were made by companies from outside the housing industry buying well-known names *in* the housing industry. More deals, and better deals, were made at a 10 to 15 multiple as good builders took a lower initial price but got good growth stock.

Returning to the earnout, its underlying principle is that the selling company gets less initially but is ultimately paid more than it would ordinarily get, in exchange for sharing the acquirer's risk and gearing part of the sales price to subsequent performance. It's worth it to the acquirer to pay the builder a bonus price for an investment that proves itself to be safe. Oftentimes, as it works out, buying a company on an earnout basis is also cheaper than it appears. A hypothetical merger of the 1969 period illustrates the point.

Let's say that you're the founder and chief executive of a hot little development firm that is turning out $1 million in earnings and you're positive you can produce a 30% compounded annual growth in earnings over the next five years. You're not greedy, but we're still in 1969 and when you talk with a prospective acquirer you figure that your kind of company *has* to be worth at least 20 times earnings, so that's what you ask for. The acquirer thinks this over and then says, "I'll tell you what: I'll give you a chance to get not just 20 times earnings but 24 times earnings if you're willing to take the risk with me and put your performance where your mouth is: I'll pay you 12 times earnings now and another 12 times your initial earnings if you bring in your projections below the line." You, being a plucky fellow, agree. Over the subsequent five years your earnings go from $1 million to $1.3, $1.69, $2.20, $2.86 and finally to $3.72 million. At the end of this period, your acquirer has accumulated roughly $12 million in earnings from your company. You're $4 million richer for having taken the gamble, and the acquirer is satisfied he's paid the right price. Meanwhile, your five-year earnings stream has performed miracles for the acquirer's stock. (However, it should be remembered that the earnout itself could become a source of problems if it resulted in sloppy or otherwise uncontrolled growth.) It is for reasons like these that acquiring companies have liked to load up developers with as heavy an earnout as possible. But for the 50-50 rule on tax-free merger transactions, which specifies that the earnout cannot be greater than the number of shares initially given to the seller, some of those earnouts would have been gigantic, I'm sure. Earnouts also can't run over five years, but this gets us into a complex tax rule. Note the maximum earnout, equal to the initial number of shares paid, in each of the three examples in Table 8.1.

THE USES OF FUNNY MONEY. A subject truly complex and various, and limited only by the ingenuity of the brilliant gnomes of Wall Street who come up with new twists all the time. But the essential principles governing the use of funny money in merger deals are simple. Convertible preferreds and debentures make for wonderful earnings leverage on acquisitions. In former years such securities could under certain circumstances be used to expand the company's earnings base through acquisitions without at the same time expanding the number of shares of common stock against which

Table 8.1 High Earnouts at the Height of the Merger Boom

Acquiring Company (Acquired Company)	Date of Agreement	Stock Price of Acquiring Company (b)	Securities Issued by Acquiring Company	Value of Shares Received	Earnings of Acquired Company (c)	Ratio of Price to Earnings	Book Value of Acquired Company (c)	Premium Paid Over Book Value	Total Dividends on Securities Issued	Maximum Contingent Future Payments
Lear Siegler (Trousdale Construction)	8/28/69	19-5/8	500,000 shares of common stock	9,812,500	N.A.	N.A.	(814,209)	N.A.	250,000	500,000 shares
International Paper (Donald L. Bren Company)	7/21/69	37-3/4	960,000 shares of common stock	36,240,000	571,590	63.4	1,122,110	3,130	1,440,000	960,000 shares
CNA Financial (Larwin Group Companies)	6/16/69	25	3,745,318 shares of common stock	93,632,950	4,726,000	19.8	19,910,000	370	1,872,659	3,745,318 shares

the increased earnings are applied. The use of convertible instruments thus enabled a number of major corporations to make costly acquisitions without suffering dilution, and to show handsome jacked-up earnings for their shareholders. By the time preferreds are convertible into common stock, the added earnings provided by the acquired company neutralize dilutive effects.

Since convertible preferred stock may be restricted, or "stiff," stock, and may likely pay a lower rate than common, in a merger its value could be discounted from market value by the acquirer who lays it out for purposes of the transaction. This lets him suppress the actual value of the acquired company and its assets by carrying them on his books at the discounted rate. When the acquired company subsequently reports earnings, these earnings appear proportionately larger than they would be otherwise, because they're flowing in part from the suppressed values that don't appear on the corporate books. As an example, one acquiring company bought a developer with preferred stock convertible into something over 300,000 shares of common valued at roughly $12 million. But after valuing assets and because of restrictions on the preferred, it booked the transaction at about $8.9 million, or a 25% discount from the market value of the common. This raised the acquired company's earnings stream by a corresponding 25%. There have been many other sophisticated ways to establish the value of stock for bookkeeping purposes. Their common purpose has been to increase reportable earnings by understating values on acquisition. That's funny money for you. The builders, by the way, really liked the convertible preferreds. Rain or shine, with a convert there was no downside risk. The coupons paid a clockwork 4% interest, whereas common-stock dividends could be feast or famine. Convertible debentures have the added attraction of paying tax-deductible interest.

A CLOSER LOOK AT MERGERS UNDER THE OLD POOLING RULES

Having examined some of the clever tools for the creation of profits in merger deals, we can now see how they bear on the issue of pooling. Pooling of interests is the accounting method that lets one company acquire another without revaluation of the acquired company's assets to fair market value. When acquirer and acquired are "pooled" into a single unit, the assets of the acquired firm (carried at initial cost rather than their presently higher market value) are consolidated right into the acquirer's balance sheets at their original cost basis. These historical values are subsequently used in calculating profits. Pooling has thus been a favorite method for acquiring assets with a low historical cost but high present value, because it allows the acquiring company to report high profits based on the low book cost of such assets.

This factor, of course, made many realty and development companies highly desirable candidates for acquisition because of their large holdings of land carried at low initial cost. Land can rise in value pretty rapidly, and particularly so when it is in areas perceived by canny builders to be ripe for development. Corporate acquisition officers, dazed with lust for profit, dreamt of letting all these suppressed values bloom on their balance sheets when such assets were sold to a third party in the normal course of business.

Poolings could be particularly attractive under the old rules when you consider that the acquirer could also bring to bear the entire clever apparatus of profit-expanding and investment-protecting mechanisms — the very concepts of synergism, earnout and funny money leverage that we have already discussed. The combination of all these instruments of merger together with pooling could really sweeten reportable earnings. The earnout was particularly important for two reasons. It of course served a valuable function in giving the acquirer some assurance over the performance of his acquisition. But it also guaranteed to the acquirer that the suppressed market value he was buying was actually there. Acquirers would structure the earnout to pay off additional shares to the builder if and when he sold land he owned and brought in the expected profits. (The earnout thus functioned to pay a builder off for existing suppressed values instead of serving as an incentive to generate new values and profits — something of a departure from the conventional notion of its function.) In short, under the old rules every element appeared to work in favor of giving the acquirer maximum earnings with maximum control over the acquisition at a minimum of risk. As one builder sighed nostalgically: "Before 1970 it was a beautiful world."

THE POOLING RULES ABUSED

There was only one major problem in this beautiful world. The synergy approach is not a bad idea if it is just one part of an overall plan for the production of sustained earnings from the acquisition itself. But the temptation was too strong for many companies in American industry to resist. Many acquisitions were plainly undertaken not for their own merits but because the combination would hype the acquirer's earnings. This was the "instant earnings" technique whereby an acquirer, who has sat around all year and suddenly sees that the cupboard is bare and annual earnings report time is coming up, quickly acquires a smaller company with a lower P/E ratio to produce some instant earnings at year's end. Of course, once on this treadmill, the acquirer has to continue with other fast earnings to sustain his stock's rising P/E, until one day he trips and the whole Rube Goldbergian structure collapses.

I've already cited one example of a synergistic merger's effects on stock values, but here's one from Ken Leventhal which make the point very clearly: Assume Company A has 1 share outstanding, earns $1 and sells for $30, and Company B has 1 share outstanding and earns $2. Because Company A is publicly traded, it is able to acquire Company B through the issuance of 1 share. Therefore, Company A now has 2 shares issued and outstanding and the earnings of the surviving company is $3 or $1.50 per share. So Company A has increased its earnings by $.50 because of the acquisition. Now, if it still enjoys the multiple of 30, the market price of the stock will rise from $30 to $45 per share, the stock increasing by $15 per share just because of the acquisition.

There was another method of "one-shot" earnings. Carrying the assets of an acquired firm at *cost*, the acquirer in most cases had in fact issued securities enough to pay the sellers the full *market* value of the asset. Hence, in principle, he had already discounted the actual profitability from his own future sale of the asset at market value to zero (i.e., from such a future sale he would only recover enough to balance the "paper" he issued to buy the asset in the first place). Yet, when he did sell the asset, he would report the difference between book cost and market value as "earnings."

A couple of examples will clarify this. Assume the selling company carries land on its books at $1 million, but the buyer and seller agree it has a market value of $5 million. The buyer pays the seller $5 million in stock or funny money and takes over the asset, still carrying it at its $1 million cost basis. Under the old rules, there was nothing to prevent the buyer from turning around and selling the asset the following day for $5 million, and then reporting the difference between cost and market, or $4 million, as extraordinary earnings. He's got his "one-shot" earnings, conveniently disregarding that he has already paid $5 million in securities for that asset. A case of heady earnings reports full of sound and fury but signifying nothing, it was a device of the old gunslingers to fill the earnings gap.

Another similar example of such flexible use of the pooling-of-interest concept: Assume that Company A's financial statement reads as follows: Asset, $10; Net Worth, $10. Let's further assume that the fair market value of the asset is $100. Along comes Company B, whose stock is selling for $50 per share, and Company B issues two shares in exchange for the stock of Company A. The shareholders of Company A, instead of owning a company that had an asset worth $100, now own stock in Company B that is worth $100. If Company B then turns around and sells the asset for $100, it will recognize in its financial statements a profit of $90.

Let me emphasize that there's nothing inherently bad about the pooling concept whereby the asset (i.e., land) held below its market value on the books of the selling company is not written up to market value at the time of the combination. If the merged company develops and builds on this acreage and takes the profit flowing from its submerged value as additional profit in the course of developing and selling land and homes, it is simply doing what companies like Lennar, Shapell and Larwin do all the time. This is a repeatable function, booked as ordinary income, and whether it is done by a company before or after it is pooled into a larger company does not make it any more or less wholesome. But while this concept is not *inherently* bad, it did offer the *potential* for abuse in those cases where the merged company carrying substantial land assets did not have the desire or ability to earn the potential profit in the ordinary course of business (by developing and selling the land as a finished product for an end use to many purchasers) and would thus realize it as extraordinary income.

An example: Say a developer owns acreage which he carries on his books at the cost of $3,000 per acre but which is now worth $10,000. If he is bought by a conglomerate which has immediate income needs and the land is sold to a single user merely to enhance the conglomerate's earnings, the sole reason for the transaction is to make the parent company look healthier than it is. Fortunately the accounting principles now force this to be shown as extraordinary income in the income statement, and it can be spotted with relative ease.

The changes in accounting rules on poolings attempted to eliminate the *potential* for such wheeling-dealing abuses, and to differentiate between the productive uses of the pooling concept and the nonproductive ones. The point is, the responsible developers have to use the same principle of pooling as the gunslingers. There are only two ways to account for a merger, either by the pooling-of-interest method or the purchase method. Either one has potential abuses and can be used in examples to show improper intent by the acquirer. But just because responsible developers have to use the same merger principles as did the gunslingers doesn't mean they use them to the same ends, and these developers should not be assassinated by inference. This is largely the error that a certain otherwise honored professor of accounting committed in a widely read 1971 *Barron's* article on homebuilding accounting practices. Accounting abuses were bound to occur in some cases. But although relatively few acquiring companies availed themselves of the gross extremes of abuse made possible by permissible accounting practices, all were to be affected by the ensuing reforms.

POOLING RULE REVISIONS

The Accounting Principles Board began to move in 1969 by insisting that common-stock equivalents be included in all earnings-per-share calculations, thus taking the bloom off earnings flowering through funny-money and contingent-share acquisitions. When the APB published the proposed reforms in accounting principles for mergers early in 1970, these were so stiff that the business community blanched as one man and raised a storm of protest. In the ensuing intensive debate some of the more extreme proposed provisions were eliminated. Among these was the proposal that no company acquiring another would be eligible for the pooling method of merger accounting if the acquirer was more than three times as large as the acquired. The proposal was first revised to permit an acquirer to pool a company at least a tenth of the acquirer's size, but was later thrown out altogether on the grounds that such a size test has no basis in economics and would force the 400 largest corporations, along with many others, to avoid the pooling method of accounting entirely. The provision would have eliminated all major companies from acquiring the relatively small builders by the pooling route. But despite such victorious skirmishes, the main battle was lost and the new rules that became effective on October 31, 1970, spelled the end of much hanky-panky.

In order to qualify for the pooling-of-interest method of accounting, a merger henceforth had to meet the following condition:

1. Each of the combining companies is autonomous and independent and has not been a subsidiary or division of another corporation within two years before the plan of combination is initiated.

2. The combination is effected in a single transaction or is completed according to a specific plan within one year.

3. A corporation issues only common stock with rights identical to those of the majority of its outstanding voting common stock in exchange for substantially all of the voting common stock interest of another company.

4. Each of the combining companies maintains substantially all the same voting common stock interest; with virtually no exchanges, retirements, or distributions to stockholders in contemplation of effecting the combination.

5. The ratio of the interest of an individual common stockholder to those of other common stockholders in a combining company remains the same as a result of the exchange of stock to effect the combination.

6. The voting rights to which the common stock ownership interests in the resulting corporation are entitled are exercisable by the stockholders; the stockholders are neither deprived of nor restricted in exercising those rights.

7. The combination is resolved at the date the plan is consummated and no provisions of the plan relating to the issue of securities or other considerations are pending.

8. The combined corporation does not agree directly or indirectly to retire or reacquire all or part of the common stock issued to effect the combination.

9. The combined corporation does not enter into other financial arrangements for the benefit of the former stockholders of a combining company, such as a guaranty of loans secured by stock issued in the combination, which in effect negate the exchange of equity securities.

10. The combined corporation does not intend or plan to dispose of a significant part of the assets of the combining companies within two years after the combination except to eliminate duplicate facilities or excess capacity and those assets that would have been disposed of in the ordinary course of business of the separate company.

THE IMPORT OF THE NEW RULES FOR REAL ESTATE MERGERS

The reform thus eliminated acquisitions arrived at quick asset turnover and "one-shot" earnings. But the practical effect of two of the foregoing rules changed the whole ballgame for realty mergers in a far larger way:

The rules eliminated the use of funny money from pooling transactions, thus wiping out a favored method of acquiring realty companies by convertible preferreds or convertible debentures. From thence onward, pooling transactions had to be an exchange of voting common stock for voting common stock.

The rules eliminated the earnout from mergers accounted as pooling of interests by specifying that such mergers be initiated and completed within one year with no further plan pending for the issue of other securities.

The net result, as Stan Ross of Kenneth Leventhal & Company points out, was that many of the pooling mergers effected prior to the rules change by the use of preferred stock and earnouts would have been impossible under new rules. Among these are the Bren-IP, Larwin-CNA, Watt-Boise Cascade, and Lyon-American-Standard deals. The restriction of merger securities to common voting stock could of course lower the prices a pooling acquirer might pay for a builder without suffering immediate dilution, as well as eliminating the acquirer's discounting of the deal for bookkeeping purposes to leverage his income stream. But most grievous was the loss of the earnout on mergers by pooling of interests, which had given acquirers a means of protecting their investment and lowering the acquisition risk, as well as the potential to lower the actual acquisition cost. With a big earnout the builder could be locked in and make things go right for up to five years, working for the incentive of added payment. Without the earnout, the potential acquirer suddenly felt naked to the whim of fortune. All those submerged values in a development company had to be paid for in advance, without the assurance of subsequent performance. With no control over the builder, the prospect of paying out a huge amount of stock suddenly assumes a terrifying risk — especially if the buyer is an outsider to the development business.

(One sees why acquiring companies took pains to hustle a number of merger deals under the wire just prior to the rules change. CBS's acquisition of 49% of Klingbeil as of October 31, 1970, also benefited by the "grandfather" clause: If and when CBS decides to pick up its option for the other 51% of the company in 1975, it can do so under the old pooling rules.)

The alternative to the pooling of interests accounting method for mergers is *purchase accounting.* But, alas, so far as the potential acquirers looking at companies with lots of submerged values were concerned, this was jumping from the frying pan of pooling into the fire of purchase. The purchase accounting method not only permits the use of convertible preferred stock in acquisitions but also allows the welcome harness of the earnout. So far so good. Unfortunately, however, *the assets of the acquired company have to be revalued to fair market value at the time of the acquisition* so that the value of the shares issued matches the asset value of the acquired firm. Such write-ups from cost to market value of course wipe out the very submerged values many acquirers look for and result in lower profits on future sale of assets.

Nor is that the only stricture of purchase accounting. Under this method, *any amount paid out for an acquisition that is not allocated to assets at fair market value has to be allocated for bookkeeping purposes to the intangible called "goodwill." Goodwill under the new accounting rules has to be amortized against earnings.* The most favorable — i.e., the lowest — rate of amortization for which a company may qualify is the rate of $2\frac{1}{2}\%$ a year over a forty-year period. But the amortization could be accelerated if the acquired company does not continue to perform regularly and well. And this write-off is *not* tax-deductible. The import of this provision is that any amount an acquirer pays for a builder's ability and earnings capacity, as distinguished from his material assets, becomes an amortizing item which whittles away at the builder's future earnings.

For example, an acquirer paying a seller $1 million more than the value of his assets must, at the very minimum, deduct $25,000 a year from the acquisition's earnings for forty years in order to write off the excess paid over asset value, with no tax offset to minimize the bite. In actuality, since merging builders can command high prices based on their earnings capacity rather than their assets, the price paid can substantially exceed the fair market value of assets, and the size of the write-off can be a substantial drain on earnings. The impact of the write-off on earnings can be lessened by paying the builder less initially and putting him on a big earnout, but the factor of amortizing goodwill is nonetheless a big damper for corporate merger seekers looking for big earnings.

The net effect of the purchase method of accounting for mergers is to force submerged values into the open right at the outset and to relate reported earnings more directly to real earnings production — which means, compared with pooling, lower earnings. It does provide the acquirer with the security of the earnout, which also makes the sales price dependent on the builder's real earning power from development and construction. The permitted use of convertible preferred stock in such acquisitions opens up some possibilities for leveraging the builder's income stream. But with lower earnings in prospect under the purchase method and with the rule concerning the amortization of goodwill, there is a downward pressure on prices paid to selling builders.

Potential acquirers are thus forced to make a difficult choice. They can go the pooling route, buying the submerged values of a development company by paying a higher price on the downstroke (to compensate the builder for the lack of earnout), but having no control over their investment and the builder's future performance. Or they can go the purchase route, which provides them with control but at the price of surrendering high earnings by the required elimination of submerged values from the deal. In a nutshell, it is a choice between peril or lower profits. This is usually resolved by pooling the larger, more seasoned companies and purchasing the smaller ones where there is less goodwill and more risk with less track record. There's less "submerged value" in a newer company, thus less is lost writing up assets to market value.

In any event, the new merger rules quickly made it plain that something new would be required from potential acquirers looking at the development field: a genuine understanding of the development and construction business, along with a genuine commitment to staying in this field for the profits that it (and not numbers-juggling) could generate. So long as an earnout was permitted in combination with pooling, the built-in profits were substantial enough and the protection comforting enough to make it a breeze to decide to get into real estate.

The earnout especially, offering the salve of protection, bred a sloppiness of mind about acquisitions. It successfully seduced merger-makers away from a thorough and painstaking examination of each other's motives, management skills, personal fit, long-term commitment, and merger price. There was the comforting, if illusory, feeling that it was pretty hard to go wrong, so what the hell, let's shoot craps. It is ironic, if not surprising, that so many of the big-gun merger deals founded upon the illusory protection of the big earnout ran into trouble — and often with that same earnout as one of the instruments of their affliction.

The absence of the earnout from pooling mergers refocuses attention where it should have been all along, and that is on the structuring of a sound, lasting merger. That takes both an understanding of the business and a demonstrable long-term commitment to it. Mergers by the purchase accounting method, placing their emphasis on real future earnings, likewise demand that the acquirer be able to judge his acquisition's earning capacity, and therefore the acquisition, accurately. Such combinations perforce require that the acquirer know the business and be willing to go in for the long pull. The upshot of the merger rule changes is thus an upgrading of the quality of mergers already made and still to be made.

As a practical matter, the rules changes thus reduce the field of acquirers to those with a serious dedication and the ability to operate a real estate subsidiary stably: those who understand the building business or can acquire the necessary understanding, who have studied the mistakes of others, and who have the talented people to work along with the acquired development firm. The acquirers need not be builders themselves, as witness Singer, City Investing and Weyerhaeuser. But building companies like U.S. Home will play a stronger role.

THE POOLING OR PURCHASE ROUTE FOR YOU?

The choice between pooling and purchase accounting depends not only on the condition of the potential acquisition but on the philosophy of the acquirer. If, for example, he is earnings-oriented and the acquisition is rich in submerged values, he will try to buy it on a pooling basis. The argument for pooling is particularly strong among some earnings-oriented acquirers I know, because the net worth of the acquisitions can be small in relation to the value of the securities issuable for the deal by the potential acquirer. As we have seen, this results in a large allocation to amortizable goodwill and a subsequent drain on bookable earnings if such a transaction is effected under purchase accounting rules. So the earnings-oriented people before the 1973 stock market decline began structuring their deals with far more care and preparing to go the pooling route without the earnout protection. As one acquirer observed: "With the pooling rule changes, the buyers aren't getting the value they got before October 1970 if they acquire by purchase. So on the larger deals they're biting the bullet and going the pooling route without the control of the earnout; they can't afford the exposure of the write-off and the goodwill." As another acquirer remarked: "These straight pooling deals are very sweet for the seller — the multiple of earnings paid stays pretty high because the buyers are up against the seller's alternative of going public and can't drop the price too much below what he would get that way."

Actually, there was ample precedent for acquirers from outside the field making merger deals without the earnout. The Singer-Besco, INA-Brock, Bethlehem-Multicon and Inland-Scholz mergers were concluded without earnouts per se prior to the changes in the pooling rules. And all of these (including Inland minus Don Scholz) have been profitable to the acquirers. But it is true that, even with such precedent to go by, every acquiring company would like some sort of control over the builder's future performance. And in place of the earnout the managerial bonus system has really come on strong, though this does, of course, have its limits; you can't exactly give the acquired builder a multimillion-dollar earnout disguised as a personal performance bonus. There are some interesting efforts being made by acquirers to devise other camouflaged controls on acquired managements in place of the earnout, but whether these will prove successful remains to be seen.

With the decline in stock multiples and the fall-off of homebuilding merger activity in early 1974, a discussion of the relative merits of pooling purchases may seem academic. Acquiring builders are presently paying extremely low prices. It is also my feeling that more non-housing corporations will be getting into real estate by investment of a passive nature (on the order of Gulf & Western's investment in Richard Wasserman's new company). While the pooling route to acquisition will be used by acquirers more knowledgeable in real estate and willing to take the risk, the *purchase accounting* method of acquisition appears to be emerging as a favored method of merger for the big, conservative corporate acquirers who are not builders themselves. It not only builds some guarantees into the investment but also, as we have seen, lowers the acquirer's cost of buying a builder. Weyerhaeuser's acquisition of Westminster Construction of Greensboro, North Carolina, in September 1971, and City Investing's buy of Denver's Wood Bros. in the same month, for example, put both builders on big earnouts. The feasibility of the purchase accounting approach depends on four factors:

1. The acquired company carries relatively little submerged value on its books, the difference between cost and market value of its assets being low. In such instances the acquirer doesn't lose much by way of built-in earnings when the acquired company writes up assets from cost to market. The acquirer may of course be primarily interested in the company's future earnings capacity, in which case it would be irrelevant to him how big the write-up from cost to market might be.

2. The difference between the acquired company's net worth and the

value of the stock issued to effect the transaction is not so great as to materially affect earnings. The acquirer must bear in mind that any stock he issues which is not allocable to tangible or intangible assets stated at market value will be allocated to goodwill and amortized without tax offset. The big risk, one that should be examined in each case, is that the earnout stock may also be allocated to goodwill, and this is not controllable in amount.

3. The acquired company has a reasonable history of continuous performance, not operations on an intermittent project-by-project basis, so as to qualify for the longest-term amortization of goodwill; that is, over a forty-year period, or at the rate of 2½% a year. Such a qualification of course lessens the impact of amortization on bookable earnings.

4. Perhaps the most important determinant of the feasibility of the purchase method of merger is the relative value the acquiring company itself places on reportable earnings as contrasted with return on investment. The acquirer's own corporate goals determine whether he's looking for the short-term contribution of high earnings from pooling or the long-term economic aspects of the acquisition. The latter include the basic viability of the acquisition and its long-term prospects, as well as return on investment.

The purchase method of accounting for merger seems to be favored by some big non-housing acquirers of building firms because they're far more interested in the builder's long-term performance in terms of growth and investment return than in any initial inflated boost he might contribute to earnings per share in the first year or two after acquisition. Even when the acquirer stands to lose a sizable chunk of "suppressed earnings" by write-up of assets from cost to market value, he doesn't mind doing this because he is essentially buying the builder's capacity to generate continuing earnings — not a one-shot gold mine. The threat of amortization of goodwill without tax offset acts to keep down the price he pays a selling builder (Wood Bros. sold out for slightly over 4 times earnings on the downstroke and took an earnout in the same amount, a far cry from the golden days of 1969). But if the builder believes the stock he's getting has a high potential to stably and rapidly appreciate in value — and if he believes in his own capacity to generate the high investment return the acquirer seeks — he will make the deal.

The builder's return on investment can be formidable compared with that of industrial companies. One large industrial company had a return on equity of 8.5% in 1970; an analysis of the return on equity for twenty building firms in the same year showed an average return of 21.6%, underscoring both the effects of leverage in the development business and the fact that it is a service business. It is not unusual for individual development firms to get a considerably better return than the averaged one.

An acquiring company may thus seek to pick up soundly managed building firms growing at a rate of 15% or so per year, trading a fraction of the builder's earnings to amortization in order to get a first-rate investment return. This factor in itself argues the emergence of a stable new breed of corporate acquirers looking for a steady and growing position in real estate through judicious builder buy-ups by the purchase method. In such instances, when the acquisition is carefully analyzed for its long-term economic aspects, the earnout both lowers the actual purchase cost and provides a backup guarantee to the acquirer's analysis of the builder's prospects.

Nor, with all this protection, do the earnings necessarily have to be considerably smaller than they might have been in former times. The rules concerning the allocation of stock to assets in the purchase accounting method of acquisition specify that the cost of the acquired assets may be determined by the fair value of the property acquired *or* by the fair value of the non-cash consideration given, whichever is more clearly evident. As a practical matter, the fair value of the asset received for stock issued, or the value of the stock given, may not always be clearly determinable. It may be difficult to assign a current market value to preferred stock which is "stiff," i.e., not marketable for, say, three to five years. It is also a valid question as to what constitutes "fair market value" for land the seller carries at cost. Is it the price he can get for it if he were to sell it tomorrow? Or is it the land's retail value when developed and sold complete with housing? The effect of this is that in transactions involving restricted stock without readily ascertainable value and assets whose "fair market value" can be open to interpretation, the acquired assets may be revalued to a *wholesale* market value instead of a *retail* market value, when allocating the stock to assets. The acquirer preserves and submerges a retailer's profit for himself when revaluating the assets carried at cost. The net effect is that the acquirer can now afford to make a purchase because the differential between retail and wholesale fair market value will find its way into the income stream after development. This differential can be substantial, conserving $2.5 million and turning it into bookable earnings in Table 8.2.

On balance, the advantages of the purchase method of merger ac-

Table 8.2   Assets of Developer X: Fair Market Value

	Retail	Wholesale
Cash	$ 1 million	$1 million
Land	2 million	1.5 million
Houses	10 million	8 million
(Liabilities)	($ 4 million)	($4 million)
Total	$ 9 million	$6.5 million

counting appear more attractive than the pooling method for an acquirer newly entering the real estate field. Better some assurance of the future at the cost of lower earnings than higher earnings with unknown future risks (assuming no problems with earnout stock allocated to goodwill). Few are the companies that, once having ascertained the builder's quality, will pool as readily as they purchase, with the choice dependent not on protective strategy but on maximum advantage to all parties. One such company is U.S. Home. In October 1971, for example, USH bought Norwood Homes of Houston and Witkin Homes of Denver by the pooling method, and at the same time accounted Page Corporation of Washington, D.C., as a purchase. The purchase route is simply used to harness the smaller builders whose assets don't have much of a write-up from cost to market value and which cost USH little in built-in earnings. The pooling route enables USH to get those submerged values carried at cost by the bigger builders converted into handsome earnings. The pooling acquisitions, as in the case of Norwood, also show a nice touch of synergism.

HOW LONG WILL THESE ACCOUNTING RULES LAST?

As our closing note, it is only fair to warn the reader that the entire foregoing discussion on the alternative merits and demerits of merging by the pooling or purchase accounting methods may be obsolete at any time. The rules have changed once, and the reformed rules may change again. A hot rumor went the rounds in 1972 to the effect that the Accounting Principles Board retained the present rules only by the narrowest of margins — a 9–8 vote. Rumor or not, a sizable body of experts in such matters is unhappy with the respective restrictions of the pooling and purchase methods, and feels that these restrictions are pretty much arbitrary formulations that serve no logical purpose. In a nutshell, these people are questioning the logic of amortizing goodwill in the purchase method of acquisition. What is being sought is either (a) the elimination of amortizing goodwill from the purchase accounting method, or (b) the restoration of the earnout to poolings (a wan hope), or (c) both, while also avoiding the former abuse of merger rules. And the fundamental question is being asked again: Why have two different accounting methods of acquisition at all? Why not just one? Late in 1973 the Accounting Principles Board decided again to review the acceptability of pooling of interests in merger accounting. The outcome of this debate is uncertain, but it does underscore the fact that the present rules are not finished business and that the search for more responsive merger accounting rules goes on.

Meanwhile, the Securities and Exchange Commission in August 1973 on its own initiative tightened up pooling-of-interests accounting in acquisitions. The commission spelled out the circumstances under which a company can use such merger accounting in cases where it has reacquired its own shares two years preceding initiation of a merger agreement. The effect was to severely curtail this popular format for acquisition, not only in the future but also for companies that have acquired their own shares in the preceding two years. Companies by the hundreds were buying their own shares in late 1973 because of depressed market conditions that drove down prices to bargain levels.

It was a tough rule. The SEC ruling held that shares purchased as much as two years prior to a merger, through an exchange of shares, may be tainted. If the SEC considers this to be the case, it would rule that the merger involved the use of cash and must be considered as under the purchase method of accounting. The purpose is to block a company from buying its own stock and using the stock in a merger, instead of just buying the other company for cash on less favorable terms. The rule permitted the reacquisition of shares only if the company intended to use them in stock-option programs, as stock dividends, or in conversion of convertible securities into common stock.

To prove that it wasn't contemplating a merger when it acquired its own shares, the company must show a "systematic pattern" of reacquisitions in connection with stock option or compensation plans. The SEC also noted that previous Accounting Principles Board rulings on pooling of interests do not mention possible reacquisitions of stock following a pooling-of-interest merger. Such subsequent acquisitions "may be so closely related to the prior combination that they should be considered part of the combination plan" and this would invalidate a pooling of interests. Although the SEC ruling went into effect immediately with its two-year retroactive clause, the SEC said it wouldn't require mergers that have already occurred to revise their accounting treatments.

Homebuilding merger activity in 1972 continued to be substantial, and many acquirers were going the pooling route without the earnout. As of that year, the multiples of earnings paid for acquisitions were still pretty juicy, compensating the acquired builders well for the lack of an earnout bonus. Typical was U.S. Home's acquisition of Norwood Homes late in 1971 for fourteen times earnings (though management problems were reported with this acquisition later). Horizon Land Company also acquired Tucson's P.A.T. Homes early in 1972 for something over nine times earnings. The stock-for-stock deal brought P.A.T.'s Mel Ritter $6.5 million for an organization that had earned $700,000 after taxes on sales of $15 million. The Singer Company, parent of Singer Housing, extended its homebuilding activity to the hot Southeast market by picking up Mitchell Corporation of Mobile, Alabama. And Lane Wood, a mobile home manufacturer, announced plans to buy Miami-area homebuilder Jim Kay Homes for about $2 million at mid-1972.

We should observe in closing that as 1973 was ushered in and home-building stocks took a beating on the market, builder-acquirers with lower P/E multiples were tightening up considerably on the multiples they could and would pay for other builders. But true to our projection, there was intense questing for merger partners as the big public builders sought to shore up and expand their volume. Many mergers were talked of (horrors) in terms that sounded more like book value rather than earnings multiples. The main point is that the mergers and acquisitions continue; the prices paid will wax and wane with the general condition of the acquirers' earnings multiples and the real desirability of each particular deal to the acquirer.

How the multitudes of sellers who had merged during the early 1970s felt about this new development is another story. Assuredly, as their bubbles of inflated stock burst and they were left clutching only air, they were not happy.

9

Why Mergers Go Bad

Veni, vidi, vici.

—Caesar

Did this in Caesar seem ambitious?

—Shakespeare's Mark Antony
(Caesar's funeral oration)

During the first exhilarating period of exploration and discovery we heard a great deal about the advantages that bigness brings to real estate. The principal claims were as follows: The big corporations can supply the smaller developer with the financial resources that he indispensably needs. They can raise more money at lower interest rates and are seldom in the same squeeze to pay it back as a small developer with limited resources. Moreover, theirs is the patient capital, able to wait for a return down the road; they don't have to pull out of a project before the real payoff. Financial strength enables corporations (or their subsidiaries) to take on many projects simultaneously, so that the successes will always make up for the near misses. Most importantly, to an industry that up to then flew by the seat of its pants, the big corporations were said to bring modern management methods, including the gamut of analytical, planning, marketing and financial techniques.

Although we have already seen that things haven't always worked out for the developer because of such corporate contributions, there is much that is at least theoretically true in such an assessment of corporate strengths. The formidable analytical and management skills by which big industries operate and which they were in a position to contribute to real estate development are particularly worth pointing out. Through such means the entrepreneur-builder could, in principle, gain the ability to expand his organization beyond the personal level of operation and increase his involvement in development while, hopefully, at the same time decreasing his risk. The principal error in such an optimistic evaluation of the reforming role of big money and big business was, however, the unstated assumption that the force of bigness itself could eliminate the tradi-

204

tional risks of the development field and transform a volatile and highly differentiated industry into a single, smooth — inhuman — production-line process.

Unfortunately, and much to the consternation of business-school systems theorists, the industry remains tied to that vexing and changeable factor which we may call people. People have a very annoying way of getting into system-planners' hair by obstinately insisting on their own ridiculous tastes and preferences. Certainly, they form a very rich housing market. But they form markets that are so varied, even within the boundary of a single metropolitan area, that generalizations concerning all of them are not possible. And, difficult though it may seem, considering the rich pickings, a corporation can go broke by ignoring this fact in a highly competitive industry.

Thus we find that a developer succeeds to the extent that he discerns what it is that a highly defined group of people want and then is able to provide them with it, within the bounds of reasonable economic realities. A fixed, unvarying formula, while it may be successful in a particular time and place and with a particular group, quickly becomes obsolete because our culture and the wants of individuals within that culture are constantly in flux. It takes a very uncommon individual or group of individuals to size up a particular locale at a particular moment in time and translate it into a viable program that encompasses the gamut of subjective and objective wants, moods and conditions of a community, and then to bring that program to a completion at a profit. It takes, in short, a person who can describe things as *they actually are*, draw the the proper inferences therefrom, and constantly realign the production organization to serve his perceptions as time goes on.

Not that this formulation doesn't describe the ideal for any business organization, but it is an ideal that of necessity has to be more closely adhered to in the real estate industry than in any other, if the organization is to remain profitable. A builder operates on a project-by-project basis, and his future is only as assured as the next project; each one had better be right. Energy in enormous quantities is thus required if one plans ahead and stays attuned to the multitude of potential markets: the effort to keep the organization responsive bumps straight into that monumental law of human inertia which says that any organizational form, once established, tends to blindly perpetuate itself without regard for the realities. (This law is also, by the way, known as systems planning.) Corporate types serving a production mechanism which they do not create and reshape, and which assumes an existence of its own, tend to overlook how a builder continually creates his own future. A too-high bureaucratic regard for channels and other forms of buck-passing and responsibility-shrugging are quickly reduced to their proper perspective in a builder's organization when his own survival is constantly on the line. Many corporations entering the development field, attempting to apply corporate management styles to this essentially entrepreneurial art, learned their lessons the hard way.

Take, as an example, that vaunt about the big corporation bringing economies of scale to the homebuilding business. The corporations discovered to their surprise that there are actually *reverse* economies of scale in real estate: a small builder "flying by the seat of his pants" can usually create more profits with less overhead per project because of better knowledge of the local market, closer supervision and lower startup costs. Likewise, the security of corporate financial strength has, by and large, not proven to be attractive enough where the trade-off is the builder's loss of the cherished right to make fast decisions. A number of giant industrial corporations have thus found that the talented entrepreneur not only doesn't want them but doesn't need them. Some corporations have taken the money and run when their operating methods were threatened. As one dismayed corporate officer observed with a glimmer of belated awareness, as he beheld the shambles of a former homebuilding subsidiary: "It's very difficult, running a tract builder operation, to be all things to everybody throughout the United States. There are differences, especially as they relate to buying patterns, growth patterns, and zoning. It's much more difficult to standardize a lot of things."

With this we can focus on the unresolved problems that have faced the big newcomers to real estate. The majors, many of them serving stable secondary manufacturing markets, entered the builder's domain with a principally production-oriented viewpoint. That is, the cycle of response to their market changes is perhaps far longer and can be effected in a far more organized and leisurely fashion because of the stability of their markets. Thus, their emphasis is on volume and uniformity of product with relatively few major management decisions compared to real estate development. But the real estate field, as we have seen, is dominantly market-oriented and highly competitive and requires a complex set of major management decisions with every new project. To make such decisions, the builder keeps himself loose and his bureaucratic constraints minimal. His repeated experience enables him to make major decisions quickly in a way that would astonish the conservative corporate type used to polishing numbers rather than taking responsibility for them. In joining the two — corporation and builder — we are thus faced with the philosophical problem of fitting a round peg in a square hole.

In those instances where the newcomers were dominated by production thinking and chained the builder in corporate protocol or disregarded the realities of the market, they predictably ran into severe trouble. On the other hand, where the builder ran free of corporate management controls, the risk factor attending typically large investments was terrifyingly unascertainable to your corporate type. In sum, it became apparent that in many circumstance the bigness of money and management not only could not minimize the risks of development; it could actually increase them, by either too much control of the builder or not enough. It would almost seem that a major outsider who wanted to get into real estate would paradoxically have to know more about the business than the builder he was working with, if he wanted to succeed.

Somewhere along the line, of course, it should be possible for both parties to benefit from their respective strengths and achieve the ideal *modus vivendi*: a sophisticated development firm with a highly streamlined management apparatus that is subject to and controlled by marketing considerations only, and operates by a system of financial checkpoints for its performance. Within such an organization, sophisticated and creative market research can play an important role in formulating and verifying management decisions to the satisfaction of both the builder and his corporate partner; its importance has too often been ignored, only to be regretted. The question remains how to arrive at such a working relationship, how to structure the right organizaton, and how to balance the liberties and controls by which it will operate. And perhaps we can arrive at the best answer to such a queston by focusing on its reverse: How do mergers go bad?

HOW MERGERS GO BAD: A VIRGIN'S GUIDEBOOK

In every instance of a troubled merger relationship, the reason is the same: the acquired builder does not meet his profit projections. Here the similarity ends, for the roads to that common failing are multitudinous.

Underlying all the ways that a merger can go wrong there is a profoundly important cause: insufficient communication between the acquirer and acquired as to the objectives of the acquisition and the optimal mode of operation to achieve those objectives. Two alien entities — the nonhousing corporation and the builder — come together because they have the same bottom-line objectives. All too often they have optimistically mistaken the initial *bonhomie* accompanying the deal as a satisfactory equivalent for the hard decisions that make a merger viable. It is only afterwards that the two begin to realize what sort of planning should have gone into the acquisition and the sort of policy that is required to successfully translate the entrepreneurial art of development to the bigger corporate plane.

The awakening can be quite drastic. One would expect that a corporation which has spent anywhere between twenty million and one hundred million dollars in stock to buy a builder would have learned in advance what sort of business it was entering. But it is surprising many did not. Says one manager formerly with a major builder now troubled by friction with the corporate parent: "The learning process required by Corporation X since the acquisition has been enormous. It underestimated the amount of financing the building business takes. It doesn't understand the entrepreneurial outlook — the fast response to opportunities, the quick response to problems. They just didn't know what they were getting into." When a corporation like this one *does* find out what it has gotten into, the contrast between its first expectations and the subsequent realities makes it liable to get extremely disenchanted.

This brings us to one characteristic difference between non-housing corporations and builders. Major corporations are geared to minimizing losses *after* they've gone ahead and gotten into a venture. If they don't like what they've turned up in the middle of, they cut their losses and get out. Characteristically, in their entry into the homebuilding business they did not judge well in *advance* of the entry. A builder, conversely, may size up a project more carefully in advance of getting into it but has a harder time getting out if it starts to go bad. He will tend to throw good money after bad instead of cutting his losses. Between the two approaches there should be room for a balanced one that appraises any venture carefully both in advance and after the start. The "second-generation" corporate acquirers have gone a long way toward learning this art in their builder-merger ventures. But the early acquirers, panicking at the first sign of letdown from rosy predictions, tended to shoot from the hip.

The major characteristic of such management was intervention by corporate fiat in the operating formulas which had made the entrepreneurial builders successful. Of course, as everyone knows, when you violate a successful formula the operation goes downhill. For many builders the violation came in the form of intolerable delays in communications and decisions they had been accustomed to making rapidly as a response to the dictates of the business. (For a number of corporations it was primarily a case of when in doubt, stall.) Accordingly, the builders' operations suffered. Eli Broad sums up this form of attrition well:

"Success in housing," he says, "rests to a great extent on the flexibility and the capability to make decisions quickly and to carry out the appropriate actions without delay. Delays in housing cost money — lots of money — and often the difference between profit and loss is the amount of time taken for decision-making and then following through." But, he continues, "Even the most sophisticated and best managers in American industry do not understand housing and the care and feeding of industry managers. Layers of vice presidents, decision review boards, formal communications channels, committees — all the trappings of textbook organizations — are anathema to the entrepreneurial style of management. Instead of making decisions and moving forward, housing entrepreneurs who were acquired by non-housing corporations were thrust into traditional desk-bound orthodoxy."

To be sure, there are other reasons that mergers can go bad. Sometimes these do not reflect on the parent company so much as on the acquired builder. Understandably, these are less talked about by homebuilders. In such cases the builder was already in trouble and succeeded only in postponing his collapse by latching on to a naïve but rich acquirer to buy him out. Two major Southern California builders that I know personally were hailed as entrepreneurial geniuses and that got them a good merger price. But by the people in their industry, both were broadly known to be headed for trouble before they ever sold out. One started a recreational-land program that was causing him headaches before he merged, and he was also burdened with many poorly bought, overpriced pieces of residential land. The other's lackluster performance after acquisition did not need a corporate relations problem to justify it. The projects which got him in trouble were already mapped out and in planning before he ever merged, and they had to be written down substantially after the acquisition because they weren't worth what was paid for the land.

In short, in both these instances (and there were others), the failure didn't stem from corporate relations problems but from built-in flaws in the builders' own operations. There is no blaming excessive expansion through infusion of new capital or lack of communication. Expansion after acquisition in such cases only compounded the builders' problems as additional ill-conceived projects turned confusion into outright disaster. In some instances, corporate stalling on further expansion was really a blessing because it saved the parent from suffering further losses. This point is real, and it is too often forgotten.

A merger may also occasionally terminate not from failure but simply because the parent company decides to change its long-term priorities. I cannot think of an immediate example, but many companies that have gone into real estate directly (without acquiring a builder) can and do pull out as they decide to pursue other investment alternatives. Atlantic-Richfield (now ARCO) was, for example, involved in the Coronado Cays project in San Diego, California, and also had ventures in Hawaii. Later it made a corporate decision to shift its priorities to development of Alaskan oil pipeline opportunities, finding that the return on investment there would be better. The company sold Coronado Cays to Signal, which, for one, had decided to get into real estate just as ARCO was getting out.

But notwithstanding these exceptions, it is still most often true that mergers go bad from a lack of careful planning and thinking through the corporate venture into real estate. Mission Viejo Company's president, Philip Reilly, believes that corporate incompatibility is largely a myth and that any well-planned and well-considered merger will work if both partners pay attention to what the other is saying and to the realities of conducting a professional real estate operation. Reilly's comments are reserved for the chapter dealing with his own merger, in the following section. Let's look here at some of the basics of working out a good marriage.

DECISIONS UNDERLYING A SUCCESSFUL MERGER

In order to make a merger go right it takes, in short, considerably more reflection and planning than was evident in certain of the major mergers which sailed in on a high wind of enthusiasm and charitable "pooling" rules. The corporate acquirer has to be aware of a number of critical decision areas simultaneously if he is truly dedicated to taking a permanent position in the housing field. The decision areas imply that he has thought through his reasons for getting into housing and that he understands the entrepreneurial nature of the business.

I shall set out these decision areas in schematic form, but they are of course closely interrelated. For purposes of this analysis, one assumes that the builder who is the candidate for the acquisition is a sound one. We focus here on the more difficult question of structuring the proper environment and operating basis that make a merger successful. After we have looked at the key decisions to be made, we shall examine how various acquirers have handled them to their credit or detriment.

Senior Policy Governing the Acquisition

1. Are we acquiring the builder because we count heavily on him to boost our per-share earnings? Or, do we basically want him because he can provide us with a high return on invested capital compared with our other operations? If our own business is capital-intensive are we wise to acquire another capital-intensive business? Are we prepared to make thoughtful and serious contributions to the builder's management operations, as well as capital? Are we willing and able to learn the real estate business so that we can make worthwhile management contributions?

Corporate Commitment to the Business

1. Are we prepared to earmark a specific sum of money for the builder's use, so that he doesn't have to battle for finances with the corporate financial officer every time he's starting a new project? How big is our financial contribution going to be?

2. Does the financial structure of our corporation permit the acquired builder to leverage his capital maximally? After all, we're getting into the business for the leverage potentials in it. Or are we locked in from borrowings beyond a certain point by senior debt agreements we've made with lenders? If so, what sort of structure should we consider for the acquisition to get around these?

3. What kind of rate of growth are we going to expect from the acquired builder? Is 15% a year ample? Do we want him to expand into types of construction other than those he has formerly specialized in, in order to increase this growth rate?

4. Are we confident enough about the long-term value of the acquisition to take in stride an occasional mediocre or poor performance stemming from causes basically beyond the builder's control, such as when markets get overbuilt and housing slumps? Or is our move predicated on the happy notion that the builder will never have less than a phenomenal earnings year, and are we liable to get unhappy if things go otherwise?

The Operating Relationship with the Acquired Organization

1. How shall we resolve the question of corporate control vs. builder autonomy? Do we make him go through our own corporate channels, or can we figure out some way whereby he can basically run his own show without undue interference from us? (After all, *he's* the expert and we're off base telling *him* what to do.) On the other hand, just because he knows the business is no reason to let him run hog-wild. Many undercapitalized builders have overexpanded with an infusion of capital; a plain case of overeating. They have to be intelligently guided. So, what do we have to do to learn the industry well, so as to guide and control him intelligently?

It takes mutual participation to plan well, and much mutual teaching. It's not a matter of dispassionate observation à la Harvard case history. The builder should be able to credibly document why some millions should be spent, satisfying not just the corporation but also himself on the value of the project; he should be able to really test and analyze his deal before putting it into action. (A good example of such successful cooperation is the Philip Morris-Mission Viejo merger.)

2. How do we motivate the builder to do his very best for us now that we're making him a millionaire (maybe many times over) by buying out his company?

3. Do we recognize sufficiently that the builder's top management team commands a higher pay scale and greater incentives than management of industrial corporations? The builder's earnings will, after all, only be as good as his team's performance. Are we willing to set up the kind of

incentive program that will get the best results, even though it might give some of the key building execs a higher income than that of the president of the corporate parent?

Now, as it happens, it is difficult to make a success of a housing acquisition unless the corporate acquirer can somehow come up with the right answer for *all* of the foregoing questions. And that is a difficult art in itself in view of the fact that some of the right answers will appear to contradict one another. For example, the acquirer will want to harness the builder's incentive by putting him on an earnout. (The concept of the earnout is discussed in some detail in Chapter 8.) But he will also want the builder to go slow when housing markets slump, while the builder strains at the leash in order to get the additional earnout payment. How do you avoid unpleasant conflicts in this case? The successful merger is a delicate and complex dynamic of forces that ultimately works because of the specific people involved, not because of schematic plans. Nevertheless, the chances for its success are considerably enhanced if the acquirer has thought through all the key decision areas and comes up with an operating philosophy that anticipates as many problem areas as possible.

EPS OR ROI ORIENTATION?

It is my own belief that the seeds of most merger problems are planted when the acquirer makes the decision to get into real estate for the per-share earnings game without having given careful thought to all of the vitally important key decision areas which govern the success of the merger. Real estate, to begin with, truly makes sense only when viewed in light of return on investment. Because of the high leverage, the ROI substantially exceeds 20%, while industrial companies' ROI usually falls considerably under 10%. Viewed as a return on total assets, real estate is a mediocre or poor business: compared with one industrial company's return on assets of $6\frac{1}{2}\%$, a group of twenty builders averaged a return on assets of only 5%. When the acquisition is undertaken primarily on the basis of the builder's return on total assets and expected earnings contribution to the parent corporation's stock, that decision sets up a pressure-cooker operating environment in which — even with the best planning and finest of intentions — communications problems multiply; many fast, forced decisions have to be made; and reported earnings can be slim. This being the case, for a non-housing acquirer to rush headlong into the earnings race without a considered policy and sound operating structure, and with unrealistic expectations to boot, is to literally invite failure.

The acquiring corporation can compound its problems and set its own trap by linking its own earnings performance projections too heavily to the builder's performance. This has been often true where the acquirers themselves have been capital-intensive businesses. This puts a double onus on the builder. First, he must perform not only for his own account, so to speak, but is also in effect responsible for the entire corporation's earnings performance. Secondly, he finds himself competing with the parent corporation for scarce capital. With the acquirer's future heavily dependent on the builder, and with money in short supply, corporate management gains a strong (if not well-conceived) reason for intervening in the builder's operation when his earnings look imperiled. Such interventions by a management essentially untutored in real estate almost always have exactly the opposite of the intended effect; they bypass and snarl the builder's own decisions and operations in the name of help. And, as a capper, if earnings then fail to materialize because of operational chaos engendered by such interventions, the acquirer gets panicked and may decide to pull out of real estate altogether. The write-off is a painful but wondrous tool for wiping the slate clean of massive screw-ups and moving on to greener pastures. The important lesson in this is that capital-intensive industries should stay out of real estate development altogether, unless staged with exceptionally talented management versed in that business. This is one reason why companies like INA and CNA, which have large recurring cash flows to invest, have fared better than manufacturers buying into homebuilding.

The demand for big earnings on a clockwork basis, when made by an acquirer who doesn't understand real estate, leads to rapid expansion of the building operation. Rapid expansion in such situations leads to poor decisions and a loss of control over the operation. As each quarter rolls around with its demand for an ever-larger earnings statement, the pressures mount and the temptations multiply to make expedient instead of sound decisions. Marginally feasible projects get approved and, with communications problems, feasible ones get bogged down in channels. Longer-term investment opportunities are sacrificed for the chance to book immediate profits. Capital pours out for overhead and is dribbled away in the crevasses of inefficiency that gape throughout the rapidly growing structure of the builder's operation. Communication and controls become devilish problems for the builder himself as he attempts to ride herd on the burgeoning apparatus. Middle management, without the benefit of the boss's direct control, gets disheartened because it is out of touch with him or is infiltrated by incompetents who'd just as soon stay out of touch. But the builder's communication problems with the parent corporation may be even more difficult, as on the one hand it drives him on while on the other it constantly brings him up short by subjecting his own decisions to sometimes absurd deliberations and delays bred of ignorance.

The abrupt corporate decision to go slow likewise creates problems when it overrules the builder's own plans or the initial merger agreement. Here, one of the key elements that has underlain the problems of the earnings-oriented acquirer is, ironically, the earnout itself. Having paid extremely high multiples of the builders' earnings to acquire them, the corporate parents loaded up the builders with heavy earnouts to insure the best possible performance. The agreements were made in times of strong housing markets and with the expectation that such strong markets would continue to exist. But housing markets can and do change radically within a year or two, calling for increased financial commitment, increased marketing skills — and increased risk — if earnings are to be wrung out of them. When some corporations decided to pull back in face of these conditions, their earnings orientation resulted in an extreme disenchantment with the real estate subsidiary, not to mention the builder's disenchantment with the corporate parent.

Generally speaking, the relationship between acquirer and acquired will be healthier if the builder is not impelled into the race of directly supporting the non-housing acquirer's stock with his own earnings; for, as we have seen, that sets up a tyranny over the builder's operaton which can defeat both him and the earnings goals. Housing remains a project-by-project business, and builders produce the highest eventual return on capital and greatest profits if they are free of external pressures governing the timing and the volume of their projects. This suggests that the acquirers with the greatest chance of finding happiness in housing will be those who have plenty of surplus cash to invest, and which are already growing well enough to let the builder do his own thing. When the acquirer is solely interested in rising earnings per share on a quarterly, semiannual and annual basis, this maximizing of earnings over short periods conflicts with a builder's objective of keeping taxes down, accumulating property, and gaining lead time — leading to other problems. The builder's long-term survival directly depends on his ability to control his own growth, and this is the essential element which is hazarded when he gets on the EPS treadmill. Inevitably, he has to start racing to keep up with himself. And when he carries the responsibility for the parent corporation's performance as well as his own on his shoulders, well, that sort of pressure nobody needs. For such reasons, non-housing acquirers modifying their policy of ROI and settling for a moderate growth rate instead of concentrating solely on EPS in their ventures into real estate have a fundamentally better track record.

Related to the basic decision of EPS vs. ROI orientation, several problem areas arise in troubled mergers, most of them stemming from faulty or inadequate communication and planning. These are worth examining individually.

FINANCIAL COMMITMENT

The question of an acquiring corporaton's financial commitment to its builder subsidiary is really a question of whether it knows what it is doing in real estate in the first place and how much it is willing to trust the builder to make his own decisions. The reason the builder merges is to get access to the acquiring corporation's capital resources so he can continue growing. But the acquirer, having paid a large chunk of stock for the builder, can sometimes be quite hesitant about providing the capital the builder asks for, or can get scared and shut off the flow. Review boards in the financial department can and do pick apart feasibility reports submitted for projects, in effect taking the decision-making capability entirely out of the builder's hands. This situation puts the builder in an adversary position with corporate management and, far from having his capital base assured, he is reduced to competing with other divisions or subsidiaries for working capital. As one builder put it: "Since the corporate management didn't know beans about real estate, where do you think they put their money when they had a choice between financing a new paper mill or a subdivision?"

One classic example of the lack of corporate commitment to financing support was the Deane Brothers merger with Occidental Petroleum. In the three years that Ben Deane worked under Oxy's corporate controls, he says that the financial department approved only a single new project. Ben himself is very careful to qualify how he feels about that merger. "I must tell you," he says, "I have no regrets about it. It has been good for Occidental, and it has been good for me." But then he goes on: "But one of the things I should have gotten was a commitment to capital. You merge in order to get capital, so you can do new things. Be sure that the capital is going to be available. A mere statement that the acquirer will back you up in the things you want to do is not enough. You want to have him committed to put up capital, with some sort of penalty if he doesn't do it." Don Scholz likewise learned that a handshake and a general understanding that Inland would support him in his ventures by no means guaranteed that capital would be forthcoming when he sought it. Since Scholz had counted heavily on Inland's financial resources in his plans to buy up land and develop apartments to the tune of $100 million, this impasse led to his quick departure.

The solution to this kind of problem is, as Ben Deane suggests, to get the commitment to financing in writing right in the merger documents. This sort of commitment can take two basic forms. The acquirer either agrees to supply a specific amount of working capital within a specified time frame and subject to pre-agreed principles of project feasibility, or he commits himself to a direct loan to the acquired builder at the time of the merger, with the developer then exercising his own controls over the money. When

Larry Weinberg sold Larwin Group to CNA, for example, he negotiated a $20 million loan at a rate slightly above the prime interest rate as part of the merger deal to assure himself adequate working capital. But by no means have all merger deals involved equity financing commitments.

LEVERAGE

Real estate is a leverage business that customarily operates with far higher ratios of debt to equity than those of industrial corporations. But a few industrial acquirers have precluded themselves from taking advantage of the full leverage potentials of the development business by consolidating the acquired real estate operation in the overall corporate statement instead of running it as an unconsolidated, separately incorporated subsidiary. In such instances, the developer's borrowing ability may be severely hampered by the corporation's existing senior debt agreements. Concluded with the major lenders, such agreements control the financial structure of the corporation, among other things specifying permissible debt/equity ratios. Since industrial debt/equity ratios are conservative by comparison with those generally accepted in the real estate business, a corporation carrying a consolidated real estate operation may be unable to leverage its equity adequately.

The acquirer should strive to have the senior loan agreements amended to exclude his real estate subsidiary from the guidelines governing the debt/equity ratio. This avoids the embarrassing situation of a strongly earnings-oriented corporation demanding rapid growth of its homebuilding subsidiary without being able to finance that expansion. Real estate subsidiaries should be introduced to financing sources as independent conventional development operations. If the corporation's lenders do not recognize this distinction, the acquired real estate operation can be prevented from effective operations by an industrial debt/equity ratio. In such a case, either the acquiring corporation is obliged to pour a far higher proportion of equity dollars into development or the real estate operation limps along with a chronic shortage of financing — an unwelcome choice any way you look at it. Analysts point out that Boise Cascade faced this sort of situation with its consolidated homebuilding operations, as the parent company's senior debt restrictions precluded an effective use of leverage.

The reverse of such a leverage-limiting situation occurs when a parent corporation helps a small, independent real estate subsidiary to expand its leverage beyond that normally available to a real estate operator. Certain-Teed, for example, used its credit rating to enable its Valley Forge subsidiary to buy a large chunk of acreage near Atlanta for a 25% down payment on better financing terms than it might have been able to get independently.

Land development loans for 50% of value then recoup the subsidiary's down payment and subsequent construction loans provide most of the needed working capital. This is an example of maximizing the leverage potentials of real estate. (Other major corporations in large-scale development have attempted to buy large land parcels free and clear to keep corporate balance sheets free of debt, giving up the benfits of leverage. When they did leverage, the carrying costs on vacant land were sometimes so large they wiped out profits for years.) Of course, Certain-Teed's approach increases the risk in the parent company's balance sheets, and since it runs up against its own senior loan agreements there is a limit to the purchase obligations it can be liable for. The ideal scene is an entirely independent real estate subsidiary with its own capital structure and with adequate borrowing power to operate without the parent corporation's credit backup.

MARKET PENETRATION

The message here is that it is difficult for an acquirer to convert his builder-tiger into an octopus without coming up with corned beef hash. This is one of the big difficulties that subsidiaries held by profit-hungry parent corporations, and publicly held building companies, have run into. The builders are usually good to very good in one particular type of development (such as single-family housing) and in one particular market. But, driven by demanding profit goals, they expand rapidly, both in terms of new markets and new types of real estate product. As a result, instead of concentrating on what they're good at, they spend a great deal of time attempting to learn new activities (mobile-home parks, apartments, etc.) and new market areas. The results are often sad and the best of companies bomb out. The irony is that most builders never scratch more than the surface of their local market before they start branching out geographically and by product type.

The delegation of new activities and markets to able and trusted lieutenants is no answer, only a crapshoot: it's one thing for a chief to recognize the strength of a subordinate in his own ballpark, but how can he evaluate the competence of his boy to handle a new product or new market when the chief himself doesn't understand the product and/or market? Certainly if an experienced homebuilder is going to have this problem with his own lieutenants, the company owning or acquiring the builder is going to have far larger problems of judgment if it wants him to expand profitably and safely.

The acquisition of developers who are already large and diversified by market and product type also does not present a satisfactory answer. If you want to operate in several markets with several types of product, you'll do far better by buying four specialized builders, each of whom is expert in his line and knows a market inside out, than one big operator who's scrambling all over the lot, attempting to be all things to all people. I could have purchased, for a lower price, a half-dozen excellent specialized development firms (possessed of lower overhead and greater profits) than one acquiring corporation paid for one large developer. And I would have had experts, while the major developer was spending further tons of money looking for specialist lieutenants who would create still further problems.

You should be aware that small builders are as a rule more excited and receptive about incorporating new programs, management controls and methods than are the bigger builders. They generally welcome the opportunity to receive help and the management tools to help them grow bigger. The bigger ones have the tendency (though not in *every* case, of course) to act on the principle of "If I've already grown so big, I'm good; so bug off." One major acquirer for whom I have evaluated a number of building companies encountered his greatest problems not with the smaller builders that he picked up but with the largest one he acquired. This big fella just bucked at every management suggestion, including some very good ones to improve his record-keeping and cost controls.

As a final alternative, you can quite possibly create a development company from scratch by staffing it with knowledgeable entrepreneurial types who can be attracted away from other firms because they're unhappy with improperly assessed incentives that are their current lot. Lee Davis, who heads one executive search firm, the Goodkin Executives of Westlake Village, California, calls this tactic the "rescue" of top-notch executives from development companies who've overlooked their true potential. A corporation must of course evaluate the comparative risk in starting up an operation as compared with acquiring a tested, ongoing one. But as Lee points out, it is not always necessary to spend millions for a company when a successful operation can be created from the ground up by finding three or four key men to run the marketing, advance planning/land acquisition, construction and financial ends of the business. Judging by the fact that most of the major builders and developers in the Western United States, as well as a number of industrial corporations, work through Lee, he does a great deal of such "rescuing."

CORPORATE CONTROL VS. BUILDER AUTONOMY

The question of corporate controls over the acquired builder operation is a delicate one and is closely interrelated with the question of motivating the acquired management, which we shall look at below.

For all acquirers, the basic controls start with the setting up of a budget, profit projections, and guidelines in sale and purchase of assets. The acquired builder usually has to go through a readjustment period, getting familiarized with corporate accounting systems and reporting procedures that may be highly sophisticated. He may not have been used to living with a monthly profit-and-loss statement, for example, and thus may have to readjust his entire accounting system to accommodate the corporate parent. The acquirers also sharpen up the analytical tools to define return on investment more closely, forcing the builder to tighten up his operations. The result is that the acquired builder has a lot more paperwork to do each month to report on the status of the operation. But this need not be taxing. As one developer puts it, after going through an adjustment period, he now has his reporting procedures down to two and a half hours a month. With a financial control system to monitor his activities, so long as the builder stays within his budget and meets his projections, everything is fine.

But the real problems of control arise not from financial systems but from the people involved and their ability to make the correct decisions at the right time. A growing realty subsidiary submits a constant flow of project plans, financial requests and corporate planning ideas for approval. Good control must thus start with a good understanding of the acquired builder in particular and of the development business in general, in order to direct and support the subsidiary's growth intelligently without at the same time killing the builder's enthusiasm and motivation. The single most important rule concerning a successful merger is to make sure you start off on the right foot in the first place; i.e., that the deal basically makes sense and the people are compatible and competent. You can get good support in such evaluations from competent consultants. Having satisfied yourself on this basis, two other rules become evident:

First, if you trusted the builder's ability enough to buy him in the first place, accord him enough trust to permit him to run his operation autonomously, reporting monthly but consulting you only on the most major decisions. You must understand that real estate is a very creative business which depends on individual skill of judgment and fast responses to local situations. It cannot be well operated if every decision must be run through a highly structured, multilayered corporate apparatus. By the time everyone involved gets through pecking at the proposal or request or whatever, the opportunity is usually dead. This is really just another way of saying that you must be willing to delegate to your acquired builder the authority or power to match his responsibilities. If you don't, you've paid but you're afraid to play the game, and you won't be in it long because the builder will work out his contract and split.

And second, make one top corporate officer entirely responsible for the realty subsidiary, so as to segregate and shelter the realty operations from the corporate bureaucracy and to give the acquired builder an identifiable terminal to deal with in the corporate structure. The corporate officer should understand the real estate business well enough to evaluate major decisions affecting the builder's operation properly and promptly. His authority should be large enough to rule on major decisions and to influence the executive committee of his corporation when a corporate vote is called for. Such a corporate officer in effect serves as the acquired builder's ambassador plenipotentiary to the corporate kingdom, taking on the burden of translating the builder's language and requirements and dealing with the corporate bureaucracy.

A clear line of responsibility and command to a single authoritative source is indispensable to a builder seeking to operate efficiently. Without such precaution, he is too often caught in a corporate crossfire from various corporate officers who score points with the president of the parent corporation at his expense. This problem stems from the essential difference in viewpoint that separates an entrepreneur who is also an owner of a business from the professional manager who is merely employed by a business. The owner will only be concerned about making the best decisions to enhance the survival of his company. But the professionals without stock who are clawing their way up the corporate ladder are, as a rule, more concerned with power and with the need to make a good impression than with the question of a building subsidiary's optimal survival. If the acquirer has not guarded against this fact of life by giving only one officer the authority to deal with the builder, the corporate bureaucrats can make life miserable for the acquired builder. Decisions will emerge after long delays, and only by a vague consensus, because no one corporate officer is fully responsible for them. But meanwhile, all of them, unburdened by excess knowledge of real estate, will have had the opportunity to pick apart the hapless builder because they're all *somehow* involved.

In the real estate industry, and particularly among development companies who have become subsidiaries of industrial corporations, this phenomenon is known as the "seagull syndrome." As one expert who has long observed this phenomenon describes it, "The seagull is the guy from corporate headquarters who flies in, shits all over you and flies back out again. Most builders are unfortunately deluged with seagulls. When you're wrong they make you know it; if they're right, you know it. And they always have to know everything that goes on, even though it doesn't concern them; they're always interfering. They're a pain in the ass and can kill a deal anytime."

The effects of the seagull syndrome can be truly insidious. In the instance of one corporation that expanded its subsidiary's building operations rapidly, all of the corporate officers and the board approved the expansion step by step. But when earnings faltered, both the officers and the board members suddenly weren't responsible and everybody was pointing fingers at everybody else. The builder, a sensitive and dignified man, was seagulled to death in executive meetings after having been pressed into rapid growth by the same executives. The board itself never did know what it was doing, composed as it was of elderly gentlemen serving mainly for purposes of prestige. They were mouthpieces for the opinions of corporate officers. Each officer had a favorite board member into whose ear to whisper self-serving gossip, and to curry favor with in hopes of advancement. When the acquired builder was finally brought down by the board, it may be that he never did know the third parties who were the real agents of his humiliation.

This episode underscores the basic truth that most if not all merger problems ultimately resolve to the particular people involved, their strength of character and their ethical qualities. But some of these human frailties can be anticipated and avoided by structuring the corporate relationship with the subsidiary through a single corporate officer and compensating this man in direct proportion to the success of the subsidiary he's responsible for. This way, the builder reports to only one person vitally interested in his progress and not to a half a dozen uninterested guys trying to kill him. The half-dozen similarly have to go through the responsible corporate officer in order to reach the builder. Meanwhile, the builder gains the clarity of decision-making and the freedom of movement to do his entrepreneurial thing successfully.

Not all merger relationships are structured this way, but one that did follow this format exactly is the Singer Company when it acquired Besco (now Singer Housing Company) of San Leandro, California. The housing entrepreneur, Wayne F. Valley, is responsible to only one corporate officer, Joseph Smith, a vice president at Singer. The relationship has worked extremely well, with none of the red tape that has characterized many merger relationships. Once the subsidiary's goals and capital requirements were approved by the parent corporation, the builder was left to operate with an ideal degree of autonomy. The success of the relationship stemmed from Singer's recognition of the unique nature of the housing business.

It should be understood that the corporate officer to whom the builder reports must have a strong capability in real estate, if they are to make a good team. This is the real key. Such individuals can occupy various posts in the corporate hierarchy. Sometimes, as in the case of Cerro Corporation, it is the chief executive himself who is the real estate expert. The company's president, Gordon Murphy, had acted quickly in the fall of 1970 to buy Leadership Housing Division of Macco Corporation from the tottering Great Southwest empire after Penn-Central declared bankruptcy. And he has presided protectively over Leadership's expansion into a major building company.

As Harrison Lasky, Leadership's president, puts it: "Gordon doesn't run this place like a concentration camp. We have the autonomy to deal on a large scale at the local level without going through fourteen commissioners." At the same time, Murphy smooths the road for ventures that do need corporate approval by his own authoritative ability to evaluate the specific venture, thus creating an inviting operating climate for the subsidiary and coming up with the answers it needs without delays. "It's all the difference between having to sell the executive committee on a deal and handing the committee a deal which it rubber-stamps," Lasky says of Murphy's contribution to the operating relationship between the parent corporation and the subsidiary.

MOTIVATING THE MANAGEMENT

The proper motivation of a builder takes some understanding of his character. So far we have mostly envisioned him as an anonymous person, but in real life he usually turns out to be an all-too-real dynamo of action and intuition with the same leadership style and regard for bureaucracy as the late General Patton. I am sure that even in the best relationships there are days when board chairmen of prestigious firms, after a nerve-shattering session with an irascible builder-partner, seriously wonder whether they should have gone into the garment business instead of real estate.

The well-adjusted response by a builder who's been bought is a continuing leadership role on the battle lines—and wise is the acquiring corporation that does not attempt to tie such a man to a desk job. But there are two other types of post-merger reactions that it pays to be aware of. The first is that of the man who relaxes so completely that he becomes a dropout. He's been so busy surviving and never quite having enough (even if he was worth a million or two) that when he suddenly finds himself worth ten to fifty times a million through a stock transaction, his desire to live really turns on. How do you motivate such a man to produce profits for you, even on an earnout? The other type is the megalomaniac. One taste of power and big money and he's convinced that he's another Jimmy Ling. Suddenly, he's brilliant. Suddenly, his hunger is for more money, more power, more status. Suddenly . . . he wants *your* job as president of the acquiring company. One major developer whom I know well showed some symptoms of the latter contagion. He tipped his hand when, on being acquired by a very large corporation, he remarked: "Any company that paid this much for me needs new management "

In truth, acquirers have had far more reason to be concerned about insufficient motivation than excessive zeal. Some advocate acquiring only younger builders, preferably under age forty, who still have a world to conquer and will not cash in their chips. The earnout is of course a powerful tool for enlisting incentive and it continues to be in use under the purchase accounting method of acquisition. When the seller has the opportunity to receive as much on the go as he did on the come his performance and tenure constitute far less of a question than they might otherwise. Most acquirers also work out some sort of a package of frills, such as placing the builder on the board of directors and giving him an opportunity to identify with other top management of the corporation, in order to boost his status and thus, hopefully, his desire to perform well.

But the best of the entrepreneurs are in the business for more than money or superficial status. What they seek is satisfaction, a sense of achievement, following a desire to control their own destiny. It is here that the issue of good corporate control of the building subsidiary intersects with the issue of proper motivation. For the best builders the real estate operation they run is a vehicle for the expression of long-term aspirations. When the corporate acquirer understands the real estate business well enough to structure a control relationship that will not cramp the builder's freedom and creativity, this factor in itself can motivate the entrepreneur far more than frills or earnout. In the absence of such a relationship, men like Ray Watt, Ben Deane and Don Scholz leave the scene, often becoming competitiors of the companies that acquired them in the first place. The real essence of the art of merger is to match a capable builder with a corporation that will truly understand him. The import of this is that proper motivation of the builder *starts* with the establishment of the right control relationship. And only when that is satisfactorily accounted for is it appropriate to consider the further financial incentives that will make the builder move. Most acquirers have gone about this backwards.

Given the right relationship, the acquirer can set up one of two basic types of financial incentive. The first is the earnout, as we have seen. The only possible disadvantage of the earnout is that it may put the acquirer and acquired in an adversary position by locking the builder into a program of rapid growth for a period of up to five years without regard for market conditions. The builder may be accused of using corporate capital carelessly and subordinating the basic interests of the parent corporation to his own drive to earn the contingent stock. As noted, the tension between acquirer and acquired becomes particularly apparent when market demand for housing falls while the builder is still on the earnout; the two engage in a tug of war, one wanting to keep expanding, the other wanting to hold back. But such conflicts can be minimized or avoided if the developer pre-plans an intelligent geographic diversification and is strong on marketing. The earnout is then an excellent way of harnessing incentive.

The other method of harnessing the builder's incentive, and one that is increasingly popular in the Seventies, is to have the builder continue as a partial owner in the building subsidiary. Ownership encourages the builder to plan every investment as his own because it directly reflects on his profits, thus inspiring a greater unanimity of interests between acquirer and acquired. With his earnout completed, there's nothing to keep the now-rich builder from getting the itch to move on and start another organization if the long-term relationship with the acquirer doesn't jell. But as a partial owner of the subsidiary, his interests remain rooted where he is, and he is also in a position to exercise some measure of influence or control over corporate policy governing the subsidiary.

The underlying virtue of the partial-ownership arrangement is that the corporation acquiring an interest in the builder now looks less like an owner and more like an investor. The builder gets a greater measure of autonomy than he would in the usual merger relationship and is at the same time inspired to do his best because he can't hurt the corporate parent with-out hurting himself. A number of acquirers who have gone this route have found it a very satisfactory way of reducing or eliminating many of the problems that accompany conventional mergers. Cerro Mining owns 80% of Leadership, while the subsidiary's management has options to buy the other 20%. Potlatch Forests likewise purchased only 80% of Brown & Kaufman, and Bethlehem Steel bought only 80% of Multicon. CBS, own-ing 49% of Klingbeil (for the time being) surrenders decision-making con-trol to the subsidiary entirely. Philip Morris, owning approximately 50.1% of the Mission Viejo Company, has a theoretical edge on control but is in a true partnership with the subsidiary.

One particular event that focused broad attention on the shift from the conventional merger relationship to an investor relationship between acquirer and acquired was the formation in December 1971 of the Richards Group, Inc., a new housing company 50%-owned by the conglomerate Gulf & Western. The organization was formed by Richard M. Wasserman and Richard P. Bernhard, who had held the top two posts at ITT Levitt, Inc., before quitting earlier in the year. Wasserman, who had been the president of the ITT subsidiary, underscored the difference in the investor relationship: "It's *our* business in which Gulf & Western has invested in this case. We'll have no interference in our company's operations. We're not a wholly owned subsidiary." The relationship gives him the best of both worlds: the freedom to run the company according to the dictates of entrepreneurial talent along with strong financial backing from Gulf & Western ($10 million for openers).

MOTIVATING KEY PEOPLE

Motivation planning in the building business doesn't stop with the builder-owner but must also include the top management which is responsible for producing the company's profits. Corporations entering the real estate business, and indeed many a builder, sometimes fail to recognize the critical distinction between manufacturing executives and building management. The difference is, there is nothing proprietary in the developing business. The major asset of the company is not a physical plant but the talent of the executives who make the important decisions and create the successful housing projects — identifying markets, assembling land at the right price, developing marketing programs and arranging the financing. So the management must be sufficiently motivated to perform at its best effort every day. Building management thus cannot be put on a salary structure equatable with that of manufacturing executives. You can get the best industrial manager for $80,000 but you can't necessarily get a good divisional manager for a housing company for the same salary.

Since the top four to six managers of a building company are literally responsible for creating the profits, they justifiably demand compensation in line with their ability. The successful developers have worked out various formulas to hold on to their good men, but one of the best compensation packages I know of is offered by Leadership Housing to its key executives. There's nothing like ownership, or the potential of ownership, to bring out the best in individuals and convert a "seagull" into a hardworking member of an ownership team. At Leadership, Harry Lasky took care that options to buy 20% of the company were spread among the top six executives, insuring a dedicated team effort. In addition, a bonus system rewards the managers with as much as 100% of their annual salary if they meet divisional projections. Salaries for the division heads are roughly on par with or slightly lower than salaries paid by the major developers in the industry. A Leadership division manager earned $45,000 in 1971, compared with about $50,000 paid by other firms for a comparable job. But with the bonus system, the Leadership manager who brings in his projections earns an additional $45,000, thus bringing his income for the year to $90,000. That is quite an edge on the competition's pay scale and is calculated to produce outstanding performance for Cerro's housing subsidiary. Major stock options have also made a number of millionaires among managers in such rapidly growing, expertly managed companies as Kaufman & Broad. Dick

Wasserman of the Richards Group is another entrepreneur who was thinking along stronger lines than even Harry Lasky when he said: "We expect
to get the best guys who exist in this industry and to give them an equity
interest in the business, and I don't just mean stock options."

In light of the foregoing, I am always wryly amused when I hear the
broadly voiced complaint that it is difficult to attract highly motivated, aggressive middle- and upper-rank executives to staff building companies. It
is only difficult because the homebuilders in question are trying to buy a lot
of talent on the cheap by putting their profit-winners on straight salary with
relatively insignificant stock options. The developer's or the corporate
acquirer's niggardliness regarding executive compensation can defeat the
senior purpose of turning in an excellent performance. The organizations
that larded in the overhead by filling themselves up with second-rate
$12,000- and $20,000-a-year men learned that quantity is no substitute for
quality. As Lee Davis of the Goodkin Executives puts it: "The key men in
the successful building organization are understaffed, overworked and
overpaid."

The closer one looks at the actual elements of a successful real estate
operation, in fact, the more the human element dominates and the impressive statistical recitations of the security of bigness ring hollow. Real estate
is a people industry and projects succeed or fail based on the judgment of
a very few individuals, no matter how many milllons of dollars are involved
or what ingenious management controls are devised. *Risk varies in inverse
proportion to the talent of the few key people making the decisions in the
organization.* This is the closest you can get to a slide-rule formula for a
successful merger or a successful real estate venture of any type. Perhaps
the underlying message of this chapter has been that it is worth paying
close attention to the care and feeding of the subsidiary's talent. If they're
taken care of, the earnings and the success will follow.

TOMORROW'S MERGERS

Real estate mergers will continue throughout the Seventies because of
the independent builder's need for ever-larger capital resources if he is to
survive in the consolidated future. But the character of the combinations is
changing even today. Because it is difficult for a non-housing corporation
to understand the prospective builder acquisition properly, or to structure
a productive relationship with such a subsidiary, there will be considerably
fewer outright purchases of builders. Rather, the non-housing corporations
will follow the lead of Gulf & Western by partially buying or *investing in*
outstanding independent building organizations, thus providing an experienced management with the autonomy and incentive to act as it sees fit. For

the corporations it is a case of regressing slowly to their original role as passive investors. This shift from an ownership and active management role to what (though still an acquisition, in many cases) verges on a joint-venture relationship foreshadows a broader usage by the entire industry of the joint-venture relationship.

Two other types of acquirers will continue to make acquisitions. The first of these is the corporation looking for an excellent return on investment from the large cash flows it generates. This acquirer will have an in-house real estate expert who can set up and operate a real estate subsidiary successfully, having studied and profited from the experiences of the earlier acquirers. The second type of acquirer — and a dominant one during the Seventies — will be the company that is already engaged in the housing business in one form or another. A housing congeneric already has the requisite understanding of the subsidiary's business to keep the merger relationship happy.

I do foresee that even the congeneric companies may run into organizational and management difficulties eventually. The concept works because the independent builder acquired by the bigger company has a direct line to the top men in the congeneric. But as the company grows to the point where it operates, say, forty builders, you get a breakdown in communications with all these people attempting to report to, and secure the ear of, the top men. It's at this point that bureaucracy gets too large and builders might be expected to splinter from the group with the entrepreneurial environment lost. There's a solution to this problem, however. Instead of organizing the group horizontally, so that every builder is equal to every other and all report to a single channel, a congeneric could organize itself in a self-reproducing cellular structure. In a nutshell, here's how this works:

A controllable number of major builder-members of the congeneric report to the corporate headquarters. When further acquisitions are made, it is these key builders who make them, *not* the parent corporation. Each of the key builders acquires a controllable number of smaller builders. These report not to the parent corporation but to the builder who acquired them. Thus, a direct line of communication between the bigger, successful entrepreneur and the smaller one is always preserved. As each of the smaller builders expands his operation he, in turn, acquires a controllable number of newer builders who report to *him*. This process of acquisition would enable the overall congeneric to grow rapidly without jamming the communication lines at the top, while maintaining a strong line of communications at each vital entrepreneurial link of the growing chain. It's a *building-company* solution, rather than an industrial-type solution to the problem of managing expansion.

With homebuilding stocks generally in a bear market from early 1973, many non-housing firms stayed away from acquisitions in this field. But, in accordance with our predictions of a general trend to congeneric-type mergers, in 1973 there were more money-laden building companies on the prowl for further homebuilder acquisitions. With their own P/E ratios depressed, they weren't paying the high multiples of yore (indeed, many of the offers were closer to book value), but dealings were still moving at a fast clip. Some of these activities were postponed as the stock market declined sharply in 1973, but with a turnaround, the congeneric merger would again come into its own. Edward C. Birkner of the Marketing Information Network made some astute observations about the congeneric merger form in his *Professional Builder* column early in 1973, and I want to borrow the quotes he got from two builders.

Art Rutenberg, who left U.S. Home Corporation to start his own congeneric, said: "The homebuilding industry is wide open to the formation of congenerics — basically because of the industry's fragmentation, on the negative side, and the prospect for the synergism which a building congeneric generates, on the positive side." He believes that synergism can help a builder reach a six-year goal in three years by better management systems, easier access to more capital, and fewer mistakes. Don Scholz, after leaving Inland Steel, is still set on forming a congeneric on his own. Says he: "If the Sixties can be said to have been the decade of the mortgage trusts, the Seventies will be noted for the formation of the building congenerics." I should also add that Dick Wasserman, who left the presidency of Levitt to form the Richards group with Gulf & Western as a financial backer, was also reported to be moving his new company in the direction of the congeneric format early in 1973, with plans to acquire other builders.

The major industrial corporations who have achieved a solid foothold in real estate are, willy-nilly, likewise following the congeneric mold. The emerging pattern for success in corporate acquisitions works like this: the acquirer acquires one star builder who then becomes the head of the building subsidiary and chief consultant on all other building acquisitions. The latter become subsidiaries of the star builder's acquired company. There are several examples: Cyanamid began by buying up the Ervin Company of Charlotte, which now heads Cyanamid's newer acquisitions (Edmund J. Bennett & Associates of Bethesda, Maryland, and Sunstate Builders of Tampa, among others). Singer's acquisition, Wayne Valli of Besco, oversaw its second acquisition, Mitchell Corporation of Mobile, Alabama. Olin found a leader for its housing activities by buying out Robert H. Young of Young/American Corporation of Dallas. Although acquired later than some previous Olin acquisitions, Young now heads the subsidiary Olin-American Corporation, to which the other Olin subsidiaries, Maryland Housing Corporation, Morrison Homes and Yeonas Bros., report.

Bigger, as it turns out, *is* better — but with the proviso that the acquirer must know what he's doing. The enthusiastic acquirers who thought they were going to reform the curious and "backward" practices of real estate by button-down corporate procedures learned that there were good reasons for such practices. In the end it was not they who submerged real estate but real estate that submerged them.

A WORD ABOUT OUR FRIEND THE BUILDER

And now that we have polished off the sins of corporate acquirers, let us say a few words concerning the builder delegation. The builders come off looking pretty good in this book: innocent entrepreneurial virtue ravished by coarse corporate lust, etc. But these pristine chaps aren't all that free of, shall we say, *peccati minori* themselves. In this chapter, and elsewhere in this book, the rise and fall of many a good builder is sung. But let us establish clearly at this point that in every instance where a merger went on the skids it was ultimately, in one way or another, the fault of *both* partners. It takes two to make something go wrong, by an act of omission or commission. This entails bad judgment and subsequent bad performance by the party of the second part, as well as of the first.

For all their bumbling, the big corporations entering the housing field were in it to make money. The builders convinced them they could perform and then through their own shortcomings let them down. And because they didn't perform, they didn't get capital. Or because they didn't establish in advance what kind of operating environment they'd need, they got into bottlenecks. The acquirers were, after all, looking to the builder to guide them. The acquirers, for their part, failed to distinguish between the builder's making a profit when he had a strong (and therefore nonrecurring) price advantage on land and his real, basic competence to make a profit under ordinary conditions. The acquirers did not measure accurately the quality of the developer's team and its ability to handle rapid expansion. You had lots of sophisticated numbers, but no sensitivity to the quality of people and ability. (Those sophisticated numbers, by the way, had their origins almost entirely outside the homebuilding industry. Where building companies were criticized for their accounting procedures, the critics almost uniformly overlooked this small fact.) Lacking this judgment, a corporate acquirer would get a builder and right from the outset expect too much of him. The builder let the corporation down by going along with unrealistic estimations of his own ability. And the builder came out of the wreckage of a merger far better than the corporate parent. In most cases he'd walk off with all those millions in stock tucked away in his pockets and start over elsewhere.

The key element that an acquirer must be able to perceive in evaluating the quality of a builder is the builder's real performance as contrasted with his performance on advantageously priced land. The best way to distinguish between the two is to watch the builder's track record when he moves into a *new* market area, where he starts from scratch just like every other builder. This is the test that counts; it provides a new perspective on the performance of even the very best companies.

Pardee Construction Company has a reputation for being terrifically successful in San Diego, but this is because they inventoried land there for years. Shapell in 1972 did very well at Bixby Ranch near Los Angeles, but it was the only company in the area and in a strong market. Mission Viejo has performed outstandingly at its new town in Orange County, where it has a great advantage on land. In Phoenix, where it bought land dearly, the competition is stronger. The Bren Company did phenomenally well in the new town of Valencia until lot prices were raised substantially. Boise Cascade Building Company bought a lot of land at prices that precluded success. The Lyon company overpaid for particular parcels or bought without regard for market conditions. Kaufman & Broad didn't do very well in California's San Fernando Valley, and Larwin had problems in Newhall-Saugus. The larger, better-capitalized builders could afford to make many unobserved mistakes; their percentage of successes kept them going. The smaller builder, who couldn't afford to make a *single* mistake, came off looking unwarrantedly worse.

It is the value of product offered that sells, and in the right market conditions. When it is no longer offered because of high land cost and in a tough market, nearly every builder who looks very sharp based on a non-recurring advantage can lose the special touch. This highlights the importance of in-depth research to keep a company from losing its shirt on bad land deals in bad markets, and to keep it from wasting incredible amounts of valuable management time that could be otherwise profitably used. In the early mergers, the builders were not intensively sized up by such tests.

Perhaps the early corporate acquirers had no way of knowing these facts. In the hot California market there were years when anybody who threw up housing could sell it, because of enormous demand. Perhaps the builders themselves, sold on their own local success, didn't appreciate these facts sufficiently. It all came out in the wash of mutual inadequacies. The acquirers are now learning that the key to successful expansion lies in the *specific ability* of the builder's management both to evaluate marketing conditions and to buy land at the right price.

In the earlier mergers, the level of expectation was too high on both sides without a sufficient estimation of realities. The builder didn't expect any discipline; the acquirer didn't expect anything but brilliant performance.

Both discovered they lacked the necessary sensitive understanding of each other's responsibilities and requirements. The builder, disillusioned, found no fount of money; the corporation, disillusioned, found no profits. By contrast, one reason why the congeneric concept of merger has on the whole worked better is that each acquired builder stays in his own backyard, where he knows the market, the land, the landowners and the zoning councils inside out. The congeneric thus bypasses the acquired builder's need to suffer the trials of expansion into new markets.

A REVIEW OF SOME DON'TS

It is evident that arranging a workable merger (or even joint venture) with the right builder can be a tough proposition even for a skilled acquirer. So a short review of a few commonsense don'ts that may be observed with profit will not be redundant:

Don't judge the company very heavily by its history. In the real estate field, because of very diverse markets and a multitude of rapidly shifting circumstances, past performance has less bearing on present success than you might think. Many builders look like geniuses because their product happens to be selling marvelously in their own regional market. Underlying the success is not brilliance but a competitive advantage on land costs that allows (a) a better product for the money, or (b) plenty of lard in the overhead without going broke. Put the same builder into a new market, though, and he suddenly loses that magic touch, or is exposed for the cretin that he may be. The costs of land, labor, financing and materials also change so rapidly that a successful product can be priced right out of its market in short order, transforming the inflexible formula builder into a lemon. Numerous other acts of foolish man and an angry God can also convert the apparently vast success of an operation into a rather half-vast one. Zoning can be changed, an engineering report by the most competent firm in the business can be substantially off. Any number of unforeseen elements can arise to cripple sales.

Don't settle for anything short of a complete analysis and justification of the financial and marketing merits of the builder's proposed program. "Do I contradict myself? Very well, then, I contradict myself." A builder needs to be his own decision-maker, true. But you want to verify his projections at the outset. Once you've done it, *then* leave him alone. It might seem tough to make a thorough evaluation, as you may be a stranger to the industry and could kill your builder with unanswerable objections. But you can find reputable and expert outside talent to guide you until you get the hang of it. Among the most important questions you have to ask with regard to a specific project proposal: Is the land worth as much as we're paying for it? Will the proposed program perform well in the specific market? Why? What is the absorption potential of this market? What alternate plans are there if the proposed program fails to take wing?

Don't be guided solely by the bottom line and return on investment, or by the tyranny of quarterly earnings reports. The former will drive you to apparent economies, the latter to poor decisions and insane expediency, and both to an early grave. Don't rush; proper timing is of utmost importance to success in a market. Concentrate on making sure that the builder's operation and product have the right ingredients of sensitive judgment and market-responsive product; the profits will appear on their own and will be all the bigger for your not having forced them.

Don't, when considering the acquisition of a builder, get saddled with a phantom organization. Some well-known corporations, after paying great sums for what they believed to be large building companies, have found themselves in the embarrassing position of clutching air when the principal of the building firm departed. Despite appearances, management strength may often run no more than one or two execs deep; the rest are not decision-makers but order-takers. In this situation, when you lose the king, as Alexander shrewdly perceived of the Persians, the entire army scatters. In evaluating your potential acquisition, if you wish it to survive healthily the anticipated or unanticipated departure of its chief, you have to have some means of judging the strength of individual departments. Again, this is tough but can be done with outside help from people who know the industry.

Don't make the mistake of thinking that the builder is a wage serf like the corporate type, but don't think that he's invariably such a smart guy, either. You have to understand that the top real estate executives are more entrepreneurial in nature than the typical corporate executive. But an entrepreneurial nature doesn't automatically confirm wisdom or success. Some big operators stink, and when *they* bail out of an acquired organization, that can be a godsend. When one of these undergifted builders teams up with some hapless corporation wanting to make money in real estate, it becomes truly a sad case of the blind leading the blind.

Don't be a know-it-all, but there is an area in which you can help the builder: planning. For the most part he has no history of being a good planner. His goals are to find the land and build the product — now. He also has a tendency to underestimate the effect of competition and general economic factors. But if he is going to grow he needs top-notch marketing information for product design; the finest market analyses; and sharp appreciation of business cycles and their effect on his labors. He needs to plan what he'll be doing a year, three years, five years ahead — and where — and how much land to inventory. He needs to be apprised of new product types and potential markets. In all these areas the management skills and technology of big corporations can help by setting up a structure for these functions that will be responsive to him without choking him. This will also ease the builder's burden of self-reliance; it's easier to find the right people for well-defined functions than for poorly identified or broadly overlapping ones.

Now that you have achieved a modicum of confidence about the ways in which the real pros profit in real estate, a last point — made by a big West Coast builder in connection with defining joint ventures (though it also applies to mergers) — will summarize the essence of the art of real estate: "Joint ventures," said the builder, "are a partnership to which the corporation brings money and the developer brings experience. And at the end of the deal, the developer has the money and the corporation has the experience."

10

Structuring for Your Merger Deal

Nolite id cogere, cape malleum
majorem.*

—Inscription found on wall of
ancient Roman chariot shop

There is no mystery about the essentials. The single most important factor determining your success or failure in seeking an affiliation is your ability to grow profitably. The ways of judging your future potential profitability are your past record of profitability and the age and depth of your management. You should fully consider exactly what you have, what you have achieved in the past, and what you are capable of doing in the future. Is the merger route a valid one for you? If you believe that your company scores well on the aforementioned points, you should be able to interest several larger companies (whether builders or non-housing corporations) in talking with you.

Your ultimate success also depends on your ability to identify exactly what *you* are looking for in a partner, so that you don't just grab the first deal to come along but select the situation that will be right for you. Ask yourself if you want a small or large company to work with and define in advance exactly the kind of operating relationship you would like to have. The ideal is to pick out a company whose goals reinforce yours and whose management is compatible with yours. You will want to know such things as the suitor's earnings history and prospects for the future. How good is *its* management? (An important question, since you'll most likely make a deal by means of a tax-free stock-for-stock exchange. You don't want a stock that will deflate when the hot air is out of it, but one that will grow.) Ask yourself: Three years from today, what will my holdings in the acquirer be worth? What would be my net worth five years from today if I pursued other alternatives — one by one? What are the pros and cons of each alternative? If merger still looks interesting, does the suitor understand your business well enough to provide the right operating guidelines for you without overcontrolling you?

* Don't force it, get a bigger hammer.

YOUR FIRST STEP: FIND OUT WHO YOU REALLY ARE

Any sound plan for the future must begin with an honest evaluation of the present. It may take you one to three years to prepare yourself for a merger, so you can't start planning too early. If you have begun thinking about hitting the merger trail, take a day or two off with your key managers and spend the time asking yourselves some rough-tough questions.

1. What business are we really in? Is this the business that we *want* to be in? What are our company's strengths and weaknesses? What are our own shortcomings as manager-owners? What can we do about this?

2. What are our personal goals in life? Do we have a deep and driving desire to give our most highly motivated efforts to promote the growth of our organization? Are we willing to work *hard?*

3. What are the areas of opportunity in this business? What do we want our organization to achieve this year, in the next two or three years, in five years, in ten years? What product lines should we be entering? What geographical markets? What do we need to do to develop the appropriate management? What does it take in terms of skills, people, money, personal dedication and strategy to get us where we want to go?

4. Five years from today, what will my personal role be in the business if I (a) merge (b) go public (c) stay private? Which do I like best?

5. What are our real motives for considering a merger? Are we afraid we won't survive? Or are we really looking for a larger partner with an integrity as strong as our own, so that we can both get out there and rewake the world according to *our* sense of values, and thus survive better? Be honest with yourself.

Define exactly where you want to go and the steps that it takes to get you there. You will want to examine your firm's marketing ability, your financial capacity, your management and control systems, your building technology, your ability to buy land. In the course of your analysis, you will come up with a much clearer picture of your company's strengths and weaknesses, in light of the goals that you want to achieve. If, after evaluating yourself thoroughly, you feel that an affiliation with another company would be helpful to your long-run objectives, the same analysis becomes a helpful source of strong points to use in merchandising your company with a prospective suitor. Do you have an ability to move into new markets and/or new products? Can you outsell your competition anytime? Are your profit margins better than most? All such points become selling points that increase the value of your firm. Your knowledge of your strengths will also help you to define what kind of company you would be happiest with.

Don't let the uses of that analysis end there. If you've been frank with yourself and have really given your operation the thought it deserves, sometime in the course of your intense soul-searching with your key people you'll ignite with a spark of intense excitement and begin to glow. Your attention will have been freed from the narrow vision of day-to-day involvements and small defeats and you'll suddenly begin to see broadly and into the future the full range of what you can *really do* with your company. The message is: *Do it.* Write out your goals (by sales, profits, product and market) for one, three, five years. Then write out both your strengths and a program for improving the weak areas of your organization to meet your goals. If you know what's needed, set up a strategy to bring it into existence; if you don't know how to handle certain areas such as management or reporting systems, make a point of finding out what it is you don't know, and then how to do it. Start shaping your organization in response to the goals of your long-range vision. You may even discover that you don't need to merge.

If you stay on the track of your exactly perceived purpose you will maintain your enthusiasm and your long-range view of the company's aims; you'll always have the energy to keep molding your company in the direction of the ideals you've set up for it. By following out your plans you achieve several other things. First, if you've decided that you should join forces with another company sometime down the line, the record of active building up and improving of your organization is the best recommendation for any acquirer. Enthusiasm and clear purpose are infectious and, when supported by a demonstrated record of achievement, make the acquirer hungry for you. Second, since you know where you want to go, you will see with clearer eyes the compatibility of potential suitors and be able to select a few to keep an eye on while you're still grooming your company.

At the time you feel you're ready to talk merger/acquisition, there's nothing like taking the initiative. There was once a Kievan prince by the name of Vladimir Monomakh, who, when the ferocious Pecheneg steppe-dwellers threatened war, would always act first; he always sent his enemies the message, "Prepare yourselves, I march on you." Put yourself into Vladimir's frame of mind. Acquirers have many reasons for buying a company. The buyer may be looking for a foothold in new markets or good management or good assets or some talent that will make his investment worthwhile. It is reasonable to assume that a good acquirer almost always knows why he wants to buy. This usually gives him a number of advantages: of initiative, of timing, and of strategic advantage. A seller, on the other hand, far less often sells with as clear a plan in mind. He may sell for the wrong reasons or at the wrong time or to the wrong buyer — or he may fail to sell. He may sell defensively, needing capital or management or access to new markets; he may look for an easy out by selling. He may be, simply, overawed. None of this helps him because he is essentially *reacting* instead of making a sound case for himself and choosing his own acquirer. But when you have a positive plan that defines in action your own strengths and goals and already defines to some extent the kind of acquirer you would be happy with, you can begin to meet the acquirer on his own terms. Take the initiative by anticipating what he wants and making a sound case for it. Let him know you're prepared. Don't leave it to him to perceive your strengths and goals; *sell him*. That's sending Vladimir's message.

REORGANIZE YOUR COMPANY — AND BALANCE SHEETS — TO SHOW TAXABLE PROFITS

Packaging your company for sale to a corporate investor requires not only a clear definition of your present business and future goals but also a balance sheet and an income statement that will show off your company in the most favorable light and maximize its value. Builders historically have kept accounts and measured profits on a project-by-project basis instead of on a per-year-earnings basis. Since most acquirers, whether major builders or non-housing corporations, operate on an annual-accounts basis — and, indeed, keep score of quarterly performance — you will have to recast both your accounting methods and your operations on a basis consistent with theirs. For one thing, your project planning may have to be better co-ordinated so that you have new projects coming onstream in rising volume as others are sold out, with the result that your sales and earnings will show a steadily rising curve. You will find yourself placing more emphasis on marketing and paying more attention to the timing of closings. The idea is to regear your operation into a steady producer from a project-by-project operating basis. The steady measure of quarterly performance provides the discipline for whatever improvements may be required in your organization's management.

Your earnings history is important. The acquirer will want to review your past achievements in accounting terms that are comparable to his. Therefore, you will have to get a competent accounting firm to restate your old project-by-project accounting records on an annual-accounts basis compatible with that of the acquirer. Remember, you want to establish convincing proof of a rising earnings trend in your past activities. Include in the consolidated recast earnings statement of your past performance all predecessor companies and realty assets that you may have spun off into separate entities for tax purposes. A privately held building company usually does everything possible to shelter income from taxes, but since an acquirer will look for your earnings power, you will have to restate your past performance on the "as if" principle: as if the multiple entities had been a single company and realty holdings were sold for taxable profit instead of being tucked away. The job of recasting is a sophisticated one, but it has often been done.

Recasting your records and your operation to reflect earnings is a sizable but necessary task if your business has been to build and hold apartment properties. Apartments, with their depreciation, are greatly desired as a personal tax shelter but become a liability to a company interested in maximizing annual profits, because the depreciation eats into earnings. This is one reason why homebuilders were the first to be snapped up in the merger wave in real estate: the homebuilder (or mobile-home manufacturer) makes a product for immediate sale and can report an income statement that investors can easily equate with earnings of other companies. But the company whose earnings consist mainly of cash flow from ownership of income-producing real estate has a more difficult time. As acquirers are interested in recurrent high earnings, the developer who has been accustomed to building and holding apartments must usually switch over to a build-and-sell type of operation. (Many private builders run their business on the basis of their own convenience. They take very substantial salaries and have depreciable assets to shelter them. The company may be showing no profit while the president is taking out $300,000 in annual pay. A business that serves as a personal convenience structure must be restructured to be attractive as an acquisition.)

The proposed tax revisions on apartment tax investment complicate the picture, but prior to 1973 there were ways to handle this by segregating your assets. For example, let's say you were a developer holding 700 apartment units with depreciation flowing from them. You could create leasebacks for the apartments, putting them into a separate entity or leaving them in partnership or in private hands, thus segregating the depreciable assets from the cash flow. Your company now became a profit-reporting organization as the result of its lease position with respect to those apartments. This entity could become a developer of future apartments, collecting a construction fee reportable for tax purposes and selling off apartment projects to syndicates or private or institutional investors.

Ronald Rosenfeld, president of Multiplex, Inc., a Cleveland apartment developer which in 1969 merged with Titan Group, provided a hypothetical illustration shortly after his own merger of an apartment development company restructuring itself for merger purposes:

1965: A and B form a partnership, the X Company. During this year they build 200 units, which they retain.

1966: The X Company added C to the staff to obtain mortgages for the X Company and any other developer that wanted to use his services. D was added to the staff to be in charge of construction. E was added to build condominiums. In 1966 the X Company built 400 apartments, which were retained, and built and sold 50 condominium units.

1967: In this year money was tight, so X Company built 600 apartments for outside investors on a fee-per-suite basis. The X Company built

100 apartments for its own account. The company sold the 200 units it built in 1965 and put the profits into Treasury notes. This year the firm added F to the staff to manage its properties and the properties of outsiders. The company also added G to do architecture for the firm and for outsiders.

1968: The X Company built 700 suites for outside investors, 300 for its own account plus 200 apartment units for the elderly under the HUD program, and sold 200 condominiums.

1969: A and B decide they want to enter a stock-for-stock merger. They form the Y Corporation, which will derive all its income from fees paid by outside investors for apartments that the Y Corporation will build for them — fees from mortgage procurement, fees from architectural services, management fees, profits from sale of condominiums, profits from work done under the HUD program. The Corporation is capitalized with the Treasury notes that the X Company possesses. The real estate holdings are kept out of the Y Corporation, since the depreciation would cause a dilution of the earnings.

In effect, Rosenfeld concluded, A and B restructured operations to be attractive to a corporate suitor. They had the ingredients and through restructuring achieved the appropriate form.

THE ROLE OF THE ACCOUNTANT

Your accountant is an important part of your operation at any time, but he becomes positively invaluable at the time you begin preparing yourself for a merger sally. In most instances he is not only the person who sets up the sophisticated reporting techniques that you need to run your business well but also the one who will prepare and recast the financial statements showing your performance, monitor the company's accounting principles to be consistent with the most recent rulings of the American Institute of Certified Public Accountants and advise you on the optimal consolidation of your multiple entities at the time you start planning for a merger.

A good accountant is, in fact, usually better equipped to evaluate a merger than anyone else from the pure numbers angle and, working from an audited statement of your financial performance, should play an important role in merger negotiations as a technical consultant. He could help both merger principals to develop a sales price that will be the best one possible. He may be familiar with the tax consequences of a transaction, and how securities laws affect the reporting and structuring of the transactions, as he works alongside your tax and SEC attorney. The accountant whose business it is to stay on top of all merger trends in the industry will, in short, package you up and advise you financially so that you can make the best deal. Not all perform complete consulting services. But, the ideal, as one of them says, is to supply information that will "relate the deal to the real world. Is your client getting a good deal or a bad deal in relation to other things going on and other deals being made?"

The accountant will work from two important financial tools that you will normally need to have him develop before you implement any merger venture. The first of these is a certified or audited financial statement showing your organization's performance for at least the preceding three years. A certified statement that shows you at your best is one of your best tools in estimating your value and thus securing a good price in merger negotiations. Without it, the acquirer will conduct his own audit of your books and you'll have to take whatever offer he makes without knowing if it is adequate. (After U.S. Home's experience with its acquisition of 3H Building Corp., the acquirer may go over your numbers for himself, no matter *how* certified your statement is.) Relatively few privately owned building companies before 1970 had any history of certified statements, and when they did it was on a basis more suitable for income-tax purposes than for a merger foray. A good accounting firm can give you a statement that will present your company in the best light, consistent with generally accepted accounting principles. The bigger companies that went the merger route in the late Sixties and early Seventies prepared for this eventuality by having certified statements for years beforehand. And the certified statement is increasingly required for joint-venture deals and other financing arrangements. If you haven't started getting your financials independently audited and validated, it would be a good idea to do so now.

The second important tool is a three-year projection and strategy plan for your company and its performance, including projected earnings and cash flow. This will be the financial vertebrae of your written documentation of future projects and profits. It is the timetable that shows the acquirer how your business will become more valuable. It takes a great deal of hard thinking and planning to project your activities three to five years ahead, project by project. But this develops a clear track for your future activities, as well as a clear case for your future earnings power. Your accountant translates this into earnings projections, and, of course, these establish a value for your company. Be cautious and realistic in these projections. They are viewed as having little meaning if projected further out than your presently available inventory of land. You could lose your credibility with a knowledgeable acquirer by showing him a three-year projection without any inventory in hand.

A CHECKLIST ON GROOMING FOR MERGER

1. Decide and define in writing what business the company is in. Homebuilding? Land development? Apartments? This will help future

analysis of profits, so that an occasional high-profit land sale is classed as an extraordinary and not recurring item.

2. Define your short-term goals for a one- or two-year period. These should include the approximate rate of diversification geographically and by product type. What percentage of your efforts will be devoted to residential housing, rental or other?

3. Develop realistic long-term goals for your company, covering at least ten years, and set up the strategy for achieving them.

4. Plan for in-depth management, because your company will normally not be appealing unless key positions of marketing, finance, forward planning, and construction are well filled and backed up by good understudies. Start developing good management early. Consider a profit-sharing pension trust or stock option or other appropriate incentive plan that will enlist management's incentive for the long term.

5. Very early and very clearly separate your personal real estate holdings from company properties. This is also the point at which to enlist a national accounting firm to advise you, and to begin getting audited statements.

6. Develop a total corporate image, including a corporate logo, and distinguishing motifs of advertising and publicity. Consult your accountant on the best timing for eliminating your multiple corporations and putting them under one roof prior to merger.

7. Prepare an internal company profile, including the description of activities, product lines and depth of management, including backgrounds of your key people.

8. Get your house in order with respect to general organizational responsibility. Organization, procedure, management and control techniques should be clearly delineated.

9. Prepare a condensed summary of earnings for a minimum of five years, plus a comparative current short period and a balance sheet on revised accounting principles making appropriate restatements and recastings where necessary.

10. Prepare a three-year projection and strategy plan including projected earnings and cash flow.

11. Review the company's accounting principles and differences between financial and tax reporting, considering the following questions:

   a. Have all corporations and partnerships been consolidated?
   b. Have predecessor companies or assets that were included in your name which would be part of the earnings trend been included?
   c. Has a decision been made with respect to presentation on the balance sheet of current and non-current assets?
   d. Have major accounting decisions been made with respect to real

estate inventory, including allocation of land and related improvement costs; what costs should be capitalized (i.e., interest, taxes,
overhead); and sales costs — are these product costs or period
expenses?

e. Has an accounting principle been established with respect to when
   a sale is a sale, and the related reserves, including imputing interest?

f. Have deferred taxes been considered with respect to differences
   in reporting between statement and tax; i.e., installment sales, cash
   vs. accrual and capitalization policies?

HOW THE ACQUIRER GOES ABOUT HIS WORK

A look at the basic principles by which the sophisticated corporate
acquirer operates will provide a starting insight on preparing your company
for the merger gambit. This setup exists more in theory than in practice.
What happens is that after all the corporate rigmarole of abstract analysis,
the way an acquisition is formed is by somebody happening to mention to
somebody else that this or that company is available. But the theoretical
approach is still useful to see.

The Acquisition Department has the job of searching for companies
to acquire along lines laid out by corporate policy. Its functions include:

1. Monitoring markets and industries the company presently serves
and developing projections of future performance of these markets and
industries and the company's performance in them.

2. Monitoring markets and industries in which the company doesn't
operate but in which it has a policy interest, to be aware of their growth
rates and of any unusual economic and technological developments. This
includes watching individual performance of companies in each market or
industry to be aware of how well they're doing relative to their industry.

3. Taking on investigative projects leading to recommendations of
specific companies as acquisition candidates.

4. Making up priority listings of companies to be approached as
acquisition candidates and preparing reports in support of such recommendations.

5. Investigating candidates for acquisition, coordinating the activities
of various departments of the company called in on such investigations.

6. Preparing final recommendations on the acquisition candidates, including recommendations on how much the company should pay, the form
of the transaction, and the best way to approach the deal.

7. Conducting acquisition negotiations.

WHAT THE ACQUIRER LOOKS FOR: BASIC FACTORS

1. *Management.* Management is critical. Homebuilding is a local market business. A large number of key management decisions are made at the local level. As a result, it is extremely important for a company to have strong, experienced entrepreneurial and professional management at the division level.

The acquirer will prefer those companies which have been able to reduce the entrepreneurial functions at the divisional level by such factors as regional buying of key land parcels, regional production facilities, centralized financing, etc. He will also prefer those companies which have anchored their markets with at least one large long-term project. These policies reduce the company's dependence on one or two divisional people and provide a stability to operations.

There is a definite shortage of senior divisional management in the industry. It is essential that candidate companies provide career opportunities for middle and top management. In addition, most management should already be in place. Homebuilders that will succeed will be managed by experienced, well-motivated professionals with high morale. Rapid turnover in a management organization is a danger signal for future problems.

2. *Market analysis.* Market analysis should focus on local market position. It is essential to evaluate the opportunities and risks involved in attempting to increase share of market in each specific area. Total national housing starts or national vacancy rates may not necessarily present a meaningful index to measure the outlook for a particular homebuilder. Total statistics for a metropolitan region could also be misleading. Each metropolitan market area is really comprised of at least thirty to forty submarkets, each of which have their own demand patterns. For example, a homebuilder building single-family homes in Florida would certainly not be influenced by a slowdown in rental housing demand in California. In addition, a company building low-priced, single-family homes in the southwest quadrant of Miami may not be affected by a slowdown in the demand for high-priced condominiums in the northeast sector of Miami.

The following factors are important in market analysis: (a) A homebuilder should have at least some multimarket operations in order to reduce exposure to any one market and a proven history of successfully expanding into new markets and submarkets. Only a few builders have successfully expanded into new geographic market regions. Therefore, the acquirer should be very wary of those companies which are expanding into new markets without a prior record of multimarket success. (b) A home-builder's market penetration in each of its markets should be determined. If possible, the total penetration of all the major builders in the market should also be estimated. (c) One of the key factors for success in any local market is the ability of divisional management to consistently identify the specific submarkets within a given area. Most homebuilders build only the most popular priced, average housing product and have very little talent for identifying and capitalizing on the submarkets. (d) The acquirer will also be impressed with homebuilders which have demonstrated the ability to achieve a dominant position in a major market. In many cases, this is the result of long-term consumer loyalty which has evolved because of the company's ability to produce a quality product in a quality location and environment. The development of such a consumer franchise provides the homebuilder with a significant competitive edge. Assuming sufficient management depth, it is reasonable to expect that the company can de-velop similar consumer loyalties in other markets in subsequent years.

It is difficult to precisely define the optimum level of penetration in a specific market. Historically, it has been assumed that the maximum pene-tration of a specific geographic market by a major builder was approxi-mately 10% to 15%. However, as of the early Seventies there have been an increasing number of cases where a major builder has obtained 20% to 30% of a market. For example, Ryan Homes in Pittsburgh, Centex in Dallas, Lennar in Miami, and Robino-Ladd in Delaware have all achieved and consistently maintained penetration in excess of 15% in these markets. One of the key factors in enabling these companies to sustain their market penetration has been their ability to develop a consumer franchise. Kauf-man & Broad in Toronto and U.S. Home in western Florida are other companies that have developed consumer franchises, which are enabling them to obtain a consistently increased share of these markets.

(e) Companies which have demonstrated the ability to profitably enter the secondary markets, such as Louisville, Indianapolis, or Gaines-ville, have an excellent long-term outlook. There are a great number of these markets in the country and they provide an unusual opportunity for future growth with limited major homebuilder competition.

3. *Product.* Analysis of product mix is important. Similar to market analysis, it is dependent on the local market situation. For example, if total starts in Houston are expected to decline, the decline may only be occur-ring in multifamily rentals. If demand declines for single-family detached homes in New Jersey, it is quite possible that demand for condominiums near New York City would continue to be strong. Demand for high-priced units may decline while demand for low-priced units may increase. Product analysis requires consideration of a number of interrelated factors such as:

(a) *Diversity of product line.* A homebuilder should have the capability to produce and market a diversified product mix in order to be able to switch emphasis from one product line to another if consumer demand shifts. Such products would include single family, condos, low priced, high priced, rental apartments, land, etc.

(b) *Complementary products.* Homebuilders should have a complementary product mix to their homebuilding operations in order to provide a greater degree of diversity. For example, these products would include insurance, commercial development (shopping centers, office parks), and building materials. The earnings of the pure stick homebuilder could be vulnerable to a severe decline in housing starts.

(c) *Product quality.* The ability to consistently provide quality housing for the consumers in a specific market can result in a consumer franchise. More important, the failure to consistently provide quality housing can be one of the most important factors in loss of market share.

(d) *Product differentiation.* As the major homebuilders continue to enter new market areas, a key factor to success will be the ability to differentiate its product from that of its competitors. The key factors in product differentiation are location, cost and quality.

(e) *Customer analysis.* Similar to product diversity, a diversified customer mix is also necessary. For example, those companies which have a significant portion of their product mix directed toward retirees have a distinct advantage during periods of high mortgage rates and tight money because retirees usually pay cash (or mostly cash) and require either no mortgage or a very low mortgage.

(f) *Price.* An analysis of household incomes indicates that about 50% have incomes under $10,000. Therefore the homebuilders must be able to develop a low-cost product mix in order to penetrate the majority of the market.

(g) *Interior/exterior amenities.* Properly designed amenities can result in product differentiation. Exterior amenities such as open parks, tennis courts, clubhouse, etc., are desired by many consumers.

(h) *Quality Control.* Quality control is an important factor in assuring a high quality product. Many builders are beginning to develop and implement quality control procedures.

(i) *Environment.* It is important to realize that many consumers are now demanding more than just a house. They want a total environment. Therefore, those companies which can provide attractive and real communities will have a significant competitive advantage.

4. *Financing.* Financing is a broad category that includes the major categories of capital financing, construction financing, and mortgage financing. Sophisticated and skillful financial management is one of the most

important factors for success in the industry. Homebuilding is a capital intensive business and may become increasingly more capital intensive. Therefore, access to long-term capital will be a critical factor to long-term profitability and success.

A strong balance sheet is essential. However, a careful analysis of balance sheets and company operations is necessary to obtain meaningful comparisons. For example, some companies use option agreements rather than purchase money mortgages (non-recourse debt). Both techniques achieve the same objective and have similar risks, but the purchase money mortgage is carried on the balance sheet as debt while an option is not. With non-recourse debt the company is not directly liable as the lender has recourse only to the particular property. So, adequate balance sheet analysis requires a careful evaluation of both the stated liabilities and footnotes in order to obtain a clear picture of how current and future operations are likely to be financed and the real exposure the corporation is assuming in financing its activities.

Some homebuilders have developed and retained ownership of income producing properties such as shopping centers. These properties are carried on the asset side of the balance sheet at cost even though they would produce a gross profit of at least 20% to 25% if sold. In addition, long-term debt (approximating cost) is carried on the liability side of the balance sheet. However, this debt is also non-recourse debt. In addition, the ownership of these properties results in unrealized profit which is not reflected in net income, thereby understating the company's net worth. In effect, what appears to be increased leverage could be a hidden source of real equity and cash which may actually facilitate the ability to finance future activities.

5. *Cost controls.* Most small homebuilders have ineffective cost control systems. Unfortunately, however, even an excellent cost control system does not prevent serious cost overruns caused by rising material prices and shortages, weather delays, labor unrest and environmental delays. Even the most well-managed companies have certain projects which do not meet original cost expectations. The effective solutions are: cost control systems which provide an early warning so that corrective action can be immediately taken, and multiproject operations which enable a few bad projects to be balanced by many good projects.

Necessary controls include monthly income and balance sheets, cost, and cash controls per division and operating, inventory, and new order controls per project per week. The acquirer may prefer those companies which subcontract almost all of their operations; this procedure provides known fixed costs before the houses are sold. However, it is important to note that in-house control of certain operations can be both desirable and necessary. Ryan Homes, for example, controls much of the prefab building procedure at company lumber yards. Development Corp. of America controls its own land development work in its markets where good land development subcontractors are at a premium.

A key factor in controlling operational costs can be the homebuilder's relationship with his subcontractors. Those companies which have long established relationships with the quality subcontractors in a market can have competitive advantage. Most of those companies which have lost control of their costs in new geographic markets have done so because of the difficulties of working with new subs.

6. *Land.* Some acquirers have been unfamiliar with land and consequently feel uncomfortable with companies utilizing land in their operations. This has been compounded by the wide publicity received by the retail land sales companies (such as Deltona) in recent years. Corporate acquirers probably have been further confused because, until recently, very few companies dealt in land as part of their on-going operations. A land sale by a manufacturing company was always considered an extraordinary item. So, it is important to clarify three points in the analysis of a builder for acquisition:

(a) A homebuilder is not a retail land sales company.

(b) A homebuilder uses land as a raw material. In fact, land is the most important raw material in homebuilding and is the only natural resource the company can control.

(c) A homebuilder creates value in his land by building houses and thus also creates important residual by-products such as shopping center sites or surplus housing sites. The sale of these residual land sites creates income for a homebuilder because it is an on-going natural portion of its business. This function can be abused, to be sure, but it can also be a valid source of profit. It will be up to the acquirer to analyze the builder's residual land sales carefully, in order to establish whether such sales have reflected real or bloated values. Properly done, development does create added value on residual sites. The function is analogous to an oil company which processes crude oil and sells the product at various stages depending on an analysis of values. In addition, the oil company creates and sells chemicals as a by-product of its oil operations. The sale of oil products at various refining stages or of the chemical by-products are normal recurring income for the oil company as is the sale of land by-products for the homebuilder.

Long-range land planning has become extremely important because of increased environmental and complex zoning considerations. Communities are now more concerned about the type of growth they will tolerate. More time is required for planning, research, and municipal approvals. The developer who builds the usual subdivision tracts may find it increasingly difficult to obtain community approvals. Most homebuilders are volume-oriented merchandisers. They lack either the capital resources or the integrated management skills and experience necessary to develop a sophisticated land strategy.

The competitive, environmental and aesthetic demands of the Seventies will result in the greater emergence of the fully integrated community developer, a trend discussed in Chapter 2. The land strategies of these companies will be characterized by the following factors:

(a) Large parcels of land (300–3,000 acres) will be acquired for a four to ten year building program.

(b) The land will be analyzed and planned to achieve the maximum results for both the community and the company.

(c) The land design will include commercial, industrial, and recreational park sections as well as the traditional residential sections. The master plan will be developed in accordance with population growth and community requirements.

(d) The companies will have substantial capital resources. Access to long-term capital will be a critical factor to long-term success.

Homebuilders having the skills to become community developers will obtain the following advantages from such a land strategy:

(a) Large projects provide a degree of stability to operations since the project is operational over a long period of time. The company does not have to search constantly for new land parcels and new and improved locations.

(b) The long-term development of the large project will create additional land values from the steady increase in population. The company benefits from rising land values. Land appreciation is maximized and provides an important earnings by-product. In addition, the company will derive important cost and competitive advantages as the land surrounding the project increases in value and becomes more costly for other builders to buy. This cost advantage can produce a lower product cost or result in higher profit margins.

(c) The problems of immediate land availability will be reduced because of the long-term nature of the project.

(d) The company will be providing a well-planned community environment, which should appeal to many consumers and result in additional competitive advantages.

(e) Many merchant homebuilders have very little expertise in complex community planning and large project development. In addition, the capital requirements of such projects can be substantial. These factors create additional competitive advantages for the community developer.

However, because of the risks and capital requirements of large projects, a homebuilder must diversify his land and project mix as he does his market and product mix. In other words, the company should also be developing a number of smaller projects. Because local market conditions can be quite different, a unilateral land strategy would not be rational. For example, a land strategy in the rapidly growing markets of Florida and New Jersey would probably be quite different from the strategy in Western Pennsylvania.

7. *Production.* Most homebuilders utilize subcontractors for on-site lot development and housing construction. Companies which are able to obtain a high unit volume per project or market area are able to utilize volume buying which provides a number of advantages including:

(a) Lower raw material and product costs per unit.

(b) Lower lot costs.

(c) Lower subcontractor costs per unit.

(d) Ability to obtain raw material products when demand is strong.

(e) Better control over costs because of long-term firm commitments.

Most homebuilders build speculative houses, i.e., the houses are started before a new order is received. For the small, undercapitalized companies, this philosophy can result in serious financial difficulty when demand slows down. However, for the larger, well-capitalized homebuilders, a rational inventory program is a sound procedure for the following reasons:

(a) It enables the company to better program its production flow. In other words, if a project is selling ten houses per week and should continue to do so, it would appear logical to start ten houses per week even though the houses started may not be sold. If sales continue, the houses would soon be sold.

(b) Those markets which are characterized by heavy in-migration of population require inventory housing to meet the current demand for immediate housing.

(c) A homebuilder is a retailer and, as do other retailers, should have some inventory on hand to meet the immediate demand which is a submarket in itself.

An inventory program should be carefully monitored from both product and market factors.

Homebuilders are not modular home companies. Most homebuilders have understood that modular home construction will not occur in the industry for at least the next ten years. However, a number of companies, such as Ryan Homes, have been able to develop efficient in-plant production of prefab housing packages. Ryan Homes and the Fox & Jacobs division of Centex are probably the industry leaders in low-rise housing production techniques. These companies produce interior and exterior wall panels, stairs, prehung doors and windows, roof trusses, cabinets, flooring systems, and various interior and exterior trim. In-plant production provides the following advantages over on-site housing: The average in-plant wage is less than half on-site wage costs; better cost control; better quality control; improved production flow; better inventory control and less shrinkage.

Many homebuilders have stated that, according to their analysis, in-plant production does *not* offer any cost advantages over volume on-site production. However, based on an analysis of Ryan Homes, Centex, and Forest City Enterprises (in-plant production of high-rise core units), in-plant prefabrication can offer many advantages. In addition, because of escalating on-site labor costs, the cost advantages of in-plant production should increase in subsequent years. This is particularly relevant in high-rise construction. Most of the typical homebuilders do not build high-rise construction and, therefore, a complete review of this topic is not included here. However, those companies which can develop a building system to reduce high-rise construction costs will have a significant opportunity for growth during the next decade. Currently, Forest City Enterprises is the only domestic company which appears to have an effective high-rise system. Their system is based on prefab modular core units, precast concrete components and cast in place concrete. Forest City's system has been in operation for more than a year and has resulted in a savings in time of up to 67%.

An important long-term advantage of in-plant production and prefabrication could be the ability to penetrate many smaller cities by selling housing packages to the small homebuilders and/or directly to consumers in those cities. National Homes has been relatively successful in developing this marketing/production strategy. Kaufman and Broad and Ryan Homes also initiated operations to serve these smaller markets.

The mobile home does not offer a competitive product to a conventionally built house and is *not* a cheaper form of housing. Even though a mobile home may cost only $7,000–$9,000, significant monthly costs (in addition to the mortgage) are incurred because:

    (a) The mobile home purchaser must either lease ($70–$80 a month) or buy a site ($5,000–$6,000).

    (b) Monthly financing costs are quite high because of a higher mortgage rate and shorter amortization period. The interest rate on a mobile home purchase is typically 10–12% versus 7–8%

for a house; the length of the loan is usually 8–10 years (with some FHA financing up to 15 years) compared to 20–30 years for a house.

(c) A significant hidden cost for a mobile home is depreciation. Mobile homes depreciate while well-located conventional houses usually appreciate.

(d) In addition, a mobile home offers less value, less construction quality (mobile homes could not pass rigid construction standards required for houses), and less square footage than a conventional house.

Those homebuilders who can build townhouses, condominiums and quadplexes in the $15,000–$24,000 range can offer residential housing at a real monthly cost equal to that of most mobile homes. Therefore, most of the growth potential for mobile homes must result from those consumers who prefer that form of housing and style of living and who cannot obtain the necessary financing for conventional housing.

However, the real profit potential is in the marketing, retail, and land sectors of the business rather than in the production sector. Therefore, it is the merchant homebuilders who have the opportunity to capitalize on the demand for mobile homes because the homebuilders are *consumer* oriented. U.S. Home and Centex, for example, began developing mobile home parks and retailing mobile homes.

8. *Income statement.* The accounting practices of homebuilders have received a great deal of publicity during the past two years. Two basic points should be clarified:

(a) Homebuilders sell their houses for *cash*. Generally, their net income is *cash* income. Profit is recorded when the house is built and delivered to the consumer, not when a sales contract is signed.

(b) Most companies follow sound accounting procedures. But, as in any industry, quality of earnings is important. The earnings statements and balance sheets should be closely inspected for bogus land sales, second trust deeds, expressed vs. capitalized taxes, etc.

It should be emphasized that, fundamentally, quarterly EPS results are not necessarily relevant to total year's earnings or to a company's actual progress during the year.

9. *Balance sheet.* A strong balance sheet and adequate sources of capital are essential to continued growth because homebuilding is a capital intensive industry. The acquirer will prefer those homebuilders which utilize bank lines of credit, permanent funds and their own working capital rather than high-cost construction loans. He will also prefer those com-

panies which have demonstrated the ability to successfully buy large tracts of land in quality locations. Since land is quoted on the balance sheet at cost, many homebuilders may have understated equity accounts because the land may have appreciated sharply in value as a result of the homebuilders' skill in zoning, community planning, initial development and inflation. In other words, the intangible, value-creating skills of a homebuilder can be extremely important in creating values for the company which are not fully reflected until the product is sold, even though the value is well established prior to the sale.

10. *New orders/backlog.* These are two of the key items to monitor in determining a homebuilder's short-term future progress. If the new order rate declines for two or three consecutive months, the homebuilder is probably experiencing demand difficulties in its markets. The continuation of such a trend would inevitably produce declining revenues and profits. A rising new order pattern usually indicates increased future revenues.

Backlog is also important as a determinant of future activity. However, backlog is a function of both new orders and the production rate. Therefore, an unusual trend in either direction could signal problems. For example, a declining backlog could be a reflection of declining new orders or an increased production rate. Conversely, a rising backlog could be an indication of production problems which would ultimately cause cost overruns and lower profit margins. The acquirer will look for companies whose backlog is approximately four to six months of production. The major exceptions would be those companies which have price escalators in their new order contracts or have secured all product costs.

11. *Investment building.* A number of homebuilders are recognizing the inherent quality of recurring income and are starting to build and develop a small portfolio of income-producing properties such as rental apartments, shopping centers, recreational leases and land leases. In most cases, this is the highest quality cash flow a builder can generate since the leases provide a recurring income stream.

Even though the builder may develop these properties one year and expense all associated overhead, the company's income statement for that year would not reflect the profits from the projects if these projects are not sold. In effect, the builder has deferred a certain portion of his income into some future year.

In summary, there are a number of significant benefits which occur to a builder utilizing this concept.

1. It creates a recurring income stream.

2. It creates a substantial deferred income for future years and, therefore, enhances the possibility of continued future earnings gains.

3. It lowers current year earnings in order to enhance future year earnings and, therefore, raises the quality of the current year's income.

4. It provides a substantial source of future cash flow and capital. Since the leases pay the mortgage each year, the builder benefits from the equity buildup in the project and from a continued rate of inflation.

5. It strengthens the builders' balance sheet, because of the increase in equity values.

Builders utilizing this concept should be carefully analyzed to determine the buildup in equity values and resultant deferred income which is being created.

MAJOR PROBLEMS AND RISK FACTORS

As previously emphasized, homebuilding is a local market/product business. National trends do not necessarily provide meaningful information with which to analyze a particular homebuilder. However, national data do provide information which should be considered, particularly if such data indicate unfavorable trends.

Some of the risks and problem areas which must be considered follow:

1. The availability and cost of money is one of the most important factors in determining the actual level of demand. During 1973 the money markets reacted to both the high rate of inflation and a tightening of monetary policies. Consequently, both short-term interest rates and mortgage rates sharply increased. The savings flow into thrift institutions declined 27% through May 1973.

In order to bolster the savings inflow into savings and loans and to stem possible disintermediation, the interest rate levels that savings & loans and banks could pay their depositors was increased. However, the basic result of this program was that S&L's had to charge significantly higher mortgage rates to cover the higher cost of obtaining funds. In addition, the S&L's began requiring larger down payments. In many states these mortgage rates rose above the state usury limit. The higher rates definitely priced many consumers out of the market and resulted in a sharp decline in housing starts.

Total mortgage credit demands in 1973 exceeded the availability of mortgage money even with the secondary mortgage market (FNMA, Federal Home Loan Bank Board, etc.) providing $12 billion in mortgage money. This further contributed to the housing decline. A reasonable government monetary policy was expected to swing into effect, resulting in a housing starts level of approximately 1.6–1.8 million units in 1974. However, since the supply and cost of money are only *short-run* determinants in the level of housing demand, the temporary dislocations in demand caused by expensive money must be made up in the future.

2. Because of their rapid growth, most of the companies do not have

an adequate supply of management. Therefore, the ability to attract and retain capable top middle management is a critical factor in assuring the future growth of a homebuilder.

3. The price of houses has increased rapidly in the past few years. The price index increased 6.3% in 1972 and was expected to increase by a minimum of 8% (per sq. ft.) in 1973. The cost of land, labor, and materials have all increased sharply since 1970. In early 1973 the median price of a home was $32,800 compared to $26,700 in April 1972. A higher priced house eliminates consumers from the market because of higher down payment and monthly carrying charges.

4. Increasing environmental pressures have made it more difficult and more costly to open new housing projects. Such factors as increased fees for utility connections, sewer moratoria, restrictive zoning, excessive land for parks and schools are all affecting the availability of buildable land. Even though these pressures and restrictions have increased the difficulty and cost of operations, they have also accelerated the demise of many of the smaller homebuilders. Therefore, the major builders could benefit from this trend. However, it should be noted that these restraints can cause unexpected project delays which influence earnings on a quarterly basis.

5. Housing production will be adversely affected by the elimination of many government housing programs, as the powers-that-be plan an urban orientation to future subsidy programs. Therefore, if the demand for conventional housing declines more than expected, the homebuilders will not be able to rely on any government programs to support their earnings.

6. In April 1973 the ratio of homes for sale to homes sold reached 7.9, the highest level ever and substantially above the 5.7 ratio of April 1972. This ratio indicated slower sales and, therefore, overbuilding. It is emphasized that a market and product analysis is necessary to determine the implications of this ratio for any particular homebuilder. However, it appears reasonable to expect over-building to occur in certain markets in the mid-Seventies. In April 1973 it took 4.8 months to sell a house compared to 3.2 months in April 1972, a further indication that supply caught up with current demand and that potential overbuilding was a real threat.

7. The major homebuilders are now operating from much larger bases. So, the opening of a new market or a new project does not have the same large favorable impact it had in 1969–1970. Consequently, it will be more difficult for these companies to grow if demand declines simultaneously in three or four markets.

8. Expansion into new geographic markets has always been very difficult for a homebuilder because of the local nature of the industry. Many public companies have experienced profit difficulties as a result of such attempted expansion. The acquirer should carefully monitor any company

which is attempting to expand into unfamiliar markets without the necessary management.

9. Many large homebuilders (both public and private) have been expanding into the same major markets. Profit margins began eroding as the competition increased. The expertise of the national multi-market public homebuilder does not necessarily provide any advantage in such a competitive environment. The experience and skill of the particular division management is the key factor. The establishment of a consumer brand name could provide an important competitive advantage.`

10. While profit margins expanded or remained at high levels for most companies in 1971 and 1972, as of 1973 and 1974, volume increases will be more difficult to achieve, resulting in margin erosion and profit declines for many companies.

In evaluating the merchant homebuilders, the following factors should affect long term investment considerations:

1. Homebuilding is one of the nation's largest industries. In 1972 annual industry revenues exceeded $43 billion.
2. Demographic factors have created the potential for significant housing demand during the next ten years. Demand should exceed 2.0 million units per year.
3. As a result of inflation, the dollar size of the housing market should increase to $70 billion by 1982.
4. Despite negative developments in the mortgage market in 1973 and 1974, the well-managed homebuilders should be able to increase their earnings, though at a slower rate than formerly.
5. The stocks of most homebuilders have declined to extremely low values.
6. Many homebuilders are selling for *less* than their real net worth; a net worth comprised of land and houses, both inflation protection assets.

The potential does exist for the well-managed companies to sustain a high level of earnings growth over the longer term. Excluding a severe and prolonged period of tight money, the well-managed companies could still be able to double their earnings during the next four years.

HOW THE ACQUIRER WILL INVESTIGATE YOU: A CHECKLIST

Financial Condition
Financial Statement
1. Verifies the validity of its preparations and determines if an independent audit is required.
2. Obtains an objective opinion by another accountant.

Balance Sheet — including, among many other factors, these actions:
1. Evaluates accounts receivable.
2. Checks and analyzes the method of evaluation of inventory.
3. Evaluates contingent liabilities, if any.
4. Analyzes tax and depreciation history.
5. Analyzes contractual obligations.
6. Analyzes profit-and-loss statements.

Status of Assets
1. Conducts a physical inspection of facilities, inventory and equipment.
2. Performs a comparative analysis of inventory and production with company's competitors.
3. Reviews contracts, bids, etc.
4. Analyzes insurance coverage and executive and employee insurance retirement programs.
5. Investigates leasehold interests; patents and trademarks; outstanding liens such as chattel mortgages and deeds of trust; and title policies.

Position in the Marketplace
1. Analyzes the relative position of the company in its industry, labor situation, strength of management and current position of industry in the economy, plus its long-range future.
2. Determines that candidate has a reputation as responsible and respected member of the business community where he is located.

Corporate Examination — These items are covered by warranties in final written contract. If combination structure calls for a transfer or exchange of shares, the following should be investigated:
1. Legal review of corporate charter.
2. Name.
3. Validity of issuance of stock through compliance with federal and state securities laws.
4. Review of corporate documents for possible restrictions of transferability of shares or buy-out provisions.
5. Verification that the candidate is not under any litigation involving substantial potential damages.

THE ACQUIRER'S METHOD OF ACQUISITION

Corporate acquisitions as a rule have been consummated by means of non-taxable exchange of voting securities wherever:

1. The price/earnings ratios of the acquired company are comparable with, or lower than, those of the acquiring firm (if the acquired company is public).
2. The exchange basis does not dilute earnings per share of the acquiring company.
3. The tax basis of the assets of the acquired company is substantially above market value of the shares to be given, or an offsetting earnings capacity has been demonstrated. (Although not required, this is desirable.)

The foregoing sets out in a *schematic, generalized* form the way an acquirer operates. After you have digested this, you are ready to look at the very *real* and specific criteria of a specific acquirer who has been making quite a splash in the homebuilding/development industry. Test yourself against the guidelines as you read them, and we shall have some comment on them when you have gone through them. The following is the acquisition policy that U.S. Home formulated as of November 16, 1970. As this major company made more than a dozen acquisitions between 1969 and 1972, this policy was extensively implemented. The company's acquisition criteria, although revised somewhat since the issue of the following guidelines, can be regarded as quite representative of the guidelines of other major organizations seeking acquisitions among builders and developers. But USH has refined and articulated them perhaps more fully than any other organization.

HOW ONE BUILDER-ACQUIRER HAS OPERATED

U.S. Home's Acquisition Program for the Three-Year Period Ending February 28, 1974

I. *Objective:*
   To increase the long-term earnings per share of U.S. Home by a program of external growth.

II. *Preferred acquisitions are those that meet the following guidelines:*
    (The guidelines listed below should not be considered a checklist where failure to meet one or more criteria would automatically reject the acquisition. These values, however, are to be considered in proposing an acquisition to the Board. The ultimate recommendation would be based upon the opinion that the company to be acquired would increase our long-term earnings per share.)
    1. Company should be in the real estate or construction industry (see Appendix One). The total mix of U.S. Home consolidated sales should remain under approximately 20% in supplies, service, or vertically related business.

2. Personal chemistry of the principals is satisfactory. The seller's long-range goals are compatible with those of U.S. Home.

3. After-tax profit of $250,000 minimum ($500,000 for companies listed west of the Rocky Mountains).

   Where the company is located close enough to another U.S. Home subsidiary to be controlled through that subsidiary should it be deemed necessary by U.S. Home, then after-tax profit may be less than $250,000 but not less than $100,000.

4. *Projection for the next three years believable to U.S. Home of growth equal to or better than U.S. Home internal rate. If only equal to, then all of our profit must be in the purchase price. For companies where we can project considerably higher growth rates than U.S. Home internal, we can pay up to the point of dilution.* [Author's italics.]

5. Selling company should be able to specify its own management deficiencies.

6. *It is desirable that ROI (return on investment) be equal to or better than our own.* [Author's italics.] If below ours, there should be reason to expect that after acquisition we can bring it up to the U.S. Home planned ROI.

7. Operational quality of the business, quality of the product, and reputation in the community should be equal to or better than U.S. Home.

8. *The price paid should yield a projection which will increase our earnings per share over the five year, earnout period.* [Guidelines were formulated prior to elimination of earnout from poolings.] We seek anti-dilution at purchase and a projection of increase in our earnings per share due to projected growth of the new acquisition.

9. The principals of the company are willing and able to increase the acquired company's rate of growth by entering new segments of the industry.

10. Start-up risks are past.

11. Incoming company is less than half the size of U.S. Home.

III. *Volume of external growth desired:*

	Internal Volume	External Growth	Total Volume
Fiscal '71	$ 52	$ 55	$107
Fiscal '72	125	65	190
Fiscal '73	225	100	325
Fiscal '74	390	110	500

IV. *Method:*

1. Determine which segments of the industry U.S. Home wishes to enter.

2. Determine which are the growth markets in the coterminous United States and determine our target areas. Where U.S. Home can identify the leading builders in target areas, personal knowledge and contacts will be used to make approaches directly. Where U.S. Home cannot readily identify leading builders in target areas, an association with an investment banker in those areas will be established. Whereas U.S. Home desires to use only one investment banker in an area, the exclusiveness of the arrangement will depend upon performance. The investment banker may assist in finding, screening and negotiating. U.S. Home is willing to pay a fee based on services rendered.

V. *Geographical Approach:*

It is the policy of the company to expand into any of the good markets in the coterminous United States. Whereas it is desirable for the company to enter states in which it does not now operate, the primary consideration will be the quality of the company to be acquired rather than the location.

SEGMENTS OF THE REAL ESTATE CONSTRUCTION INDUSTRY IN WHICH U.S. HOME OPERATES

1. Custom home building on owner's lot
2. Conventional single-family tracts
3. Retirement tracts
4. FHA and VA single-family tracts
5. Vacation-home developments
6. Condominium villas
7. Garden condominium apartments or townhouses for sale
8. Garden rental apartments
9. High-rise condominium apartments
10. Government-subsidized apartment buildings
11. Modular-home tracts
12. Mobile-home parks
13. *Office parks (see note, p. 260)
14. *Shopping centers and development of other commercial properties (see note, p. 260)

ACCEPTABLE SEGMENTS OF THE INDUSTRY IN WHICH U.S. HOME DOES NOT NOW OPERATE

1. High-rise rental apartments
2. Turnkey projects

3. *High-rise office buildings
4. *Industrial parks

Companies in industry segments new to U.S. Home would have to meet higher standards if they are in a market also new to U.S. Home. They will require closer scrutiny in the following areas:

1. Size
2. Second-line management
3. Track record
4. Distance from general offices in Florida

CRITERIA: FOCUS ON CHEMISTRY PLUS NUMBERS

U.S. Home's former chairman, Robert H. Winnerman, puts emphasis on what he terms "instinct" in arriving at an evaluation of a prospective acquisition. "To the trained accountant or corporate executive most of the weight in the final decision-making process is given to the tangibles. But long before the time for final decisions arrives, intangible factors may swing the balance one way or another," he says. The intangibles include the personal affinity or "chemistry" of the principals, their long-range goals and the compatibility of their operating policies. The most important gut decision, however, is judging the company's ability to manage itself.

Winnerman adds that having management deficiencies doesn't rule out an acquisition, so long as management recognizes its own problems. But strong second-line management is of major importance to him. "Equally important," he says, "is the fact that a strong management team reflects the company's awareness of the need for depth; it reflects a realistic attitude to the essentials of growth; and it indicates that the company has developed a long-range program for its own growth." Among other major factors that have to be sized up by "feel" rather than statistically are the firm's ability to react to new markets and the aliveness of its merchandising concepts for the Seventies.

Says Bob Winnerman: "A business merger must start with strong personal attraction between the people involved. If basic philosophic differences exist which will widen in time, problems will arise which can diminish profits, erode efficiency and stymie growth." But, as the U.S. Home policy statement indicates, the economic underpinnings of the merger must be sound. The candidate's net after-tax profits as a percentage of sales must be at least as good as U.S. Home's. The acquirer earned $4.6 million on revenues of $91 million in fiscal 1971, so its profit as a percentage of sales came in at a little better than 5%. This figure varies with the particular product mix by company, but overall is excellent by national industry

* Acceptable segment as part of a company which produces residential units.

standards. The candidate's return on investment must also be as good as that of U.S. Home. While the acquirer has never published its figure for ROI, we can arrive at a reasonable estimate of what it was for fiscal 1971. The company worked with equity of about $39 million during the year, but of this amount $21.5 million came in at the very close of the fiscal year. The workable equity for the period thus amounted to about $18 million; taking a weighted average of the working capital for the year, U.S. Home's return on equity must have been substantially higher than 25%.

U.S. Home was aiming for a long-run internal growth rate of 20% compounded annually, but had actually been doing better. Thus, a candidate for acquisition who wants a good multiple of earnings had better be able to demonstrate an even better growth; otherwise U.S. Home has paid well below its own P/E and picked up the kicker. The price paid for a builder is based on inside calculation of management as to the builder's potential contribution to earnings. The one unsettled question that U.S. Home, like many acquirers, faces is at what point to fix the price of the stock to be handed over to the acquired builder: when the agreement is made in principle? when it is signed? or when it is closed? In their negotiations, some builders going the merger route have fixed a floor by specifying a *dollar value* of shares to be delivered to them, rather than *number* of shares, to protect themselves against fluctuations in share price before the deal is closed. Presumably, however, if the acquiring corporation's prospects are good, and its sales and earnings are rising through internal growth and acquisition, the stock will go up. So this is not a major problem. (It does get hairy sometimes, though, when the stock is dropping between contract and closing time or between the time a letter of intent is signed and a merger contract is negotiated.)

COMPARE YOURSELF AGAINST THE BIG BOYS

For the builder who wants to compare his performance by key accounting indexes similar to those of UH's net profit and ROI percentages, here are a handful. How does your own organization compare with the major national organizations in housing and development?

Inventory Turnover on Residential Construction
The top 37 companies in 1970 ranged between 2.0 times a year (for Kaufman & Broad) to 3.7 (Ryan Homes, which buys only prefinished lots to build on).

Turnover of All Inventory by Top Companies in 1970
Cousins Properties   0.5%   (apartment developer)
Rossmoor   1.0
Shapell Industries   1.3

McKeon   1.4
Centex   1.5
Kaufman & Broad   1.6
U.S. Home   1.6
Ryan Homes   3.0
U.S. Financial   3.3 (accelerated by joint ventures)

Gross Pretax Income for 1970
National Homes   5.2%
Kaufman & Broad   8.1
Ryan Homes   9.5
U.S. Financial   9.7
U.S. Home   9.8

On-Site Construction as % of Sales
Single-family housing construction runs 46%–52%.

Land Improvement Cost Per Lot As % of Sales
About 22%–25% of sales, for single-family housing.

Financing as % of Sales
About 5%–8% of cost of sales.

Land Ownership
The company may hold a 1–3 ratio of owned to optioned land
(1 owned and 3 optioned), but this is not a rigid formula.

Acceptable Growth Projections for Top Companies
15% annual growth   —acceptable
20% annual growth   —good
30% annual growth   —very good

Acceptable Return on Investment
20%   —minimum
30%   —good
40%   —very good

HOW GOOD DOES YOUR ORGANIZATION "FEEL"?

It bears repeating, however, that what Bob Winnerman describes as
"instinct" — a direct and knowing *feel* for the acquisition candidate's
operation based on a close first-hand knowledge of all aspects of homebuilding—is indispensable and perhaps dominant in any builder-acquirer's
evaluation. If it doesn't *feel* right, then it's no go, no matter how handsome
the numbers might be. In this regard the non-housing corporations that
have formerly bought into the field and are still occasionally buying are at
a sizable disadvantage. The industrial acquirer will get some bright Harvard

MBA to do a fancy mathematical model of an economic study encompassing every possible statistic concerning a builder-acquisition but failing to say a single meaningful thing *about the builder himself*. Stan Ross of Kenneth Leventhal & Company showed me one of these studies once and we both had a good chuckle. I solemnly swear that the great roll of paper that Stan unfurled with a flourish streamed across the office in an awesome banner fully twenty feet long. It was both a microeconomic and a macroeconomic model skillfully relating almost everything in the universe to homebuilding and quantifying the effects. But it never got to a *qualitative* analysis of the builder or his operation.

Perhaps this sort of educated boondoggling goes on all the time out there in the big wide business world; I can't say, being just a little old buffalo-chip kicker who packages up real estate projects, provides market consultation and does some development by joint-venturing. If it were me, however, I would focus less on the candidate-builder's position within the overall industry, and evaluate his management from an *operating* level. The builder's long-term plans are good evidence that he has thought ahead, but I would take a close look at what he has *now*, for openers.

One very strong indicator is the builder's aliveness to people as reflected in his "market sense." Is his product competitive with the best? Does he — judging by his product — have the knack of spotting the unique "hole" in the market and filling it? Is he *alive* enough and aware enough to constantly be delivering a unique and freshly conceived product that is based on a discerning perception of subtly shifting consumer preferences, economic realities, and competitive actions? Does he, in short, have a *market* sense, or is he a robot cranking out a cookie-cutter product that will go on even when the buyers have long gone?

Closely connected with a marketing orientation is another vitally important factor in the evaluation of any builder: the ability to perceive, evaluate and buy *land* at the right price and for the product that will find price and consumer acceptance in the market. The ability to acquire land is vital because the survival and continuity of the business depend on it. And it is an ability closely related to the marketing sense: from his long years of experience, the successful builder can either work from a knowledge of the market to select the right property or, conversely, on seeing a particular parcel at once envision the exact product for it that will meet a particular consumer and price demand. It is a subtle ability because it incorporates knowledge of cost and price feasibility and market and submarket tastes and demands, plus the ability to envision and combine these factors into the right product at the right price in the right place at the right time on inspecting the land.

Market research, of which I am always a strong advocate, is extremely helpful in helping you to define the product, price, volume, and market; and it is therefore extremely valuable as an aid in indicating locations and prices you can pay for land. But research alone won't do it; the builder's own market sense ultimately comes into play in inspecting and making the final decision on the given parcel. As Jerry Snyder of the Loew's/Snyder partnership says: "If I like the land and the research also recommends it, I buy it; if I like it and the research recommends against buying it, I sometimes buy it and sometimes don't; if I don't like it and the research recommends buying it, I don't buy it."

Beyond the prime requirements of market sense and ability in land acquisition, you can tell enough about the quality of the builder's operation to make up your mind about buying him just from poking around the organization for a couple of days. Are people doing what the builder's presentation book says they are supposed to be doing? Are the salesmen selling and the construction people building? Are sales reports accurate and is construction on schedule, judged by the critical path program? Do the managers, administrators, sales and construction personnel look like they're *pulling together?* Is there a good feeling about the place?

The potential acquisition must have a strong ability in the very important areas of product development and marketing. This is an area that smaller builders can often be deficient in; but large non-housing corporations have been very guilty of it too. The financial, or so-called bottom-line, orientation is as deficient as the pure "hammer and nails" approach when it comes to a successful homebuilding enterprise.

In 1972 I had the opportunity to evaluate for acquisition a young homebuilding company located in the Southwest and operated by a very bright young man just a few years out of law school. He was tremendously talented in financing and land acquisition, but had not placed enough importance on product development and marketing. Thus we spotted a very serious problem that might have been disastrous if we had not caught it in time. The bottom line in the long run means nothing without care, attention and responsive innovation in housing product and marketing skill. This young fellow just didn't understand the essentials of developing an excellent product. But fortunately, the problem was identified and its satisfactory solution was made a condition of consummating the merger with a congeneric operation.

Before this, the young builder had been trying to get as good a bargain on architecture as he had been getting on land deals, failing to recognize that the best bargain in architecture is good design regardless of cost. He felt it a sign of weakness to seek expertise outside his own firm; and he pretty much overruled the counsels of his in-house people. While he was building single-family homes his basic formula had been to find out what had been selling well in the same neighborhood and to steal the plans. It was a successful formula because his ability to buy land enabled him to offer a better value than the guy he'd stolen the plans from. At the time we came in to evaluate and improve his operation, however, he was embarking on a substantial program of attached housing. Therefore, despite his impressive track record, he was in many ways a beginner all over again. And in this venture he would have landed flat on his backside — and broke — had his operating formula on architecture and marketing not been altered in time.

Stan Ross of the Kenneth Leventhal & Co. accounting firm has also been involved in acquisition for major clients and he summarizes very well how some builder-acquirers size up potential acquisitions:

"The builder or developer making an acquisition makes the toughest deal because he knows the business. Not always, but usually he will evaluate the builder by his *assets*, which are very important for a continuing inventory. The builder should have about a three-year supply of land; maybe five at most. *Plus*, very important, he should have the ability to acquire land. He should look around at the builder's tracts and developments and find out not only how the builder bought the land but *when* he bought it. If he bought it thirty years ago and is making a profit on it today, that doesn't indicate the kind of ability we need.

"Next, he looks over the product. How good is it? How good is the builder's planning and ability to get land rezoned? How good is he vis-à-vis the market competition? His margins are analyzed and profits should come in somewhere about 8% to 10% pretax after all overhead.

"Last but not least is the management; very important. The acquirer checks their numbers and follows their logic. How do they reach a conclusion? Is the quality of their thinking and ability a sound basis for their overall economic plan? To really get this, the acquirer should walk their tracts. This is the difference between a builder buying another builder and an industrial company buying one. The builder gets the feel for how they build, how they sell — their style.

"The builder-buyer asks for the builder's sales report and his sales projections for the week, then gets into the car and sees his tracts. He talks to the salesman and sees if such-and-such a number of homes are really in escrow as the sales report says. He would check out the critical path program to see if construction is on schedule. He gets to know the feel of the company by these unexpected small tests. That's the real difference in style between analyzing an acquisition by a macroeconomic model and knowing what it's really like from the inside."

WHAT SHOULD YOU LOOK FOR IN YOUR ACQUIRER?

You will want to satisfy yourself that he really understands the real estate business, has prepared the necessary managerial environment for it, and will be truly committed to it in terms of capital and the support of top management. I am assuming that you will be able to show the prospective acquirer how he can make more money with your business than you could alone, and that you will be able to arouse his desire to buy. But while you're selling yourself, you are also buying a partner; you may fit him but make sure he fits *you*.

You have two basic choices in going the merger route. You can go with a builder or with a financial or other corporate giant. It takes a good knowledge of yourself and your motivations, abilities and goals to make the decision on which way to go. You might begin with the following considerations:

The big builder will want to acquire you to enter a new geographical market, or a new location within a market he's already in, or for your land, or because you're good at a particular housing product or housing technology. He will look for a local, independent entrepreneur who is going to be a hard-core operating man, helping the parent organization capture a larger percentage of some market. The acquirer doesn't always want a tycoon who is going to turn into another Eli Broad and jostle him for primacy in the hierarchy. If you go with a larger builder, you become — and stay — *middle management*. Is that what you want?

The acquirer will drive a hard bargain with you. But you can still make out well, perhaps even better than elsewhere. In the early 1970s, the builder acquired by a larger builder (1) cashed out; (2) had more upside potential in the stock he received because the parent company's P/E could rise much higher than the P/E of non-housing acquirers; and (3) had the opportunity to make a lot of money as the operator of a regional subsidiary, since salaries and bonuses tend to be very handsome.

The financial or other corporate giant will want to acquire you to enter the development field newly. There are advantages to going with one of these, instead of a builder. As a rule, the acquirer pays more of a premium to buy your expertise. And, instead of losing your own identity, you have the opportunity to be the Big No. 1 in your own scheme of things; you can still dream of being the kingpin and making your organization into one of major national scope. The negative in this situation is the risk of ultimately mortal conflict between you and your corporate parent after the honeymoon is over. (You may also find that the stock you received when you sold out doesn't grow very much, no matter how well you perform, because the P/E ratios of almost all companies are conservative by comparison with those prevailing in the housing field.) You may, of course, make a deal with a corporation whereby it *invests passively* in your company, like a limited partner, taking 50% or so of profits in exchange for putting up the equity capital and leaving all your operational decisions to you. In any case, your choice of going with a major corporation will be primarily the result of your continued desire to carve out your own building empire rather than becoming a cog (a very entrepreneurial cog, to be sure) in a larger builder's operation.

What do your inner heart, your temperament and your abilities tell you about which route is right for you? Do you really need to sell yourself at all? If you do, at least pick a stable firm operated by people with real integrity and not one that is merely "consistent with generally accepted operating principles." Once you have made the basic decision as to the partner who will fit your own goals, you can apply some essential tests to your prospective acquirer (whether builder or non-housing corporation). Each merger is unique and can ultimately be considered only on its own merits, but certain basics apply to them all:

Is the acquirer operating out of fully defined goals in undertaking the merger/acquisition? A soundly based merger will result in gains for both companies. The acquirer should be able to spell out for *you* exactly how you can benefit from the parent company's assets and exactly how you fit into a long-term growth plan. This should be backed up with the willingness to put into writing the agreements on the appropriate operating environment. Mergers founded on a vague good feeling alone don't last long.

Does the acquirer have someone in top management who understands real estate fully and to whom you will report exclusively? Is the chief executive *really* committed to you, for example, and capable of making the necessary decisions to back you up? Management by committee is disastrous, particularly in a business like development. And assuming you find the acquirer's management competent, do you *like* them as people? Is there a feeling of enthusiasm and spontaneity coupled with accomplishment in the acquiring firm? Or have you got a bunch of stuffed shirts bucking decisions around the table, harrumphing ever so discreetly and politely, and all busily stabbing each other in the back. I've seen some corporate environments where there was as much spontaneity and sincere goodwill among top managements as in a meeting of the Politburo under Josef Stalin. That kind of environment you don't need.

What is the acquirer's position in *his own* industry? Is he doing poorly, so-so, or well? Too often the builder did very little homework in evaluating his acquirer, entering the deal mesmerized by the size of the company. Is the acquirer a worthy partner? Does he have a record of sound growth? What are his gross and net profit margins, his return on book value, his working capital ratio? What do his competitors and the fraternity of investment bankers think of him? What has been his record of bringing off other successful merger/acquisitions? Does *he* have a record of keeping good management, or have his people all been hired away by the competition? Can he really afford to commit the capital it will take to support a growing real estate operation? The proper evaluation of an acquirer is a critically important task that the seller should not slight.

Take a hard look at the acquirer's stock price. How vulnerable is it? In selling your company for stock you are putting the product of your life's work on the block. You don't want to get paid in inflated securities that will vanish to nothingness when the bubble bursts. This is always a difficult decision area and I return to it at the end of this chapter. But, generally, a little conservative thinking will do you good. As Ken Leventhal says: "You must evaluate the future value of the stock. Would you rather have $10 million in the stock of Esoteric Convalescent Hospitals, selling at a P/E ratio of 100, or $500,000 in GE stock selling at a multiple of 13? Look long and hard at that piece of paper you'll get."

Just as an example, it may be that the acquirer's stock is traded over the counter and the marketable assets aren't very liquid, so that a strategically placed bid will maintain the market at an unusually high premium. Is that real market value? How does the acquirer's P/E ratio compare to other companies in the same business? Does his past record of growth indicate that the acquirer's P/E is warranted? Has he tapped out his growth potentials, or is there plenty of "upside" left in the stock? Maybe you should enter the deal from the viewpoint of "How much can I *lose?*" — and then work out ways to minimize the vulnerability of the stock you will receive.

Mergers can be unmade — witness the Bren-IP deal and the less fortunate conclusions to the Lyon-AmStan and the Boise ventures — but the price of the unmaking is a heavy and psychologically damaging one. Better you should make a sound deal in the first place; look over the merger more coldly and objectively than any investment decision you have ever made.

A WORD ON TAXES AND MERGERS

The subject of taxation with regard to mergers and acquisitions is a complex one on which many folks more capable than I have written extensively. For our purposes, we can cover the subject briefly.

One of the first decisions made in a merger/acquisition is whether you should opt for a taxable transaction or a nontaxable transaction, or whether you might structure a combination of taxable and nontaxable elements. There are advantages and disadvantages to each situation and the option is usually based on the particular objectives of buyer and seller in a specific situation. The various factors are too complicated to list and require the careful analysis of expert tax counsel and your accountant. Most often, the merger will be set up as a tax-free exchange. But on occasion, some element may be taxable; e.g., the building and related corporations comprising the Larwin Group were merged on a nontaxable basis, while investment-type assets (apartment and other income-producing properties) went in as a taxable transaction.

As a rule, you will want to go the nontaxable route. It is more difficult to structure a nontaxable transaction, but there are three basic methods. First is the statutory merger: two corporations desire to combine; they obtain stockholder approval; the merger is carried through under the statutory framework. Basically, the stockholders of the merging corporations exchange their stock and obtain stock of the newly merged corporation. The second form of tax-free combination is the stock-for-stock exchange. The acquiring corporation issues its voting stock for stock of the acquired corporation, and the acquired entity continues to operate as formerly, but now as a wholly owned subsidiary. The third form of tax-free transaction is the stock-for-assets acquisition. In this case, the acquiring corporation takes over the assets of the acquired corporation in exchange for voting stock. The acquired corporation can distribute the stock it has received to its shareholders in liquidation; or it can continue operating as a holding company or personal holding company. If the acquiring corporation wants to operate the asset acquisition as a subsidiary it may transfer the assets to a new wholly owned subsidiary.

Another type of tax-free exchange involves transfer of assets — owned individually or by partnership — to a corporation. This is a step usually taken by a builder who operates through multiple entities when preparing for a public offering or a merger/acquisition. Among the holdings transferred may be apartments or office buildings or shopping centers (or the net leases on such properties), or land acquired in individual ownership or a partnership. Property may be transferred to a corporation if immediately after the transfer the transferrors own 80% of the corporation stock .

I do not suppose I need to emphasize that the tax implications of mergers/acquisitions are very complex and that a qualified, experienced team of merger-wise lawyers and accountants is an absolute necessity when you start contemplating the merger route. Get the best; don't let a regular lawyer or accountant pick up his merger experience at your expense.

KEY ISSUES IN NEGOTIATING YOUR MERGER

At the time you've finally located a good prospective acquirer and you get down to serious negotiations, you will find yourself working toward agreement on a number of key issues covered by an acquisition contract. The first phase of your negotiation will be agreement in principle. This produces a letter of intent, which is basically a non-binding document saying that you agree to agree on a merger/acquisition and giving the ballpark terms of the prospective deal. The second phase gets you into the negotiation of the contract (or acquisition agreement), and is far more detailed. Let's look at the skeletal outline of the points such a contract might cover.

*TERMS FOR INCLUSION IN ACQUISITION
AGREEMENT*
  1. General statement of agreement and description of transaction
  2. Description of purchase price and method of payment, including interest, default, allocation, security, reserve for taxes
  3. Representations and warranties of seller
     a. Good title
     b. Due organization and valid existence of seller
     c. Capitalization
     d. Stock ownership (if sales of stock)
     e. Correctness of financial data
     f. Absence of undisclosed liabilities
     g. Correct list of material contracts
     h. Description of real property interests
     i. Litigation, pending or threatened
     j. Tax liabilities
     k. Accounts receivable (appropriate reserve for doubtful)
     l. Inventory — pricing method, etc.
     m. Identity and relationship of customers and suppliers
     n. Description of intercompany transactions
     o. Changes in condition of seller from date of most recent financial statement to date of agreement signed
  4. Representations and warranties of acquirer
     a. Funding of acquired entity with equity and/or debt
     b. Stock option plan
     c. Buyer's agreement to register stock received by seller
     d. Employment agreements with selling principals
     e. Others (as appropriate)
  5. Assets to be acquired by acquirer
  6. Acquirer's assumption of liabilities
  7. Seller's indemnification of buyer and remedies upon default
  8. Seller's covenant not to compete
  9. Seller's conduct of business pending closing

10. Conditions precedent to closing
11. Plan of reorganization
12. Brokerage fees (if any)
13. General provisions

I will focus on what I believe to be the four or five key areas where you will find good negotiation the most rewarding:

REGISTRATION RIGHTS. It is relatively easy to structure a non-taxable transaction on a stock-for-stock basis, but the important question has been, when can you get actual cash out of the deal? When the acquirer buys you out, exchanging some of his stock for all of your shares, almost always what you receive is "investment stock" — that is, stock not yet registered with the Securities and Exchange Commission. Under the old rules, you could usually have bargained to sell immediately at least 25% of the shares you received (taxed at the capital gains rate at the time of sale) by having the acquiring company register that number of shares with the SEC at its expense, without affecting the deal. Under the new rules there are no limitations on when and how many you may sell. However, check with your tax adviser if your sales approach 50% in the initial year.

You should make sure that your subsequent registration rights are clearly set forth in the acquisition agreement. Registering stock can be pretty costly, and it's also a good idea to try to get the acquirer to pay for as many registrations as possible; one acquirer agreed to pay for three of the builder's, for example. (If your acquirer will be planning security issues of his own in the future, you may negotiate so-called "piggyback registration rights" — that is, the right to register and sell portions of the shares you hold at the time of the corporate stock issue. It works out to be cheaper for the acquirer to register portions of your stock when he's floating an issue of his own.) It may take you five years to dispose of your stock, if that is your wish. In the ideal merger you would, of course, happily hold it for its "upside" appreciation, but the real world doesn't always work that way, as the 1973 stock market demonstrated. So make sure your rights on converting stock into cash are clearly specified.

REPRESENTATIONS AND WARRANTIES. Anything you disclose in negotiations you're not liable for. The big problem is what you *don't* know — that underground stream on one of your subdivisions, for example, that ruins forty-seven homes. The acquired wants the builder's money-back guarantee on values; the seller's philosophy is *caveat emptor*. So in negotiating warranties, they both strike a middle ground. The builder's approach in negotiating warranties is, first of all, to try to avoid them altogether; but if the acquirer is insistent, to work for the broadest protection possible. Your negotiator should try for the biggest cushion first, whereby the buyer has to suffer a loss of 10% of the seller's gross assets before he can turn to the seller for recourse. If this is not acceptable, retreat to a cushion of 10% of the purchase price. And if this doesn't go through, retreat to 10% of the seller's net worth. By way of illustrating how these negotiations go, one builder's cushion amounted to the first $2 million of any loss, damage or unexpected expense; he delivered enough shares of common into escrow for a two-year period at the time the deal was made to serve as security for agreements of indemnification he had made with the buyer.

COVENANT NOT TO COMPETE. As a rule, the builder must sign a very tough noncompetitive agreement with the buyer which restricts him from any activity on his own for anywhere from two to five years. Should he decide to bail out early because the merger isn't going according to his liking, he could have nothing to do but sit on a beach until the noncompete agreement covering his area of operations expires. This happened with Jack Bertoglio of Kansas Quality Construction, for example, when he left shortly after his company was acquired by Redman Industries. It's a good idea to try to plan the merger well enough so that you don't run the risk of being restricted from your area of expertise during your best years.

WHAT PRICE P/E? You are naturally going to try for the highest possible price for your company. The multiple of earnings that the acquirer will pay on a merger accounted as a pooling of interests will be partly set by your demonstrated earnings capacity and the *quality* of your earnings (do you jack them up with occasional land sales, etc.?). But other factors enter into the decision. We have covered these in Chapter 8, but it's worth reviewing them briefly. The typical acquirer these days usually sports a pretty conservative P/E multiple compared to the 1970–71 period in the housing field, and he's not going to pay you at a higher multiple than his own because that would dilute his earnings per share. As one major builder recently acquired says: "The dollar value of the stock is meaningless. You've got to find out what the acquirer's P/E is and then come in lower, because they've got to have that kicker."

THE IMPORT OF THE EARNOUT. The earnout originally became popular because in negotiations it often became difficult to set exact value for the acquired firm. The contingent-share arrangement includes compensation for past, current and future performance. The downpayment is based on historic and current earnings. Then, as part of the purchase price, acquirer and acquired establish an earnout formula which produces a multiple of earnings over three to five years. The theory is that in this way not only is potential growth recognized but an added incentive for growth is put into the deal because the acquired company will work hard to get the added shares and at the same time, by increasing overall corporate earnings, raise the value of the stock it receives.

The change in accounting rules governing mergers (see Chapter 8) had the effect of lowering the P/E multiple of a builder that acquirers can shell out if they want to go the earnout route by the purchase accounting method of acquisition. They now have to write the builder's assets up to market value and amortize without tax offset whatever they pay him in excess of amounts allocated to his assets. Since such a write-off constitutes a drain on reportable earnings, the net effect is to lower the prices acquirers initially pay, in order to avoid such a drain. Thus, when City Investing acquired Wood Brothers of Denver ($40 million revenues) in the fall of 1971 for $10 million in stock, the acquirer paid slightly over 4 times the builder's net earnings (with another 4 times earnings as the earnout). Wood was also put on an earnout worth another $10 million. Quite a difference from the old wild and woolly days of the CNA-Larwin and Bren-IP deals.

How MUCH ROOM FOR GROWTH IS THERE IN THE ACQUIRER'S STOCK? With the change in the accounting rules on mergers and the advent of lower P/E multiples paid for builders, an important new consideration emerges in negotiating your merger deal. You can make big bucks by pooling. But whether you pool or purchase *you are no longer going to make the fattest gain on the initial value of stock paid for your company but on the subsequent appreciation of the stock you receive.* This means you are going to join a fast-growing company if you want to maximize on your sale. In a way this increases your risk, because a stock that moves up rapidly can also move down — way down. The whole thrust of many earlier builder mergers was toward major corporations with very stable stock prices, in which the builder constituted less than 10% of the surviving entity and the value of his stock was isolated from the vagaries of his own performance.

Many conservative builders would still blanch at the prospect of joining a fast mover, no matter how attractive the "upside" potential of the stock, out of the fear that something might go wrong and the value of the stock would plunge to zero, cleaning them out. Still, unless you're very conservative, this is an element of risk you'll have to face if you want to make a lot of money on your sale. It's at this point that really expert judgment of the acquiring company is necessary, to select a partner firm that will grow without hitting occasional lows proportionate to the previous highs. As of 1972, Bob Grant appeared to have made a successful selection with Santa Anita Consolidated, and City Investing kept on growing, as did U.S. Homes. Use them as your criteria in evaluating other acquirers.

THE ROLE OF THE MIDDLEMAN

Why get involved with a middleman at all? Frankly, you don't always have to. Most of the builder-acquirers I know are pretty forthright and spontaneous people, and if you think you might be well matched with one of them you can readily initiate a contact without a great deal of corporate pussyfooting to find out what you've got in common. However, as there are many types of acquirers and you will want to evaluate every possibility and present yourself in your best form, a professional middleman can be a genuine help to you. If he is good, he earns his fee by helping you in many ways that your own accountants and attorneys normally cannot.

He can help you get the best deal from the right company, making sure of its soundness, evaluating its stock and analyzing its growth potential.

He can keep your company from being shopped.

He can research prospective buyers for proper criteria on goals, finance, and compatibility of management.

He can guide you past pitfalls of merger/acquisition negotiations, particularly in the important factors of securities laws.

He can help you determine what you really want when you seek a merger, and then help you achieve it by coming up with a creative solution that will meet your desires without slighting the acquirer's.

He can serve as a valuable third person with an exterior view in the negotiating process, playing a key role in helping seller and buyer over obstacles to achieve their merger successfully.

A formula in common usage sets his fee based on the total value of the transaction and payable either on closing or in periodic payments over a specified span, usually negotiated in advance. The total fee runs something like this:

5% of the first $1 million
4% of the second $1 million
3% of the third $1 million
2% of the fourth $1 million
1% of everything over $5 million

A good middleman is often distinguished from a "finder" — a person who merely introduces merger prospects to one another. The professional may be an investment banker or an accountant or attorney with a thorough knowledge of real estate and of mergers and acquisitions in this field. Most of the larger investment banking firms have one or more good people to handle such functions, but many of the best middlemen are also found elsewhere. One example is Art Winston of Los Angeles, who has acted on the Besco-Singer, Grant-Santa Anita and the Klingbeil-CBS mergers.

Talk with the people who know the industry. For the builder or acquirer who wants to get a thorough acquaintance with the range of merger/acquisition possibilities in housing and real estate, Ken Campbell, president of Audit Investment Research of New York, is an expert analyst of the industry and its capital sources and keeps a close observation on all developments. Probably one of the best-known men in the industry is also

Edward C. Birkner, director of the Marketing Information Network of New York, which provides consulting services to housing. Ed's remarkable series of major seminars on the infusion of corporate capital into real estate have, since 1969, brought together the leading cross-section of the nation's developer/builders, corporate acquirers and investment specialists in semi-annual powwows on the state of their art. Probably more real estate mergers were made in those seminars as a result of this interdisciplinary rubbing of shoulders than in any other way. I would be remiss not to include my brother, Sanford R. Goodkin, in this list, though it opens me up to the charge of nepotism. Operating one of the best-known market research and consulting firms in the housing industry, and also sponsoring a number of significant corporate/builder seminars, Sanford is always a good man to be tuned in to and has played a direct role in some major mergers.

For the builder just starting to think about the possibility of the merger route and wanting to learn more about who's doing what in the field and with what result, there are several good ways to start. You can attend the conventions of the National Association of Homebuilders, and the National Apartment Association, the Pacific Coast Builders Conference, *Professional Builder*'s major housing seminars and its INBEX (Industrialized Building Exposition), as well as the ACN Conference/Exposition. Each of them usually has specific seminars devoted to the subject of mergers/ acquisitions.

The key men of the business journals covering the industry are good starting sources of helpful information and insight. Wes Wise of *Apartment Construction News*, and John Goldsmith of *House & Home* are two such people. Having long known Marsh Trimble, who publishes *Professional Builder* magazine. I can assure you of his courtesy and helpfulness. *Professional Builder* also publishes two outstanding annual reviews — by far the best in the industry — of who's who in the housing and development field. The two statistical and performance reviews do for real estate what the *"Fortune* 500" and the *Forbes* reviews do for American industry — and these are indispensable guides to any merger-bound builder or acquirer. One is *Professional Builder*'s "Annual Review of Housing Giants," including both private and publicly held companies. Many merger-bound builders seek to get listed in an appendix to this review called "Tomorrow's Giants?" The other is Ken Campbell's annual earnings and performance survey of "The Public Builders," an acute financial analysis of all publicly traded corporations in real estate. Both analyses are published in the summer editions of *Professional Builder*.

PART THREE

Vignettes from the Masters of Merger

Call to mind, say, the times of Vespasian. It is the same old spectacle—marriage and childbearing, disease and death, war and revelry, commerce and agriculture, toadyism and obstinacy; one man praying that heaven may be pleased to take so-and-so, another grumbling at his lot, another in love or laying up treasure, others, again, lusting after consulships and kingdoms. All these have lived their life and their place knows them no more. So pass on to the reign of Trajan. All again is the same, and that life, too, is no more.

—Marcus Aurelius

Prefatory Note

The tide of the big glamor mergers in real estate receded by the close of 1972, leaving a curious and slightly disheveled flotilla of building companies on the beach of the American business scene. These were the high-rollers, the masters of merger, who caught the tide to fame and fortune. Some were wrecked by the consequences of their rapid rise when the wind went out of the housing promotion boom. Not all fared poorly, to be sure. Many astute merger partners have worked out viable formulas — Leadership Housing, Mission Viejo, City Investing, and Brock among them — that kept them on the upswing even when the economic climate turned harsher. But the difficulties of other giants in decline cast a pallor over the industry nevertheless.

There are a million stories out there about mergers failed and mergers true. This section presents a baker's dozen of them. The profiles of their rising and/or falling fortunes make for nostalgic reading to anyone who has lived through the housing merger age. But these stories may also be informative and useful to anyone engineering housing merger combinations in the future.

As a related point, the reader should bear in mind that the events he reads about are quite distant from him in time — a passage of even two or three years is considerable. All of the firms discussed herein have changed a great deal — some very radically — from the time they may have posed for their snapshot here. In no instance, positive or negative, would it be fair to assume beforehand that the company's condition remains static.

11

Larry Weinberg Makes a Deal

> All men dream: but not equally.
> Those who dream by night in the
> dusty recesses of their minds wake
> in the day to find that it was van-
> ity: but the dreamers of the day
> are dangerous men, for they may
> act their dream with open eyes, to
> make it possible.
>
> —Lawrence of Arabia

Lawrence J. Weinberg had some fast figuring to do along about the end of 1968. Was he going to take his Larwin Group public or merge it into a larger corporation? It was a critical decision for a man who, starting in homebuilding in 1948, had become two decades later one of California's biggest developers and certainly one of the most sophisticated marketeers. The immediately succeeding events favored the belief that Larry made the right choice. He became a legend in the industry by negotiating one of the highest-priced mergers ever consummated with a nonhousing corporation, becoming fabulously rich in the process.

As earlier stated, Larwin was acquired in July 1969 by CNA Financial, the insurance holding company whose assets of $3.6 billion in 1971 ranked it the fifty-ninth largest corporation in the nation. The merger deal gave Larry and his brother Bill (who between themselves held 95% of the Larwin Group) $100 million in CNA stock, plus the potential to earn another $100 million's worth on a five-year earnout. The combination put Larry under pressure to bring in earnings and control Larwin's rapid growth. But it also made him the biggest shareholder in CNA Financial and opened up the possibility that he could hop from homebuilding to a bigger-league ballgame. There was speculation in the industry during 1971 that he was in line for the role of chairman and president of CNA Financial.

279

LARWIN IN THE CONTEXT OF CNA

The way for the Larwin acquisition in mid-1969 was actually paved on December 31, 1967, when Continental Casualty Company and Continental Assurance Company formed CNA Financial. It was one of the more than four hundred holding companies to be created by insurance firms during the Sixties. The main purpose of the reorganization was to facilitate the insurers' redeployment of capital into profitable ventures.

The insurance base: Continental Casualty and its affiliates, formerly known as the Continental National American Group and now usually called CNA Insurance, rank as the nation's seventh largest casualty insurance group. (Continental Casualty has been nicknamed "Lloyd's of Chicago" because of the unusual events it sometimes insures through its commercial risks division. Though this is a small portion of the division's overall business, it has underwritten such events as a thousand-foot cable

Table 11.1   Combined Income of the Larwin Group (thousands)

	Year Ended December 31,				
	1968	1967	1966	1965	1964* (Unaudited)
Revenues					
Sales	$49,599	$31,668	$21,788	$18,329	$24,768
Financial service income	760	774	68	72	369
Other	212	606	(93)	406	142
	$50,571	33,048	21,763	18,807	25,279
Expenses					
Cost of sales	40,621	25,360	18,164	14,465	19,515
General and administrative	1,501	1,812	1,455	1,809	1,724
	42,122	27,172	19,619	16,274	21,239
Income before taxes on income and extraordinary item	8,449	5,876	2,144	2,533	4,040
Current federal and state taxes on income	3,487	1,799	588	1,015	1,700
Deferred federal and state taxes on income	236	765	83	127	201
Total	3,723	2,564	671	1,142	1,901
Income before extraordinary item	4,726	3,312	1,473	1,391	2,139
Gain on sale of marketable securities, net of taxes on income of $394,000	–	1,183	–	–	–
Net Income	$ 4,726	$ 4,495	$ 1,473	$ 1,391	$ 2,139

*Revenues and net income in 1964 benefited from a large number of housing completions reflecting an unusually high backlog of sales at the beginning of the year in a new housing development.

walk by aerialist Karl Wallenda across a high gorge in Georgia; the setting of a speed record by a jet-powered automobile, the Blue Flame, which roared across Bonneville Flats, Utah, at 622.407 mph, driven by Gary Gabelich; a thirty-mile free-fall by two daredevil skydivers; the test voyage of the first nuclear submarine; and other peacetime events like rattlesnake hunts.) Continental Assurance is the seventeenth stock life insurance company in the nation by assets. The CNA insurance group also includes Valley Forge Life Insurance Company, Valley Forge Insurance Company, Transcontinental Company, and American Casualty Company. In 1969, CNA also bought Canadian Premier Life Insurance Company of Winnipeg.

Overseas, the corporation is associated with the Winterthur Group of Switzerland. Winterthur has a small ownership position in CNA Financial, and CNA, through Continental Casualty, owns a small portion of Winterthur. There is a further connection with Provident Life Association of London, Ltd., and United Standard Insurance Company, Ltd., of Britain, both partly owned by Winterthur. CNA also shares a majority ownership in Stronghold Insurance, Ltd., a London-based reinsurer, with Winterthur. With Provident Life, CNA recently launched a program of hospitalization and life insurance for members of British professional groups.

CNA's EXPANSION PHASE. Consolidating its insurance operations, CNA Financial between 1968 and 1970 embarked on an aggressive acquisition program to profitably employ surplus capital generated by its insurance activities. This was the period in which it embraced interests in consumer finance, mutual fund investments, nursing home and medical services, the whole field of real estate and tax shelter, as well as smaller but promising areas such as nuclear core leasing. Prior to his retirement as chairman, Howard C. Reeder explained the acquisition philosophy in the following terms: "Our operation revolves around this one point — personal financial security and planning for the family and the individual." He described the concept as a one-stop financial center.

Because CNA was born out of the insurance business, insurance plays a big part in the concept. But since the home is the biggest investment for most families, CNA sought to broadly expand its services in that field. As a result of the acquisition program, it is theoretically possible for a family to deal exclusively with CNA-controlled companies to buy all of its insurance coverage, buy or rent housing, negotiate consumer credit loans, invest in mutual funds, obtain medical and nursing home services, work in a CNA-owned office building, and buy a vacation retreat or spend a vacation at a CNA-developed resort hotel.

Among the present CNA subsidiaries are the following:

General Finance Corporation, a personal-loan chain that opened 28 new offices in 1971, bringing its total to 435 offices in 21 states. General Finance reported pretax profits of $5.6 million for the first half of 1971, compared with $1.5 million for the comparable period in 1970.

Kane Financial Corporation, which own 87% of Quechee Lakes Corporation, a 5,000-acre recreational community in Vermont, and has a major investment in Healthco, one of the country's bigger and more diversified health-services companies. Kane is also involved in venture capital investment through its SBIC, Massachusetts Capital Corporation, and a small group of commercial, industrial and residential real estate developments.

Tsai Management & Research Corporation, which manages five mutual funds, the largest of which is the Manhattan Fund. The mutual funds took a bad beating at the hands of the stock market in 1970 after some glamorous years, and Tsai's funds suffered along with them.

CNA Investor Services, Inc., a nationwide securities broker-dealer selling insurance, mutual funds and variable annuities. One of the new packages touted as of 1971 combined life insurance, savings and loan deposits and mutual fund investment.

CNA Realty Corporation, a real estate investment company.

CNA Actuarial Consultants, Inc., which assists corporations in developing and maintaining employee benefit programs.

CNA Nuclear Leasing, Inc., which leases nuclear cores to electric utilities, as well as vehicles and data processing and other equipment to other corporations. The firm's first three core leasings, for a total of more than $50 million, were announced in 1971. (Private industry stepped into this field because of federal law prohibiting the Atomic Energy Commission from leasing nuclear fuels after December 31, 1970.)

Employee Benefits Consultants, Inc., which designs and administers tax-sheltered pensions and profit-sharing programs and counsels large trade associations on insurance problems.

Modern America Corporation, a mass-marketer of financial planning services. The Dallas-based firm became a CNA subsidiary in 1971.

Into this corporate picture we now introduce Larwin. The insurance

Table 11.2   Five-Year Record of Home Sales

Year	Detached Houses Sold	Townhouse Units Sold	Total Single-Family Residences Sold
1964	1,228	0	1,228
1965	705	65	770
1966	485	277	762
1967	671	329	1,000
1968	1,305	436	1,741

companies account for the majority of CNA Financial's earning and will probably continue to do so. (Net operating income for the insurance companies and other principal subsidiaries for the first half of 1971 was $28.6 million, up nearly 44% from the comparable period in 1970.) But CNA's bosses counted on the performance of the Larwin Group for the next largest contribution to the holding company's future earnings growth, more so than any other CNA subsidiary. CNA could of course also get an excellent return on its invested capital by funneling equity money into Larwin operations, but it is earnings that count with this earnings-oriented acquirer. And it was the expectation of substantial earnings, along with the premium that an outsider usually pays for a housing company at any time (but especially during the buy-a-builder rush in 1969) that encouraged CNA to fork over such a big merger price.

WHAT KIND OF A COMPANY DID CNA GET? Prior to the merger, the Larwin Group comprised twenty corporations and subsidiaries. It also included the unincorporated Larwin Fund, a partnership set up to develop and hold commercial and apartment properties. Although Larwin was primarily known as a builder of single-family homes in the $19,000-to-$40,000 range, it was also engaged in other activities. These included FHA and VA financing through its Brentwood Mortgage Corporation, insurance coverage, merchandising of home furnishings, and development of shopping centers and other commercial and industrial facilities. At the end of 1968 it owned or managed 1,000,000 square feet of floor space in six shopping centers and other commercial facilities, and was planning on developing several other similar facilities. As the following exhibits from CNA's proxy statement at the time it acquired Larwin show, the combined income of this heterogeneous group for the last full year prior to the acquisition came to $4,726,000. The net worth of the group amounted to $24,610,000 just prior to acquisition.

The balance sheet item "Investment in non-combined financial affiliates" represented the principals' equity in Brentwood Mortgage Corporation, Alliance Escrow Corporation, and Rexford Financial Corporation.

Table 11.3 Supplementary Profit and Loss Information (thousands)

| | Charged Directly to Profit and Loss | | |
	To Cost of Sales	To General and Administrative Expenses	Other Revenues (See Note)	Total
Year ended December 31, 1966				
Maintenance and repairs		$ 45	$ 44	$ 89
Depreciation and amortization		111	453	564
Taxes, other than federal and state income taxes				
Payroll and related taxes	$ 46	77		123
Property taxes	136	6	175	317
Rents		55	16	71
Year ended December 31, 1967				
Maintenance and repairs		26	100	126
Depreciation and amortization		55	376	431
Taxes, other than federal and state income taxes				
Payroll and related taxes	52	57		109
Property taxes	144	8	150	302
Rents		101	46	147
Year ended December 31, 1968				
Maintenance and repairs		44	35	79
Depreciation and amortization		62	445	507
Taxes, other than federal and state income taxes				
Payroll and related taxes	141	94	29	264
Property taxes	82	2	210	294
Rents		187	6	193

Note: Included in other revenues in the accompanying financial statements are rentals net of operating costs from commercial operations.

Members of the Larwin Group (not including subsidiaries)

Alliance Mortgage Corp.	Seagate Investment Corp.
Brentwood Mortgage Corporation	Service Management Corp.
Guild Homes	Sound Homes, Inc.
Laret Investment Corp.	Standard Development Corp.
Larwin Company	Valiant Investment Co.
Larwin Development Corp.	Westwood Advertising, Inc.
Larwin Home Center, Inc.	Wilshire National Corp.
Larwin Realty, Inc.	Wilshire National Life Insurance Co.
Maiden Fair, Inc.	Wilshire Park Corporation
Savoy Homes, Inc.	Wilshire Supply Corporation

Unincorporated:
Larwin Fund

Table 11.4 Combined Balance Sheet of Larwin Group, December 31, 1968 –
Assets

Cash and certificates of deposit	$ 5,250,000
Notes and accounts receivable–less allowance of $168,000 for doubtful accounts	3,105,000
Lease contracts receivable–less unearned income of $952,000	1,668,000
Real estate projects–at lower of cost or market	51,241,000
Investment in non-combined financial affiliates–at equity in net assets	1,793,000
Commercial properties–at cost–less accumulated depreciation and amortization of $1,941,000	9,182,000
Furniture and equipment–at cost–less accumulated depreciation and amortization of $303,000	264,000
Other assets	475,000
	$72,978,000

Table 11.5 Liabilities and Net Worth

Accounts payable and accrued liabilities	$ 4,547,000
Trust deed notes	24,248,000
Construction loans payable	13,902,000
Other notes payable	1,980,000
Federal and state taxes on income–including $1,168,000 deferred*	3,280,000
Co-venturer's interest in combined partnership	411,000
Net worth	24,610,000
	$72,978,000

*The company changed its method of accounting for state taxes on income to conform with accounting principles adopted in 1968 by the American Institute of Certified Public Accountants. This change had the effect of reducing net earnings and net worth previously reported for 1967 by $124,000. The effect for the years 1964, 1965 and 1966 is not material. In addition, previously reported net worth at the beginning of 1967 has been reduced by $106,000 of additional federal income taxes on income resulting from an Internal Revenue Service examination completed in 1968 for prior years.

Deferred Federal and State taxes on income were provided for differences between tax and financial reporting, and include $236,000, $765,000 and $83,000 provided in 1968, 1967 and 1966 respectively. These differences principally arose from capitalization of interest and property taxes on real estate and the timing of profit recognition on land sales.

The company provided for estimated federal taxes on income applicable to partnership income as though such partnerships had operated as corporations. In the accompanying financial statements, these amounts totalling $515,000 were presented as contributions to partnership capital in the year 1968.

Table 11.6 Statement of Changes in Combined Net Worth, Three Years Ended December 31, 1968

Balance at December 31, 1965	$10,722,000
Net income for the year	1,473,000
Partnership withdrawals–net of capital contributed to corporations and partnerships*	(202,000)
Balance at December 31, 1966–as restated*	11,993,000
Net income for the year–as restated*	4,495,000
Capital contributed to corporations and partnerships– net of partnership withdrawals*	4,862,000
Balance at December 31, 1967–as restated*	21,350,000
Net income for the year	4,726,000
Partnership withdrawals–net of capital contributed to corporations and partnerships*	(1,466,000)
Balance at December 31, 1968	$24,610,000

*The company changed its method of accounting for state taxes on income to conform with accounting principles adopted in 1968 by the American Institute of Certified Public Accountants. This change had the effect of reducing net earnings and net worth previously reported for 1967 by $124,000. The effect for the years 1964, 1965 and 1966 is not material. In addition, previously reported net worth at the beginning of 1967 has been reduced by $106,000 of additional federal income taxes on income resulting from an Internal Revenue Service examination completed in 1968 for prior years.

Deferred Federal and State taxes on income were provided for differences between tax and financial reporting, and include $236,000, $765,000 and $83,000 provided in 1968, 1967 and 1966 respectively. These differences principally arose from capitalization of interest and property taxes on real estate and the timing of profit recognition on land sales.

The company provided for estimated federal taxes on income applicable to partnership income as though such partnerships had operated as corporations. In the accompanying financial statements, these amounts totalling $515,000 were presented as contributions to partnership capital in the year 1968.

A condensed, combined statement of the financial position of these affiliates as of December 31, 1968, looked like this:

Table 11.7

Assets (thousands)	
Cash and marketable securities	$ 673
Trust deed notes held for sale	16,242
Construction loans to affiliates	12,113*
Other assets	1,271
	$30,299
Liabilities (thousands)	
Notes payable–collateralized by trust deed notes and construction loans	$28,102
Other liabilities	404
Stockholders' equity	1,793
	$30,299

*Net of undisbursed funds of $12,863,000.
Note: At December 31, 1968, the above affiliates were committed to purchase, principally from Larwin Group companies, approximately $30,000,000 of loans collateralized by first deeds of trust. In addition, these affiliates had agreements with investors for the sale of such loans in the aggregate amount of approximately $49,800,000. Further, these affiliates were servicing 17,801 loans totaling $329,000,000 and had trust funds and escrow deposits totaling $5,625,000 on deposit in trust accounts and with various mortgagees which have been excluded from the preceding condensed combined financial statement.

CAPITALIZING ON THE UPSWING

If the merger price is computed in some way as a multiple of the seller's earnings, it is interesting to observe that the performance of the Larwin Group in the three years ending December 31, 1968, probably earned the Weinbergs about two-thirds of the price they ultimately received when they sold out to CNA. Assuming a 20 times multiple as an initial payment and another 20 times based on an earnout, Larry added roughly $120 million to the merger price by virtue of Larwin's earnings increase between 1966 and 1968. It was a virtuoso example of capitalizing on the upswing. Larwin's earnings had gone from $1,473,000 on sales of $21.8 million in 1966 to $4,726,000 on sales of $49.6 million in 1968. At the same time, net worth more than doubled, rising to $24.6 million, as the rising earnings were plowed back into the company along with capital contributions. Much of the new capital went into further land acquisitions. CNA's price paid for the Larwin Group partly reflected the future earnings buried in such land carried at cost.

The largest single asset of the Larwin Group at the end of 1968, according to the CNA proxy statement, was its real estate, having an assigned value, at lower of cost or market, of $51,241,000. Of this sum, $21.0 million reflected work in progress — houses completed or in various stages of completion, including land and improvements and model homes. But the other $29,319,000 represented undeveloped land that Larwin carried on its books at lower of cost or market. At the end of 1968, the company owned 3,050 acres of undeveloped land, of which approximately 74% was located in the greater Los Angeles area. Before the end of March 1969, when the merger with CNA was first announced, Larwin further amplified its landholdings by buying or taking options to purchase another 887 acres in the Los Angeles area for $13,650,000. And it signed contracts to buy 500 acres in the greater Chicago area for $2,250,000. It also owned or had options to buy 400 acres in San Diego County and 200 acres in the San Francisco Bay area for total purchase prices of approximately $2.6 million and $2.9 million, respectively.

THE MERGER DEAL

The merger of Larwin into CNA followed a three-step process. Prior to the acquisition by CNA, all the Larwin Group Companies except the Larwin Fund were merged into Larwin Company. CNA then acquired

Larwin by merging it into a wholly owned subsidiary, The Larwin Group, newly formed for this purpose. Larwin Fund was then acquired by CNA through the sale of its business, assets and liabilities by Larry and Bill Weinberg to Larwin Properties Corporation, a newly formed subsidiary of CNA's Larwin Group. The merger of the Larwin Company into CNA's Larwin Group was a nontaxable reorganization treated as a pooling of interests. The acquisition of the Larwin Fund was a taxable transaction.

The merger of the Larwin Company and the sale of the Larwin Fund closed concurrently. On the closing date the Larwin stockholders and Larwin Fund partners received 3,745,318 shares of CNA common stock which, at the time the agreement to merge in principle was made, had a value of $100 million. Of the total number of shares, 209,288 shares of CNA common were paid for the assets of the Larwin Fund, while the balance was exchanged for stock in the Larwin Company. Each of the 26,250 outstanding preferred shares of Larwin were converted with 3,745,318 shares of CNA common, and each of the 3,086,397 outstanding common shares of Larwin were converted into (1) 1,113,827 shares of CNA common and (2) 32,400,238 shares of CNA preferred (Series B) stock, which latter were deposited in escrow.

And this brings us to the earnout. Both the Larwin Company stockholders and Larwin Fund partners (in both cases, Larry and Bill Weinberg) were entitled to receive further blocks of stock depending on the earnings performance of the merged entities. But the Larwin Company stockholders were to receive the additional shares in the form of convertible preferred stock held in escrow, while the Larwin Fund partners were to get theirs contingently in the form of CNA common. From the recipients' point of view, this made little difference, since the preferred was convertible into common anyway. But, as we have seen, it makes a difference in the acquirer's cost of acquisition for bookkeeping purposes. So let us maintain the distinction.

THE ORIGINAL EARNOUT FORMULA

At the time the deal closed, 1 million shares of preferred convertible (Series B) stock, each share valued at $100, were issued to Larwin's stockholders and delivered into escrow. This $100 million in stock thus formed the earnout pool. From it, depending on Larwin Group's earnings between 1970 and 1974, Larwin Company's stockholders would receive additional shares of convertible preferred. Basically from the same pool, Larwin Fund partners would also receive additional contingent shares of CNA common (converted from the preferred), dependent on earnings of Larwin Properties over the same five-year period. The release from escrow of the preferred stock to Larwin stockholders and the delivery of contingent

shares of common stock to the partners of Larwin Fund could not together exceed the lesser of $100 million in value of 3,745,318 shares of
common stock (or the equivalent shares of preferred stock before giving
effect to its conversion).

The specific earnout formula employed was a two-tier one, with a
higher payoff in the first two years, according to the CNA proxy statement:

1. If the combined net of Larwin Group and Larwin Properties exceeded $5,829,410 in 1969 ($5,451,581 for Larwin Group; $377,829
for Larwin Properties), the number of preferred and/or common shares
to be delivered in 1970 was to be determined by multiplying the excess
earnings by 17 and dividing the product by $26.70 if common stock was
to be delivered, or by $100 if preferred stock was to be delivered.

2. Likewise, if the combined 1970 net exceeded 1969 earnings or
$5,829,410, whichever is higher, the same formula was to be applied in
delivering additional shares.

The maximum number of shares deliverable on this basis in each of
the first two years was set at $25 million in value, using $26.70 as the
value of CNA common and $100 as the value of the preferred. This maxi-
mum imposed an annual limitation of 936,330 shares of common stock
(if only common stock was delivered), or 250,000 shares of preferred
stock (if only preferred stock was delivered).

3. Beyond this, CNA set up a second earnout tier. If Larwin stockholders and Larwin Fund partners really hustled and got combined earnings in excess of $7.3 million ($6,826,856 for Larwin Group; $473,144
for Larwin Properties), for each of the two years 1969 and 1970, they'd
be entitled to an additional payout beyond that already stated. The additional number of shares, if any, to be delivered for 1969 were determinable
by multiplying the excess combined net earnings over $7.3 million by 7
and dividing the result by the average market price of CNA common stock
during the month of December of the year preceding the year in which
delivery was to be made. If earnings exceeded $7.3 million in 1969, this
would become the new earnings base for 1970.

4. For the years 1971, 1972 and 1973 the combined earnings base
was again set at the lower figure of $5,829,410 ($5,451,581 for Larwin
Group; $377,829 for Larwin Properties) — though, of course, earnings at-
tained over that level in any year become the earnings base for each succeeding year until a higher earnings base is achieved. The additional shares,
if any, to be delivered for 1971, 1972 and 1973 are also determinable by
multiplying the excess combined net earnings over the earnings base by
7 and dividing the result by the average market price of CNA common
during the month of December of the year preceding the year in which
delivery is to be made.

As already stated, this plan called for Larwin stockholders to get convertible preferred stock based on excess earnings of Larwin Group, and for Larwin Fund partners to get common stock based on excess earnings of Larwin Properties. In any case, however, the maximum number of shares deliverable under the earnout agreement is limited to the lesser of (a) the number of shares having a value of $100 million, or (b) 3,745,318 shares of CNA common stock (equivalent to one million shares of preferred stock). The shares deliverable in 1970 and 1971 for excess combined net earnings up to $7.3 million were fixed at a value of $26.70 per share for common stock and $100 per share of preferred. Any additional shares deliverable in 1970 and 1971, as well as any shares deliverable in 1972, 1973 and 1974, were to be valued at the average market price of CNA common for the month of December preceding those respective years. So that the foregoing maximum cannot be exceeded, the number of contingent shares of CNA common stock delivered to partners of the Larwin Fund each year are convertible into preferred stock equivalents and are deducted in that year from any shares of preferred stock to be released from escrow and returned to CNA for cancellation.

For purposes of the earnout agreement, Larwin and CNA defined "net earnings" as determined in accordance with generally accepted accounting principles and after state and federal taxes, including profits on sales of commercial, industrial, residential and other real property. But they wrote the following prohibitions into the agreement against fast, one-shot earnings. A computation of net earnings for purposes of the earnout agreement would exclude profits on sales of vacant land zoned residential to unrelated persons, other than to a governmental agency or sales of individual lots retailed to the ultimate consumer. Also excluded would be profits in excess of $800,000 in 1969 and 1970, and $950,000 in 1971, 1972 and 1973, from sales of commercial or industrial properties whose development was completed on or before December 31, 1968. Finally, also excluded until 1971 were any profits on the sale of Larwin's office building, located at 9300 Wilshire Boulevard in Beverly Hills, if the building was sold prior to 1971.

WHAT'S A MERGER REALLY WORTH?

In one sense it is impossible to pin a specific price tag on a merger. When the Larwin deal was agreed upon in principle, the number of common shares earmarked for the front-end transaction had a value of $100 million. At the time the merger closed, the shares had fallen in value to $93 million. But stock-market values can swing upward as well as downward, expanding a fortune as well as contracting it. The Weinberg fortune was back on a considerable rise in 1971 and 1972. The exact value of the deal at the moment of the transaction thus assumes a smaller importance. What mattered to CNA was that it was buying roughly $1.40 in 1968 earnings for each of its 3.745318 common shares initially delivered, plus a reasonable assurance of higher subsequent earnings. What Larry Weinberg was getting was a stock that, if quickened by rising earnings, had the potential to rise in value over a long term.

One nice thing about the preferred stock in escrow is that, so long as it remains unconverted into common stock, it is exempt from fairly short-term stock-market fluctuations. The 1 million shares of CNA's Series B stock were given a stated value of $100 per share, giving the Messrs. Weinberg some measure of protection from downside risk, assuming that they could attain earnout projections and claim the stock. Each share is ultimately convertible into 3.745318 shares of CNA common stock, but this conversion is spaced out over five years. The Series B stock was divided into five classes of 200,000 shares each, with one class becoming convertible each year, starting April 1, 1970. Because spaced over a long period, this sort of conversion formula permits stock values to appreciate and lessens the chances that the successful earnout recipient will get less than $100 million in common stock, following the formula that the total earnout is limited to the lesser of 3,745,318 shares or shares having a value of $100 million.

There were further benefits. In addition to receiving cash dividends on the 3.7 million shares of stock initially exchanged by CNA, the Weinbergs are also entitled to annual dividends of $1.00 per share on the preferred stock held in escrow — and such dividends are payable regardless of whether Larwin achieves its earnout projections. That translates into dividend payments of an additional $1 million per year prior to the conversion of any of the preferred into common. It was an extra benefit of the merger that was much appreciated by Larwin stockholders in 1970, when the company apparently fell short of meeting the earnout. CNA also provided that any contingent common shares delivered on earnings of Larwin Properties would be entitled to the cash dividends which would have been paid on such additional shares if they had been held of record on any record date for the payment of dividends during the period from January 1 of the year of such delivery to the delivery date of the additional shares.

Having made such a substantial commitment to the homebuilding business, CNA likewise committed itself in the merger agreement to provide Larwin Group with loans of up to $20 million at 1% above prime rate between 1969 and the first quarter of 1971. The loans were made for terms of seven years and, subordinated to bank borrowings of the Larwin Group, were used as additional working capital and for the acquisition of more land. It is one of Larry's strong beliefs that the financial ability to control and carry land is a vital key to success in the increasingly competitive industry. In addition to enlisting the incentive of Larry and Bill Weinberg with a strong earnout, CNA also tied them closely to its bosom by means of five-year employment contracts as chief executive officer and executive vice president, respectively. As a condition of the sale of Larwin Fund, the partners Larry and Bill withdrew from it $4.7 million in cash and certificates of deposit. This sum, coincidentally approximating the 1968 earnings of the combined Larwin companies ($4,726,-000), was excluded from the merger. The finder's fee paid by CNA amounted to $1 million and it went to two gentlemen named Bertram J. Cohn and Stephen A. Lieber for their services in bringing together the parties to this transaction.

In the aftermath of such a strong merger parlay it was widely said that Larry Weinberg was in line for the top post to CNA Financial itself, at the same time as he was driving after the big earnout. From the time it was organized as a holding company in 1967, CNA had been steered by Howard C. Reeder, a gentle-spoken and distinguished man who held the titles of chairman, president and chief executive officer. But Reeder planned on retiring at the end of 1971 and the impending vacancy raised tantalizing possibilities. Reeder stimulated the guessing game about his successor in the fall of 1970 by publicly all but ruling out mutual-fund head Gerald Tsai, operator of another CNA subsidiary, as the man to follow him. Tsai, who was CNA Financial's second-largest stockholder, was ultimately to leave the company at the end of 1972 as his mutual funds were being battered by a screwy stock market. Reeder's 1970 statement temporarily propelled Larry, who was now CNA's largest stockholder, into the forefront as a possible successor. However, in the fall of 1971 Elmer C. Nicholson, former president of Fidelity Mutual Insurance Company, was chosen as the new boss of CNA Financial, reflecting the present dominance of CNA's insurance operations. Reeder retired to the chairmanship of CNA's executive committee.

A RAPID GROWTH TO SUPERSIZE

Larry Weinberg and the hot-shot group of top management — including Richard Weiss, president; Mike Tenzer, head of residential housing; Lou Fischer, former president of Levitt; Dick Earlix, head of market research — began pushing the Larwin Group all the way into 1973. In the process, the earnout was achieved and the firm hit revenues of nearly $300 million. There was apparently a temporary hitch, with the firm not able to start collecting its earnout entirely on schedule but things worked out with a bang. Larwin performed well in 1969, as pretax earnings rose to $13.1

million (subtract about 46% for net) on sales of $72.6 million — a great upsurge from 1968 performance. But in 1970 — a generally bad year for homebuilders — sales rose by another 17.1%, to nearly $85 million, while pretax earnings fell off by 27.5% to $9.5 million. The inability to fully meet earnout specifications in 1970, as stated in the proxy formulas, thus put great pressure on Larwin Group to achieve higher earnings ratios in subsequent years in order to recoup for the earnings setback in 1970. The year 1971 was a dramatic comeback. First-half earnings reached $5.8 million pretax, up 59% over the $3.6 million reported for the first half of 1970. Final volume in 1971 reached a towering figure of $188.4 million, and earnings heaved upward to nearly $26 million pretax. Larwin had expanded rapidly to the Midwest and the East Coast in both residential and apartment construction and sales, producing a total of 7,793 units in 1971. It was a phenomenal performance. Larry made that earnout, and he made it good.

Larwin was able to achieve its earnings goals up to 1972 because it has always been a master of marketing. How many people in housing really understand the influence of social and economic phenomena on our business — the immediate impact of lower birthrates, war-baby booms or longer deferrals for marriages — and how these translate into building opportunities in the local market area? It is in this that Larwin is a master and deserves all the credit that has been indicated by its impressive sales performance. This company typically spends more money on market research than any other builder in the United States. Its people are not just observing market conditions but are always out there digging for all the small facts and analyzing them. For example, some years ago Larwin was among the first of the building companies to initiate the family-oriented apartment boom. It saw the opportunity to develop family-oriented apartments in California's San Fernando Valley and did so — very successfully — at a time when the apartment market there was so soft that other builders thought Larwin's collective head was addled to risk it. It was no risk; it was well-backed by research data. Some of these breakthroughs begin as a hunch, but then sophisticated research approaches document the volume and potential of various types of housing demand.

For a company to expand nearly sixfold in just five years — going from sales of $49.6 million to nearly $300 million in 1973 — was an incredible achievement. But the problems of sustaining and managing such a growth rate beyond that period looked very difficult. The turnover of personnel at Larwin was indicative of the pressure under which the company labored. The kind of growth rate it was shooting for could only be predicated on a stable economic environment and a continuing large demand for housing. And so the times caught up with Larwin in 1973.

Not only did a bearish climate affect sales. The advent of percentage-of-completion accounting along with the rollback of subsidized housing programs and the probable introduction of investor tax shelter restrictions suddenly rendered Larwin's apartment and recreational land sales unfeasible. Retrenching strongly in 1973, the company decided to take a non-recurring loss of $8 million to $9 million by writing off all these activities. In the future, it promised to focus on residential housing, commercial mortgage banking, and REIT management. The firm also got caught in a zoning rollback on a large piece of property in Oxnard, California, which resulted in an "open space" designation and necessitated the recording of another extraordinary loss of about $4 million.

These write-offs hit Larwin as its sales were slipping on divisions that remained profitable. For the first half of 1973, it showed earnings of $1 million, down from $2.8 million in the same period of 1972. In the third quarter, profits were down to $3.4 million for the period from the $25.4 million recorded in the third quarter of 1972. The upshot was that Larwin projected a net loss of about $8 million to $9 million in 1973 on sales estimated by company personnel to approach $300 million.

This was bad news for parent CNA because its own profits had begun slipping, and it had actually reported a loss resulting from write-offs in the third quarter of 1973 — the first in its history. The loss, including pro-rated Larwin write-offs and sizable casualty-insurance underwriting losses, amounted to about $7 million. For the same period a year earlier, CNA showed profits of $26 million. For the first six months of 1973, the company had reported profits before capital gains and tax credits of $38.8 million, down from $40.5 million for the same period a year earlier. For all 1972, CNA's earnings before capital gains and tax credits were $94.7 million. Nine-month 1973 earnings were off 53% to $37 million.

The parent company's third-quarter 1973 loss was announced just one day after CNA Financial and Gulf Oil Corp. had called off merger talks that had commenced a month earlier. Gulf, on an upswing from a five-year profit decline, had wanted to acquire CNA as a means of diversifying into insurance and financial services. But it may have shied off from taking on CNA's recently emerged difficulties in insurance and real estate. Thus, CNA was left to solve its own problems as the savior on the white horse rode by.

LARRY WEINBERG TALKS ABOUT TWENTY–FIVE YEARS AT LARWIN

The problems of sustaining and managing such rapid growth would have defeated nearly anyone else. The years of the early Seventies will in particular be remembered as the time when Larry Weinberg's unique talents and entrepreneurial genius were pitted in the greatest test of his career; and he set up that challenge himself, by acting his dream with open eyes, to make it possible. An insight into the man and the company is provided by an extensive interview he had with Ann Griffith, managing editor of *The Group*, a Larwin publication, early in 1973 on the occasion of the twenty-fifth anniversary of the company he founded.

LARRY WEINBERG: You asked how I got into the business of building houses. In the fall of 1947, my wife and I were students at UCLA. It was my senior year, and I realized I had better make plans to support ourselves. We had been married the previous January in Arizona. Neither of us was originally from California, but we loved it here and we wanted to stay. We had about $10,000 — from gifts to me as a child and from what I'd saved in the service. Around that time, laundromats had first appeared and become quite popular, and I thought it would be a great business to get into. Ultimately we thought we'd operate not just one laundromat, but a chain of them so that if one location didn't do well, the others could compensate. We would add other services such as dry cleaning, shoe repair, and — our secret weapon — hat blocking! The idea was to have something unique and better. I went to see the manager of a company that sold laundromat equipment, and after I told him what I wanted to do, he said, "Gee, that sounds great. How much money do you have for a down payment?" I told him I had $10,000, and he began to frown. "Well," he said, "how much experience do you have?" I said, "I'm a student at UCLA." He really frowned then and asked, "How old are you?" I told him I was twenty-one, and he said, "Get lost!" That was the end of my venture into the laundromat business.

AG: Did you make plans to go into something different?

WEINBERG: Yes, I began to look for something else. It was about two and one half years after the end of World War II. Most of our friends were either students or just starting to earn a living. Social conversations would frequently turn to talk of the scarcity of homes they could afford to buy, so I thought that going into the building business could be a great opportunity. I had a cousin who was a "veteran builder" (he had been in the building business for about six months). I asked his advice, and he said, "Gee, Larry, I think you're making a big mistake. It's been a few years since the war, and they've already built enough homes to satisfy the demand. From here on, it looks as if building will be a slow, draggy business."

AG: Why didn't you take the advice of a "veteran builder"?

WEINBERG: I must admit I was disappointed. We then spent many weekends looking at tracts of houses being offered for sale, and finally convinced ourselves that he was wrong. My father-in-law came to Los

Angeles for a visit around January 1948, and he suggested that the first thing I should do in getting into the building business was to get a good lawyer. So he introduced me to a nationally renowned law firm. They assigned one of their young lawyers to my "big" account, and he promptly asked for a $1,000 retainer. One of the attorneys knew an architect who was a general contractor and had been in the business for some time. I met with him, and we worked out an arrangement to work together. His office became the "company headquarters" — it was a desk in a tiny addition onto a building on Canon Drive in Beverly Hills. I arranged my schedule so that my classes at UCLA were over about noon, and I spent the afternoons working at the office. One of my fondest memories is that of planning the kind of company we would become. We wanted it to be a company that would strive and be known for excellence. On February 2, 1948, we incorporated under the name of Guild Homes. We thought that "Guild" would imply hard work and pride of craftsmanship. We planned special ways to merchandise our homes. For instance, we would install a stylized pennant in front of each house. I recently rummaged through some old files — and lo and behold — there was the little notebook I used when we were just getting started, and on the fourth page was my wife's sketch of the pennant.

AG: What was your first housing "development"?

WEINBERG: Well, first we had to find some land. We bought four small lots in Mar Vista, in the 3600 block of Stewart Avenue, which cost a total of $6,000 or $7,000. My associate and I then designed four houses. We finally settled on one particular floor plan with four different elevations. We felt we could afford to have different exterior designs, and from that learn which were the most popular. A wonderful thing about the housing business is that you can learn how to work on floor plans rather quickly. You may not be able to engineer a house, but you can work on the arrangement and sizes of rooms.

AG: Did you have a basic philosophy regarding your homes from the very first?

WEINBERG: Yes, from the beginning we wanted the homes we built to be the very best on the market in their price range — in design, features, and livability. Whatever we were going to do, we wanted to do it best, to be unique.

AG: Were you still working on your original $10,000?

WEINBERG: Yes, we couldn't get a building loan until after we began construction, and we had only our savings. As you can imagine, we were very cautious about how we spent every dollar.

Our associate started to advertise for subcontractors to come and give us bids on the various trades. He would talk to them in the mornings, and

I would see them in the afternoons. I got a great kick out of making comprehensive lists of all the elements that go into a home, estimating their costs, and then negotiating the final contracts.

My associate had a policy that later became an important point of difference between us. He said that we were the general contractor, and that it was inappropriate for us to "fraternize" with the subcontractors. We should give the plans to several subcontractors and accept the lowest bid — he felt no discussion was necessary or appropriate. I knew nothing about running a business, but felt instinctively that communication — a give-and-take with the subcontractor — could benefit us both.

I remember when a plumber came in once and said, "Mr. Weinberg, if you'll move the sink over six inches, I can save you $25 because I can eliminate certain fittings." That $25 was an awful lot of money, so I told my associate about it, and he became upset because I had discussed the plans with a subcontractor. But I continued to talk to subcontractors, and in several other instances learned that we could save money or improve the plans by making minor adjustments.

This difference of opinion between us continued and became more and more pronounced. Finally we agreed to separate.

AG: So then you no longer had an office to work from?

WEINBERG: Right. I moved the office to our apartment at 1277 Oak Street in Santa Monica. In those days, there was a shortage of phone cable in certain areas, and we weren't able to get a phone. My brother Bill joined us about that time, and got an apartment only a block away where phone cable was already installed, so we used his telephone. I recently found one of our first business cards which shows Bill's name and title with the phone number typed in.

AG: How did you arrange the financing to start construction?

WEINBERG: While at UCLA, I maintained a small bank account at the branch of a major bank in Westwood Village. I went to the loan officer there and asked for an FHA loan. He went through the usual questions as to experience and age, and then he said, "Why don't you get into some other business that doesn't require borrowing money?" After a couple of other attempts, I went to the California Bank, which is now the United California Bank, and spoke to a young loan officer in the Beverly Hills office named John Van der Zee. After careful evaluation, he granted the loan. Johnny has just been promoted to executive vice president of the United California Bank. I've sometimes wondered what would have happened if I hadn't been able to get that first loan.

AG: Who did you get to handle the construction end of the business?

WEINBERG: After looking for some time, I met Frank Neilson, who became our first superintendent. Fortunately, he not only worked with the carpenters and trades, but was also adept at drafting. Bill worked with Frank and learned the construction part of the business. He later was in charge of our construction and purchasing operations.

AG: Were you still using your apartment as an office?

WEINBERG: We moved our "operations" to Bill's one-room apartment at 1307-A Ocean Park Avenue. It had a bed, a small desk, and two chairs, so that if two people came to see me, one had to sit on the bed. Obviously, we couldn't afford a secretary or a bookkeeper, so my wife handled all the paper work. She would type up all the myriad forms that had to go to the city, county, utility companies, and especially the FHA and VA. This was long before Xerox, and there was one particular form that required five or six copies. I can still see my wife struggling with all those carbons, trying to keep the sheets aligned and to fit the type between lines that seemed too narrow for the type face.

AG: How did you go about selling your first four homes?

WEINBERG: During the week, production of the houses and the regular business operations took place, and on the weekends we'd sit in front of those houses and wait for prospective buyers. That was in the fall of 1948, and we would sit in the car listening to football games. When we got cold, my wife would go to the nearby drugstore and bring back some hot soup. I remember that when we were ready to sell the first house, I went to the hardware store and bought a For Sale sign. Now, when you put up a For Sale sign, you have to attach it to a stake, and I don't want to shatter any illusions, but I'm not exactly adept at "do-it-yourself" carpentry. I started to nail that poor sign to a stake, and after a while it looked as if both stake and sign had been through a war.

One Saturday afternoon my brother-in-law, Dick Weiss (now president of the Larwin Group) who was then practicing law, came out to "sit on" the houses with me. A young couple came by, and after they started to look through the house, I introduced myself. I wanted to establish some mutual identification with them, but I didn't want to be too obvious about it. The woman was noticeably pregnant. Coincidentally, so was my wife at that time, so I said, pointing to Dick, "You know, his sister is pregnant, too." When that went over okay, I said, "He's my brother-in-law." Anyhow, I sold them the house. That was our first sale.

We sold those first four houses for around $7,500 each, and today they're reselling for more than $27,000. After the houses were completed and sold, we calculated that we had made a total profit of $32.00, or about $8.00 each. I recognized that our real profit was the experience we had gained. That was the last time we intentionally built houses only for experience. I had just barely recovered my $10,000 from the sale of the first four houses, and I used that as a down payment on ten acres near Coldwater

Canyon Avenue. We divided the land into lots and were ready to get started on our first "big" development — thirty houses.

AG: Did you have something in mind that would make your houses different from others in that area?

WEINBERG: Yes, after the first four houses were sold, we spent every weekend looking at other houses that were for sale, evaluating their best features as well as interesting construction techniques. We discovered that almost all the houses in the Valley were in the $8,500 to $9,500 price range. Most of our friends couldn't afford those prices, and we felt there must be a demand for less expensive homes. We decided that the unique element in our first project in the San Fernando Valley would be to build houses that would sell for around $7,500. We spent months developing those plans, trying to include as many desirable features as possible that were usually found only in more expensive homes.

We finally had three really good floor plans, and then we ran into a problem — the government insuring agency didn't want to insure homes in that low price range. I had a long to-do with them, and was at times really afraid they would never approve the tract. Finally, I convinced them to use our thirty houses as a "test case," and if it worked out well, they would consider doing it again.

AG: Did United California Bank provide the financing for these homes?

WEINBERG: No, they were not lending on tracts of homes at that time.

In 1949, most tracts were financed by savings and loan associations, and almost all of them were then located in downtown Los Angeles. I tore out the "Yellow Pages" that listed the savings and loans — there was just one page — and I went downtown and walked, in alphabetical order, from one association to the next. Finally, I reached Western Federal — yes, all the way to the "W's" — and I was lucky enough to meet Hugh Evans, who was later to become the head of Western Federal. He looked at the plans, then looked me over, and finally said, "Let me take a look at the property this weekend, and I'll let you know on Monday." When I phoned him on Monday, he said, "Come on into my office. I think we can work something out."

We called that development Coldwater Park. It turned out to be quite profitable and a great success — the houses sold very well. It was exciting to bid them out, to see the construction actually take form, and afterward, watch as the families moved in. We got that special satisfaction that comes from building homes that are well received and realizing that we had touched the lives of thirty families hopefully for the better.

I learned another lesson — as our houses began to sell well, other builders in the area who had been watching the success of our "test project" started to build homes in our price range. We had spent a lot of time pioneering something while others stood on the sidelines, adapted what they learned from us, and then profited by jumping into the field. Doing things best is what really counts, whether that means developing original plans, or adapting and attempting to improve upon a worthwhile concept from somewhere else.

When we started building in the Valley, we moved our office to the site of the development. At Coldwater Park, our office was about twelve feet by twenty feet. The size was dictated more by the dimensions of the plywood we used to build it than by any more scientific factor. We used unfurnished models there, and converted one of the one-car garages into a sales office.

AG: You were building under the name Guild Homes. When did Larwin come into the picture?

WEINBERG: When we were in the San Fernando Valley, Guild Homes was the building company, and we decided to set up a company that would act as sales agent. I remember discussing this with Dick Weiss, who was our outside counsel then, and we came up with the name "Larwin" for the second corporation.

During 1949, we bought a group of seventy-two finished lots in Downey from a developer for about $1,250 each. I guess today, those lots are worth around $15,000 each. I recall telling a banker about our new lots, and he said, "Downey? Who in the world would want to live that far out? Nobody will buy those houses — you're out of your mind!"

Our plan for Downey was to build houses similar to the ones in the San Fernando Valley, but with certain refinements. Again, we spent a great deal of time comparing homes in the area and trying to make ours the very best. That was our basic philosophy — we had to feel that ours were the very best that were being built.

We put our office structure on a truck and moved it from the San Fernando Valley to Downey and began to develop Downey Park. An interesting development took place just before we started construction in Downey. In mid-1949, I was in the fathers' waiting room at Cedars of Lebanon Hospital, waiting for my wife to give birth to our first son. I started talking with another prospective father, who turned out to be an accountant. As we discussed taxes and the building business, we gradually developed a concept whereby a building company could retain the mortgages on the homes. By doing this, the builder didn't have to pay taxes until the collections were made over the twenty-year period of the mortgages. In a sense, the profit would be distributed over a twenty-year period as we made the collections on the mortgages. It was a whole new idea in project development.

We established a company called Downey Park Investment Company, which had to become an approved mortgage lender in order to carry out this new plan to hold the mortgages. We have subsequently changed its name to Columbia Mortgage Company, then to Brentwood Mortgage Corp., and now to Rexford National Corporation. So our mortgage banking business really started in the fathers' waiting room at Cedars of Lebanon Hospital in 1949.

I recall July 4, 1949, my wife and I, with our son in a bassinet, and Sue and Dick Weiss and their daughter Nancy had a picnic near where the first houses in Downey were being framed. After we ate, we took a walk through the orange grove — it was a wonderful time. In those days, I would work six days a week and on the seventh, I'd be out selling houses or looking at the competition. I hardly took a day off, but we were young, enthusiastic, and full of hope for the future — just about as happy as anyone could be. And we felt the houses we were building were the best around.

AG: I take it you proved you weren't "out of your mind" to build in Downey?

WEINBERG: Right. The seventy-two homes in Downey Park sold very quickly. We then bought forty-seven more lots which became Downey Park No. 2, and they sold rapidly as well. We were making a profit of about $1,700 per house on a $7,500 sales price. I was delighted because it proved once again that you can incorporate a superior profit with a superior product if you really work at it.

AG: What was the next development after the two in Downey?

WEINBERG: We bought 122 lots on Anaheim Telegraph Road which we called Anatel Park. We converted our movable office into our first non-garage sales office there and opened up a regular office in a store front on Second Avenue in Downey.

After we had developed two tracts at Anatel Park, the Korean War broke out. The building business in Southern California slowed down for two or three years. Labor was very difficult to get because of the draft and defense work, and without a priority one could not get materials. I bought an aircraft business and operated both businesses concurrently for seven years. I learned much about production and operations in the aircraft business which helped me at Larwin.

We expanded building activities in 1953, and early in 1954, after a great deal of planning and preparation, we put together a development in the Covina area that was really special — we called it Arrow Park. We developed some of our first sophisticated merchandising concepts there.

It was the first time we had completely furnished our models. To the best of my knowledge, we were the innovators at Arrow Park of the "trap" concept — that is, a prospective buyer had to go through the sales office to get to the model homes, and then back through the sales office in order to leave. In the model complex we erected a large comparison chart which listed the major developments in the area as "A," "B," and so on. We compared them to Arrow Park on the basis of features, cost, available transportation, etc.

AG: What sort of advertising did you use for Arrow Park?

WEINBERG: We started using display advertising in the major newspapers, but the ads were extremely crude by today's standards. There might be a small rendering with lots of copy that listed all your features. We also had "teaser" ads prior to the opening, and there were several large billboards in the area surrounding the project.

We began sales at Arrow Park on a Saturday morning. I recall arriving around eleven A.M. — we were mobbed. The minute we got there, my wife started typing the processing forms in the sales office. We were reluctant to go out for lunch or dinner — it was one of the most exciting weekends I've ever had, and by the end of it we had sold sixty-eight homes. After going through months of sweating over plans, moving walls six inches here, three inches there, trying to fit special features into this or that home, deciding on the best placement of a window or a door — then the grand opening, and at last you see the enthusiasm of a family that falls in love with your house. It's great!

AG: What was the price of the homes in Arrow Park?

WEINBERG: These sold for $10,750. By that time, Larwin had become the principal company, and Guild Homes the sales company. Arrow Park became a springboard for Larwin. We had become leaders in merchandising and marketing concepts. We then developed Arrow Gardens and Arrow Square in the vicinity of Arrow Park, and those homes sold well, too. They totaled about seven hundred houses. Our next large development was Mirada Park in La Mirada. Again, we spent months analyzing all our competitors and trying to put together the best plans possible. Our houses were a bit larger than the Arrow Park homes. We developed a more sophisticated trap and included three furnished models, each done by a different well-known decorator. I remember that it was pouring rain the weekend we opened for sales, and we were all afraid no one would come to see the houses. We had to put boards across the puddles in front of the sales office. But people had come to expect something special when Larwin opened up a new development, and they came in droves. The houses sold beautifully, and over the next two years we sold over seven hundred homes in La Mirada.

AG: Was it at the end of the 1950's that you began building in Orange County and then in Simi Valley?

WEINBERG: Yes, we started to acquire some land in Orange County about that time, and our first development was called Town and Country Square. Brentwood Park in Buena Park was a 2,000-home community that became one of our largest and most successful developments. Most people thought we were crazy to start building homes in Simi Valley. We had bought a good-sized parcel of land and felt we could design a larger home that could be merchandised at a lower price than the homes offered in the San Fernando Valley. In the early sixties, Simi Valley was practically undeveloped, and we had a difficult time getting the VA to approve our first tract. They had good cause for concern, as about the only other VA tract was directly across the street and was in foreclosure. Finally, they agreed to go along with us on a test basis, and our first development, Simi Park, sold beautifully. We then built Valley West in Simi Valley, and it, too, was a great success.

I had confidence that we had developed the expertise that would enable us to go a little farther out, and by doing a better job of researching the market, we could develop an exciting community that the public would buy. We tried to analyze what people there really wanted and needed and could afford, and then we did our best to perfect our "package" for them.

Toward the end of the 1950's, we were getting into larger developments, and I felt we should start broadening our operations and building an organization that would allow us to be more efficient in our business. I didn't want to take over any of the sub-trades, but there were certain complementary operations which would have an impact on growth and profitability, and I felt we needed these capabilities in-house.

We were one of the first developers to have and train our own sales force. We were one of the few to provide escrow and mortgage services. It wasn't that we made a lot of money from escrow services, but it is a crucial part of processing a sale and reinforcing the buyer's decision. We began our mortgage business as brokers and planned to establish close relations with those located in the East who made the market in mortgages. Through the office we opened in New York, our contacts enabled us to anticipate trends in the mortgage market. This helped the single family business as well as our mortgage operations. In 1961 we began servicing mortgages and became a full-fledged mortgage banker.

AG: Following the establishment of mortgage banking services, what was the next major area that Larwin entered?

WEINBERG: We then went into commercial and shopping center developments. We had sold a few of the commercial corners in our developments, and I felt that there was potential for a separate profit center by developing our own commercial properties. We would also have greater control over the quality and timing of these developments, which could help the marketing of the overall community.

AG: What prompted your decision to merge with another company?

WEINBERG: By the late sixties, we had become the largest and, I believe, most profitable privately owned builder in the country. Our goal was to continue our growth aggressively, but soundly. I wanted to expand geographically and to establish new divisions. As a private company, our available capital would severely restrict these plans.

Faced with these expanded needs for capital, I felt there were two ways we could go — either become a public company on our own, or merge with another company. We tried to evaluate all the possibilities open to us. As a matter of fact, we were preparing an application to go public at the time we merged with CNA Financial Corporation, so we were going down both tracks at the same time.

From the merger standpoint, we had to decide what we needed from a potential parent company. The only thing we really required was the availability of long-term, relaxed capital. The kind of company that typically has that resource available is an insurance company, so that's where we concentrated our efforts.

AG: Did you ever consider merging into another building company?

WEINBERG: No, not unless they were willing to become a subsidiary of Larwin. In one instance, however, a major conglomerate approached us and asked if we would become a part of their large homebuilding division. I said that I would be willing to enter into a five-year arrangement whereby Larwin and their homebuilding company would remain separate. At the end of the five years, they could evaluate both companies, and the one with the best track record would be the surviving company. But the chief executive officer of their homebuilding company wouldn't agree.

AG: Why did you decide to merge rather than take Larwin public?

WEINBERG: I was concerned at the time that Wall Street didn't fully appreciate or understand the housing industry. At the time we merged, home building was a hot industry, and a lot of builders were going public. My feeling is that the lion's share of the building companies won't make it in the long run. There is a price-earnings ratio by which Wall Street typically values an industry, and that ratio is crucial to the value of the stock. I was concerned that, if many of the building companies didn't make it, the price-earnings ratio for the industry would go down. When that happened, the value of Larwin's stock might be dragged down with it.

AG: Why did you decide to merge with CNA?

WEINBERG: CNA was basically an insurance holding company and could provide Larwin with the long-term money we required. I felt that with this support Larwin would be able to reach its long-range goals of volume and profit and would thereby prove to be a very valuable subsidiary for CNA.

AG: At what point did you decide to expand Larwin's single family operations to national regions?

WEINBERG: In the mid-Sixties, we embarked on a program of planned growth. An integral part of that plan called for each of our operations to become a major factor in every important housing market in the country.

Our first single family region outside the Los Angeles area was in San Diego. We then opened Illinois, Northern California, the New York area, and now metropolitan Washington, D.C. Our ability to succeed in these and other regions which we will establish will depend to a great extent upon our ability to transfer from region to region the areas of expertise that Larwin has and will develop in the future.

AG: Do you have any plans to consider regions in international markets?

WEINBERG: Yes, I feel that there are exciting opportunities for us in Europe and in other overseas markets. I expect that we'll see such a move within the next few years.

AG: What new regions will be opening in the United States?

WEINBERG: We expect to be averaging one new geographic region each year. We will be starting a new region by the end of 1973, or the beginning of 1974. In a sense, we opened two regions in 1972 — New York and Washington, D.C.

AG: What part does Larwin's Multiple Family Division play in your growth program?

WEINBERG: Getting into multiple family was a natural part of our plan to be in the total real estate development business, and it will be an increasingly important part of our business operations as time goes by.

Sophistication in the development of apartment communities is still in its early stages. But I believe that Larwin has now and will continue to develop the proper expertise in design, marketing, management, financing, and ability to consummate the ultimate sale that will enable us to excel in developing those multiple family communities of the future.

The market here is unlimited for Larwin just as it is in single family housing.

AG: There has been a lot of talk about "overbuilding" in the apartment industry. Does that concern you?

WEINBERG: It is of some concern to us, but it's not really a key factor. Our job must be, through careful and incisive marketing research, to identify specific needs in a market and then to develop a superior product to meet those needs.

AG: Does Larwin plan to retain management of its apartment communities?

WEINBERG: We have, for the main part, been retaining management. This enables us to stay close to our customer and more fully understand his needs which aids us in developing ways to make our existing and new apartments the most appealing and desirable ones to live in.

AG: What do you feel is the long-term potential for the Urban Housing Division in providing housing for low- and moderate-income families?

WEINBERG: To quote the title of a popular song, "We've only just begun." The private sector of our industry can provide new housing for less than fifty percent of the total population. As time goes by, the inflationary effect on housing costs, plus higher taxes, are increasing more rapidly than is the consumer's ability to pay. Our nation will not long ignore this worsening condition. One way or another, be it federal or state, government will in the long run find it desirable to help the majority of Americans who now cannot afford to buy or to rent new housing.

Larwin has a responsibility and an opportunity to be of help. This market will ultimately be enormous and urban housing may someday become one of our most important and largest divisions. In the short run, however, this division will suffer its ups and downs until the fundamental needs of our society get more solidly locked into our national priorities.

AG: The area of recreational communities development has been a controversial one in the last few years. What plans do you have for Larwin in this area?

WEINBERG: Here, too, the industry is in a period of transition. A decade ago, a few fly-by-night operators gave the recreational-communities industry a bad name. It has now matured to the point where both the developer and the consumer are more product- and use-oriented. That's all for the good.

As time goes by, new concepts in recreational communities will be developed that will make obsolete older existing developments. Larwin has the qualities and the determination necessary to succeed, and, we believe, to lead in this changing environment.

We'll have to find more effective ways of marketing our product, and we'll have to find better ways to finance these communities for the consumer. The market here, too, will be unlimited. In addition, there will be opportunities for us to develop all kinds of corollary services and profit centers related to these communities.

AG: How did Larwin get into the real estate investment trust field?

WEINBERG: We were convinced that Larwin had, because of our experience and organization, the necessary expertise to understand the needs of the developer, and that we could do a better job of tailoring a lending program to satisfy those needs. We also understand the risks that a developer faces and are better equipped to design our loans in such a manner as to minimize or eliminate those risks for our trusts.

As is the case in our divisions, the growth of our trusts has boundless potential. We've now come out with a closed-end investment company whose principal objective will be to invest in other REIT stocks. Again, our experience, in this case as a REIT manager, enables us to better evaluate other REIT's and to do a superior job of managing this new investment company. It's all part of our plans to develop the most proficient management in our field, and then adapting their expertise to new corollary businesses that are synergistic to our existing operations. This helps the existing businesses in addition to establishing new, self-sufficient profit centers.

AG: Do you have plans for expanding Larwin Home Center operations beyond current capabilities?

WEINBERG: Our eventual goal for the Home Center is to provide for the customer any and everything he might need in and around his home or apartment. This operation is again typical of our concept of developing an added service for our customers, and thereby creating a new profit center and helping our existing businesses. We will one day offer a full line of furniture, appliances, landscaping, swimming pools, and even kitchenware, dishes, and linens. All this will also help us to sell more homes and rent more apartments.

We expect to be able to sell to our customer at better prices, because we will have lower costs for selling, lower costs for inventorying, and no additional credit checks will be necessary. We will be better able to help him finance his purchases by adding some of the costs on to the mortgage and by providing the necessary financing for the balance. The customer can then include furnishings as a part of his monthly home or apartment payment.

AG: In a broad sense, what are your plans for Larwin in the coming years?

WEINBERG: Our next major long-term goal is to do 25,000 housing units per year — approximately $1 billion in annual volume. I believe we will reach that goal before 1980.

Reaching a volume of about 25,000 units a year would bring certain fascinating concepts into play. At that volume, we could allocate a certain number of dollars per house for meaningful research and development. One of my theories has been that a program of continuing R&D on the total house will enable Larwin to accelerate our penetration of major markets.

Until now, most of the research and development has been done by manufacturers, but for a very narrow product line. Builders have never had enough volume to be able to allot substantial amounts of money for ongoing programs year after year. Now, when you are producing 25,000 units a year, and if you allocated $50 per unit, you would have $1,125,000 annually for research and development on a continuing basis. It's very exciting to realize that at that level, we could develop entirely new concepts of design and construction that have never before been feasible.

Ultimately, we could reach the point where we may very well have brand-name products designed specifically for Larwin homes and apartments. For example, we might go to General Electric or Westinghouse and say, "We want to develop a very special kind of Larwin kitchen that has appliances that are different and better than those sold in the stores." And it becomes feasible because you can order 25,000 of them year after year. We could do the same kind of thing for many other elements of the house.

With volume that large, our land planners and architects could develop innovative design concepts and exciting new ways of living for our customers that are undreamed of even in today's most advanced communities. We could also test and develop different systems and procedures that would enable our managers to really focus in on the key, "gut" elements that affect our business.

On a broader scale, Larwin has the potential of becoming an important factor in every major housing market in the world. I don't really know whether there will ever be a General Motors of the housing industry, or even a Ford or an American Motors. There is, however, no question in my mind that there will evolve a small number of extremely large producers, and my personal goal is to see that Larwin becomes one of them — possibly the leader of them.

AG: In a company that has grown as rapidly as Larwin, how do you infuse a sense of personal pride at every level of operation?

WEINBERG: A company that is expanding, developing, and planning the kind of exciting future that we have at Larwin provides great opportunities for advancement and a sense of fulfillment for all its employees. Each of us, if he really wants to, can help Larwin achieve these ambitious goals and at the same time get the special satisfaction and rewards that come from being part of a championship team. Larwin is not one man or woman, or ten, or even a hundred, but it is the sum total of each of our efforts. Each person affiliated with Larwin makes a valuable and significant contribution toward our success. I hope every one of us understands and appreciates that.

The homebuilding business itself is thrilling and challenging, and I get tremendous personal satisfaction from knowing that Larwin is excelling as a leader in our industry. We have tried from the start to be the best in whatever we attempted—to have the best product, the best profit, and the best people. I hope that we will be able, even as we continue to grow in size, to transmit that feeling of pride-excitement-fulfillment to each of our employees. We are trying to find ways to retain, at 25,000 units a year or more, the entrepreneurial quality and personal identification with our company and our product that we had when we were building 250 units a year.

AG: There's one last thing I'm curious about. You have worked very hard for twenty-five years, and now your company and you personally are tremendously successful. Why do you keep at it? Why do you continue to work such long hours?

WEINBERG: I get enormous satisfaction out of my work. Over the years, I've gotten as much, or greater, delight from looking at one of our developments the night before it opened, and saying to myself, "This is the best — the most exciting group of houses in town," than I have from looking at our profit at the end of the year. Every man has a personal goal for himself, and mine has been to do the best job I could, and to continue to learn and to grow.

Whenever I can, I drive through the communities we've developed. I can't tell you how gratifying it is to see families living in homes that we built and realize that to some extent, we have hopefully helped them to a better life.

Being active in our business means exposure to a very broad spectrum of our society — from the farmer whose land we purchase to the producer of basic materials used in construction; from the myriad activities involving our federal government to obtaining building permits in a local municipality; from the subtle impact of foreign trade deficits on interest rates across the country to the reinvestment experience of a neighboring savings and loan; from industry-wide bargaining in same basic trades to a wildcat strike that affects a large subcontractor; and from the influence of various consumer communications on the public to fundamental changes in the homebuyer's style preferences. We are affected by them all, and we must keep in touch. That keeps us alert, involved — it's always stimulating.

The people I work with have a major impact on the enjoyment of my work. I am familiar with the management of most of the larger developers, and I know that the best operators and managers in our industry today make up the Larwin senior management team. Dick Weiss, Lou Fischer, Mike Tenzer, Irv Adler, Larry Farmer, Fred Gale, Ted Rhodes, Chuck Horne, Herb Grossman, Lou Weider, Mike Keston, Bill Avella, Howard Borde, Dick Earlix, Irv Rosen — all are tops in their fields.

And finally, the housing industry is really special. We are at the center of crucial issues affecting our society. What we do really counts — we can directly touch the lives of many thousands of people and influence the quality of living throughout America. What more can one aspire to?

12

What Ben Deane Learned from the Wizard of Oxy

In the long run men hit only what
they aim at. Therefore, though
they fail immediately they had
better aim at something high.

—Thoreau

The merger of Deane Brothers into Occidental Petroleum represented the coming together of two entrepreneurs. They weren't playing the same game, but you couldn't mistake either one for anything but a master in his own field.

THE BUILDER

Ben Cady Deane started his homebuilding career in 1940 as a carpenter in Alaska. A resourceful, quick-thinking man, he early perceived the coming opportunity in housing development. Shifting his operations to Southern California after the war, he caught the tide of rising demand for housing and began to build up a homebuilding company. Brother Jim worked along with him, and as their sons grew up, they, too, entered the business. Under the tutelage of their fathers, Ben's son Larry and Jim's son Bill both became experts at parlaying hefty chunks of capital into successful housing projects at an age when other boys were still looking for their first serious jobs. The family enterprise, named Deane Brothers, throve. By the mid-Sixties it had become one of the nation's five largest homebuilding firms, with sales of $25 million in 1966.

The company was known as a developer of extremely attractive residential communities, and for its exceptional merchandising. The Deanes' Garden Kitchen home, uniting indoor and outdoor living space, revolutionized subdivision home design in the sunny California climate and became one of the most copied ideas in housing. Ben also pioneered the building of single-family housing on leased land, building in Huntington Beach, California. And, working in association with M. J. Brock & Sons, another major builder who was later to go the merger route, he developed Barrington Plaza in Los

310

Angeles as a private urban renewal job. It was the first residential high rise building to receive an FHA commitment.

THE CORPORATE WIZARD

Dr. Armand Hammer is quite a different sort of entrepreneur. As the head of Occidental Petroleum Corp., he emerged as practically Henry Kissinger's commercial envoy to the Kremlin in the early 1970s, so few readers will not be familiar with his name. Hobnobbing with Premier Kosygin, Dr. Hammer signed a series of gigantic oil and gas deals with the Soviet Union, to be financed through U.S.-subsidized loans. Perhaps less well known is the fact that Dr. Hammer had a long history of association with the U.S.S.R., and that he once hobnobbed with Lenin as he later met with Kosygin.

New York born, he received a medical degree from Columbia, but his talents for wheeling and dealing from the outset seemed to dwarf whatever inclinations he might have had for the healing profession. Even before he graduated from medical school, he had already banked his first million dollars by successfully helping his father to run the family pharmaceutical business. On graduating the young doctor went to Soviet Russia with a field hospital in 1922. But he soon launched into a whirlwind sequence of such intensely capitalistic wheeling and dealing in that Communist land that Karl Marx must have rolled over in his grave. He started trading in wheat and ended up with a pencil factory in Moscow. By the time he left in 1930, after an eight-year stay, he took out of the U.S.S.R. another million dollars in cash and a priceless boatload of Czarist art treasurers.

It was in the U.S.S.R. that Dr. Hammer formulated his credo: "When you don't have all the money in the world, you have to do something else, like finding out what people need." On his return to the United States, he went on to make fortunes in other ventures, including an art gallery, a whiskey distillery, and breeding prize bulls. By 1957 he was fifty-nine years old and had already retired from active business. But it was only at that time that he launched another venture which was to dwarf all his preceding accomplishments and become the capstone to a brilliant entrepreneurial career. In 1957, the good doctor invested $1.2 million in a small wildcat oil outfit — Occidental Petroleum — and in a period of ten years built it into an industrial giant.

Occidental Petroleum (or "Oxy" for short) became what they call a Cinderella story. Steered by Dr. Hammer, who became its chairman and president despite his "retired" status, the company burgeoned from an unsteady driller of wildcat wells with sales of less than $1 million in 1957 into a dynamic, diversified operation whose revenues in 1971 reached nearly $2.7

billion. At the end of that year, the doctor owned about 3% of the company. Since Dr. Hammer was no oilman, his quick success and unorthodox tactics irritated other oil companies. He struck his first big gas field on land abandoned by one oil company, and his biggest oil strike came on land another oil company had given up as worthless. The annoyed oil industry jumped on him for publicizing oil finds quickly. There was likewise much disgruntled feeling about his offer to build an agricultural complex in Libya and hotels in Morocco in order to win oil concessions. But Dr. Hammer's biggest battle with the oil industry came over his plan in 1969 to establish a free-trade zone in Machiasport, Maine, where he wanted to refine crude oil and undersell the majors. The oil companies fought the plan, and it fell through. Notwithstanding, Occidental prospered as Libyan oil became its biggest profitmaker.

Starting in the mid-Sixties, Occidental's chief accelerated the growth of the oil giant by engineering a vigorous acquisition program, diversifying the company's operations considerably. He made Occidental a major chemical producer by buying up big Hooker Chemical Corporation, which in 1970 accounted for 25% of Occidental's sales and 20% of its earnings. Occidental likewise took a strong position in the coal industry with the acquisition of Island Creek Coal Company, which in 1970 accounted for 10% of Oxy's sales and 15% of its profits. Dr. Hammer also acquired Permian Corporation, which buys and sells crude oil in the United States, and Jefferson Lake Sulphur Company. Reaching to Europe, he bought the continental refining and marketing operations of Signal Oil & Gas Company. Finally, he branched Occidental into real estate.

It was at this point that the paths of Ben Deane and Armand Hammer began to converge, though neither of them knew it yet. Hammer's first venture into homebuilding came in July of 1964 when Oxy acquired S. V. Hunsaker & Sons (Sunshine Homes) for about $4.8 million in stock. The doctor was acutely perceptive and could spot both the profit opportunities in housing and the boom fever that housing was to enjoy on Wall Street from away down the pike. The Hunsaker operation had reported sales of $42 million in the year it was merged and looked like an excellent bet for Oxy's foray into building. As it turned out, however, the doctor had bet wrong. Hunsaker sold homes on the installment contract method, recording profits from sales at full value when the homebuyer made a small down payment. S. V. Hunsaker, founder of that homebuilding firm, was an extremely talented man and pioneered this concept in Southern California. However, it worked only as long as the economy was buoyant; when California nosed into a bad housing slump, homebuyers began abandoning hundreds of homes after the contracts, worth millions of dollars, had already been booked by Oxy as profits. Moreover, each repossession cost up to $2,000. Meanwhile, unsold Hunsaker inventory also began backing up. Dr. Hammer needed to do something to bail out of this situation. He began looking around for another homebuilder. His intention was not known, to be sure. But an acquisition at this time could have had the practical effect of killing two birds with one stone by satisfying Oxy stockholders with another homebuilding acquisition and repairing the errors of the first one during the excitement generated by the second.

THE DEANES MEET DR. HAMMER

Thus it happened that Ben Deane got a phone call from Armand Hammer up in Los Angeles in June 1966. Would the Deanes like to come up to the office to discuss a development venture that the doctor had in mind? From that moment events moved quickly. As Larry Deane, who is now in his early thirties, recalls it: "Dr. Hammer called us up and said he wanted to talk to us about a joint venture. We went up to his office. The discussion on the joint venture lasted about four to five minutes, and then the topic was switched to the merger proposal. That man does not beat around the bush. The deal was put together in a very short period of time." A short time, indeed. The meeting with Dr. Hammer took place on June 28, 1966. One week later, the two parties signed a letter of intent. On August 3, 1966, they traded stock, completing the deal. As part of the merger agreement, the Deanes negotiated the right to retain the Deane Brothers name on becoming an Occidental subsidiary, unlike many other acquired builders who took on the names of the corporate parent.

What motivated the Deanes to join Occidental? There was, of course, the incentive of $8 million in Occidental stock (including the earnout) which made them independently wealthy. One could speculate that Ben might have received many many more millions for the company had he waited until 1969 to merge his building company, when sky-high multiples were being laid out by anxious industrial corporations; still, $8 million is nothing to sneeze at. But perhaps even more important than the idea of cashing in was the Deanes' desire to link up their company with a strong capital source that would enable them to transcend the entrepreneurial hazards of undercapitalization and really take advantage of the opportunities they could perceive in the development business.

Every builder is familiar with the costs of entrepreneurial freedom, which is often the freedom to take all the risk. Larry Deane sums it up this way: "If I as a builder develop a project with my own money plus leverage and it's a success, I'm only generating equity capital for other projects. But if the second or third project is a flop, all my past capital is down the tube. Every time a builder goes after a new project he's putting all his past capital

on the block; if the project is bad, he loses everything. But a large corporation has the staying power an individual does not have. It can take you
through the highs and lows of the market. And a builder can also cash out
for all his past work. Thus a merger becomes a tantalizer for a builder —
he sees the potential to convert all his past work and his future potential
into hard dollars." Or as Ben puts it: "On merging, you get through that
period when every morning you get up and all your chips are on the table.
You change all that."

A MERGER THAT GOES NOWHERE

The Deanes got financial security, all right. But if they believed that
Oxy would come through with working capital to finance the growth of that
homebuilding business and take advantage of profit opportunities in apartments, high-rises and mobile homes, they soon learned they were mistaken.
Deane Brothers did start one new housing project after joining Occidental — Lake Forest, a beautiful residential project located on approximately
1,400 acres halfway between Los Angeles and San Diego — but that was it:
the money tap was thereafter dry. The Hunsaker inventory was the corporate
financial department's responsibility, not the Deanes'! But, the Deane boys
say, the financial problems of that Hunsaker inventory became part of the
rationale for Oxy's corporate finance people to deny further investment capital to Deane Brothers because of the "unprofitability" of the real estate division! During the more than three years of the marriage, the Deanes time
and again submitted project proposals to the financial vice president, and
time and again these were shot down. It amounted to a crushing letdown after the magical, whirlwind courtship and the quick merger agreement.

"It's very easy for a financial department of a corporation to find many
reasons why a real estate project is not feasible," recounted a wiser Ben
Deane. "You will go many times through the exercise of feasibility reports
and prepare what you are sure is a fine analysis of a fine project, and they
can still shoot it full of holes. They can frustrate and stop your operation
just by coming up with a rationale, proving in effect that your project is not
feasible. Then you're stopped and not going anywhere, and now all you've
accomplished is that you've taken care of your estate, and are maybe ready
to die. You have not gotten yourself into position where you can create continuing growth within your company which you've worked so many years
to create."

Meanwhile, Oxy's problems stemming from the Hunsaker deal did not
show signs of abating for quite a while, either. A close observer makes a co-
gent observation on the contrasting corporate and entrepreneurial styles in
handling the large Hunsaker inventory of land and houses: "For an individ-

ual entrepreneur, the obvious way to handle this situation would be to get rid of the burden in one year, taking the loss and starting anew, rather than continuing to carry it and have it weigh you down each year. But a public corporation can't withstand this; it has to carry the burden for an extended period of time, trying to hide it. And that is the right way for a public corporation to do it, but not the way for a real estate division. Anytime you have land or houses on the books, you have money tied up. They're very expensive to hold, with a further cost in taxes and upkeep on land and homes. Weighing the market costs against holding costs, you're better off selling below market to get rid of the burden. This way you release operating dollars and don't have them tied up in frozen assets."

Occidental did eventually succeed in trading off most of the Hunsaker homes for land, making some good swaps along the way, both during the time of the Deane merger and more recently. But it is important to note that Ben Deane did not have specific responsibility for handling the Hunsaker inventory; that situation affected Deane Brothers indirectly, coming into service as a partial excuse for the refusal of operating capital to the real estate division for proposed Deane projects. The Deanes' own operation, though limited to Lake Forest, prospered extremely well: during the first two years of the project, they booked $2 million in profits from it. However, this successful performance did not seem to impress Occidental when Ben came knocking at the door with proposals for other projects.

Nobody can say that the Deanes didn't make every effort to make the merger work. But after three years of futile efforts to get working capital, and with an atrophying housing company on their hands, "it became apparent to us that Oxy didn't want to be in real estate," as Larry puts it. What really clinched this observation was Oxy's intervention in the Deane's successful Lake Forest operation. "They decided to shut it down and sell the real estate," says Larry. "We drew the conclusion that they wanted out of real estate: why else would they want to shut down a going concern?" After extended frustrating dealings with Oxy's financial department, Ben finally confronted Dr. Hammer. "He's the most brilliant man I ever met," he told Frank Lalli of *Forbes,* "but we had some horrendous arguments. In the end I said, 'Either I run the housing division alone, or you can run it alone.' " Shortly afterwards, the Deanes resigned.

THE LESSONS OF THE MERGER EXPERIENCE

The Deane-Occidental merger can serve as an archetypal example of the problems and conflicts that arise when an industrial corporation acquires a builder without careful prior consideration to the success of that venture. The Deanes could probably qualify as experts at counseling other builders how to avoid merger pitfalls. Four key points emerge from an analysis of the Deane merger itself:

1. The conflict between the corporate and the entrepreneurial merger styles. "You have the one problem that arises in a marriage," observes Larry Deane, "and that's the problem of the two different ways of operation. The corporation is an extremely large organizational machine which, due to its size and the objectives it must accomplish, adopts operating methods suitable to itself. For a decision to come out of the machine, it has to go through many more processes than in the case of the individual entrepreneur." Larry emphasizes that a more formal and thoroughgoing decision-making process proved instructive. "From the standpoint of time and ease of decision-making, it imposes a burden," he says. "But, on the other hand, it teaches the entrepreneur an awful lot: that the processes, though time-consuming, are useful; that they can provide a proper focus for the management of the development business." The corporate process can lead to excessive wheel-spinning, he concludes, but the art in tailoring a merger is not to eliminate it but to incorporate it within an entrepreneurial framework.

2. The problem of communication and understanding. "You have the problem of an oil company trying to understand the intricacies of accounting and cash flows peculiar to real estate," Larry says. "So for a while, there is a learning process as the acquiring corporation and the builder each learn how the other operates and what each other's special problems are. Until the financial department understands real estate — and maybe they never will — you'll have trouble. This was basically our situation. Oxy either did not understand the problem of real estate or didn't want to."

3. The "Seagull Syndrome" (for definition, see Chapter IX). In a typical large corporate structure, the professionals without stock in the company face the problem of climbing the corporate ladder. Their operations decisions may therefore be partly or wholly monitored by a concern for how they may maximize their own reputations with a minimum of risk. This situation creates an unstable political environment to which, unless specifically guarded against, the builder's operation is subject. The Deanes are understandably unwilling to air the small details of much meddling stemming from this situation, but it should be obvious that when managers unacquainted with real estate have absolute control over what a builder might do, such strife is inevitable.

4. But all of the problems resolved to the single most important issue: access to, and control of, investment capital. "This was our major area of misunderstanding," says Larry. "We had a lot of minor ones, too, but none of these in themselves would have created a falling-out. Commitment to capital and decision-making ability with regard to that capital are the requirements for a successful operation. It should work this way: We set certain

goals and criteria. If projects we later submit meet these criteria, we get a commitment from a pre-committed pool of capital automatically. I admire and respect the doctor and his team, but at Oxy there was a lack of [housing] industry knowledge and support; a lack of a desire to continue in the business."

This last was a lesson that Ben Deane learned very well from the Wizard of Oxy. I remember how, at a 1970 conclave of the National Association of Homebuilders, during a panel session on mergers, a tense, expectant stillness fell over the packed audience of builders when Ben Deane — fresh from the breakup of his merger deal—arose to speak. Ben did not refer to the breakup. In a sonorous voice that rolled across the hall, he began to describe the merits of his merger: "I must tell you I have no regrets about it. It's been good for Occidental, and it has been good for me." But everyone there *knew,* everyone was reading between the lines. Here was Ben Deane, one of the building industry's leaders, come to tell them what had gone wrong. The utter stillness continued and Ben's voice rang out clearly and steadily: "But one thing I should have gotten was a commitment to capital. You merge so there will be an availability of capital, so you can do new things. Be sure that the capital is going to be available. A mere statement that they'll back you up in things you want to do is not enough. You want to have them committed to put up capital, and if they don't do it, there should be some kind of penalty." And when Ben was through speaking and sat down the stillness still reigned. This was no consultant or financial professional speaking on the mechanics. This was a man who had *done* it, gone the route, and who was now making sure that nobody else would repeat his own mistake. His words drove like an arrow finding its mark.

But why was Occidental in real estate if it was not prepared to finance development and get profits from it? Speculation is idle, but knowing Dr. Hammer's brilliance leads one to consider that there might have been a method underlying the apparently disorganized handling of Oxy's forays into housing. It was an observable fact that a lot of key Occidental investors were very satisfied when the oil company acquired Deane Brothers. Perhaps the acquisition itself was the sole objective. Says one observer close to the scene: "The doctor will never be foxed or fooled. Perhaps the question is best answered this way: Real estate becomes a glamour issue and the company's officers get investor pressure — 'Gee, real estate looks good.' So perhaps the doctor bought into real estate to show that he saw the boom coming and to satisfy his investors. Maybe that was all he wanted. And with that achieved, Occidental later made the decision that it didn't want to be in real estate."

Despite their falling-out, the Deanes maintain a very large respect for Dr. Hammer's abilities. "I'm not knocking Occidental, or saying that it treated us badly. The problems arise from differing criteria: they have one set, we have another," says Larry Deane. "Occidental's people are probably making the right decisions for Occidental — Dr. Hammer and his boys are too smart to do otherwise — but by the same token, those decisions, although right for Oxy, were not right for the building arm. The real estate arm's earnings are not a major part of the corporation's earnings, so it doesn't make much difference if real estate doesn't make a profit. Real estate is regarded as a speculative issue—and a cheap one, too—in the corporation's portfolio of investments. Occidental is going to support the larger investments like Hooker Chemical. We don't make a ripple compared to an outfit like Hooker so far as earnings go, so why support us at their expense? But I also feel," Larry goes on, "that corporate homebuilding divisions can and do get the kind of support they need in order to blossom: large dollar volume and staying power. If you get a situation where the parent corporation upholds the real estate division in the manner it needs to be upheld, the merger will be successful."

THE DEANES BEGIN ANEW

The Deanes left Occidental in January of 1970, but they were back in the building business within four months. Ben and his son Larry founded Deane Homes in Huntington Beach and started planning their first project. It was nothing like the old days of high-volume construction, but very satisfying. The project took form in 1971 as a luxury-priced attached-housing condominium development in Newport Beach. Ben Deane as usual surprised housing people by his keen ability to spot a market that others had overlooked, and to create a successful product for it. Called Big Canyon, the residential community consists of 230 units priced from $65,000 to $120,000. By the fall of 1971, as the Deanes were completing the construction of the models, they had already sold out the first section of 32 such townhouses. The project was a smash success in 1972. "We're very concerned to keep this project a success, so 90% of our attention will be on that alone for the next six months," Larry Deane said at the time. Afterwards, they were to be moving on to other ventures.

Jim Deane and his son Bill had meanwhile gone into a major joint-venture project with Westinghouse Corporation, developing 8,000 acres of oceanside land south of San Francisco on Half Moon Bay. Westinghouse put up the capital and they put up their talents. The development program is a diversified one for the big master-planned project. It includes recreational home and lot sales, apartment and mobile-home park construction, commercial development, and low and high-priced residential housing. The

Northern California Deanes also set up a homebuilding arm of their own, called Deane & Deane, Inc., and by the fall of 1971 were constructing models for a residential project named Frenchman's Creek in San Jose, with plans for other developments in that city, as well as in Cupertino, California, and (reaching back south to an old stomping ground of the original Deane Brothers company) at Diamond Bar. Working with Bill and Jim was Robert Hardesty, who has headed marketing operations for Ben and Bill since 1962. In 1973, Jim Deane terminated the partnership with Westinghouse.

Occidental, for its part, reformulated its real estate holdings under a corporate real estate department and hired Lawrence Kagan, brother of another big developer, to head it. But Kagan also didn't stay long. The real estate department suspended building operations and began to sell some of Oxy's real estate and to revalue and hold other parcels. It's a pity that Lake Forest didn't get completely built out by the Deanes. It is a beautiful piece of land, halfway between Los Angeles and San Diego. It gets its name from a 25-acre lake developed by the Deanes as its focal center (complete with $250,000 clubhouse for community residents), and from a large grove of eucalyptus trees originally planted by the Union Pacific Railroad in the 1870's for eventual (and unrealized) use as railroad ties. The Deanes were building at the focal point of the project, creating a viable residential community and thus creating a market for other development on surrounding Lake Forest land. At the time the Deanes were active, this land was also sold off in selected parcels to other builders, creating more market activity and another source of profits to Occidental.

OXY GETS A NEW DEAL IN THE U.S.S.R.

After the dissolution of the Deane merger, Dr. Hammer soon found other matters to preoccupy him. After ten years of spectacular earnings growth, Occidental in the third quarter of 1971 reported the first earnings loss in its history: $13.5 million. Sales increased 20% to nearly $2.1 billion for the nine months, but earnings fell 56% to $54.4 million, or 72 cents a share. Wall Street was disillusioned by the setback and bid the price of the stock down as low as 10 from its 1971 high of 23, and way down in the deeps from its 1968 high of 55.

Occidental's problems stemmed from several factors, according to *Business Week*. Notably, profits from Libyan oil operations got tightly squeezed as the revolutionary military government there boosted oil royalty rates by 85% since it had deposed the monarchy in 1969. And now it was demanding even higher rates along with a 51% equity in foreign oil companies. At the same time a glut of oil in Europe, Oxy's biggest market, depressed prices. Oxy also found itself with three times as much tanker tonnage under charter as it needed, a costly excess. Moreover, its domestic operations in coal were hurt by a strike.

Finally — and this was not the least of its problems — a complaint by the SEC accused the company of overstating its profits from real estate transactions, as well as from coal leases. Oxy subsequently changed its accounting method, but several stockholder suits were pending based on the SEC complaint. The good doctor did not take kindly to one investment analyst's labeling of Occidental as "an unending flow of bad news and misfortunes." Joel Fisher, analyst with Burnham & Company, told *BW* late in 1971: "It looks like Hammer is presiding over a disaster."

The securities analyst spoke too soon. Dr. Hammer was soon to find a major new lease on life for Occidental by his deal-making in the U.S.S.R. In addition to its Soviet ventures Occidental was pinning its main hopes on Venezuela, Peru, Nigeria, and on oil leases it was expecting to get in the North Sea. Occidental is also hopeful about the future of its coal production, which Dr. Hammer sees as potentially the company's No. 2 profit source, after oil.

At the end of 1973 he was seventy-five years old and was nowhere near retirement. His employment contract with Occidental, at $200,000 a year, doesn't run out until mid-1975. But with his new duties keeping him globe-trotting, in November 1973 he appointed a thirty-eight-year-old London banker, Joseph E. Baird, as president and chief operating officer. It is likely that Baird, formerly the chief executive of Western American Bank (Europe) Ltd., will take Dr. Hammer's place as chairman and chief executive officer of Occidental when Hammer retires.

And Ben Deane? By comparison with his earlier days, he was taking it easy as a "small" builder again. Other giant corporations have approached him for a merger, but, as he says, "Who needs it? I can make more money by accident on my own than I ever made as a big builder with Occidental." The relatively small size of his operation gives him flexibility to roll with the market instead of jumping into projects to keep up overhead. And he and Larry can make the future as big as they want by carefully culling through the welter of joint venture and other real estate proposals that the Deane name keeps attracting, on the off chance the Deanes might find a particular deal especially interesting.

Ben is also having a lot of fun. He recently built a $750,000 beachfront home for himself and his wife. He's invested in three oil wells, real estate and a new record company—the last just for the hell of it. "I spent my whole life converting half-opportunities into real opportunities," he says. "Now I want to enjoy myself. Besides, otherwise I'd just gamble the dough." And evenings, he spends a lot of time sculpting and singing.

13

The Metamorphosis of Don Scholz

It is true . . . that you have only
known one side of my fortune,
and that the better side. It has
remained with me longer than is
usual, and perhaps this fact has
deceived you as well as me. But
we must remember that we are
mortals. We must bear what has
happened and again put fortune
to the test. One may still hope
that, just as I have fallen so low
from such a height, so from these
depths I may rise again.

—Gnaeus Pompey Magnus
(after defeat by Caesar)

When Donald J. Scholz merged the Scholz Homes group of Toledo, Ohio,
into Inland Steel in the fall of 1969 for something like $87 million in cash
and stock, to outsiders it looked like the latest and biggest coup for the
gentle-spoken but powerful entrepreneur who had started the company in
1946 on a bankroll of $15,000 and had taken it to sales of $58 million at
the time of the merger. It appeared that the acquisition not only enabled him
and other major stockholders to capitalize handsomely on their labors, but
also gave the building organization access to a wealth of the parent corporation's capital by means of which Scholz Homes could expand further still at
an assured pace. The inside story was, in fact, something else.

A GOAL TO REACH THE TOP—AND PROBLEMS FROM A SURPRISING SOURCE

In 1966, when Scholz Homes was an $11 million publicly traded com-
pany OTC dominating the luxury prefab market with superb home designs,
Don had reevaluated his goals and set up a truly challenging one: to make
his company into a General Motors of housing (as he liked to call it) that
would build housing nationwide for every price range. This goal led him to
formulate an ambitious acquisition program of his own and to diversify into

321

apartment construction. The acquisition program ultimately outlined a series of twelve mergers with other housing-related companies. The word wasn't used in those days, but what Don Scholz was in fact planning on was the creation of a mighty builder "congeneric" which would transform his operation into the biggest building company in the United States. And indeed, had the plan gone off fully, it would have been: in 1970 the combined sales of the twelve building companies that were to have comprised the Scholz operation were approximately $220 million, matching the sales of the then biggest builder, Levitt & Sons. But a heartbreaking thing happened on the way to the General Motors goal. Instead of continuing to be an acquirer, Scholz was himself acquired by Inland Steel before his own program of merger-making was complete.

Scholz's hunt for building companies had led him in 1967 to a Chicago investment banker and merger expert, Bertel Malmquist, at McCormick & Company, and a close association developed. Working closely with Scholz, Malmquist closed three acquisitions for Scholz Homes in 1968 and 1969, enlarging the company into a giant with sales of $58 million. The acquired companies were Schult Mobile Homes, a mobile-home maker with a reputation for quality, and two builders, Public Facilities Associates (a Wisconsin turnkey builder) and Detroit's Allstate Homes. The acquisitions diluted Scholz's own control of the company by creating powerful new shareholders. Foremost among these was Schult's Walter O. Wells, who actually became the dominant partner by virtue of stock ownership, as well as becoming the board chairman and chief executive of the combined operation. Another was Malmquist himself, who along with close associates received $713,250 plus 50,000 shares of Scholz common stock ultimately valued at more than $2 million for services performed between 1967 and 1969. While Don Scholz continued to line up further acquisitions for his General Motors (and by the fall of 1969 he had nine additional candidates, ranging from a $1 million sectional-house manufacturer to a $15 million apartment developer), his new partners decided on another plan — to sell Scholz Homes to a giant industrial corporation.

That move came totally out of left field, so far as Don was concerned, and it was both surprising and deeply shocking. For Scholz has the quality of absolute loyalty and was used to getting it in return — at least from his key lieutenants. That was Don's strongest quality, in fact: the effortless ability to infuse his co-workers with a fanatic drive (20-hour workdays) and devotion to him, by the example he set. Withal, he had always been Boss.

How did Inland first get into the picture? The steelmaker, seventh largest of its kind, started shopping for likely acquisitions outside its own line after announcing a diversification program in 1968. This diversification program was in itself reported to be a defensive one: in the hurly-burly days of intense merger activity in the late Sixties any company with ample cash holdings and a moderate growth pattern could be a target for a takeover. Inland decided to diversify after Wall Street analysts began describing the cash-rich and sluggish company as an attractive candidate for a takeover bid by another industrial giant. Thus, a merger with a large building company, already doing something like $60 million in sales annually and growing at a rate of 35% a year, was right up Inland's alley. Such a move could help convince Wall Street and restive shareholders that Inland was accelerating its growth and discourage takeover attempts. So when a banker referred David Carley of Public Facilities Associates and Bertel Malmquist to the Inland regarding a potential merger, it was perfect timing.

That is, it was perfect timing for everyone but Don Scholz himself. A merger with Inland (or with any other major company for that matter: General Development and Gulf & Western had also been looking Scholz over) was at first clearly a second choice for the entrepreneurial developer. He had been dedicatedly moving toward the goal of his life's work — a plan to acquire nine additional building companies and take the whole combine public. Even after he signed the merger agreement in principle with Inland, he doggedly attempted to preserve his original acquisition plan with a twist that would satisfy his partners, thus making the consummation of the merger unnecessary. The idea was that, after Scholz had acquired the nine companies, the new combine would float stock, allowing Wells, Malmquist and others to sell their shares at $32 each, or $10 above Inland's price. Inland had offered about $87 million, or about 25 times Scholz's earnings, in cash and stock for the 3.9 million Scholz Homes shares outstanding; this translated into an offer that was an option to exchange each Scholz share for $22 in cash or one-half share of Inland $5\frac{1}{2}\%$ preferred stock, convertible to Inland common at $44 and non-callable for six years. But Scholz was unable to persuade his board on the merits of the alternative plan and the Inland deal went through. Reflecting on the eagerness of his partners to go with Inland instead of the congeneric route, Scholz observed a year later: "They wanted the bird in the hand, and they were smart. With delays to close all the mergers, we would have run smack into the 1970 bear market. No one knows where we would be today."

Scholz's partners did indeed want the bird in the hand. They pressed the merger with Inland for a variety of reasons that seemed sound to them. With Scholz Homes short on cash and its short-term debt rising, Don was looking for another $100 million for land and apartment construction, so the partners felt the company would need a big corporation behind it for that kind of borrowing power. But perhaps equally importantly, they also wanted to cash in their Scholz shares for blue-chip stock. Wells and others feared that the Scholz stock, at 25 times earnings, was overpriced and would soon level off. The merger gave Malmquist, for example, a good way to cash in his Scholz holdings valued at about $2.4 million. It was Malmquist, himself by now holding almost as many shares as Don Scholz, who was instrumental in engineering the Inland deal more than any other of the major Scholz Homes stockholders. As Frank Lalli (now West Coast bureau chief for *Forbes*) repeated in his excellent coverage of this episode in *House & Home* magazine, Malmquist backed up his power by getting Wells's proxy as well, while Wells went off to Switzerland during the final merger negotiations. As Scholz himself observed, "The swing man was Malmquist at McCormick & Company in Chicago. He pressed me to go with Inland. So I reconsidered and was completely convinced it had tremendous potential." Asked if there was no way he could resist the investment banker's pressure, Scholz replied, "If it became a matter of losing the support of your investment banker . . ." and left the rest of the sentence unfinished for the listener to make his own inferences.

It is true, Don was at first extremely unhappy about the derailing of his own plans, but when he confronted the situation fully he decided to make the best of it. Some published reports left the impression that he went into the merger believing it would not work, but this is not true. Having taken his lumps, Scholz entered into his role as an Inland company with complete dedication to making the merger go right. His revived optimism was based on the belief that he could still achieve his objectives as an Inland subsidiary, if not as an independent entrepreneur. He had the understanding that Inland had consented to create a mortgage system to finance the expansion of Scholz Homes and buy land for future development, as well as acquiring the nine companies that Scholz had originally sought.

THE PROBLEMS OF UNEXPECTED MERGERS

And here we enter phase two of the Scholz story. For, alas, instead of ending, Don's travails had only begun. Thrown off his original purpose and into a merger that he had decided to make function right, Scholz was now confronted with a parent company that was unwilling to let him operate in the manner that he had expected to. In latter reports, Inland officials denied that there had been any promises to accede to Scholz's grand design for the expansion of the building group. That basic misunderstanding laid the groundwork for subsequent difficulties arising between Scholz and the officials of the parent corporation. The merger agreement had been concluded very quickly, and none of the details of financial commitment and right of control had been spelled out in writing. As Chet Stare, Scholz's divisional vice president for West Coast operations, put it: "The understanding with

Inland was that there would be general financial backing. At the time, though, Inland didn't understand how this would jeopardize their own financial statement." In short, when Inland officials, more used to running a steelmaking operation than a development business, discovered that every banker wanted the parent corporation to assume contingent liability for Scholz's credit operations, they conservatively put a brake on Scholz's expansion plans.

The post-merger period is a difficult time for both the parent and the acquired company even in the most carefully planned situations. In a merger such as the Scholz-Inland one, where the financial commitment, operation policies and areas of decision-making authority had not been spelled out in the merger negotiations, the transitional period became even more difficult. To complicate matters, Don Scholz, who has walked with the aid of canes since a childhood polio incident, broke a leg in five places shortly after the completion of the merger and was bedridden for four months. That kept him out of the action, and when his lieutenants, attending weekly board meetings at Inland, began coming away empty-handed, his frustration increased. Chet Stare gives a good running description of the situation:

"There is no question that the Inland people were all sincere as hell about the desirability of the merger. Then, immediately after the merger, Don broke his leg and that left only us underlings to attend the board meetings. Inland had assigned the Scholz acquisition to its corporate development department for handling, and we met with them. It's just a corporate department — its members aren't even officers in the parent company — so how important can it be? It's an expense department — not a profit-maker — so its influence in the parent corporation is highly questionable.

"They said many times, 'We don't want to hinder you.' But they began to put restrictions on us that were impossible. If Don had been able to be there, perhaps he could have handled the situation. But by the time we'd report to him and get back to Inland, maybe the latest suggestion would already be policy. Essentially, the corporate development department got itself into the position of really running our company and *not* making any decisions. Everything had to go through them, but they had no expertise and were afraid to make decisions. So it was death for our company. Our operation needed instant communication and instant decision. It was an untenable situation."

One complicating factor impeding clear communications at those weekly board meetings, according to Chet Stare, was the presence of Walter Wells without the countervailing influence of Don Scholz. Wells, who was by this time the board chairman and chief executive of the steelmaker's housing subsidiary, was very content to let the company run slowly. And, says Stare, "at board meetings, since he held a dominant position, it was hard to make a point forcefully without appearing to bypass him. If Don could have been there, it might have been different."

THE MERGER BREAKS DOWN

The specific points on which the merger broke down ultimately came down to two:

1. Inland vetoed Scholz's plans for certain apartment programs. In at least one instance — it was a tight-money period — the Scholz people wanted to proceed with an apartment program with construction loans and, contrary to more conservative practice, without at the outset securing a permanent loan. The thought behind this practice was to avoid paying unduly expensive interest in a period of tight money, with the expectation that the money market would relax and interest rates would drop by the time the project was completed. Inland rejected this approach. Generally, says Don Scholz, "what sank the merger was their decision not to go on with certain projects. They couldn't arrive at the conclusion that, starting projects in the tight money period, we could sell them to investors. But the market goes up and down like a yo-yo; you have to start in a down period in order to be ready to sell in the turnaround. We did in fact start the programs after leaving Inland, and the market did turn around by the time we were ready to sell."

2. Inland turned down Scholz's program for the acquisition of the nine companies. The clear indication of the parent company's feelings about his General Motors concept came when Inland rejected a merger Scholz had set up with Rainer Manufacturing Company of Oregon, one of the companies in his acquisition master plan. Inland did acquire Jewel Builders, Inc., of Columbus in June of 1970 on Scholz's recommendation, but that was it. Jewel's president, Julie Cohen, took over Scholz's role when Don himself departed. Said Scholz at the time: "The executives are making the right moves for their shareholders. But I had to decide whether to become a guardian of the public trust, or return to being a builder." A year after his departure, he reflected, "The problem is that the Inland operation just didn't know enough about the business. They'll learn eventually, but I didn't want to hang around until they learned."

THE END OF A DREAM

So Don Scholz made a momentous decision which was to leave the company he had founded and had flawlessly nurtured into a national organization. And he implemented that decision on September 15, 1970. As a close associate recounts it: "Don was very honorable. After six months of attempting to make the deal work and having the effective control of the company's future removed from his hands, he went to the top management and said he didn't want to destroy a company he had spent twenty-five years building up. His employment contract with Inland was for one year, and he told the top people that he'd leave at the end of that time no matter what, so why wouldn't they just let him leave immediately." Both Philip Block, Jr., Inland's board chairman, and its president, Fred Jaicks, argued that he hadn't given the merger enough time to shake out, but Scholz stood firm, and in the end they acceded to his request.

One might have thought that this would be the end of a major builder's career. All he had at the time was his Inland stock, which was yielding him a dividend of $150,000 a year, and some plans to reenter the development business in what appeared to be a small way. For many an individual, of course, that kind of financial well-being would be sufficient. But for Don Scholz, dreamer of empire, who had stood within sight of his dream's achievement, it was a long and bitter fall. Who can be happy running a power station in the Urals after almost grasping the scepter of a life's ambition?

And it is here that the latest chapter in the life of Don Scholz began. For where another might have succumbed to a massive sense of failure or to a life of resigned obscurity after such a setback to a life's work, Don, with the vision of his goal still burning fiercely within him, immediately plunged back into the work of building up a brand new national company from scratch. Within a month after leaving Inland, he had formed a new company, Donald J. Scholz & Company, based in the Toledo suburb of Sylvania. And his purpose rang out the same as ever: "Through expertise gained in past experience — also mergers, investments, acquisitions and employment of key personnel — it's our intention to become the General Motors of the housing field." His immediate goal was to build a track record to take the company public in mid-1972. With that achieved, he expected to resume his growth plan exactly where he had left off in the fall of 1969. And here the bear market for housing stocks again intervened to abort his program.

DON SCHOLZ COMES BACK

The speed with which he generated a comeback would have enabled him to achieve the goal of a "General Motors" rapidly, had the market not plunged. Within a year after he left Inland, his new company had fifteen major projects underway in twelve cities. Four of the apartment projects are in Toledo, Ohio; the others are in Chicago; Cleveland; Detroit; New York

City; Washington, D.C.; Buffalo and Syracuse, New York; Newport and Santa Ana, California; and Charlotte, North Carolina. Total volume of projects in planning or underway represented sales in excess of $400 million, with 13,000 units on 1,650 acres of land.

Scholz was aided in cutting down the lead time on generating new construction by the fact that much of the land he was using for the fifteen projects had been previously lined up. His old contract with Inland had permitted him to deal with properties as an individual, and he also came to an amicable agreement with Inland that let him pick up some properties it didn't want. (Inland felt it would be better to stick closer to Chicago and Toledo, so Scholz's new company took over most of the projects outside the Midwest.) But even taking this into consideration, the speed of Scholz's comeback is amazing. In the same period he also built up an entirely new national organization. Four of the key positions in his company are held by old Scholz Homes hands who joined him when the Inland housing subsidiary cleaned house of "overloyal" employees after Scholz's own departure, as they say, terminating them "involuntarily." But the rest of the staff is new.

The fruits of the new company's first efforts immediately propelled it back into the select company of major development companies. For its fiscal year ending May 31, 1972, Scholz estimated that pretax profits would be in the range of $5.3 million to $8.0 million on sales of approximately $30 million. Conservatively estimating a pretax profit of $6 million for the year would bring the company a pretax return of approximately 20% and a return on investment of approximately 100%. This was still the period of rising housing demand and a buoyant stock market. Headily, the new company projected a continuing *minimum* 30% annual increase, compounded, in sales and profits over each of the succeeding three years. Sales from projects in planning and/or development as of early 1972 were projected at $50 million, $77 million and $95 million for the fiscal years ending 1973, 1974 and 1975, respectively.

AN INITIAL FOCUS ON APARTMENTS

The new company's first area of concentration was on apartment construction and the sale of projects to investors. One of the most unusual of such projects is Versailles-on-the-Bluffs, a 997-unit enclosed apartment community in Newport, California, and it serves as an example of the product that Scholz turns out. What's unusual about it is its French château and Southern colonial architecture in a state where the Spanish and Mediterranean influence is paramount. Will Scholz reverse the traditional pattern of exporting California styles East by bringing Eastern styles West?

The first 255-unit phase of the project, finished in January 1972, was sold to Pacific Plan of Menlo Park, California, on a syndication sale for $8.5 million before construction even began. Scholz's guarantee on the sale to the syndicator was to rent up the project to 95% occupancy and to manage it for one year after completion. "On our syndication sales," says a Scholz associate, "we insist on at least 20% hard money as a down payment. Then, we like to retain the management of the property whenever possible in order to take tip-top care of it. Although we didn't do this with Pacific Plan, we even like to participate in the turnover of the property whenever possible; that is, get an option to buy the building back in five or six years for the original purchase price plus an escalation, because we can have another buyer in the wings at a higher price. We give the first investor an ironclad guarantee that he'll make money — say an 8% return plus all the depreciation — and for this we get an option to repurchase at a fixed price. We can then resell at a profit. We can do this because of the quality of our product and because of the importance we place on continuing maintenance."

Unfortunately, it was not until considerably later that substantial problems emerged with Versailles-on-the-Bluffs. These focused on the project's high-density construction and on its appearance: it had been an error of some magnitude to believe that Midwest-type architectural plans could be transplanted to the West Coast without first consulting local tastes and preferences. As of mid-1972 the project's rental projections had apparently not been maintained; the first increment was said to have only 30% occupancy. More dramatically, the Newport Beach Planning Commission rose up in arms against the project in a startling and unexpected move, essentially on the grounds that it was architecturally incompatible with the city. At heated City Council meetings the massive Versailles structure — situated on a hill overlooking the softer and lower-rise cityscape — was referred to as "Attica West."

The affair became quite heated. The Planning Commission decided to cut the permitted density for the second increment to half of what it had earlier allowed: to 18 units from 37 dwelling units per acre. And Scholz contemplated a suit against both Planning Commission and City Council for damages on grounds that he had already made a substantial investment in utilities and would be reft of his profit by the zoning rollback. It appeared that he might switch to less massive condominium structures for the balance of the Versailles project and possibly at a density lower than the original zoning of 35 units per acre overall.

The situation muddied Scholz's plans to grow rapidly without a recurrence of problems. And it illustrated once again the imperative of never underestimating the importance of good market research in new market areas.

An even greater problem, however, was the probable emergence of tax-shelter restrictions to apartment investors by 1974. If such legislation is enacted, it would minimize sales of apartments to investors (where the tax shelter is used to offset other income). It was for this reason, as well as a result of newly introduced percentage-of-completion accounting, that many developers began getting out of investment building in 1973. Where these events would leave Scholz is unclear.

AND A SOLUTION TO THE PROBLEM OF LAND

Don Scholz did solve in an efficient way the problem of land for future development. The key to continuing expansion of sales in a building and development company is, of course, a continuing and expanding supply of land for future development. The typical two-year lead time between land acquisition and start of construction makes this mandatory. Also, the planning and development of raw land into zoned land with facilities is the single most profitable phase in the entire housing production cycle. As we have seen, a company like Larwin thus takes one approach to assuring itself of an adequate supply of developable land, which is to tie up large acreage well in advance of need. But the holdings of large amounts of land can have a negative effect on a company which is earnings-oriented because large amounts of capital are tied up in static landholdings, the land produces no income, and interest and taxes eat into the company's cash flow.

Scholz worked out a method whereby his company carries no land in its inventory other than that used for immediate development, but still maintains a large supply of land for future development and derives much of the profit from appreciating land values accruing from the enhancement of the land. The Scholz company does this through two specific programs: (a) the "land sale program," which is usually used in the development of assemblages of very large tracts of unzoned farmland which must be master-planned and zoned for ultimate development of small "new city" communities; and (b) the "land bank program," which is used to hold land in multi-phased developments which are already zoned and ready for immediate building activity. A brief explanation of each program will illustrate the merits of their use.

LAND SALE PROGRAM. In this program the company acquires large-acreage farmland on as favorable low-down-payment, long-term-installment and low-interest-rate terms as can be negotiated, with title taken subject to a purchase-money mortgage represented by these terms. The land is then processed through land planning, zoning procedures, and civil engineering — on completion of which this land will have substantially increased in value. The land is then sold to a limited partnership at a price substantially in excess of its cost. The investor partnership pays the company a down payment (usually in the 10% to 20% range) and the company takes back the difference in a mortgage in the amount of the sale price less the amount of the investor purchaser's down payment and the original purchase-money mortgage. In this program, the company thus makes a complete sale of the property, in which it realizes a substantial profit. However, as the investment partnership which purchases the land is composed of passive investors with every interest in a continuing relationship with the company (to direct the future development of the land), the company is in a highly favored position to participate in the further profits from the ultimate development and subsequent building operations on the land.

Don Scholz's Toledo land for the project known as Eastpointe was acquired and developed by this procedure. The property, 170 acres in all, was acquired by the company at a cost of about $270,000. After land planning, zoning and engineering, the company sold the land to a limited partnership for $2 million, with $200,000 down, taking back a 7%, thirty-year amortizing mortgage due in ten years. (The original purchase-money mortgages are at 5% to 6% interest.) The company thus receives approximately $126,000 per year in interest income in the early years. A qualified investor in the 50% tax bracket will probably receive in excess of 20% after-tax annual return on his investment. Moreover, the company during the projected ten-year development of the property will in all likelihood be the one to develop the land and provide design, engineering and mortgage banking services for the property, as well as construction and marketing.

LAND BANK PROGRAM. In those situations where "mature" sites are "banked," the property is sold to a limited partnership and a wholly owned subsidiary of the company becomes the managing general partner of the investor partnership, with rights to all residual profits from the sale of the land by the partnership in excess of the agreed-upon return to the limited partnership — usually in the range of a 20% return on their investment. The managing partner may direct the sale of the land to the company in stages, in accordance with the progress of development (in which the company picks up its normal building and associated profits), or it may direct the sale of the property, all or in part, to other parties if such a course looks better, in anticipation of the profit over and above the return due the limited partner. This type of land bank program was adopted by Scholz for the Versailles-on-the-Bluffs development, as well as for such other projects as those located in Chicago and in Washington, D.C.

In either program, the company retains only a minor, if any, cash investment in the land while retaining effective control over it, as well as realizing a profit on the sale of the land to the investor. At the same time, it eliminates interest and tax payments which would otherwise reduce cash flow. And the company gains earnings on annual payments of interest made to it by the investor on the mortgage held by the company. The company may even realize a profit on the interest on the original purchase-money mortgage, since the company mortgage is a "wraparound" mortgage and is invariably at a higher rate of interest than the original purchase-money mortgage. The procedure is also advantageous to the investor. He gets a high percentage rate of return (made possible by the relatively low-down-payment, highly leveraged cash investment), typically in the 20% range if he is in the 50% tax bracket, and this is taxed only at the capital gains rate. He also gets substantial tax deductibles in the early years from his interest and tax payments, making his purchase for the most part with after-tax dollars.

ONWARD TO THE GENERAL MOTORS GOAL

To be sure, apartment construction is not the sole purpose of Donald J. Scholz & Company. Don also expanded into condominium and townhouse construction and into fourplexes. And to fulfill his goal of building housing nationwide for every income range, he is also set to resume his master program of key acquisitions of leading builders to speed him on his way to the General Motors goal whenever economic conditions might permit.

By mid-1972 he had already put together the nucleus of a diversified congeneric group as affiliates of the firm, including a mortgage banking firm and an engineering and planning organization. The new Scholz company held options for the acquisition of these companies prior to the time it would go public. Scholz's agreement with Inland permitted him to return to the prefabrication field after September of 1972, and Scholz was expected to make a heavy commitment in this field again, acquiring a specific modular housing manufacturer based in Grand Rapids, Michigan, after that date to further round out the new organization's activities.

The mortgage banking affiliation itself gives Scholz & Company a sound financial base for the expansion of its operation. Founded in 1971, the company is Connolly & Jones, Inc., operating nationally, with headquarters in Bethesda, Maryland, and a branch office in Chicago. Edmund V. Connolly, the president, was formerly the director of FHA's multifamily housing division. Robert N. Jones, vice president, is the former deputy assistant director of FHA's multifamily housing division. Before founding Connolly & Jones, the two men were operating heads of First Northern Corporation, a mortgage banking subsidiary of Kaufman & Broad. Eugene Ford, another participant in the founding of what was eventually to become the Scholz mortgage banking subsidiary, is president of Mid-City Developers, a major Washington, D.C., developer which is wholly owned by Development Corporation of America. He's also the director of American Housing Partners, a publicly held limited partnership; president of Nationwide Management Company, a wholly owned subsidiary of Kaufman & Broad (and the managing general partner of American Housing Partners); and a member of the advisory board of FNMA.

Don himself is an acquisition expert, and he had two others working with him, Dan Sydlaske and Jack A. Burke. In the old days, at Scholz Homes, they had acquired other building and development companies using a pooling of interest formula whereby the acquired companies received Scholz Homes stock based on the acquired company's current and future earnings. In the formula used, the acquired company received 30% fewer Scholz Homes shares than its earnings would have entitled it to had the distribution been on an equal earnings-per-share basis. This formula insured that the acquisition itself contributed to rising earnings per share, aside from the added earnings potential inherent in the expanded future operations of the acquired company. The ability to accomplish the acquisition of such companies by Scholz Homes partly stemmed from strong personal relationships Scholz held with many of the builders who would have been acquired under his general plan.

WHAT MIGHT HAVE BEEN — SHALL BE AGAIN

At the time that Scholz Homes was acquired by Inland, Don was in the process of preparing for the filing of registration statements for the acquisitions of four additional building companies by Scholz Homes, out of the total of nine that he had already lined up (in addition to Rainer Lumber Company). The principals of each of the companies were longtime personal friends of Don's, and each already knew the other's operation intimately, an invaluable factor for future compatible relations. When Inland Steel decided not to proceed with this program, the deals of course fell through. But, as Don observed in 1972, it is interesting to speculate what would have occurred had the General Motors concept been realized at that time. "Each of those companies was doing in the neighborhood of $10 million in sales," Scholz later reflected. "Now each of them, a year or so later, is doing in the neighborhood of $25 million." A comparison of the performance of these companies supports his point (Table 13.1).

The original blueprint still remains Scholz's clearest statement of his goals. Fredericks Development was acquired by Pacific Lighting Corporation in 1970, and Mitchell Corporation was bought by the Singer Company in mid-1972, while L. B. Nelson Corporation also in mid-1972 announced plans to go public. But several other builders would be ready to talk to

Table 13.1   Blueprint for Don Scholz's General Motors of Housing—1969

New Entity Operating Divisions	Sales 12 Months Ending 12-31-69 ($ million)	Estimated Sales 12 Months Ending 12-31-70 ($ million)	Earnings 12 Months Ending 12-31-69 ($ million)	Estimated Earnings 12 Months Ending 12-31-70 ($ million)	Net Worth 12-31-69 ($ million)	1970 Initial Share Distribution*	1971 Contingent Share Distribution*	Shares to be Cashed Out*
Scholz Group:								
1. Schult Mobile Homes	$ 30.0	$ 45.0	$1.20	$ 1.8	$ 9.0			500,000
(a) W. Wells						800,000		
(b) Other Officers						440,000	360,000	
2. PFA	6.5	8.0	0.30	0.6		116,354	23,000	
3. Allstate Homes	3.0	4.0	0.13	0.2		1,431,815		
4. Scholz Homes	20.0	45.0	0.75	2.0				220,450
(a) B. Malmquist								
Jewel Builders of Columbus	7.0	10.0	1.00	1.0	4.0	600,000	59,000	
Stiles-Hatton of Grand Rapids, Mich.	1.0	9.5	0.10	0.5	0.3	30,000	350,000	
Republic Development Corp. of Detroit	14.6	20.0	1.00	1.3	7.0	850,000	145,454	
Fine-Bilt Homes of Lansing, Mich.	2.7	3.0	0.14	0.2	3.8	87,000	500,000	
L.B. Nelson Co. of Palo Alto	15.0	20.0	1.00	1.3	5.0	500,000	350,000	
Betker-Fredericks Co. of Los Angeles	10.0	12.0	0.50	1.5	3.0	350,000		
Ranier Manufacturing Co. of Oregon	13.0	18.0	0.60	1.2	3.4		120,000	318,200
Imperial Components of Chicago	6.0	10.0	0.20	0.4	0.6	120,000	350,000	
Mitchell Corp. of Mobile	14.3	18.0	0.80	1.1	3.0	350,000		
Totals	$143.1	$222.5	$7.72	$13.1	$39.1	5,675,169 Shares	2,257,454 Shares	1,038,650 Shares

Source: House & Home.

*[Based on $22 a share value, as of Nov. 1969]

Scholz anytime. These same builders, or others similar to them, are typical of the kind of company that would be considered in a new program of acquisitions.

Neither has Scholz given up on the idea of adding a timber company to his General Motors. First, unlike the Sixties, when lumber companies sold at low multiples, the projected high demand for lumber during the Seventies (coupled with restrictions of supply from environmentalists' pressures) will make such an addition very profitable. Second, there's a lot of hidden value in a timber company, since timber reserves are carried on the books at the original very low acquisition cost in relation to current value, and with rights to cut on government land assigned no value at all. Third, the production that would be added to the volume of a timber outfit like Rainer by captive orders from the Scholz operation could increase volume by 50% and profitability by a greater figure. And finally a company like Rainer (with an unbroken fifteen-year history of profits) may be acquired reasonably. Rainer itself could have been acquired at a figure of 7 times earnings in 1969.

Table 13.2 Subsequent Performance of Companies Whose Merger Negotiations Were Interrupted

Company	1969	1970
Fredericks Development Corporation Los Angeles (Fullerton), California Builder of Apartment Communities in Southern California	$10,000,000	$29,900,000
L.B. Nelson Corporation Palo Alto, California Builder of Apartment Communities in Northern California	15,000,000	25,600,000
Republic Development Corporation Detroit, Michigan Single and Multifamily Builder	14,600,000	26,500,000
Mitchell Corporation Mobile, Alabama Home Manufacturer and leading Builder in the South (La., Ala., Ga., Fla.)	14,300,000	23,050,000

Source: *Professional Builder.*

14

Bill Lyon Visits the Plumber

> O Captain! my Captain! our fear-
> ful trip is done!
> The ship has weather'd every
> rack, the prize we sought is won. . . .
>
> —Walt Whitman

The star-trails of William Lyon and American-Standard first crossed when, in the late Sixties, they undertook a successful joint venture in Ventura County in Southern California. Bill was at that time one of the three biggest builders in the state, operating a highly efficient construction and sales organization. He specialized in single-family homes, and he was one of the best. His two chief companies were Luxury Homes, building homes in the $30,000-and-up range, and Dutch Haven Homes, providing homes priced from $18,000 for the moderate-income market. Over the years, Lyon had plowed most of his profits back into his building activities; by the late Sixties he was building in eight to ten locations throughout Southern and Central California. A quiet man from whose deceptively placid exterior flowed a strong dedication to win (he was, and still is, a colonel in the Air Force Reserve), he also had the craftsman's meticulous attention to detail. He ran all aspects of the organization personally, regularly piloting his own airplane to his scattered subdivisions.

A "TOTAL APPROACH TO SHELTER"

Bill Lyon's organization was to become the keystone in a rapid program of expansion and diversification undertaken by American-Standard in 1967. The big corporation, one of the nation's one hundred largest, makes and markets plumbing and heating equipment and is also involved in transportation systems, industrial and construction products, security systems and graphic arts. In the course of three short years American-Standard went from no direct involvement in the housing field to a diversified shelter giant rivaling Boise Cascade. In the same period, 1968 to 1970, the Lyon organization's sales skyrocketed from an estimated $20 million to about $135.2

336

million. Bill Lyon, who had been exclusively a builder of single-family homes, found himself at the head of a shelter and land empire in which the construction of such homes had become only one of perhaps a dozen major activities of international proportions.

The architect of AmStan's overnight growth into a shelter giant was William D. Eberle, who joined the plumbing-ware manufacturer as president in 1966 and rose to chairman and chief executive officer in 1967. A dynamic and personable man, Eberle had gone far since getting degrees in both business and law from Harvard. Before he was thirty-five, he had parlayed his private investments (a Hertz franchise, hotels, motels, a taxi company, real estate) into his first million in his home state of Idaho. Turning to politics in 1953, he won a seat in the Idaho House of Representatives and rose to the top as house speaker by 1961. In 1962 he joined the Boise Cascade Corporation as secretary and became one of the young management group that catapulted the company into the big time. It was no surprise when, on becoming the head of American-Standard, he formulated a policy of expansion and management which echoed that of his former company.

The philosophy of the company became one of a "total approach" to the shelter industry which it was already serving with its products both domestically and internationally. As Eberle explained it at the time: "Our motivation is to improve our position as a supplier of building products and to broaden our market as a supplier of a total housing package. We, of course, expect to make a fair profit and improve our position as an international shelter supplier." Part of AmStan's reorientation under Eberle was to move away from what he described as low-return, high-cost operations and into "low start-up, high-return markets such as air conditioning and electronics." But the corporation's major new departure was to enter the housing field directly, both because it represented a large captive market for its products and for the profits inherent in development itself.

The rocket ride for Bill Lyon began when American-Standard acquired his organization early in 1968. Bill and his brother Leon received 350,000 shares of AmStan stock, then trading in the mid-30's, plus another 50,000 shares contingent upon subsequent earnings. The corporation booked the initial acquisition at about $8.85 million, or about a 25% discount, because of stock restrictions. Other merged builders might have had difficulties in getting their parent to back them in their plans, but not so Bill. Working closely and amicably with Eberle, and in fact encouraged and aided in the most ambitious plans, the Lyon organization began to grow rapidly, both by internal diversification and by further acquisitions, as well as by an extensive program of joint ventures. The high points of this growth follow.

THE LYON EXPANSION PROGRAM

The Wm. Lyon Development Company, as it was now named, continued to build and sell single-family homes (and later, fourplexes and condominiums. But it also diversified heavily into built-for-sale apartments. By 1970, the company had a ninety-man apartment division and was knocking out 3,500 to 4,000 apartment units throughout Northern and Southern California and in Phoenix, Arizona. (Many of the sales were on the all-inclusive first and second mortgage arrangement whereby the project developer issues notes secured by all-inclusive first and second trust deed and assumes payment of a smaller first mortgage on the property. This can result in paper profits but impose a cash drain on the developer. At the end of 1970 the Lyon Company was contingently liable for $10.7 million of loans resulting from such sales.) At the same time, Bill expanded his organization into recreational-land development and second-home sales, and got several such projects going. The company also got involved in mobile home park development.

Twin Rivers Holding Corporation was next formed in 1969 as a joint venture with Kendall Development Company of Hightstown, New Jersey, for the development of Twin Rivers, a 719-acre, $120 million "new town" located halfway between New York and Philadelphia in New Jersey. The project, which is one of the largest new developments in the country to be devoted primarily to rental units and condominium-type dwellings, worked out quite successfully. During the first fifteen months, 500 townhouses were sold at an average price of $28,000; 100 garden apartments were rented at an average rental of $200; and 50 condominium townhouses were sold at an average price of $22,000. The total housing mix at Twin Rivers was projected for 1,680 townhouses, 480 garden apartments, 420 condominium townhomes, 220 high-rise apartments and 200 single-family homes, plus 253 acres devoted to light industrial and commercial uses. Lyon's joint-venturer, Kendall Development, subsequently became the eastern anchor of the Lyon land and shelter group, as the Lyon organization acquired the remaining 50% interest in the joint venture in 1970.

Builders Homes of Dothan, Alabama, a major producer of modular housing, was acquired in 1970, giving the Lyon organization access to assembly-line modular production. At the end of 1970, Builders Homes was producing nearly 1,000 homes a year and had started a modular plant with a capacity of 10 units a day. Athough it is a manufacturer of housing, the company also joint-ventures with smaller builders throughout the South, particularly on the development of subsidized (FHA Sec. 235) housing for low- and moderate-income markets. American-Standard acquired this company and the remaining 50% of the Twin Rivers joint venture for a combined total of 249,353 shares.

Continental Homes, based in Washington, D.C. became the international building arm of the Lyon organization when it was acquired by American-Standard in 1969. Headed by Don Carmichael, Continental pioneered housing programs in Latin America and the Caribbean, as well as in Africa. Working with local joint-venture partners, the company developed middle-income housing in Argentina, Chile, Ethiopia, Jamaica, Paraguay, Panama, Colombia, Barbados and Puerto Rico.

The reasoning behind AmStan's acquisition of Continental was clear enough. As one of the top ten U.S. firms in foreign investments, the company had the usual problem converting foreign-earned currencies into dollars before inflation ate away profits. With funds lying idle, the answer was to utilize them locally in an active, inflation-hedging business such as real estate. Enter Continental. The association with an international builder also gave the Lyon firm the opportunity to advertise itself as a "worldwide builder," along with Levitt & Sons and Kaufman & Broad. The comparison is not exact, since the latter two firms are building in highly developed Western European nations and Continental operated in less-developed equatorial countries under dissimilar financing and construction conditions, but it is close enough.

What's it like to build abroad? Development in parts of Latin America can be an unstable venture because the American developer may be squeezed by restrictions both Stateside and in the country where he wishes to operate. Continental's project in Chile, for example, represented the most publicized form of Latin American housing — the loan guarantee from the U.S. Agency for International Development (AID). AID provides a guarantee similar to an FHA guarantee, protecting the original investor against default for financial or political reasons. But by 1970 the future of AID had come into question. A White House task force recommended scrapping AID in favor of international-type agencies like the World Bank, substituting more of an international cooperative effort for bilateral aid. And in that year pressure was also put on AID to go slow on committing its full authorization of $550 million for mortgage guarantees because of America's balance of payments problem. So much for domestic problems. On the foreign side, Continental found itself faced with another restriction in 1970. A new Colombian law limited

U.S. housing investments to urban-renewal-type development. The law did not affect projects the company had under way but made future investment, even via joint ventures, difficult. This reason underlay the company's subsequent moves into Puerto Rico and Ethiopia and its exploration of programs beyond AID.

Typical of Continental's Latin American projects is a 400-home development done in 1970 in Concepción, Chile (400 miles south of Santiago). The project was funded with a loan of $1.8 million from Fidelity Mutual Life Insurance of Philadelphia. Of the mortgage financing, 25% was provided by a local steel company, Compañía de Acero del Pacífico, which also provided urbanized land for the venture. This participation satisfied an AID requirement that a local company be at least 25% financially involved. Continental joint-ventured the deal with a local Chilean builder, Carlos Valck. Once the AID paperwork was approved, the sales operation proceeded quickly. The three-bedroom, 650-square foot homes sold for $6,000 — $1,200 down with a twenty-year mortgage — and half the units were presold to the steel company's employees. The biggest stumbling block in housing sales was overcome when the steel company made the down payment on behalf of its employees, based on their seniority. Chilean law requires every company to set aside 5% of its annual profits for housing; the down payments came from the housing fund held in escrow by the company.

Another project Continental handled was one named "Tres Esquinas" in Bogotá, Colombia. Entirely locally financed, it consisted of a 144-unit three-bedroom condominium development undertaken by joint venture with HOLCOL, a local firm. Continental's Colombian partner obtained financing from Colombia's Central Mortgage Bank, which will lend between 50% and 80% of the project cost; the balance of the funds came from American-Standard's investment of pesos generated by product sales in Colombia. HOLCOL paid 17% interest on the loan from the country's central mortgage bank, which could be construed as modest by Latin American standards. The condominium units, selling for $10,000 each in 1970, required down payments of 40%, but many middle-income families can swing this with the aid of a Colombian law providing that major corporations in the country must set aside one month's salary in reserve for a down payment on a house; an employee can get this reserve anytime he presents a letter of intent to purchase. HOLCOL general manager Alonzo Castelblanco expected to make a 20% profit on buildings and land and to have the original investment returned in three years.

To stabilize its investment portfolio, Continental in 1970 expanded into Puerto Rico and Ethiopia. Their first project in Puerto Rico was located at San Sebastian, a city 100 miles west of San Juan. Financed under FHA Sec. 235, the development consisted of 107 single-family units priced from $17,000. Again there was a joint-venture partner, Frank Kier, president of Atlantic Quality Construction and one of the island's most successful condominium builders.

The general formula for cooperation between Continental and the parent Lyon organization was described by Don Carmichael as follows: "Lyon provides working capital loans to us on a project-by-project basis. Not only do we pay interest on these loans to the parent, but also our projects must show an ROI in excess of similar developments in the U.S. due to political exposure and higher risks." Carmichael expected a 10% net profit on sales when a foreign housing program is developed. "Invariably, we find that a cost of building a house equals about 50% of the sales value. Urbanized land will equal 25%, and the remaining 25% is for profit and overhead."

Guy Hatfield Homes, of San Diego, California, also became one of the substantial joint-venturers with the Lyon organization, benefiting both by AmStan's money and Lyon's marketing expertise. Starting in 1967, with corporate financial backing Hatfield in three years built up a homebuilding organization with $15 million in sales derived from the marketing of single-family homes to young moderate-income families.

American Mobilehome Corporation, a major Southern California developer of mobile-home parks, also entered into the widening ring of the Lyon organization's activities in 1970. In that year, Lyon advanced $1 million to and bought $4 million of convertible debentures from this organization, among whose shareholders is Ray Watt. At the time, Lyon also agreed to increase the investment in AMC to $8 million, convertible into 50.1% of American Mobilehome stock.

This lineup summarizes the disparate parts of the Lyon corporate building organization. There was, however, one other major involvement in development undertaken by American-Standard, though Lyon himself was not directly connected with it. This was the joint venture that American-Standard formed with Celanese Corporation in 1969 to build urban housing for low- and middle-income families in New York. The venture was enthusiastically named "Construction for Progress" and·reflected Eberle's strong interest in urban problems (he was chairman of the National Urban Coalition at the time). CFP built a 66-unit apartment building as its first venture. It was financed by the company itself and purchased by the New York Housing Authority. Eberle said at the time: "The project was undertaken for the first time by a private industry. It had the special advantages of being completed in less than half the normal time it takes the local housing authority — twelve months from concept to occupancy — instead of twenty-one to twenty-four months. It also cost 10% less than it would have cost the city."

In 1970 CFP accordingly expanded its program, undertaking four additional buildings for a $7 million building program. One of these was to have an experimental site-cast concrete structure. Said Eberle: "These new methods will allow CFP to complete more buildings, in less time, for low- and middle-income families. The cost-savings factor, including the differential in interest charges, is expected to be about 15% of construction costs." The European system meets the most stringent building codes and has built 70,000 apartments utilizing the site-casting technology.

A CORPORATION CHANGES ITS MIND

But American-Standard had hardly spread its wings in the development business before it began having second thoughts about what it was doing. The official line was that the parent corporation's management had begun to get concerned about Lyon's profit margins after advancing more than $28 million in loans to the subsidiary over the three-year period. But if profitability was the yardstick, then AmStan had little ground for basic dissatisfaction. It is true that at a later time Lyon did register a loss: for the first nine months of 1971 the subsidiary showed a loss of $500,000, compared with a profit of $1.5 million for the comparable period in 1970. But during this period its corporate support was questionable; at the time American-Standard began reevaluating its role in the building business, that is to say at the end of 1970 and early in 1971, the Lyon organization still looked pretty good.

Lyon's earnings went from $1.3 million in 1968 to $2.0 million in 1969. They did decline in 1970, falling to $1.7 million while sales shot up to $90 million (excluding all joint ventures), indicating that Lyon was having problems keeping overhead under control. But it was still a creditable performance and it looked all the better when you consider that this income accounted for *more than half* of giant American-Standard's reported profit in 1970. The corporation's sales for that year rose to a record $1.049 billion, but profits plunged from $39.3 million a year earlier to a mere $3.1

million (including Lyon's contribution), after extraordinary charges. If Am-Stan was worried about profitability, it might have been hard pressed to explain why it began getting concerned about Lyon, who turned in a better profit on sales of $90 million than the parent corporation did on sales of almost $1 billion. Although the building subsidiary's 1971 performance was tarnished (and it may have been strongly affected by corporate disruption of its activities), that in itself would not ordinarily be a sufficient reason to reverse course entirely: many acquired builders have weathered a year or two of losses without losing the confidence of their parent corporations.

The real reason American-Standard began looking at the Lyon organization askance was that the entire "total shelter" philosophy, guided by which the parent company had expanded for three years, now came up for reexamination. What had looked like a flawless approach to growth when corporate profits looked good became expendable, if not entirely with logic, when hard times hit the parent company. It bears noting that the Lyon hierarchy itself did not account for the parent corporation's major losses. AmStan had a write-off of $47 million before taxes in 1969 due to problems in its plumbing and heating lines. In 1970 it had further write-downs to account for shrinkage in its French subsidiary and to cover receivables losses in Penn Central accounts, and its main plumbing and heating lines performed poorly.

CASH FLOW IS KING

What happened was that AmStan found itself with a rising debt load and falling cash. The corporation's cash and equivalents had declined from $51.6 million to $37.6 million during 1970, and working capital had fallen to $320 million from $364.8 million. Examining its capital outlays, the company essentially decided that it no longer wanted to support real estate, which requires substantial capital ($28.3 million in loans to Lyon in three years), though it can produce relatively good profits.

Simply stated, this translated into a lack of basic commitment to the building business. With corporate profits down and debts rising, the management decided it would shed the newly acquired activities which had a way of gobbling big money, and devote its cash to a business it understood — plumbing and heating. Lyon's following profits for 1970, however good when compared with overall corporate performance, provided the justification for pulling back in the capital commitment for a business unrelated to their main concerns.

Along about this time, a change of management was also underway. Bill Eberle ultimately left American-Standard in October 1971 to become President Nixon's newest special representative for trade negotiations; William A. Marquard, who had been the company's president under Eberle, now became the chief executive.

American-Standard was not the only major corporation supplying the housing field that found a direct role in real estate distressingly capital-intensive. In May 1972, International Paper announced it was divesting itself of its high-priced acquisition, Donald L. Bren Company — selling the company back to Don — and began pulling out of some other of its direct housing involvements. Bren bought the company back for $3.5 million cash (as well as giving IP secured interest-bearing notes for $18.5 million to cover IP's cash advances to the development company). Had this been the entire divestiture arrangement, IP would have got about $30 million less for Bren Company than it paid for it. But Bren also gave IP warrants to repurchase 49% of his company's stock within a five-year period, starting in mid-1975, at its *book value* at that time. Bren will probably go public before this, and IP, by having access to the developer's stock at the low, book-value price, may recoup. Don Bren at least made a satisfactory deal to get out from under his merger connection and take away his excellent company intact. Bill Lyon was not so fortunate.

With the advent of Mr. Marquard as chief, not only was AmStan's involvement in real estate halted but the parent corporation itself was to undergo considerable shrinkage. Shortly after Eberle's departure, Marquard announced a far-ranging two-to-three-year plan to sell off one-fifth, or $250 million, of corporate assets and to close down and consolidate other facilities involving total assets of $130 million. The reason given for the move was to cut out activities that "haven't been earners" and to generate cash to reduce AmStan's indebtedness as of October 1971 almost in half, reducing it to about $250 million from $450 million and bringing total indebtedness from 50% of capitalization to 35%. At the same time, the company set up a $100 million reserve for losses in connection with the write-downs in 1971 and projected a substantial loss, after that extraordinary item, for the year. It was plain that the old regime was over and the new boss had gone to work with a broadly swinging scalpel, though the general character of the company would remain the same. Whether rightly or wrongly, one of AmStan's officials under Marquard laid the corporation's problems at the door of the acquisition policy the company had followed from 1967 to 1970, saying the company had spent more money than it had taken in on the growth, as well as being hurt by the poor economy.

BILL LYON SAYS GOODBYE

In any event, the new regime did not include real estate on its list of favorites: the new motto became "cash generation." One of the first Am-

Stan real estate ventures to go was its 50% partnership in "Construction for Progress." This was sold to Cushman & Wakefield in mid-1971, a few months before Eberle's departure to cut down on AmStan's "steady flow of invested capital." Next in line was Wm. Lyon Development Company and its building subsidiaries. Bill Lyon made a deal to buy his organization back from the corporate parent in May 1971 for $44.7 million, agreeing to pay 65% cash and the balance in short-term notes. It would have been a profitable sale for AmStan, since its total investment in the Lyon organization came to approximately $42 million. Lyon had formed a group of investors into a company known as the WL Corporation for this purpose and had until October 15 of the same year to close the deal. It was widely expected that on buying out the company he would take it public, perhaps entering into a direct association with that other entrepreneurial builder departed from a corporate giant, Ray Watt.

Thus it was very unfortunate for both Lyon and American-Standard that he was unable to arrange for the financing. His deal with AmStan fell through. The corporation was left in the development business against its will. It planned to go on operating the subsidiary but at a greatly reduced pace. Already, before the start of 1972, it had sloughed off the recreational-land sales, mobile-home park and apartment development program. Bill Lyon was back to being a builder of conventional homes.

Bill stuck it out for a few months longer after the denouement, just as he had stuck it out in earlier times through the cross-purposes of management policy and the stop-go driving. But he knew when the bottom had been plumbed. Early in 1972 he quietly resigned his vice presidency of American-Standard, leaving behind him the now-shrunken building company he had founded and taken to national prominence. He was on his own again, but in that end was a new beginning.

Bill resigned from AmStan a few weeks after it reorganized its land and shelter operations into A. S. Realty, Inc., with him as chairman, amid reports that AmStan began negotiating to sell A. S. Realty's western operations. Forming a new venture in the spring of 1972, WL Builders Corporation, based in Newport, California, he bought property for initial projects from his former parent and, much like Ben Deane, began building again, hammering out townhouses and fourplexes in the $20,000 to $25,000 range. His feelings about the merger gone awry were quite plain to those of us who operated with him in the Southern California housing market, but he gave them for the record:

"I left American-Standard because its management and its whole philosophy of business changed; American-Standard couldn't make up its mind what it wanted to be in the real estate business. I wouldn't trade the time I spent with American-Standard for anything. But the other conditions in major corporations and the other things they're doing inevitably reflect in their attitudes toward their building operations. The companies that seem to be going in a really big way are the ones that kept their autonomy. Every morning they know what the name of the game is. And they know where their financing is coming from and how large their commitment is."

But if Lyon was through with American-Standard, he was by no means through with homebuilding. After buying three projects from his former parent company as the initial investment for WL Builders, he continued buying unfinished developments from American-Standard. Early in 1973 he bought five of its land projects in San Jose and Union City, California, along with 530 homes that had been sitting in inventory. As a capper, he even managed to reacquire his old company's name, William Lyon Development Company. As of mid-1973 he had ten projects underway in California and planned to achieve $20 million in sales for the year.

As a reminder of its realty heydays, American-Standard through its A-S subsidiary still had fifteen projects going in a half-dozen states.

15

How Harry Lasky Saved His Baby from the Wolves at Penn Central's Door

> And I in deeper spring have seen
> Greenness emerge in autumn.
>
> —David Ross

Harrison M. Lasky may not have to hurry quite so much these days, but he still does. A blond-complexioned, balding man of forty-one years, he looks so engrossed in the concerns of his business that one gets the impression of him almost puffing from his exertions. What Harry tries to keep up with is his mind. You realize this when he talks to you, as he does with speed and abrasiveness, with great precision and wit. You feel the inexhaustible power of his mind, its keenness, its especial quickness. The sense is of a large, crackling, electric energy which instantly perceives all aspects of any problem, defines it precisely and homes in sharply on the exact and correct solution. You feel his impatience that language, however precise, is an inadequate instrument to convey the exact rightness and simultaneity of Harry's perception; that only action will suffice. And so Harry is all action, forever striving to make real the perfection of his perfect vision. If he puffs, it is because he drives his corporeal body hard.

It should come as no surprise that in an industry where exceptional entrepreneurial ability is common and brilliance is not uncommon, Harrison M. Lasky is a sheer and true genius, the entrepreneur's entrepreneur, combining the tactical brilliance of Stonewall Jackson with the strategic and organizational abilities of a Rothschild. In an industry where great empires can collapse overnight with no warning, Harry, a former mortgage banker, has demonstrated an astonishing ability to survive and prosper by clear thought and effective action which converted disaster into opportunity. He has demonstrated an ability to create one of the finest and biggest housing organizations in the U.S., fairly sparkling with an almost Germanic brilliance and efficiency. And he has demonstrated perhaps the rarest ability of all, which is the knack of spotting the exact and right abilities of others and putting those to work; he showed this quality not only in the selection of his

347

working team but in his choice of a corporation to merge with and the
right sort of corporate boss.

HARRY LANDS ON HIS FEET

In the summer of 1970, Lasky suddenly almost found himself out of a
job when the Penn Central declared bankruptcy and the rumble of falling
dominoes hit Great Southwest, a subsidiary of the railroad, and then ripped
on to GSW's subsidiary, Macco, before descending in a crash on Leadership
Housing Systems, which Harry was heading as a Macco division. Leadership, founded in 1968, had a bright future (sales of $63 million in 1970),
and Harry wasn't about to let it go under. In a display of brilliant footwork,
tugging against the fatalism of Great Southwest people and working under
tremendous pressure, he disengaged the housing division from Macco and
sold it to the Cerro Corporation. During 1971 he committed himself to the
task of developing what had been a division into a complete company, setting up tight management controls and full-fledged housing, apartment/mo-
bile-home-park and modular divisions, as well as diversifying operations
geographically well beyond California to the Southeast, the Southwest and
to Hawaii. He turned in sales for the year of about $72 million.

And early in 1972, in another lightning stroke, he took advantage of
another unexpected misfortune — somebody else's this time — to enlarge
his organization substantially and to go public at the same time. Acting on
the advice of Lasky's team, parent Cerro swooped in to buy control of
troubled, AMEX-listed Behring Corporation, a major Florida builder with
substantial assets that Lasky could well develop. Leadership Housing Systems was merged into Behring, with Harry becoming president and his team
assuming the key positions. That combination put Lasky at the head of a
public building corporation whose sales for 1971 exceeded $100 million. It
also gave him a brand-new job of organization to develop the full potentials
of a company that he still regards as embryonic.

To be sure, Lasky's ability to act as fast as he did in the case of Behring
and at the time of the Penn Central collapse owes a great deal to the abilities of C. Gordon Murphy, the president of Cerro Corporation, and to Cerro's own urgent desire to diversify into new markets because of the uncertain future of its South American mining operations. But Harry deserves the
credit for picking out the right corporate partner in the first place. Murphy,
who had been brought in as president of the giant mining corporation to get
a diversification program going mighty quick, just happens to have been an
expert in real estate and was formerly head of a Litton Industries division.
As Lasky has that precious ability to analyze and communicate the exact

merits of an opportunity, so he is well matched by Murphy's equal under-standing and his readiness to act.

HARRY MEETS PENN CENTRAL THROUGH A GO–GO OPERATOR

Harry Lasky is an element of continuity between the tortuous and com-plicated history of Penn Central's real estate activities and the emergence of the Behring Corporation as a major national building subsidiary of Cerro. The story has its genesis in the railroad's acquisition of Great Southwest Corporation back in 1964. GSW then was a developer and operator of in-dustrial and amusement parks in the Dallas-Fort Worth and Atlanta areas. The company was 92% owned by Pennsylvania Company which was in turn held by the holding company also owning Penn Central Transporta-tion, the railroad operators. Penn Central later also acquired a 58% interest in a Miami land developer, Arvida Corporation, and a 25% interest in Madison Square Garden Corporation. Macco, which then owned 130,000 acres of California land, entered the scene as a Penn Central subsidiary in 1965 when the railroad paid $38.4 million to add it to its collection.

Great Southwest and Macco were at first unrelated subsidiaries of the railroad, but that was one of the first things to change in 1967, a year of many changes. The action began when Macco's executives in the fall of that year projected that the company would show a loss of $3 million for the year, instead of the $10 million profit originally anticipated. The alarmed managers at Penn Central asked another of their subsidiaries, Great South-west, for help. GSW's head, Angus G. Wynne, Jr., sent in a protégé, a bril-liant thirty-four-year-old lawyer named Bill Baker, to look the situation over.

Baker was a superb operator and he launched such a thoroughgoing era of reform that the old guard at Macco reeled, and most of its members either quit or got fired. His first action, with three months remaining in the fiscal year, was to convert the projected $3 million loss into a profit of $6 million by pulling off a series of major land sales. He then merged Macco into Great Southwest as an operating subsidiary and set about converting the sluggish, land-rich company into a major developer through acquisitions and the hir-ing of experienced top-notch personnel.

Macco had previously been in the housing business itself, but this as-pect of its activities lacked both marketing expertise and spirit; it had made most of its money by speculating in California land. While Baker proceeded to convert the company into a first-rate diversified housing developer, he pared down the company's landholdings from 130,000 to 36,000 acres by a series of ingenious land sales, thus also keeping reported profits on the up-and-up. In 1968 Macco's profits rose to $10.5 million on sales of $66.1 million. In 1969, Baker ran them up to $33 million on sales of $122 million.

One of Bill Baker's strokes of marketing ingenuity was his plan to syndicate the 4,928-acre Bryant Ranch for $30 million to private investors after he tried and failed to sell it for $7 million in 1967 (and that lesser sum was $1 million below Macco's total investment, which with carrying charges had risen to $8 million after the company paid $5 million for the land in 1963). The ranch had substantial drawbacks. The management of the new town of Mission Viejo, its prosperous next-door neighbor in Orange County, declined to sell a strip that would have reduced access to the San Diego Freeway from sixteen to four miles. The ranch also lacked water and sewer lines to support full residential development, though there were enough facilities for a recreational project. Plus, it had carrying charges of $500,000 a year.

So Baker came up with the idea of selling the ranch as an exclusive horse-and-gun club called Coto de Caza. The buyers were to be individual investors who bought lots and shared 45% of the Coto de Caza recreation club's profits. By mid-1968, 400 investors agreed to pay $75,000 each, with a down payment of $15,000 in cash. The resulting $6 million in cash ($15,000 × 400) was tax-deductible prepaid interest on a $30 million note ($75,000 × 400) held by Macco. And Baker was able to borrow another $7.5 million against the note from a financial institution.

Thus, the ranch that Baker couldn't sell for $7 million generated $13.5 million in cash ($6 million in down payments plus $7.5 million advanced against the note), with the note yielding a further $1 million yearly and the prospects of 55% of the club's profits further sweetening the deal. Baker was so enthusiastic about this success that he started building $5 million worth of clubhouses, motels and stables at Coto, though he was obligated to spend only $2 million by the terms of the syndication agreement. Later, he pulled off another major deal, selling for $19 million Macco's minority interest in the new town of Rancho California.

HARRY GETS THE GO-GO

Simultaneously with legerdemain, Baker pushed Macco strongly into a development role to establish a sounder base for earnings than land sales alone could provide. Many of the plans for the galloping growth that Macco was to start on came up from Baker's executive vice president and indispensable right-hand man, Bill Ray. And they dug in the spurs together. On approving the expansion plans, Baker told Ray: "Go till you hear glass breaking."

The year 1968 saw the start of the Leadership Housing Division, which then handled only single-family homes. Coming aboard as head of the division, Harry Lasky had to start virtually from scratch, setting up marketing and purchasing operations, developing new architectural approaches and nailing down loan commitments. Within ninety days, a remarkably short time for start-up, Lasky had men building round the clock getting homes into production (they worked under lighted tents by night). Lon Rubin, an alumnus of Kaufman & Broad also came aboard as head of a newly formed Macco Apartment Division and swung into frenetic activity. By 1970 Leadership had a 115-man staff and was selling 2,100 units, up from 1,250 in 1969, throughout Southern California and in Dallas. The apartment division built and sold 2,086 units in 1969 and planned on 3,500 for 1970. Commercial and recreational divisions were also established, and the company evolved a philosophy of picking up, where possible, 500 to 1,000-acre parcels which all the divisions would develop cooperatively. The 1,180-acre Scripps Miramar Ranch near San Diego, bought by Macco in late 1968 for $4 million, was handled this way.

Through a series of acquisitions, Baker and Ray looked forward to giving Macco's total housing production a further boost. For 1970 some 17,400 units were projected as a result of both internal growth and acquisitions, up sharply from Macco's 9,000 units for 1969. Great Southwest brought big mobile-home manufacturer, Richardson Homes of Elkhart, Indiana, into the fold late in 1969 for $15 million in stock, plus another $5 million contingent on earnings. Richardson, planning to double plants from eight to sixteen, projected 10,000 units for 1970, up from 5,700 in 1969. In 1970 GSW also acquired the I.C. Deal Companies of Dallas for about $22 million in stock. Irving Deal, a top-notch apartment developer who specialized in swinger apartments, built 1,250 units in Dallas in 1969 and planned on 1,800 in Dallas, Houston and Atlanta for 1970. Macco also rounded out its building program by introducing a modular-home division during 1970, in expectation that 70% of residential and apartment construction by 1975 would be built with modular components. In theory, the various divisions and acquisitions were separate operations, but Lasky was coordinating the company's move into modulars and mobiles and Rubin shifted to handle both single-family homes and apartments. In practice, the two worked together even more closely, since responsibilities outran organizational charts.

It was a period of exuberant growth and fast action, with the sky appearing to be the limit. Hooked by large incentives and big salaries, executives worked twenty-hour days and ran every minute. There was a feel of awesome opulence to the operation: of high-rolling wheeler-dealers who had style, limousines, a company yacht and leased jets; an assistant to the apartment division head was ferried to and from work sixty miles each day by company helicopter. Nothing was too good for the team that was putting Macco on the map. And that was in all probability true. Had Macco been an independent entity, it might have kept on growing stably; it certainly had absolutely first-rate talent. Unfortunately, it was connected by a long chain of ownership to the fortunes of Great Southwest and the Penn Central. And when the railroad folded, Macco was also kaput.

CANCELED MEETING AND THE WORM OF AMBITION

It was known that Penn Central had problems, but the end of the railroad was, to say the least, unexpected. From a retrospective view, however, there were one or two incidents to foreshadow the calamity. One of these was the waning fortunes of Great Southwest itself in the spring of 1970. Even as GSW undertook a nationwide promotional campaign to advertise itself and trade publications boomed with stories of Great Southwest and Baker's success at Macco, GSW's stock began to fall. The company's fortunes seemed to turn sour for a couple of reasons. The first of these was a footnote in its 1969 annual report which disclosed that the company had changed its policy to enter the business of "constructing, developing, selling and operating" major regional amusement parks. Previously, the company had constructed parks and held them — a very different strategy. The shift in policy let GSW book two large transactions as ordinary income: a 1968 deal yielded a $4.8 million profit on a $23 million sale and a 1969 transaction raised a $17.5 million profit on a $40 million sale. Without those sales, 1969 income would have dropped 26% to $16.8 million. In 1970 the company started developing two more parks with the intent to sell them, but the question was whether the market for major amusement parks was large enough to permit GSW to build and sell a park each year.

The second reason for GSW's stock downturn in that spring of 1970 also, ironically, precipitated Penn Central's declaration of bankruptcy. In mid-March, Great Southwest canceled a series of scheduled meetings with New York security analysts on a half-day's notice. The company had wanted to make a favorable impression to raise its stock's P/E ratio and pave the way for a stock offering later in the year. The abrupt cancellation angered some influential analysts and brought out speculation of a corporate-wide breakdown in management, and the stock started falling — from 13¾ to 5 at mid-1970. As the stock fell in March, it adversely affected a plan of Penn Central's for a security issue of its own. The railroad was forced to abandon a plan to add GSW shares as a sweetener to a contemplated $100 million debenture offering. Ironically, as Ken Campbell reported in his *Audit* stock advisory newsletter on housing investments, those cancellations of the analysts' meetings that started GSW's stock decline and made it unappealing as a stock offering were ordered by Pennsy executives who had wanted to safeguard their own offering; the railroad's attorneys wanted to avoid any hint of illegal preregistration publicity, and so vetoed the meetings. Inadvertently, Penn Central thus cut its own throat. Without the stock sweetener, the financial community spurned the offering. And then, without the debenture money, the railroad was forced to go to the government for a loan guarantee. When the loan fell through, the company declared bankruptcy and filed for reorganization.

CAN BANKRUPTCIES MULTIPLY?

The immediate effect of the Penn Central's collapse was to push Great Southwest to the brink of bankruptcy, taking Macco with it. Banks in the U.S. and Europe immediately cut off all credit and withheld pending loans, including mortgage financing for the heavy program of apartment construction. GSW was not, of course, legally involved in the railroad's bankruptcy, but as a 92%-owned subsidiary it was pretty hard for any banker to view it as a separate entity and its chances of survival were deemed nil. Factually, while most of GSW's stock was pledged by Penn Central for loans made to the railroad, GSW itself appeared to be in good shape — but tell that to a banker in the crisis air of a major bankruptcy. Pennsy worsened GSW's situation after filing for reorganization, by draining off all available cash from it to meet its weekly payrolls. So the amusement-park developer was teetering periously close to immediate reorganization itself under Chapter 11 of the bankruptcy laws in the summer of 1970.

This unhappy situation was complicated by another major sideshow: a wideopen war for control of GSW that had broken out between Bill Baker, by now president of the company, and Angus Wynne, the chairman, who had been Bill's mentor and main factor in his earlier ascendance. Siding with Baker was his executive veep, Bill Ray. The backroom power struggle had been disrupting some company operations for months as Wynne and Baker vied for the affection of Pennsy's new chairman, Pal Gorman, and it broke into the open when the railroad went into reorganization. Baker and Ray tried to get loans from a number of New York banks but failed. As GSW was about to go under, Wynne announced that *he* had succeeded in lining up some interim money, and then quickly displaced Baker as chief executive officer. Campbell reported that Wynne announced his victory by walking up to Ray and saying: "You're fired." Baker left shortly afterward to form another concern, headquartered in Newport Beach, California, specializing in real estate.

Some of that interim money that kept Great Southwest out of bankruptcy, as we shall see, may have come from Cerro Corporation. But GSW's severe liquidity problem was scarcely abated and had a devastating effect on the Macco subsidiary. GSW sustained a $3.5 million loss in the first half of 1970, compared with a $20.7 million profit in the 1969 period — the performance a compound of internal disorganization and the external pressures of the railroad's bankruptcy.

GSW temporarily stayed alive by passing up payment of dividends on two series of preferred stock, thus saving $1.8 million, and cutting down severely on its staff of 1,000. It also put substantially all of Macco's 35,000 acres on the block and cut the Macco staff from 800 to 500, in order to reduce Macco debt load and provide funds for operations of Six Flags, Inc., the GSW subsidiary operating amusement parks. Macco had meanwhile stopped all activities as its financing lines had been cut.

HARRY RUNS LIKE THE DICKENS

And at this point we reenter upon the universe of Harry Lasky, who sat back one day and recalled the course of his peripatetic hustling from the moment when he first heard the Penn Central was going under:

"Penn Central made its announcement on June 26, 1970, a Friday afternoon, at 4 P.M. I heard about the bankruptcy at 9 A.M. the next day, a Saturday. Lon Rubin and I were in Beverly Hills selling an apartment to an investor, and I was badly shook. I didn't realize until subsequently, however, how bad off Great Southwest was — I didn't realize that the railroad was going into Chapter 11 on the next day, a Saturday — and I thought it wouldn't hurt us. This hit Great Southwest at the absolute wrong time. We were just in for financing. All our major bank credit lines, including large Eurodollar borrowings, needed to be revolved into longer terms and one-year master lines were to be drawn up. They included a $45 million unsecured loan from Chase Manhattan and Eurodollars for massive sums. It was all brilliantly conceived, and then the bankruptcy hit and everything stopped incomplete. The open war between President Baker and Chairman Angus Wynne, and Bill Ray, compounded the situation. The banks didn't have any confidence in us anymore. The bankruptcy of the railroad came at the absolute wrong time. The parent even took our construction loans to pay its bills.

"We at Leadership Housing waited thirty days. Suddenly, we got *really* scared as our receivables got higher and higher. Finally, I had to do something. I initiated the idea of us selling ourselves; the railroad probably didn't believe that we could do it, but they said OK. So we assembled a presentation book on ourselves and went out on our own. We had put the apartment and single-family divisions into one group, under Lon Rubin and myself, and went out to start talking. [Richardson Homes and I. C. Deal were not included in Lasky's presentation or in the subsequent sale of Leadership to Cerro.]

"I saw five to seven companies and four were really interested. I went to New York on Tuesday morning, on the eleventh of August, to see Gordon Murphy of Cerro; he had been recommended to us by a finder who was Gordon's next-door neighbor. On Wednesday, I went to Milwaukee to see MGIC. They were also very interested, but what I wanted was 20% of our company for ourselves — for the management — in our own stock, and they wanted us to take stock in MGIC, the parent company itself. On Wednesday I was back in New York for a late afternoon meeting with Gordon again. He was pretty goddamn knowledgeable and sophisticated in real estate; he quickly recognized the essentials of the situation. On Wednesday he said, in effect, 'Super! I'll be out in California the following Monday to review the situation.'

"I flew back to California Wednesday night because my father had passed away, arranged the funeral Thursday morning, and left for New York again Thursday afternoon. On Friday, I saw both Olin Mathieson and CBS and both said, in effect, that if Gordon doesn't buy you they would have a definite interest. On Friday night I came back to California with the sense of a job well done and waited for Gordon.

"On Monday morning Gordon started working with Great Southwest. He stayed with it from the eighteenth of August straight through till he bought the company. That's quite a feat, considering that Great Southwest was a completely disheveled company. In this period, Leadership owed over $6 million. The deal was cut on September first, and closed on September twenty-second. Gordon stayed in California the whole time and did a really unbelievable job. He knew he had to act quick or the situation would disintegrate.

"So we sold Leadership to Gordon because he acted quicker than anyone else. He recognized a bargain when he saw it. Cerro bought the net equity assets for $9 or $10 million — that is, it paid book value on an audited book basis — plus, it paid $5 million over book, payable over ten years. Gordon even advanced money to Great Southwest to keep them in business during the course of the negotiations — $3 million in cash — and this really saved Great Southwest. They were teetering then; if they had gone into bankruptcy, everything would have been involved, and Cerro wouldn't have been able to buy Leadership.

"Both Cerro and we as stockholders got a helluva good deal. Cerro bought houses in construction, inventory, land and sites ready to start on construction, an entire ongoing situation. So even though it bought only assets, it was go from the start instead of waiting two years to start from scratch. It took a strong chief executive who knew an opportunity when he saw it, who had the ability and the knowledge in real estate, and who was a guts ball player; he had to believe in us, the group of guys who were management."

Technically, the sale to Cerro was a straightforward sale of assets by Great Southwest; Leadership had existed only as a division of the selling firm. The terms of the transaction called for $11 million cash and Cerro's assumption of $34 million liabilities. It was, as Lasky said, a good deal for Cerro because a top-flight management came along with those assets.

LEADERSHIP GROWS UNDER HARRY

The period after the Cerro acquisition was a busy one for Lasky and his team, but also productive. While they were busy organizing the company anew as a subsidiary of the mining giant, they also sold 350 single-family homes and 700 to 800 apartment units between September 22 and December 31, 1970. Cerro had indeed bought well, because Lasky had a strong team and he put it to work with ample incentives based on his philosophy that "building management can't be put on an equatable salary structure with executives. There's nothing proprietary in real estate — you build one project and then you have to build a new one; you're only as good as the last project. So, management has to be creative and motivated every day." The key men at Leadership, all survivors of Harry's team at Macco, were Lon Rubin, executive vice president, thirty-eight; Darrel Wright, vice president for California single-family housing, twenty-nine; David Riese, vice president of the apartment division, forty; Allen Condon, director of the company's Florida operations, thirty-two; and Fred Sattes, Jr., head of modular development, thirty-six. Wright later left the company to found his own homebuilding firm backed by Trammel Crow. Among themselves they owned options on 20% of the company and worked on a handsome bonus system based on meeting their performance projections.

During 1971 the company made a strong push to diversify geographically out of the Southern California market, where it has been traditionally strong. It opened branches in San Diego, San Francisco, and Honolulu, in addition to getting a first exposure in the Dallas and Houston markets. It also set up a full operating division in Hollywood, Florida, under financial officer Allen Condon. And it decentralized its operation away from the Newport Beach headquarters, naming managers for each of its new areas. LHS Financial Corporation, a wholly owned subsidiary, was set up to provide mortgage financing and insurance for the company's real estate operations.

"In 1971, 80% of our business was still in Southern California," Lasky said. "But by the following year only 65% or less will be." The long-term strategy was to create a major diversified organization which would adhere to a fifty-fifty production of apartments and single-family homes. And it looked as if Harry had succeeded. Sales reached $72 million in 1971 and pretax earnings exceeded $4 million (under old accounting rules); for 1972 Harry projected sales of $90 million on 1,200 single-famly homes and 2,300 apartment units.

But in December of 1971 the whole picture changed abruptly again when the chance to buy the Behring Corporation suddenly presented itself.

SERENDIPITY STRIKES HARRY AGAIN: BEHRING

Behring Corporation, also located in Broward County, had been the beneficiary of considerable Wall Street publicity as one of the major modular-housing and development companies on the national scene (1971 sales: $38 million). The AMEX-listed corporation rose to a sky-high multiple on the wave of appeal for modular housing companies but tumbled badly as investors recognized that no magical advantages were implicit in modular housing and profits were dependent on the general merit of the particular builder. The extent of the company's problems with modular production became obvious when, for the nine month period ending September 30, 1971, Behring reported that modular-plant operations had a deficit in excess of $2.2 million, resulting in an $811,000 loss for the company. By the end of the year the company had a peck of worse financial and marketing difficulties, though it also held substantial assets and could perform well as a conventional developer.

What's Wrong with Modular Housing?

Nothing, intrinsically. In high labor-cost areas of the Northeast, conventional builders for the mass market can achieve some economies by prefabricating parts or all of their on-site housing at a nearby factory. But the problem is that many industrialized housing plants, particularly those outside the Northeast, can build units a lot faster than they can sell them. A small builder can cut down his overhead quickly if business falls off. But a housing factory, to be profitable, must maintain a steady production and a high rate of capacity utilization. And so, despite 1972's housing boom, many independent modular producers functioned at less than 50% capacity. Increasingly, such industrial housing manufacturers are expanding into land development and even on-site construction (or merging with large builders, like Donald J. Scholz & Company) to gain better control over the market for their product. But as the case of Behring Corporation illustrates, not even this move is foolproof.

Production and marketing of the homes has to be closely coordinated with site acquisiton, zoning, site preparation, architectural design and distribution economics. Due allowance must also be made for the price and quality of the competition's conventional product, as Behring learned. His $6 million factory turned out an award-winning two-bedroom home of exceptional design and sold it in several complete communities developed by the company in the fast-growing Florida market. But production exceeded sales, while high overhead and an unskilled work force inflated production costs. On-site installation of the steel-frame modules also proved much more time-consuming and costlier than anticipated. To cap things off, Behring was locked into a low competitive price — $19,000 to $23,000 — which didn't begin to cover his production costs. Even then, the homes were not regarded as competitive with conventionally built models of other builders in the market.

There's no question that the modular housing industry is the fastest-growing segment of the field. But most of the three hundred companies who entered the field between 1968 and 1972 have put too much emphasis on exotic building materials and "overkill" sophisticated technology and not enough on the economics of marketing and distribution. The problems appear to be more readily solvable in the Northeast when a modular or prefabricating plant can tie in with a high-volume housing developer operating in several cities, so as to minimize fluctuating factory production, and where the product can be competitive with or more economical than conventionally built on-site production. This is the bane of industrialized housing: unlike other manufacturers, it has to stay competitive with on-site housing.

As Eli Broad observes: "The necessary technology has long been available to build all of our homes in a factory. The problems are not those of technology but putting the technology together with the economics, distribution and consumer acceptance of housing. Many people believe that producing homes assembly-line fashion will realize significant cost reductions. This is not true at this point in time when compared with efficient on-site, mass production, using the many prefabricated sections and components available today. The amount of on-site labor in the past ten years has actually declined from 26% to 16% of the selling price of a home."

Unless one operates in a truly high-cost area for on-site labor, the economies of factory production of a complete home have not proven to be very significant before 1971. Promised cost savings on a $20,000 home have materialized not in the range of 20% but 5% to 10%. And these savings can be offset by high transportation costs, inventory backups and delays in site preparation by developers. The practical range for truck shipments is about three hundred miles. Local code variations which require interruption of runs for retooling lower production efficiency and raise costs. But at the same time the industry is under consumer pressure for enough design variety to eliminate the factory-made boxy look of its product. At this point, transportation codes also conspire to limit creativity, as twenty-five states limit load widths to 12 feet, thus confining design variety. But there is a trend toward allowing shipment of 14-foot-wide modules, and this will promote greater design flexibility.

For the present, the mobile home is the only form of housing that in the early Seventies meets the criteria for successful factory-built housing: economy, delivery system, volume production and consumer acceptance. Prefabrication of housing parts has gone a long way as an aid to the on-site builder. But the benefits of modulars nationwide are still in the future.

Incidentally, Behring was not the only major modular producer to encounter serious troubles at about the same time. In March 1972, creditors of McGrath Corporation and its subsidiary, McGrath Modular Corporation, filed petitions asking that the companies be declared bankrupt. McGrath, headquartered in Bellevue, Washington, was the largest residential builder in the Pacific Northwest (1969 sales: $14.3 million). The company was badly hurt when the region slumped into a severe recession with the failure of the aerospace economy — particularly when Boeing cut its payroll of 100,000 by two-thirds — and McGrath's switch from on-site to modular housing hastened the company's decline. McGrath had switched to modulars as its on-site market dwindled, but the company bogged in unprofitable overhead and operations. McGrath Corporation went public in 1969. The company lost $900,000 on sales of $7.2 million in fiscal 1971. It had a 3 to 4-year land inventory. Modular Housing Systems of Pennsylvania, which at one point was going to buy the Behring modular plant from Leadership, also followed McGrath in the modular shakeout.

In July 1972 the modular shakeout continued with the financial collapse of Stirling Homex, which in 1971 was regarded as the leader in making factory-built homes for low-income families. Stirling filed for a Chapter 9 bankruptcy after an overly ambitious expansion program and narrow marketing targets brought it up short. The company booked profits when each unit came off the assembly line, but due to a heavy lag in deliveries it suffered a heavy cash drain. It had two years of production — 10,000 units valued at $100 million — unsold and $37 million of short-term debt when it declared bankruptcy.

Here was another opportunity for Cerro to pick up a major ongoing organization and its land inventory — an organization which, shorn of its unprofitable modular operations, could prove as successful as Leadership. Behring was a rich plum in terms of landholdings. As late as October of 1971, the distressed company was making a series of extensive land acquisitions, including a 2,319-acre lakeside tract north of Tampa-St. Petersburg which cost $2.6 million and was to be zoned for 11,740 housing and apartment units. Harry had, incidentally, hoped to have Cerro take a portion of Leadership public along about 1973, but the merger of his company into Behring would back him into the public market at least a year sooner and infuse the Behring stock with new vigor and P/E from the juice of Leadership's rising sales and profits. The Behring name disappeared from the merged corporation, and Leadership Housing, Inc. (the name "Housing Systems" was dropped) appeared on the American Stock Exchange. As earlier, C. Gordon Murphy was not dilatory about snapping up a good thing like Behring — particularly in view of the fact that Cerro's mining operations were getting shakier. In October of 1971, for example, the entire Peruvian mining operation was closed in a strike by 13,000 workers, signaling an intensification of a bitter dispute between the government, the unions, and Cerro.

By January 24, 1972, Cerro and Behring had reached agreement in principle whereby Cerro would acquire a majority interest in Behring; and Behring and Leadership would subsequently merge. On February 1, Cerro's Murphy and Behring's chairman Kenneth E. Behring announced that Cerro completed the purchase of 3.4 million shares of Behring Corporation's common stock owned by Behring at a price of $4 per share. The purchase gave Cerro a 65% equity interest in the Florida company for a total of $13.6 million in cash and notes. The boards of directors of the two companies also approved in principle Behring's acquisition of the business of Leadership Housing Systems in a tax-free exchange of shares, with the final OK to have been ratified by Behring shareholders in April of 1972. On the completion of the transactions, Cerro was to own over 80% of the outstanding shares of common stock of the combined company, whose sales for 1971 reached about $114 million. And the mining company held an option to purchase an additional 400,000 shares of Behring's stock at varying prices up to 1978.

On August 28, 1972, the stockholders of Behring Corporation as a majority-owned subsidiary of Cerro approved the combination with Leadership as a wholly owned Cerro subsidiary. This combination, effective as of September 1, 1972, resulted in the issuance by Behring of some 4.6 million shares of common stock, $.10 par value, and 4 million shares of Series B Preferred stock, $.50 par value, in exchange for all of the common and preferred shares of Leadership Housing. Right after the merger Leadership became a wholly owned subsidiary of Behring and the name of Behring was changed to Leadership Housing, Inc. Harry Lasky had meanwhile been elected president and chief executive officer of the newly recombined company. Ken Behring continued for some months as chairman before resigning, succeeded in this role by Cerro's Gordon Murphy. Even prior to the combination Behring's nine-man board of directors had been loaded up with seven Cerro people, including Lasky, Murphy and Lon Rubin.

BYE-BYE MODULES

Behring had earlier announced a 40% cut of personnel at its modular housing plant and introduced other cost-cutting measures. But the new board of directors early in 1972 went into a review of modular problems and, to no surprise, immediately decided to get out of that business. By February 1972 Behring had announced the company was quitting that field and setting up a $4 million reserve to cover possible 1971 losses. In March the company's 300,000-square-foot modular housing plant at Fort Lauderdale went on the block for $4.3 million asked. Thenceforth Behring would function only as a conventional on-site builder.

HARRY LASKY EXPANDS HIS NEW-WON EMPIRE

Leadership's effective absorption of Behring's considerable assets immediately enlarged it into one of the few real estate firms operating in the $100-million sales category and the company overnight became an industry giant by every standard. At the head of this impressive realty group stood the indomitable Harry Lasky, who had survived in bad times and was now back on top in a remarkably short time and running hard to develop the full potential of his newly won empire. During 1972 Leadership flowered under his unrelenting generalship in the field. Sales for that year ran up to $116.4 million and income shot up to $4,967,000 (52 cents per share), contrasting sharply with combined 1971 results of the predecessor Behring and Leadership companies, which were sales of $83.4 million and a loss of $861,000. (An original 1971 profit for Leadership was converted into a loss through a voluntary restatement of Leadership's 1971 operations in accordance with stricter accounting rules governing the timing of profit recognition on apartment sales.) During 1972 the new Leadership took orders for 3,027 single-family houses, closed sales of 1,984 homes, and entered 1973 with approximately $63 million in backlog. In the same year it completed 1,166 apartment units and had another 1,764 under construction at year's end, all previously sold to investors.

The sales and earnings leap in 1972 was particularly commendable in view of the fact that all of Behring's modular housing production and sales had been curtailed and the focus shifted to conventionally built homes. Leadership's housing sales in 1972 were $44,635,000 compared with a total of $62,232,000 for the two predecessor companies in 1971. It is true that 1972 apartment sales rose to $22,004,000 compared with $12,539,000 for 1971, but this was primarily due to the adoption of the percentage-of-completion method of accounting revenues during the construction period.

What really made it possible for Leadership to come out ahead in 1972 was the fact of its expansion into an entirely new line of business: investor land management and land sales. This represented an expansion beyond Lasky's earlier policy of keeping company activity equally balanced between housing and apartment construction and served, in fact, as another testament to his genius. For by this move he not only accelerated sales and earnings beyond the combined previous efforts of Leadership and Behring (all of the latter's marketing programs, don't forget, had been dropped) but also opened up his company to a major new source of future development capital and future joint venture projects with majors. This takes some explanation.

When Leadership took over the assets of Behring Corporation it found itself with three major properties on its hands, extremely valuable for future development but in view of their size also representing a drain in carrying costs and future construction financing. Leadership turned the tables neatly, also in the process expanding its sales and earnings, by selling two of the three properties in December 1972 and taking them over as a manager. First, a group of private trusts purchased 1,706 acres in Tamarac, Florida for $22.4 million with Leadership receiving $17.9 million in cash. Then a Leadership subsidiary sold 2,305 acres in Palm Beach County to a partnership composed of Leadership and Texaco Boca Del Mar, Inc., a subsidiary of Texaco, Inc., for $23 million, with Leadership receiving $14.7 million in cash. As a further bonus these sales enabled the company to retire the major portion of its corporate debt. Perhaps most importantly, however, through the buyer agreements Leadership will continue to participate in a further 50% of the profits as the land is improved and sold to other developers. The two properties were zoned for some 22,500 dwelling units at the end of 1972. That's quite a deal! And in view of the continuing future earnings potential to Leadership from these properties, it differs entirely from the type of one-shot land sales deals that some companies used to make to push up earnings. Rather, it represents a finely wrought joint venture and variant on a land-banking scheme arrangement whereby Leadership is dispossessed of carrying charges on major parcels and supplies only the necessary management expertise to turn its share of the profits. No wonder Harry Lasky was the darling of the *Wall Street Journal* early in 1973.

The concept has met with such enthusiasm (local builders fell all over themselves when they heard they had a chance to buy subdivided parcels on the Boca Del Mar Property from Leadership-Texaco) that early in 1973 Leadership also began negotiating, on similar terms, the sale of its third major property, the 2,300-acre Tarpon Lake Villages, which has already been planned for 11,500 dwelling units. In expectation of further similar deals, the company also at that time acquired another 1,650 acres in Florida's Broward County and had another 2,350 acres under option. Several prospective corporate partners were reported to be negotiating with Leadership for joint venture agreements to develop this property. It looked like a sure bet that a substantial part of Leadership's efforts in the future would be devoted to the development of gigantic master-planned communities on this type of program. Harry provided the tip-off in observing: "There is every expectation that more major investors will want to enter the housing industry this way. To activate an organization to undertake the development of a 10,000-unit community would be prohibitively costly for a non-housing company. Leadership's role as a partner supplies the management expertise necessary for timely and well-planned realization of the potential which major land resources offer."

As of early 1973 Harry was also intensively exploring both foreign markets and foreign capital sources to assure Leadership's future performance. One early product of this activity was a new corporation formed by Leadership and a Japanese panelized house manufacturer to experiment with construction of low-cost housing in Hawaii. The Japanese partner, Misawa Homes, Ltd., got about $200,000 of Leadership money as the latter's contribution to the new entity. Two prototype housing units — a single-family detached house and a resort condominium — were to be developed for use in Hawaii, using methods of panelized construction now employed by Misawa in its twenty manufacturing plants in Japan. If they prove feasible, the new company will build the Misawa-Leadership house in a 100-home project now being developed in Kailua-Kona by the Leadership joint venture with C. Brewer & Company. If the homes were found acceptable in the Hawaiian market, a manufacturing facility was to be established in Hawaii. A second phase of the agreement also gave Misawa-Leadership exclusive license for the use in the United States of Misawa panelized construction for a twenty-five-year period.

The firm also began intensive explorations for other joint ventures abroad with foreign and domestic corporations and began planning its first European housing project near Lisbon. Late in the year, Cerro said it would in effect gain complete ownership of the building company by buying up the 893,777 outstanding common shares of Leadership that it didn't already own for about $4.9 million. The building company was thus to become a wholly owned subsidiary and a major profit-maker for Cerro.

Leadership entered 1973 with nineteen home developments and a sales backlog of $63 million in residential housing, compared to a $19 million backlog when entering 1972. While intensively exploiting the Florida market (St. Petersburg, Lake Tarpon, Fort Lauderdale) and steadily building in both Northern and Southern California (Los Angeles and Orange counties, Scripps Miramar, Bay area), Leadership also broadened its activities in the housing and tourist markets of Hawaii. One of its programs there is a joint venture with C. Brewer & Company, Ltd., one of the Islands' "Big Five" companies and a subsidiary of International Utilities Corporation. The co-venture, organized as Pacific Environments Company, began a development of 100 single-family homes in Kailua-Kona in 1973. Four new apartment projects totaling 1,000 units were to open early in 1973 in Northern California, Houston and Tucson, with another underway in Las Vegas and six more in initial design stages. It was a good foundation for future growth. And who knows what other gains will pop up?

It's all on account of Harry, folks. Take it from me.

16

U.S. Home Pilots a Congeneric of Builder Barons

Shoulder to shoulder
And bolder and bolder we
Grow as we march to the fore.

—Song "Stout Hearted Men"

It really must be the most immense round table in the world, down there at the U.S. Home offices at Boca Raton, Florida. King Arthur's would have seemed like a barstool by comparison. It is a table of such proportions that fifty men could sit around it and would have to stretch hard to toss a football to the other side. The building was designed with this table in mind and a special conference hall was built to accommodate it. And it is at this table that U.S. Home's growing legion of acquired entrepreneurial builder-partners gathers several times each year to discuss strategy and to cheer on the growth of what may in all probability be the nation's first housing firm to reach sales of $1 billion and annual profits of $50 million by 1976.

A NEW LANGUAGE FOR BUILDING

U.S. Home is a unique corporation, which has contributed two new terms to the language of the housing industry: "congeneric" and "peer group." As a building company that grows by internal expansion as well as by the acquisition of other builders, it qualifies for the former (as contrasted with "conglomerate," a company making acquisitions among unrelated industries). As a company that eschews the corporate hierarchical setup and permits — indeed, encourages — each of its acquired builders to run his own show semi-autonomously, and is in turn steered by the group of its subsidiary member-builders, it qualifies as a "peer group."

At last count, in late 1972, U.S. Home had gathered to itself, through its acquisition program, a constituency of some seventeen builder-partners in twenty divisions selected for their long-term performance histories and management strength, and more were to come. The company's sales for fiscal 1971 were $91.6 million and hit $200 million in fiscal 1972, a 100%

growth in a single year made possible by a combinaton of rapid internal growth and a number of acquisitions. This performance considerably exceeded UH's announced long-term program of at least 40% compounded annual growth — half through acquisitions and half through internal growth — through 1975. The real goal is even bigger; as stated, the company was shooting for the $1 billion sales mark by the end of that target year.

The company's problems with one or two acquisitions and bearish housing conditions in 1973 resulted in a decline of its growth rate in that year. Chairman Charles Rutenberg said earnings were to decline by about 10% from the 1972 level of $16.2 million. Wall Street, turning into a big bad bear on housing stocks in general, also sold off U.S. Home stock to low levels. But U.S. Home remains distinctive and will be a major factor in the industry during the 1970s. In a period when industrial corporations lost their uncritical appeal as merger partners for builders, this company set the definitive pattern for a new type of acquirer: a merger partner who, because he is already a builder, provides a congenial environment based on mutual understanding of entrepreneurial requirements.

The architect of this strategy was Robert Henry Winnerman, who was chairman of the company until his resignation in May 1973. The highly successful strategy was implemented both by Winnerman and Charles Rutenberg, who was and remains president of the firm. Discussing the U.S. Home concept before his departure, Winnerman credited much of its success to the members' ability to communicate freely and effectively with one another and to make most of their own decisions. "We have combined the ingenuity of private entrepreneurs with the national support required in today's housing environment," said Rutenberg. "Our philosophy provides continuing recognition of the entrepreneurial instinct which is vital to success in this industry."

"In formulating U.S. Home," said Winnerman, "we rewrote the plan sixteen times. We selected about fifteen markets in the U.S. which will be growing markets over the next five to fifteen years. We may ultimately add up to five companies in each market area and may even start satellite operations within each market. With a big distribution of $100 million or $150 million or $200 million in each market, we may have fifteen product mixes. Each division (an acquired builder) can teach the others to do what it does. When modular housing becomes effective, we can drop a plant in the center of each market area and distribute to four or five builders."

THE BLUEPRINT FOR GROWTH DEVELOPED SLOWLY

U.S. Home had gone an enormously long way by mid-1972 since embarking on its acquisition strategy in 1969, when Winnerman envisioned a giant company with total housing capabilities and relatively immune from shifts of local construction and financing markets. In little more than three years the company grew from a local New Jersey operation to a nationwide firm, making Winnerman the unquestioned king of builder acquisitions. It was quite a leap for the man who in 1954, while still in his late twenties, first organized the homebuilding company originally known as Accurate Construction. The company first went public in 1959 and by the end of 1968 it was still a modest local developer, with sales of $7.6 million and profits of $365,000 in that year. By this time, however, Winnerman's congeneric merger plan was in an advanced stage of germination.

U.S. Home took its first giant step by acquiring Imperial Land Corporation and Rutenberg Homes of Florida in 1969. This move raised earnings for that year to $1.4 million on sales of $36 million. Winnerman moved up to chairman and Charlie Rutenberg, founder of Imperial, became the president — a fruitful partnership in which the acquisition program took final form. The flurry of a dozen major acquisitions followed in 1970 and 1971 based on criteria of successful track record and strong management. Winnerman recounts some of the key considerations that led to this program:

"In developing a viable growth plan, we carefully weighed the feasibility of growth by expansion and growth by acquisition. From a financial viewpoint, it became apparent that even if the most experienced team were sent into a new market area, it would take at least three years before we could really determine whether or not we could operate profitably there. This represented a substantial risk factor which was far too inhibitory to the rate of growth which we had in mind." So U.S. Home opted to acquire builders with good track records over several years who had a high degree of familiarity with local markets.

"But these geographic markets were only one side of the coin," Bob Winnerman goes on. "The other side was a different type of market — perhaps industry segment is a better term. We foresaw significant changes occurring in the housing industry of the Seventies, a coming need for a wider product mix as housing markets narrowed and became more specialized. No one builder can be a specialist in all these product types. But by acquiring builders specializing in one or more varieties of each, we communicate the expertise of each throughout the entire structure of U.S. Home."

WHAT'S IN IT FOR THE MERGED BUILDER?

While the advantage to U.S. Home of acquiring successful builders in important market areas around the nation is apparent, what advantages are there for the merged builder? The key points merit review. The merger gives the local builder, who may fear an industrial partner or the rigors of the public market, the ability to capitalize his efforts and develop a meaningful

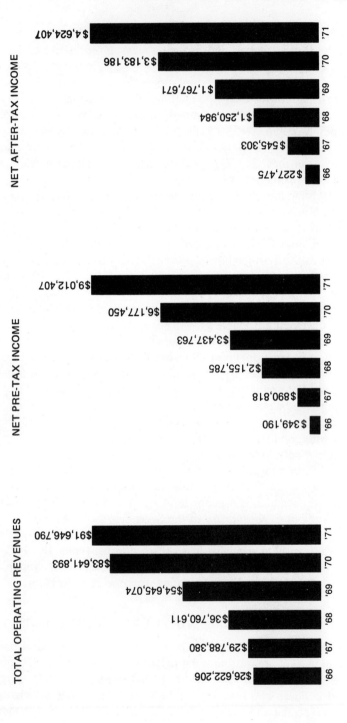

NET AFTER-TAX INCOME

'71 $4,624,407
'70 $3,183,186
'69 $1,767,671
'68 $1,250,984
'67 $545,303
'66 $227,475

NET PRE-TAX INCOME

'71 $9,012,407
'70 $6,177,450
'69 $3,437,763
'68 $2,155,785
'67 $890,818
'66 $349,190

TOTAL OPERATING REVENUES

'71 $91,646,790
'70 $83,641,893
'69 $54,645,074
'68 $36,760,611
'67 $29,788,380
'66 $26,622,206

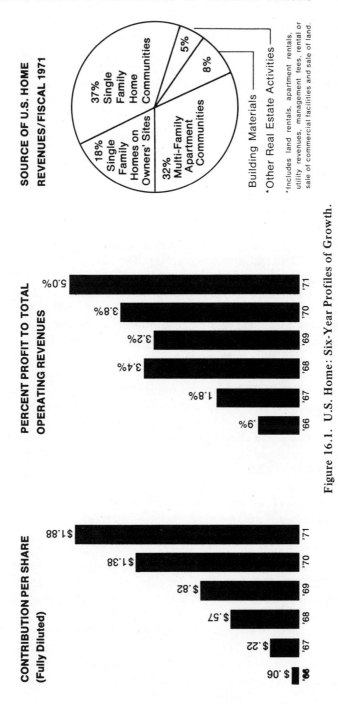

Figure 16.1. U.S. Home: Six-Year Profiles of Growth.

estate. The association with a major national organization and its added financial stability enable him to take on expansion programs he would be unable to start otherwise. The acquired builders themselves point out that one of the strongest advantages is the gain in flexibility and broader capabilities with new products and markets as a result of the access to the expertise of other builders within the company. UH doesn't promote it, but one strong incentive for each to perform is the prospect of appreciation in the value of the stock they hold as co-owners of the rapidly growing company.

One prime reason why UH was attractive to seventeen builders as of early 1972 is that the company offers them otherwise unavailable low-cost financing. In fiscal 1972 UH obtained more than $40 million in working capital from debt and equity offerings in the public market. A December 1971 offering of $5 million was earmarked exclusively for future land acquisitions, development and construction. The company's emphasis is on low-risk development, with a substantial portion of fiscal 1972 income derived from multifamily, retiree and other markets not affected by a rise in consumer interest rates. Late in 1971 UH also started up U.S. Home Mortgage Company to initiate and place consumer mortgages, with an initial unsecured line of credit for $55 million from Continental Illinois National Bank and Trust at close to prime rate. This organization, eventually serving all of UH's divisions, will broaden the market for their housing customers. A corporate services department of fewer than sixty people provides corporate planning, accounting and legal assistance, all tax work, guidance on federal programs, central purchasing and marketing assistance.

Winnerman's own approach to management by the parent corporation was to keep it passive, long on analysis and evaluation and short on actual interference if the builder is producing on target. Each constituent builder-peer controls his own cost control, cash flow, profit and sales. Land purchasing, land use, financing arrangements are locally controlled. The only standard rules touch on reporting. Income statements, balance sheets and operating statements are submitted on a monthly basis; sales figures are on a weekly basis. And each builder pays $\frac{3}{4}$% of gross sales to UH as a management fee. The budget for each division is worked out jointly with parent UH staff, and UH also approves major extraordinary expenditures. Budgets must meet profit guidelines: the minimum is a $5\frac{1}{2}$% net after-tax profit and 20% increase in sales annually.

Jack M. Soble was to have provided us with one example of a big builder who opted for a merger with U.S. Home. A director of the parent corporation and, as president of U.S. Home Communities Corporation (renamed from Soble Construction Corporation), one of the largest builders of government-assisted housing on the East Coast, he was a warm, witty and sensitive man. Tragically, after this chapter was largely prepared, Jack Soble died on April 16, 1972, when his company plane crashed into the ocean on takeoff from Atlantic City, New Jersey. I think it would be a most appropriate memorial to reproduce his interview here as it was originally written, keeping it in the present tense.

It took Jack Soble some time to make up his mind whether or not he even wanted to merge. As he says: "At first we thought, what the hell do we need this for? We're making money; we've got a big yacht down in Florida; we've got automobiles and we go on vacation. We have a $20 million company and plenty of real estate." But he became concerned about estate problems, properly reasoning that real estate itself is quite inflexible. And he came to the conclusion that he would feel better about having negotiable securities for a second reason: "I would be very much concerned about the fact that I had millions of dollars on paper and I was in the position where someone could pull the rug out from under me. I didn't want to be in that position. I wanted security."

But when Jack Soble began looking for a merger partner, he quickly learned a lesson he regards as important: It's not only a matter of finding a company, but finding the right company. The story of his negotiations with a large conglomerate firm, while it may not be representative of all industrial firms by any means, is a chuckle. He was informed that on merging he would be placed in charge of a "whole division" within the corporate structure. It turned out that the "division" he would be in charge of was his own company and that of another builder. Pressing further Jack Soble discovered that *his* "division" would be placed within a still larger division. When he asked for an explanation of the logic of the fit, the reply was that his "division" would be part of the service division. To this day Jack Soble professes to be puzzled how his organization would have fitted with a division which, among other things, made oilcans and fishing rods.

"U.S. Home came along quite by accident through a friend of ours," Jack Soble says. "We met with one of their people and he was able to see the future of our company." That sold him on a major merger point: "It's not the size of the company that's important, but rather it's being able to be with someone in your own industry." The merger with U.S. Home enlarged his borrowing ability and thus his building program. But what he stresses is his ability to communicate with the principals of U.S. Home (other builders) and deal in an atmosphere of professional understanding. "When I complain now that a mortgage man charged me an extra half-point," he observes wryly, "the chairman of the board, the comptroller, the vice presidents and everyone else know what we're talking about and they don't feel sorry for us. They leave us alone and let us worry about getting our own half-point back." But he adds: "What we have is a coordinated team. You lose a little bit of your autonomy, but if you merge with the right company, you form a team and you feel you're dealing with people and not numbers."

THE ROSTER OF U.S. HOME'S BUILDER BARONS

Following Jack Soble's logic, the roster of U.S. Home's subsidiaries has grown steadily. The pattern does not show any standard financial formula for the acquisitions. U.S. Home has used both the pooling and the purchase accounting methods, with and without earnout, using stock or cash. The specific approach is based on the builder's own desires, the company profile and its production record. Some acquisitions, like Orrin Thompson's, involved cash; the mergers of the bigger companies after the merger rules changed have seen straight pooling with no earnout. Smaller firms go the earnout route. Among the members of the U.S. Home confederation are the following:

Ellis Suggs Construction Co., Inc., Phoenix, Arizona, a major marketer in the greater Phoenix area specializing in single-family community development. It began diversification into townhouse programs under U.S. Home.

Brown Homes, Inc., Clearwater, Florida, which has concentrated on single-family projects in the Clearwater area for fifteen years, focusing on the middle-income market. The company moved into multifamily construction with a 100-unit condominium project after joining U.S. Home.

Clearwater Concrete Industries, Inc., Clearwater, one of two examples in U.S. Home of an acquired organization not directly engaged in housing production. The company produces ready-mix concrete, blocks and other building products on computerized programs. U.S. Home bought it to support its multifamily activities in the Florida area.

First Development Corporation of America, Sarasota, Florida, a diversified builder/developer with operations in Sarasota, Bradenton and Fort Myers. Its projects in 1972 included single-family developments, cluster-duplex condominium units, a golf course/country club residential community, and a vacation community at Bald Mountain, North Carolina.

Imperial Land Corporation, Clearwater, the most diversified subsidiary of U.S. Home. It builds single-family homes, condominium garden apartments, retirement-oriented homes, condominium villas, mobile-home parks and waterfront recreational communities.

Rutenberg Homes, Inc., Belleair Bluffs, Florida, which builds custom single-family homes on the customer's own lot, as well as developing single-family subdivisions and condominiums. The condominium program is a recent expansion, involving projects in Naples, St. Petersburg and Largo aimed at the retirement market.

Port Builders, Inc., Belleair Bluffs, engaged in development of mid-rise and high-rise luxury condominium apartments and shopping centers.

U.S. Home of Greenbriar, Inc., Clearwater, formed in 1970 to plan, develop, and build planned residential communities, with two projects underway in 1972: Greenbriar, a 1,000-acre development, and Imperia, a 300-acre, 1,700-unit project.

Orrin E. Thompson Construction Corporation, Minneapolis, Minnesota, one of the largest single-family home builders in the Minneapolis-St. Paul area. The company in late 1971 was developing four large projects and adding townhouses to its product line.

Dee Wood Industries, Inc., Linwood, New Jersey, a manufacturer of prefabricated window units, prehung interior and exterior doors and prefabricated stairways, as well as a marketer of lumber and millwork. The operations are centered at the company's 75,000-square-foot plant in Linwood. But this U.S. Home subsidiary also began moving in the direction of a direct role in construction in 1970. It built a 56-unit garden-apartment complex in Ocean City, New Jersey, and had another underway in 1971, with further units planned subsequently. Rental and management functions are handled by a subsidiary set up for that purpose.

Soble Construction Co., Pleasantville, New Jersey (renamed U.S. Home Communities Corporation), one of the largest builders in the Eastern U.S. of low and moderate-income multifamily communities under subsidized programs, building in New Jersey, Maryland and eastern Pennsylvania.

U.S. Home-New Jersey Division, West Orange, New Jersey, Bob Winnerman's original company, building single-family homes and residential adult communities.

East Construction Company, Cincinnati, Ohio, builds and develops garden apartments in the greater Cincinnati area, most of which are sold to investors.

Norwood Homes, Houston (renamed U.S. Home Corporation of Texas), the biggest homebuilder in this major Texas city.

Witkin Homes, Denver, a major diversified developer of apartments, townhouses, subdivisions and planned-unit communities.

Marved Construction, Tucson, Arizona, which builds homes and town-houses with a twenty-year history in Tucson.

Stuart Golding, Inc., Tampa, Florida, a shopping-center developer.

Papparone Construction Company, Moorestown, New Jersey, a developer of single-family home communities and apartments with a twenty-year history of operations in the Cherry Hill section of New Jersey.

U.S. Home Corporation of Tampa, formed in February 1972 to build single-family homes in Tampa.

U.S. Home Mobilife, formed in 1972 to develop mobile-home parks.

3H Building Corporation, which entered into agreement in principle with UH in mid-1972 for a tax-free merger into U.S. Home. This marked the entry of UH into the metropolitan Chicago market.

THE IMPACT OF TOGETHERNESS

The cumulative activities of the U.S. Home subsidiaries are impressive. During 1971 they had twenty-five single-family home projects in various stages of construction in Florida, New Jersey, Minnesota, Arizona and North Carolina. Seventeen apartment projects were under way in Florida, New Jersey and Ohio. Another fourteen apartment projects involving various governmental programs were also in progress. Nine additional single-family projects and nine multifamily developments were in planning stages. Two planned-unit residential communities were scheduled by Greenbriar. And at Pinellas Park, Florida, construction started on U.S. Home's first mobile-home park.

The cross-pollination of ideas between the builder-members of U.S. Home is more than a slogan. It has operated to boost production substantially. For example, as a result of the exchange of expertise, Brown Homes, Rutenberg Homes, and Dee Wood Industries went into apartment construction. Rutenberg also went into single-family projects, a departure from the company's longtime specialization in scattered-lot custom construction. U.S. Home-New Jersey drew on the experiences of Imperial Land in retirement housing to develop viable marketing and sales programs for its major Greenbriar program.

In early 1970 U.S. Home was still heavily concentrated in single-family housing. But then, says Fred Fisher, UH's executive vice president, "We began experiencing an extension of trends that we had recognized a year earlier. And responding to these trends, we shifted our total emphasis away from single-family, conventionally financed housing to a substantial mix of single-family, retirement housing, multifamily housing and government-sponsored programs. By February of 1971, approximately 58% of our units and 32% of our operating revenues were from multifamily sales, versus 48% of our units and 23.8% a year earlier. As for government-sponsored programs, approximately 45% of our units and 32% of our operating revenue were in these programs, versus 40% of units and 23% of operating revenue the previous year. All our subsidiaries together produced about ¼% of all housing built in the U.S. in 1970."

U.S. Home streamlined itself by changing its name to the present one on June 22, 1971, from the older, longer version — U.S. Home & Development. And on July 6 of the same year its shares were listed on the New York Stock Exchange. In mid-1972 it moved its corporate headquarters to New York City from West Orange, New Jersey, though the builder-peers still continued to meet at its Florida base. For the future, Winnerman planned a combination of two strategies: "At present we hope to continue this growth through both internal expansion and further acquisitions. As we continue to acquire capabilities in new industry segments, cross-pollination among divisions will create new internal growth for each division. This, in turn, will diminish emphasis on acquisitions, with greater portion of our annual growth stemming from internal expansion." The company's projected annual rate of internal growth did, in fact, prove to be very conservative. As an example, in 1971 nine-month figures showed that "in-house" growth rose by 51% — from $65 million to $98 million.

HOW DO YOU MANAGE AN ENTREPRENEUR?

The way Winnerman saw it, you didn't have to have any problems managing a growing empire with the right viewpoint. Charles Rutenberg, the president, has always been operationally oriented and plumped for closer control of the sprawling network; but in Winnerman's eyes the company's strength was based on the antithesis of the concept of central decision-making authority. Winnerman felt he was shedding himself of an entire vexing dimension of problems by not having to oversee builders in the field or ruling on their own entrepreneurial judgment. "The best way to handle a builder," he says, "is to let him build. The reason we acquired a company in the first place was because it *had* strong highly developed management capabilities.

"The management functions of the parent company were developed along the lines which provided comprehensive observation — with minimal interference. Our controls and data analysis are accurate enough to pinpoint possible weaknesses and help dissipate them, but under normal conditions operational control and local decision-making are left in the hands of the division.

"We recognize that these are all entrepreneurs, not corporate types. We buy only builders with track records, and then let them continue in the same vein. They continue autonomously, except that they're now in a mutual fund of builders. The builder-peers get together several times a year to trade knowledge and problems. This approach keeps up entrepreneurial incentive; they have a good deal of friendly competition among themselves and a lot of pride about meeting their projections." (Rutenberg calls this "quota attainment by embarrassment: no one wants to report he hasn't met his budget.") "Overall," Winnerman would add reflectively, "management by millionaires is very successful; they *are* all millionaires. It's fun, and if the management is good, you don't change a winner."

END OF THE MERGER PHASE: WINNERMAN LEAVES U.S. HOME

Bob Winnerman's liberal management philosophy and congeneric concept were spectacularly successful. Perhaps even too successful, for in 1972, despite its entirely excellent internal growth record, the company found that many Wall Streeters viewed its growth with some distrust as coming primarily from acquisitions. U.S. Home toned down its merger image severely and put the spotlight on its operations. But with the exuberant growth period over, the creator and architect of the grand strategy now looked out of place. Policy differences between Winnerman and Rutenberg began to crop up more frequently, as the latter drove to emphasize the nuts and bolts of operations as against larger strategies such as new market penetration. "We both agree that if you have good management you leave it alone," said Rutenberg. "But it's my responsibility as the operating officer of the company to look at the specific parts of the operation as well as the whole, which is how a chairman tends to look at it." (Not all of the builder-peers were appreciative of the closer control: the three top officers of U.S. Home of Texas, formerly Norwood Homes, quit early in 1973, alleging a poor fit.) The centralized management policy of Rutenberg vs. the laissez-faire policy of Winnerman came to a head in May 1973, when Winnerman unexpectedly resigned.

It was right about the time of Winnerman's resignation that U.S. Home also encountered its first major problem with an acquired company: 3H Building Corporation, which it had acquired in mid-1972 for 525,000 shares of stock worth $15.5 million. What happened was that a post-acquisition audit of the subsidiary's books turned up problems that looked is if they might turn 3H's anticipated $1.2 million profit contribution to U.S. Home's profit into a $3 to $4 million extraordinary loss. U.S. Home typically runs a close audit of a company's books prior to acquisition, but 3H is a publicly held company and U.S. Home accepted its figures without feeling the necessity for its own audit. The company went to court to attempt to rescind the acquisition and claimed $18 million in damages. As one alternative, it sought to change the acquisition from a pooling to a purchase basis.

Both Winnerman and Rutenberg said that the problems with 3H were not related to his resignation. Winnerman, in fact, observed that "to make a mistake or so in seventeen or eighteen acquisitions is a very small thing."

There were few immediate changes, U.S. Home closed up the New York corporate offices it had opened a year earlier (putting Winnerman's 5,000-square-foot, 67th-story executive suite on the block), and Charlie Rutenberg assumed the offices of both chairman and president. And Bob Winnerman? He pocketed $5 million from the sale of his U.S. Home stock and went off for a six-month jaunt to the Orient and Northern Europe, dreaming of new empires to build on his return. "At this point the architect is no longer needed at U.S. Home," he remarked ebulliently on his departure. "What he wants to do is to go on and create more masterpieces."

17

The Building Blocks of Building Systems

"We decided to throw all our eggs
into one basket."
—Stan Rothenfeld, former BSI
President

There are more ways than one to use the merger route to get into the big time. Would you believe, for example, that putting together two construction companies, a component manufacturer and a masonry contractor can produce a centrally operated, vertically organized organization with clout in the national homebuilding market? Those are the constituent parts of Building Systems, Inc., of Cleveland, a vertically integrated firm with both factory and on-site housing capabilities, which achieved the $83.7 million mark in annual sales by 1972. The company was formed at the end of 1969 from a combination of several old-line organizations in the Cleveland area — Zaremba Construction Company, Thomas G. Snavely Company and Palevsky Industries.

On of BSI's principal activities was planning, development and construction of government "turnkey" housing by taking advantage of Zaremba's experience as a builder of apartments for private investors. The BSI subsidiary building public housing began operating nationwide, often undertaking projects others did not find feasible. The company also built a high volume of apartment projects for private investors. With its capabilities in component housing and its integration of management skills, BSI was one of the few companies in the early Seventies which had put together "total systems capability" and was going to grow rapidly to national prominence.

The times caught up with Building Systems by 1973, however. A crippling combination of management problems, accounting-rules changes, a bearish economy, and rising interest rates plus the great decline of the stock market conspired to knock the company's building blocks askew. In August 1973 the firm disclosed that four of its directors had resigned and that Leonard S. Jaffee, executive vice president, succeeded Stanley Rothenfeld as president and chief executive. The president of the multifamily group, Alan Gressel, also resigned. In September 1973 came the bad news about the firm's financial performance. The company said its consolidated

378

net loss for the year ended May 31 could exceed $25 million. This was to result in a negative net worth of $11 million for the firm. It was quite a swamping after the year-earlier performance of $1.4 million in earnings on $83.7 million in sales.

Announcing emergency measures, Building Systems, at the time it released its loss projections, began meetings with creditors to restructure its debt. Earlier, it had refinanced $17 million in debt with a group of banks led by Union Commerce Bank of Cleveland. But at the same time another creditor, Ziegler Co. of Milwaukee, launched foreclosure proceedings against two of BSI's building subsidiaries. While he didn't disclose the disputed loan volume, R. D. Ziegler said that it represented about 9% of Ziegler Financing Corporation's outstanding loans, involving BSI public housing projects in Toledo and Rochester and Cleveland.

Late in 1973 it was not clear how Building Systems would fare in the future.* But its travails were ample testimony to the dangers of putting all the eggs into one basket. It seems that the component parts of BSI were stronger than the whole.

OLD ACQUAINTANCES POOL THEIR EFFORTS

How did the diverse elements of BSI come together? The Zaremba company dates back about three generations in Cleveland; in the five years preceding the formation of the new company it built over $90 million of housing. Palevsky was a major Midwest firm distributing building products over the region and producing components. Snavely was was one of the biggest masonry contractors in Ohio. With the key operations centered in Cleveland, the three firms dominated much of the area's building. As they were the biggest, they were often one another's customers; it seemed only logical that as time went on they would get together to create a super-sized building organization. Stanley Rothenfeld headed Palevsky Industries prior to the merger. He described how the genesis of BSI came about through the principals' extended contracts with one another over the years:

"Zaremba had been a big builder here for many years. Over those years we (as Palevsky Industries) supplied them with most of their building materials and Snavely, who has also been in the area for a long time, completed most of Zaremba's masonry work. Snavely and Zaremba worked very closely and eventually began to joint-venture some projects and more or less tied up together about four years ago. On many of the projects, Palevsky also invested with the other two. Through this, we all became closely associated both from a business and a social standpoint.

"Around the time that money began to get tight, all three of us began

* It has since begun bankruptcy proceedings.

investigating various government programs that were becoming available," Rothenfeld went on. "We realized then that turnkey housing might offer us a great opportunity. We formed a joint company called Housing Development Company, which specializes in turnkey projects. This company was the forerunner of BSI where we tied in completely together. In 1969 it occurred to us that because we all had plans to go public it might be worthwhile to form one company and all go public together. We sat down and tried to analyze exactly what direction the building industry would take in the Seventies. We decided that because of all the problems associated with shelter production today, the future would be industrialization."

Based on that decision, the BSI structure integrated the production of factory-built housing with land development, construction and professional property management, all under a single roof. It became a vertically integrated housing organization. Unfortunately, Rothenfeld's periscoping of the 1970s did not foresee the economic upheavals that would shatter this concept.

THE COMPONENTS OF BSI

Unlike U.S. Home, which operates semi-autonomous decentralized organizations, BSI's group consolidated operations fully. It built everything from single-family homes to townhouses, garden apartments and high-rise buildings. Although the company didn't have a mortgage banking firm, its vertical integration was nearly complete. It produced most of the components needed for construction, either concrete or wood. It designed, developed and built the structures and then managed them on behalf of investors when the structures are completed. The integrated operations were handled through five subsidiaries, each of which functioned as a semi-autonomous profit center. They are as follows:

Palevsky Industries, Inc., manufactures such factory-produced housing components as exterior wall sections, interior partition walls, roof trusses, stairs, complete floor deck systems, interior and exterior pre-hung door units, millwork and plastic laminated products. It also distributes a wide range of building products to contractors in eight states, as well as selling hardware, kitchen appliances, cabinets, windows and doors through three distribution and retail centers. In 1971 the subsidiary invested in an addition to its housing manufacturing plant, more than doubling production.

Building Systems Housing Corporation planned, developed and built projects for private investors and was also the company's turnkey public housing developer of low- and moderate-income projects.

This subsidiary was created from the consolidation of two other organizations at the start of 1971: Zaremba Construction and Housing Development Corp.

The Thomas G. Snavely Company provided contracting services for other developers as well as doing the masonry walls of BSI projects. This subsidiary pioneered the construction of masonry, wall-bearing buildings and was one of the first to introduce automated materials handling equipment to speed up production at the site. It also developed precast and cast-on-site concrete systems used in project development.

Concrete Building Systems Company is a contracting subsidiary which uses the Van de Heuvel Concrete System, one of two used by BSI for high-rise structures. BSI was the exclusive licensee in the U.S. for this system, successfully pioneered in the Netherlands, Sweden and Belgium. It cuts building costs by a third and enables a building to be completed in a quarter less time, thus also saving on construction loan interest.

The John David Management Company is BSI's property management and marketing arm. The subsidiary handles leasing, provides tenant services, supervises maintenance, collects rents and provides property owners with income and expense records. The man whom the company is named after, John David, was a pioneer in computerized resident billing. In 1971 this subsidiary increased its management rolls to 10,000 units.

MINORITIES INVOLVED

One interesting aspect of the company's operation was its strong program of involvement with minorities, principally Negroes. Alan E. Gressel, former vice president of BSI's building subsidiary, observes: "BSI is committed to equal opportunity, and our program of minority involvement became a sales asset in our activity with sponsors and housing authorities. Our positive approach to minority opportunity has made us welcome in model cities areas and the ghettos of large cities.

"During field erection many BSI subcontracts go to minority contractors, returning profits as well as wages to the black community. In areas where minority contractors in the critical trades are not strong enough to bid our large jobs, we encourage — and if need be arrange — joint ventures in those trades. In these joint projects we provide bonding, packaging, and our systems. The minority contractor provides all construction management and we split the profit over his fee for supervision. Such joint ventures allow the minority contractor to learn the techniques of a large contractor and to familiarize himself with our systems so that he may bid the next job with knowledge, experience and confidence not otherwise available."

Approximately two-thirds of the company's work in early 1971 was in the Federal Turnkey Housing Program because the forerunner of BSI, Housing Development Company, started in the program early. But BSI's aim was to reduce Turnkey activities to about half the company's work, while increasing involvement in other government-assisted programs to 25% with conventional development work accounting for the balance. "We want to create this type of situation," BSI's President Rothenfeld, said at the time, "so that if money again becomes tight, we can move back into Turnkey heavily. But if money dries up here, we can move heavily back into conventional."

18

Everybody Prays for Eli Broad

So live as on a mountain.

—Marcus Aurelius

In the heyday of the homebuilding industry's expansion, Kaufman & Broad has created an enviable reputation for itself as a permanently rising constellation in the industry's firmament. K&B achieved the longest record of unbroken growth, the most consistent history of clockwork profit increases, the best record of anticipating the industry's trends. It is certainly still one of the best managed building companies in the United States, and it did the best job of communicating both its own corporate story and the realities of homebuilding to the nation's financial community. In the ruthless glare of public ownership the company withstood endlessly detailed examination exceptionally well. Thus to Wall Street, Kaufman & Broad came to stand for the homebuilding industry itself.

One result of this reputation is that any company entering the public market inevitably found itself compared with and judged against the standards that financial analysts derived from their familiarity with K&B. Another is that Eli Broad, now K&B's chairman, became in effect the guardian of the homebuilding industry's reputation with the investment people, since his company was (and is) regarded as a prime indicator for the potentials of that industry. So far as the public market is concerned, it wasn't inaccurate to say that as Kaufman & Broad went so went the housing industry. Admirers of the firm often said that if the company were ever to report a loss, the reverberations from the massive loss of confidence among the investment analysts would hit every publicly listed building company hard. Conversely, so long as K&B could keep on turning in those 25% annual increases, it created a glowing aura for homebuilding from which other companies profited. That's why at least one publicly listed builder only half-jokingly, confessed that every night he got down on his knees and prayed for Eli Broad. That's why everybody in the industry still prays for Eli Broad.

Even Eli's record was not entirely impeccable, of course, There was a period, during a severe tight-money crunch that hit the homebuilding indus-

383

try in 1964 and 1965, when K&B's profits did fall off from their usual climb. Kaufman & Broad was a considerably smaller company then; its sales in 1964 were just over the $30 million mark and they fell to $27.2 million in 1965. But in 1966 Eli really got it together and announced his goal of 25% compounded annual growth, and the company, easily overcoming the tight-money period of the late Sixties, boomed along without a hitch all the way into 1974. Scanning the company's overall history, sales rose from $1.7 million in 1957 to $284 million in 1972. Earnings kept pace, rising to $19.5 million in 1972.*

With the coming of 1973, however, Eli could use those prayers. Long the darling of Wall Street's institutional investors, even Kaufman & Broad with its excellent performance record could not withstand the panic atmos-phere engendered by Watergate, the financial scandal of Equity Funding, suspicions concerning accounting practices, and the bear market. With homebuilding industry stocks nosediving across the board, Kaufman & Broad's stock fell sharply — though it still commanded a relatively far better price/earnings ratio. In K&B's case, at any rate, the sell-off was attributable purely to emotional factors, as the firm had not shown any slump in performance and was still projecting a solid growth rate for the year despite higher interest rates and more inflation. But jittery institu-tional investors felt differently, and the realities of K&B's continued per-formance somehow seemed purely irrelevant. There was no love lost for Wall Street's darling as it was unceremoniously dumped.

K&B suffered the harrowing experience of sharp sell-offs on several occasions in 1973. On April 30 the company had complained to the SEC about a raid that had knocked its stock off the year's high of $45⅞. Some days later, it was hit again as a few hedge funds and other short sellers blitzed the shares all the way down to $14½, though the stock recovered to about $20 shortly afterward. In the fall, just as the fuel scare began to be felt, K&B's stock was hit once more. The final jolt came in November when the firm announced its 1973 sales and earnings and 1974 projections.

To be sure, the growth in 1973 earnings was again dramatic, but there was an undercurrent of unease because K&B also revealed that the earnings gain was achieved despite a $1.5 to $1.6 million after-tax loss in its big mobile home division. Eli announced immediate plans to sell, restructure, or liquidate this unit. With company figures restated for 1972 and 1973

---

* The 1972 sales figures do not include $44 million in unconsolidated revenues from Sun Life Insurance Company, the wholly owned subsidiary acquired at the end of 1971. But $5.25 million of the earnings figure is attributable to Sun Life. Thus, the net income from the company's housing divisions alone came to $14.25 million, a 44% increase over 1971. Profits rose faster than sales because K&B concentrated on higher profit areas such as the East Coast and Europe, and stopped building subsidy housing, as well as getting a lower tax rate because of Sun Life. It is this sort of performance that makes Eli Broad and K&B indisputable industry leaders.

to exclude the mobile home division, sales rose to about $275 million from $232 million in the previous year, a gain of about 20%. Excluding the mobile home unit, fully diluted earnings rose to an estimated $1.45–1.50 per share from $1.09 per share achieved in 1972. In absolute terms this performance still amounted to a sharp gain over K&B's 1972 record, when the fully diluted per share net, including mobile home operations, stood at $1.18. "Net income per share rose faster than sales in 1973," said Eli, "because our growth came from our highest margin areas."

More significant and somehow poignant, however, was Eli Broad's effectual abdication from his long-held standard of 25% annual sales and earnings growth for 1974 and beyond. "We will have a good year and an increase, but not of the 20% variety," he conceded. "The way things look now, we will have increases in every quarter, but we will not have as dramatic an increase in 1974 as in 1973." Noting that Wall Street analysts forecast earnings for the company of $1.60 to $1.80 per share in 1974, Eli elaborated: "At this point we feel a little more comfortable at the lower end of that spectrum." Such a projection left Kaufman & Broad still one of the strongest homebuilding firms in the business, but it also marked the end of an era. For Eli, as for the entire industry, the boom days were over and the days of the long hard grind in a harsher economic environment had come.

ELI'S EXPANDING DOMAIN

During the 1960s and early 1970s, Eli's company went from a small local home builder to a multimarket broadly based housing producer. At the end of 1971, the firm had sixty major single-family and apartment developments underway in the metropolitan areas of Los Angeles-San Diego, San Francisco-San Jose, Chicago, Detroit, New Jersey. It qualified for the title of "international housing company" by virtue of projects in Toronto, and its successful homebuilding ventures in Paris, where Eli set up shop in 1968. K&B's announcement during 1971 of entry into the homebuilding markets of Munich and Frankfurt in West Germany (along with a similar move by Levitt & Sons) also foreshadowed the advent of the period when, like major American industry, the homebuilding industry had to begin thinking of expanding internationally into less developed markets in order to shore up its sales curves as the domestic potentials were tapped out.

Through its now-abandoned mobile-home subsidiary, Kaufman & Broad Home Systems, K&B had emerged as one of the nation's major producers of mobile homes, The number of plants producing mobiles rose to eight during 1971 with the opening of factories in Durham, North Carolina, Lancaster, Pennsylvania, and Sebring, Florida. With other plants operating

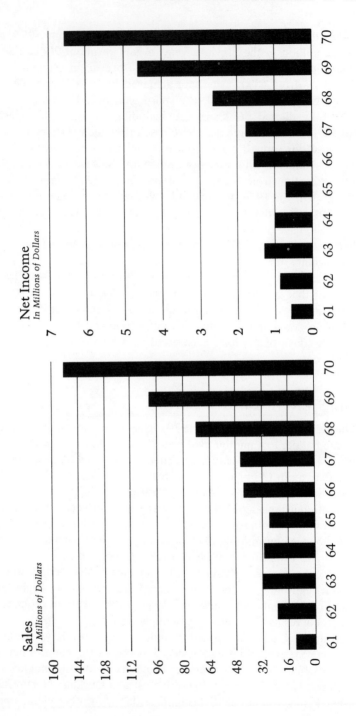

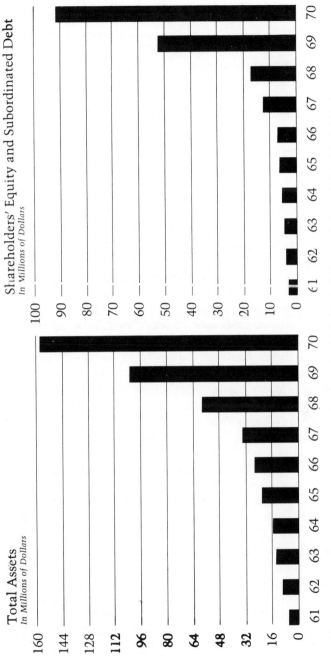

Figure 18.1. Ten-Year Record: Kaufman and Broad, Inc. and Consolidated Subsidiaries.

in Chino and Sacramento, California, Phoenix, Arizona, Boise, Idaho and Fort Worth, Texas, K&B covered the territorial map pretty broadly. The eight plants reached $40 million in sales on 10,500 units in 1971, more than twice 1970 production. While the company did not go into modular production per se, it became heavily committed to the use of prefabricated components and parts — such as wall panels, roof trusses, doors, kitchen cabinets, windows and other items interchangeable from house to house — in its on-site construction.

Eli viewed his company's off-site manufacturing of such components as the "logical link between total on-site production and the complete factory-built house." The company still operates a 100,000 square-foot prefabrication plant in Livermore, California, which produces components for its largest division, the San Francisco-Jose group. It did get its foot into modulars as a member of a team headed by TRW Systems which was one of the Operation Breakthrough finalists, though Eli was long known to feel that the country isn't ready for them. The company's nationwide in-plant manufacturing capacity through its mobile-home subsidiary was to put it much farther along the road to becoming a major industrialized producer, but as of 1974 these plans were obviously changed.

Widely recognized for many industry "firsts" (some of which are mentioned in this chapter), Eli Broad achieved another major "first" in April 1973 by announcing Kaufman & Broad's move into the odd-lot building market. The company formed a new subsidiary, Kaufman & Broad Custom Homes, to sell precut homes directly from the factory to consumer. The new subsidiary, headed by Max Zamansky, formerly president of the Homes Group Division of Evans Products, operates out of Minneapolis. It will tap a market that, as Eli says, has a greater potential for long-term growth "than all our current U.S. on-site housing operations." Broad has often pointed to the fact that no one housing company has gained even 1% of the market by building on-site because more than 70% of American housing is produced in areas that are too small for major building companies to enter. K&B had been serving a portion of this market with its mobile-home operation. In November 1972 it almost made gigantic merger news because of a proposed merger with housing titan National Homes; that merger didn't go through, but the motive for it was also a desire to get at the custom market.

Although in the new ballgame of 1974, Kaufman & Broad's projected slower growth rate was attributable primarily to a severely unsettled economy, the bête noire of the homebuilding industry's accounting principles also contributed to its problems. Not that K&B has not always been meticulous in its adherence to the rules. But the accounting rules themselves have permitted so many variations on reporting of sales, assets, and profits that in the early 1970s they came under severe attack. Critics like

Abraham J. Briloff, writing stinging articles in *Barron's* singled out industry leaders such as K&B to illustrate — not always fairly — alleged accounting rules inconsistencies and distortions. While K&B cannot be blamed for applying the rules as they've been laid down, the probable continued revision of such rules by the accounting fraternity and the SEC will shift reporting in a more conservative direction. This will result in more conservatively stated sales and profits in the long term.

Conservatively stated sales and profits are, of course, lower sales and profits. That's another reason why Wall Street, anticipating this trend, began unloading housing stocks well before the general plunge of the stock market in the fall of 1973. The May 1973 bear raid on Kaufman & Broad's stock, for example, followed the appearance in *Barron's* of a highly critical article about the company's accounting practices by Briloff. Briloff blasted K&B and its auditors, Haskins & Sells, on several points. He questioned the company's assertion that 95% of its sales are collected in cash. He suggested that K&B had tried to play down the importance of the sale of remnant land left over from project developments. And he sniped the validity of the accounting followed in K&B's acquisition of Sun Life Insurance Co. — especially the calculation and disclosure of the amount of intangible "goodwill" acquired in the transaction and which, under accounting rules, must be written off against income over a period of years.

K&B's defense, presented at mass meetings with analysts in New York and Boston, seemed to satisfy Wall Street at the time. Several brokerage firms issued special reports supporting Kaufman & Broad and criticizing the Briloff piece. One of Briloff's main points, for example, was that in a 1971 prospectus K&B stated it would acquire $8.8 million in Sun Life "goodwill," while in the 1972 annual report it stated the figure at only $1.6 million. Briloff suggested that K&B had hidden assets that were not being amortized against earnings, in violation of accounting rules. Writing in response, Harvard professor David F. Hawkins said in an accounting bulletin published by Drexel Burnham & Co. that the original goodwill projection was only an estimate and was changed after K&B revalued the Sun Life assets, all in accordance with accounting rules.

This battle was more symptomatic of the industry's underlying problems in agreeing on a uniform set of accounting principles than of problems with K&B's accounting. But although K&B appeared to win that particular go-round, it wound up eating its words in another way. At their defensive meetings with analysts, K&B's officials gave assurances that the accounting controversy would not affect corporate goals to increase per-share earnings at the rate of 20% a year for the next five years. But by early 1974, with a groaning economy and further accounting rules changes in prospect, even that growth goal fell. It remained a question how Eli Broad and his president, Eugene S. Rosenfeld, would respond to the rapidly changing conditions. Even in adversity, their company remains the industry's leader. As it goes, so will go the entire homebuilding sector.

FROM CPA TO INDUSTRY "PROFESSIONALIZER"

Eli Broad's steady climb to the position of industry leader began shortly after he completed college. Graduating with a business degree from Michigan State University in 1954, he became, two years later, at the age of twenty-two, the youngest CPA in Michigan. On receiving his certificate he started his own practice in office space provided by Donald Kaufman, a Detroit homebuilder. That gave Eli his first exposure to homebuilding. In January 1957, after analyzing the opportunities with a characteristic thoroughness, Eli at the age of twenty-three, pooled his resources with Kaufman and established Kaufman & Broad with capital of $25,000. Two months later they opened their first model homes. Sales the first weekend totaled $250,000, giving the young entrepreneurs a profit of $25,000 and launching fifteen years of meteoric growth for the company. The company was one of the first housing producers to go public, as it did in November, 1961. And it was the first major housing company to get a listing on the New York Stock Exchange — in May, 1969.

Concurrently with the emergence of Kaufman & Broad as a major national housing company, the housing industry itself embarked on the most expansive and dynamic growth period in its history, undergoing radical changes that will revolutionize its character by the end of the decade. This book has remarked on the swift changes in the technology and the financial institutions of housing with the advent of prefabrication and the entry of the federal government into a dominant role in the mortgage market. The third major change was, of course, in the composition of the housing industry itself. We saw the emergence of large, better-managed and well-capitalized firms at the opposite end of the spectrum from the common image of the homebuilder as an undercapitalized, inefficient one-man operator. Despite setbacks experienced by many of them, on the whole these companies are as sophisticated in financing, management and operations as those in any other industry.

Kaufman & Broad has been one of the companies that has played a major role in advancing the emerging professional image of the housing industry. Foremost in contributing to this has been the company's initial viewpoint of approaching housing as a producer or manufacturer, and basing its operating policies on that premise. Eli Broad also pioneered the policy of decentralizing management in order to give the organization maximum flexibility. The approach, recognizing the intensely local nature of the housing business, delegates maximum responsibility to entrepreneurial divisional managers. K&B also pioneered the introduction of complex cost controls and management information systems in 1966, permitting decentralized management to function efficiently.

One might list several other firsts achieved by Kaufman & Broad. Awfully sharp in marketing, the company established the first five-year warranty on its homes in 1967. It was the first major firm, noting the inflation of housing costs, to introduce townhouses to the mass housing market. It was one of the early participants in almost every government housing program — including the development of the first project under Sec. 221(d)3 in Detroit in 1962 — and was the first on the West Coast to receive funds for Sec. 235 subsidization program. Approximately 15% of K&B's sales have been financed under the Sec. 235 or Sec. 236 interest-supplement programs. And Eli broke at least one other barrier. K&B was the first housing producer to sell its own prime-rated commercial paper as of 1969, thus avoiding the high-interest, short-term construction loans then used by most builders. Even before 1969, Eli was a genius at developing unsecured lines of credit and sources of long-term debt. Given this sort of originality, he will be watched closely for his responses to the revenue and marketing decisions of the mid-1970s.

AN UNDERSTANDING OF MEN AND MONEY

It has been my pleasure to know Eli Broad, as well as the company's president, Eugene S. Rosenfeld, for a good many years now. And in all the time I've watched them, I have come to the conclusion that Eli and his key men — but particularly Eli — have the rare genius that would put them at the top of *any* industry. Eli himself is an unassertive but exceptionally clear-minded man who has never assumed he knows all the answers but who has always striven for excellence and has always known exactly what he wanted to achieve. His particular strength in corporate planning is the ability to take the long view and to guide the corporation toward a very clearly perceived goal, anticipating major obstacles. But the key to this is that Eli thinks in terms of *organizations*. The great strength and greatest weakness of many exceptional homebuilders is that they are essentially a one-man show. Eli is that relative rarity, an entrepreneur who is also a first-class professional *manager*. And his exceptional managerial abilities are founded, as it happens, on a base of positive genius in corporate finance and on a profound understanding of how to attract, motivate and keep an equally first-class entrepreneurial management team.

SECURING A FINANCIAL BASE. Eli has well understood, for example, that housing's future belongs to those companies who can secure for themselves a strong base of both equity and mortgage capital. On-site housing is a capital-intensive business and relatively few homebuilders have managed to develop resources they would regard as adequate. Kaufman & Broad had gone a long way from 1965, when it had a capitalization on only $6 million and relatively limited access to credit. By the end of 1970 its capitalization was $91 million; it had credit lines with eleven of the nation's biggest banks; it could issue its own commercial paper at prime or near-prime rates; and it had warrants outstanding which will generate an additional $16 million of equity capital when they are exercised in 1974. But to support K&B's continued growth, Eli anticipated that the company would have to get more extensively involved in the growing field of housing-related financial and mortgage services.

These thoughts culminated in 1971 with the establishment of a Financial Services Group at Kaufman & Broad, bringing under a single umbrella several newly organized financial activities. Said Eli: "We strongly believe that financial services related to housing is a logical area in which to expand our activities. As a result of our corporate planning efforts in the past year, we delineated strong competitive advantages available to us from housing-related financial services in three to five years, as well as deriving a continuous stream of income from our homebuyers." He also pointed out that the ability to offer financing to others should be a significant competitive advantage for K&B's mobile-home subsidiary as a viable distribution system evolves for factory-made housing. "By supplying financing as well as a good product," he said, "Home Systems [the subsidiary] will be able to compete effectively for the business of small builders who do not have access to equity markets or other sources of stable funds."

The first step in the establishment of K&B's Financial Services Group came in March of 1971 when the company's subsidiary, International Mortgage Company, expanded its activities to include mortgage servicing and sale of GNMA-guaranteed certificates. The mortgage company's 1972 volume in arranging financing for K&B customers hit $150 million.

The second step was the formation of Kaufman & Broad Asset Management, Inc., a wholly owned subsidiary, to buy, sell and manage tax-sheltered housing for investors.The cutback of subsidized housing and the probable advent of legislation limiting the tax shelter feature of income property was later to crimp this program. But, as Eli outlined at the time of its promotion, the new subsidiary was going to serve two major functions. First, it acquired and managed federally subsidized housing developments, primarily Sec. 236 projects, for American Housing Partners, a publicly offered limited partnership for tax-motivated investors. The 1968 tax law made subsidized housing one of the most attractive tax-shelter areas, but there had been no simple method for broad public participation. American Housing Partners, sold through E. F. Hutton & Co. in mid-August of 1971, became the first public offering to tap broad public money. As its second major activity, K&B's Asset Management sold K&B's conventional multifamily housing developments to institutional and other investors also looking for tax shelter, and provided management when required. Among the investors were a number of the larger banks in the country, with most of whom K&B already had credit or investor relationships.

But the third major element in K&B's financial group is the one that shook up the industry the most at the time of its occurrence. On July 6, 1971, K&B reached agreement in principle to acquire Sun Life Insurance Company of America for approximately $67.6 million in stock, or roughly 10 times its earnings. The agreement called for each holder of 10 Sun Life shares to receive K&B common stock with an aggregate market value of $240 and one share of 5%, $60 K&B convertible preferred. Sun Life had 2,254,560 shares outstanding, with the majority owned by the company's management and members of their families. K&B had previously gone outside its own field to acquire Nation-Wide Cablevision, a subsidiary serving about 45,000 subscribers to community antenna television. But the Sun Life acquisition by the homebuilding firm was the first instance in the building industry where a major financial-services firm was not the acquirer but the acquired.

Based in Baltimore, Sun Life was founded in 1890. It is qualified to conduct business in thirty-eight states, including every area in which K&B has housing operations. At the end of 1970, Sun Life had assets of $211 million and over $1.5 billion of life insurance in force. On a statutory basis, the company earned $2.96 million before taxes and $2.86 million after taxes in 1970, or $1.27 a share compared with $0.85 in 1969. On an adjusted basis, Sun Life earned $1.83 a share in 1970 vs. $1.63 in 1969. By 1973, Sun Life was contributing about 22% of K&B's pretax operating revenue.

The significance of the acquisition is that it gave K&B control over a large pool of long-term investment funds available from life insurance cash flows. The insurer's funds were to enable K&B to provide a total financial package to other builder-customers three to five years hence, when distribution of factory-made housing would be more a reality. The tie-in with the insurer was to prove to be an extremely important one for Kaufman & Broad in ways other than already stated. There is the sale of insurance to K&B's large annual volume of homebuyers (there were 15,000 of them in 1971). Young homebuyers present a large captive market whereby the K&B subsidiary can boost its own and thus the parent corporation's profits. But Sun Life has also had a substantial investment in mortgage loans over the years, and it might be a significant source for the placement of mortgages taken out by buyers of conventional K&B homes.

The insurer with an average growth record, has also had considerable experience in direct development and derived substantial investment income from it. Sun Development Corporation, a subsidiary, had more than 1,000 apartment units in development in the Washington-Baltimore area in 1971. If anybody can, Kaufman & Broad can put Sun Life's investment capital to work even more profitably. Eli suggested as much in saying, "It is our intention to give energetic support to Sun Life's management in its efforts to improve earnings by the development of new product and marketing strategies to increase investment income, especially from housing-related areas."

Reviewing Eli's financial activities, one can thus say that in the first phase of Kaufman & Broad's growth he concentrated on the development of equity capital and credit lines to enable his firm to produce housing. In the second phase, he expanded to create a strong base of financial services in order to broaden and assure the company of a market for all the produce it can deliver. Financial services is a profitable area in itself, but the real reason for getting involved in mortgage servicing, sale of GNMA-guaranteed certificates, sale and management of apartments, and insurance and investment activities was that thereby Eli took under direct corporate control the company's future. By making sure of adequate financial sources for his buyers, and by broadening and finding new markets for his company's product, he laid groundwork for future growth that, even after the bad experience of late 1973, should serve him well.

A MANAGEMENT TEAM OF ENTREPRENEURS. Financial strength aside, the most important factor in K&B's growth has been its policy of operating through decentralized management. Each of the company's housing divisions operates as a semi-autonomous profit center, with so much independence that it is practically a company within a company. There's a limit to how much growth centralized control can efficiently support, and by going the decentralized route Eli can expect the company to keep on growing for many a year, assuming economic conditions permit it. The ability to delegate decision-making power, and to select the right men for major responsibilities, has been a basic characteristic of his success.

K&B's consistently successful performance over the years has, in turn, attracted entrepreneurs of high caliber to join its ranks as division presidents or middle-level managers. Often, they have been independent homebuilders themselves who have preferred to run on a shorter leash in the employ of a big corporate builder than to savor the pangs of undercapitalized independence. Through handsome incentive compensation plans and stock options these executives have a meaningful proprietary interest in the company. Several who joined in the late Sixties are now millionaires; one who got an option for 1,000 shares on coming aboard in 1966 found it worth $500,000 by mid-1971. Not everyone survives the intensely competitive pressure-cooker environment of the public building firm, for above all the emphasis is on performance. But this competitiveness has operated to attract top-caliber people; those who leave to join other firms always find it an asset to have been "K&B men."

Typical of K&B's managers is Jim Hintz, who presides over the Los Angeles Division and undertook eight major community projects in 1971. A successful builder of moderate size for many years, he signed up with K&B two years ago and has performed outstandingly. Another example was that of Robert Charlton, one of the best-known builders on Staten Island, New York, who joined Kaufman & Broad in the fall of 1971 as project manager for K&B's new home development activities on the island. Another is Bill Meeker, twenty-eight, who in 1971 left a vice presidency with his father's Southern California building firm to become general manager of K&B's newly opened New York operation on Long Island. K&B, which embarked on a plan of opening one new division each year, opens them in markets that it believes will support sales of at least $20 million annually. Its first Long Island project is a $6.5 million, 300-unit condominium project in the $20,000-$23,000 range in Islip, Suffolk County. Each division is supported by a skilled corporate staff and operated within policy guidelines and financial controls established and monitored by corporate management.

In passing, it is interesting to compare K&B's approach with that of U.S. Home. Although the two companies begin at opposite poles, one growing primarily internally and the other placing a strong emphasis on acquisitions, both end up with a very similar operating format; that of semi-autonomous divisions (subsidiaries) operating within a framework of guidelines and controls. K&B, however, has "grown its own" management, while U.S. Home has been buying it lock, stock and barrel with a successful, ongoing business operated by the acquired entrepreneur.

ELI BROAD LOOKS AT MERGERS

As mentioned, Kaufman & Broad's past growth was primarily internal. But over the years Eli has engineered a series of strategic acquisitions to aid the company in entering a new market more efficiently or to acquire trade names, product lines or plant facilities. In most, but not all, instances the company has supplied the management team to operate the business after acquiring it. Thus, for example, K&B first moved into mobile homes in October 1969 by acquiring Biltmore Homes. Biltmore's sales were about $18 million in 1969, from three plants, and it became the nucleus of K&B's subsequently developed industrialized housing group. As another example, K&B in February of 1970 bought 80% of Victoria Wood Development (1969 revenues: $17.5 million), including 44% from financially beleaguered Revenue Properties. Victoria Wood, which became the Toronto

Division, produces single-family, apartment and high-rise housing, and had substantial surplus land which K&B profitably sold off. The company also owns 80% of Leisure Industries, developer of a large recreational community in Northern California.

(K&B also owned a 50% interest in Mid-City Developers, Inc., a Washington-based firm specializing in development of government-assisted housing. The company sold its interest in mid-1971 for approximately $2.15 million of the stock of DCA Development Corporation, a Boston-based organization involved in government housing. But in October 1971, K&B sued to cancel its sale of Mid-City, charging that DCA had made material misrepresentations about results of its operations and had not performed all its obligations under the agreement. Kaufman & Broad is also involved in joint ventures. One notable one was its joint-venture deal with the outstanding apartment building organization of Ring Brothers to build an 800-unit, $12 million complex outside of Chicago.)

So far as merging Kaufman & Broad itself into a large industrial giant, Eli Broad prior to 1973 had always ruled that out, rejecting the route of Big No. 1, Levitt & Sons. As he said: "Through the years, Kaufman & Broad has been approached by the largest American industrial and financial firms seeking a merger, but our directors and management have made the decision to remain an independent public company. We feel that the disadvantages of being a part of a large corporation which does not understand the entrepreneurial and special nature of our business far outweigh the headaches of being an independent public company, especially since we have undergone a ten-year learning curve." However, with all options wide open as of 1974, who knows what partner K&B might link up with in the future to enhance its survival?

Perhaps looking over his shoulder as well as into the future, Eli has not, however, rejected the idea of acquiring smaller builders intact with their operations. As he points out, among K&B's acquisitions, "we have successfully acquired two homebuilders to supplement our internal growth. In one, we bought inventories and a good name but in the other (Kay Homes in the San Francisco area) we acquired a management group which has really thrived in our corporate environment."

Thus, in December of 1971, Eli let it be known that K&B might be considering acquiring smaller companies, though it is not primarily acquisition-oriented: "For the housing-company entrepreneur who doesn't want to get crunched in a corporate mold or who shuns the responsibility and risks of his own public company, there is a third alternative: join an established large public housing company. If you become part of such a company, with a proven track record, you can enjoy all the advantages of a public company, which it has taken many years to achieve, without the responsibilities and risks. At the same time, you will be associated with a management that understands you and knows how to provide an environment in which the housing entrepreneur can thrive. There are several large public housing companies who are interested in acquiring proven companies with good management."

But you can be sure that any deal that Eli makes is not going to be one of those exorbitantly high-multiple giveaways that characterized the mergers of 1970–1971. "We are not foolhardy enough to reach to the blue-sky limits that other industrial companies did in paying for housing producers," he says. "We are looking for value and are willing to pay a fair price for net worth, earnings and a good management team. Over the longer term, we think this arrangement could be more satisfactory to the housing entrepreneur than any other."

Applicants who might feel that Kaufman & Broad has gotten too big to sustain further rapid growth are advised to inspect Eli Broad's and Gene Rosenfeld's statement at the end of 1970: "At $152 million in sales, there's unlimited growing room for us in our $30 billion, soon to be $60 billion, a year industry. If sales reached $1 billion annually we still would not have a significant share of the industry when compared with the market shares held by leading companies in other major industries. As exciting and successful as our past has been, it is really prologue." If the K&B boys can see their way clear through the complications of the national emergency, they can still make the sky the limit.

19

George Scharffenberger Kept on Buying

> He who perceives clearly may find much opportunity in a domain that others, having been tried and found wanting, declare to be inhospitable in order to justify their failure.
>
> —Lucius Cimber Voorhies

The year 1971 was not one to engender confidence in the stability of major diversified corporations to successfully operate entrepreneurial housing subsidiaries. The travails of Boise Cascade and American-Standard, to name two, set off a widening circle of opinion that conglomerate mergers for housing were passé. And yet, just when the negative publicity concerning such combinations was thickest in the fall of that year, a major NYSE-listed-company — a highly sophisticated conglomerate, at that — announced that it had bought a major homebuilding firm to expand its real estate holdings. Furthermore, the acquiring company's president said that his organization has every intention of becoming a giant in the shelter industry that some corporations were so assiduously trying to get out of.

MOVING AGAINST THE CORPORATE SWIM?

The speaker was George Scharffenberger, the urbane, razor-sharp president of City Investing Company. City in September of 1971 acquired Wood Brothers Homes, a Denver homebuilder with estimated sales of $39.4 million and earnings of $2.74 million in that year. Wood is a company Scharffenberger viewed with cheerful certainty as "the ideal candidate for national, if not international, growth." Considering Wood's strong performance — it had tripled sales and quadrupled earnings in one year — City's president had reason to be cheerful. Wood Brothers in 1970 earned $651,000 on sales of $13.8 million. The builder rapidly began expanding operations beyond Denver and Phoenix to Tucson, Dallas, Oklahoma City, Houston and Albuquerque in 1971. Although both City Investing and the Wood Bros. sub-

398

sidiary were buffeted by general economic stresses occurring two years later, the conservative acquisition formula put them in better shape to weather the storm than many other merger partners.

The homebuilding acquisition was not City's first move into real estate: it was already a shelter giant by some definitions. The company owned 53.6% of Guerdon Industries, one of the largest manufacturers of mobile and modular homes; 49% of General Development, the Florida land developer and builder; and land-sales operations and recreational developments in California and New Mexico. But, curiously, City had not moved into entrepreneurial homebuilding itself (General Development is primarily a land developer, selling lots in large planned developments) until its Wood acquisition — rather late in the acquisition game, but indicating that there was plenty of juice left in the business. The timing of City acquisition, going against the popular grain of corporate movement out of entrepreneurial development, may have been disconcerting to some corporate plungers because it carried the suggestion that plain mismanagement and not intrinsic incompatibility was the key to other merger breakups — breakups that City could well avoid by handling its affairs properly.

Scharffenberger was always unique, or nearly so, not only because he set his own course and went against the grain but also because he has never been a homebuilder himself along the route to the creation of a housing empire. He is similar to Cerro's C. Gordon Murphy, a financial wizard whose strength also lies in the selection and the proper management of men and organizations. That is a rather portable talent, encompassing but not limited to the housing industry. The comparison with Murphy is, in fact, appropriate. For, like Murphy, George Scharffenberger also came from Litton when City Investing, then a staid, sixty-two-year-old company, hired him away to become its president in 1966.

Scharffenberger mapped out a plan to diversify by acquiring companies with revenues of at least $20 million a year and a predictable annual growth rate of at least 15%. This program took City into three majors areas: financial services, manufacturing, and housing and land development. Between 1966 and 1971 City acquired Home Insurance, Southern California Savings & Loan Association and Westamerica Securities in the financial services field; Rheem Manufacturing, Hayes International, Wells Marine, American Electric and World Color Press in manufacturing; and Guerdon, General Development and Wood Brothers in housing and land.

As a result of these acquisitions, City's revenues, including unconsolidated subsidiaries, rose from $167.5 million in the year ended April 30, 1967, to $1.4 billion in fiscal 1970. Income climbed from $4.6 million to $44.8 million. City then went on a calendar year, earning $47.7 million on revenues of $1.5 billion for 1970. Total net sales and revenues, including consolidated and unconsolidated companies, were $1.64 billion in 1971. Net income rose to $57.3 million. Housing and land development, which accounted for 0.9% ($1.4 million) of the company's sales and a pretax operating deficit of $493,000 in fiscal 1967, contributed 20% of sales ($306.5 million) and 27% of pretax operating income ($28.2 million) in 1970. In 1971, housing and land development sales totaled $476,220,000, up from $391,381,000 in 1970. Income rose to $40.2 million from $34.2 million the previous year.*

A CITY BOY MAKES GOOD IN REAL ESTATE

City's first move into its present broad role in real estate was back in 1966, when it bought 16% of General Development Corporation, the Florida land developer. It bought another 33% a year later, bringing its ownership to 49%. General Development, operated by a retired head of Sears, Roebuck & Company, Charles H. Kellstadt, earned $4 million on sales of $41.5 million in 1966. The company develops and sells homesites and builds homes in seven planned communities totaling some 200,000 acres, including the big projects of Port Charlotte, Port Malabar and Port St. Lucie. Sales in 1971 were $141 million vs. $120.5 million for the same period a year earlier, and income rose to $20.5 million from $17.1 million.

City next moved into the savings and loan field by acquiring Southern California Financial Corporation in 1967. Expanding, Southern California has become heavily involved in joint ventures on shopping centers, apartments, commercial buildings and land sales. Revenues rose from $13.5 million in 1967 to about $38 million in 1971, while profits more than tripled. A typical Southern California involvement is its partnership with developers Robert A. Brindle and Clifford A. Hemmerling to develop a 40-acre Old Towne Shopping Mall in Torrance, California, including two high-rise buildings.

In 1969, City acquired a piece of Guerdon Industries and by 1971 brought its interest up to 53.6%. Sales were $180 million in 1971 vs. $158.8 million in 1970. Net income totaled $6.4 million in 1971 vs. $4 million in 1970. Guerdon produced about 26,000 mobile units in 1971, up from 22,500 in 1970; 2,400 sectional units vs. 1,750 in the previous year; and 2,500 modular units vs. 3,100 in 1970.

During 1971, City consolidated other of its diverse land development activities under a new real estate management team. The group holds Sterling Forest, a 30-square-mile (22,000 acres) tract of land 30 miles from New York that City acquired in 1954 for $850,000. Also included: the 6,300-

---

* The total sales figure includes certain housing-related products such as water heaters, heating and air conditioning. The total sales figure also includes total revenues of both Guerdon and General Development.

City Investing Company

	1971				1970			
	Sales		Earnings		Sales		Earnings	
	(Dollar figures in millions)							
Housing and Real Estate	$ 476.2	29%	$ 40.2	34%	$ 391.4	26%	$ 34.2	32%
Manufacturing	435.8	27%	18.3	15%	439.3	29%	21.1	20%
Financial Services	727.3	44%	60.7	51%	669.9	45%	51.8	48%
Total	$1,639.4	100%	$119.2	100%	$1,500.6	100%	$107.1	100%

*The total sales figure includes certain housing-related products such as water heaters, heating and air conditioning. The total sales figure also includes total revenues of both Guerdon and General Development.

acre Hendrick Ranches in Riverside County, California; 82,000-acre San Cristobal Ranch in Santa Fe County, New Mexico; Kelly Ridge Estates, a 500-acre recreational-land project in Oroville, California; and other properties located in California, Texas, Florida and New York.

One of the company's fastest-growing investments is the chain of budget motels called Motel 6. Between 1968 and 1971 the chain expanded from 3,000 rooms, mostly in California, to 7,000 rooms in twenty-three states. Included in the conglomerate's Financial Services group is C. I. Mortgage Group, a real estate investment trust created late in 1969 and advised by C. I. Planning Corporation, a wholly owned subsidiary. The trust's assets had grown to $181 million and closed loans and commitments to $303 million by January 31, 1972, compared with $76 million in assets and $94 million in loans and commitments two years earlier.

A KEY TO HAPPY MERGER MARRIAGES

Up to the economic crisis of 1973, City successfully operated this diversified collection of companies and activities by a personal management style and a strong emphasis on financial incentives. Scharffenberger strove to achieve a personal relationship with the managers of the acquired company from the outset and made clear that their entrepreneurial prerogatives and incentives were not diminished by the merger. This approach can yield an even greater success for the company than it had formerly, he says.

To harness the incentive, City's merger agreements, since the accounting rules change, have usually been structured on the purchase accounting method, setting up earnouts with strong rewards contingent on performance. In the case of Wood Brothers the seller received $10 million in stock as a down payment, with another $10 million in stock laid up in escrow and deliverable subject to promised growth. The purchase accounting method for mergers may take the extra kick out of initial earnings by gearing them more closely to actual production and sale of homes, but it does provide the kind of buyer's safeguard that City conservatively wants. City gears what it pays to what the subsidiary earns; the sellers have the chance to get more than they might for an outright acquisition by the pooling method if they really perform well.

City's management method was quite similar to that employed by Bob Winnerman at U.S. Home or Gordon Murphy of Cerro in the early 1970s; that is, decentralization and management by minimum interference. City would merely add one or two of its officers to the subsidiary's board of directors to make contributions as individuals, while it maintained the continuity of the subsidiary's management. Its primary active role was to act as a source of funds for the subsidiaries. It is interesting that because of this approach City could run its $1.5 billion business with only about seventy people, including secretaries. The company's person-to-person management style does place a limit on how far it can expand; Scharffenberger has said that handling more than ten major subsidiaries would get unwieldy. Such an informal, intimate structure, almost resembling a homebuilder's entrepreneurial operation, is one reason why City's earlier ventures into real estate have been successful.

THE ALMOST-WAS HOUSING JUGGERNAUT

At the time he acquired Wood Bros., George Scharffenberger was a strong advocate of the wisest operating philosophy for any major developer: letting the subsidiary carry its own burden of management within a system of entrepreneurial incentive and financial monitoring. But as recently as July of 1970 he seriously contemplated and nearly implemented a plan to do the exact opposite: to group all of City's housing and land development activities into a single large company. That company was majority-owned Guerdon. Guerdon was to acquire City's interest in General Development and all the real estate assets of SoCal in a $120 million stock swap. F. L. Cappaert, Guerdon's president, was to have been president and chief operations officer of the revamped company, and Scharffenberger himself was to become chairman and chief executive.

It is surprising that this consolidation plan, which was published, did not attract major attention in the housing industry. Had the plan gone through, it would have immediately created by far the largest housing corporation in the U.S. Sales of the combined organization for 1970 would have been in the neighborhood of $325 million and earnings in the $25 million range. The new Guerdon would have dwarfed the estimated $225 million sales of the biggest builder of 1970, Levitt & Sons. Guerdon would have been operating twenty-eight housing plants in seventeen states; building conventional single-family, mobile and modular housing; and developing land and mobile parks. Assets would have totalled $175 million and net worth $150 million.

But Scharffenberger finally changed his mind and never actually implemented the plan to regroup City's holdings into a single mammoth organization. He saw housing as the largest single market of the Seventies — larger than the automotive industry — but he came to believe the concept of "synergism" had been overplayed. City's subsidiaries would do better each on its own than lumped together. As it happens, the choice may have been fortunate. With modular housing a tactical disaster for the industry and with mobile home sales also affected as of 1973, a conglomerate structure such as the one temporarily envisioned could have fallen apart with a crash as a result of the unprecedented economic stresses that the industry faced after 1973.

CITY AT THE CROSSROADS

City Investing took its time getting into a direct role in homebuilding. While other acquirers leapt for the stick builder, George Scharffenberger contented himself with manufactured housing, land development and financial services. But when City finally did enter the merchant builder field via the Wood Brothers acquisition, it became a major competitor in the U.S. housing industry overnight with potentially the same impact as a Kaufman & Broad or a U.S. Home. In fact, with the exception of its manufacturing operations, City looks more and more like a modern, diversified, decentralized homebuilder. Kaufman & Broad has backed into financial services out of a housing base; City moved into housing out of a financial base. At the same time, the conglomerate incorporates the "congeneric" principle of autonomous subsidiary operations.

There may be more acquisitions in store for City Investing. At one point, the company said it was negotiating for the acquisition of Estes Brothers, a Tucson apartment developer, and Batir S.A., one of France's largest on-site and modular builders. Apparently these ventures didn't materialize because, in June 1972, City vice president John Silver said: "To date, Wood Brothers Homes has been the only company which met our tests for management, product, geographical reach and visibility of earnings prospects in the three- to five-year period ahead." But he pointed out that "we will continue to search for additional ways to participate in conventional building along the lines of another Wood Brothers Homes." Scharffenberger underscored this with the observation that homebuilding is "the area of our business that will grow the most."

Concurrent with the emergence of a stronger orientation to conventional homebuilding, some major changes were contemplated in the status of City's two big partially owned subsidiaries, Guerdon Industries and General Development. These had been producing the bulk of the company's Brothers Homes has been the only company which met our tests for management and real estate revenues. True enough, in May 1973 City Investing moved to buy the outstanding 52% of General Development for about $63 million in debentures to give it complete ownership. Earlier, in the fall of 1972, it also brought its ownership of Guerdon to 100% by buying up the 46% that had been publicly held. How the fast pace of changes in the national economy was to affect Scharffenberger's subsequent plans remains to be seen.

20

Philip J. Reilly Smokes Philip Morris

> We have no art. We do everything as well as we can.
>
> —Balinese saying

"It is said that real estate mergers don't work because the entrepreneur and the corporate types inevitably clash. This is not true. The key execs of Philip Morris are as dynamic and innovative as anyone. Man, they're *hard-charging* execs! And we get on beautifully with them. The problem isn't that the real estate entrepreneur is a unique breed of cat. The problem, where mergers fail, is that the relationship was not adequately explored to begin with so that the two could live well together."

That's Phil Reilly, the president of Mission Viejo Company, talking. A dynamic, hard-charging man himself, he literally overflows with enthusiasm when discussing the acquisition of his company by the giant, diversified cigarette manufacturer Philip Morris. Mission Viejo, developer of the Orange County, California, new town of the same name, went the merger route early in 1970. At that time, PM laid out $15 million in convertible debentures to buy about a quarter of the development company plus another $5 million for an option to purchase controlling interest (roughly 51%) within three years. The honeymoon bloomed into a good marriage and toward the end of 1972, nearly three years of experience behind them, PM and Mission Viejo began the negotiations that were to lead to full 100% ownership of the developer by the cigarette manufacturer for a price undisclosed at that time. Although the economic outlook for homebuilding has changed since that time, the key measure of this merger is that it has continued to thrive. That is the real proof of its success.

TOBACCO GETS INTO HOUSING

It was truly a marriage of the great corporation and the development entrepreneur. PM is a giant multinational corporation that is the world's third largest manufacturer of cigarettes (headed by the Marlboro brand) and owns, among other firms, beer companies (Miller) and paper and packaging manufacturing operations. And it was a company growing rapidly.

Revenues for 1970 hit $1.51 billion and net earnings came to $77.5 million, up 32.1% and 32.8%, respectively, over 1969 results.

Mission Viejo is a development and construction company formed in 1966 to transform approximately 11,000 acres of land lying midway between Los Angeles and San Diego into a "new town." Although the California economy slumped, the project prospered with a steadily rising sales and earnings curve. By the start of 1971, more than 3,800 homes were occupied by a population of 14,000 people, making it probably the most successful new town in the U.S. Plans call for a population of 100,000 people at Mission Viejo by 1990.

Since the time of its 1970 merger, Mission Viejo Company sharply accelerated its growth. While continuing to increase sales at the new town, the company in 1970 and 1971 took on its first ventures outside Southern California. One was a 450-acre, 850-unit planned community in the Phoenix suburb of Tempe, undertaken as a joint venture with El Paso Natural Gas. Another was the start of land development and construction on a 640-acre, 4,000-unit planned community in Denver's Cherry Creek Dam area. Late in 1972 the company was also finalizing plans for a major lake-oriented community at the site of its first new town. Meanwhile, Reilly was sifting through increasing numbers of joint-venture proposals from major landholders and financial sources throughout the country.

"The important thing about our relationship with Philip Morris is that it has been extremely positive." said Reilly in 1973. "I get comments like 'From the looks of your transaction it looks like it was made in heaven.' It really works." Perhaps the strongest reason why the merger proved to be so workable is the compatibility of the management teams of the parent and subsidiary companies. Perhaps more than virtually any other marriage, it seems to be a truly "synergistic" relationship. Each side has educated the other and both have improved as a result. Philip Morris brought to the developer a measured conservatism of thorough long-range planning and controls; Mission Viejo taught its parent the real estate business. Together they have been successfully building a soundly based pattern of growth. It appears to be an ideal combination of professional planning and performance orientation.

A MARRIAGE OF MANAGERS

One high-placed insider summarizes the three years of the working relationship with the parent company: "Philip Morris's influence has been very beneficial to our management. PM is one of the best-managed firms in the country, but it is also down-to-earth and very people-oriented. They're not impressed by frills and they think clearly. Thus we got direct exposure to highly professional people who would be outstanding in any field. They brought to us a deliberate balance of realism and conservatism that is pretty unusual in an industry that has been so notoriously freewheeling.

"The area in which we benefited most was finance and accounting. Here, PM has been a tremendous influence on us. Jim Gilleran, who is now our vice president for administrative services, covering these areas, was formerly assistant controller for Philip Morris. They have also been of great influence in getting us to evaluate programs and opportunities on a completely rational basis, making allowances for contingencies and so on.

"In some companies there is a tendency to yield to stockholders and press for rapid earnings. But nothing is more destructive to a good plan than not allowing sufficient time for it to work as a result of impatience. Philip Morris is unique in this respect. They appreciate good careful planning. They always ask a lot of acute questions and force you to think things through. As a result, we are planning very conservatively and expanding very carefully. From 1970 onward there has been a tendency for small firms in real estate to diversify geographically at sometimes a fantastic rate. The problem is, will they be capable of handling and supporting such diversification over larger periods of time without severe strains. We have already seen that some companies have difficulties surviving their own success; without management depth, without control, they go from high profit to deficits. This is a very real danger and we are very aware of it as a direct result of Philip Morris's influence. So we are planning our expansion very conservatively.

"Somehow, we immediately hit it off with PM, felt intuitively that the match was right from the beginning. And it has worked out extremely well. Their people are both performance-oriented and people-oriented, and that's a combination hard to beat."

A "JOINT VENTURE" TYPE OF ACQUISITION — AS A FIRST STEP

What entices a non-housing corporate giant like Philip Morris into real estate development? Leaving aside Mission Viejo's excellent management team and its impressive, sustained performance record, housing is still a risky business during the parent company's initial learning period in the first years following a merger. In this case, Philip Morris decided to test the waters gradually before plunging in by making only a partial purchase of Mission Viejo at first. By remaining part owners, indeed majority owners, Mission Viejo's stockholders stayed in what might be called an earnout situation. As one of them says, "We envisioned retaining a major interest so that we wouldn't take unusual expansion risks to increase the price of the parent company's stock but harm our own company by increasing its risks down the line." In short, the parent company couldn't get hurt without the subsidiary's stockholders taking a major bath themselves. As Reilly himself observed late in 1972: "The rationale for the partial purchase decision is that it adds great credibility to the builder at the outset." When the trial period passed successfully, Philip Morris moved to buy out the entire company.

The form of the Mission Viejo–Philip Morris deal thus anticipated to a degree the changeover of merger pattern from outright acquisition and a direct corporate role in development management to a more tactical, almost joint venture form of investment. This particular merger moved on to full ownership of the subsidiary by the parent company, to be sure. But — in its first stage at any rate — it foreshadowed the rise of such corporate involvements as the 50-50 Wasserman deal with Gulf & Western.

"We reached a decision to affiliate with someone in order to add dollars to our operation and to spread our risk," Phil Reilly says. "We commissioned Merrill Lynch and they counseled us on the way to go. We decided that the 'going public' route was not for us: we were operating only in Orange County and had no geographic diversification of the sort that would be looked for; we held 11,000 acres of land on option, and this asset and its appreciation is not reportable for a public company to give a truer picture of its value.

"So we went looking for a merger partner. We were like a cute little sophomore at the Senior Prom and got asked to dance by many candidates. We were pleased, but we also weren't pressed to make a decision. We had a chance to look over the dance cards. The dollars would be the same from any of several potential partners. What we looked for were the specific management characteristics of the acquirer and his willingness to let us stay in the picture. Philip Morris recognized the benefit of our strong continuing interest as a 49% owner. We made a deal."

ON THE PRIMACY OF GOOD MANAGEMENT

Phil ticked off two basic reasons for the success of his relationship with the cigarette manufacturer as of early 1973:

1. "Philip Morris did an awful lot of investigation before they got into the business. They satisfied themselves as to the risks and opportunities they would face in carrying their share of the marriage."

2. "Philip Morris management pays attention to understanding the people and the business involved. There is no intrinsic reason why a merger between real estate and a corporation shouldn't work. If it doesn't work, it's because somebody isn't paying attention. Philip Morris manages 151 corporations in other countries. The pretax profits from those corporations went from $3 million ten years ago to $30 million or $40 million in 1971. You don't do this unless you can manage people. They're good people managers. They know how to work with us and do it well."

Economic crises notwithstanding, the experience of Mission Viejo Company seems to be a sure proof that a corporation from outside the housing field can succeed as a merger parent in this business — if it bases its involvement on an understanding of the realities of the business and direct, people-to-people communication.

PHIL REILLY TAKES AFTER THE MYTHS OF CORPORATE INCOMPATIBILITY

Reilly is, in fact, certain that the alleged basic incompatibilities between builders and non-housing parents nearly always resolve to a simple problem of human understanding and communication — just as in any other industry. He spoke at some length on the misleading or outright erroneous myths that becloud this simple fact at Ed Birkner's Marketing Information Network Seminar in San Francisco on December 9, 1971. The speech may have been prompted by an article in *Forbes* dated November 1, 1971 which pointed out that of the top twenty builder mergers none had lasted five years and seven lasted less than a year. We have analyzed many of the aspects on which Reilly touches in the preceding chapters, but his comments are so perceptive that they are directly quoted in the following paragraphs.

Let's look at the most often cited reasons for lack of compatibility of the homebuilding company with that of large corporations. The reasons given are:

1. The top executives of homebuilding companies are high-flying seat-of-the-pants, one-man operators who are unwilling to operate without total authority.

2. The real estate industry indulges itself in accounting practices which are technically proper but not in keeping with the conservatism demanded by Wall Street and therefore would taint a large corporation's image.

3. The homebuilding executive loses his motivation when he gets his money, because he is now financially independent.

Those are the three reasons most often given for lack of compatibility. They are heard so often they feed on themselves. There is an interesting common ground among those three reasons — all of them lay the blame on the homebuilder, or on the practices of the real estate industry. Perhaps that is not where all the blame lies at all. Let's examine the reasons given for lack of compatibility and maybe some positive points can be made.

There is the claim about lack of motivation because of financial independence: I cannot buy that. If this is true, why do any rich men work? Any good management consultant will tell you that beyond a certain relatively low level, dollars cease to be the prime factor. The president or chairman of many corporations is a man of financial worth whose real motivation comes from accomplishment — either directly or indirectly by helping others within his influence to accomplish. Most of these men are not only motivated, they are also motivators — or they should be! To infer that a homebuilder folds up when he becomes financially independent is to look for the easy answer. Perhaps the real answer is that the chief of the acquirer has forgotten some of the old-fashioned principles of motivation — or perhaps the people in his lower echelon never really knew or practiced them.

Next, they say the exotic accounting practices of the real estate industry are not compatible with the conservatism demanded of the big companies and this causes friction. I am the president of a homebuilding company — I am not an accountant, so I cannot take on the professional in all the details. Nevertheless, my experience with the homebuilding and land-development industry indicates that the genesis of exotic accounting practices did not occur in the office of the homebuilding executive. We may have come up with some exotic forms of finance that tended to help the cash flow — but I do not think we invented the earnings curve or the ramifications thereof.

I certainly do not know all the merged homebuilders, but I know several. Most see the benefits of leverage to them because of their original cash flow struggles. Cash flow — not profits — required the imagination. Sometimes — often — cash flow needs controlled sales techniques to the disadvantage of profits. The homebuilders that I know were not used to calling things "sales" for profit purposes until the escrow closed and title went to an independent entity. Most of those escrows got that builder at least 90% of his money when he transferred title. Perhaps he was too busy building houses or developing land to see the opportunities he was missing with respect to profits accounting. Those who are still in the real estate business, and report the way they used to report, seem to be able to stand the bright lights that are now turned on. If the builder was purchased because of the paper profits his business was capable of showing, assuming certain reporting techniques were available, there may be some disenchantment now that the lights are on.

I wonder . . . was it the real estate entrepreneur who suggested the alternative profits approach that was available, or was it some sharp member of the acquisition team that saw the potential, suggested the approach, and quickly expanded to capitalize on it? The answer may vary in every case, but in making our evaluation on compatibility — the lack of it — and where the fault may rest, it seems superficial to conclude that it was the real estate industry that authored the now questionable systems.

Perhaps the most frequently given reason for incompatibility is that the real estate executive cannot wear a corporate uniform — he is too loose, high-flying, seat-of-the-pants oriented to accept his role as a team player. He is an entrepreneur and entrepreneurs and industry do not match. What the hell does "entrepreneur" mean? Webster says an entrepreneur is one who organizes, manages and assumes the risks of a business. Yes, that is the president of a homebuilding company. But the definition does *not* say he is a "seat-of-the-pants" "one-man-show" kind or guy. In fact, most of those I know who have built their companies into a position to be merged are definitely *not* seat-of-the-pants, one-man-show guys. I must admit that there are some of *those* in the list, but they are few and far between.

Is a real estate executive who takes his company public, such as Eli Broad or Randall Presley, generically that much different from Ben Deane, Bill Lyon or Larry Weinberg, who merged their companies? Different in style, different to some extent in priority, but I would class all as entrepreneurs and *none* as seat-of-the-pants, one-man shows. It again seems too easy to say that the mergers have been unhappy because the real estate guy cannot wear a corporate team uniform. I have talked to lots of real estate men who wear them and they find them uncomfortable. Could it be that the problem lies not with the mannequin but rather with the tailor?

HOW ABOUT GOOD OLD UNDERSTANDING?

Now then, if there *have* been acquisitions by big companies, and if there has been a fair amount of incompatibility and if the three most often stated reasons seem to lack total credibility, then where is the reason? I believe that *Forbes* magazine, in its November 1, 1971, issue came the closest to hitting it — though its comment was hidden away in one paragraph. It said, in effect, that big firms really did not understand the real estate business and how it operates before they acquired. There is room to expand upon that reason for lack of compatibility. That is a basis for the problem which can be grappled with — a basis that offers a solution by a technique other than surgery!

People tend to talk about the real estate industry as though it was a one-product industry. It isn't! It has many major segments. Some segments, by their very nature, tend to defer profits; other segments require relatively small equity but large debt; yet another facet of the industry has larger front-end equity. Most acquisitions occur after skilled and detailed accounting review, but little real evaluation of what the business requires. Unfortunately, a large firm's middle-management "barn-burner" sees one company doing something and wants to jump in with his new acquisition and try to do the same thing, yet refuses to understand there is not time, or capital, or present management, or land. *Lack of understanding.*

As a lawyer, I found that better, sounder, more workable deals were made when both lawyers knew the field in which they were operating. Neither felt insecure and both were, therefore, more flexible. Both were knowledgeable of the risks — really knowledgeable — and were, therefore, ready to accept those risks that were reasonable.

If you have merged and have a problem, open up a university — help to educate your partner — and that goes both ways. Education breeds understanding and that leads to compatibility. Honest inquiry is not necessarily a slur upon ability. Closing off the avenue of communication will cause suspicion, more inquiry, and the circle can be vicious. You know, confident management does not mind *real* questions. On the other side of the coin, confident management only *asks* real questions.

If you are considering an association, let me suggest that you carefully and honestly evalute what you want. I was asked to speak to a group of brokers, analysts and clients recently. One of the people said that he felt the reason for real estate mergers was to get the unlimited supply of capital that big firms could pump in. There is no such thing — two or three recent episodes prove that no company can afford those ideas. Look at your real reasons, then evaluate your prospects and look for the fit . . . and it better be a two-way fit. In that regard, I would like to speak a word against the workout (i.e., the earnout) form of acquisition.

Frankly, I feel that this form of acquisition creates a conflict of interest almost from the start. It can make it tough to maintain objectivity when it comes to evaluating risk of loss. Work to a price going in, if possible; if that is not possible, then look to why. Therein may be the basis for future problems. A workout for purposes of management motivation may well motivate, but not to the long term interest of the company.

There is no wizardry in corporate compatibility — just understanding and hard work. The reasons being given for incompatibility are too superficial — too easy. Real estate executives have the same pride of accomplishment as do top executives of large companies — and often they work for that reason just as hard as for the dollars. It is too easy for the acquirer to simply say his real estate executive left because he got financial independence. It seems too easy to allow the blame to be hung upon some supposed generic characteristic that says real estate executives are all seat-of-the-pants, one-man shows — there is too much evidence that there are some team players, some sharp team players. It seems unfair to say that the *opportunities* for accounting variations in the real estate industry make it incompatible with the conservative practices of big business. It is the big corporation that has the option of selecting the variation.

Real estate acquisitions and the men on both sides are really no different than in any other acquisition. If there is not a full understanding of the goals of each side and a willingness to accept the limitations of both sides, the deal may fail because of a lack of mutuality. It is just that simple — or just that complex. The sooner we realize it, the sooner we can get back to the business of increasing the efficiency, the product, and the reputation of the real estate industry.

21

Whither the Empire That Levitt Built?

> Nel mezzo del cammin di nostra
> vita
> Mi ritrovai per una selva oscura,
> Che la diritta via era smarita.
>
> —Dante

Say the name of Levitt and almost any man in the street will know whom you're talking about, for the firm of Levitt & Sons occupies a unique niche in the American culture. As in the case of Ford and Xerox, the name does not only represent a specific product or company but has been swept into the stream of popular language to become a generic term, designating an entire style or way of life. To many people, the entire postwar housing industry and its product — the American suburbs — is summarized by "Levitt." In a very real sense, Levitt & Sons *created* the pattern of the present housing industry, setting the standard of mass-producing moderate-cost housing for the millions, and pioneered the required organizational and marketing techniques. From the moment it started building the first of its Levittowns on Long Island in 1947, Levitt & Sons entered history.

Within the housing industry itself the company has also been regarded as the traditional leader, and this was particularly true at the time that it was a publicly held firm. Formed in 1929, the company is perhaps the oldest housing company in the U.S., and it was also the first to go public after World War II. It has always commanded the special authoritativeness that comes from being the *biggest* housing producer in the country, as well. For many years there was no one to compete for the dominant role of Levitt's marketing excellence, organizational professionalism and sales volume, until Eli Broad came along in the latter half of the Sixties with fast-growing, publicly listed Kaufman & Broad as the "We're No. 2. We Try Harder" company. Perhaps it wasn't so, but to many observers it looked as if Eli was taking dead aim at capturing the No. 1 spot among the publicly held companies; Kaufman & Broad also paid Levitt the compliment of following it into the European market. Eli's firm did become the biggest publicly listed housing organization when Levitt & Sons delisted and merged into International Telephone & Telegraph early in 1968. But Levitt as of 1971 was still the *biggest* housing firm, with sales estimated at close to $300 million in that year.

Unfortunately, the times were not kind to the company from 1972 on. To begin with, the firm's future was cast into doubt by the fall of 1971 when the Justice Department ruled that IT&T divest itself of Levitt & Sons by the close of 1974. That put the whole relationship on an interim basis and deprived it of any opportunity to develop meaningful growth and management goals. Disputes with the IT&T hierarchy led to a game of musical chairs in the Levitt president's office, resulting in the departure of the best top management. The dismembered subsidiary seemed to lose its forward motion well before the economic dislocations of 1973 that forced it out of modular housing and put the screws on the housing industry in general. At this writing, it was reported that IT&T would keep the most profitable Levitt division (land sales) for itself, while selling the homebuilding group's assets to another large firm, such as the Kaiser-Aetna Realty partnership.*

Levitt & Sons was truly a great organization, the giant and the great innovator of its time. The man behind the company is William Jaird Levitt. The achievements of the man and his company deserve to be known.

BILL LEVITT STARTS A CAREER: THE AGE OF LEVITTOWNS

Bill Levitt started in the building business at the age of twenty-two with his father and brother by way of taking over a piece of property at Rockville Center, Long Island, as collateral on a defaulted loan. In 1929 they built and sold 18 homes at an average price of $18,000; the following year, 40. The young company grew slowly until 1934 when Levitt and his boys sold 200 homes at their Strathmore project in Manhasset, Long Island, for prices ranging from $8,900 to $14,900. (By 1970 the same houses were worth $40,000 to $60,000.)

Levitt got his first real feel for high-volume production techniques when he left Long Island in 1942 to plunge into the construction of 750 units of low-cost military housing in Norfolk, Virginia, followed by another 1,600 units. Then he closed up shop and spent the rest of the war in the Seabees, but soon afterward the Levittown was born. The first of them, built on a Long Island potato patch, caught the towering postwar housing shortage head-on, and flung Bill Levitt into the big time. Starting with 300

---

* Apparently this feeler for the sale to Kaiser-Aetna didn't work. In Spring of 1974, William Levitt announced he would be rebuying the homebuilding group.

acres, Levittown ultimately expanded to 5,000; in five years, Bill Levitt's organization built and sold the unheard-of volume of 17,447 Cape Cod homes (complete with range, refrigerator, washer, and landscaping for $7,990 each). Next came another Levittown, in Pennsylvania near the Philadelphia metropolis, and Levitt put up 17,311 homes there between 1952 and 1958. A third Levittown was started in New Jersey and took Levitt & Sons into 1960.

Along the way, Bill Levitt introduced innovative materials-handling systems to facilitate production in those booming years, systems that revolutionized large-scale housing construction for years to come. "We developed a top management team that was effective," he says. "We devised mass production techniques — a sort of assembly line in reverse — and gave 40% more value. Through volume purchase we attracted and featured top brand products. We gave the buyer a better house with quality products and improved installation methods. We pioneered the advertising techniques. I wrote most of the ads myself in the early days; you have to be sincere, know your product."

The Levittowns, especially the first one, aroused a cacophony of angry cackling from America's aesthetic peanut gallery, as prominent culturati called them "the future slums of America." But it was not so: the Long Island Levittown, for example, has become an attractive community for 68,000 people and the resale prices of those Cape Cod homes have doubled and quadrupled. On the occasion of the company's fortieth anniversary in 1969, Bill Levitt gave this estimate of his firm's achievement: "We showed the way to build good, standardized lower-cost housing and complete communities. In short, a better way of living." He didn't think that everyone unstood this, "But our accomplishment — the inexpensive houses we built and the landscaping we added at our own expense — provided its own reward. Some years ago a woman wrote to say that every night her son recited a little prayer: 'God bless mommy and daddy and Mr. Levitt.' That mother and her son understood our accomplishment."

It *was* a great accomplishment, but the days of the Levittowns ended in 1960 when Levitt was among the first to discover that with the ebbing of the postwar housing boom he could no longer afford to put all his eggs into one basket at a time. As Norman Peterfreund, the company's vice chairman and chief financial officer and an old Levitt hand, observes: "We learned in 1960 that you have local market conditions changing from year to year which don't overall reflect the national market conditions. We were in Levittown, New Jersey, all alone. We had no place to go to make up for the unfortunate market conditions there. So we began to diversify geographically."

THE NEW-TOWN BUILDER MOVES TO
NATIONAL MARKET FLEXIBILITY

Thus, during the decade of the Sixties Levitt & Sons entered what might be termed the second phase of its history, opting for greater flexibility by a broad geographic and product diversification program which transformed it into the biggest of decentralized national firms. The geographic diversification started with a move into the Washington, D.C., market and throughout the decade has expanded until the firm in 1972 found itself building homes in twelve major market areas throughout the U.S. and abroad. The company was the first to crack the foreign market by entering Paris in 1965 (where in 1972 it was selling 500 to 600 units annually). And late in 1971, Bill Levitt himself announced in a Paris press conference that Levitt & Sons would open markets in Madrid and Munich, selling 400 to 600 homes yearly in each. It also builds in Puerto Rico and in 1971 confirmed it had plans under way for starting up a homebuilding operation in Japan.

(Other homes are also moving toward Japan. Nippon Homes and B. A. Berkus Associates, subsidiary of Environmental Systems International, began joint-venturing on 181 homes in the spring of 1972. And Mitsui Company, a worldwide trading company, joined with West Coast Orient Company of Portland, Oregon, a lumber exporter, to ship pre-cut American-style homes to Japan.)

NEW MARKETS. Throughout its diversification period, Levitt was one of the first companies to rely extensively on sophisticated market research as a guide to consumer demand and preferenes and in locating its expansion targets. Under the irascible and brilliant Dr. Norman Young, who was Levitt's head of marketing during this period, the company perfected sophisticated computer techniques and analyzed more than five hundred markets and market segments to pave its way. It is my own occupational disease to point out that such market research helped. When Levitt entered the Chicago area in 1967, the company's Strathmore project, located in then far-out Buffalo Grove, Illinois, outsold all other Chicago area housing developments for eighteen months. When Levitt entered the metropolitan Detroit market with Windmill Pointe project in Troy, it sold $3 million worth of houses in three weeks.

FLEXIBILITY A KEY. As it was expanding, Levitt simultaneously scaled down the size of the homebuilding projects the company would be handling in each market area. A *major* housing project in a metropolitan market progressively became defined as one selling 400 to 600 homes a year. And through the late Sixties and into the early Seventies the company worked out a so-called "satellite" approach to give itself still greater flexibility. The emphasis now falls on projects of 100 or so houses a year. Each of the smaller jobs is peripheral to at least one major project in each metropolitan area. The management of the big project handles the smaller ones, thus making them viable. "You can go in and pick up 100 or 150 zoned lots, for example," says Peterfreund, "and build them out in a year's time." That provides Levitt & Sons with the capacity to respond quickly to changing market conditions and gives it what Peterfreund terms "an important new flexibility."

This approach, giving a giant developer the flexibility of a small one, took "a lot of adaptation" in a company that had geared to assembly-line construction of on-site houses, but the concept has taken root. In incorporating the flexible "satellite" approach into its operating philosophy, Levitt & Sons was in effect following the pattern of a basic changeover in the entire housing industry which began to be evident along about 1966: the shift from a construction-oriented to a marketing- and market-oriented philosophy, prompted by increased competition, rising prices, unstable credit sources and volatile markets.

NEW PRODUCTS. Product lines also multiplied as a response to changing economic conditions. Like many other major builders about this time, Levitt in 1969 organized Levitt Multihousing Corporation to build townhouses, condominiums and garden apartments and projected an annual volume of 6,000 units by the mid-Seventies. It was a less than happy turning point for Bill Levitt, whose entire career had been dedicated to single-family housing, and he said at the time: "Every family is entitled to a house of its own. Unfortunately, land costs have forced us into multifamily construction." In the same year the company also moved into industrialized housing. One of Levitt's key men at the time, Louis E. Fischer, saw it as a major answer to housing's problems and predicted that by 1977 "at least half of all Levitt production will be coming out of a factory — and I don't mean trusses," but entirely modular or sectional homes. "Whether we buy from others, or more quickly expand our own operation, we're going to have to buy houses from the plants instead of going through the continuing suffering of trying to find the available manpower for on-site construction of housing," Fischer said.

That plan, unfortunately, did not last, and Levitt had to fold its modular program in 1972. The company had a substantial foot into industrialized housing with its Battle Creek, Michigan, plant, which turned out mobile/modular units for the company's Operation Breakthrough commitment. But, as the company did not actually sell mobile-home-type modulars as mobile homes but incorporated them in on-site housing, the volume of demand as of 1972 was relatively small and Levitt's people were still working on getting the plant "on line the way we would like to see it" when the word came down to close up and pull out of modulars. It is one significant and very interesting difference between Bill Levitt and Eli Broad that Levitt did not pursue a major role as a mobile-home manufacturer. In retrospect — considering Kaufman & Broad's decision to get out of mobile homes in 1973 — it was a smart choice.

Levitt's reluctance perhaps stemmed from a distaste for mobile homes as a substitute for a house; he could accommodate his "a home for everyone" philosophy by stepping into apartment construction, but at mobile homes he drew the line. His comments endeared him to no one in the mobile-home industry, and wounded those who thought they had converted the conventional mobile home into a suburbanite's palace by better design and larger sizing, but Bill Levitt always spoke his mind: "It is a sad commentary on this country that at this time, with our standard of living, people are settling for mobile homes. They are nothing but trailers without wheels. That is only shelter, just as a tent is only shelter. I cannot imagine anyone really wanting to own a mobile home."

CAPITALIZING ON NEW-TOWN EXPERTISE. As the final step in its diversification program, Levitt & Sons also moved into major land development programs. One could say that this is really a continuation of its role as a builder of Levittowns, but it takes new forms. Having gotten its eggs out of one basket and established a stabler (i.e., more diversified) sales base, it was only natural for Levitt to put to work the organization's strong expertise as a developer of archetypal "new towns" in master-planned major land projects. The company follows the role of many corporate new-town developers, planning major parcels for complete communities and developing the land, then constructing the preplanned mix of residential, apartment, commercial and industrial buildings. While the front-end investment in such projects is, as is the usual case, substantial, the rewards are large. This approach also permits the use of joint ventures with other builders. At one point in the late Sixties, Levitt's Dr. Young even discussed the possibility of his company's building scores of self-sufficient "new towns" and worked up a detailed computer model identifying the economic feasibility for such a program.

One of Levitt's major land projects is Belaire Village in Maryland, a 2,400 acre community with clustered residential neighborhoods built around a lake and a 200-acre "downtown." The company also put two years into planning a $13 million, 1,270-acre community of 4,235 dwellings for Loudon County, Virginia, but early in 1971 the county's board of supervisors turned down Levitt's rezoning request on grounds that a tax increase would be required to support new schools, which Levitt had volunteered to build. The company planned to sue, and was optimistic about winning, though this necessitated at least a year's delay for the project's start. But in April 1972, a Virginia circuit court unexpectedly upheld Loudon County's ban on the $112 million new town, located thirty-eight miles from Washington. And Levitt's attorneys appealed to the Virginia Supreme Court.

Early in 1971 Levitt also began house sales at Palm Coast, a 100,000-acre planned community located midway between Daytona and St. Augustine in Florida. The project, exceeding the 93,000 acres of Irvine Ranch in California, shapes up as the biggest planned land development in the world. The head of the Levitt Land Development operation became Dr. Young, and he promised to maintain strict control over every stage of planning and development to insure "environmental balance." Levitt picked up most of the parcel after it became a subsidiary of ITT, getting it from ITT Rayonier, a cellulose manufacturer with its own timber lands. With a brisk business in lots and a growing one in houses, the project is expected to gross $200 million by 1980.

A GIANT COMPANY REORGANIZES

By March 1971, the company had grown to such an extent that a restructuring became necessary. Under the old table of organization, Levitt & Sons, Inc., was doing all the single-family homebuilding as well as managing the six major divisions set up since the company had started diversifying in 1960. So, a new manager-company, ITT Levitt, Inc., still head-quartered on Long Island, at Lake Success, New York, was organized to oversee six Levitt operating corporations. The old Levitt & Sons, Inc., became an operating unit concerned totally with developing residential communities. Richard Wasserman, the forty-four-year-old president of Levitt & Sons, stepped up to become president and chief executive of ITT Levitt, the manager-company, with Bill Levitt as chairman. Joining Wasserman as second-in-command were Richard P. Bernhard and Norman Peterfreund, executive vice presidents of operations and finance, respectively. Louis E. Fischer moved up from a senior vice presidency to become president of Levitt & Sons, Inc. The other operating divisions were Levitt Multihousing Corporation, Levitt Building Systems, Inc., ITT Levitt Development Corporation, Levitt United Corporation (previously acquired by ITT as Herman Sarkowsky's United Homes), and Levitt France S.A. Two months later, the name of the manager-corporation was changed back to Levitt & Sons, Inc. Figure 21.1 shows the way the final realignment looked on paper.

Thus the Levitt organization rounded out the decade of momentous expansion and diversification of the Sixties. Enthusiasm and energy fairly crackled in the air around the brilliant young management team that Bill Levitt had assembled and promoted to high posts as the organization had gathered momentum in the late Sixties. And central to that enthusiasm was management's optimism about the fruitful possibilities of the linkage with

ITT early in 1968, which was to have provided the capital strength and corporate support to back up Levitt's expanded growth plans. Levitt's brilliant team projected a 20% compounded annual growth through the Seventies and Eighties, predicated on the threefold strategy of (1) the "satellite communities" concept, (2) expansion into new market areas at home and abroad, and (3) major land development. It looked as if things were going well. In early 1971, sixty-four-year-old Bill Levitt felt he could afford to relax and let the younger men do some of the hard driving. He organized the Levitt-Pickman Film Corporation with Jerome Pickman, former head of American Continental Films, to produce and distribute films. (The company started with distribution of Federico Fellini's *The Clowns*.)

A PROMISING MERGER — AND A TIME OF TROUBLES

Levitt & Sons had merged into ITT in February 1968 for $92 million of the conglomerate corporation's stock. This step, taken by the $120-million homebuilder, rocked both Wall Street and the housing industry and had undeniable influence in promoting the ensuing scramble of builder-industrial mergers. ITT redoubled its bet on housing by acquiring United Homes of Federal Way, Washington, a $25-million builder, in February 1969, for about $11.2 million in stock plus a $1.9 million earnout. But what began for Levitt as a promising marriage that should have enhanced its role in the ranks of housing's leaders became instead a source of disruption and imperiled the stability of the company's future. Problems external and internal arose, each aggravating the other; in the process, Levitt lost some of its best men. As of early 1972, the company did not even know to whom it would belong in 1975.

One of the external and visible uncertainties began in the fall of 1971 when ITT, ordered by the Justice Department to divest itself of several companies, announced that it would unload the Levitt organization by September 24, 1974. This came about as the result of the ITT-Hartford Fire Insurance Company merger — the biggest merger in history — which was completed in December 1968. Hartford Fire, with its more than $1 billion annual cash flow, was a great plum for an expansion-minded, cash-hungry conglomerate like ITT. The Justice Department brought an antitrust suit but on July 31, 1971, abruptly announced an out-of-court settlement: ITT had persuasively argued that it should be allowed to keep cash-rich Hartford Fire if it were willing to divest itself of $1 billion worth of other companies. The theory was that by so doing ITT "wouldn't get any bigger." Along with Levitt, ITT decided to give up Canteen Corporation, Grinnell's fire protection division, Avis Rent-A-Car, and two small insurance subsidiaries.

Subsequently, of course, one of the juicer election-year controversies boiled up in Washington when it was learned that ITT had offered to pick up part of the tab for the GOP presidential convention to be held in San Diego. Democratic critics asseverated that the latter event was a direct result of the former (the out-of-court settlement) and ITT was publicly pilloried for alleged political influence-peddling. The storm quieted down because, of course, no proof of connection between these events was ever summoned, but boiled up again in 1973 as part of the Watergate investigation. The significance of the whole thing to homebuilders was that Bill Levitt was left without a corporate roof over his head.

ITT's FORMULA FOR ACQUISITIONS. Why were earnings important, perhaps even especially important, to ITT? Conglomerates like ITT have grown by a complicated financial process which uses the assets of the company acquired to help finance the purchase. In the case of Avis, for example, ITT agreed to pay premiums of 53.2% above the market value of the company's stock in order to entice it into the merger. It paid 32.9% over the market for Continental Baking and 29.9% over market for Sheraton Hotels. In eight of its ten major acquisitions, ITT's price exceeded the market value of the acquired firm. To make these purchases, ITT borrowed money and used the profits of the corporations acquired to service the new debt (i.e., pay the interest). It got Levitt on this basis, plus more than forty other companies with combined assets of $1.5 billion. When Levitt's profits did not match expectations (the company's sales ran at about $225 million in both 1969 and 1970, as it failed to meet its stated 20% growth projection), it was lost love because presumably ITT's debt service on Levitt's acquisition cost continued.

There were, by the way substantial risks in ITT's intermittent overpayment for an acquired company. The approach works so long as the company keeps on acquiring additional firms to create a "synergistic" growth of its stock, but this imperils the acquirer's financial statement. For the thirty Dow-Jones industrials, for example, the ratio of earnings to interest owed is a healthy 17 to 1. But for ITT, as it went into debt to acquire new companies at premium prices during the merger boom of the Sixties, its interest coverage fell at one time to 4.52 to 1. As debt ratios increased, financial stability suffered; ITT's ratio of long-term debt to net worth rose from 26.3% at one time to 36.1% and stockholders' percentage of equity declined.

One reason why ITT was able to pay large premiums for acquired firms without whittling down its own profit picture was that it could permissibly "lower" the acquisition cost for bookkeeping purposes. A House antitrust subcommittee, issuing seven volumes of hearings on conglomerates after three years of study, asserted that ITT had paid $1.278 billion for the companies acquired but listed them on its books at their net-worth value of only $534 million. Walter Adams, an economist of Michigan State University, says: "By thus 'lowering' the acquisition cost by a simple stroke of the pen, ITT was able to overstate its profits by 70.4% in 1968."

It was also asserted that one reason the Justice Department's antitrust division finally decided not to divest the Hartford Fire Insurance Company from ITT was that, at the prices on which it had been acquired, stockholders might suffer as much as $1 billion in market losses on a forced sale of Hartford Fire. Any bets that ITT winds up making a profit on its impending divestiture of Levitt?

How Big Is ITT?

International Telephone & Telegraph is one of the biggest of the giant multinational corporations, with assets of $6.7 billion in 1972. Although it has "telephone" and "telegraph" in its name, it gets only one-sixth of its income from communications. *Moody's Industrial Manual* for 1971 describes the International Telephone & Telegraph Corporation as a company "engaged in development, manufacture, sales, and service of electronic and telecommunication equipment, and industrial and consumer products and related financial activities; in the production of chemical cellulose, wood pulp, lumber and wood derived from chemicals; in mining . . . ; in consumer and business services; in manufacture and distribution of food products; and utility operations."

Some of ITT's subsidiaries as listed in *Moody's* are: American Building Services, Inc.; American Electric Manufacturing Corporation; Federal Electric Corporation; G. K. Hall Corporation; G. K. Hall & Company; Grinnell Corporation (ordered divested July 31, 1971); H. M. Harper Company; Hartford Fire Insurance Company; Howard W. Sams & Company; Industrial Credit Company; ITT Avis, Inc. (ordered divested); ITT Canada, Ltd.; ITT Canteen Corporation (ordered divested); ITT Continental Baking Company, Inc.; ITT Education Services, Inc.; ITT Electro-Physics Laboratories, Inc.; ITT Export Corporation; ITT Farnsworth Research Corporation; ITT Federal Support Services, Inc.; ITT Financial Services, Inc.; ITT Gilfillan, Inc.; ITT Rayonier, Inc.; ITT Systems Constructors, Inc.; Intelex Systems, Inc.; International Standard Electric Corporation; Pennsylvania Glass Sand Corporation; ITT Sheraton Corporation of America; United Building Services, Inc.; U.S. Telephone & Telegraph Corporation; ITT Industries. Inc.; ITT

Europe, Inc.; International Telephone & Telegraph Company, Ltd.; ITT Far East and Pacific, Inc.

This is just a partal list of the more than 100 companies either wholly or partially owned by ITT. Into this happy company of communications specialists went Levitt & Sons.

A GOOD MAN IS HARD TO FIND

Far more unsettling than the uncertainty of Levitt's next owner had been the abrupt departure from the company, as of July 1, 1971, of the building company's two strongest men. Richard Wasserman, the dynamic president of ITT Levitt & Sons, Inc., and Richard Bernhard, the executive vice president for operations, both gave two months' notice and then quit their jobs after having been loyal Levitt men for many years. The timing of their resignations — coming about three months before the public announcement of the Levitt divestiture — left it an open question as to whether it had any bearing on their departure. What is known is that Wasserman was a loyal Levitt man who was said to be working for advancement in the ITT hierarchy, and only the gravest discontent could have caused him to abandon both his $150,000-a-year job and the company in which he had grown up. His departure came only two months after Levitt had reorganized itself into its newest corporate firm.

Wasserman himself was mum on his reasons; a patently diplomatic ITT press release quoted him as saying: "After twelve years with Levitt, I feel that my personal growth and development require that I now seek new challenges and explore new opportunities." The New York Times, quoting an unnamed Levitt insider, attributed the departure to a personality conflict, growing lack of communication and different ways of doing things. *My* own inside source on this matter, placed impeccably at the highest level, tells me the source of the conflict was ITT management's insistence on telling Wasserman how to run his show; plus its inability or unwillingness to give sufficient weight to the building subsidiary's performance based on ROI (return on investment), where it performed exceptionally, and evaluating it by the sole industrial concept of EPS (earnings per share). Earnings, while not disclosed by Levitt, were reported to have disappointed the ITT people in 1970. Levitt's sales, reaching the 1969 level, stayed at $225 million. Many builders would have been happy to maintain their volume in 1970, a generally bad year for housing. But perhaps ITT, having seen a 20% annual growth goal for Levitt, was not so happy. If it was happy, its brave offer to the Justice Department to divest itself of the building company must be viewed as a courageous act of self-sacrifice.

In the spring of 1972 there was still another surprise. Testimony at the Senate's inquiry into an ITT antitrust suit settlement revealed that just before ITT was ordered by the Justice Department to divest itself of the ITT Levitt & Sons subsidiary, the Justice Department allowed ITT to buy Levitt's Development subsidiary. The sale was approved less than two weeks after the corporation learned of the divestiture ruling on June 29, 1970. On September 17, the name of ITT's new subsidiary was changed to ITT Community Development. At the time the divestiture agreement was published, the land development subsidiary's sale was not mentioned. The development entity's sales and earnings were estimated at $50 million and $8 million, respectively. The overall Levitt corporation was estimated to have earned about $15 million on sales of nearly $300 million in fiscal 1971. So, the development subsidiary that ITT retained contributed about half of Levitt's total earnings, or one-sixth of total sales. ITT's divestiture thus took on less of a hardship aspect than ever.

Wasserman, while admitting that 1970 was "mediocre," took pains after resigning in 1971 to point out that Levitt was in no financial trouble. "Even though last year's volume was mediocre, we made a substantial profit," he said. "This year is going to be our best ever. I expect our volume to hit $300,000,000. If the company had been in financial trouble, I wouldn't have left."

A NEW ROLE FOR LEVITT'S EX-PREXY

Wasserman was deluged with job offers. When the Levitt divestiture was announced, it was also speculated that he might (a) head a group of investors to buy it from ITT or (b) be hired back by his mentor Bill Levitt, with whom he parted on a friendly if minor note. But Dick wasn't having any of it. In December 1971, the conglomerate Gulf & Western announced it had a new investment: $10 million in passive cash for a 50% in a newly formed real estate and development company named the Richards Group. Richards Group? Sure. Richard Wasserman and Richard Bernhard: so why not Richards Group for a name?

"It's *our* business in which Gulf & Western has invested in this case," crowed an ebullient Dick Wasserman. "We'll have no interference in our company's operations." He anticipated running the new organization's sales up to $100 million by its fourth year. This projection could possibly be attained much sooner, as it became known early in 1973 that the Richards Group was reportedly moving in the direction of a congeneric format: it had plans to acquire other builders with the apparent blessings of Gulf & Western. So Dick Wasserman was off to a new start to make some more history in the building industry.

Wasserman says he did not know that Levitt was going to split off from

ITT when he resigned. He says he might have left anyway, since he had already helped to take it from sales of $15 million to over $300 million in his twelve years with the company. "I think a lot of the juice is out of it at this point," he said. "With a $300 million company, you've got to add $70 million or $80 million a year in volume. You start getting into so much paperwork, so many layers of people, so many other problems, that it isn't the kind of exciting situation that the Richards Group is."

In the aftermath of Wasserman's departure, Bill Levitt came out of his chairman's role and resumed active management of the leaderless company. In the fall of 1971 he named Louis E. Fischer president of the manager-company. About the same time a new chairman and chief executive was also named, and for the first time in its history Levitt & Sons had a top manager at its head who did not come from homebuilding. The man appointed was Gerhard R. Andlinger, who came to Levitt through ITT after resigning as chief executive of Esterline Corporation in New York. Bill Levitt, reaching the age of sixty-five, retired and was designated founder-chairman of ITT Levitt & Son, Inc., and Levitt & Sons Inc. Lou Fischer occupied the post of president under Andlinger until early 1972, then quit. He shortly thereafter reemerged as a top industry figure by becoming vice chairman of the executive committee for the Larwin Group, while Andlinger took over his former post.

22

Bob Grant Goes to the Races

> I can also assure you for a fact
> that on this day the Great Khan
> receives gifts of more than
> 100,000 white horses, of great
> beauty and price.
>
> —Marco Polo

Robert H. Grant is one of those blond-haired, square-jawed men with a strong, level gaze and a hearty handshake who wind up on the cover of *Fortune*. And Bob might well do it. After graduating from Worcester Polytechnic Institute in Massachusetts and serving as a naval officer in World War II and the Korean War, he set up shop in Southern California and started his career as a homebuilder in 1953 with a partnership. In 1956 he formed his own company to build attractive "Stardust Homes," and with partner Dick Owen subsequently diversified into commercial construction and land development. By 1970 the Grant Corporation was doing a $35 million volume in residential construction alone. In mid-1970, Grant merged his organization with Santa Anita Consolidated, the diversified company up to then perhaps best known as the operator of the Santa Anita racetrack in Southern California.

It was a true merger, not an acquisition, as Bob emerged dominant in Santa Anita and his company accounts for 60% or more of the merged entity's revenues. For fiscal 1971, Grant racked up sales of $56.1 million and projected further rapid growth for the decade of the Seventies. With Santa Anita in 1972 contemplating a listing on the New York Stock Exchange, Bob Grant stood on the verge of his greatest growth. True, the glum economic climate of late 1973 had a negative effect on Santa Anita's race track revenues, as people became more conscious of inflation and spent less on recreation. But the consolidated firm's homebuilding group continued to perform well.

A merger with a racetrack operator? The combination seems unusual, but it is not unique in the real estate business. Santa Anita Consolidated's major commitment to real estate reminds one of at least one other big organization, recently formed through a three-way merger with major holdings in entertainment and development. This is the Madison Square Garden Corporation, formed early in 1971 after the old Madison Square Garden and Transnation Development Corporation merged and then acquired 89% of Long Island's Roosevelt Raceway via tender offer. MSG's entertainment holdings thus came to include Madison Square Garden itself; two professional teams, the New York Knickerbockers basketball team and the New York Rangers hockey club; 80% of the Holiday on Ice show; and three racetracks, Roosevelt Raceway plus Arlington Park and Washington Park in the Chicago area.*

RACING CASH POWERS DIVERSIFICATION

In a word, it is the *cash* generated in a large stream from racing that underlay the logic of such mergers as the MSG-Roosevelt and the Grant-Santa Anita combinations. Both real estate and leisure/entertainment fields like racing have been rapid growth sectors of the economy in the early Seventies. And the ponies came bearing gifts that are well utilized in real estate: a high, recurring cash flow that can be invested for an extremely high ROI in development of office buildings, houses and land, with the additional benefits of subsequent tax shelter.

With its Los Angeles Turf Club subsidiary providing a strong asset base for diversification, Santa Anita in 1966 embarked on an acquisition in fast-growing fields that culminated in its merger with the Grant Corporation. It was distinguished from Roosevelt Raceway in that it was the country's only old-line racing company to reorganize into a holding-company setup and broadly diversify, rather than remaining static or choosing to be acquired by a larger company. Thus, through 1970 — and not including the full impact of Grant's 1971 sales performance — its revenues shot to $66 million from $27 million four years earlier, reflecting a compound growth rate of 30% per year and annual earnings increases of nearly 35%. From 1967 to 1970 its asset base grew from $20 million to $48 million. An original investment of $5,000 made in 1934 when Santa Anita built its racing plant came to be worth more than $400,000 by 1971. By that same year, Santa Anita's non-racing subsidiaries provided more than 70% of the company's revenues.

Two of Santa Anita's first moves beyond the racing field took it into

---

* MSG's realty holdings include an 80% interest in the joint venture operating Pennsylvania Plaza, the 29-story office building built over Pennsylvania Station in Manhattan; an entire block of Manhattan formerly the site of the old Madison Square Garden; 1,650 acres between Pensacola and Fort Walton, Florida; 450 acres in Chicago, and many smaller parcels. But Roosevelt Raceway became the plum of the new entity, bringing not only 192 valuable acres of land to the merger but also a strong cash kitty. Its net income growing 12.7% on a compound annual basis over the preceding six years, the raceway netted $5.5 million (pretax) on revenues of $25.9 million in 1970, and it came into the merger with a $4.8 million cash balance.

transportation and related services and into investment in corporations engaged in energy exploration and computer techology. In 1968 the company acquired Hadley Auto Transport, a contract carrier delivering automobiles for Ford in fifteen western states for nearly forty years. About the same time, SACO Investment Company was formed as a division of the parent corporation, buying a 17% interest in General Exploration, a gas and oil exploration company. Santa Anita had $1.28 million (representing 320,000 shares) in the company as an equity investment, plus a $1 million loan due in 1976 or convertible into another 86,000 shares of common stock. At the end of 1970, SACO also bought a 9% interest in Magnetic Head Corporation of New York, a computer-components maker.

SANTA ANITA BECOMES A REAL ESTATE GIANT

But Hadley Auto Transport in 1971 provided only about 10% of Santa Anita's revenues (about $13 million in 1971) and only 3% flowed from its investments in technology and oil exploration. As the business climate turned adverse, in fact, Santa Anita closed out some of these peripheral operations. The major source of the company's revenues increasingly became real estate. The direction was plotted out when the SACO investment division began planning the development of a $25-million regional shopping center on 70 acres of the racetrack's 396-acre plant. Called Fashion Park, the enclosed mall got underway by the fall of 1972 as a joint venture with Ernest Hahn, a major Western shopping-center developer. But Santa Anita's biggest move into real estate, of course, came with the Grant merger. Bob Grant brought to Santa Anita a thoroughgoing capability in all aspects of real estate — not only homebuilding but also major "new town" development expertise, plus mobile-home and commercial development strength.

The Grant Corporation had been going through some pretty rapid growth of its own and it, too, was structured as a company with five semi-autonomous subsidiaries operating within a framework of corporate guidelines and support on marketing, finance and land acquisition. As of 1972, these were as follows:

> Grant Company of California, the nucleus of Bob's organization, has built some 9,000 single-family homes in the Los Angeles-Orange County area in the $19,000–$40,000 price range.
>
> Grant Company of Hawaii sprang into existence in 1969 and by 1972 was one of the three largest residential developers in the state with major projects on the islands of Hawaii, Oahu and Maui. In 1971 the company acquired $10 million in development rights on Oahu

for the construction of 1,100 single-family and condominium residences over a three-year period.

Grant Company of Nevada entered the Las Vegas and Clark County markets in 1969 and also made a hit with planned-unit communities incorporating sophisticated California marketing, design and construction techniques.

In January of 1970 Grant entered the mobile-home manufacturing business. The subsidiary, which subsequently became known as Santa Anita Mobile Homes, produced 450 units in 1971 and projected 600 for 1972. It was a modest begining, and it was unclear how it would fare as of 1973,

Anaheim Hills, operating as a division of Grant Corporation, represents the company's most ambitious undertaking in land development: the creation of an entire city on 4,000 acres of land in Orange County. Grant acquired the property, known as the Nehl Ranch, when the company merged with Santa Anita, and the land development project became a joint venture with a Texaco real estate subsidiary. Texaco bought a 50% interest in the deal for $5.5 million in cash and agreed to provide another $8.5 million in loan assumptions and working capital, thus eliminating the need to use Santa Anita funds for the development of the land. The 50/50 arrangement with Texaco is on the land only — not in homebuilding or in commercial development. The plan calls for the development of up to 15,000 homesites in a planned environment over a period of ten years, with lots sold off to smaller builders for construction. This leaves 67 acres of commercial development plus the opportunity for further profits from residential construction to Grant Corporation itself. Grant plans to build a $250,000 clubhouse at its new town. And some 300 acres were sold off to the cities of Anaheim and Orange, which will construct a 235-acre golf course in the new project.

Said Bob Grant of the joint venture with Texaco: "We felt that with a financial partner we could make as much money as we would alone because of the faster rate of development made possible by the added capital, as well as minimizing our own risk; in the long run the ROI will be about the same. It'll take ten years to complete the project and build out the ten thousand or so homes. We'll develop the land and let other builders buy parcels to build on; and maybe we'll build some, too."

Commercial development rounds out Grant Corporation's capabilities. It builds, leases and sells or manages a variety of commercial structures and properties. For example, it has developed fifteen neighborhood shopping centers in Orange County, two hospitals and four medical center buildings, and owns and manages a $2.5 million, 14-acre industrial park in Santa Ana.

THE MAKING OF A PERFECT MERGER

Bob Grant has always been delighted with his Santa Anita merger. "I would have done nothing differently," he says. "We have excellent relationships with the parent corporation's management and no problems regarding our own freedom of operation." But as in all such successful and stable relationships, a great deal of planning and analysis went into making it so. The preplanning culminated in Bob's finding a merger whose own corporate growth goals matched and dovetailed with his, and with whose management a spark of personal affinity kindled into a close rapport.

Grant's search for a merger partner began after he ruled out going public. "I think that the responsibility of going public is so great for a small company that it drains the time and energy of the president," he says. "It drains it to the point where he's diverted from conducting his business and lets it slip out of control because he spends most of his time running around promoting the company with financial types."

Instead, Grant sat down and worked out a careful philosophy to guide him in the search for a corporation to merge with. His company was in first-class shape; it had audited statements of performance for several years, excellent management, good geographic and product diversification. Grant had also written out the company's goals for the next decade and had a clear picture of where he wanted to go and what he wanted to achieve. His next job was, as he says, to look for "an acquirer who wants what you want rather than take any deal that comes along. Mergers go bad because an acquirer doesn't understand the financial requirements of the business and its entrepreneurial element. So I wanted to avoid a merger with a company that would restrict capital or overcontrol to the point where the builder can't operate."

As it was, Grant had armed himself with formidable talent, so didn't have to look long. He brought in Art Winston, a top merger specialist who had been Norton Simon's right-hand man for fifteen years, to help him hunt for a partner. Kenneth Leventhal Company was Grant's auditor, and Ken Leventhal also came in on the merger negotiations. Winston put Grant in touch with Santa Anita Consolidated, and they all sat down and started negotiating, with a battery of lawyers rounding out the retinue.

The prospect of a merger with Santa Anita appealed to Grant for several reasons. The company was looking for diversification into real estate and already had large real estate holdings. It was small enough so that Grant's performance would substantially influence the value of the parent corporation's stock — and Grant wanted that kicker because he believed his company would keep on growing rapidly. (It's an interesting difference of viewpoint from that of builders who have taken stock in large corporations chiefly from the motive of stability, so that their own performance could not influence it appreciably.) Moreover, Grant already knew the horse-racing business. He had been involved in it for ten years as an investor, and in the year preceding the Santa Anita merger had also become an owner of Del Mar racetrack, another Southern California racing facility located near San Diego. So, as he says, "I know the business from both sides of the track — both building and horse racing." And as he understood both aspects of the business, so did Santa Anita. The merger followed.

Summarizing the reasons for his choice of corporate partner, Bob Grant says: "I went for this merger because I wanted a company where we wouldn't be swallowed up: I wanted to own a large percentage of the acquiring company. Owning one-half of one percent of a giant company means that no matter how much volume or profits I generate I would not particularly advance the shares I'm holding in the parent corporation. I wanted a company, also, whose stock was not overpriced and with assets behind it. I wanted a company with a record of declaring dividends so that my key people and I had something more to work for than just salaries. I also wanted a company in which I could have autonomy for my own operation. Santa Anita met all these criteria."

THE SPECIFIC MERGER FORMULA — AND AN EARNOUT JACKPOT

The Grant Company merged with the racetrack operator in July 1970 for a multiple of 10 times earnings, with an earnout based on another 10 times earnings over a five-year period. In the negotiations, Santa Anita's preferred stock was pegged in advance at $40 as of March 31, 1970, regardless of earnings, thus setting the price. At the time of the merger Grant and his partner received 267,540 shares of Santa Anita's preferred stock convertible into 1,112,160 shares of common, valued at $10.7 million. Another 267,540 went into escrow for release over a period of four years and seven months under the following formula: Whenever Grant's income exceeded $1.2 million, Santa Anita would pay in stock worth 10 times the excess, each year of increased earnings then becoming the new base. The formula is not unlike the one agreed to in the Larwin-CNA merger.

"This is the deal we both wanted," Grant says. "Santa Anita thus didn't have to pay cash, and also didn't get locked into paying a high price, because it put us on earnout. I didn't want the cash, either, because it would have given me a tax problem, plus having to reinvest the money and spend time looking for investments with good earnings. I felt I would rather take the Santa Anita stock and rely on my own earning power as an investment."

As part of the merger deal, Grant also negotiated a loan of $2 million cash from Santa Anita "to help expand my operation and help my earnout."

And he took part of the earnout and set up a stock plan for key employees, as well as putting each on a profit-sharing plan. A strong part of the acquired company's motivation to perform stems from the fact that it plays a key role in the parent corporation's expansion plans and can appreciably influence the value of the stock the key employees hold.

Reviewing Santa Anita's nine-month earnings in 1971, the corporation's president, Robert Strub, noted that the net after-tax income of $3.86 million for the period was 59% greater than the company's performance for the comparable period in 1970. And he said: "A major part of this increase was generated by the excellent performance of the Grant Corporation. As a result, we anticipate that President Bob Grant and Executive Vice President Dick Owen, the former owners of the company, may earn out the 267,540 contingent shares which have been held in escrow under the terms of the agreement consummated when Santa Anita acquired the company last year. These shares were to be released upon attainment of increased earnings based on a formula to run over a period of a maximum of four and a half years. The company has done so well this year that there is a good possibility that all of these shares will be earned out."

This is exactly what happened. In fiscal 1971, Grant revenue was up 63% over 1970, from $38.7 million to $61.3 million. The building company contributed 63% of Santa Anita's total revenues of $96.7 million and 49% of its net earnings of $5 million. Without the appearance of strain, Bob Grant thus achieved in one and a half years an earnout that was to take four and a half years. The Grant Company's earnings for the fiscal year ended September 30, 1971, were $2.5 million. This amounted to $1.3 million more than the 1970 base. Following the earnout formula, a payment out of escrow at a multiple of 10 times the excess amount exceeded the entire $11 million earnout.

It should have come as no surprise. Grant's earnings had increased by an average of 50% annually in the preceding five years. Starting out with a loss of $979,000 in 1967, he thus attained $1.2 million in 1970 and $2.5 million in 1971. And in the first quarter of 1972 the company's net was $150,000 on revenues of $10.4 million, up from $25,000 on revenues of $7.9 million in 1971.

A MATTER OF STYLE

Santa Anita counts on its greatest gowth in the Seventies from real estate. Internally, the growth will come from Grant's expansion in Hawaii and a move into Northern California and certain Midwestern markets, as well as from the development of the 4,000-acre Anaheim Hills project. In 1972 Grant projected construction and sale of 2,000 single-family homes, up from 1,400 in 1971. Beyond this, Santa Anita has made it known that it is interested in further acquisitions among companies in the real estate and leisure fields. Such companies would most likely come under the umbrella of the Grant Corporation. In 1973 Bob Grant moved up to chairman of the board of the company he founded, continuing as chief executive officer; his old-time partner, Dick Owen, moved up to the presidency.

It is a characteristic of Bob Grant that he gets very personally involved in the affairs of his business. He is also the rare individual who can establish a strong and imaginative centralized management team that will maintain a very orderly, secure, unhurried control without lapsing into footdragging or, alternatively, going hog-wild. If the Grant Company's past growth is any indication, I know Bob Grant has the talent to become the very biggest of builders. But that's not his style. He only wants to be the best. Unlike many builders I know, Bob is a true gentleman from the spirit outward. He has achieved himself and needs to prove nothing, and so he is free to enjoy his life. And he does, whether it is creating a fine housing product, traveling to Europe, enjoying his horses, or appreciating his many friends. For Bob, the *quality* of life counts more than quantity of money. Perhaps not surprisingly, with that kind of philosophy he will end up with a better home builder's track record during the 1970s than many of his contemporaries.

23

Milt Brock, Jr., Helps INA Invest Its Cash

> I never advise anyone to play
> poker or not to play poker, but I
> always advise them to keep the
> limit down.
>
> —Clarence Darrow

M. J. Brock & Sons became a wholly owned subsidiary of INA Corporation in September 1969. Although the Brock organization is a substantial one, so far as comparative sizes go it was a marriage of the gnat and the elephant. Brock's combined commercial and home building revenues in 1971, for example, were somewhere between $40 million and $50 million, and it operated in six market areas of the U.S. INA's revenues for 1971 were in the neighborhood of $1.25 billion and it operated more than fifty direct and secondary subsidiaries in more than a hundred countries. INA had a net income that year verging on $80 million, assets of $2.75 billion and a net worth of $900 million.

It has been a stable marriage. Throughout the heady days of empyrean booms and busts in real estate, the INA-Brock merger has remained an isle of harmonious calm. That is enough to recommend a close look at the underpinnings of the relationship between a conservative, old-line Los Angeles-based building company and the casualty insurance giant that dwarfs it as a benevolent parent. As one discovers, the success of this relationship offers one more proof that good mergers are made in the planning and only ripen thereafter. The conservative basis of this merger also placed it in a sound position to weather the economic downturn of 1973 and 1974.

AN OLD-LINE BUILDER DIVERSIFIES

Let's first take a look at the kind of company we have in M. J. Brock & Sons. Formed in 1922 primarily as a commercial builder, the organization in subsequent years expanded its capability both as a major commercial/industrial contractor and as a developer of single-family communities. The company grew not rapidly but steadily. It was tightly and expertly run by Milton J. Brock, Sr., its founder, with a combination of Yankee conservatism and establishmentarian finesse which are not usual in the homebuilding industry. The senior Brock was an outstanding contributor to that industry, including service as president of the National Association of Home Builders in 1948. He retired from the company at the time the INA merger was concluded and passed away in 1971. During the elder Brock's long management his sons, Milt Brock, Jr., and Carroll E. Brock, grew up in the company and it bore the character of a conservatively run, family-controlled business. Rounding out the nucleus of the Brock family was a small staff which included executive vice president Richard C. Chenoweth, an eighteen-year man with the organization, and Lester Goodman, vice president of marketing, who was elected as "Marketing Man of the Year" in 1971 by the Home Builders Association of Los Angeles.* The reputation that the company thus built up for itself over the years rested on the Brock characteristics of stability, outstanding product and making haste slowly.

HOUSING. The Brock organization first went into residential housing in a major way in 1940. One of its first geographic diversifications was to the Sacramento market in Northern California in 1953. Headed by Carroll Brock, that division has sold nearly 7,000 homes and in 1971 was accounting for 20% of Sacramento's housing sales. Expanding from its California base, M. J. Brock & Sons in the late Sixties and early Seventies took on the coloration of a national operation. It developed communities in Colorado Springs and in Denver; in 1971 it undertook a joint venture with the land subsidiary of Gates Rubber Company for the development of a 500-unit resort condominium project in Colorado Springs. It opened divisional offices in Clearwater, Florida, and Philadelphia, Pennsylvania, for development of both housing and commercial projects. It handled a project in Honolulu and later started an award-winning 942-unit condominium community at Lake Tahoe, Nevada. A project was initiated in Tucson, Arizona. Meanwhile, the company's single-family housing activities in Southern California diversified into apartment construction at Thousand Oaks, California, and into mobile-home-park development.

CONTRACTING. But as Brock's housing activities expanded so did its work as a major commercial/industrial contractor. Through 1971 the company built more than $200 million worth of commercial, industrial, office and hotel structures, and these activities provide approximately half the firm's revenues. The general contracting division has built such structures

---

* Chenoweth moved up to the presidency, with Milt, Jr., becoming chairman in 1973, while Les Goodman took the position of senior marketing vice president with Art Rutenberg's Florida-based housing congeneric, Omega Housing. The Brock company got itself an excellent new project manager in the person of George Sheridan, who formerly handled responsibilities for Standard Oil's subsidiary, Chevron Land.

as the Kaiser-Sunset Hospital and Barrington Plaza Apartments in Los Angeles; Beckman Auditorium at Cal Tech in Pasadena, California; Magic Mountain Amusement Park at Valencia, California; and in 1972 it began work on the $25 million million Logan Circle hotel complex in Philadelphia. Unlike most contractors, Brock does not bid its projects, working under negotiated contract procedure only.

COMMERCIAL DEVELOPMENT. In 1970 the company formed its third major division, entering a direct role in commercial development. The division acquires and develops neighborhood and community shopping centers as well as motor hotels, restaurants and service stations. Four sites for small shopping centers were under development at the end of 1971 and the company planned to expand this operation swiftly by 1972. As Dick Chenoweth, the executive vice president, observed, "Commercial development is contracyclical to residential development and evens out our inflow."

MILT BROCK, SENIOR, PLANS AHEAD

As an example of the care with which Milt Brock, Sr., planned the company's future, the steps that culminated in the firm's acquisition by INA in 1969 began eight years earlier. Well in advance of the merger boom in real estate, Brock recognized the two limitations of a closely held private company: limited ability to secure additional equity capital, and difficulty in placing a value on the company and capitalizing it for purposes of estate planning. "So, as far back as 1961," says Chenoweth, "we started organizing the posture of the firm that would one day provide the basis for selling it to an acquirer or going public. When a firm is privately held, it does all it can not to pay taxes; but a public company or a subsidiary does everything it can *to* pay taxes to provide earnings per share. We recast our accounting methods in accordance with this principle and for many years before merging compiled a visible track record by securing audited reports of our work. We also strengthened our management structure, introduced sophisticated controls and developed good product lines to create a continuing earnings stream."

But far more significant than merely organizing the company for public view was Brock's astute comprehension of the criteria that a potential acquirer would have to meet in order to operate a real estate subsidiary successfully. He had early ruled out going public. As the merger boom neared and it was all too characteristic of many builders to *sell* themselves for the highest bid, Brock went into the market looking to *buy* the right corporate parent. The principal standards that Brock management had in mind for the "right" acquirer separated out in this fashion:

1. The acquirer's stock must be conservatively priced, at close to book

value, to minimize the risk of loss to the seller after he parts with ownership of his organization. It is better to take a lower price in secure stock with a low P/E and selling at or near book value than a high-multiple stock that can crash and wipe out the seller's gains.

"Unless they've been raiding the company for salaries and stripping it, the owners have their entire lifetime in the company they are putting up for sale; they have all their blood and guts on the line," observes Chenoweth. "So, they must make a value judgment on what they want. If they are a prudent, conservative organization in their philosophy, they look at it one way. If they are a high-roller, they look at it in another. With us, it became a selection process among potential acquirers. If your fiancée's stock is selling at 25 times earnings and you find that's about 20 times its book value, you get another date. The question becomes: Do you want to take three times your worth in funny money, or less with a company that has strong downside protection?"

The Brock people saw one conglomerate acquire a builder for something like 35 times earnings when its stock was selling for a flashy multiple. The handsome paper price gave pause, but the Brocks' conservatism was vindicated: the underlying book value of the stock was something like $1, and the P/E subsequently plummeted to nowhere. The acquired builder was wiped out, losing his life's investment. In another instance, a major general building company acquired a smaller Los Angeles firm with high-multiple stock which subsequently dropped by 66%, denuding the sellers of their gains.

2. The acquirer must appreciate real estate for its high return on investment and not place the complete emphasis on contribution to per-share earnings. Earnings criteria should be compatible with the seller's philosophy of conservative, steady growth. Inordinate pressure for earnings is to be avoided, as it results in loss of control over one's operation and thus financial reverses. Hence, no agreement should be made involving an earnout, as it has a tendency to pressure the management's judgment.

Brock management's concern about the pressures of an earnings orientation was prescient, in view of events that overtook a number of major firms by 1971. It is clear, for example, that the Lyon organization ran into problems at American-Standard at least partly because it failed to meet the parent company's earnings criteria. And Boise Cascade was a classical example of a company trapped by the necessity to create earnings for shareholders. As one insider described it: "In the mid-Sixties, Boise saw residential housing suffering from both oversupply and lack of credit. So it began selling recreational land. On the contract sale, it took 5% to 10% down but booked 100% profit, as its own expenditures rose from front-end costs and bonding for future completion of improvements. But the profits for accounting purposes resulted in a quick jacking-up of earnings per share, and this was like a guy taking heroin: the Wall Street analysts call up and say 'Great! What'll you do for me next week?' So Boise took on two such projects, and then on and on. Very little cash flow was coming in, as the salesmen alone got 30% of the cash flow. Soon, Boise was selling financing, issuing debentures to get cash back in to do the improvements on the projects. All Boise got, in sum, was earnings with negative cash flow."

The acquirer should recognize that incentives other than an earnout may be preferable, and even necessary. The acquirer buys *management* — not a proprietary item — and this management must be *motivated*. A homebuilder can use stock options as strong incentive because in a single-product company (housing) the value of the stock directly reflects performance. Outfits like Kaufman & Broad, Pulte and Ryan use stock options well. If a builder is acquired by an industrial or financial giant, however, incentives can be bonuses tied to goals on internal rates of return on invested capital, in order to reward specific performance. An earnout, while not rewarding all management — only the sellers — also may push the company into unwise growth, according to Brock's line of thought.

3. The acquirer should have capital resources sufficient to support a continuing commitment to real estate, providing a sound equity base for the growth of the subsidiary. The acquirer should not himself be in a capital-intensive business because this may lead to conflict over scarce capital between parent and subsidiary. He should recognize that real estate is a capital-intensive business and that he'll need a lot of capital, or access to it, if he wants performance.

Again using Lyon as an example, both the real estate subsidiary and American-Standard, running capital-intensive operations, were placed in fundamentally unsound competition for a limited supply of capital. By opting for association with a corporation not having high capital requirements, the Brock organization avoided such conflict.

The conservative Mr. Brock found his criteria for a satisfactory merger partner fulfilled in INA. Acquirer and acquired were introduced through the accounting firm they have in common, the Arthur Young organization. After a breakfast meeting with John T. Gurash, chairman and president of INA, and the top Brock management the deal was made. "There was an element of chemistry; we found we had basically parallel philosophies," says Dick Chenoweth.

INA met the first criterion — that of a soundly supported and conservatively priced stock. Very conservatively, in fact. At the time that M. J. Brock & Sons was merged, INA's stock was selling for less than book value. INA also had a strong history of stability, not having missed a dividend payment in 179 years. Brock opted to have the stock grow historically from a conservative base and it has been doing so, rising above book level since the acquisition.

INA likewise met the second criterion — that of placing a strong emphasis on return on invested capital and not primarily on earnings per share. The stated policy governing the initial organization of the giant corporation and its subsequent purpose is (1) to maximize return on its resources and (2) to diversify and get into businesses with a high ROI both through internal development and acquisition. The primacy of investment return in the company's philosophy is demonstrated by the fact that the Brock acquisition involved no earnout. The sellers sold for a lump amount of stock. The subsidiary has not gone into the driving pace of an earnout situation.

The Brock organization acquires an importance in the INA structure beyond the impact that it makes on earnings per share. Says Chenoweth: "If we were measured by earnings as a subsidiary of a major earnings-oriented public company, we would impact their earnings by at most seven or eight cents per share. Why go this route and get lost in the shuffle? At INA our actual contribution is higher than is reflected in our contribution to the stock. We provide a return on investment that is better than the corporate rate, as well as contributing to earnings. But investment return is the key; we are not under pressure to create a market for INA stock.

"If we can create an internal rate of return that is substantially higher than their rate of return on invested capital, we raise the overall return on the parent corporation's investment portfolio. If their rate were, say 10%, and we were giving them a return of 20%-plus, we earn a place in the sun without making a major impact on earnings per share. Ours is a capital-intensive business and we can use their equity."

INA also met the third criterion — that of possessing ample capital for investment in real estate. Unlike solely life insurance companies, casualty insurers like INA Insurance must retain high liquid reserves. Life insurers can actuarily determine how much is available for long-term investment and thus place their funds into long-term mortgages. But a casualty company has to keep a large reserve for the unexpected; as of 1971, INA's was in the range of $900 million to $1 billion. These funds are plowed into a variety of short- to medium-term investments, ranging from one-week commercial paper long-term bonds, and spanning the range of high-return equity investments like real estate. The Brock organization's own guidelines on the use of corporate equity capital are, as Chenoweth says: "The money in and out with the investment return in three to five years."

Suggesting that the merger has proven workable is the fact that most of the Brock company's expansion beyond California occurred after it merged into INA; revenues went from $15.1 million at the time of the merger to more than $40 million by 1971. The builder found itself grouped in INA's real estate division along with two other organizations, INA Properties, Inc., and Richgart, Inc. Real estate is just one of eight divisions for the financial holding company that is known as INA Corporation. The others cover property and casualty insurance, insurance services, life and group insurance, financial services, protection products, computer services and participation investments. Among the latter is a 10% interest in the Suez Financial Company, the original owner of the Suez Canal and now a $600 million insurance, banking and industrial complex in Europe with extensive real estate activities of its own. Among INA's wholly owned subsidiaries are the investment banking firm of Blyth & Company, Banque Blyth & Cie, Insurance Company of North America (casualty) and Life Insurance Company of America, to name a few. The Brock company's apparently painless transition into subsidiary status within such a diversified environment suggests the match was well made.

INA REORGANIZES FOR MORE GROWTH

INA Corporation on September 30, 1971, announced a major organization intended to further the company's diversification program and strengthen top management coordination of its multiplying involvements. In the process, INA created three new posts of executive vice president and M. J. Brock & Sons got itself one of them as its boss. The man is Donald E. Meads, who assumed responsibilities for the "Finance and General" group, one of three major operating groups created by INA. Meads came to INA after resigning as chairman of the board and chief executive officer of the International Basic Economy Corporation (IBEC), the Rockefeller-founded organization supplying financial services and developing food and shelter enterprises in thirty-three countries. IBEC's 1970 net income was $8.15 million on consolidated net revenues of $282 million. Among the subsidiaries in the INA group headed by Meads are Blyth & Company Banque Blyth in Paris, Philadelphia Investment Company, AID (which builds and operates hospitals), Star Sprinkler, Safety First Products, Air Balance, and Suez Financial.

"Our new structure," Chairman Gurash explained, "is designed to make the most of our great human and financial resources. This reorganization enables us to delineate more clearly to our executives what we expect of them." At the same time, INA enunciated some broad guidelines for the diversification program INA would be following in subsequent years. The company will be hewing to the following criteria in its activities:

Financial orientation: a policy of balanced capital generation and utilization, avoiding involvement in manufacturing because of long-term capital requirement to fixed assets.

Quality and reputation: a policy emphasizing INA's stability, integrity and credibility, avoiding "flamboyance and excessive speculation."

Scope and magnitude: a policy of acquiring companies "with significant and meaningful industry positions."

Total majority ownership: a policy of moving "rapidly" to majority ownership of acquired businesses.

Although Brock might have functioned satisfactorily within the earlier framework, the new structure improves the subsidiary's long-range planning capability and systematizes access to capital allotments. With a group executive vice president representing overall realty objectives in his management committee of the three group heads who now develop the overall planning of INA capital, a truly corporate-wide coordination between real estate and other activities became possible. With this reorganization, the Brock group developed a new program for increased use of INA capital in an orderly, though not rapid, expansion of all three areas of its business and in further geographic diversification. The Brock plan has "not precluded acquisitions" of other builders. Neither, for that matter, has INA's though as of 1972 the holding company was not involved in any such merger ventures. Real estate is an important activity in Gurash's estimate, however, and the pace of INA's activities in it will no doubt be increasing through the Brock organization and other entities. INA was, for example, at one time exploring possible real estate interrelationships with Suez Financial.

The route that M. J. Brock & Sons took to merger would not have appealed to everyone in homebuilding, but the firm's conservative approach has been thoroughly vindicated. No longer do builders and acquirers regard with disbelief the absence of an earnout and the company's philosophic opposition to the hell-for-leather expansion which has been more characteristic of the industry. The merger price, though not disclosed, was also known to be conservative compared to going rates in 1969, and set this company off from the prevalent style. In virtually all respects the Brock-INA merger was at the opposite end of the spectrum from the nearly concurrent Larwin-CNA deal (thus neatly rounding out our tales from the masters of merger). But the Brocks got exactly what they wanted: the continuity of their stable operating pattern, and almost ironclad protection from downside risk on their sale, and access to the equity capital they have needed. Milt Brock, Jr., who now runs the company, is happy to help INA invest its cash, and is, relatively speaking, snug as a bug in a rug while other empires are collapsing.

PART FOUR

Joint Ventures

Supple and turbulent, a ring of
men
Shall chant an orgy in the summer
sun.

—Wallace Stevens

24

The Flexible Flyer

Infinite shapes of creatures there
are bred.

—Edmund Spenser

The joint venture can be generally defined as a one-time association between two unrelated parties for the purpose of bringing off a successful project. This organizational device has proven extremely valuable in the field of real estate development because, all too often, no single entity commands all of the elements necessary to develop a project; by bringing together partners with similar goals but with different capabilities and resources the joint venture permits them to handle a deal that neither of them could undertake separately.

The classic joint-venture arrangement is a marriage of capital and entrepreneurial talent. With the acceleration of the building industry's chronic capital shortage through the Sixties, the perfect situation was created for a massive fusion of corporate investor capital with the expertise of cash-short developers for the purpose of profits that neither could achieve otherwise. Corporate investors were enamored of the leverage and consequent high profits they could achieve in real estate ventures. The undercapitalized builders and developers were delighted to find financial partners who could back them. As of the mid-1970s, the joint-venture vehicle is more significant than ever, with not only domestic but also foreign corporations seeking competent partners to undertake real estate projects in the United States as well as in Europe and the Far East.

AN ALTERNATIVE TO MERGERS

The joint venture also emerged as the great prelude and alternative to mergers. A prelude because, by working through a few specific deals, a prospective acquirer and the builder would get a chance to know one another without undue exposure to risk before making the critical decision to merge. An alternative because, with many mergers failing, both builders and acquirers have discovered the joint venture as an instrument that permits them to take fullest advantage of one another's strengths while eliminating the weaknesses inherent in a more permanent association.

445

There can be many advantages to the corporate investor in going the joint-venture rather than the merger route. In the first place, he really gets the builder's incentive working for him. A builder who has been bought out, even at a handsome price, may or may not perform with enthusiasm and total commitment; but a builder working with you on a joint-venture basis has a reputation that is only as good as his last project: should he fail, he knows he does not face much of a future. The joint venture can also get the corporate investor a return on his capital faster than in any other aspect of real estate. Instead of staffing up, buying and zoning land, and drawing up plans over a two-to-three-year period — or making a great investment by buying a company — the joint-venture investor can usually take his pick from among the best "ready-to-go" packages in the country. By the joint-venture route he can spread his risk by investing in fairly short-term projects scattered over various markets. And if he knows what he's doing, he can run a whole series of such joint ventures with just a few men.

This arrangement makes many builders happier, too, freeing them from the constraints and strictures of an industrial-oriented management hierarchy that comes with so many mergers and letting them be their own bosses to run the business as they think best. Men like Ray Watt and Ben Deane, for example, make excellent joint-venture partners and are eagerly sought by corporate suitors though they did not find a corporate environment to their liking as merger partners. At least one other builder opted to maintain a continuing joint-venture relationship with a prospective acquirer instead of merging. This was Merrill Butler of Southern California's Butler-Harbour Homes who, after long discussions with San Francisco-based Foremost-McKesson (acquirer of two or three successful homebuilders), decided that both companies would be better served by a joint-venture relationship than by outright acquisition.

The joint-venture route is a prominent one for large landowners, too. In some situations, as with Irvine Ranch, all development is by joint venture; Irvine won't sell off lots to builders. (The procedure for getting a joint venture agreement from Irvine is like an elaborately rehearsed audition. The builders make an extensive formal presentation for which the company brass often assembles. If they pass the screen test, they're in.) The j-v is popular with large landholders because it enables them to generate greater profits than they would normally create from land sales alone. Their leverage is increased: if the market for housing goes soft, they can make it up on the land; if they become too heavily committed on land, they make it on the housing product. Several large landholding companies have, to be sure, gone on to start their own building companies after going in via joint venture first; it is certainly less profitable to split those profits with the builder. Among the recent companies going this route is Newhall Land &

Farming. But not all big landowners possess the experience or dedication that it takes to become a competent builder.

BUILDER JOINT VENTURES MULTIPLY

One of the more intense applications of the joint-venture concept, however, only began coming into its own with the advent of the Seventies. This is the use of the joint-venture format by major building and development firms to increase their sales volume (and earnings) beyond what the in-house management team can itself produce from its own development operations. A major, fast-growing organization can enhance its own performance considerably without getting top-heavy on management by taking on a number of joint ventures with selected smaller builders and developers in addition to its own activities. If it selects these ventures carefully, it solves the two key problems that big organizations inevitably run into as they try to maintain their growth curve: good management and good deals.

Ideally, in each instance the major picks an already-prepared development package offered to it by a smaller operator who is a reliable entrepreneur capable of developing the deal. The smaller builder/developer is committed to the success of the venture for the profit share he will receive from it; the major corporation thus gets the management it needs to handle the deal. By supplying the necessary financial backing plus whatever marketing help may be needed, and putting the smaller joint-venturer into a framework of sophisticated controls, the bigger builder can considerably enlarge his total volume of operations without building up his overhead or running into the chronic problem of getting good people.

One of the increasingly evident advantages of working with a small joint-venturing builder (particularly if you're a remote and mighty financial or superhousing corporation) is the local joint-venturer's ability to "front" for the big partner in a local market. With various problems relating to ecology and zoning increasingly critical, the local builder's store of community goodwill can be a priceless asset. Big multimarket developers have been learning from bitter experience that they are shunned or suspiciously greeted in many local markets as "the outsiders" or "the L.A. high-rollers" or "the New York boys." But in a joint venture where a local builder serves as local representation, it is quite often possible to get the zoning that an outside builder wouldn't be able to get. For example, Mike Towbes of Santa Barbara, California, has proven to be an outstanding example of what a small local developer can achieve. He has an excellent reputation in the community and the highest batting average of any developer for achieving rezoning in one of the most difficult counties in the state because he has proven himself to be reliable. All his projects are joint ventures with corporations or such individuals as Leo Rosen, formerly the head of Puritan Fashion Industries.

In my opinion, the number of joint ventures between such small, local builders with excellent reputations and major outside capital will be growing rapidly. Quite often it is the small builder of this type who has by far the keener sense of awareness and greater sensitivity than the large "outside" developer concerning local land prices, zoning, and community attitudes affecting development, not to mention marketing. Often such small builders can tie up all or nearly all the good parcels of land and then really capitalize on the entry of the majors into their markets.

There are new problems of development today that go well beyond the marketability of a project. They include zoning rollbacks (downgrading zoning to reduce development) and moratoria on development that can tie up precious capital. This problem is only exacerbated by the recently emerged oil crisis, heating up the "environment vs. development" battle to a new pitch as developers focus on higher-density housing closer to urban centers, while environmentalists fight to keep densities down. Many major companies hesitate to get involved in anything that will even remotely smack of controversy or uncertainty. So the smaller local-market developers will be filling an increasingly valuable role as their expert partners because they are close to the local scene and have the know-how to handle it.

In September 1972 a zoning rollback was announced for the entire sprawling city of Los Angeles, for example. To the extent that it needlessly stopped or slowed development, it was a frightening circumstance that made the builder's life precarious. In such situations it is the small local builder, with a strong local reputation and in good rapport with the local officials, who stands to get hurt least by this situation. Being trusted and having a reputation for credibility, he usually has a better chance of getting projects through where the larger builders get jammed up in red tape. The Los Angeles situation again focused more interest and emphasis on the role of the local builder as a joint-venture partner.

A good example of a joint venture between a larger and a smaller building organization was the investment of ALODEX Corporation of Memphis in William Bone Company's 24-acre, $10 million Deep Well Ranch condominium project in Palm Springs, California. Thirty-year-old Bill Bone, a Harvard MBA and second-generation builder, runs one of the sharpest development firms in Southern California. He turned in sales of $15 million in 1971 and projected $25 million for 1972 from his overall operations. In addition to builder-investors like ALODEX, he has co-venturers who include U.S. Gypsum, John Hancock Life Insurance, as well as the president and chairman of the board of Holiday Inns. But Bone himself learned the definition of moratorium at first hand in one unfortunate instance. Developing Benedict Hills, a luxury project in the lush Benedict Canyon area of Los Angeles, he ran across a court ruling forbidding his heavy equipment to cross a public roadway. Thus his project was obstructed and he had a serious problem on his hands for a while, complicated by a bad market.

Many homebuilding firms have taken the principle of joint-venture operation to substantial lengths. Outfits like Weyerhaeuser have set up subsidiaries to pursue joint ventures. Many other big organizations, while not heavily committed to the joint venture as a primary source of profits, are finding themselves steering in this direction. Edwin N. Homer, president of Chrysler Realty, runs a company that as of 1970 invested $2 million to $4 million a week in real estate. He typified the attitude of many major developers in preferring the joint-venture route to the creation of a super-giant housing corporation. Said Homer: "It is not possible for a manufacturer to build a real estate operation by itself. We look for established builders where we will both benefit by having our names together."

Homer's formulation of the assistance that a major developer can provide to a smaller co-venturer is representative of all such joint-venture efforts, and is worth restating here as he first described it to *House & Home*:

"Our 150 employees bring expertise in financial planning and control, engineering supervision, purchasing, legal taxes, public relations and advertising. We can provide equity capital and help a developer arrange the financing of large projects. Because the projects are large, a developer who works with us can achieve economies of scale.

"The builder who works with us can supplement his own organization by calling on our management resources. For example, we have applied the same computerized-systems approach to some of our real estate projects that our manufacturing organization has used in building automobiles. Usually, on a project — whether it be joint-venture or completely our own — we become involved in financing, have our own engineer supervising the job, process all construction payments and handle all purchasing. In other words, we act as developers taking an active part and not as passive lenders."

The implications of a widespread use of the joint venture are manifold. First, because it solves the two major problems of big organizations — the supply of good local management and/or the supply of good deals — the joint-venture format can permit a company to grow far beyond the size it could attain on its own. It's the optimum decentralized operation, with profit-motivated local entrepreneurs, who know their own markets inside out, making key operating decisions within a control framework provided by the "big brother" partner. Theoretically, a major company could expand into a gigantic, nationwide network of joint-venture arrangements without the same risk of losing control that it would face if it attempted to grow to a comparable size by expanding its own management internally.

The second implication is that corporate investors looking for joint-venture deals with builders and developers are running into much more competition. A few years ago they were all alone in the field with their equity capital; today, they're competing with several dozen major building organizations who are also looking for the same joint-venture deals. This brings up the old truism of the building industry that although money is tight, there is always more money than good deals. More outside capital flowing into this industry finds fewer qualified builders to joint-venture with, as the industry streamlines and consolidates. Prompted by competitive pressures, it's going to be easier to make a mistake by taking the marginal deal or going with the marginal builder.

The third implication is that with the broader use of the joint venture, we are again back to asserting the ultimate dependency of this industry on the smaller builder-developer. Despite all the consolidating tendencies of this business, it is still a business that depends on a knowledge of local markets and local expertise. The industry's age of evolving giantism is paradoxically founded, in part, on the continued survival of the smaller operator working in a large skein of joint-venture relationships. The competent smaller operator may strengthen himself by means of a congeneric merger, but he need not have concerns about his future. He is increasingly in demand. And, as it takes a strong share of the equity in a project (roughly 50%) to motivate him to perform successfully, he is not going to come cheap.

For a while, a second group of major joint-venturing housing companies arose, which gave the smaller builder-developer another whole dimension of joint-venture options. These were the manufacturers of modular housing, who began turning to a direct role in development to assure themselves of a market for their product. Modular Housing Systems of Northumberland, Pennsylvania, for example, operated a joint-venturing company to assist sales of its modular units by co-venturing on deals. Another firm of this type was Diversified Communities of Newport Beach, California, formed as a joint-venturing operation to assist the marketing of homes produced by Fleetwood Enterprises. However, the modular housing shakeout pretty much ended this idea, also driving Modular Housing Systems into bankruptcy.

Joint-venture deals are not without their risks, of course. No matter how good the deal looks, every estimate of profits depends entirely on the builder's reliability. You can cut down the unpredictability by choosing a builder with a sterling track record, but ultimately you don't know how good your venture will be until after you've committed your capital. One way in which a number of deals have gone bad is that the investor goes in on a project that either is too big or takes too long to complete. Projects always have a way of growing beyond the planned completion date; it is better to pick small deals and realize that they might take longer than anticipated than to go after a big one that will stretch beyond all expectations and result in heavy expenditures in carrying costs. A long-term project also exposes the venturers to uncertainties of future market conditions and economic factors, whereas a quick in-and-out deal of a year, or at most two, minimizes such risks. Land development projects almost invariably pay off, for example, but the trick is to get them to pay off in the expected period of time or suffer a lower return on investment. The builder or developer isn't always at fault: many joint-venture deals go bad because the investor doesn't know enough to keep his nose out of the entrepreneur's decisions and overrules him on key issues. The best rule is to get yourself a real estate expert in analyzing and setting up the controls for joint-ventures, let him handle the whole show; once he has approved a project, he should know enough to monitor the project passively without unnecessarily injecting himself into the builder's operation.

First-rate experience is worth far more than gold to a corporate investor getting into real estate. I am often shocked by the methods that sophisticated companies resort to in buying land, sometimes paying all cash and/or exorbitant interest rates. It is all too common. For example, it is my opinion that Shelter Group of Southwest Forest Industries overpaid for a parcel of land in Phoenix a few years ago. They bought nearly two sections, not only overpaying but also purchasing on terms that were a dream for the seller and a nightmare for the buyer. As another example, a major oil company I've worked with bought several sections of land and overpaid by *at least* several thousand dollars per acre; and it was an all-cash deal, to boot! In this case the buyer lost whatever bargaining position he might have had because his name was also disclosed to the seller.

There is no better financing available than from the landholder who finances the sale of his land. When the seller finances the purchase, the knowledgeable buyer has a good chance of getting both a longer repayment term and a lower interest rate than he can get from any financial institution. When you borrow from banking sources you sign corporately and take responsibility for payment in full with no flexibility; if you buy right from a landowner and get him to finance the purchase, your flexibility can be far greater. For example, buying 3,000 acres at $7,000 per acre you might be able to negotiate a fifteen- or twenty-year payment term — certainly better than you could do at a bank. The only time to finance an acquisition through a bank is when it offers a tremendous price advantage that will more than offset any inherent risks and you can't make a better deal with the landowner. In any event, economic and marketing considerations — *not* buyer competition — should dictate the deal that is made. Too often, this is not the case.

The major non-housing corporations are primarily the only remaining buyers of large land parcels, and they are the ones who often need real help in making such acquisitions. The big builders don't as a rule want large positions in land anymore; they've shifted to more frequent acquisitions of smaller parcels to hype up their turnover. This situation leaves the field wide open for some bad bargaining on the big acreage. Most major acquisitions are properties that lay dormant on the market for years without a buyer; when they're bought up it's because the timing is right for development, if the deal is perceived soundly. But the big buyers, while they will often fight hard to establish the critically right price on a small parcel of land, lose their judgment on the large purchases. They overpay and think they got a bargain because the average price per acre tends to be low (compared with small-parcel prices) on large parcels. They overlook the fact that the tremendous costs of carrying the large parcel, as well as the cost of development loans and front-end outlays for amenities, can eat up their imagined price advantage. There's no substitute for good, hard bargaining when making a major land acquisition. Every dollar saved (or longer terms gained) eases the load of the subsequent carrying and development costs. But in no case is there ever a justification for overpaying in the first place.

It's overpayment on the land that leads to shenanigans and problems with it down the line. I admit that certain big builders I know have been just as guilty of this (if not more so) as anybody else. Overpaying for a large parcel, they master-plan it and assign various values to the component parcels — some of the values utterly unrealistic and nowhere near what the market will pay. One Southern California builder who resorted to this device thus achieved a very low lot cost for the parcels assigned to single-family development; to compensate, he assigned an exorbitant value to commercial and multifamily properties marked for development in future years. The houses sold well, but when they were gone the remaining land was priced completely out of sight and eventually had to be written down drastically. So the net result of this affair was zero — or less than zero — profits. It's trick mirrors like this that one must watch for. A corporate purchaser shouldn't be afraid to bring in an outside consultant to determine the feasibility of the land acquisition. Not to recommend myself, but too often I've been called in only after the fact, and at that point it was like operating on a terminal patient.

Every acquisition should be thoroughly analyzed in light of market demand for housing. The most capable developer can become arbitrarily optimistic or pessimistic concerning the market area and the particular land deal. In-house research is very important but in the case of major decisions it should be tempered by outside judgment to corroborate or correct it — it is well worth the cost in either instance. There are a number of first-rate consultants in the land acquisition business around the nation; but make sure you get one who really knows the business and is not riding on a wave of hot air and firewater — a public relations image instead of performance. I was recently called in to consult on a major land purchase and the market planning of it for a condominum project. The client, as it happens, was a certain major railroad and had started off the project with another group of consultants. The head of the consulting group was a real *maven* (Yiddish for the man who happens to play golf with the president of the client company). Unfortunately, the consultant's experience had been limited to industrial properties and high-rise buildings, while the railroad's project consisted of low-rise condos and apartments. To remedy this defect of knowledge, the maven called in other mavens of his acquaintance, and they called in still others. Thus when I was finally called in to clean it all up, I met a never-ending chain consisting of the entire membership of the maven's club, his lenders, and the chairman of his church building fund. That is no way to run a railroad. In this case my advice went unheeded and a major writedown of the land was decided upon. I might add that a number one maven got an exclusive to sell the written-down land package. I have often told smaller builders not to be mesmerized by polish or bigness as a criterion of expertise. The sophisticated corporate investor needs to be reminded of a similar point. Don't be mesmerized by your consultant's social veneer or his country club membership; it is not necessarily concomitant with the talent you need to get your real estate project handled right.

Some of the smaller builder/developers make excellent joint-venturers on corporate land and can often provide sound local marketing judgment. They do not always appear polished but some of them have incredibly larger statements of net worth for their efforts than the operators of the giant building companies that went belly-up. And in a joint venture they pay far greater attention to detail because each project means far more to them than to a big multimarket developer. They're committed to their locale and reputation, and thus to successful performance. One relatively small developer who has worked his way to great success is Arnold Stubblefield of San Bernardino, California. An unassuming, resourceful man, he has piled up a greater net worth than most of the big builders had before they converted via merger or the public market. His type is not unique in this business.

"PERMANENT" JOINT VENTURES ON THE RISE?

Because builder-partners of proven performance are in demand (and because mergers between builders and non-housing corporations have not always worked), we have also been seeing the first significant stirrings of another significant trend in the industry: major corporations have begun locking up long-term relationships with successful builders either by the mechanism of the "ongoing joint venture" or by becoming something like limited partners through passive investment in successful building firms. In both instances, the builder remains his own boss and retains the incentive to perform to the best of his efforts. The Los Angeles-based Loew's/Snyder partnership was one example of a diversified corporation pumping equity funds on an ongoing project-by-project basis into a successful building operation, and will be discussed in more detail elsewhere. Another ongoing joint venture has been the relationship between Justus Enterprises of Indianapolis and Browning-Scott of Nashville, turning out highly successful apartments for the "senior citizen submarket" in a number of Southeastern cities. (Walter Justus, who turned thirty in 1972, has been building for eight years and holds 2,350 units in Indianapolis alone.)

The investment deal that Dick Wasserman and Dick Bernhardt made with Gulf & Western will also be growing as a type. The conglomerate became a 50% owner and passive investor in their Richards Group for an investment of $10 million, illustrating the passive investment type of "partnership." Boston's Alpha Industries, way back in 1969, bought a minority interest in Curtis F. Peterson's Briston Corporation of Tacoma, Washington. Gulf Oil is another corporation that made a similar investment in the Pittsburgh-based apartment-building firm of Mathews-Phillips, Inc. In 1971 they paid more than $4 million for a 45% passive ownership in the company. The two builders, Gordon Mathews and Howard Phillips, have been turning out about 1,000 apartment units a year, and many of them on a joint-venture basis with companies like ALCOA and Chrysler Corporation. Their formula is to conceive and create the project, including design and zoning, and then take it to the co-venturer, giving up 50% of the action for the capital requirement. Nothing in Mathews-Phillips's agreement with Gulf prevents either party from forming joint ventures with any other party, and both companies take on deals of their own in addition to their own relationship.

A WORD ON FINANCIAL CO-VENTURERS

Of course, this sort of survey cannot begin to do justice to the full variety of the joint-venture's uses. It is, for one thing, the principal route of most financial and institutional investors to real estate profits. The nation's major insurance firms have used the joint-venture vehicle extensively. The joint venture is the key mechanism by which the fast-rising savings and loan service corporations (essentially, S&L holding companies) are getting into direct development. During 1971, for example, a joint venture between High Point Development Corporation, a subsidiary of Building and Land Technology Corporation, and Unisave Service Corporation, a service corporation established by twelve of New Jersey's federally chartered S&L's, resulted in a 320-unit condominium project in Lakewood, New Jersey. It was the first such venture for an S&L service corporation in that populous eastern state, but such deals are common in California. Great Western S&L, for example, is very active in the San Diego market. In Chicago, a joint-venture was formed between New Vistas, a real estate firm, and Allstate Insurance to redevelop 100 acres of inner city with near-luxury housing.

Some builders are so pleased with S&L joint ventures that they are calling them the wave of the future. The new S&L service corporations were rapidly emerging as building partners, taking advantage of changes in federal regulations that permit them to utilize up to 1% of their assets for ventures and loans not permitted to S&L's formerly. The service corporations can provide the joint-venturing builder with front-end money as well as short- and long-term financing and a guaranteed builder's fee. They may even identify the deal for the builder.

Here's a typical S&L/builder joint venture for a condominium project negotiated by a New Jersey institution in 1973. The S&L, a state-chartered institution, arranged for construction financing with a federally chartered S&L for 8.5%. The builder's contribution to the $2.25 million project consisted of the land, which was acquired by providing the original owner with a percentage of the profit. Cash investment was zero. The S&L service corporation's investment was $200,000 for 50% of the ownership. The builder received a developer's fee (guarantee for non-construction activities) of $125,000. Institutional presence in the venture helped to secure beach privileges for the project at a nearby beach and reduced bond prices to a minimum level. In addition, normal condo holdback (delay of financing until a certain number of units are sold) was waived. The service corporation received a finance fee of about four points or $88,000. The profit for the condo development came to $1.2 million and was divided as follows: The original owner of the land got 25% or $300,000; the builder, a 37½% owner, got $450,000; and the S&L service corporation, also a 37½% partner, got the remaining $450,000.

Many of the financial co-venturers err on the side of excessive conservatism in the ventures they pursue. This industry literally begs for innovation, and there are many market gaps to be identified through perceptive and creative research, even in the most saturated markets. McKeon was selling a lot of product for a long time before the industry woke up and realized that he had identified a gigantic gap in the market for low-priced housing. There are all kinds of opportunities waiting out there for the firm that is willing to invest the time to ferret them out and to trust good logic and good research. There is so little innovation, so fantastically much copying in this industry that I never cease to be astonished — particularly because only a *bit* of fresh perception and imaginative analysis will almost always yield a greater reward. Too many builders work on a sheer stimulus-response basis — doing only what is "tried and true" — and even the innovators become guilty of the worst kind of imitation — imitating themselves. A continually fresh perception of the everchanging marketplace brings to light continually new housing needs and thus new and better opportunities for profit.

Another error too frequently encountered is basically one of belief — the belief that if you have enough money you can overcome all the problems of any joint-venture project. Things don't work out this way. A bad deal will be just as bad later in time, and to think that time will make it better indicates a badly managed development company. There are just too many really fine opportunities existing today to justify the statement that the stockholders' grandchildren may expect some profits out of a bad project that one is committed to unreasonably. Notwithstanding, bad deals continue to be made. Some of the properties acquired are not to be believed. One highest-and-best-use study that I performed on a high-priced chunk of land discovered that the property's highest and best use was to hold the world together.

And a number of financial and financial service companies with subsidiaries already in the building field do a land-office business by financing further joint ventures. Among these is Milwaukee-based MGIC Financial Corporation, a subsidiary of MGIC Investment Corporation, which has entered into multitudinous deals such as its co-venture with Varient Investments of Whittier, California, for a 180-unit garden apartment complex in Newport Beach. At the same time another of MGIC's subsidiaries, MGIC-Janis Properties, was in one of its many joint-ventures — this one with First Realty Investment Corporation, of Miami Beach, Florida, for the development and operation of two golf courses and a country-club complex on an 1,100-acre Sunset Lakes project in Dade County, Florida. First Realty Investment, for that matter, has been one of the big joint-venturing companies in its own right.

Formed in 1969 by the founders of First Mortgage Investors, the biggest real estate investment trust, FRI tied into a single package both development skills and equity and mortgage finance capability. The company has worked on improving internal development capability through acquisitions of successful developers, but has been doing about ten joint-venture deals each year. One of its unique distinctions from other financial houses is FRI's access, via First Mortgage Investors, to a source of mortgage funds. Said one of its officers: "If a deal comes in with a sizable equity requirement, FRI can restructure the deal to diminish this equity requirement because of our mortgage capability." FRI also felt that it operated with greater flexibility in joint-venture arrangements than some financial organizations. One organization, for example, provides all the equity in a deal but demands it back in full before any division of profits and offers no guarantee of additional financing if the builder gets caught in a cost squeeze; but "not so with FRI."

FRI created many of its own joint-venture situations by searching out the need for a product and then filling it by putting together the capital and skills needed. In 1970 the company also acquired, among other organizations, the firm of Johnson-Loggins, Inc., which was engaged in ten joint ventures with mortgage banking firms, public corporations or capital investment groups in and around the city of Houston. This subsidiary substantially expanded FRI's joint-venture and development capability. Largest of the Johnson-Loggins joint ventures is a 4,300-acre new-town development undertaken in partnership with a subsidiary of Ideal Basic Industries and incorporating three subdivisions in separate price ranges, apartment complexes, commercial structures and an office park complex. Another project involved Johnson-Loggins as development contractor for a 656-acre residential project known as Cypresswood, owned by a subsidiary of Humble Oil & Refining Co.

THE JOINT VENTURE ALSO UNITES
COMPLEMENTARY TALENTS

One very important use of the joint-venture vehicle is not just a pairing of money and talent but of complementary talents. A perfect example of this was Kaufman & Broad's bringing in the perfectionist, Los Angeles-based luxury apartment builders, Ring Brothers (subsidiary of Monogram Industries), to develop an 800-unit, $15 million apartment project in northwest suburban Chicago. Kaufman & Broad had the expertise as a high-volume housing producer, but Seldin Ring was the man with the track record for the type of apartments K&B envisioned. In this case, K&B wanted the Rings' talent enough to give them 25% of the action for their development guidance while it put up both the land and the equity financing. The project was developed through a subsidiary, Barrington Properties, 75%-owned by K&B and 25%-owned by Ring Brothers. This sort of cooperation is very prevalent in the building industry, and not just for apartments. Often, you get a situation where one entity controls the land, another has the packaging and development expertise and a third has the financing; they combine in a three-way joint venture to make a deal go.

The pooling of talents and monies can be on a pretty gigantic scale. Witness the formation of the Kaiser-Aetna partnership in 1969 with a net worth of $160 million for openers, and including seven operating projects covering 100,000 acres. It may be stretching the definition to call this a mere joint venture, but it does qualify if we view it as an association of unrelated entities for a specific profit objective. Aetna Life & Casualty of Hartford, Connecticut, owns 50% and Kaiser Aluminum & Chemical owns the other 50% (a third partner, Kaiser Industries, was originally in for 38% but sold its share in a stock swap to the other Kaiser firm). The Kaiser Companies brought to the partnership their 66% interest in the 87,500-acre Rancho California, situated south of Los Angeles. They also contributed Hawaii-Kai, a 6,000-acre resort complex in Honolulu; Aliso Ranch, a 6,000-acre farm near Fresno, California, and Port Westward, an 835-acre industrial development near Portland, Oregon. Aetna threw the 630-acre Warner Ranch in San Fernando Valley near Los Angeles into the deal for industrial and residential development, plus industrial parks near Santa Clara and San Diego, California.

One of the new partnership's first acts was to buy out the remaining one-third interest of Rancho California from Macco Corporation (see Chapter 15) for $19 million cash. And it began expanding into a welter of real estate activities: agricultural, commercial, industrial, residential and recreational land development throughout the United States. Subsequently, the Kaiser-Aetna partnership itself got into the acquisition business, picking up several builders. By 1971 it had projects totaling 190,000 acres in the Western United States, Hawaii and Guam. And it was operating three divisions specializing in residential construction in California: Mackay Homes, Ponderosa Homes and Northern California Shelter Division.

About this time the Kaiser-Aetna partnership formed still one more partnership relationship with another developer, the Dallas-based I. C. Deal Companies. Deal had been acquired earlier by Great Southwest as part of the same expansion phase into residential development that saw the expansion of GSW's subsidiary, Macco. But when GSW's parent, the Pennsylvania Company, went into bankruptcy Deal's construction operations were suspended. Fortunately, Irv Deal — a superb developer of apartment complexes with market appeal — was able to disengage himself and later to join up with the Kaiser-Aetna giant. Deal's partnership was named Kaiser Aetna Texas and swung into the development of residential and commercial projects in Dallas, Houston and in the Lake Tahoe area. The partnership essentially amounts to another example of the on-going joint-venture relationship mentioned above.

CAN YOU MERGE YOUR WAY INTO A
JOINT VENTURE?

Big corporations often make willing partners for independent developers of big master planned projects where the potential return on investment is large enough to offset the risk of longer exposure. This is particularly true in cases where profits flow not only from construction and sales but also from the greatly higher values that successful rezoning of land can achieve. A good developer can raise the market value of land by perhaps 400% or more, taking a rough figure, by assembling enough property through options and then providing an integrated development plan on the basis of which the overall parcel is successfully rezoned. The co-venturing corporation thus makes a profit not only on the construction and marketing, but also a handsome markup on the revalued land designated for commercial, industrial and residential uses.

In some instances this sort of joint venture is actually handled as a *merger* because of favorable tax consequences to the developer and the corporation's ability to use its stock to make a deal with him. Once the developer has lined up his properties on options, has provided the master plan, and has successfully achieved the desired rezoning or can satisfactorily demonstrate that it can be achieved, he organizes a new corporation with the land options as its assets. He nails down the specifics of the entire development program including permits, final plans and costs for the first section, as well as developing detailed projections of cash flows and profits over the life of the program. A corporate investor buys the new corporation under a corporate reorganization on a stock-for-stock basis, trading its stock for the stock of the developer's entity. The value of the stock the developer ultimately gets is approximately half the total projected profit from the project to be developed, because as a rule these are earnout situations. But his stock comes in two installments. He gets about half of it at the outset, while the other half is put into escrow and is delivered to him in three to five years if the project lives up to its profit expectations.

The transaction is handled in all ways exactly like any other merger. For its part, the acquirer (corporate joint-venturer) requires certified statements of the developer's past performance and a good reputation; the developer must provide able second-level management and sign a non-compete agreement. For his part, the developer negotiates a financial commitment (whether direct investment or financing guarantees) sufficient to complete the project, plus an employment contract that puts him on salary for the duration of the venture. Since, as in any merger, the stock the developer gets is restricted investment stock, he must also negotiate for the right to dispose of up to 25% of the shares he initially receives by having the company register that number of shares (preferably at its own expense), plus the right to piggyback on other company registrations subsequently. The advantage of this format over a straight joint venture is that it permits the developer to make more money on the real estate deal because his profit (now converted into stock) is taxed at the lower long-term capital gains rate when he sells the stock instead of at the higher ordinary income rate that he'd pay on a cash profit flowing from a joint venture.

Major land development projects, so often called "new towns," are, of course, classically undertaken by joint ventures between capital-rich corporate investors and talented building entrepreneurs. Many of these have been cited in Chapter II. One example is the $250 million New Century Town located thirty miles north of Chicago and undertaken jointly by Sears, Roebuck & Company and Mafco, Inc. (a subsidiary of Marshall Field & Company), the two merchandising giants, which came in as financial partners, and Urban Investment and Development Company (another subsidiary of Aetna Life & Casualty), which came in as the developer. The Marshall Field and Aetna Life subsidiaries also in 1970 formed a joint venture for the development of a $60 million urban complex in Chicago. It's actually been a very long-range relationship between them: Aetna's subsidiary, UI&D, is operated by Philip M. Klutznick, and in 1955 — long before he joined Aetna — he had teamed up with Marshall Field & Company for the development of Park Forest, south of Chicago, one of the earliest postwar large-scale communities.

(The big land developers, such as Kaiser-Aetna and the Sears-Mafco-UI&D team, often concentrate on land development and sell off finished lots, as well as undertaking considerable construction on their own; but they also often farm out residential building to smaller builders on a joint-venture basis. This factor accounts for another large stratum of joint-venture activity in the building industry. Examples of such arrangements in new towns like Reston, Columbia, Westlake Village and Valencia have been numerous.)

JOINT VENTURES TO DEVELOP SURPLUS CORPORATE LAND

Joint ventures are formed between corporations and developer-entrepreneurs not only for the purpose of developing new properties but also to develop surplus properties held by the co-venturing corporation. Oil, timber, railroad, and manufacturing corporations with large land holdings have often gone the joint-venture route to translate their excess lands into profits. The structure of such co-ventures varies enormously depending on the specific requirements and tax ramifications of each deal, but it might be interesting to illustrate the procedure followed by one corporate venturer we have worked with in accomplishing one specific deal. The company is a real estate subsidiary of a major oil company, originally formed for the purpose of developing higher uses for the oil company's vast land holdings on the West Coast. The particular joint venture was undertaken in corporate form, for the development of surplus property, and it followed this format:

1. "Pre-incorporation agreement." Parties agreed to form a new 50-50 owned corporation for the purpose of acquiring from Standard all or a portion of the remaining 185 acres within Section _____ and developing such property for industrial and commercial purposes.

   A. Attached to the pre-incorporation agreement were the articles of incorporation, form of bylaws and form of minutes of first meeting of board of directors.

   B. A "project plan" was also attached. This Project Plan was adopted by the new corporation and recited in general development plans, sales plans, project objectives, financing methods, and the scope of operation for the new corporation to be administered jointly by Chevron Land and its joint-venture partner.

   C. A "land development agreement" was also attached. This agreement was executed by the new corporation, between Chevron and its joint-venturer (or in other cases between the two of them and a third party who possessed the necessary expertise). Under this agreement the joint-venturer or third party agrees to assume functional responsibility at cost plus overhead and administrative fee (and, in the case of a third party, some reasonable profit) for certain items. These may include services, labor, materials and equipment required for planning, zoning, improving, as well as building and marketing any industrial or commercial facilities constructed on the property.

   D. An "exchange agreement" was also attached. This agreement was executed by the new corporation and the oil company's real estate subsidiary, whereby the parties agreed to the terms and conditions under which acreage owned by Standard was to be exchanged for certain properties acquired for this purpose by the new corporation at its sole cost and conveyed to Standard.

   E. The pre-incorporation agreement stipulated the amount of stock to be subscribed for by the two parties. (This might be a nominal amount initially, but the total stock subscription must be accomplished prior to the acquisition of the first parcel from Standard pursuant to the exchange agreement and should amount to at least 25% of the exchange value of such a parcel.)

  F. The pre-incorporation agreement also stipulated any conditions to be negotiated between the parties which established a basis for abandonment of the project and dissolution of the new corporation (for example, zoning conditions).

2. Formation of new corporation. Parties formed the corporation pursuant to the pre-incorporation agreement.

3. On fulfillment of these conditions referred to in item 1-F above, the new corporation adopted the project plan, executed the exchange agreement with the oil company, and executed the land development agreement with the joint-venturer (or a third party brought into the venture in other instances, as outlined in item 1-C).

THE REAL ESTATE PROFITS OF CORPORATE GROWTH

Growing corporations also have a particular potential to develop and exploit creative joint-venture opportunities in real estate that are tied to their own expansion. Many of these potentials are still not being tapped nearly as well as they might be. For years I have watched one industrial firm or another plan and develop a new plant or factory in a new location without paying attention to the effect of such commercial or industrial development on surrounding real estate values. It is almost axiomatic that by such industrial development the expanding company creates more profits for other real estate entrepreneurs and speculators than it will ever make from its new plant alone.

Walt Disney Enterprises learned this lesson when the late Walt Disney and his brother Roy first developed the hugely successful Disneyland in Anaheim in Orange County, California, in 1955. The 230-acre amusement park, drawing some ten million visitors a year, set off a major real estate and development boom in the Anaheim vicinity, which resulted in countless millions in profits for speculators and developers. The Disneys, who were responsible for this fountain of wealth through their own daring and imaginative entrepreneurial efforts (they hocked themselves up to the eyeballs to finance the project, even borrowing on life insurance) not only did not get a penny of all those profits, but were also dismayed at the unplanned, helter-skelter development that soon hemmed in Disneyland from every side. They were later to say that they had made "one major mistake . . . : The company did not control the development of the property surrounding this great tourist magnet."

The Disneys learned well and corrected their error. When they began planning the East Coast super-equivalent of Disneyland — the $400-million complex called Walt Disney World, near Orlando, Florida — they tied up no less than 27,400 acres, or about 120 times the amount of property used in the California project. Of this amount, the actual Disney World Park and attendant hotel-motel and service facilities occupy only about 800 acres. The rest of the property has been attractively master-planned for coordinated commercial, industrial and residential development; the parcels are either sold off or joint-ventured with droves of small and not-so-small commercial and residential builders and developers. Land values, maximized by good planning, have leaped tremendously: from $700 per acre to as much as $4,000; $8,000; $15,000; and $60,000 per acre, or more, depending on the land use. The Disney company is also developing much of the property directly through its Buena Vista Construction subsidiary, a major organization in its own right with some 4,000 employees. Disney World opened successfully in October of 1971, expecting at least a third of Florida's yearly flow of 20 million tourists to visit. And the Disney company has this time reaped for itself the great fortune from the rapidly appreciating land values surrounding the park.

It doesn't have to be on the same scale, but any expanding corporation planning new commercial or industrial development can profitably borrow the Disney technique. Neither does it take extensive in-house expertise; development consultants skilled in real estate dynamics, market and economic analysis and project packaging can be retained on a consulting or co-venturing basis. The object would be to analyze the probable impact of the new plant or facility on surrounding real estate values and on the local economic base, and to estimate the optimal course for the maximization and exploitation of those values in light of the highest and best uses defined for the surrounding real estate once the facility is in place. Having a clear picture of the probable values and uses of properties adjacent to the proposed plant, the corporation has several courses of action available to it. At a minimum, such properties can be tied up on option at a low price and sold at a substantial profit when they have appreciated in value after the facility is in place: the prices fetched are always highest when an exact use for the property is defined and the right user is located. Or the corporation may wish to share in the further profits of development of such appreciated properties. It's worth remembering that a company moving into a new area is usually the recipient of much good feeling because of its expected economic impact. Its leverage gives it the power to get rezoning approvals that others wouldn't always get. But it should use that goodwill early on, while it is still being courted; good feelings often turn sour when the company has been in town awhile.

To handle this type of project, the company could organize a joint venture with a competent co-venturer who can credibly establish the feasibility and market potential of such development, package the properties and oversee their completion. The corporation can invest its own equity capital in such development or, with the assistance of its co-venturer, locate and introduce another financial partner into the joint-venture to fund the development of the project or projects. Such an approach can result not only in a maximum financial reward but also in an aesthetic one; it eliminates haphazard land use and helter-skelter building, creating through expert advance planning an orderly and attractive environment in the vicinity of the new facility.

VARIATION ON A THEME

A variant of this technique permits a corporation to speculate successfully on rising real estate values by joint-venturing with a builder/developer in such speculation. The key to the success of this type of deal is the builder's own development activity, which raises the values of surrounding real estate. In such a joint-venture effort, the investing corporation coordinates its land acquisition activities with the builder's development plans, buying up cheaply properties which are immediately adjacent to a proposed major development program that is still unknown to the world at large. The development of, say, a 1,000-unit apartment complex, immediately raises the value of surrounding properties. The joint-venturers then may sell off the properties and split the profits.

A developer, no matter how successful, can occasionally use a joint-venturer who has the capital to invest in this type of land acquisition in order to control the full profit potentials of a major parcel of undeveloped real estate. A 1,000-unit apartment complex located near a major freeway intersection, for example, creates a further potential in the same area for an office park, a light industrial plant, service stations, a shopping center, and further apartment development. Land values thus rise proportionately in the aftermath of the first successful project (the apartment complex). In a joint venture, to take advantage of this appreciation in value, the developer would normally handle the negotiations for the purchase and resale of land while the investor puts up the capital necessary to tie up the properties on option or buy them. The corporation's share of profits can amount to a return of several hundred percent of its investment. Of course, the success of the speculation depends very much on a *good* initial project and a continuing strong local market, plus factors such as availability of the right zoning. But it's hard for the co-venturer to actually lose the money (other than on small options) that he puts into real estate; at worst, he's stuck with a non-liquid asset for a while. As in the earlier example, to be sure, the co-venturer also has the option of entering into direct development of the appreciated properties for further profits, instead of selling them.

JOINT VENTURES IN LAND PACKAGING

The emergence of multimarket homebuilding firms that operate under the pressure of handling more and more successful projects to support their rising sales curves creates a further opportunity for corporate investors in land packaging. The major builders do not always have adequate staff to explore market opportunities in various local markets in as much detail as they would like. And it is not feasible for them to accumulate large land inventories because of the heavy carrying costs. Carrying a lot of unzoned land for future development is also dangerous these days for another reason: the increased effectiveness of conservationist and ecological groups in blocking rezoning applications. A builder buying a big chunk of land on the assumption of future profits from rezoning faces the hazard of a considerable loss if his application fails (and I've known of several to whom exactly this happened). So a builder is going to try to pass on the zoning risk to someone else if he can and pay more for a property already zoned. As a result of these factors, the big builders are nearly always under pressure of operating on a very short-term basis: locating new markets, defining the need for some successful housing product in such markets, locating and acquiring land that will meet market criteria, and (when they buy new land) rushing the land through planning, zoning and development stages.

It especially needs to be stressed that today the entire zoning problem has become exceedingly complex and the achievement of desired rezoning can in no way be taken for granted. This factor, arising with increasingly activist communities fighting tooth and nail against encroaching development, has contributed to builders' unwillingness to hold land. Not only is rezoning more difficult to get, even existing zoning may be disallowed. It has happened in many instances, including that of Don Scholz. This has never been truer than today when the thrust of development is headed inward toward the city as a result of higher gasoline costs and already-crowded communities resist further development. Prior assurances from politicians and even the passage of zoning ordinances no longer count. The definition of a local political leader is one who holds office by popular vote; and when he sees crowds of protesters in his office, his assurances to the builder vanish.

For those developers who have to continue buying land, my suggestion is to reduce your risk wherever possible by providing for adequate contingency clauses offering escape from the deal or a penalty price reduction in the event the required zoning is not achieved or if existing or newly achieved rezoning is rolled back. The idea is to get the seller to share as much of the risk as possible. Healthy profits on land acquisition are still possible if the land is attractively priced relative to its current zoning and the chance of getting upgraded zoning is an opportunity to land a windfall profit instead of merely breaking even. The real danger comes of buying property whose seller anticipates rezoning and prices it accordingly. In such instances he should take as much of the risk as the builder can pass on to him. It is not surprising, with all these factors to consider, that the big, high-volume developers are not always happy to carry a lot of land.

It is at this point that the person generally called a land packager steps in, meeting the builder's need for land by presenting him with properties which have already been zoned and in some cases developed for utilities, lots and roads. He offers what he's got to the builder, and if it more or less meets the builder's cost criteria he buys it and works out his own building and marketing program. He forgoes much of the profit on the land itself by paying a premium for land already zoned. But this is worth it to him because it spares him carrying costs (enabling him to increase the turnover of his working capital) and still lets him make a profit on the construction and sale of homes. The packager makes most of his profit from the rezoned value of the land. At least one public company, New Jersey's Building and Land Technology Corporation, does this type of work. FRI of Miami successfully joint-ventured with a group of young Denver businessmen on a similar deal, and they created millions of dollars in added values by tying up and rezoning various parcels.

Actually, what is termed "packaging" is very loosely defined and changes depending on whom you talk to. It can range from the sheerest speculation in land to a pretty sophisticated process based on zoning, financing, marketing and development skills. One form of packaging is called *land banking*. A realtor or developer or builder or investor acquires property he feels may be in the path of development and plans and rezones it, raising its value. He then flips it over to a limited partnership group which holds the property for a two- to five-year period for a guaranteed fixed return. At the right time, the land is sold to a builder who is now hot to go with the development of the parcel. If the builder is the one who set up the limited partnership (like Don Scholz), he makes most of the profits showing from appreciated land value; if it was any non-building investor who set up the deal, he's the one to take those profits, leaving the builder to make money only from the construction and sale of homes.

There's nothing new about land speculation or even packaging: Alexander Hamilton was packaging and speculating in properties in western New York in 1801; George Washington earlier reaped profits from subdividing land in Virginia. But none of the approaches I have seen over time truly taps the full profit potentials of packaging as they might be exploited on a timely, market-oriented, national basis; each program has some limitation. In some instances, land is rezoned speculatively without a sound regard for thorough market research to demonstrate the marketability of the property. In other cases the rezoning may not achieve the property's best use. Frequently, parcels are rezoned without relating the planning to the best needs of the community or the specific needs of potential acquirers, to the disadvantage of both the community and the builder. Some programs are good, but they are regional or even local in nature. None have been structured to take full advantage of the complete potential of this field, however successful some of them have been.

I say this because I believe that we developed with some of our clients in the firm I previously headed a comprehensive packaging approach that refined the term "packaging" by relating land acquisition to both marketing skills and the best needs of a community, and it did so on a national basis. The program is so designed as to be capable of providing the greatest number of builders in the largest number of markets with the most *marketable* development packages, consistent with local community needs. The approach was grounded in our firm's multimarket research capability and our experience as marketing and planning consultants to major builders on market and feasibility research, building program design and land acquisition and zoning, plus our own packaging activities. In this program, the whole nation was in effect under survey for development opportunities, and each package conceived was far more closely related to the immediate market's planning concerns and needs, as well as the builder's needs, than has formerly been the case. We sold the builder not just a rezoned piece of land but a complete project concept to go with the land, taking into account the local community's concerns for planned growth and the key housing needs and tastes of the local market.

A FORMAT FOR A NATIONAL PACKAGER

Here are the key elements of this program approach:

We conduct a continuous detailed monitoring program of the top twenty-five housing markets in the nation for regional and local planning concerns, economic factors, present and anticipated housing demand, consumer preference characteristics, and competitive activity.

We take on thorough economic and marketing analyses of areas entering a growth phase to develop a sensitive awareness for the unique aspects of the local market. The demographic and economic characteristics are placed in the perspective of real people and their actions and concerns. Problems of zoning, utility development, school facilities, road networks and transportation facilities are closely analyzed. Commercial and industrial development is examined. The area's concerns and objectives for planned growth are studied in detail, so that development planning will reflect the best interests of the community. Present and anticipated residential construction activity is examined. The entire market area is closely inspected for locales and features that have built-in marketing advantages of price, advantageous location or desirable amenities in terms of the types of housing demand we would perceive.

A close analysis of the economic base and statistical housing demand is only the first step. It gives way to a close analysis of *people* and their tastes and preferences, and the various potential submarkets they form by price, housing type and location. It takes into account how well the competition is perceiving the same people and the submarkets they form, and how well it is catering to them. And it takes into account the local planning concerns, and its special problems and special features. Every problem can be an opportunity if you know your market well enough.

What emerges is a very clear picture of the dynamics of the local market; you can begin confidently identifying specific development opportunities. You begin to observe that one type of housing product incorporating particular design features will beat competitively priced projects all hollow in a particular area; or that a condominium development with a price advantage in a given area will sell like hotcakes; or that a high-priced residential development is a natural for an area others have missed because now a golf course and lake are planned nearby; or that an apartment complex near an urban center would fill a big unmet demand for housing for the elderly; and so on. The accumulated experience of operating in many markets over many years often enables us to perceive specific opportunities overlooked by local operators or those newly arrived — opportunities based on design, product type, price ranges, consumer tastes, location, and marketing and sales methods.

Strategic parcels of land would then be optioned or acquired, with the acquisition based on our prior definition of the product to be built on them and a complete prior definition of an *existing* market for this product, consistent with the community's general plan and its ecological concerns. Unlike other, more general packaging approaches, we worked from an entirely completed definition of the anticipated end user in formulating a land acquisitioned program. The property is rezoned and planned. The final package consists not only of a zoned piece of property for development that will serve a genuine community need, but also a complete marketing and development plan. This defines the housing product type, the number of units, the specific price ranges, the specific design criteria, the architectural treatment, the financial analysis of the proposed development, and the recommended marketing program. We worked with associate planning and architectural firms as required in tailoring such packages. The approach not only tailored a package exactly to the market we discerned for it, but in doing so, also heightened its desirability to a major builder because the development concept and the marketing program for it came with the land. In instances where such packages were sold to other developers, they bought not just a piece of rezoned land but a completely market-planned project that was "ready to go" and acceptable in the current market.

Builders moving into new markets can commit the error of paying too much for land in terms of the final product they have in mind, or selecting land poorly in terms of location, or coming up with a product that does not meet the market demand because of local taste and preferences. A builder's big size does not exempt him from such flaws. Thus, a skillfully prepared package based on a close study of the market and on a strong input of marketing skills can be appealing because it reduces the builder's own chances of making a major error.

Locating and controlling the strategic piece of real estate is the key to profits from both land appreciation and construction. The greatest values in development are created at the stage of defining and creating the project concept, which establishes the higher land values. The major builders, in their search for construction volume, forgo profits of concept creation and become *users* of land as a processed industrial commodity, making their profits solely from the marketing of dwellings they construct. If they have a demonstrably reliable project package presented to them they'll pay the premium for the real estate for the sake of getting a successful building program. The sale price of the project package still lets them make a good construction profit from the development and sale of the housing product defined by the package.

Such a packaging program has three important underlying bases. It must be based on an expert forecasting knowledge of the active markets the major builders will favor, accurately anticipating the evolution of "hot" markets. The proper timing is of the essence in this business. The program must also be based on close continuing relationships with major developers to anticipate and stay attuned to their particular requirements. And, very importantly, such a program must perform a genuine service to both the responsible developer and to the local community. It should do so by preparing development packages consistent with the foremost ecological and planning concerns of the area, and by carefully marrying the particular project with the developer most capable of executing it successfully in accordance with the community's interests.

I see it as inevitable, by the way, that financial sources joint-venturing with smaller builders must eventually extend their operations into the area of such responsible land packaging. They will have to do so to exercise a greater control over the selection of their joint-venture projects (number and quality), as competition for good deals increases and mounting environmental and municipal planning concerns make good project planning an increasingly more comprehensive process. This step will also get the funding sources in on the profitable concept planning end of each deal. As fine an organization as Builders' Resources Corporation is, for example, I think it did not tap its full profit potentials prior to 1972. Up to that time, it got only the deals that smaller builders chose to bring to it instead of going out and creating them; and it passed by the profit in land appreciation from a newly defined land use, leaving it to the builder. It could have been out in the field creating very choice packages of its own and then joint-venturing them with builders *it* would select. BRC could thus have shared in profits from both construction *and* land, as well as assuring itself of the high quality of each venture by originating them itself. This is the way the funding sources will take charge of their own future on joint-venture deals, instead of waiting for independent builders to originate their deals.

THE FLEXIBLE FLYER

The range of opportunities in real estate almost always exceeds the capabilities of any single organization. By bringing together the needed talents (management, marketing, development, architecture, sales) with the resources (money, land), an infinitely flexible range of combinations is achievable to take advantage of the uniquely perceived development opportunity. The joint-venture mechanism enables the players of the real estate game to home in from any angle on the broad range of opportunities for profit. The joint-venture form is also especially attractive because it provides corporate investors the opportunity to work with the best people in each type of real estate development; it is far more flexible than the alternative of acquiring a residential developer and trying to make him an all-round genius.

25

Joint-Venturing Giants

Every man a king!

—Huey P. Long

The union of capital and entrepreneurial talent through the joint-venture vehicle takes a number of forms. Two of these forms set a dominant pattern for the building industry in the early Seventies. These are: (1) joint ventures between homebuilder-oriented financial houses established expressly for this purpose and small independent developers; (2) the ongoing joint-venture format between a major corporate partner and an established building company. In this chapter we'll take a closer look at two of the organizations that have been among the pioneers in these forms of joint venturing.

THE EVOLUTION OF BUILDERS' RESOURCES CORPORATION

Builders' Resources Corporation, now headquartered in San Mateo, California, was one of the earliest and most developed examples of the new financial organizations that began springing into existence in the late Sixties to funnel money to the capital-starved housing industry on a joint-venture basis. The company was initially capitalized by eight major corporations: CNA Financial, American-Standard, National Gypsum, Stanley Works, U.S. Plywood (later merged with Champion Papers), Whirlpool, Property Research, and the investment banking firm of Donaldson Lufkin & Jenrette. BRC's avowed purpose was to undertake joint ventures with the smaller builder, typically grossing less than $2 million a year. And in the pursuit of this policy, during its first three years of operation BRC got into 54 joint-venture deals with 31 builders, producing 9,600 units and a sales volume of over $300 million.

THE SMALL BUILDER'S FRIEND. What particularly distinguished BRC from other joint-venturing giants in the field was the way it merchandised itself as a financial source for joint ventures. It was from the outset identified as the financial partner that gave the smaller builder a better break. BRC at the start of operations adopted a single formula: it would provide up to 80% of the builder's equity requirement (up to a ceiling of $500,000) for 50% of his profits. The formula has actually been more flexible. In some instances, BRC negotiated a smaller than 50% share of itself — perhaps as low as 35% — when working on a highly profitable deal with a strong partner. But the repetition of the primary joint-venture formula had its advantages in calling attention to BRC in the homebuilding industry. The company has been successfully operated since its inception in 1968 by president Bob Medearis, who combines a civil engineering degree from Stanford and an MBA from Harvard with the expertise gained from an earlier career as a builder-developer in the San Francisco area. Medearis has also been a vice president of the Lusk Corporation of Tucson and president of the Arizona Association of Homebuilders.

Bob Medearis and his team refined a number of appealing examples in educating smaller builders to the advantages of joint venture. These turned on the benefits of increased leverage and diversification that a co-venturing financial source makes possible. A typical project of 100 homes priced at, say, $25,000 will cost $2.25 million. A builder could probably borrow $2 million from conventional sources, but this still leaves a requirement of $250,000 that he must come up with as "front money." With such a project taking up to three years to build out, he multiplies his capital needs if he wants to start additional projects in this time. Joint-venturing lets him leverage his funds to get into more projects faster and thus grow more quickly. According to BRC's calculations in one example, a builder can run up his volume to five times that which would be possible with his own funds when he joint-ventures. Starting with $250,000 of his own capital, the builder could develop one project of 100 homes and get a net profit and contribution to overhead of $250,000. But with the same money and with BRC as a joint-venture partner, he can get into four separate projects and run his profits up to $812,500. He also picks up the added advantage of possible diversification in product, price range and market area.

These builders who had been exposed to joint-venture proposals from insurance sources where the financial partner keeps all the profit accruing from a project for the first five years, appreciated BRC's profit-sharing formula. BRC would begin splitting profits 50-50 as soon as the equity capital was recaptured. When the cash flow from project sales began, BRC collected its 80% contribution by taking 80% of the cash flow (the builder in the same period would retrieve *his* equity contribution by taking 20% of the cash flow) until the project reached a break-even point. In a project with a $250,000 equity investment, for example, BRC would pull out $200,000 while the builder took $50,000. Thereafter, the returns would split equally. If for some reason *additional* capital would be required while the project was under way, by BRC's rules it would also be provided on an 80-20 basis.

A STRONG ASSIST WITH MANAGEMENT. BRC's financial assistance was paramount, but other forms of help were valuable in less obvious ways. BRC's reliance on expert economics and market-research experts provided it with insight on national and regional housing trends in finance, technology and marketing. The company's broad exposure to a variety of housing projects gave the BRC staff a broad capability in evaluating new products, materials and construction and marketing methods. When necessary, the company provided management skills to help market the housing a builder-partner produces. Specific assistance includes market, site and feasibility analysis, cash flow, budgeting and scheduling, cost-performance controls, relations with lending institutions, and marketing and promotion. BRC occasionally even supplied a partner with good people to improve his staff. It generally has served as a strong partner with the capacity to analyze and improve the weak areas of a local entrepreneur's business.

One benefit of joint-venturing with BRC is that many builders came out of the relationship as much better managers. BRC requires strict cost and performance controls on its projects, and partners report on a regular basis. A comparison of actual performance with projected financial, production, and sales schedules provides an exception-type monitoring system that gives early indication of needed corrective action. As Medearis observed, once a builder recognizes that the process of standardized reporting actually helps him to operate more professionally, he welcomes the opportunity to work with it.

THE PAYOFF FOR BUILDERS. Joint-venturing with BRC has paid off for a number of smaller builders. There's Charles Beattie of Beattie & Associates, San Jose, who was building 30 units a year in 1969 and by 1971 was building at an annual rate of 400. Don Dixon, of Dallas, was able to get Raleigh Blakely, another builder, to go with him in a merger of their smaller companies that resulted in the organization of Raldon Corporation, which rapidly boosted its volume to more than ten projects. From a staff of six people, Dixon increased the roll of employees of Raldon to fifty in a year's time and grossed about $14 million for fiscal 1971. Moving from five to ten subdivisions in the same amount of time, Raldon also branched into apartments.

One of Bob Medearis's more exciting stories about the potential success of joint ventures is the caper BRC pulled off with Westport Home Builders in Orange County with two lower-priced housing developments. Westport built a $21 million fourplex project of 831 units under the FHA condominium program, priced from $15,995, and a 362-single-family project with homes priced from $21,995 in San Juan Capistrano. The overall project was named Capistrano Villas. On opening day more than 4,000 people showed up and sales the first day ran to $4.5 million, representing nearly 260 units sold. BRC considered the two project packages as part of the same joint venture, but split them into two financial sections. In financial projections the BRC investment in the single-family subdivision was set at $204,000 and its profits at $349,000. For the fourplex project, BRC's investment was $281,000 and its profits ran to $967,000. BRC's total profits on the deal thus came to $1,325,000 on an investment of $485,000.

TOO MUCH OF A GOOD THING: A CHANGE OF POLICY FOR BRC

As good an organization as BRC has been, however, the management decided it was operating under some restrictive limitations. Under its policy of joint-venturing deals that smaller builders brought to its door, BRC was, first of all, essentially in a passive role. It was dependent upon outside developers to conceive the right deals, with no assurance that it would get the best deals. BRC likewise had no assurance that the developer who worked successfully with the company on one or two ventures would stay with it after BRC had underwritten his successes. The company also did not always share in the high profits occasionally accruing to developers from their upward revaluation of land at the time they sold it to the joint venture. Management of fifty or so builders could also get to be a problem. BRC formed each of its ventures as a partnership, with itself as the limited partner. As one insider observed, "A lot of these builders didn't know what they were doing, and it's hard to control them without becoming the general partner." Perhaps most importantly, however, it became apparent to BRC that it was missing entirely a very large source of potential profits — from collateral financial services supplied for the development activity it was financing. Unlike U.S. Financial, whose fortunes are also discussed in this chapter, BRC had not ventured into the related financial services that can supply as much as another 150% of profit in the course of a development venture.

Accordingly, BRC's orientation began changing as of early 1972. The changes started when Bob Medearis arranged the transfer of the company's ownership by sale from the original stockholder group to New York-based Moller Industries on March 10, 1972. The new owner of BRC became a subsidiary of A. P. Moller, Inc., a Danish company based in Copenhagen and engaged primarily in shipping. Stanley Works is the only original stockholder retaining its one-eighth ownership share. The change of ownership expanded both BRC's financial lines and working capital. Simultaneously,

BRC began implementing plans to enter into and expand its financial service capability both by start-up and acquisition. As Bob Medearis put it, "We will provide total financial services." The company would thus in a short time be providing all short-term financing, insurance, bonding and mortgage banking activities connected with its joint-venture activities. At the same time, BRC began to move heavily into multifamily housing construction and set about establishing a syndication arm to function as a major part of its operations. And it indicated that it would be more involved in direct project creation, instead of waiting passively for developers to present potential ventures.

"The basic format of our operation remains the same," Medearis said. "The difference is, we will be doing more projects with fewer builders. We will always be open to working with new builders, but we would like to have all their work now." The trend to more projects with fewer builders was in evidence by June of 1972, when BRC had 69 projects underway with 20 builders. One benefit to the joint-venturing builder under the new regime at BRC is that, with a good deal, he can probably count on getting more than mere 80% of the front-end equity money. He will also get one-stop shopping service for all required financial services. But he is going to have to be a better and bigger builder and, as indicated, he'll probably expect to have an on-going relationship rather than one or two in-and-out deals.

YOU SAY YOU WANT TO JOINT-VENTURE WITH BRC? As of 1972, BRC set four criteria for developers to meet in order to get past the first screening. (1) You have to control the land you propose to develop for your project, either through outright ownership or option. (2) Your proposed project has to be located in a market area that can absorb at least 10,000 units annually. (3) Your project has to be a minimum of 50 units — whether single-family, townhouse, condominium or apartments. (4) You need to have a completed engineering feasibility study and development plan. Beyond this there were no hard and fixed criteria, though BRC sought some convincing demonstration of a record of past achievement in the types of projects a potential partner presents to the company.

Assuming your project proved feasible on detailed analysis, you have to show that you can successfully plan, construct and market a project on schedule and achieve profit projections. A track record of building similar projects successfully is usually a must. Beyond this, BRC would examine a builder's motivation to expand his business and his capacity to handle management of a growing business. You don't need a big management staff to sell BRC, but you must prove you're not a chronic one-man band by showing a staffing capability or demonstrating that you can and have successfully subcontracted key functions such as sales, accounting and

construction. BRC has typically checked past records for operating overhead tests to see what kind of manager you really make. Bob Medearis's
selling point has been that BRC provides equity and strengthens your management because the firm is not just a moneylender but a true working
partner. But you've got to prove one thing: that you're the *able* local entrepreneur who makes a good partner for the financial big brother.

THE LOEW'S/SNYDER JOINT VENTURE:
STEADY AS SHE GOES

Jerry Snyder, forty-two, has been box-office business for Loew's The-
atres, Inc., the diversified conglomerate with which he's joint-ventured on
residential development since early 1969. The venture was set up to start
five projects in California on land Loew's bought for $2.9 million in stock.
By the start of 1972 Snyder had nearly $500 million of housing in process
in sixteen projects. The company's California sales were projected at $35
million in 1972. The Loew's/Snyder operation as of 1972 penetrated six
major market areas: New York, Los Angeles, San Francisco, San Diego,
Tucson and Chicago. It has a reputation as one of the sharpest privately
held marketeers in the country today.

The joint-venture formula between Loew's and the J. (for Jerome) H.
Snyder Company was a simple one: the builder gets the corporation's equity
capital without restrictions for projects that meet criteria the two had set
up at the beginning of their relationship, and later the profits are split up
on a 50-50 basis. As Snyder says: "I tell Loew's what and where I want to
build, estimate the construction cost and outline the projected return. Then
Loew's has the option of accepting or rejecting. So far, Loew's hasn't rejected anything." After three years of working with his financial partner,
Snyder regarded the relationship as still in the "honeymoon" stage. Naturally enough, he was a strong advocate of the joint-venture format as the
best method of linking corporate financial strength with a building company.
"A merger can't do it," he said. "The joint venture is the best form to keep
up a builder's incentive: to make money, you need to keep producing."

Jerry Snyder should know. Back in 1961, he was one of the first to
sense the trend to mergers with larger companies and merged his Signature
Development Company into Pacific Coast Properties for $750,000 in stock.
But after Pacific showed losses in 1963, '64 and '65, he formed Signature
Homes, bought $9 million worth of residential land from Pacific and began
building on his own again. Having been on both sides of the fence, as an
independent builder and as a corporately owned subsidiary, he saw the
problems builders encounter in mergers at a time when most of them still
regarded the corporate marriage as the perfect way to go. Throughout the

late Sixties he worked at formulating a concept for linking his company with corporate capital without the disadvantages that might accrue to both in a merger. Often, he would kick his ideas around with his buddy Eli Broad when the two got together socially, and Eli pitched in with his own experience and perceptions. Out of this emerged the pioneering concept of the ongoing joint-venture format, and it was implemented when Snyder was introduced to Loew's boss, Laurence Tisch, through "a mutual acquaintance."

Perhaps the most important reason why the Loew's/Snyder relationship worked during the early 1970s was Jerry's ability to deliver profits consistently. The man is one of the industry's most talented people when it comes to spotting promising markets and buying land at the right price for the right housing product. The talent began showing early. Brooklyn-born Jerry Snyder, youngest of a family of five children, first got into homebuilding in 1950 at age twenty, after serving as apprentice to his father in the remodeling business, when his family moved to Southern California. Snyder was one of the first builders to see the enormous potential of Orange County as a housing market, and cleaned up with a 1953 subdivision in Garden Grove. He pioneered the development of Newhall with a 3,200-home project, an area north of Los Angeles that had previously been used primarily as a setting for movie Westerns.

Jerry was also among the first builders to home in on such growth areas as Lompoc, near Vandenberg Air Force Base; Goleta, north of Santa Barbara; and one of the first Southern California builders to extend northward to San Francisco. Throughout the period preceding his venture with Loew's he showed a knack for sizing up a market other builders had overlooked or bypassed. An example was a North Long Beach project that other builders turned down because of what they regarded as insoluble problems of the site. Snyder solved the problems and sold out the entire package of 220 homes in two days. By the time he entered into his joint-venture deal he had piled up a record of 15,000 homes sold.

Snyder has continued to demonstrate the knack for selecting the right piece of land and putting the right product on that land during his relationship with Loew's. Although his company grew considerably — by 1972 including four operating divisions scattered from San Diego to New York — he set things up in such a way that he always controls what he properly regards as the key function: land acquisition. As he said: "I always make the final decision regarding land. If the property's not right, nothing will work; you can't put a $25,000 house on land for a $35,000 house. But if you're right on the land in your initial selection, then at least you've got a chance of good project execution." Coupled with a sharp eye for the right land deal, Snyder is a first-class marketer of shelter who is not locked into turning out any particular housing type, but who flexibly produces whatever product may be desired to meet market needs. Although single-family housing for the mass market ($20,000 to $30,000 price range) represents a major segment of sales, the company broadened its operations to townhouse and garden-apartment type condominiums, as well as both high-rise and garden apartments.

Across the bay from San Diego, at Coronado, Loew's/Snyder have built Coronado Shores, two luxury high-rise condominiums, 15 stories each and incorporating a total of 285 units. In the San Francisco area, varied projects include the 500-unit Westborough Hills duplex townhouse complex; the San Carlos development, a mix of 434 condominiums and 150 single-family homes (including the first "child care and development center" ever put into a private project); and a 510-unit apartment complex at Burlingame. The Chicago division, opened in 1971, started on a 280-unit townhouse project for the mass market as its first venture. In the big Los Angeles market, seven projects were going that bracketed every housing type and price range. Homes in the $20,000–$30,000 price range were going like hotcakes in projects situated in Yorba Linda, Simi Valley and Lancaster, north of Los Angeles. Closer in, Beverly Glen Park was underway — a high-priced residential community of single-family homes overlooking Beverly Hills and Bel Air. And the company's Ocean Towers project in Santa Monica, scheduled for completion by the end of 1972, is a twin 16-story high rise structure incorporating 317 rental apartments, all with an ocean view. Early in 1972 Jerry also expanded to Bakersfield, California, and Sierra Vista (near Tucson), Arizona, by entering into a joint venture with Tenneco West to build more than 1,000 fourplex condominiums and single-family homes on Tenneco land. Tenneco West, California's big fruit grower, is a subsidiary of Houston-based oil conglomerate Tenneco, Inc.

A good example of Snyder's exceptional marketing ability is the success story of his penetration of the New York market with a planned, 2,025-unit townhouse development on Staten Island in 1970, inspiring other major multimarket builders (including Kaufman & Broad) to chase in pellmell after him. When Jerry first looked over Staten Island, it was a puzzlingly moribund market. Despite its proximity to Manhattan, its thousands of undeveloped acres, and a huge pool of potential buyers from among apartment dwellers in Brooklyn, the Bronx and elsewhere, the island had only 2,000 home sales in 1969. But Snyder correctly perceived that it was the housing and merchandising that were uninspired, not the buyers.

Noting that few builders had changed from the 1920's-type grid plan that unappealingly jammed row upon row of single-family homes at eight to the acre on 40-foot-wide lots, he bought 165 beautifully wooded acres and created a magnificently designed, mixed-density community of attached townhouses selling in the $32,900-$43,900 range. Raising gross density to twelve units per acre to lower per-unit land costs ($50,000 an acre) also enabled Snyder to leave 80 acres free for greenbelts and recreation areas, a startling innovation for staid Staten Island. Local builders watching the action clucked their tongues, saying that attached units would never sell, that a density of twelve to the acre was too high, and that the price range was also too steep for the market. But when the project opened in August of 1970 (with the entire recreational complex still unbuilt), Snyder sold more than 150 units in the first month, with the buyers willingly forking up down payments of from $3,000 to $11,000. The planned-community concept, sharp California architectural and interior design, and a broad range of floor plans, instead of a fixed subdivision pattern of one or two plans, had done their work.

Snyder confesses that being a pioneer was taking quite a risk. But, he says, "I'm convinced that no matter where you build and no matter what the local market is used to, doing the best possible job and giving it the best possible merchandising is the only way." In 1971 Loew's/Snyder expanded their Staten Island operations, opening a second project of 440 garden-type condominiums in the mid-thirties price range, called Fingerboard Square. And they added a set of five lower-priced models to Village Greens, their first community, with prices starting at $29,000 as total project sales passed the $17 million mark.

For all the multitude of activities involved in the operations of a growing homebuilding firm, it prospers or falls on the basis of a very few key decisions. Snyder himself quipped: "The development business is like flying a jet plane: hours and hours of boredom interrupted by moments of stark terror." So to free himself up for making those key decisions, he has put a lot of thought and effort to getting the J. H. Snyder Company to run like clockwork. The central Los Angeles office was built up into a corporate organization with accounting, construction and planning departments that act as problem-solvers for the divisional operations. Snyder worked on a policy of taking each new division through an incubation period before expanding to others. As he said in 1971, "San Francisco's now going very well. New York two years down the line will be well run. There will always be a division that's a baby. We don't start any new ones, though, until the last is totally operative. Each one goes through the same problems of getting staffed properly with the right personnel and getting familiarized with company procedures." Jerry also began beefing up his staff with some bright young talent. Starting in 1970, for example, he and his corporate staff journeyed East to winnow Harvard and Wharton MBA's to add to the management group.

By 1973, Snyder was shooting for $100 million worth of construction completed in that fiscal year (ending August 31), up from $85 million in the prior year. He was well on the way to attaining that goal, with a total of $410 million of work in progress at eighteen projects from coast to coast early in 1973. In keeping with his plan of opening up one major new market area yearly, the company moved into Chicago in 1973 and targeted about 3,000 units in four suburban projects. Other major projects beefing up the totals were the $100 million Village Greens on Staten Island, which in 1973 started its third section; Coronado Shores, the 1,500-unit, 10-tower highrise condominium venture in San Diego; and the Tenneco West joint venture to build a 1,000-unit project near Bakersfield, California. Reviewing the four-year relationship with Loew's, Jerry Snyder observed: "Our relations are smooth, and we have benefited. It's a marriage that has worked."

Whether this relationship would survive the strains of the economy in the mid-1970s only time could tell. But up to 1973, it was regarded as an ideal set-up.

26

The Institutional Joint-Venturers

Don't look back; something may
be gaining on you.

—Satchel Paige

Builder joint ventures with insurance companies in the early 1970s were considerably fewer in number than during the tight-money years of the late Sixties and into 1970. Most builders want to sell their project, while most lenders want to keep them. The builders also found they could often line up 100% financing more cheaply with other sources. An insurer in 1972 putting up money at 9% and making a 70% to 80% loan wanted a higher return on its equity because of the greater risk. But at that time, at any rate, there were lots of equity investors around who were willing to take an equity return lower than the "constant" (9.02% to 9.67% as of early 1972). For their part, the insurers became very choosy about whom they'd joint-venture with. It takes a very strong developer and a very large project to qualify to do business with such a co-venturer.

This is not to say that insurance companies are not a major force in U.S. real estate. They have long played an important role as investors in and owners of developed property, and they continue to expand this role. But their *joint-venture* activity in the field of residential real estate has turned back from a high-water mark as other sources of equity have become available. At the time the insurers were most active, however, their impact on the industry was so significant and so controversial that no reference to the joint-venture form would be complete without including them — not only as a lesson in history but also an indicator of what might come again, now that the housing industry faces another crippling round of high interest rates.

The rise of insurer joint ventures in the late Sixties was a function of tight money and inflation. With the money market in a shambles and both equity and long-term mortgage funds in critical demand, the insurers began taking advantage of their financial strength to take a "kicker" or "participation" on every project for which they provided a mortgage. This gave them a portion of the income from the property. Beyond ceasing to lend money

481

on a fixed-interest basis, the insurers also began taking a cut of developers' profits as co-venturing partners by taking an outright ownership position in the project to be developed. They worked out a variety of financing or "joint-venturing" techniques that gave them a 50% ownership of the property, plus, in many instances, 100% of its cash flow for up to five years, as a condition of providing 100% financing for such development.

DRIVING THE TOUGHEST BARGAIN

The favorite joint-venture vehicle among insurers was a formula based on some variation of the package providing 100% financing through mortgage debt with subordinated sale-leaseback. The package would ordinarily consist of a ground lease, a leasehold mortgage, equity participation, plus 50% ownership of the project. John Hancock Mutual was a leader in developing and refining this approach, but Prudential, Connecticut General and other major insurers also set the pace.

Here's how the deal was illustrated in the July 1970 issue of *Fortune*: A developer with land worth $5 million on which he wants to build a $25 million building could raise $22.5 million (75% of value) by mortgaging land and building together. But he could raise more by separating the land and structure. Hancock would buy the land for 5 million and lease it back to him. The developer would then mortgage his leasehold estate to Hancock for 75% of the value of the building, or $18.75 million. This way, the developer would get a total of $23.75 million, or $1.25 million more than if he had mortgaged land and building together. As a third step, Hancock usually got the right to buy a 50% equity interest in the building through a wholly owned subsidiary. The purchase price would run to about 10% of the size of its mortgage loan, or $1,875,000 in this example. Hancock would put up no cash; it would pay for its equity with a commitment to provide funds once the project was completed. This three-level commitment for 100% of financing then enabled the developer to get a full construction loan from a commercial bank. Only the strongest developers had the bargaining power to withstand the insurer's demand for a 50% equity ownership.

The return to Hancock would be fourfold. First, the insurer received a ground rent, which ranged between 9% and 9½% of the value of the land paid annually. Second, it received an interest payment of about 9¾% on the leasehold mortgage. Third, it received an equity kicker tied to the ground lease. After deducting mortgage and rent payments, taxes and a predetermined amount for operating expenses, Hancock got 25% to 35% of the remaining cash flow as its kicker. Since the ground lease usually runs twice as long as the leasehold mortgage, and the equity kicker continues throughout its life, this is quite a bonus for Hancock. Fourth, as its return on its own equity investment of $1,875,000, Hancock did not split profits 50-50. It would take a 12% cumulative preferred dividend before the developer got anything. That is, it would take the first $225,000 before allowing the developer any part of cash flow. If the project should yield less than $225,-000, Hancock would take all there is and then add the unpaid amount to the next year's $225,000 payment. After all these payments the developer was not likely to see any cash return for the first five years of a project's life. (See Chapter 2 for REIT techniques of 100% financing.)

What was in it for the developer, then? He might get a substantial management fee for overseeing the construction of the project. He might make a good profit initially on the sale of the land to the insurer. He could also be in a position where he'd reserve for himself the rental income from boat slips (if building a water-oriented apartment complex) — a non-depreciable item. His chief remaining reason for wanting to go on a deal like this, however, was the possibility of capital gains. Since a good project will appreciate in value, the long-term gain can be substantial. But it was the insurer who made the profits in the early years of the project, leaving the developer to carry the risk and to wait for cash flow a long way down the line.

Many developers were thus very unhappy with insurer deals. "It just doesn't seem to be worth the effort anymore," a Chicago developer lamented in 1970. "We can build them. We can rent them. But it's getting tougher and tougher to build and rent apartments at a profit. And if there is a profit, the insurance companies who lend us the money are creaming it off first." The annual return to an insurance joint-venturer on a joint-venture package like the one described above ranged from 13% to 20% depending on whether it leveraged its equity investment by using another insurer's mortgage money or provided its own mortgage funds.

REFINING THE CONCEPT OF JOINT–VENTURING SUBSIDIARY

Most insurers would carry on their joint-venture deals through real estate subsidiaries, or through even smaller subsidiaries of the realty subsidiary. This shields the assets of the parent from debts or losses the joint venture might unexpectedly incur. The subsidiary has also proven to be a clever device for circumventing legal limits on the percentage of assets that insurers can invest in real estate. Most state laws put this ceiling at 5% to 10% of total assets. But by reorganizing themselves as holding companies — with both the real estate subsidiary and the insurance firm as unrelated subsidiaries of the holding company — the insurers that are stock companies have achieved an unrestricted access to real estate. Companies like Aetna and Connecticut General have effected such reorganization. (Mutual companies, owned by their policyholders, cannot use the holding-company mechanism and are somewhat more restricted as a result, but also operate through subsidiaries. In New York State, the mutual-company parent and subsidiary together cannot invest more than 10% of assets in real estate. But other states are more liberal in their interpretation of statutory limits on real estate investment; insurance examiners may charge only the equity portion of the mutual insurer's investment against the asset limitation, enabling it to expand its involvement by three to ten times.)

Operating through a corporate subsidiary has had only one drawback: the subsidiary has to pay the full corporate tax rate, 48%, and a second tax must be paid on profits when they are passed to the corporate parent. To lick this problem and take advantage of the much lower effective tax rate that the life insurance company usually pays, the insurers along about 1970 began using a new joint-venture format involving *both* the parent company and its realty subsidiary. *Fortune* explained this development in the following terms:

> According to this plan, an insurance company might negotiate a 50 percent equity interest and enter the joint venture itself as a 49 percent *limited* partner, while putting its subsidiary in as a 1 percent *general* partner. A general partner is entitled to participate in the management of the joint venture, but it is also liable for all the venture's debts. A limited partner has no liability, except for its initial investment, but neither has it the right to manage. By sharing its partnership interest with its subsidiary, the parent has the best of both worlds — the right to manage without exposing its own assets.
>
> This arrangement also provides a tax bonanza. As a limited partner the insurance company has an ambiguous relationship with the joint venture. On the one hand, it is a lender to the venture, receiving interest income from its mortgage; on the other hand, as a partner, it pays out mortgage interest — in effect to itself. The income it gets as lender is taxable; the interest it pays as a partner is deductible. The key to the tax advantage is that, for many insurance companies, the marginal tax bite on interest income is generally about 30 percent, while deductions for interest paid are usually worth close to the full corporate rate of 48 percent. The difference arises because the investment income, of a life company is divided into two parts: the policyholders' share and the company's share, it is not taxed on what belongs to the policyholder. So its effective tax rate is lowered substantially.
>
> If the joint venture paid the insurance company $100,000

in mortgage interest, the company's tax liability on that would be $30,000. But when the insurance company is a 49 percent limited partner in the fifty-fifty venture cited above, it is entitled to deduct $49,000 as its share of interest paid. That deduction would lower its tax from $30,000 to $6,480 (48 percent of $49,000 equals $23,520). If the insurance company were a 74 percent limited partner — in a seventy-five to twenty-five deal — its share of interest paid by the partnership would more than wipe out its $30,000 tax obligation on the mortgage interest it received (48 percent of $74,000 equals $35,520). In other words, the more substantial its equity position, the more the insurance company makes on its loan. And if it takes a big enough equity position, it can even raise its after-tax yield on interest income above its pre-tax yield.

A number of insurance companies have only just discovered this bizarre tax wrinkle and are planning to use it for the first time this year (1970). If the Internal Revenue Service acquiesces, those companies may become even more insistent in demanding equity participations. And as long as mortgage money remains scarce as it has been, few doubt their ability to enforce this demand.

Those percentage contributions by the parent insurance firm as a limited partner can actually get much larger than Sanford Rose describes. In one deal I know of — not atypical — the insurance company's subsidiary put in something like $500 into a deal as the general partner; the insurance parent put in $3,350,000 in capital as a limited partner with a 49.999 interest in the joint venture. That's maximizing the after-tax yield on interest income for you.

THE INEQUITIES OF THOSE EQUITY DEALS

It was unpleasant enough to give up five years of cash flow for 100% financing. But some insurers exacted essentially the same conditions for providing 80% mortgages during the tight money period, and did *that* make builders unhappy!

There seemed to be something terribly inequitable about an insurer demanding 50% ownership of a project and 100% of its cash flow for five or more years as a condition of making say an 80% loan at a 10% interest rate. The only reason insurers were able to make deals like this is that they became the smaller apartment developer's primary source of long-term financing at a time when such financing was hard to get. They would take a half-ownership without getting involved in either the entrepreneurial preparatory work or in the property management following the completion of the property. The builder would conceive, organize, build, rent and manage the project without the insurer's venturing a penny of its own front-end capital. Then the insurer would walk in and take over 50% of the deal and 100% of the rental income during the project's best years.

Moreover, the insurer's approach often promoted only mediocre construction. Many of the insurance co-venturers have typically evaluated deals not by the experience and expertness of the developer and the quality of the project, but solely by inflexible paper formulas of yield criteria. Typically, they projected operating expenses at 42% of gross income and vacancy rates at 5% to 7%, then setting the loan at 75% to 80% of projected value based on net income. These inflexible yield formulas, ignoring quality, have often left the insurer holding a project with a high paper yield but an actual cash drain. Good projects have been passed up for inferior ones for the sake of an added interest point. The developer's ability to *manage* — crucially important to the insurer's turning a profit on the deal well after its completion — has often been overlooked. A good property-management record actually has worked against a developer seeking apartment financing. If loans are inflexibly set on an assumption of 42% of gross income for operating expenses, management ability that holds expenses consistently at 32% to 34% is not well recognized.

The insurers' formulas also tended to work against enhancing the quality of projects by not allowing for the extra amenities that a good developer usually builds into a project. Money spent on landscaping, recreational facilities, interior design and layout has been kept within the bounds of the insurers' standard income-expenses-vacancy formula. Put another way, the best way to meet the lender's requirement has been to lower the quality of a project.

The only people for whom many of these "joint-venture" deals appeared workable were the speculative developer with a speculative project, working for the capital gain down the line. Relatively few serious developers considered taking on a venture that entitled them to all the work and no profit for years. Thus, a number of insurers found their projects foundering. But it has been their own fault, for they chose to support the weaker developers who haven't the bargaining power to go elsewhere for a better deal. Some say they don't care if the developer folds because they can get the project back at 85 cents on the dollar, but unsound properties are often worth less than that. And to save his equity the lender must get into a very active unwelcome role in property management to rescue the project.

Underlying many of these problems was the insurers' unwillingness or, through long years of habit, inability to see themselves as co-venturers rather than as lenders. One principal in an apartment development firm has successfully joint-ventured with several insurers, and he notes:

"Our most difficult job in the past has been to convince the men at the insurance company to think not as lenders, but on a risk-taking basis. After all, they have been trained as lenders. Sometimes I have thought I had convinced John Doe at the insurance company, which is our partner, that his position is taking a risk, rather than lending. Then, the next thing I hear from him is that they plan to take the information we send and put it through a computer and 'work out a commitment.' Now, we are all familiar with 'commitments,' but that is a lender term. Too often, even when the insurance company is involved as a co-venturer in a risk position, we will hear some of their officers talk about commitments and 'let's see if it flies,' as they put it, referring to computing a loan."

THE INSURERS START REVISING THEIR JOINT–VENTURE FORMAT

By 1971 with ample money again flowing into the industry, it was evident to several of the insurers operating in the field with prohibitive joint-venture formulas that they would have to revise their mode of operations. A number of them also had ruefully discovered that the developers had ways of getting even with their financial joint-venture partner, either through neglect or cunning, when there was no prospect of cash flow for years. The cost of developing a property also would unexpectedly grow without its being the developer's fault. Yields came in lower than expected because of underestimated construction and rent-up periods and overestimated rent levels. Some insurers found that they could not always use the depreciation flowing from property ownership. A trend began to build apartments to sell rather than for long-term holding, and the big Wall Street syndication funds created a market. And with this the requirement to produce top-quality projects also reasserted itself. Some insurers suspended their joint-venture programs outright and went back to straight mortgage loans (with equity kickers), recognizing that greedy yield requirements gave them only weak partners and troubled projects.

As might have been expected, many of the big projects didn't work out too well. Particularly with regard to apartment complexes financed during the tight-money period, the costs based on the formulae employed would get so high that feasibility was difficult for all but the most unusual situations. A project had to have some special feature to make it work — such as a low land cost, or an unusual market area with premium rents (in the San Bruno area near the San Francisco area, for example, rents are 20% higher than in nearby San Jose without a difference in operating expenses). Such added leverage was necessary because of the inordinately high interest costs.

In 1970, a good job cost for a project was $5\frac{1}{2}$ times gross rent un-furnished (and by 1972 it had risen to more like $5\frac{3}{4}$ times gross). When a developer wanted to borrow $5\frac{1}{2}$ times gross (or a $4\frac{1}{2}$ million loan on $1 million), he got a $9\frac{1}{2}\%$ loan with a $10\frac{1}{2}\%$ constant. The land, valued at, say, $750,000, came in at a ground rent of 9% or $67,500. And the de-veloper's $250,000 "equity" cost him 12%, or another $30,000 in a 100%-financed deal. This amounted, in sum, to $570,000 in combined debt service and equity return — or, in short, what amounted to a 57% debt service. If the project's expenses were computed at another 35%, the break-even point was 92%. In this period, it was not unusual to get a break-even of 92%–95% no matter what the appraisal. This left precious little room for error and put a number of projects in hot water when money got plenti-ful and projected rent rises did not materialize because of increased supply of apartments. As interest rates dropped and the "constant" dropped to $9\frac{1}{2}\%$, the debt service in this example declined to $522,500, providing a 5% lower breakeven. When other builders could begin building more cheaply, the older projects were placed at a competitive disadvantage be-cause they were locked in at high break-evens without prepayment clauses.

With a growing awareness on the part of the co-venturing insurers that the developer would have to get a better deal, the standards concerning repayment of equity have also been relaxed. The developer negotiating a joint venture with an institutional investor could get a better deal in 1972 than he could in 1970. But John C. Opperman, vice president of United California Mortgage Company in San Francisco, suggested that he must watch several key issues, including:

1. Repayment of equity. There were wide discrepancies between the insurance companies on formulas for repayment of their share of the equity in the deal (the amount over the first mortgage or leasehold mortgage). At one extreme of the scale, the insurer still gets his equity with interest on a preferred basis before the developer gets any cash flow. But more insurers became aware that the developer needs *some* cash flow to operate. Some came up with formulas for amortizing their equity over periods of fifteen to twenty years, pretty much on the same basis as debt. More insurers began offering a plan to split cash flow on an 80–20 or a 90–10 basis, with the majority portion going to the lender to reduce his equity investment and pay him a return on it until the equity is repaid, at which point profits are split on a fifty-fifty basis. Where the cash equity of the financial partner approximated the "soft" equity of the developer (for example, increased land value contributed by the developer to the joint venture), cash flow was often split proportionately to ownership interest without recapture of equity.

2. Insurers' Leverage. Some lenders insist on making the long-term

mortgage and include a prepayment prohibition. But the majority of insurers began preferring to increase yield and thus make an effort to get mortgage financing elsewhere. They could often find it. Not every source of long-term financing wanted a piece of the action as a condition of making the permanent loan. Opperman observed that some companies felt a high-rate loan backed up by the equity of another large institution was a desirable investment; they preferred the security of a priority position to the uncertainties of an equity position. What if the insurer in the joint venture couldn't find another source of long-term financing right away? Opperman suggested the fairest approach is for the financial partner to issue a "livable standby" at terms in the current market but with the hope that when the building was completed and rented a larger and/or lower-rate and/or longer-term loan could be obtained elsewhere.

3. Cost Controls and Builder's Fee. In the past some insurers contributed front-end equity only rarely, fearing that they would have to put up extra funds if a project ran over budget. Cost overruns have thus been met by the developer, and if he couldn't get the extra cash the insurer could refuse to fund its commitments. While the guaranteed maximum contract is used, with cost savings to be split by the venturers, the financial partners also realized that for a number of reasons beyond the developer's control (strikes, bad weather, interruption by governmental agencies) costs can increase. The safety valve included in the joint-venture agreement should provide for an equitable coverage of these costs by the financial or developer partner. The increased costs can be added to the equity repaid to the financial partner out of cash flow, or be put up by the developer with a return and returned to him pro rata with the financial partner's equity. Some insurance co-venturers also paid the developer a fee for superintending the process of construction; some few others may still feel the developer's contribution in putting the package together is adequately rewarded by participation in ownership alone.

NEW DIRECTIONS FOR THE INSURERS

Several smaller life insurance companies continued to joint-venture profitably with builders on the basis of more livable formulae. Following the trend of competing financial sources, the insurers have also begun venturing beyond apartments into condominium development. The lender will put up various classes of money, amounting to 100% of financing. This will include: (a) land acquisition funds, for which a deferred rate of return is charged; (b) all development funds for architecture and overhead; and (c) any funds required in excess of the mortgage loan. The developer and insurer will agree on a developer's profit, but this is earned on a percentage-of-completion basis. When the cash flow starts, the first money out pays back the pro rata computed interest for contributions. Next, it is allocated to the respective investments. Thereafter, cash flow is split 50–50. This still leaves the developer with little cash flow on the front end, but he can try to make up for it by retaining ownership of boat slips, etc. Typically, these days, if the insurer provides the equity he will prefer to have another lender make the mortgage loan, or vice versa, in order to leverage the return.

If a number of major insurers have withdrawn from their former level of joint-venture activity on apartments, as of 1972 they were actively pursuing another tack: buying up income-producing properties that are built to order for them on a free-and-clear basis. Prudential's equity arm was among those actively involved. Apartment projects in 1972 were purchased at prices yielding 9%–9½% cash flow after vacancy and expenses. Free-standing commercial and industrial properties were being bought to yield 7½% to 8¼% income. There are several advantages to buying this way. The developer handling the project gets a construction loan at 9% and no points to pay — because the lender who'll be buying the building makes him the loan. There are no points to pay for a permanent mortgage. And there are no real estate brokerage fees involved, as there would be in most other sales. So 7% or thereabouts of a project's cost is saved in this fashion.

A BUILDER TALKS ABOUT INSURER JOINT VENTURES

The Ponty-Fenmore organization has engaged in several joint ventures with insurers. This company was one of the first to start developing apartment projects in Marina Del Rey, the big recreation-oriented residential project just south of Los Angeles. Ponty-Fenmore built Tahiti Marina, a $4.5-million 149-unit complex with 230 boat slips as a co-venture with John Hancock. The company's $14 million Pacific Harbor Apartments and Marina Point Harbor Apartments, with 848 units and 1,000 boat slips between them, were the products of a partnership with Travelers Insurance. The company has also built apartments in the Westwood and Brentwood sections of Los Angeles. It put up a 312-unit, $6 million project in Santa Barbara, California. It built about 1,500 units in 1970, and started about 1,500 in 1971.

On most joint ventures, Ponty-Fenmore has become the general partner together with the insurance subsidiary. The parent insurance company becomes the limited partner. In a fifty-fifty deal, the developers would own 50% of the joint venture. The insurance subsidiary is usually a small one (capitalized for a million or two) and comes in as owner of anywhere from

½% to 5%. The parent insurance firm then owns from 49½% to 45% of the deal as a limited partner. By sharing the general partnership between themselves and the subsidiary, the co-venturers share in active management, each having veto power over the other's actions. The subsidiary is small enough not to hazard much in the way of assets if the project gets into trouble. The big limited partner doesn't share in active management; but, of course, it has its own subsidiary looking after its interests. It should be noted that the developers insist on having no personal liability when they go into such a deal. In some cases the co-venturers set up partnerships so that both share in depreciation.

Several basic points also emerge for an operating formula on joint ventures, based on a talk by partner Max Fenmore in the early 1970s:

1. Build in a liberal contingency factor when preparing the cost figures for your co-venturer. When a developer calculates the costs in applying for a loan, he might tend to show low expenses and high income in order to get the highest possible loan. But when working the numbers as a co-venturer it pays to be realistic. "It is very important that we present absolutely honest cost projections," Max says. "Put in every penny you think you are going to need for interest during construction, then add to it. If you are going to have leasing costs, rent-up costs, advertising, and so on, put it in and add something to it. As developers, we have a tendency to be conservative on those costs; we must not be in a co-venture arrangement with our partners. What you save is fine. But what you come up missing in a co-venture deal is murder, because you are stuck for it."

2. Add a builder's fee to your cost projections. The Ponty-Fenmore organization generally gets a builder's fee ranging from 5% to 8%, depending on the size of the project.

3. Negotiate a management fee for the completed project. For Ponty-Fenmore this runs anywhere from 3½% to 5% of gross revenues.

4. Define your partnership goals clearly. On allocation of profits and losses, the worst deal Ponty-Fenmore had was a 60–40 distribution, with the majority going to the co-venturer. Generally the distribution runs 50–50. The developers also pay special attention to cash flow distribution. "If the insurers want to get their capital back before you get any money out of the deal, pass the deal by," Max Fenmore says. "In our deals the insurance partner's capital stays in until all financing occurs. Then of course, they get their capital back. Until that time, they might get a return of someplace from 8% to 11% on their capital contribution."

5. Provide for estate problems. The term of the Ponty-Fenmore partnerships is "longer than any of us as individuals will live — for example, till the year 2025. Then, of course, we provide what happens in case of death." In some partnership agreements, Ponty-Fenmore have arranged to

give their families up to 49% of their respective interests in the project in the form of trusts or gifts.

6. Get a mortgage finance guarantee from your co-venturer. The co-venturing insurance firm usually provides Ponty-Fenmore with a guarantee that it will finance the project if the developers cannot get mortgage financing elsewhere. Then both co-venturing parties have the right to shop for permanent financing at any time until the project is finished. In some instances the insurer will want to be the financial partner but no longer wants to issue the permanent mortgage loan, so he can leverage its investment. In one instance, an insurer co-venturing with Ponty-Fenmore secured a long-term mortgage from a New York savings bank.

7. Insist on a specific individual to represent the co-venturer. "This is important," Max Fenmore says. "We want to always deal with an individual — somebody we can talk to day or night, or on weekends if necessary. We have that arrangement with each of the insurance companies and it works out well. In large cities, most insurance companies have correspondents. But my advice is to try desperately to deal with somebody at the home office who has the authority. He is then your partner. It can save weeks of time and lots of aggravation."

27

The Builder: So You Want to Put Your Own Deal Together

> He which that nothyng undertaketh, nothyng n'acheveth.
>
> —Geoffrey Chaucer

Let's assume that you're neither a big-gun developer who's been turning over joint-venture deals for twenty years, nor a well-heeled financial wheeler-dealer. You think you know something about real estate. And you're sitting there in Centerville wondering how to get in on the action by putting your own joint-venture deal together with a financial source for a partner. What do you need to know?

This subject can be extremely detailed, but let's make it simple. Keep in mind the basic principle of the joint venture: that it brings together partners who contribute different capabilities and resources to the common goal of making a profit. The joint venture is formed between two or more otherwise unrelated parties when they achieve a mutuality of interest, each bringing to the venture what the other can't supply. The basic question you have to answer for yourself is this: What can I contribute to a joint-venture deal that would make me a desirable partner? Your answer will indicate your best method of approach to structuring a deal.

In formulating the answer to your question, make a thorough appraisal of yourself and your capabilities in light of the essential elements of any joint-venture deal. The basic ingredients of a successful joint venture organized for the purpose of developing and selling a housing product are:

1. Identification of a specific profit opportunity
2. The land required for development
3. Capital
4. Builder-developer capability
5. Marketing capability
6. Management capability to superintend the venture

Depending on your particular situation, you can become part of a joint venture by bringing one or more of the above elements to it.

It will, of course, help you considerably if you already have a per-

493

formance record of some kind, demonstrating your competence to conceive and execute a project successfully. Consolidated financial statements (certi-fied) showing your score in this area are a strong sales tool with a financial source. But your route still need not be blocked if you don't have such a track record. The key to your success can be your entrepreneurial role in identifying a specific profit opportunity, perceiving the appropriate partners who will make the project viable, and then bringing them together in a credible package to present to the financial source. You bring them together by showing each partner how he benefits by contributing his skills and re-sources to the deal.

Don't forget that a joint venture doesn't have to be a gigantic one. They can be minute in size, ranging from a project as small as a single duplex or fourplex. We can get mesmerized by the big deals and forget that there are profits in small deals too, as well as an excellent way to build a track record if you don't have one. The key for you to remember is that the j-v must answer complementary needs of the parties involved.

GAINING THE LEVERAGE TO MAKE A DEAL

Your basic leverage — your talking point — as an entrepreneur is gained by your perception of a specific development opportunity and your control of the land for the prospective venture. You earn your right to par-ticipate in the deal by perceiving a particularly strong housing demand and tying up the land for the housing product (by lease option, lease, purchase option or fee simple ownership). You may also enter the entrepreneurial role by controlling a housing concept that is ascertained to be highly mar-ketable in given markets because of price advantage, density advantages or other features (McKeon Construction Company's fourplexes are an ex-ample). Starting from one of these two approaches, you would develop a valid pro forma financial model of the project and then begin assembling the team of partners who can successfully translate the project into reality.

Here, you must begin thinking like a *creator*. In lining up your part-ners, ask yourself: What skills and talents does this package need to be credible to a financial partner who will be asked to contribute the equity funding for the deal? Many builders, particularly the smaller ones, have not been very sophisticated financially and have operated on an adversary basis: the conduct of the business is one long battle between the builder and his lenders, subcontractors, leasing agents, realtors, and so on. But you should begin looking at all of these entities as potential allies and *partners* who can contribute the skills and resources to make the joint-venture deal come alive. Search for the common interest that can bind you together to make a whole working team.

Supposing you own or have tied up land that you believe to have a strong potential for development, but you need to define the specific housing product and to credibly document a strong local demand for that product. This immediately suggests selecting a credible marketing organization to define a housing demand and the right product for it, on the basis of which a reasonably valid financial pro forma can be prepared and preliminary architectural plans drawn. Supposing you have credibly documented a strong housing need but lack the development expertise. This suggests bringing an established contractor or developer into the deal as the co-venturer who will supply the needed stable element of ability and knowhow. Supposing you need sales-marketing talents; this suggests bringing in an established marketing organization to serve this function as a co-venturer.

Especially, do not neglect the financial source you already know, be it an insurer, a savings and loan service corporation, a mortgage banker, or a title insurance company. There is more interest among financial institutions of all types today in participating in an equity role in development than ever before. If you bring a financial service organization a credible package — perhaps showing it how it can make money on refinancing the land and on construction and mortgage financing in addition to profits flowing from an equity position in the deal — you may get yourself a strong partner. A major developer, perhaps a publicly listed firm, can also become a joint-venture partner supplying you with the required equity capital, and providing some sharp controls to boot. It's important to get a financial partner who already understands the building business inside out and can recognize the merits of your team and your deal as well as providing you with the support you may need, rather than breaking new ground with investors untried in the field. For this reason some types of lenders, mortgage bankers and major developers can make good co-venturers.

Savings and loan associations through the vehicle of their holding companies make excellent joint-venture partners for many small builders. Developers like Roger Boyar and Murray Ozer of California's San Fernando Valley have successful histories of such relationships. Harris Laskey (not to be confused with Harrison Lasky), of the Los Angeles-based Laskey-Weil Company, began developing a substantial condominium project in the Pacific Palisades area with an S&L as a partner in 1972. The number of savings and loan associations actively seeking equity-type relationships with smaller builders continues to grow. Unlike insurers, they tend to get more involved on smaller projects and in primarily for-sale ventures such as single-family housing and condominiums. The S&L's increasingly have the attitude that if the deal is good enough to put 90% financing into, it's good enough to be financed 100% by the S&L for half the profits. It's a good deal for the builder, too, offering him 100% financing on advantageous terms for something like half the profits of the venture (although the percentage distribution varies with each deal).

JOINT VENTURES FOR THE LANDOWNER

Many landowners go the joint-venture route because they find it difficult to locate a private or corporate investor substantial enough to buy their property. For the big landowner, the joint venture can be an excellent solution. It can make substantially more money for him with very little more risk than he might incur in selling the property outright. The landowner continues to inventory the land, reducing the developer's own carrying costs; an attractive feature even to well-capitalized firms. If the market softens, the developer can usually make adjustments on the portions of the property that he is obligated for. But the joint venture permits the landowner to participate in profits not only from the sale of land but also from the profits of development and sale of housing. If the landowner is smart he can also get very involved with the builder and thus control the latter well; on an outright sale he loses all control of the land and what may be done to it.

A joint venture may be a slower way for the landowner to dispose of his land, but when he does sell it (and it is subsequently developed and sold with housing on it) it stays sold. On a bulk land sale to a major purchaser, however, there is always the possibility that the seller would end up with the land back in his lap if the purchaser is not able or not willing to continue his payments. With the flexible arrangements often made on such sales, this can happen. It could prove disastrous to the landowner if in the meantime he made other financial commitments predicated on income from the sale — he could wind up losing both his land and whatever other ventures he had become involved in. I know of at least one instance where a very large parcel of several thousand acres reverted to the owner, Camarillo Ranch in California's Ventura County. The property was bought by Great Lakes Properties, subsidiary of Great Lakes Carbon, and again ended up with the original owner when the purchaser perceived adverse market conditions.

As already noted, purchases of large parcels on any terms are becoming rarer and the landholders go into joint ventures for this reason if not for any other. The only time an outright acquisition of a major property makes sense for a builder any more is when there is a decided advantage in price that largely offsets any risk of adverse market conditions. Such a sale might be structured in the following way: the builder arranges to have released to him only whatever land he needs for immediate development, with the minimum release (or "takedown") set at an extremely low fraction of the total acreage for any given year. Some developers have a requirement for a takedown of 50 acres annually, fully anticipating that they can absorb twice to ten times that much but hedging very conservatively against downside risk in bad years.

Buyers these days may not even pay interest on the principal balance as a condition of purchasing an *entire* parcel at once. But the wise developer will obligate himself for as little as possible; he will set up realistic release clauses and secure options to buy additional increments at a higher price. The price set in the option agreements may be higher than the cost of buying the additional parcels and paying their carrying costs. But the conservative, bit-by-bit approach is actually cheaper. The developer avoids the carrying costs that come with the purchase of the entire parcel; $100,000 or so payable as interest can usually be used much more profitably in other projects. At the same time the developer eliminates his downside risk by staying clear of obligation for the whole property. When he can actually use the land it's worth it to him to pay the higher incremental price. It's not really a higher price when you take into consideration the alternative use of the dollars that would have gone toward interest payments, and the lowered risk.

WHAT THE FINANCIAL PARTNER LOOKS FOR

Your prospective financial partner will look, first of all, at your team's *proven ability* to execute the project you are proposing. So, a strong marketing plan and the involvement of a competent construction capability is essential in the proposed venture. You can generally get the prospective financial partner's indication of interest of the basis of a preliminary cost and profit analysis for the project (such as the one included later in this chapter). But you will have to create a detailed economic analysis for final approval. Your presentation need not be complex or voluminous. You must include the sponsors of the venture, a *complete* marketing analysis for the project, detailed pro formas, and a presentation that will answer all questions pertaining to the deal.

The basic data in the presentation should include:

1. Location map identifying the site.
2. Sketch plot plan indicating dimensions of site.
3. Zoning information.
4. Availability of utilities.
5. Photographs of site and adjacent sites.
6. Copy of option or purchase agreement.
7. Legal description.

8. Market demand projections based on a marketing study analyzing the economic, competitive and consumer characteristics of the area. These projections are extremely important to the prospective financial partner. The study should be conducted by an independent third party that has credibility with lending institutions.
9. Overall project financial analysis, showing required equity capital, the length of time for its use, site development and improvement costs, and projected profits.
10. Land use plan and building design concepts.
11. Names and addresses of the project's sponsors and their principal businesses and activities.
12. Bank references of the sponsors, together with current personal and business financial statements.
13. Background data on sponsors, including all previous experience in the field, together with delineation of their respective responsibilities in the proposed venture.

The structure of the joint venture is generally determined by legal limitations (e.g., role of lender) as well as by tax consequences and responsibilities of the participants in the venture. The deal can be a limited partnership if one partner has a non-managerial, passive role and wants to limit his liability. If both partners participate in the management, it will be set up as a general partnership. Usually, when a financial partner comes into a deal and is the one to provide guarantees to lenders, he automatically becomes a general partner along with the other principal co-venturers. A corporation formed for purposes of joint venture has the liability of double taxation; the profits are taxed at the corporate tax rate in the venture itself, and taxed again when they are passed on to the co-venturing parties. Some major corporations occasionally form incorporated joint ventures on major development deals (see, for example, joint-venturing by the merger route in Chapter XXIV), but as a rule most joint ventures for residential development have been of the unincorporated variety. In some cases an incorporated joint venture may be the best way of limiting liability to the venture itself.

SOLVE PROBLEMS TO PUT A DEAL TOGETHER —AND CONTROL THE LAND

The key to putting together a successful joint-venture deal is not, however, a polished presentation. If the project is speculative or is not *demonstrably* going to meet a documented strong market demand, you can forget it. No financial partner is going to take a flier with you unless the venture looks exceptionally strong from the initial presentation. The numbers have to work and the market for the proposed housing product must be a strong one. I say this to warn you away from putting in considerable time packaging up deals that may be regarded as marginal. Even experienced builders are not exempt from this sin, which illustrates the degree of their competence. It is because of many builders' incompetence that a lot of financial people have bypassed them and have gone into direct development and construction themselves, figuring they could do it better and deserved the profits.

Assuming, however, that you have a really sound deal, you are going to be successful in selling a financial partner on it and you will have a role in the venture if:

1. You control the land for the deal by lease or purchase option before you start seeking financial aid.
2. You solve the problems the various parties to the deal may have and create incentives whereby each gets the most by participating in the joint venture. This is creative financial structuring of a deal.

Structuring a joint venture is a *problem-solving* business. I can illustrate this with two examples of joint ventures in which the firm I previously headed has been involved.

Let me first qualify our own usual contribution to a joint venture. Our market research and consulting capability enabled us to identify and document specific development opportunities from time to time. Through our affiliate architectural and planning firm, Goodkin Ruderman Valdivia, we had access to the requisite architectural and planning skills. And we involved ourselves in complete marketing program design for such projects, as well as organizing and managing the sales-marketing function. We usually brought in a smaller competent contractor-developer for the construction function to work under our supervision when joint-venturing with a financial source. This typically left us with only the equity capital requirement to secure. And this we acquired by joint-venturing with both major developers and financial services organizations serving the real estate field.

DEAL NO. 1 — AN EXAMPLE

In one instance the identification of the opportunity was relatively simple. In an area of Southern California where our surveys disclosed an exceptionally strong, documented demand for homes in the under-$30,000 price range, we discovered a developer who wanted for health reasons to get out of a sound, ongoing subdivision marketing homes in the $26,000-$28,000 price range. The subdivision had a potential for another 153 home sales at a profit of about $3,000 per unit, or about $500,000 in all. Now we had a demonstrable profit opportunity and faced certain problems that had to be solved successfully to make the deal viable for us.

The selling developer had built and sold 120 homes. He held a remaining 108 acres of undeveloped land personally on a first trust deed. He felt that he had enhanced the value of this land surrounding the completed homes by about $2,000 or more per acre. So he would sell the whole package for approximately $300,000 to a new developer wishing to build out the remainder of the project. We felt we could arrange to bring a proven builder into a venture organized for this purpose, to handle construction under our supervision. But we had to solve three problems first:

1. Assuming the first trust deed held by an individual
2. Arranging for the selling builder to receive an additional $2,000 per acre (or $300,000 in all) for the land held, to buy him out at capitalized value added
3. Securing approximately $150,000 in front-end equity capital for the operating costs of the new entity that would develop the remainder of the project

We solved all these problems by bringing in a mortgage banking firm to arrange refinancing of the land at its higher value and become our equity partner in a joint venture for the development of the project. Ascertaining that the $2,000 added to the per-acre price was merited and would not inflate per-lot cost, the mortgage banker arranged for a wraparound mortgage that gave the selling developer the deal he wanted. Then, for 50% of the profits, the mortgage firm funded the equity requirement of the joint venture. As a condition of providing capital, the company also reserved for itself the right to line up the construction loans for the project and the right to secure the mortgage financing upon the sale of the homes. Our arrangement called for the mortgage broker to be the limited partner, with our building-development team acting as the general partner and handling all construction and sales-marketing functions.

DEAL NO. 2 — AN EXAMPLE

In another instance, our ongoing research activities identified an exceptionally strong market for high-density apartment condominium units in the under-$25,000 price bracket in a certain Southern California city. We were especially fortunate to locate a most advantageous piece of land in this market for the product; because of the strategic location of the parcel within the market, we knew the demand for moderate-priced, attractive condominium units would be redoubled. Thus, we identified the profit opportunity. And again, we had a series of problems to solve before the project could be made real.

Our initial analyses showed that the project could support the sale of approximately 250 units on leased ground and show a pretax profit of about $1 million. Our first objective was to demonstrate the feasibility of the project to the landowner and tie up the property on a lease option. The property was not to be sold in fee but leased to purchasers of the condominium units built on it for an average monthly lease payment of $40 per unit, or about $120,000 a year gross income to the landowner on a sixty-five year net ground lease. As a sweetener, we threw in a kicker giving the landowner a 3% share of the gross profits, with two payments of $30,000 each in advance, from the sale of the condominium units.

Having secured the lease option, we organized the sales-marketing concept and prepared the preliminary architectural materials on the basis of our detailed marketing and financial analysis of the proposed product. We introduced a competent local developer as a second party to the venture, to handle construction activities under our marketing supervisor. As a final step, we took the package to a major corporation engaged in development throughout the Southwest to provide the equity funds for the project. We had ascertained the interest of the funding source early in the game, based on a preliminary analysis of the project's profitability, so we weren't knocking on the door in the dark.

The funding source for a net equity capital contribution of approximately $250,000 (though never exceeding $125,000 on a cash-flow basis) became a 55.9% partner in the joint venture through a subsidiary corporation. The contractor became an 8.8% partner. And our Goodkin Group became 35.3% partners in the venture, principally for our skills in packaging the venture and for contribution of the lease option and architectural and ongoing marketing skills. The venture was organized as a general partnership.

This joint venture moved along at a more rapid pace than we expected it to and generated a substantially greater profit than initially projected. This was due to a higher actual demand for the units than our initially projected absorption rate, which in turn enabled us to increase prices without materially affecting the sales route. The philosophy has been to be conservative on projections and be pleasantly surprised rather than trying to make the highest profits on paper and suffering the consequences of reality.

This relates again to the importance of good market research. Some builders use it only as a tool to get financing, but it is perhaps even more valuable as a tool in making the right decisions fast. Ongoing research gave us the edge on making rapid decisions in a highly competitive marketplace. Timing is of the essence in real estate, and as little as a thirty-day edge on the competition can provide the builder with a dominant position in his market by the momentum he creates. Good research enables the builder to make fast decisions on land purchases without sacrificing judgment. Many builders do this backwards, first selecting a project and only then getting it researched. It slows them down too much.

With a thorough understanding of the market based on prior research, the builder can not only move fast on good land acquisitions and get into construction early; he also knows where the other good parcels are located and has them as a backup. Too often we have seen a builder acquire a parcel and develop a very successful project, only to run out of land and become an observer as the competition starts hitchhiking on his initial success. McKeon, for example, gathered tremendous strength with his four-plex program in Palm Desert but had no backup parcels available in antici-pation of such success. Others passed him by. Often this situation can result from a builder's sketchy or inadequate understanding of the under-lying and real forces of the market. This is dangerous if he has overstated his position and very disappointing if he has understated it, as did McKeon.

The remainder of this chapter presents some of the working papers of this joint venture. The three key documents are:

1. The preliminary financial analysis of the proposed project.
2. The preliminary agreement governing the lease option acquired by the Goodkin Group.
3. The preliminary joint venture agreement between the parties to the venture.

It is emphasized that these working papers were drafts toward a particular venture in a specific situation, responsive to the specific needs of the parties involved. They are not intended to, and should not, serve as examples for anyone else. They are presented only to illustrate how a particular venture was handled.

PRELIMINARY FINANCIAL ANALYSIS OF CONDOMINIUM DEVELOPMENT

1. Factors Used for Project Analysis
    A. Total acreage — 13 ± ac.
    B. Total number of apartments — 251
    C. Average apartment — 925 sq. ft., 2 bedroom, 2 bath
    D. Average apartment sale price — $23,250
    E. Average monthly lease payment — $40
    F. Real estate tax — monthly estimate — $35
    G. Monthly maintenance estimate — $35
    H. 15% minimum down payment
    I. Construction finance — 80% of appraisal — ($22,000)
    J. Buyer finance — 85% of sale price — ($23,250)
2. Construction and Sales Schedule
    A. November 1, 19—— to April 30, 19——   50 apartments

B. May 1, 19—— to October 30, 19——   50 apartments
C. November 1, 19—— to April 30, 19——   50 apartments
D. May 1, 19—— to October 30, 19——   50 apartments
E. November 1, 19—— to April 30, 19——   51 apartments

Total elapsed time for total construction and sales — 30 months

3. Construction Cost Estimate — 925 sq. ft. Average Apartment

1.	925 sq. ft. @ $12 per sq. ft.	$11,100.00	
2.	Overhead and supervision	575.00	
3.	Miscellaneous labor	125.00	
4.	3% contingency and pickup	350.00	
5.	Share of on-site concrete walks	150.00	
6.	Covered parking	800.00	
7.	Rough and finish on-site grading	100.00	
	Total Direct Costs		$13,200.00
	Total Direct Costs per sq. ft.		$ 14.27
8.	Sewage disposal	200.00	
9.	Off-site streets and paving	360.00	
10.	On-site streets and paving	140.00	
11.	Water mains and meters	230.00	
12.	Flood control contingency	40.00	
13.	Electricity, phone, TV and gas	200.00	
14.	Landscape, sprinklers and lighting	500.00	
15.	1/60th share, swimming pool and deck	150.00	
16.	Engineering and legal descriptions	180.00	
17.	Architecture	200.00	
18.	Legal costs and governmental fees	100.00	
19.	1½% construction loan fee	265.00	
20.	8¼% interest on construction loan	730.00	
21.	Tax and insurance until apartment sale	200.00	
22.	1 month maintenance until apartment sale	35.00	
23.	Model costs, proration of loss	100.00	
24.	Advertising and brochures	400.00	
	Total Additional Costs		$ 4,030.00
	Total Cost of Construction		17,230.00
	Additional Contingency Fund		270.00
	Total Estimated Construction Cost		$ 17,500.00
	Total Cost per sq. ft.		$ 18.92

4. Sale Price (Leased Land) — 925 sq. ft. Average Apartment

A.	Total estimated construction cost	$ 17,500.00
B.	Sale closing costs	200.00
C.	2½% sale commission	600.00
D.	Move-in cleaning	50.00
E.	1½% take-out loan fee — builder share	300.00
	Total Estimated Costs	$ 18,650.00
	Profit	4,600.00
	Total Sale Price	$ 23,250.00

5. Construction Financing — 925 sq. ft. Average Apartment
Assume lender appraisal of $22,000 per apartment. A federal savings and loan commitment of 80% of appraised value for construction loan purposes. Construction loan of $17,600 — assume $17,500 to be actual loan commitment.

A. Appraised value of apartment	$ 22,000.00
B. Total construction cost estimate	$ 17,500.00
C. 80% loan commitment	$ 17,500.00
Construction cash required	None

6. Sale Financing — 925 sq. ft. Average Apartment
Assume lender commitment of 85% of actual sale price of $23,250.00 Take-out loan of $19,750.00, 8¼% interest, 25 years, buyer to pay 1½% loan fee — approximately $300.00.

A. 85% first trust deed and note	$ 19,750.00
B. Cash down payment	3,500.00
Total Sale Price	$ 23,250.00
C. Cash proceeds from sale:	
1. 1st. trust deed net cash ($17,500 const. loan)	$ 2,250.00
2. Cash down payment	3,500.00
Gross cash proceeds	$ 5,750.00
D. Net cash proceeds from sale:	
1. Deduct closing costs	$ 200.00
2. Deduct sale commission	600.00
3. Deduct move-in cleaning	50.00
4. Deduct builder share loan fee	300.00
Net cash proceeds from sale	$ 4,600.00

7. Buyer Monthly Payments — Ownership Costs

A. 1st trust deed and note	$ 155.73
B. Land lease payment	40.00
C. Monthly maintenance	35.00
D. Real estate tax and insurance — estimate	40.00
Total monthly ownership costs	$ 270.73

8. Cash Flow from Apartment Sales

6 months — 50 apartments	$230,000.00
12 months — 50 apartments	230,000.00
18 months — 50 apartments	230,000.00
24 months — 50 apartments	230,000.00
30 months — 51 apartments	234,600.00

9. Land Lease Income Schedule

6 months — @ $40 per month per apartment	None
12 months — 50 for 6 months	$ 12,000.00
18 months — 50 for one year — 50 for 6 months	36,000.00
24 months — 100 for one year — 50 for 6 months	60,000.00
30 months — 150 for one year — 50 for 6 months	84,000.00
36 months — 200 for one year — 51 for 6 months	108,480.00
42 months — 251 for one year	120,480.00

10. Monthly Lease Charges — Per Apartment

20 — 1 story single units — 1400 sq. ft. @ $59	$ 1,180.00
41 — multi-story units — 1125 sq. ft. @ $47	1,927.00
120 — multi-story units — 925 sq. ft. @ $40	4,800.00
70 — multi-story units — 725 sq. ft. @ $30	2,100.00
251 — total units — total lease income	$ 10,007.00
Total estimated annual lease income:	
$10,007.00 monthly × 12	$120,084.00

UNIT #1 — 50 APARTMENTS:

A. Cash Requirements Prior to Loan Recording

1. Payment to land owners	$ 30,000.00
2. Architecture	25,000.00
3. Engineering	20,000.00
4. Legal and governmental fees	10,000.00
5. Contingency reserve fund	10,000.00
Total preliminary costs	$ 95,000.00

B. Additional Costs After Loan Recording

1. Payment to land owners	$ 30,000.00
2. Off-site streets and paving	90,000.00
3. Water mains	20,000.00
4. Sewers	25,000.00
5. Flood control contingency	10,000.00
6. Electricity, TV, phone and gas	10,000.00
7. Model costs — 4 @ $8,000 average	32,000.00
Total additional costs	$217,000.00

C. Additional Costs Included in Construction Loans

1. Architecture @ $200 each	$ 10,000.00
2. Engineering @ $180 each	9,250.00
3. Legal and governmental @ $100 each	5,000.00
4. Off-site streets @ $360 each	18,000.00
5. Water mains @ $230 each	11,500.00
6. Sewers @ $200 each	10,000.00
7. Flood control @ $40 each	2,000.00
8. Electricity, phone, etc. @ $200 each	10,000.00
9. Model costs @ $100 each	5,000.00
Total costs included in loans	$ 80,750.00

D. Total Equity Capital to Start Job

1. Cash, prior to loan recording	$ 95,000.00
2. Total additional costs	217,000.00
Total gross capital	$312,000.00
Deduct costs included in const. loans	80,750.00
Net equity capital required	$231,250.00

E. Capital Investment Remaining After 50 Sales

1. Net equity capital invested	$231,250.00

UNIT #2 — 50 APARTMENTS

A. Cash Requirements Prior to Loan Recording
   1. Architecture $ 7,000.00
   2. Engineering   7,000.00
   3. Legal and governmental fees   5,000.00
   4. Contingency reserve fund   10,000.00

      Total preliminary costs $ 29,000.00

B. Additional Costs After Loan Recording
   1. Payment to land owners $ 30,000.00
   2. Water mains   8,000.00
   3. Sewers   8,000.00
   4. Electricity, TV, phone and gas   10,000.00
   5. Unit #1 — remaining investment   1,250.00

      Total additional costs $ 57,250.00

C. Additional Costs Included in Construction Loans
   1. Architecture @ $200 each $ 10,000.00
   2. Engineering @ $180 each   9,250.00
   3. Legal and governmental @ $100 each   5,000.00
   4. Off-site streets @ $360 each   18,000.00
   5. Water mains @ $230 each   11,500.00
   6. Sewers @ $200 each   10,000.00
   7. Flood control @ $40 each   2,000.00
   8. Electricity, phone, etc. @ $200 each   10,000.00
   9. Model costs @ $100 each   5,000.00

      Total costs included in loans $ 80,750.00

D. Total Equity Capital to Start Job
   1. Cash prior to loan recording $ 29,000.00
   2. Total additional costs   57,250.00

      Total gross capital $ 86,250.00
      Deduct costs included in const. loans   80,750.00

      Net equity capital required $ 5,500.00

E. Gross Profit After 100 Sales
   1. Cash income — 50 sales $230,000.00
   2. Deduct net equity capital   5,500.00

      12-Month Profit, Before Tax $224,500.00

UNIT #3 — 50 APARTMENTS

A. Cash Requirements Prior to Loan Recording
   1. Architecture $ 7,000.00
   2. Engineering   6,000.00
   3. Legal and governmental fees   5,000.00
   4. Contingency reserve fund   10,000.00

      Total preliminary costs $ 28,000.00

B. Additional Costs After Loan Recording

1. Payment to land owners	$ 30,000.00
2. Water mains	8,000.00
3. Sewers	8,000.00
4. Electricity, TV, phone and gas	10,000.00
Total additional costs	$ 56,000.00

C. Additional Costs Included in Construction Loans

1. Architecture @ $200 each	$ 10,000.00
2. Engineering @ $180 each	9,250.00
3. Legal and governmental @ $100 each	5,000.00
4. Off-site streets @ $360 each	18,000.00
5. Water mains @ $230 each	11,500.00
6. Sewers @ $200 each	10,000.00
7. Flood control @ $40 each	2,000.00
8. Electricity, phone, etc. @ $200 each	10,000.00
9. Model costs @ $100 each	5,000.00
Total costs included in loans	$ 80,750.00

D. Total Equity Capital to Start Job

1. Cash prior to loan recording	$ 28,000.00
2. Total additional costs	56,000.00
Total gross capital	$ 84,000.00
Deduct costs included in const. loans	80,750.00
Net equity capital required	$ 3,250.00

E. Gross Profit After 150 Sales

1. Cash income — 50 sales	$230,000.00
2. Deduct net equity capital	3,250.00
3. Profit before tax	$226,750.00
4. 12-month profit — before tax	224,500.00
18-Month Accrued Profit, Before Tax	$451,250.00

UNIT #4 — 50 APARTMENTS:

A. Cash Requirements Prior to Loan Recording

1. Architecture	$ 7,000.00
2. Engineering	6,000.00
3. Legal and governmental	5,000.00
4. Contingency reserve fund	10,000.00
Total preliminary costs	$ 28,000.00

B. Additional Costs After Loan Recording

1. Water mains	$ 8,000.00
2. Sewers	8,000.00
3. Electricity, TV, phone and gas	10,000.00
Total additional costs	$ 26,000.00

C. Additional Costs Included in Construction Loans

1. Architecture @ $200 each	$ 10,000.00
2. Engineering @ $180 each	9,250.00
3. Legal and governmental @ $100 each	5,000.00
4. Off-site streets @ $360 each	18,000.00
5. Water mains @ $230 each	11,500.00
6. Sewers @ $200 each	10,000.00
7. Flood control @ $40 each	2,000.00
8. Electricity, phone, etc. @ $200 each	10,000.00
9. Model costs @ $100 each	5,000.00
Total costs included in loans	$ 80,750.00

D. Equity Capital Surplus

1. Costs included in construction loans	$ 80,750.00
2. Deduct cash prior to loan recording	28,000.00
3. Deduct additional costs	26,000.00
Total cash surplus	$ 26,750.00

E. Gross Profit After 200 Sales

1. Cash income — 50 sales	$230,000.00
2. Equity capital surplus	26,750.00
3. Profit Before Tax	$256,750.00
4. 18-month accrued profit, before tax	$451,250.00
24-Month Accrued Profit, Before Tax	$708,000.00

UNIT #5 — 51 APARTMENTS:

A. Cash Requirements Prior to Loan Recording

1. Architecture	$ 4,000.00
2. Engineering	6,000.00
3. Legal and governmental fees	5,000.00
Total preliminary costs	$ 15,000.00

B. Additional Costs After Loan Recording

1. Water mains	$ 3,530.00
*2. Sewers	1,000.00
3. Electricity, TV, phone and gas	10,000.00
Total additional costs	$ 14,530.00

* NOTE: Gross sewer costs include $10,000 extra
for house laterals.

C. Additional Costs Included in Construction Loans

1. Architecture and Engineering @ $380.00 each	$ 19,380.00
2. Legal and governmental @ $100 each	5,100.00
3. Off-site streets @ $360 each	18,360.00
4. Water mains and meters @ $230 each	11,730.00
5. Sewers @ $200 each	10,200.00
6. Flood control @ $40 each	2,040.00
7. Electricity, phone, etc. @ $200 each	10,200.00
8. Model costs @ $100 each	5,100.00
Total costs included in loans	$ 82,110.00

D. Equity Capital Surplus
  1. Costs included in construction loans — $ 82,110.00
  2. Deduct preliminary and additional costs — 29,530.00

  Total cash surplus — $ 52,580.00

E. Gross Profit After 251 Sales
  1. Cash income — 51 sales — $234,600.00
  2. Equity capital surplus — 52,580.00

  3. Profit Before Tax — $287,180.00
  4. 24 month accrued profit — before tax — $708,000.00
  5. Return contingency reserves — 40,000.00

  30-month gross accrued profits — $1,035,180.00
  Deduct final payment to landowners — 55,000.00

  30-Month Accrued Profit, Before Tax — $980,180.00

PROJECT COMPLETE

PRELIMINARY AGREEMENT SECURING LEASE OPTION

A builder/developer team to be selected and managed by the Goodkin group, proposes to do the following:

1. Build or cause to be built 251 (more or less) living units, to be either for lease or for sale.

2. To provide all equity and debt monies necessary to accomplish the above. Under no conditions or circumstances will properties or lands belonging to the owner/lessor be subordinated or pledged to secure financing.

3. Builder/developer will share profits with the owner/lessor to the extent of 3% of gross sales, estimated to be $180,000 (approximately).

4. Builder/developer will advance to owner/lessor $30,000 upon entering into a binding agreement. An additional $30,000 shall be advanced owner/lessor prior to beginning construction of first increment of 251 units. All sums so advanced shall be deducted from owner/lessor's share of 3% of gross sales.

5. Builder/developer will further advance to the owner/lessor $30,000 on the first year anniversary date of the first $30,000 advance. Six months after the first year anniversary (18 months from the date of first $30,000 advance) a fourth advance of $30,000 shall be made. At this time a total of $120,000 shall have been advanced to owner/lessor. Should ground rents within the following 6 months fail to annalize at $40,000 a year, builder/developer shall contribute another $20,000. Said $20,000 shall be a builder/developer credit applied to and deducted from owner/lessor's 3% of gross participation.

6. Builder/developer will create for the owner/lessor by reason of builder/developer constructions of 251 units (more or less) of either rent or sale living units, certain ground leases. The rents accruing from such ground leases shall be for the sole benefit of the owner/lessor, and shall be spelled out in greater detail below.

7. As the aforementioned living units are sold, a ground lease shall be created between the living unit purchaser (buyer) and the owner/lessor for his sole benefit. Said lease shall be for a period of 65 years. It is the builder/

developer's opinion at this time that such leases can produce an average of $40/mo. ground rent for owner/lessor's sole account.

8. In the event sale of the units is economically unfeasible (absorption rate too slow, poor location, etc.) builder/developer will switch to a rental/lease program. It is believed that such a program would yield the same average ground rents to the owner/lessor.

9. As often happens in tract sales, some models are more in demand than others. That being the case, builder/developer reserves the right to build and sell those units that will sell the easiest and quickest. It is recognized that there is a possibility the smaller unit may be the most popular. If this should be the case, it will be impossible to yield a $40/unit ground rent average. This possibility should not reduce gross yield as the builder/developer should obtain greater density and number of units, thereby making it possible to create more leases and thus derive greater gross rentals. In the event (builder/developer considers this unlikely) larger units are to the market's demand, we will find the number of units decreasing, but unit ground rents will be greater because of the increased square footage of the units. Builder/developer does not anticipate this event would materially alter the gross yield of ground rent to the owner/lessor.

10. During that time of construction builder/developer will maintain that portion of the remaining 13 acres not under construction, but to later be built upon, in a green and verdant condition, so as not to detract from the environment, but rather to enhance same. Builder/developer further agrees to maintain the 5-acre parcel fronting on Highway _____ in a similar manner.

11. Builder/developer shall make every effort to complete a total build-out of subject project, but shall not be held responsible in the event of actions or activities beyond his control (war, strike, earthquake, etc.).

12. Upon completion and sale of the final unit of said project, builder/developer shall account to owner/lessor for all gross sales, and owner/lessor to receive all monies accruing and due by virtue of his participating in a 3% share of gross sales (less aforementioned advances). In the event the project is rented or leased by builder/developer rather than sold, no further monies are owed owner/lessor by virtue of owner/lessor's 3% participation. If builder/developer elects to rent/lease said units, he still must honor his money advance commitment to owner/lessor as stated elsewhere in this agreement, ($30,000 on signing agreement, $30,000 on start of construction, $30,000 first yearly anniversary of first payment, $30,000 six months following. Total $120,000.)

FORFEITURE

Should builder/developer be unable to complete said project, he will transfer all right, title and interest in all plans, working drawings, engineering to the owner/lessor as forfeiture compensation. Builder/developer places a conservative value of $60,000 on the aforementioned assets. Further, all legal documents pertaining to the creation of the legal entity known as a "condominium" shall become the property of the owner/lessor. Builder/developer places a conservative value of $10,000 on the aforementioned asset.

IMPROVEMENT TO ADJACENT STREET

Builder/developer will pay for all grading, asphalting, curbing and guttering arising from owner/lessor dedicating certain of his lands to the city of

_____. Said dedication to be for widening and straightening of that certain street along the subject properties westerly boundary known as _____. Under no condition or circumstance will any cost other than dedication of said land befall owner/lessor.

The owner/lessor by accepting the proposals made by the Goodkin Group, will do or cause, or allow the following to be done, and shall be binding on both parties:

1. Will allow the builder/developer to build 251 (more or less) living units, either to sell or to lease. Said sales or lease money shall be deposited solely to the builder/developer's account.

2. Owner/lessor shall draw all ground leases by and between himself and builder/developer customers at owner/lessor's expense. All leases must be acceptable to builder/developer's lenders.

3. Owner/lessor shall grant builder/developer sufficient time to build his product in a workmanlike manner, as well as sufficient time to sell or lease the same. Sufficient time is to be 48 months from the time the builder/developer and owner/lessor enter into a binding agreement.

4. It is agreed by the owner/lessor that should builder/developer lender demand a moratorium on ground rents due to lender's foreclosure action, such moratorium shall be granted by owner/lessor. The moratorium period would be for such time as it takes the lender to resell or lease the subject property. If owner/lessor demands of builder/developer a surety bond to compensate owner/lessor in the event of ground rent deficiencies by purchase/lessees, then owner/lessor shall pay the premium on said bond. Said bond not to exceed $25,000. Obligation and liability on said lease, as guarantor, ceases upon the 3rd annual anniversary of the creation of said lease.

5. All plans and drawings of proposed projects shall be submitted to owner/lessor for his approval. Such approval may not be arbitrarily or capriciously withheld.

6. Owner/lessor will restrict the use of subject 13-acre construction zone in conformance with builder/developer liability insurance.

7. Builder/developer will hold owner/lessor free and otherwise harmless from any and all accident liability arising from said construction.

8. Owner/lessor shall have no cost to himself from said project other than those stated herein.

9. Builder/developer will pay all taxes in prorate from the signing of this agreement. Said tax assessment liability shall be on the 13 acres, more or less, to be covered in a subdivision map filed by the builder/developer with the real estate commissioner for approval and recordation.

10. Owner/lessor agrees to make all necessary dedications of "right of way" to the city of _____ as regards to the aligning of (street) _____, so as to cause the city to issue builder/developer the necessary building permits.

11. Owner/lessor will at no time while this agreement is in force, construct, cause or allow to be constructed, any unit, apartment, house or facility to be sold to the public, or in any way compete with the builder/developer project.

12. All trees, foliage and ornamental plants shall remain on the subject property and shall be for the builder/developer's exclusive use.

13. In the event owner/lessor elects to allow construction of additional structures of "for sale" housing, he shall first offer said project to builder/developer under the same terms and conditions as prevail in this project.

PRELIMINARY JOINT VENTURE AGREEMENT

THIS JOINT VENTURE AGREEMENT is made this day of _____,
19_____, among: ABC Corporation, a corporation, hereinafter called "ABC";
Goodstn, Inc., a corporation, hereinafter called "GOODSTN"; and Able Contractor, hereinafter called "CONTRACTOR."

NOW, THEREFORE, the parties hereby form and enter into a joint venture upon the following terms and conditions:

ARTICLE 1

ORGANIZATION

1.1 *Name.* The firm name of this joint venture shall be: XYZ Homes.

1.2 *Purposes.* This joint venture is formed for the purposes of construction, and sale and/or leasing, of one or more condominium, apartment or similar
projects, hereinafter called the "Improvements," on certain unimproved real
property located in the City of _____, County of _____, State of California, hereinafter called the "Real Property" (the legal description of which
is contained in Exhibit A hereto). Pursuant to the terms of that certain Ground
Lease dated August 23, _____, hereinafter called the "Lease" the parties
hereto are the holders of a leasehold interest of the Real Property.

1.3 *Principal Place of Business.* The principal place of business of the
joint venture shall be located at ABC's offices at _____, Los Angeles, California, or at such other place as may be mutually agreed upon by the parties
from time to time.

1.4 *Term.* This joint venture shall have a term commencing as of the
date of this Agreement and continuing until the Improvements have been constructed and the Improvements and Real Property leased and/or sold as provided in this Agreement, or until the joint venture has been terminated as
herein provided or as provided by law.

1.5 *Powers and Limitations.* The joint venture shall have the power to
acquire, lease, develop, and dispose of the Real Property and interests therein;
to engage engineering and planning consultants in connection with the development of the Real Property; to construct or cause to be constructed the Improvements on the Real Property; to sell and/or lease all or any part of the improved
Real Property at such times and on such terms and conditions as may be agreed
upon as hereinafter provided; and, in general, to engage in all activities and take
all actions necessary or appropriate to accomplish the purposes of the joint
venture.

This Agreement shall be deemed and construed to create a joint venture
for the sole purpose of carrying out the activities and accomplishing the purposes referred to herein, and nothing herein shall be construed to create a
general partnership between the parties hereto or, except as specifically provided herein, to authorize any party to act as agent for either or both of the
other parties.

1.6 *Sale and/or Lease of Improved Real Property.* Upon completion of
the construction of the Improvements, or of an Incremental Phase of Construction (as that term is used in the Lease) the improved Real Property, or a part
thereof, shall be offered for sale and/or lease on such terms as the General
Manager of the joint venture may determine.

1.7 *Filing and Publication Requirements.* Upon execution of this Agreement, and upon any change in the parties or principal place of business of this joint venture, the parties shall execute, acknowledge, cause to be filed with the County Clerk of _____ County, being the county in which the principal place of business of the joint venture is situated, and cause to be published in said county, a certificate of fictitious name setting forth the name and residence of each party, as required by Section 17900 et seq. of the California Business and Professions Code.

1.8 *Recording Requirement.* A statement in accordance with Section 15010.5 of the California Corporations Code, executed, acknowledged, and verified by the parties shall be recorded in the office of the County Recorder of _____ County, being the county in which the joint venture intends to own an interest in real property, and such certificate shall set forth the name of the joint venture and the name of each party hereto, and shall state that the parties hereto are all of the parties to the joint venture.

ARTICLE 2
CAPITAL CONTRIBUTIONS

2.1 *Initial Capital Contributions of Parties.* Immediately following the execution of this Agreement, each of the parties shall transfer and assign to the joint venture all of their respective interests in and to the Lease. Said transfer and assignment shall be evidenced by an Assignment in the form attached hereto as Exhibit B.

The parties hereby agree that by transferring and assigning to the joint venture their respective interests in the Lease, each party shall be deemed to have made a capital contribution to the joint venture, which contribution shall have no monetary value for the purposes of this Agreement.

2.2 *Additional Capital Contributions of ABC.* ABC hereby agrees to make the following additional capital contributions to the joint venture:

(a) Subsequent to the execution of this Agreement, from time to time as required by the joint venture, ABC shall contribute cash to the joint venture in an amount equal to the amount of, or shall provide the joint venture with evidence satisfactory to the General Manager of payment of the legal fees of _____ Incorporated heretofore or hereafter incurred by the parties hereto and/or by the joint venture in connection with the preparation of the Lease and this Agreement.

(b) Subsequent to the execution of this Agreement, from time to time as required by the joint venture, ABC shall contribute cash to the joint venture for the purpose of providing the joint venture with all funds necessary to meet the working capital obligations of the joint venture as the same shall from time to time be determined by the General Manager; provided, however, that in no event shall ABC be obligated to contribute to the capital of the joint venture more than an aggregate of $125,000 pursuant to the terms of this paragraph 2.2(b).

2.3 *Additional Capital Contributions of Goodstn.* Goodstn hereby agrees to make the following additional capital contributions to the joint venture:

(a) Subsequent to the execution of this Agreement, from time to time as required by the joint venture, Goodstn shall contribute cash to the joint venture in an amount equal to the amount of, or shall provide the joint venture with evidence satisfactory to the General Manager of payment of, all architectural expenses and fees incurred by the joint venture; and

(b)   Subsequent to the execution of this Agreement, from time to time as required by the joint venture, Goodstn shall contribute cash to the joint venture in an amount equal to the amount of, or shall provide the joint venture with evidence satisfactory to the General Manager of payment of, all legal fees, other than the legal fees provided for in paragraph 2.2(a) hereof, incurred by the joint venture.

2.4   *Additional Capital Contributions of Contractor.* Contractor shall not be obligated to make any additional capital contributions to the joint venture.

2.5   *Other Additional Capital Contributions.* No party shall be obligated to, nor may, make any capital contributions to the joint venture in addition to the capital contributions described in paragraphs 2.1, 2.2 and 2.3 herein, except in accordance with the following provisions:

(a)   The General Manager of the joint venture may from time to time, and at any time, make calls upon itself and Goodstn (but not Contractor) for additional capital contributions. All such calls shall be borne as follows: 61.3% thereof shall be made by ABC and 38.7% therefore shall be made by Goodstn. Calls for additional capital contributions shall be made in writing (and served in the manner hereinafter provided for service of notices). Each such call shall specify the use to which the additional contribution is to be applied and shall state the date upon which such contribution is to be made, which date shall in no event be less than five (5) days from the date of the call.

(b)   In the event that ABC or Goodstn should fail to make any such additional capital contribution after a call provided for and made in accordance with this Agreement, then the party complying with such call may make the capital contribution of the defaulting party.

(c)   Immediately upon the failure of ABC or Goodstn to timely meet a call for additional capital contribution, the joint venture interest of such defaulting party shall be subject to acquisition by the party complying with such call, all in the manner hereinafter set forth, and such defaulting party shall no longer have the right to participate in any profits of the joint venture. For a period of thirty (30) days following the date specified in the call for the making of a contribution, the party complying with such call shall have the option to purchase the entire joint venture interest of the defaulting party for an amount equal to the sum of the balances of such defaulting party's income and capital accounts as determined at the end of the immediately preceding fiscal year of the joint venture, such option to be exercised, if at all, by giving written notice of such exercise to such defaulting party within such thirty-day period. The option price shall be paid in cash to the defaulting party within sixty (60) days after the date of such option is exercised.

2.6   *Non-Cash Capital Contributions.* In the event that ABC, pursuant to paragraph 2.2 hereof, or Goodstn, pursuant to paragraph 2.3 hereof, elects to make a contribution to the capital of the joint venture by paying any of the expenses or other matters described therein and providing evidence of payment thereof to the joint venture, then the party providing such evidence of payment shall be deemed to have made a contribution to the capital of the joint venture only following the approval in writing by the General Manager of the payment of such expense or other matter on behalf of the joint venture, and the amount of such contribution shall be equal to the amount actually paid by such party as reflected on said evidence of payment.

2.7 *Election of General Manager Not to Pay Certain Items from Joint Venture Funds.* Notwithstanding anything contained in paragraphs 2.2 and 2.3 to the contrary, in the event that the General Manager, in the exercise of its absolute discretion, determines that the joint venture has sufficient funds to pay the expenses or other matters described or referred to in paragraphs 2.2 and 2.3 hereof, the General Manager may, but shall not be obligated to, elect to pay any of said expenses or other matters out of the joint venture funds and, in such event, the party who otherwise would be obligated to contribute cash to the joint venture to provide funds for the payment of, or to directly pay, such expense or other matter shall thereupon be relieved of such obligation.

ARTICLE 3
MANAGEMENT

3.1 *General Manager.* In order to provide for the orderly conduct of the business and affairs of the joint venture, the parties shall select a General Manager who shall have general supervision, direction, and control of the business and activities of the joint venture. The General Manager may be removed from such office only by the unanimous vote of all the parties.

The parties hereby appoint ABC, and ABC hereby agrees to serve, as General Manager for the term of the joint venture without salary, except as otherwise agreed, and to devote such amount of time for such period of time as General Manager as may be necessary to ensure the accomplishment of the purpose of the joint venture; such appointment and agreement to be evidenced by execution of this Agreement by the parties.

3.2 *Powers of General Manager.* The General Manager shall have the power to directly manage the affairs and administer the business of the joint venture, including without limitation, the power and authority: to select and remove any and all employees and agents of the joint venture; to enter into contracts, incur obligations, purchase assets, materials, or supplies, and sell property; to assign, pledge, hypothecate, or mortgage any assets belonging to the joint venture, and execute any bond or lease in the joint venture name; to pledge the credit of the joint venture and cause the joint venture to become a surety, guarantor, endorser, or accommodation endorser; to cause the joint venture to borrow or lend money or property; to make, draw, or accept notes, bills of exchange, drafts, or other obligations for the payment of money in the name and on behalf of the joint venture; to release, assign, or transfer a joint venture claim or security or any other asset belonging to the joint venture; to cause the joint venture to sell, lease, or otherwise dispose of any tangible or intangible asset; and to exercise any and all rights and powers of lessee under the Lease.

ARTICLE 4
CASH DISTRIBUTIONS, PROFITS, AND LOSSES

4.1 *Distributable Cash.* The joint venture shall retain only such amount of cash as may be reasonably required to carry on its activities, such amount to be determined from time to time by the General Manager. At any time when the joint venture has cash in excess of the amount so determined, such excess shall be distributable and shall be applied:

(a) *Reimbursement of Capital.* First, to the reimbursement of the Additional Capital Contributions of ABC and Goodstn made pursuant to paragraph 2.5(a) hereof; second, to the reimbursement of the Additional Capital Contributions of ABC made pursuant to paragraph 2.2(a) hereof; and third in the ratio of 70% thereof to ABC and 30% thereof to Goodstn, to the reimbursement of the Additional Capital Contributions of ABC made pursuant to paragraph 2.2(b) hereof, and of Goodstn made pursuant to paragraph 2.3 hereof (provided, however, in the event said capital contributions of ABC reimbursed in full prior to the reimbursement in full of said Goodstn capital contributions, distributions pursuant hereto shall continue until the Goodstn capital contributions are fully reimbursed).

(b)   *Additional Distributions.* After all of the capital contributions of the parties have been returned, cash distributions shall be made to the parties in the following proportions:

Party	Percentage
ABC	55.9%
Goodstn	35.3%
Contractor	8.8%

4.2   *Profits and Losses.* The profits of the joint venture shall be shared, and the losses of the joint venture shall be borne, by the parties in the following proportions:

Party	Percentage
ABC	55.9%
Goodstn	35.3%
Contractor	8.8%

ARTICLE 5
BUSINESS AND FINANCIAL RECORDS

5.1   *Records and Accounting.* The General Manager shall, at the expense of the General Manager, cause full, true, correct, and complete books of account and business records of the joint venture to be kept and maintained in accordance with generally accepted accounting principles applied on a consistent basis. The books of the joint venture shall be kept for tax purposes in such a manner so as to minimize the current federal and state income taxes payable by the parties. The fiscal year of the joint venture shall be the calendar year.

5.2   *Location and Availability of Records.* Such books and records shall be kept and maintained at the principal place of business of the joint venture or such other place as may be designated by the General Manager and shall at all times be available for inspection by the parties and their authorized representatives.

5.3   *Capital Accounts.* A separate capital account shall be maintained for each party. An amount equal to any cash distribution made pursuant to paragraph 4.1(a) hereof to any party shall be debited against the party's capital account.

5.4   *Income Accounts.* There shall be maintained for the joint venture a cumulative income account reflecting the net cumulative profit or loss of the joint venture. There shall be maintained for each party an income account to which the party's proportion of the profits or losses shall be credited or debited, respectively. If the losses debited against a party's income account exceed the profits credited to such account, the account shall carry a debit balance. An amount equal to any cash distribution made pursuant to paragraph 4.1(b) shall be debited against the party's income account. The income accounts shall be maintained separate from the capital accounts and shall not be closed into the capital accounts.

5.5 *Financial and Business Reports.* Unaudited financial statements of the joint venture, including the statements of the above accounts, shall be prepared and furnished to the parties quarterly. The joint venture shall also render to each party such other financial and business reports as such party may reasonably require, provided, however, that in the event any such report requires the use of outside accounting or other services, the party requesting such report shall pay the cost of such outside services.

ARTICLE 6
SALE, ASSIGNMENT, AND PARTITION

6.1 *Assignment.* Any right under this Agreement, right or interest in the joint venture, or right or interest in the property of the joint venture, or any part thereof, interest therein, or right thereunder, is hereinafter called a "Joint Venture Right." No Joint Venture Right of a party, or any beneficial interest therein, shall be assignable voluntarily, involuntarily, or by operation of law, except for transfer by operation of law upon the death of a party, and except for the rights to purchase the joint venture interest of a defaulting party pursuant to paragraph 2.5(c) hereof, without the prior written consent of the other parties; and any such purported assignment, any attempt to sell, assign, transfer, or encumber, or any attempt to create or assert a lien or security interest against, any Joint Venture Right of a party, without such written consent, shall be void and of no force and effect, and such party making such attempt shall be deemed to be in breach of this Agreement.

6.2 *Partition.* Each party hereby irrevocably waives for the term of the joint venture any and all right that it may have to maintain any action for partition with respect to its undivided interests in the property of the joint venture or to compel any sale thereof under Part 2, Title 10, Chapter 4 of the California Code of Civil Procedure, or under common law.

ARTICLE 7
DISSOLUTION, LIQUIDATION, AND TERMINATION

7.1 *Dissolution.* The joint venture shall be dissolved upon the occurrence of one or more of the following events:

(a) *Accomplishment of Purposes.* Upon accomplishment of the purposes of the joint venture set forth in paragraph 1.2 hereof, unless otherwise agreed by the parties in writing;

(b) *Creditor's Proceedings.* In the event that any bankruptcy or insolvency proceeding with respect to a party is commenced and continues for a period of thirty (30) days, upon receipt by the party of written notice of any other party's election to dissolve the joint venture;

(c) *Breach.* In the event of a breach of this Agreement by a party, which breach, if continued, would have a materially adverse effect upon the joint venture, and the failure of such party to cure such breach and substantially eliminate or prevent such adverse effect within a ninety (90) day period after receipt of written notice from any of the other parties specifying the alleged breach, the joint venture shall be dissolved upon receipt by the party within thirty (30) days following the end of said ninety (90) day period of written notice of any of the other party's election to dissolve this joint venture; and

(d) *Mutual Agreement.* Upon the mutual agreement of the parties in writing to dissolve the joint venture.

7.2 *Other Causes of Dissolution.* Each party hereby waives any right to cause the dissolution of this joint venture except as specifically provided in this

Article, and any act of any party which would otherwise cause a dissolution hereof shall be a breach of this Agreement.

7.3 *Notice Requirements.* Upon dissolution of the joint venture, all notices required by applicable law shall be published and/or filed.

7.4 *Liquidation.* Upon dissolution of the joint venture, the joint venture shall not terminate, but shall cease to engage in further business, except to the extent necessary to perform existing contracts, and shall wind up its affairs and liquidate its assets. During the course of liquidation, the parties shall continue to share profits and bear losses as provided herein, and all of the provisions of this Agreement shall continue to bind the parties and apply to the activities of the joint venture, except as specifically provided to the contrary, but there shall be no cash distributions to the parties until all of the assets of the joint venture have been liquidated and all of the liabilities of the joint venture have been paid, discharged, satisfied, or otherwise provided for, at which time the total cash proceeds from the liquidation of the joint venture shall be distributed to the parties as set forth in this Article.

7.5 *Liquidation Distribution.* The proceeds from the liquidation of the joint venture shall be distributed to the parties in the manner and order of priority hereinafter set forth:

(a) *Return of Capital Contributions.* First, toward the payment of any credit balances in the capital accounts of the parties in the order of priority set forth in Section 4.1(a) hereof;

(b) *Balance in Accounts.* Second, toward the prorata payment to the parties of any credit balances in the income accounts of the parties; and

(c) *Liquidation Gain.* Third, to the parties in the proportions to which they would be entitled to any additional cash distributions in the manner set forth in Section 4.1(b) hereof.

In the event that any party's capital account, after such account has been increased by a credit balance or reduced by a debit balance in such party's income account, carries a debit balance: (i) the amount of each such debit balance shall be added to the amount of liquidation proceeds distributable, (ii) the resulting amount shall be allocated to the parties in the manner and order of priority set forth above, treating any capital account with a debit balance, as determined above, as having a zero balance, (iii) any party whose capital account had a debit balance as determined above shall be entitled to the amount so allocated to it reduced by the amount of such debit balance, and (iv) if such debit balance exceeds the amount so allocated, such party shall be obligated to pay to the joint venture the amount of such excess forthwith upon demand, notwithstanding anything to the contrary contained in this Agreement.

7.6 *Termination.* Upon completion of the dissolution, winding up, liquidation, and distribution of the liquidation proceeds, the joint venture shall terminate.

ARTICLE 8
REPRESENTATIONS AND WARRANTIES

8.1 *Representations and Warranties of ABC.* ABC hereby represents and warrants as follows:

(a) *Corporate Status.* ABC is a corporation duly organized, validly existing, and in good standing under the laws of the State of California, and has full corporate power to own its assets and carry on its business as it has been and is now being conducted; and

(b) *Corporation Authorization.* The execution of this Agreement by ABC and its delivery to Goodstn and _____ have been duly authorized by its Board of Directors and it constitutes a valid and binding obligation of ABC in accordance with its terms.

8.2 *Representations and Warranties of Goodstn.* Goodstn hereby represents and warrants as follows:

(a) *Corporate Status.* Goodstn is a corporation duly organized, validly existing, and in good standing under the laws of the State of _____, and has full corporate power to own its assets and carry on its business as it has been and is now being conducted; and

(b) *Corporate Authorization.* The execution of this Agreement by Goodstn and its delivery to ABC and _____ have been duly authorized by its Board of Directors and it constitutes a valid and binding obligation of Goodstn in accordance with its terms.

ARTICLE 9
MISCELLANEOUS

9.1 *Competing or Related Businesses.* Any of the parties may engage in or possess an interest in other business ventures of every nature and description, independently or with others, including, without limitation, businesses similar to, related to, or in direct or indirect competition with, any business of the joint venture. Neither the joint venture nor any other party shall have any right by virtue of this Agreement in and to such other business venture or any income or profits derived therefrom.

9.2 *Conflicts of Interest.* The fact that a party is employed by, or is directly or indirectly interested in or connected with, any person, firm, or corporation employed by the joint venture to render or perform services, or from whom the joint venture may buy supplies, materials, or other property, shall not prohibit the General Manager from employing such person, firm, or corporation, or from otherwise dealing with the same.

Neither the joint venture nor any party to the joint venture as such shall have any rights in or to any income or profits derived from any such employment or other dealing by any such person, firm, or corporation.

However, it is expressly understood that any such employment or other dealing shall be on an arms-length basis and on terms not less favorable to the joint venture than available from unrelated persons, firms, or corporations.

No party shall be obligated to contribute to the joint venture the use of any of the party's facilities or the services of any of its employees, or, in the case of ABC and Goodstn, any of its officers, directors, or employees.

In the event that a party provides office facilities or telephone, bookkeeping, or other services to the joint venture, such party shall be entitled to reimbursement from the joint venture for the cost to such party of such facilities or services. The amount, or manner of determining the amount, of such reimbursement shall be agreed upon by the parties in advance of the providing of any such facilities or services.

No party shall be entitled to any reimbursement for incidental services performed by any of its employees, or, in the case of ABC or Goodstn, any of its officers, directors, or employees, on behalf of the joint venture, and any such person rendering substantial services to the joint venture shall be employed by the joint venture prior to the rendering of such services and shall be compensated for such services by the joint venture.

9.3 *Insurance and Bonds.* The joint venture shall keep and maintain in force fidelity bonds covering its employees and policies of insurance, of the types, amounts, and with insurance carriers or sureties deemed adequate to cover the risks of the business of the joint venture, naming the parties as insureds or obligees, or as additional insureds or obligees, as their interests may appear, and providing for ten (10) days' written notice to each of the parties prior to the termination, cancellation, or modification of such bonds or insurance policies.

9.4 *Arbitration.* Any controversy arising out of or relating to this Agreement, or the breach hereof, shall be submitted to and settled by arbitration in accordance with the Rules of the American Arbitration Association which are in effect at the time the demand for arbitration is filed, and any such submittal shall not relieve the parties from their obligations under this Agreement. This provision shall constitute a written agreement to submit to arbitration within the meaning of Part 3, Title 9 of the California Code of Civil Procedure. Judgment upon any award rendered pursuant to such arbitration may be entered in any court of competent jurisdiction.

9.5 *Finders and Brokers.* Each party represents and warrants to the other that it has not retained any broker, finder, or intermediary, and is not paying anyone a broker's or finder's fee or commission in connection with the formation of the joint venture as set forth in this Agreement.

9.6 *Attorneys' Fees.* Each party agrees to pay to the other party or parties all costs and expenses including reasonable attorneys' fees incurred by the other party or parties in connection with the enforcement of this Agreement.

9.7 *Assignability.* All of the terms and conditions of this agreement shall be binding upon the successors and assigns of the parties, but shall not inure to the benefit of the successors and assigns of the parties, except as provided in paragraphs 1.6 and 6.1 hereof.

9.8 *Notices.* Any notice given with respect to this Agreement shall be deemed given and received 48 hours after the same is deposited in the United States mail within the State of California, postage prepaid, registered or certified mail, addressed to the person or party at the following respective address, or at such other address as a person or party may from time to time designate by written notice to the others:

ABC	ABC Corporation
	_____, California
Goodstn	Goodstn, Inc.
Contractor	Able Contractor

9.9 *Nonwaiver of Rights and Breaches.* No failure or delay of a party in the exercise of any right given to such party hereunder shall constitute a waiver thereof, nor shall any single or partial exercise of any right preclude other or further exercise thereof or of any other right. The waiver by a party of any breach of any provision hereof shall not be deemed to be a waiver of any subsequent breach thereof, or of any breach of any other provision hereof.

9.10 *Further Instruments.* The parties hereto shall from time to time execute and deliver such further instruments as the other party or its counsel may reasonably request to effectuate the intent of this Agreement.

9.11 *Counterparts.* This Agreement may be executed in one or more counterparts, each of which shall be deemed an original, and said counterparts shall constitute but one and the same instrument which may be sufficiently evidenced by one counterpart.

9.12 *Entire Agreement.* This Agreement constitutes the entire understanding between the parties with respect to the subject matter hereof. This Agreement may not be changed except in writing executed by the parties hereto.

9.13 *Captions.* Any captions to or headings of the articles, sections, subsections, paragraphs, or subparagraphs of this Agreement are solely for the convenience of the parties, are not a part of this Agreement, and shall not be used for the interpretation or determination of validity of this Agreement or any provision hereof.

9.14 *California Law.* This Agreement and its application shall be governed by the laws of the State of California.

IN WITNESS WHEREOF, the parties hereto have executed this Joint Venture Agreement the date first above-written.

> ABC:
> ABC CORPORATION
> By _____
> By _____
> GOODSTN:
> GOODSTN, INC.
> By _____
> By _____
> CONTRACTOR
> _____
> ABLE CONTRACTOR

AN AGREEMENT TO EXPLORE THE POTENTIALS OF A JOINT VENTURE

On occasion you may be approached by a substantial landowner, or may approach one yourself, with the proposal to explore the potentials of a joint venture to develop the property. At this raw beginning stage — lacking a definition of the feasible commercial or residential uses of the property, without a marketing study, and without an economic plan for the project — it may be best for you both to enter into a very preliminary (and non-binding) agreement to work together to develop the necessary marketing and economic data upon which to base a determination of the feasibility of undertaking a joint venture.

In one case, for example, we were approached by the land-development subsidiary of a major oil company as marketing consultants. We were asked to identify an innovative and highly attractive land use for two major parcels (200 and 400 acres) of freeway-oriented real estate suitable to commercial and tourist development. After a study of the state's economy, travel patterns, the unique recreational and tourist potentials of the region, and commercial users, we presented comprehensive marketing recommendations defining imaginative development concepts for the two parcels. These recommendations led to the suggestion that we enter into a joint venture with the land-development subsidiary for the execution of the concepts.

Before the joint venture could be formed, however, a great deal of further specific economic and marketing data was necessary. This included a land-use plan, development cost estimates, detailed market-demand projections, preliminary leasing negotiations and a detailed financial analysis of the proposed project. We therefore agreed to work jointly to develop the required information in order to acquire the basis upon which to determine the specific terms and conditions of the joint venture to be formed, if any. Accordingly, we dropped our role as consultants to the development subsidiary and jointly developed the required information. The venture is proceeding at present.

Following is one form of a preliminary agreement to develop the data essential to a joint venture without a further commitment until the required information is available.

PRELIMINARY AGREEMENT TO EXPLORE FEASIBILITY OF JOINT VENTURE
October 8, 1971

Mr. _____
Vice President
XYZ Land and Development Company

_____, California

Dear Mr. _____:

During the past several weeks we have held preliminary discussions towards forming a joint venture to acquire and develop certain real property owned by XYZ Oil Company in the southwest quadrant of the interchange of State Highway _____ and Interstate Freeway _____, _____ County, California (a portion of Section _____, Township _____, Range _____). The purpose of this letter is to outline an interim program to prepare, obtain and evaluate certain basic data and information essential to the formation of such a venture, some of which has previously been prepared and compiled by XYZ Land and Development Company.

Until the interim program is concluded, neither of us will be in a position to agree upon specific terms and conditions of such a venture. Accordingly, each of us reserves the right to withdraw from any further participation in the venture should the interim program fail to generate a mutual desire to proceed.

The interim program to be completed within 90 days, shall consist of the following: land use plan, building design concepts, site development and improvement cost estimates, market demand projections, preliminary negotiations with prospective tenants or buyers, and overall project economic analysis.

We suggest a budget of $25,000 to cover the elements of this program which have not already been done by XYZ Land and Development Company, with the understanding that the chargeable expenses against such budget be limited to the expense of consultants retained by mutual agreement. During progress of the program we may elect, by mutual agreement, to expand this budget.

Upon conclusion of the interim program, the costs of the program, not to exceed $5,000, shall be shared equally between Lewis M. Goodkin & Associates and XYZ Land and Development Company; provided, however, if the interim work program results in a determination that the joint venture is feasible and XYZ Land Development Company elects to discontinue further negotiations for reasons of policy or choice not related to economic feasibility, XYZ Land and Development Company shall reimburse Lewis Goodkin & Associates for its share of cost, not to exceed $2,500. If negotiations are discontinued, Lewis M. Goodkin & Associates agrees that XYZ Land and Development Company may utilize, in development of the subject or other property, any of the material or concepts reviewed by the parties during progress of the interim program without liability to Lewis M. Goodkin & Associates.

In the event a joint-venture agreement is consummated, Lewis M. Goodkin & Associates agrees that XYZ Land and Development Company will be reimbursed by the joint-venture entity for so much of the basic data and information provided by XYZ Land and Development Company as may be regarded by the entity as beneficial to the venture.

If this letter correctly sets forth your understanding of our agreement, would you indicate your approval in the space below and return one copy to us.

Very truly yours,

LEWIS M. GOODKIN & ASSOCIATES

By _____

Accepted this _____ day

of _____, 1971.

XYZ LAND AND DEVELOPMENT COMPANY

By _____

28

Elements of the Joint-Venture Agreement

But in the way of bargain, mark
ye me
I'll cavil on the ninth part of a
hair.

—Shakespeare

The perfect blueprint applicable to all joint-venture agreements does not exist: the circumstances of each deal and the participants, along with their needs and contributions, vary greatly. But the principles underlying the negotiation of a joint venture are not unduly complicated, and we can examine some of them in this chapter along with several representative joint-venture agreements.

Let me emphasize that this introductory discussion is by no means intended as a substitute for the services of a competent real estate attorney. An experienced lawyer is indispensable to steer the joint-venturing parties through the intricacies of legal and tax aspects and the host of special conditions having a bearing on the particular venture. The purpose here is to indicate some of the key issues controlling the formation of a joint venture, and to familiarize the territory for the builder confronting the subject for perhaps the first time.

The legal form of the venture most frequently chosen by builders and financial partners with an active voice in management is called the "joint venture" and can be defined as a limited-purpose general partnership. As with the general partnership, all participants in the joint venture are jointly and severally liable for the obligations of the venture. This holds true for another variant of the general partnership called "tenancy in common." The limited-partnership concept, with the obligations of the limited partner in a non-management position limited to his capital contribution, is often used for ventures to develop and/or hold income-producing property. But some joint-venturing companies like Builders' Resources Corporation have also used the limited partnership vehicle extensively for development ventures. The advantage of all these partnership forms of operation is that they are not taxable for purposes of federal income taxes and the items of income,

524

credits, deductions and losses flow through to the returns of the individual partners.

The corporate form is infrequently used for co-ventures because it is itself taxable at the corporate rate before the participants get any profit, and this profit is taxed again at the personal tax rate. An incorporated joint venture should as a rule only be considered (1) when insulation from personal liability is regarded as more important than the disadvantage of the double tax; (2) where the continuity of centralized management is necessary; or (3) where incorporation is necessary because applicable usury laws that limit the financing ability of the non-corporate forms. Occasionally, however, a venture will be organized as a so-called Subchapter S Corporation. Under Subchapter S of the Internal Revenue Code, corporate dividends can be paid directly to individuals without prior taxation at corporate rates and the recipients pay only the personal income tax on their money. To qualify for Subchapter S, the corporation can issue only one class of stock and have no more than 10 stockholders.

Corporations or subsidiary corporations are, of course, frequent partners in unincorporated joint ventures. In addition to the active management role such a form makes possible, it also provides greater flexibility in capitalization and profit sharing than is possible with the corporate form. A partnership agreement may provide the first $50,000 of profits be divided one way, the next $100,000 in another fashion, and the excess in still a third way. Potential losses can be selectively distributed among some partners for tax purposes, while all can share in profits. The timing of profit distributions and the ratio can be changed at any time without altering the capital structure of the organization. Several tiers of voting rights are also possible which are not tied to capital contribution or profit share (thus, for example, enabling a developer with a small capital contribution to control a venture largely funded by others). All of these elements make the joint venture partnership format the preferred one in real estate co-ventures.

KEY ISSUES FOR A JOINT VENTURE

The basic questions to be answered in determining the format of the venture are as follows:

1. What does each party contribute in the way of skills and resources? This sketches in the area of management control.

2. What trade-off between control and personal liability does the financial partner elect to make? The financial partner has the strongest stake in the venture. He will seek to protect his investment by imposing controls and checkpoints for the venture, and perhaps will take an active management role. But active management carries with it a liability for the obliga-

tions of the venture (operating through a small subsidiary corporation shielding the big corporate parent, the investor can still lose a million or two). A capital contribution as a limited partner protects the investor from possible debts and liabilities that may accrue to the venture, but also debars him from an active role in management. In most ventures, a knowledgeable financial partner with the responsibility for signing and guaranteeing the venture's loans will elect to take the risk of exposure by setting up a small subsidiary corporation to actively manage the affairs of the venture so as to protect his investment. The investor who is unfamiliar with real estate, or who desires to shield himself from unexpected liability for other strong reasons, will participate as a limited partner after doing his best to establish that the controls on the builder called for in the partnership agreement are satisfactory.

3. A related question is, what is the trade-off between control of, and responsibility for, the venture? Often a joint venture is set up between, say, a large landowner who is also the financial partner and the builder who contributes primarily his talent for building and marketing homes. Both parties will have an active role, and a potentially adversary situation is created. The landowner and financial source will want to control the builder closely to protect his investment. But the builder is the one who brings the expertise to the deal and feels that he is best suited to make the key decisions. The issue is resolved by a clear *prior* definition of the methods and objectives of the venture, spelling out a clear framework of each party's responsibilities and obligations. When this is properly done, the financial partner acts as a control on a program that the builder himself has provided, based on a careful consideration of unexpected events that might crop up.

Typically, the co-venturers will set up a program and agree to certain limitations on improvement costs. The builder can operate within the latitude of the agreed-upon plan, but must receive the co-venturer's approval on any sizable changes or variances. Many good joint-venture agreements incorporate the proposed budget right into the document with agreed-upon penalties for lapses from the cost or time schedule. The idea is not to penalize the builder for events occurring beyond his control, but to keep him on his toes within areas over which he does exercise control. Such agreements may also bar the builder from participating in other projects, or in competing projects, for the duration of the venture. (Others, conversely, make a point of allowing co-venturers to carry on other activities.) The matter of exercising controls is one of judgment and common sense: if the builder is very capable and the financial partner rides him with tight controls, it can be an unpleasant situation. But if the builder is mediocre, tight controls may be exactly what is called for.

4. What are the provisions for added capital contributions and for the

distribution of profits and losses? The treatment of this subject varies widely from deal to deal. In most joint ventures the partners may be called upon to contribute additional capital in proportion to their initial percentage position and share in profits and losses in the same proportion. But the timing of additional contributions and the distribution of cash flow varies considerably.

In a limited-partnership venture, the agreement may frequently provide that limited partners are not required to contribute additional capital until after they've received cash distributions from the partnership equivalent to their initial capital contribution. In such deals, the developer may want to insist that no additional contributions be required of him, but that he can make them at his option. When additional contributions are made, a special provision is usually made to return these before any distribution of profits. A limited partner may be generally entitled to some preference over the general partner with respect to cash distribution and upon the final liquidation of the partnership.

Agreements on preference in distribution of cash flow are varied. The agreement should specify periodic times on which the determination is made as to whether cash is available for distribution after provision for cash reserves for the operating requirements of the partnership. In some limited-partnership arrangements, the developer receives all of the cash flow until after completion of improvements or closing date of a long-term loan; thereafter, the investor receives a larger percentage of the cash flow until he retrieves the amount he's contributed. In other joint ventures, the investor may try to get all of the cash flow first until his contribution is returned. But the developer in a good deal should always be entitled to a significant share of the cash flow at all stages of a venture. Frequently, when substantial depreciation and other tax write-offs and losses are involved in a joint venture, one or more of the partners may elect to take a disproportionate amount of such write-offs for tax purposes in lieu of cash flow.

A builder should be especially attentive to the specification for a *timely* distribution of profits in the joint venture agreement. In many agreements, as for example between a landowning financial partner and a builder, the document may specify that profits are to be distributed after all obligations of the joint venture are satisfied. But if the joint venture is a continuing operation spanning several years, those obligations may never be fully satisfied until the deal is completely terminated. In these instances, the builder gets a nice profit on paper but has no access to it. Thus, a provision specifying distribution of profits over specific time intervals — or keyed to a completion of certain phases of the project — should be included in the agreement with a reasonable amount held back for contingencies.

The builder will, of course, attempt to limit his own financial responsibility in the type of venture where he contributes skills and the co-venturer contributes financing and land. The builder in such cases will attempt to resist additional contributions of capital. As one developer says, "I would recommend that a builder's responsibility be equivalent to that of a limited partner but with the builder still having the dominant role. The ideal to shoot for is a situation where the builder has limited financial responsibility, but *all* the authority. He's the one with the ability and the knowledge of the market."

5. How can the deal be unwound and one or another co-venturer get out of it with minimum pain if the venture goes bad? Most joint venture agreements include a "buy-sell" provision entitling one partner to buy out the other at his cost upon default of specific provisions. Because the success of the venture often depends considerably on the expertise and the personal affinity of the co-venturing parties, joint-venture agreements also often spell out very rigorous provisions governing transferability of partnership interest. There's also a problem of termination and disposition if one of the co-venturers walks off in the middle of the job, leaving it to be completed with normal costs. The remaining partner may exact penalties and certain adjustment provisions to complete the project, in addition to whatever legal remedies he might have for breach of contract.

WHY JOINT VENTURES GO BAD

The joint-venture agreement itself is a bland device. It has no character of its own and is only as good as the planning and forethought that goes into it. So the co-venturing parties should have a clear understanding of their respective obligations and responsibilities. But even more importantly, the project itself must be diligently planned out for feasibility, marketing and cost factors so that extraordinary problems of responsibility and control do not arise in the course of the venture. Most crises that pit the co-venturers against one another have their origin in unrealistic or incomplete planning at the outset of the deal which eventually involves it in problems.

A good agreement thinks out all possible alternatives. A smart businessman understands that there is an element of risk in *any* kind of investment. All the possible risks should be recited in the j-v agreement just as they are recited in SEC registrations and in real estate reports that buyers of real property get in California. So long as the co-venturers are prepared for any eventuality, the occurrence of one will not have a badly negative impact on the deal. Whatever else may be agreed to, it is always a good idea to provide for a contingency reserve of some type.

Most deals founder for one or more of the following reasons:

1. "The costs go crazy" (in the immortal words of one builder).
2. The time schedule is overrun.
3. The venture can be undercapitalized and suffer a financial squeeze.
4. The completed project may not sell or rent.
5. One of the partners may lose interest or sell his position in the venture.

Each of these elements is traceable to poor, unrealistic or incomplete planning at the start of the venture. The problems are born when a deal is proposed and made on the basis of unsupportable assumptions governing costs, marketing and financing. The agreement is based on emotions, not facts; such facts as do exist are used selectively or optimistically to support the emotional conclusion. Small wonder such deals go bad.

The joint venture agreement, and the responsibilities and obligations of the co-venturing parties, should be delineated only on the basis of complete information. This includes:

1. A thorough study of economic feasibility for a project and its acceptance in the market.
2. A detailed analysis of improvement costs based on actual bids.
3. Detailed plans for the project, complete with architectural designs.
4. A monitoring of the money market to determine the availability and cost of construction and mortgage loans. An abruptly rising interest rate for residential mortgages, for example, can kill buyer interest in the best project.
5. Based on the foregoing, a proper estimation of the builder's marketing costs. Undercapitalization can be a serious problem. One builder, for example, carried on a joint venture with the developer of a large planned community, to develop a small portion of the overall plan. The joint venture itself couldn't carry marketing costs. The agreement was that the community developer would carry on marketing for the overall community, including the joint-venture project. Later, when the developer stopped carrying on promotion entirely, the smaller joint venturer was stuck.

Many of the joint ventures that come about between a large landowner and the builder have had another type of problem. The landowner may not be realistic about the market value of his property. He may have got himself into a bad deal at the very beginning, either overpaying for the land or carrying it at too much capitalized cost. He may have overpaid because he didn't understand the long-term costs of carrying the property or the real costs of lot development with certain terrain problems. And overall development costs rose up to eat him. Or he may have capitalized the value of the land too high, hoping for a big profit on the turnover after developing and building it out himself. In either event, he's carrying too much cost on the books. When he talks to the builder to help him solve his problem by developing the property as a joint venture, the builder suffers from the same problem. Because of the inflated land price, it can be difficult to build and sell a home profitably to the available price market. The builder can cut down the value of the end product by cutting corners while keeping the price up. But oftentimes this is a big gamble because the market value just isn't in the product. This is a situation frequently encountered.

(The backside of the problem is that the joint-venturing builder developing a portion of a large parcel of land completes his work and moves on, leaving the landowner to cope with irate homeowners complaining of product deficiencies. These can range from bad plumbing and leaky roofs to driveways with severe, abrupt humps that catch the underside of home-owners' autos. Several California "new towns" that started with joint ventures on their land for economic reasons have shifted to direct construction on their own, not only because this is more profitable but also, at least in part, for reasons such as the foregoing. This includes the new towns of Mission Viejo and Westlake, even though the builders there have been generally first-rate. Westlake, for example, bought out the Deane Brothers, Shattuck-McHone, Monarch and Harlan Lee joint ventures along about 1970 and now does all its own construction through its building subsidiary, Arboles Construction.)

It should be clear, however, that the *only* time a joint venture makes sense to get into is when the land is put into the venture at a realistic price. In cases such as those described in the above paragraph the joint-venturing builders have only themselves to blame for going into a deal with over-priced land. A good venture must start on a good basis. If the owner has overpaid for the land, the j-v cannot be penalized for that error, otherwise the problem will only be compounded. It is far better for the landowner to put the land in at a price lower than he paid for it and regain the difference with some profit from a successful construction and sales program of a strongly selling product than to risk compounding his problems by putting the j-v at a competitive disadvantage with the market.

Properly planned, there are ways of arranging good "defensive" joint ventures by means of which a landholder can get out of an overpriced land situation. For example, one builder paid $35,000 an acre for a parcel of land, expecting to get upgraded zoning that would make the property much more valuable. But the zoning fell through and the property reverted to a savings and loan association. It was badly overpriced, having a market value in its condition of perhaps only $20,000 per acre. The S&L got out of the deal safely with a good j-v. The lender put the property into the venture free and clear at a value of $20,000 per acre and provided a co-venturing builder's development funds in exchange for half of the development profits. We had determined through our market analysis of the project that such profits would come to $30,000 per acre, and this was the way it worked out. The lender took half, or $15,000 per acre, which together with the $20,000 sale price of the acreage netted him $35,000 per acre. He broke even.

If, in another situation, the lender hadn't been stuck with an over-priced property he would have made $15,000 profit per acre on that joint venture. There are numerous situations where the pricing is at an unrealistic level and the j-v becomes merely a vehicle to recoup.

Realistic and complete preplanning is a real key to the success of any venture. This also means, among other things, that the financial partner does not drive so hard a bargain with the entrepreneur that the latter goes broke or gets into financial gymnastics with the joint venture's books. Voucher systems and countersigning of checks are a sound protection, but they won't save a deal from going under if it is unsoundly conceived. Given realistic planning, a basis of good faith and good communication between co-venturers is, of course, the final and perhaps most important element of a successful joint venture.

SKELETAL OUTLINE OF A JOINT–VENTURE AGREEMENT

What's included in a joint venture agreement? For purposes of this outline, let us assume that the legal form of the deal is a joint venture format with two or more parties playing an active role. The formats vary broadly, but the following provides a basic guideline to the elements of many joint venture agreements.

Preliminaries

1. The agreement is dated.
2. The name and address of each party is included.
3. The joint venture is constituted (for example, "Now, therefore, the parties hereby form and enter into a joint venture upon the following terms and conditions . . . ") and its powers and limitations are defined.
4. The name of the joint venture is given (for example, "The name of this joint venture shall be: XYZ Homes.")
5. The purpose or character of the joint venture's business is described. Usually the property to be developed and the improvements to be made thereon are described.
6. The principal place of business is stated.
7. The term of the joint venture is fixed for a specific period.

Capital Contributions

1. Initial capital contributions of the respective parties are given, including such property as is contributed (it should be specifically described, with liens, encumbrances, easements, restrictions, covenants and conditions to which it is subject). The date for such contributions may be also given. Where a builder contributes solely his skills, the partner's capital contribution is described and its treatment as a loan to the joint venture at a specified interest rate should be indicated, if this is the case.

2. Additional capital contributions. If additional contributions are required, the provisions governing them are explicitly set forth in the agreement, including the conditions on which they are forthcoming. A builder contributing skills may not be required to make additional contributions. But other forms of joint venture may require all participants to contribute specific ongoing legal, architectural and other fees. Contribution of unanticipated additional capital requirements is usually provided for by an agreement to contribute the required capital according to the venturer's percentage in the deal. When such additional contributions are made, they are first to be repaid out of project cash flow. The initial contributions are next repaid with cash flow split up according to their percentage ownership. The co-venturers then share the profits in proportion to their percentage interest. In the event he or another co-venturer does not provide the requested additional capital contribution, the other party buys him out at his cost and he loses the right to share in further profits.

Special Covenants

1. The financial partner may require the builder contributing skills to covenant that the latter will:

   a. Prepare all necessary architectural plans, designs, working drawings, specifications, cost analyses, construction schedules and marketing plans.

   b. Take full construction responsibility.

   c. Take full sales responsibility with a specified marketing budget.

   d. Make no material changes from the specified, approved program of action without the approval of the other partner, and conduct the foregoing activities only with the review and written approval of the partner.

   e. Not to enter into a competitive project within a specified distance of the joint-venture project. The builder may be required to limit other activities in general, if his co-venturer deems his talents are to be exclusively employed. Conversely, other agreements reserve the right of the co-venturers to engage in other and competitive projects.

    f. Correct his defective work at the joint venture's cost.

2. The co-venturers may also covenant as to their respective corporate status, where this is a requirement, and to the effect that the respective corporations have authorized the formation of the joint venture.

3. In limited-partnership agreements the general partner or partners may covenant to perform certain actions, such as to:

    a. Improve the property in accordance with specified plans.

    b. Pay off indebtedness in accordance with a present schedule.

    c. Reduce other indebtedness to a specified sum or keep it from rising beyond a specified sum.

    d. Attempt to close a specified long-term loan.

    e. Attempt to lease a property to produce a specified gross rent roll.

The limited partners may covenant to:

    a. Make additional loans or advances to the partnership of specified amounts on specified terms.

    b. Make or cause others to make specified interim or long-term loans for the property on specified terms and conditions.

    c. Enter into or cause others to enter into lease agreements for the property developed or for specified portions of the developed property, again on specific terms and conditions.

Return of Capital Contributions

1. The term "cash flow" or "distributable cash" is defined as an amount in excess of what is reasonably required to conduct the business of the joint venture. Periodic distribution times are indicated. In a joint venture with a builder contributing skills, payment of an overhead allowance is pegged to construction and marketing stages. A definition of direct costs of the venture is supplied, which costs are deducted from cash accruing to the joint venture before periodic distribution of profits.

2. As indicated above, additional and initial capital contributions are repaid in the ratio of the co-venturers' contribution before distribution of profits. Profits and losses in a joint venture are usually borne in the ratio of the participants' interest in the venture.

Management

1. The co-venturers may provide for shared project management, naming specific representatives. Or they may elect a general manager with power of general supervision and control over the venture. The general manager may be the financial partner who is knowledgeable in the sphere of project development.

2. Where a general manager is elected, he may have absolute discre-

tion to manage the affairs of the venture as he sees fit. This includes the right to enter into contracts, sell or mortgage property, borrow money, and sell or transfer any asset belonging to the joint venture.

Business and Financial Records

1. The builder contributing skills or the general manager agree to keep complete books and records reflecting all costs and transactions of the venture. The books are kept for tax purposes in accordance with good accounting practice to minimize federal and state income taxes payable by co-venturing parties.

2. The location of the books is specified and access to them at all times is vouchsafed to the co-venturing parties or authorized representatives. In some joint ventures the builder is required to submit monthly records to the other partner showing budgeted and actual costs along with other information requested. The records are available for audit at any time and the cost of keeping them is specified as the builder's own expense. Other joint ventures make reports on a quarterly basis, charging a co-venturer an accounting fee when he elects to undertake his own audit or request other financial or business reports.

3. The joint venture specifies that it has established separate capital accounts for each party and a cumulative income account. Some joint ventures specify the joint signatures necessary for withdrawals. Some also specify that disbursement of funds from institutional lenders be controlled by a voucher system.

Sale, Assignment and Partition

1. The co-venturers specify that their respective interests in the venture cannot be transferred or sold without the written approval of the other. In some instances, the partners may define in the agreement the qualifications for a buyer who is acceptable as a substitute for the original co-venturer.

2. Many joint-venture agreements waive the right of co-venturers to maintain any legal action for partition of their undivided interest in the property during the term of the joint venture.

3. In limited partnerships, restrictions on assignability of a partner's interest are necessary because of tax considerations. An option of first refusal may be granted, or the general partners may have the option to buy at fair market value set by agreement or appraisal.

Dissolution, Liquidation and Termination

The joint-venture agreement should state that dissolution and termination occurs in one or more of the following events:

1. Achievement of the venture's purposes.

2. Bankruptcy proceedings against one or more of the co-venturing

parties. Some agreements specify the builder must be actually adjudicated as a bankrupt; others specify that a proceeding for bankruptcy need be in effect for only thirty days before the joint-venture entity takes action to wind up the venture.

3. A material breach of any other part of the joint-venture agreement by one of the parties, so as to have a substantially adverse effect on the venture without good cause.

4. On mutual agreement in writing by the parties to the venture to dissolve the venture.

On dissolution of the venture, the joint venture is usually not terminated until it has performed to the extent necessary to fulfill existing contracts and winds up its affairs. In this period the parties to the venture share profits and losses as formerly until the venture is liquidated. Where a builder contributing solely his skills defaults, however, the remaining partner may specify the right to take possession of all assets of the venture to complete the work and the builder forfeits the right to any further profits.

Miscellaneous

1. The joint venture specifies adequate fire and liability insurance and fidelity bonds as a direct cost of the venture.

2. The joint-venture agreement may specify that controversies between the co-venturers will be submitted to and settled by arbitration in accordance with the rules of the American Arbitration Association.

3. As a rule, the agreement will specify that no broker or finder fees are involved in connection with the formation of the joint venture.

4. The parties agree that the party or parties bringing suit to enforce any provision of the agreement will also receive court costs and attorney's fees if it is successful.

5. A provision is included for giving notices by parties to one another, in connection with any part of the agreement, specifying the addresses of the parties and the time elapsed from mailing in which a notice is considered given and received.

6. In light of the facts concerning the specific venture, other agreements may also be included in the joint-venture agreement.

As stated earlier, the foregoing is a skeletal description of one form of joint-venture agreement. Such agreements can, however, vary considerably depending on the specifics of the situation and the needs of the co-venturers.

JOINT-VENTURE CHECKLIST: A QUICK REVIEW

Daniel S. Berman, partner in the New York law firm of Fink, Weinberger, Levin & Charney, provides us with an overview of points to consider when contemplating a joint venture. These call attention to many of the key issues to be resolved in putting together a good co-venture and expand on those we've raised already. Bear in mind that they only stake out the rough terrain to be covered in any negotiations and that you should get yourself a good lawyer for any particular deal to work out the minutiae of particular problems that may crop up.

Why Joint-Venture?

    a. One half of three loaves is better than no loaves.

    b. A well-funded partner supplies staying power, and staying power is the key element in the larger deals. (Compare Reston with Columbia.)

    c. Joint ventures offer the opportunity of ever-widening pools of deals. Nothing succeeds like success.

    d. The joint venture is the only way the smaller local builder can compete with the giants.

Some Joint-Venture Traps

    a. *Tax treatment.* Who gets tax benefits? Will tax benefits match cash flow? Will you pay tax on money you don't get? Will you get tax benefits you can't use? Shall tax benefits be sold to third parties for the account of the venture?

    b. *Capital requirements.* What happens if capital requirements exceed budget? Who is responsible for raising those funds? Will they be treated as loans or additional contributions? Will they come from third parties or one of the venturers? Will the over-budget capital get a special premium because it is at special risk?

    c. *Default.* What happens if the cash requirements do not come in on time? What are the rights of the innocent venturer on default of his partner? What penalty clauses? What rights to raise money from third parties? What forfeitures or rights to buy out?

    d. *"Turnkey" costs.* Responsibilities of the developer; timetable; risk of cost overruns; acts of God; rent-up; break-even point; cash flow.

    e. *Dissolution or buy-out.* Who can dissolve the venture — walk away from it — close out a "loser"? What happens in case of disagreement? Right to sell, liquidate, buy-out or walk away?

Legal Format

    a. *Entity.* Corporation; general partnership; limited partnership; joint venture or loan agreement?

    b. *Financial provisions.* Priority of return of capital contributions; priority of distribution of cash flow; allocation of tax benefits; defining cash flow and tax benefits. Priority and amount of builder's fees, management fees. What is covered; what excluded and separately billable?

    c. *Cash distributions.* Timing mandatory or optional? Failure to cover can result in moneyman squeezing out partner.

    d. *Transferability.* The business problems: Can you be put into bed with a new partner without your consent? If you are an institution, do you want to hide behind a shell? Are you ashamed to have people identify you with your developer partner? If you are developer, do you insist (for prestige and local banking and leasing purposes) that the moneyed partner be identified?

    e. *Admission of new partners.* Transferability of partnership interests; what happens in case of death, bankruptcy, insanity, etc?

Management and Capital: Decision-Making

    a. *Leasing.* Who makes decisions? Sale or refinancing? Minor leases, plans and specifications, substitution of materials, the hiring of professional consultants (lawyers, architects, marketing advisers, accountants, etc.), major repairs, improvements, insurance, accounting methods (cash vs. accrual), depreciation (maximize vs. minimize).

    b. *Disputes.* What happens if there is a dispute about those things? What are your rights as developer? As investor? Know your strengths and the investors' and be sure you protect them. Bear in mind that the institution has been brought into the deal for its money. If you are thinly financed, many of the rights you get may be academic.

Financing

    a. Exculpatory clauses; personal liability.

    b. Self-dealing and breach of fiduciary duty.

    c. Budget in form satisfactory to investor; regular comparison of budget with operating results.

Competition

    a. Developer's rights to do any other deals with the same tenants — in the same area — with the same personnel.

    b. Developer's depth of staff vs. "dividing itself too thin . . ."

    c. Rights of first refusal.

Fees to Developer

    a. What do fees cover? (internal overhead; rent of developer's office space; direct labor; secretarial services; advertising budget; etc.).

    b. Rights of investors to substitute new management in lieu of developer; objective criteria or "sole discretion"?

    c. Is right of first refusal or buy-out desirable? Remember, an institution has money; a developer may not have. A right of first refusal is not always helpful.

Tax Aspects

 a. *Developer objectives.* Tax-free going in; share of mortgage proceeds vs. ordinary income or capital gain. (see Sec. 721, IRC).

 b. *Investor objectives.* Maximizing tax shelter and construction write-offs.

 c. Conflict of the two positions.

 d. Advance decisions on depreciation, interest prepayment, etc.

 e. *Dissolution.* All cash; cash and paper; cash and kind.

 f. Basis and recognition of gain (Sec. 707, IRC; Sec. 722, IRC).

 g. Allocation of losses vs. allocation of cash flow: Orrisch.

 h. Prepaid interest (Rev. Ruling 68-643).

 i. *Limited Partnerships.* Safe Harbor Rules; two out of four; 10% or 15% net worth test for corporate general partners.

 j. Tax problem on disposition; tax on money never received.

 k. Depreciation recapture.

 l. Sec. 754 election for transfers of partnership.

 m. *Nominee problems.* Loss of deductions; usury problems; collapsible corporations.

The Appendix to this chapter presents several examples of co-venture agreements. They are:

1. An agreement between a builder and a large landowner who is also the financial partner

2. A co-venture deal between the developer-buyer and the landowner-seller, utilizing some interesting tax advantages

3. A limited partnership agreement between a builder-general partner contributing funds and a landowner-limited partner contributing a purchase option for land, plus funds

4. A partnership agreement for commercial/industrial development and long-term ownership where one partner contributes land and the other cash and know-how

APPENDIX

JOINT-VENTURE AGREEMENT NO. 1

The following is an agreement between an independent builder and a developer-landowner of a large planned community also supplying the capital for the venture. The builder bringing only his skills to the deal, in this example, worked for 40% of the net profits. The format of the agreement closely parallels the type of joint venture deal outlined in skeletal form in the preceding chapter.

THIS AGREEMENT, made on _____, 19____,
between: _____ DEVELOPMENT COMPANY,
a _____ corporation (hereinafter referred to as
"COMPANY"), and _____, INC., a California
corporation (hereinafter referred to as "BUILDER"), is as follows:

RECITALS:

1. BUILDER is an organization with extensive experience in the development, construction and sale of residential subdivisions.

2. COMPANY and BUILDER desire to join together under this Agreement to develop, build and sell residences in the development of the property described in Paragraph 5 hereof.

TERMS AND CONDITIONS:

1. Name:
   The name of this joint venture shall be BUILDER HOMES. Upon execution of this Agreement, the joint venturers shall sign, cause to be filed and publish in the County in which the principal place of business is situated, a Certificate of Fictitious Firm Name setting forth the name and residence of each joint venturer as required by Section 2466 of the California Civil Code.

2. Principal Place of Business:
   The principal place of business of the joint venture shall be _____,
   _____, California, or such other place or places as the joint venturers shall hereafter determine.

3. Purpose:
   It is the purpose of this Agreement to provide a relationship between COMPANY and BUILDER whereby the skills and experience of both can be combined to develop, build and sell residences to be constructed on the subject property. It is vital to the parties hereto that the design of the residences, quality of workmanship and caliber of the sales program be such as will insure the successful development and sale of the subject property. It is intended that the provisions of this Agreement be construed to accomplish that objective.

4. Relationship of the Parties:
   The relationship of the parties to this Agreement shall be solely that of joint venturers.

5. Property to be Developed:
   This Agreement shall extend to the construction and sale of residential units on that certain property (herein referred to as the "SUBJECT PROPERTY"), in the County of _____, California, more particularly described in EXHIBIT A attached hereto and made a part hereof.

6. Term:
   This Agreement will continue until eighteen (18) months after the SUBJECT PROPERTY is fully developed and sold as contemplated hereunder or otherwise disposed of, or eight (8) years from the date hereof, whichever is the earlier.

7. Building Design and Approval:
   BUILDER shall prepare all necessary subdivision maps, architectural plans, designs, working drawings, specifications, cost analysis and construction

schedules and sales prices subject to written approval of COMPANY and its authorized agents. All such designs and other material shall conform to the theme of the proposed development. Approved subdivision maps, plans and specifications shall be signed by COMPANY or its authorized agent indicating such approval. COMPANY shall further approve in writing all construction materials and fixtures as to cost and appearance.

8. Change Control:
   Changes from approved plans, specifications, materials and the like may be made from time to time. However, no material change shall be effective until it is submitted in writing to COMPANY or its authorized agents. Changes shall be effective after approval by COMPANY evidenced by written endorsement on the change document.

9. Construction Responsibility:
   BUILDER agrees to procure and provide labor, materials and supervision and to do all things necessary for the proper development of the SUBJECT PROPERTY and the construction and completion of residences thereon, all in accordance with plans and specifications approved as set forth above.

10. Sales Responsibility:
    BUILDER in conjunction with CORPORATE PARENT OF COMPANY, seller of the SUBJECT PROPERTY, agrees to conduct a sales and public relations program to effect the sale of said residences as expeditiously as possible. The nature and content of said program shall be approved in writing by COMPANY, which shall also approve in writing the prices and terms on which said residences are offered for sale. The sales and public relations campaign shall be initiated as early as possible in the program and not less than $300.00 per residential unit shall be expended on said campaign, which sum of $300.00 shall be paid to CORPORATE PARENT OF COMPANY as provided in the Agreement for Purchase and Sale of Real Property executed by the joint venture concurrently herewith. Said $300.00 amount is exclusive of model area costs, including but not limited to model home furnishings, decorating, landscaping and maintenance and is further exclusive of other sales expenses mutually agreed to by the parties hereto.

11. Financing:
    It is contemplated that the development and completion of this project will be accomplished chiefly with borrowed funds, and COMPANY agrees to use its best efforts to obtain such financing upon the best terms available. To the extent that capital is required, it will be furnished by COMPANY, and BUILDER shall not be responsible for any capital contributions. To the extent that COMPANY provides such capital contributions, they shall bear interest at one-half percent ($\frac{1}{2}\%$) per annum over the prime rate then being charged by the Bank of America National Trust and Savings Association in Los Angeles, California, which shall be charged as a cost to the joint venture and paid to COMPANY out of income as available. BUILDER agrees to execute all documents necessary or convenient to obtain the financing required by the joint venture, provided that BUILDER shall have no liability by reason thereof beyond the security of the SUBJECT PROPERTY and any improvements thereon.

12. Overhead Allowance and Profits:
   (a)   BUILDER shall receive an overhead allowance of $600.00 for each house actually constructed, which will be paid as indicated hereinbelow as any ten (10) or more houses reach the indicated stages of completion:
      (1)   25% upon completion of framing:
      (2)   25% upon completion of roofing and plastering and/or drywall; and
      (3)   50% upon recording of the Notice of Completion. Said overhead allowance shall be in lieu of all other charges for BUILDER'S home office general and administrative charges including but not limited to bookkeeping, purchasing and executives' salaries and any cost incurred in communicating or commuting between the office of the joint venture and the project site. BUILDER shall not be required to account for such overhead allowance received under this Subparagraph (a) of this Paragraph 12, and shall be entitled to receive said amounts in lieu of actual home office general and administrative expenses incurred by BUILDER whether or not such actual expenses shall be more or less than the amounts actually received.
   (b)   In addition to the foregoing, BUILDER shall receive forty percent (40%) of the net profit, and COMPANY shall receive sixty percent (60%) of the net profit realized on the sale of the homes constructed hereunder. Net profit will be determined by deducting from the total sales price of all residential units constructed and sold hereunder, all expenses of sale and all other direct costs. Direct costs shall include all labor, materials, the cost of each lot as set forth below, BUILDER'S $600.00 overhead allowance and all other charges attributable to the construction of a specific residence determined by standard construction industry accounting practice. Direct costs shall also include cost of insurance specified herein; salaries for full-time on-the-job personnel (except estimators and personnel taking bids) furnished by BUILDER; advertising, sales and public relations costs incurred in connection with the program specified in Paragraph 10 hereof; the cost of servicing the promissory notes secured by deeds of trust received as payment from home buyers; and such other costs as are directly incident to the performance of this Agreement but not attributable to the construction of a specific residence. No charges for labor or materials furnished by or through BUILDER shall be an allowable cost hereunder if BUILDER has a direct or indirect interest in the entity performing such services, unless BUILDER has made a prior written disclosure of such interest to COMPANY, and COMPANY has approved such cost in writing.
   (c)   COMPANY shall absorb all losses, if any, of the joint venture. COMPANY agrees to indemnify BUILDER and hold BUILDER harmless against any and all debts and liabilities of the joint venture except those which by the terms of this Agreement are to be borne by BUILDER.
13. Distribution of Profits:

(a)   Unless mutually agreed to by both parties, no profits shall be distributed unless and until the purchase-money promissory notes secured by deeds of trust on said lots executed in favor of CORPORATE PARENT OF COMPANY have been paid in full. Thereafter, profits shall be distributed in accordance with the respective interests of the joint venturers as provided hereinafter in this Paragraph 13. Upon conversion of assets into cash, such cash shall be distributed to the joint venturers in monthly or other convenient periodic installments; provided, however, that the reasonably foreseeable cash needs of the joint venture shall be always adequately provided for; provided further, however, that the joint venture shall maintain a reserve for contingent liabilities (including warranty repairs) of the joint venture in an amount to be adequate in the opinion of BUILDER but in any event not to exceed the sum of $100.00 for each house sold by the joint venture. Fifteen (15) months from and after the close of escrow for the sale of each house, said reserve shall be reduced by that portion thereof which pertains to such house so that the reserve will be terminated and distributed in accordance with the terms hereof fifteen (15) months following the sale of the last house constructed by the joint venture.

(b)   It is contemplated that payment from home buyers will be received partly in cash and partly in installment notes secured by trust deeds (the terms and conditions of such notes and trust deeds to be determined by mutual agreement of the parties), and the parties agree that payment of their respective profit shares may be made partly in cash and partly by undivided ownership in such notes and trust deeds, or a distribution of such notes and trust deeds in accordance with Section 731 of the Internal Revenue Code, all such payments to be made only as mutually agreed by the parties. The proportion of cash to promissory notes given to the parties in payment of their respective shares shall be the same, and the determination of which notes are to be distributed to which party shall be by lot, with a cash adjustment to the extent necessary; provided, however, that no such note shall be distributed until eighteen (18) months after the date of close of the sales escrow by which said note was delivered to the joint venture.

14. Books and Records:

Builder agrees to maintain books and records in accordance with good accounting practices reflecting all costs of the project, including records of all sales transactions. BUILDER shall submit monthly reports to COMPANY showing budgeted costs, actual costs and such other information as COMPANY may require. Said records shall be available for inspection and audit by COMPANY or its agents at any reasonable time. The cost of maintaining such records shall be regarded as a "home office" expense which is covered by the overhead allowance set forth in Paragraph 12 (a). Any party desiring to audit said books and records shall pay for the cost of such audit.

15. Banking and Loan Fund Disbursement:

(a)   A separate bank account shall be maintained for the payment of construction expenses, and a bank account shall be maintained for the collection and disbursement of proceeds from the sale of homes. Withdrawals may be made only on the joint signatures of _____, _____, or _____, together with _____, _____, or _____ or such other persons as may be designated from time to time by COMPANY or BUILDER.

(b) Disbursement of funds from any institutional lender shall be by voucher or such other system as the lender may impose and as COMPANY shall approve.

16. Project Management:
In management decisions related to performance of this Agreement, COM-PANY will be represented by _____, _____ or _____; BUILDER will be represented by _____, _____ or _____, or such other persons of comparable ability as may be designated by COMPANY or BUILDER. The above named persons shall serve without compensation.

17. Limitation on Other Building:
BUILDER agrees that until the SUBJECT PROPERTY is fully developed and sold as contemplated hereunder or otherwise disposed of, or until the joint venture is terminated, whichever shall first occur, it shall not build single-family residences on any property not owned by the joint venture within a ten (10) mile radius of the intersection of _____ and the _____ Freeway, or within two (2) miles on either side of the _____ Freeway from _____ Road to _____ Boulevard.

18. Correction of Work:
BUILDER agrees promptly to remove, repair and replace at its own expense all defective work resulting from its wilful misconduct. The cost of remedying all other defective work shall be chargeable as a direct cost to the joint venture and shall be performed by BUILDER.

19. Liability Insurance:
The joint venture shall procure liability insurance which will protect it from liability to others because of personal injury (including death) and property damage which may arise from operations under this Agreement, with limits of at least $1,000,000 per occurrence The premiums for such insurance shall be an allowable cost under this Agreement. Builder shall maintain for the joint venture such insurance as will protect the joint venture from claims under Workmen's Compensation Acts and other employee benefit acts, and from claims for damages because of personal injury (including death) to its employees who are direct charges to the construction performed under this Agreement. The joint venture shall obtain on behalf of the joint venture such other insurance as it deems necessary.

20. Fire Insurance:
The joint venture shall secure such fire insurance as may be required or necessary to meet the requirements of lenders to protect the structures to be erected under this Agreement. The premiums for such insurance shall be an allowable cost under this Agreement.

21. Termination
This Agreement can be terminated:

(a) By the mutual consent of both parties;

(b) By COMPANY if BUILDER is guilty of any material breach of the terms of this Agreement and fails to correct the same within ten (10) days after written notice of the nature of the breach. A material breach shall be, but is not limited to, any of the following:

    (1) Adjudication of BUILDER or BUILDER'S PARENT COMPANY as a bankrupt, execution by any one of them of a general assignment for the benefit of creditors, appointment of a receiver on account of the insolvency or any other act of bankruptcy or insolvency of any of them;

    (2) BUILDER'S refusal, without cause, to proceed with the work or any phase or part thereof required by this Agreement;

    (3) Any act or failure to act by BUILDER which is a material violation of any provision of Agreement for Purchase and Sale of Real Property of even date herewith between CORPORATE PARENT OF COMPANY and the joint venture;

    (4) Failure to build in substantial conformity with approved plans and specifications;

    (5) Violation of Paragraph 17 (LIMITATION ON OTHER BUILDING).

(c) By BUILDER if COMPANY is guilty of any material breach of the terms of this Agreement and fails to correct the same within ten (10) days after written notice of the nature of the breach. A material breach shall be, but is not limited to, any of the following:

    (1) Adjudication of COMPANY or CORPORATE PARENT OF COMPANY as a bankrupt, execution by any one of them of a general assignment for the benefit of creditors, appointment of a receiver on account of the insolvency or any other act of bankruptcy or insolvency of any of them;

    (2) COMPANY's refusal, without cause, to provide the capital and financing to be provided by it under this Agreement;

    (3) Any act or failure to act by COMPANY which is a material violation of any provision of the Agreement for Purchase and Sale of Real Property of even date herewith between CORPORATE PARENT OF COMPANY and the joint venture.

(d) In the event of termination under Paragraph 21 (b), COMPANY may take possession of all assets of the joint venture, including but not limited to all work in process and all tools, materials and appliances involved therewith, and complete all work in process by whatever method may be deemed expedient by COMPANY, and the right to any share of profits on the part of BUILDER (either undistributed, undetermined or future) as to any units of development not completed and substantially sold, shall thereupon terminate

(e) COMPANY'S right of termination under Paragraph 21 (b) is in addition to any other remedy COMPANY might have at law or in equity.

(f) BUILDER'S right of termination under Paragraph 21 (c) shall be that provided at law or in equity.

22. Approvals and Disapprovals:
Whenever COMPANY's consent or approval is required under the terms hereof, COMPANY shall not arbitrarily or unreasonably withhold its ap-

proval or consent. If COMPANY fails to give its consent or to either approve or disapprove any matter which requires COMPANY's approval within thirty (30) days after a request therefor has been submitted to it in writing, it shall be conclusively presumed that COMPANY has given its consent or approved said matter. Should BUILDER object to any disapproval by COMPANY, then upon written notice to COMPANY, BUILDER shall have the right to withdraw from the joint venture.

23. Reimbursement for Capital Advanced
with Trust Deed Notes:
In the event that the cash or other assets acceptable to COMPANY are not sufficient to provide a distribution to COMPANY of its total capital contributions or the interest thereon, there shall be distributed to COMPANY, and COMPANY agrees to accept, by way of reimbursement for such balance of capital contributions or interest thereon, trust deed notes then belonging to the joint venture in a face amount equal to the amount of the balance of such capital contributions or interest thereon then due COMPANY.

24. Attorneys' Fees:
Should either party bring suit to enforce any provision of this Agreement or any claim arising therefrom, any judgment awarded shall include court costs and reasonable attorneys' fees to the successful party.

25. Notices:
Any notice required to be given hereunder may be served personally or sent postage prepaid by certified mail to the parties at the following addresses.

BUILDER, INC.   _____
                       _____

DEVELOPMENT COMPANY   _____
                       _____

26. Assignment:
There shall be no assignment of any interest, right or duty under this Agreement by either party without the prior written consent of the other, except that COMPANY may assign its entire right, duty and interest hereunder to any corporation which has substantially the same stock ownership as COMPANY without the prior consent of BUILDER, and except that BUILDER may assign its entire right, duty and interest hereunder to BUILDER'S PARENT CORPORATION or any other corporation which is a successor to BUILDER by merger, consolidation or any other corporate reorganization on the express conditions that:
(1) said successor to BUILDER shall have a net worth of not less than $10,000,000.00; and
(2) that the management of the performance of any and all obligations and duties of BUILDER hereunder shall continue to be the responsibility of the same builder team, or such other persons of comparable ability as may be designated by BUILDER.
Any attempted assignment or transfer (either voluntarily or involuntarily) by either party prohibited hereunder without the written consent of the other shall entitle the other party, at its option, to cancel and terminate this Agreement and all of the assigning party's rights hereunder.

The limitations of this Paragraph shall cease and terminate when the SUBJECT PROPERTY is fully developed and sold as contemplated hereunder or otherwise disposed of, or upon the termination of the joint venture, whichever shall first occur.

_____ DEVELOPMENT COMPANY
By _____
By _____
BUILDER, INC.
By _____
By _____

The undersigned, being fully informed of the duties and obligations of COMPANY under the foregoing Agreement, and fully understanding the same, hereby guarantees the performance of COMPANY thereunder and guarantees that the financing required to be furnished by said corporation as undertaken in said Agreement will be furnished.

CORPORATE PARENT OF COMPANY
A Division of _____
By _____
President

The undersigned, in order to induce _____ DEVELOPMENT COMPANY to enter into the foregoing Joint Venture Agreement with BUILDER, INC., do hereby agree that neither of the undersigned will personally or through an entity in which either or both has a substantial direct or indirect interest build single-family residences in the area described in Paragraph 17 of said Agreement, during the period referred to therein.

_____
Builder President

_____
Builder Executive Vice-President

AMENDMENT TO JOINT-VENTURE AGREEMENT NO. 1

WATER REFUND CONTRACTS:

COMPANY, acting for the joint venture, at its sole option and discretion may enter into water refund contracts with COMPANY (hereinafter referred to as "WATER") or may convey to WATER, at no cost or expense to WATER, a complete system of pipes, pipelines and appurtenant facilities necessary and proper fully to supply all lots with domestic water in any subdivision to be developed by the joint venture. Any such system will fully comply with all requirements of the Public Utilities Commission and other applicable governmental authorities, as well as good engineering practice. It is agreed that if the joint venture shall enter into water refund contracts, said contracts shall be solely in favor of COMPANY and BUILDER; shall have no interest of any kind whatsoever in said contracts. It is also understood that if the joint venture agrees to convey to WATER the above described system, the contribution of said system to WATER will be without compensation to the joint venture or any joint venturer, BUILDER hereby agreeing to waive any right to enter into a water refund contract under applicable rules and regulations of the Public Utilities Commission relating to main extensions. BUILDER has been advised, and is fully aware, that WATER is a wholly-owned subsidiary of CORPORATE PARENT OF COMPANY.

AMENDMENT TO JOINT-VENTURE AGREEMENT NO. 1

Date _____ 19 _____

_____ DEVELOPMENT COMPANY

_____, California _____

Gentlemen:

Reference is hereby made to that certain Joint Venture Agreement between us executed concurrently herewith pertaining to the development of certain real property in _____, California.

This will confirm our agreement and understanding as follows with respect to the said Joint Venture Agreement:

1. In addition to the overhead allowance of $600.00 for each house actually constructed, as provided in Paragraph 12 (a) of said Joint Venture Agreement, we shall receive an allowance of $150.00 for each single-family (R-1) house actually constructed on the subject property to cover the cost of house design and decorating fees for the single-family (R-1) residences to be constructed by the joint venture. The said allowance still constitute payment in full for all such house design and decorating fees whether performed by our personnel or whether performed by others. If performed by others, we agree to pay therefor and agree to indemnify you and the joint venture against any and all liability by reason thereof except for the payment of said allowance of $150.00 per house. We shall not be required to account for such payment received by us, and we shall be entitled to receive said amount in lieu of the actual expenses incurred by us in connection with said design and decorating fees, whether or not such actual expenses shall be more or less than the amounts received.

Other design and decorating services, if any, which may be required in the development of said project (other than the house design and decorating for single-family (R-1) residences) shall be charged directly to the joint venture and shall constitute a direct expense thereof and shall not be included in the $150.00 allowance herein provided.

2. The allowance of $150.00 for each house for house design and decorating as hereinabove provided shall be paid when the concrete has been poured for any five (5) or more houses.

3 It is understood and agreed that all marketing audits or surveys performed by Sanford R. Goodkin or others shall constitute a direct expense of the joint venture and shall be paid by the joint venture provided that no such marketing audits or surveys shall be ordered without your prior written approval.

4. It is understood that we maintain a Real Estate Service Department which renders services in the disposition of homes or other property owned by a prospective home buyer, which such buyer requires to be disposed of as a condition for purchasing a home. Should the services of our Real Estate Service Depart-

ment be required by the joint venture, the charge for such services shall be deemed to be a direct expense of the joint venture; provided, however, that no charge for such services shall be incurred without your prior written approval.

Signed,

_____

JOINT-VENTURE AGREEMENT NO. 2

The following document illustrates in preliminary draft form the typical corporate structure in an advantageous tax deal between the developer (buyer) and the land owner (seller), with the development being done by a third entity — a development corporation set up by the buyer. The elements of the deal are as follows:

(1) Buyer and Seller agree on a base price per acre at 75%–80% of market value.

(2) Seller declares long term capital gain on an installment basis (as legal entity or individual).

(3) Seller takes back note and deed of trust for the amount of the base price.

(4) Seller subordinates to construction loans.

(5) The sale and development is organized as a three-way transaction. A separate corporation is introduced as the developer.
   (a) Corporation or individual — seller.
   (b) Corporation — buyer.
   (c) Corporation — developer.

(6) Seller buys $\frac{1}{2}$ of the stock of the development corporation. Buyer owns the other $\frac{1}{2}$ of stock.

(7) As escrows close, Seller is paid base price per acre pro-rated as to lot yield.

(8) Upon completion of each portion of development, the remaining profits are distributed as dividends to A and B Corporations. The corporate dividends are 85% exempt. The tax base is 7.5%.

(9) The participation agreement based on the following draft can be used for individual or syndicate investment on either an income or capital gain basis. The typical participation splits profits 50–50 between capital and management.

AGREEMENT FOR SALE OF REAL PROPERTY

Recital identifying Buyer and Seller

AGREEMENT

1. Purchase and Sale of the Property:
   Seller will sell and convey to Buyer, and Buyer will buy the property for the purchase price, which shall consist of:
   (a) Base Price equal to _____ multiplied by the number of acres in the property, the net area of which is set forth in said Exhibit A (the "base price per acre" when used in this Agreement shall mean _____); and
   (b) A sum equal to 50% of the net profits (as computed under Paragraph 9) derived by Buyer from the improvement and subdivision of

the property, the construction and/or sale of houses thereon, and any other business activity engaged in by Buyer in connection with the development of the property. Such sum is hereinafter called the profit Share.

The property shall be conveyed and the purchase price shall be paid in the manner hereinafter prescribed.

2. Escrow.

3. Preliminary Title Report: — 10 Days
   15 days approval.
   Buyer to conduct market survey, file with County tentative tract may, subject to proper zoning.

4. Promissory Note and Deed of Trust:
   At close of escrow, Buyer to deliver promissory note equal to base price. Interest shall be payable semi-annually on that portion of the face amount thereof that is equal to base price multiplied by the number of acres of property which has then been subordinated as provided in paragraph 7 of this Agreement, less the amount of the Lot Release Price payment then paid to Seller, as provided in paragraphs 8 and 12 of this Agreement. Said note shall be secured by first deeds of trust on the property.

5. Conveyance of Property to Buyer:
   Right to make conveyance if required.
   Seller shall convey the property to Buyer at close of escrow, free and clear of any liens, charges, defects, exceptions, or encumbrances except above mentioned deeds of trust executed by Buyer, conditions, convenants and restrictions, taxes, matters referred to in preliminary title report which are waived by Buyer. Seller to furnish Buyer a certificate of title, standard joint protection title policy showing title vested in Buyer. Taxes prorated at close of escrow.

6. Agreement to Subdivide and Build:
   Upon the conveyance of the property to Buyer, Buyer shall commence promptly the work of completely subdividing the property into residential lots and contracting dwelling houses on all such lots. Such work of subdivision and construction shall be prosecuted with all reasonable diligence by Buyer, to the end that all such lots, improved with dwelling houses, shall be made available for sale and sold by Buyer as soon as possible. Buyer shall have right with approval of Seller to convey, dedicate, etc., as required by public agencies.

7. Subordination of Deeds of Trust:
   Seller will subordinate its deeds of trust to all land, construction, and development loans imposed on the property by Buyer incident to subdivision and developing the property, as follows:
   (a) Within _____ days of opening of escrow, Buyer shall select any parcel of _____ acres or less to be subordinated by Seller. At close of escrow, Seller will subordinate its Deeds of Trust as to such parcel. The form of subordination to be used is attached hereto as Exhibit B and incorporated herein by this reference.
   (b) Additional land subordinated upon request.

8. Release of Deeds of Trust:

At Buyer's request, Seller will release any subdivided lot from the lien of its deed of trust concurrently with the payment to Seller of the Lot Release Price from the escrow in which Buyer is conveying the lot. The Lot Release Price shall equal the Base Price per acre multiplied by the number of acres in the tract. Lot Release Price payments received by Seller from such sub-division escrows shall be credited against the Base Price.

9. Computation of the Profit Share: Can be second trust deeds.
The Profit Share portion of the consideration which Buyer is to pay to Seller for the property shall be determined by deducting from the gross sum received by Buyer from the sale of lots in the property, from contracts entered into by Buyer for the construction and/or sale of houses and/or improvements on any of the lots in the property, and from any other business activity engaged in by Buyer in connection with the development of the property, all of Buyer's expenses as hereinafter set forth. The resulting figure shall be referred to as Buyer's net profit, and the Profit Share shall be one-half ($\frac{1}{2}$) thereof. The consideration received for the sales, condemnation, or conveyances made pursuant to Paragraph 1 shall be governed by the provisions therein contained and not by the provisions contained in this paragraph.

10. Provision for Buyer to Retain Agreed Upon Sum as Working Capital:
Buyer's expenses which may be deducted in arriving at Buyer's net profit shall be the following expenses, directly attributable to the purchase and development of the property:
   (a)   Base Price of Property.
   (b)   All direct expense incurred in the improvement, development, sub-division and sale of such lots, together with the houses thereon, including without limitation expenses for labor, materials, equipment, rental of equipment, costs of surveying, mapping, designing, and engineering, permit fees, recordation and filing fees, and such other usual and customary costs and charges as are considered proper items of cost in the subdividing and construction business. Office overhead attributed to the development of the property.
   (c)   Property taxes and similar charges paid by Buyer with respect to the property.
   (d)   All interest and financing charges for loans, including the notes referred to in Paragraph 4 above, construction and development loans procured by Buyer with respect to the property.
   (e)   Title charges, cost of necessary insurance, escrow and similar charges, including but not limited to such charges.
   (f)   Reasonable legal and accounting costs.
   (g)   All charges for post construction maintenance.
   (h)   Advertising costs, sales expenses, model furnishing, upkeep and main-tenance, and sales commissions, sales office, etc.
   (i)   Expense incurred pursuant to Paragraph 12 (d) hereof.
   (j)   Any expense incurred pursuant to the second paragraph hereof.

11. Arbitration:

12. Payment of the Profit Share:
Monthly accounting.
Final accounting 60 days after close of all escrows in each Tract.

13. Condemnation:
Base price paid to Seller.
Excess divided 50–50.
Expense deduction if price paid not equal to base price.

14. Default:
Notice, etc.

15. Force Majure

16. Default by Buyer and Other Contingencies:
If Buyer fails to perform one or more of the covenants and obligations under this Agreement, Seller shall have the right to treat such failure as a default under this Paragraph 16 by sending Buyer notice of such default. In addition to any other rights and remedies which Seller may pursue in the event of a default by Buyer, Seller may pursue the following remedy: If default not cured in 30 days, then on payment by Seller of the Default Price, concurrently with such payment, Buyer shall reconvey any portion of the property to which it then holds title. The Default Price shall consist of any expenses of development incurred by Buyer directly attributable to the portion of the property to be reconveyed, which would have been deducted in computing the Profit Share pursuant to Paragraph 9 less (a) any sums belonging to Seller and retained by Buyer, (b) any amount due Seller as the profit share which have not been paid, (c) any other amounts other than the Base Price due Seller. If the deductions referred to in the preceding sentence exceed such expense of development incurred by Buyer, Buyer shall forthwith pay to Seller an amount equal to such difference.

17. Final Date for Payment:
Property developed within 5 years? Subdivided and sold.
Payment to Seller — Base Price
                    Profit Share
                    Retained Capital Share
If not completed within _____ years, Buyer may pay to Seller Profit Share on remaining lots (based on average heretofore paid). If Buyer, after payment as above, realizes net in excess of twice previous profit due Seller, Buyer to pay to Seller difference between one-half ($\frac{1}{2}$) of net profits and share previously paid to Seller.

JOINT-VENTURE AGREEMENT NO. 3

This limited partnership agreement involved a builder as a general partner and an oil corporation contributing a land option as a limited partner. Both entities were related by virtue of the same stockholders in the background. The builder as general partner contributed $1,000.00 to the venture and then provided $74,000.00 to execute the option. The limited partner also contributed $1,000.00. As he was also the owner of the land purchased by the partnership, he subsequently also contributed the $74,000.00 received from the sale of the land as development capital to the partnership. Technically, the parties have now contributed $150,000.00 to the venture, by using the same $74,000.00 twice. This sort of deal enables a landowner to convert his contribution into a limited partnership interest to limit liability.

CERTIFICATES AND ARTICLES OF LIMITED PARTNERSHIP
OF _____ ASSOCIATES

The undersigned, being desirous of forming a limited partnership pursuant to California Corporations Code Title 2, Chapter 2, do hereby enter into this agreement of limited partnership and do hereby make and sign this Certificate and Articles of Limited Partnership for that purpose, setting forth herein the terms and conditions of said limited partnership, the rights, duties and obligations of the general partners, as well as the limit of liability of the limited partners and the duties to be attended to by the general partners, and setting forth the rights of the parties with respect to the assets of the partnership and the profits which the parties shall receive by reason of their being general or limited partners, as the case may be.

ARTICLE I
Name
The name under which the limited partnership is to be conducted is _____ ASSOCIATES.

ARTICLE II
Nature of Business
The character and general nature of the business to be transacted by this limited partnership is limited to the ownership of the option described in Article VIII below, the exercise of said option, the development of the real property comprising said option through the erection thereon of single family residences and the sale of said single family residences.

ARTICLE III
Principal Place of Business
The principal place of business of the partnership shall be at _____, _____, California, or such other place in the County of _____, California as the general partner from time to time selects.

ARTICLE IV
Name of General Partner
The name of the general partner and its residence address (principal place of business) is as follows:

Name	Address

ARTICLE V
Name of Limited Partner
The name of the limited partner and its residence address (principal place of business) is as follows:

Name	Address
XYZ	

ARTICLE VI
Capital Contribution of General Partner
1. Concurrently with the execution of this agreement, the general partner shall contribute to the limited partnership the sum of $1,000.00.
2. The general partner shall contribute an additional $74,000.00 prior to the date this partnership acquires title to any portion of the real property comprising the subject matter of the option described in Article VIII below.

ARTICLE VII
Capital Contribution of Limited Partner
1. Concurrently with the execution of this agreement, the limited partner shall contribute to the limited partnership the sum of $1,000.00.
2. In connection with the acquisition of title by this partnership of the first portion of the real property constituting subject matter of the option described in Article VIII below, the limited partner shall contribute $74,000.00 from sums paid limited partner in its capacity as Seller under the terms and provisions of said option aforementioned.
3. The capital contribution of the limited partner to the limited partnership shall consist solely of cash contributions and no other property, credit or liability is being contributed to the limited partnership by the limited partner. From and after the date the limited partner has contributed the aggregate sum of $75,000.00, as provided in Paragraphs 1 and 2 of this Article VII, the limited partner shall not be required to make additional contributions under any circumstances.

ARTICLE VIII
Option
Concurrently with the execution of this Certificate and Articles of Limited Partnership, this limited partnership shall execute an option for the acquisition of certain real property owned by the limited partner in the City of _____, State of California.

ARTICLE IX
Term
The term for which this limited partnership is to exist is seven (7) years, unless sooner dissolved or terminated in accordance with Article XV of this agreement.

ARTICLE X
Capital
1. The capital invested in the limited partnership shall be used and employed in and about the business of and for the benefit and advantage of the limited partnership and for no other purpose whatsoever.
2. There shall be set up a capital account which shall show the capital invested by the general and limited partners.

ARTICLE XI
Division of Profits and Losses

1. Profits shall be divided, 50% by the general partner and 50% by the limited partner. Losses shall be borne, 50% by general partner and 50% by limited partner, provided, however, limited partner's liability for losses shall not exceed the capital contribution required of the limited partner as provided in Article VII.

2. The profits shall be determined by deducting from the gross sum received by the partnership from the sale of houses the basic expenses hereinafter set forth. The resulting figure shall be referred to as Net Profit and shall be distributed 50% to the general partner and 50% to limited partner. Expenses which may be deducted in arriving at net profit shall be the following expenses directly attributable to purchase and development of the property:

   (a) Cost of acquisition of real property.
   (b) All direct expenses incurred in the building, improvement and sale of houses, including without limitation expenses for labor, materials, equipment, rental of equipment, permit fees and other usual and customary costs and charges as are considered proper items of cost in the subdividing and construction business in and about _____ County.
   (c) Property taxes and similar charges paid by partnership with respect to the property, all interest and finance charges for loans for construction and other purposes procured by general partner with respect to the property; such interest and finance charges shall be in accordance with the usual practice as qualified by reasonable business judgment.
   (d) Reasonable legal, accounting and insurance fees.
   (e) Charges for property construction maintenance, if any.
   (f) Sales, advertising and escrow expenses, including $_____ for single family residence to be paid to the sales manager.
   (g) Overhead allowance for each single family residence to the general partner payable pro rata as construction progresses from and out of construction loan draws which shall be in lieu of general partner's main office, including salaries and expenses of personnel assigned to such office. There will be no other overhead charges attributable to the development of the property.
   (h) Post sales pick-up expenses.
   (i) Expenses incurred as a matter of law.

3. All distributions of profit shall be made 50% to the general partner and 50% to the limited partner and in the event that the limited partner has contributed its full $75,000.00, and the general partner has contributed its full $75,000.00, and the general partner has loaned additional funds to the limited partnership, distribution shall go first to the general partner to repay such loans.

4. In the event that this limited partnership shall acquire notes secured by second deeds of trust on houses developed and sold by it, the distribution of said notes and second trust deeds to the partners shall be handled in accordance with the following principles, in the event that the general partner elects to distribute same.

(a) All notes shall be treated for purposes of distribution at par.

(b) The general partner shall divide the notes into two (2) groups which shall be as nearly equal to each other in total par value as is practicable. A difference between the two groups of $100.00, or less, shall be ignored. Any difference in excess of $100.00, shall be adjusted by adding cash to the group of lower par value to the end that the difference is $100.00, or less.

(c) The two groups shall be submitted to the limited partner and the limited partner shall within seven (7) days select one of the two groups. The group so selected shall be assigned and transferred to the limited partner without warranty by the partnership and the other group shall be assigned and transferred to the general partner without warranty by the partnership.

5. Commencing at the end of the fourth full current calendar month following transfer of title to the first residence built and sold by this partnership, and monthly thereafter, there shall be distributed to the partners an equal amount of estimated profits accruing, therefrom, provided, however, that the expenses for each tract shall be fairly apportioned to the houses and lots in each such tract and that the gross receipts from the sales shall not be accrued nor shall the expenses attributable thereto be accrued until the close of the escrow therefor. Such accounts shall reflect partnership's profits on the houses in each tract or each increment computed on a tract to tract basis during the development of the subject property. In addition to the monthly payments, and within 60 business days after the escrows have closed on all the houses in any such tract, general partner shall deliver to limited partner a financial accounting as to that tract together with a final payment of limited partner's profit as to that tract. "Tract" shall mean that portion of property included within a map filed with a municipal government and recorded after approval by said regulatory body.

ARTICLE XII

Books of Account

1. Books of the limited partnership based upon generally accepted accounting principles shall be maintained at the office of the limited partnership or at the site being developed by the limited partnership and shall, during normal office hours, be open to the inspection of the general and limited partners. Either partner at its own expense may conduct such audits as it desires.

2. The partnership shall render a monthly financial statement unaudited and an annual financial statement duly certified by a certified Public Accounting Firm.

3. The annual partnership informational tax returns shall be filed by the general partner in timely fashion and shall be prepared by a certified public accountant and copies furnished to both partners.

4. Monthly progress reports shall also be made by the general partner commencing at such date as the limited partner requests, which reports describe the status of physical construction, sales and cash flow.

ARTICLE XIII
Management

1. The general partner acting alone shall have full authority to borrow, pledge, mortgage, lease and generally manage the property of the limited partnership, including, without limiting the foregoing, the execution of deeds, conveyances and deeds of trust.

2. Before obtaining construction loans general partner and limited partners shall mutually determine the architectural and quality standards and minimum pricing of lots and homes in each incremental development.

ARTICLE XIV
Bank Account

All receipts shall be deposited in the limited partnership bank accounts and all withdrawals or payments of limited partnership obligations therefrom shall be by check or draft drawn on said accounts.

ARTICLE XV
Dissolution and Termination

1. This limited partnership shall automatically be dissolved upon:
   (a)   The adjudication of the general partner as a bankrupt.
   (b)   Unanimous decision of the partners, limited and general.
   (c)   Distribution of all assets.
   (d)   Expiration of the term of seven (7) years.
   (e)   Thirty days' notice by limited partner that said partnership is terminated, provided, however, such termination notice shall not be applicable as to any house or houses in escrow, completed and unsold or under construction on date notice is given.

2. In the event the option described in Article VIII expires, or in the event the partnership is dissolved or terminated pursuant to Paragraph 1 of this Article XV, the partnership shall as rapidly as is reasonably possible thereafter, sell its then remaining assets either as is or after the completion of single family residences thereon, and the affairs of the partnership shall thereupon be wound up and the partnership dissolved and a final distribution and accounting shall be made to all partners by the general partner.

ARTICLE XVI
Executors, Heirs and Assigns

1. The general partner may not make an assignment without the prior written consent of the limited partner. In the event limited partner assigns its interest, it shall make such assignment subject to all the terms and conditions of this agreement.

2. This agreement, the aforementioned Option for Sale and Purchase of Real Property agreement and the Memorandum Agreement of even date herewith, when taken together, constitute the total and complete agreement between the parties hereto and supersedes and takes the place of any prior written or oral agreement or agreements. This agreement may only be modified in writing and signed by duly authorized representatives of the parties hereto.

3. This agreement shall be governed, construed and enforced in accordance with the laws of the State of California.

ARTICLE XVII
Notices

Notices to be given hereunder shall be deemed sufficiently given and served when and if deposited in the United States mail, postage prepaid and registered, addressed to the limited partner at _____, _____, California, or to the general partner at _____, _____, California, as the case my be, or to such other address as either party shall respectively hereafter designate in writing.

Routine communications, including monthly statements and payments shall be considered as duly delivered when mailed by either registered mail or ordinary first class mail, postage prepaid.

IN WITNESS WHEREOF, the undersigned have executed this Certificate and Articles of Limited Partnership of _____ ASSOCIATES this _____ day of _____, 19 ____.

> GENERAL PARTNER: ABC, a Limited Partnership
> by ABC DEVELOPMENT CO., a California
> Corporation, as General Partner

JOINT-VENTURE AGREEMENT NO. 4

This example illustrates a partnership agreement between a landowner and a developer contributing both capital and knowhow for development, and a long-term leasing/rental/management of income producing property. Note that although the developer, XYZ Company becomes the managing partner, the landowner's approval is required on borrowing in excess of a specified amount, leasing/rental, selling the property or transferring partnership interest. Note also that distribution of cash flow is arranged in such a way that the partner with the dominant capital contributor (XYZ) gets a return equivalent to six (6%) per cent interest on the difference between his capital contribution and the other partner's (ABC) before the cash flow is split equally. The interest preferentially credited to the partner with the larger capital is actually computed so as to give him six per cent (6%) on the excess of his capital contribution over the other partner's throughout the year.

PARTNERSHIP AGREEMENT FOR COMMERCIAL INDUSTRIAL DEVELOPMENT

THIS PARTNERSHIP AGREEMENT, entered into as of the _____ day of _____, 19 ____, by and between _____, a California corporation (hereinafter called "ABC") and "XYZ Co." is as follows:

WITNESSETH:

1. Name:
   The name of this partnership shall be _____.

2. Capital:
   ABC shall contribute to the capital of the partnership the _____ acres

of land described in Exhibit "1" attached hereto. It is agreed that the value of the land is $_____ per acre. XYZ Co. shall contribute $_____ cash to the capital of the partnership except that XYZ Co. need contribute only $5,000.00 until such time as additional cash is needed beyond that which can be borrowed on the security of the partnership property and improvements thereon.

3. Nature of Business:

The partnership shall engage in the business of developing the real property described in Exhibit "1" and other real property for investment — principally through the construction of improvements for rent or lease. *It shall not engage in the acquisition or development of properties for sale.*

4. Managing Partner:

XYZ Co. shall act on behalf of the parties hereto as the developer, manager and operator of the partnership property and it shall be the duty of XYZ Co. to plan and supervise the grading, the design, placement and installation of streets, sewers and other site improvements, the design and construction of buildings, the obtaining of financing for such works of improvement, and the ultimate lease of all or portions of the partnership property. Promptly upon formation of this partnership, XYZ Co. shall commence the work of planning the development of the property and obtaining suitable zoning thereof, and XYZ Co. shall then and thereafter with reasonable diligence, consistent with reasonable business judgment, carry on to completion the development of the property for the benefit of the partnership.

XYZ Co. is expressly authorized, in connection with the development, operation and management of the property, to do any or all of the following things:

Engage the services of surveyors and engineers.

Prepare, and submit for the approval of governmental agencies, a map or maps of proposed development of the property.

Make application to appropriate governmental authority for zone variances or changes of zoning respecting the property.

Borrow not more than an aggregate of $50,000.00 for the purpose of developing the property, provided, however, that upon approval of ABC of previous borrowings, an additional aggregate of $50,000.00 may be borrowed without further approval.

Enter into agreements and contracts for the construction of site improvements and buildings on the property.

Upon completion of the development of the property, keep the property clean and in good order, make necessary replacements and repairs, arrange for maintenance of the buildings and improvements on the property, and do any and all other acts customary and necessary in the business of managing real estate.

5. Limitation on Partners' Powers:

The following things may be done only with the consent of both partners:

(a)   Borrowing money in the partnership name in an aggregate amount of more than $50,000.00, said $50,000.00 not to include previously approved borrowings;

(b)   Leasing or encumbering all or any part of the property or any building thereon;
(c)   Selling all or any part of the property;
(d)   Filing of a final subdivision map or final record of survey map dividing the property into lots or parcels.
(e)   Make any assignment for the benefit of creditors.
(f)   Hypothecation or other transfers of a partnership interest except (i) to another partner or, (ii) to any entity with which a partner may merge or consolidate or become affiliated with as parent, subsidiary, or sister corporation if immediately thereafter the stockholders of the transferring partner shall own in the aggregate more than fifty (50) per cent of the outstanding voting shares of the successor entitled to vote;
(g)   Cause the partnership to become a surety, guarantor or accommodation party to the obligation of another.

6. Term:
The term of this partnership shall commence as at the date first above stated and shall continue for twenty (20) years certain and thereafter until written notice is given by one partner to the other of an election to dissolve this partnership pursuant to Paragraph 17 below.

7. Place of Business:
The principal place of business of the partnership shall be any place or places as may be agreed upon, in writing, by the partners from time to time.

8. Contribution of Additional Capital:
The partners shall contribute in equal shares any additional capital that they may deem to be necessary to the operation of the partnership business. The partners shall confer from time to time to determine the need for any such additional capital and shall evidence their agreement on the subject in writing.

9. Capital Accounts:
An individual capital account shall be maintained for each partner. The capital account of each partner shall consist of its original contribution of capital increased by (a) additional capital contributions, and (b) its share of partnership profits, and decreased by (c) distributions in reduction of partnership capital and (d) its share of partnership losses. All withdrawals from any partner's capital account shall be by the unanimous written consent of all partners, and the first withdrawals shall always be from the greater capital account until the capital accounts are equal.

10. Profits and Losses:
The net profits of the partnership shall be divided, except as hereinafter provided — and the net losses shall be borne — equally between the partners. Such division of profits or losses shall be made at the end of each calendar year. In those years where the partners' capital accounts are unequal and where the partnership has ordinary income as computed for federal income tax purposes, the income, if sufficient, shall first be credited to the partner with the higher capital so that said partner receives six per cent (6%) on the difference between the capital accounts The balance of the income, if any, shall be divided equally. In those years where contributions or with-

drawals have been made during the year, the interest credited to the partner
with the larger capital shall be computed in such a manner that said partner
will receive six per cent (6%) on the actual difference throughout the year.
For the purposes of crediting interest to the partner with the larger capital,
each year shall stand alone and the right to receive the interest shall not
be cumulative.   ·

11. Management:
Except for the duties herein delegated to the managing partner, the partners
shall have equal rights in the management of the partnership business and
each partner shall devote such time to the conduct thereof as such partner
in its own judgment shall deem necessary. It is understood that each partner
is engaged in other businesses and that neither of them shall be expected
to devote its entire time to the conduct of the business of the partnership.
Both partners shall make themselves available from time to time to discuss
the conduct of the partnership business.

12. Transfer of Interest:
If either partner shall desire to sell or otherwise transfer all or any part
of its interest in the partnership — other than pursuant to Paragraph 5 (f)
— such partner shall give written notice thereof to the other partner which
shall include the price at which it is proposed to sell such interest. The
partner receiving any such notice shall have twenty (20) days within which
to commit itself in writing to purchase the offered interest at the specified
price. If the recipient of any such notice shall fail to give such written
commitment within the twenty-day period, the partner proposing to sell
such interest shall be free to do so subsequent to the expiration of such
period at any time during the immediately ensuing ninety-day (90) period
from such expiration at the specified price or any higher price. If the interest
shall not be sold during such ninety-day period, it shall not thereafter be
sold until it shall have again been offered to the other partner pursuant to
this Paragraph 12.

13. Books of Account:
The partnership shall maintain adequate accounting records. All books,
records and accounts of the partnership shall be open at all reasonable times
for inspection by the partners.

14. Financial Statement:
Financial statement shall be prepared at least annually and submitted to
both partners.

15. Banking:
All funds of the partnership shall be deposited in its name in such checking
account or accounts as shall be designated by the managing partner. Checks
shall be drawn on the partnership account for partnership purposes only
and shall be signed by such persons as may be designated in writing by
the managing partner.

16. Dissolution:
Dissolution of either of the partners, voluntarily or involuntarily, shall effect
an immediate dissolution of this partnership unless immediately thereafter
the assets formerly held by the dissolved partner shall be held and controlled by a corporation or corporations in which the present stockholders

of the dissolved partner shall own, either directly or indirectly, more than fifty per cent of the outstanding shares entitled to vote.

17. Termination:

At any time after the expiration of the twenty-year term specified in Paragraph 7 above, either partner may terminate the partnership by giving written notice to the other. The effective date of the termination shall be the last day of the third calendar month following the month in which such termination notice shall be given. If the partnership shall be terminated, the partners shall proceed promptly to wind up the business of the partnership. The assets of the partnership shall first be used to pay all debts of the partnership. If either partner shall have withdrawn funds from the partnership in excess of the other partner, then the remaining funds shall be used to pay to the partner entitled thereto a sufficient amount to equalize the withdrawals. Any remaining assets of the partnership shall be divided between the partners equally, and any losses shall be shared equally by the partners.

18. Stock Transfer:

If the ownership of the outstanding shares of either partner shall so change that the present shareholders do not hold more than fifty (50) per cent of the outsanding voting shares, written notice of such change in stock ownership shall be promptly given to the other partner. At any time during the ninety-day period immediately following any such notice, the recipient thereof may terminate this partnership by means of written notice of termination given to the other party — which termination shall be effective as of the last day of the third calendar month following the month in which the termination notice shall be given. If either partner shall fail to give written notice of a change in share ownership such as that referred to in this Paragraph 18, the other partner shall have the power of termination herein specified throughout the ninety days next following its discovery of said change in share ownership. For purposes of this Paragraph 18, change in share ownership as a result of (i) corporate reorganizations wherein the present shareholders continue to own directly or indirectly more than fifty per cent of the outstanding voting shares in the surviving corporation; (ii) gifts to members of the family or to family trusts, or (iii) transfers upon death or to family members or to family trusts shall not be counted as stock transfers.

19. Fidelity Bond:

Immediately after the signing and execution of this agreement, an application shall be made to secure a fidelity bond on the managing partner, its officers, its employees or its representatives for the benefit of the partnership. Coverage under a blanket fidelity bond shall be sufficient for this purpose. The expense of such bond shall be deemed an expense of the partnership.

20. Notices:

All notices required or permitted hereunder shall be in writing directed by registered or certified mail to the last known address of the party to whom such notice is to be given.

21. Arbitration:

Any controversy arising out of or relating to the performance of this agreement shall be resolved by arbitration in accordance with the rules of the American Arbitration Association.

22. Captions:

The captions are for convenience only and shall not be deemed a part of this agreement.

IN WITNESS WHEREOF, the parties hereto have executed this agreement on the date first above written.

_____

_____

29

Market Entry for Corporate
Joint-Venturers

Mother, please! I'd rather do it
myself!

—TV Commercial

It has been observed elsewhere in this book that no matter how tight the availability of capital for development, there is always more money around than there are really first-rate deals to put it into. This is a truth many corporate venturers are vexed to discover when convinced after a long study of the high profit potentials of this business, they begin searching for the right deal and the right builder to joint-venture with. A number, to be sure, have been fortunate enough to tie in with excellent developers who have been real money machines for them. But the results have not been, shall we say, uniformly felicitous.

The typical course of entry into the real estate business by a non-housing corporation is to set up a real estate department and hire one or two (hopefully) knowledgeable professionals to direct the entry activities. During the learning period, the corporate investor will try to minimize his exposure by keeping the initial ventures small; if the first tottering steps are successful, broader joint-venture programs are geared up. But the problem is not so simple as it appears. The corporate real estate professional is usually finance-oriented rather than *market-oriented* and may lack the capability to soundly evaluate the quality of the joint-venturing builder's own judgment or the deals the builder brings to him. The corporation's real estate performance thus may depend on the less than fully ascertainable ability of the one or two builders it lines up as joint-venturing parties.

There is no guarantee that the builder is going to be successful. There is no guarantee, moreover, that the deals he perceives and presents to the corporation are the best ventures that can be perceived and created in the given market area. The builder will argue his case persuasively because he naturally wants to start the project, but some horrible mistakes have occurred because optimism was substituted for a realistic evaluation of a deal's merits. An extreme example was one well-known major corporation that at one time started a multitude of joint ventures but had as many failures as successes and only managed to break even after several years of experience. Unexpected development and carrying costs rear up to devour the richest investor. Marketing costs balloon and homes languish unsold because planning takes everything but the buyers into account. The best ventures are the high-profit, fast-turnover smaller projects that take a year's time at most and meet a specific need in a ravenous market, but these are also the hardest to find. Most builders, operating locally or regionally, lack the flexibility to anticipate and assemble such ventures where the opportunities for them occur. Those who do possess this capability are most likely already involved with stable sources of joint-venture capital.

Let me digress on this subject of actually *finding* a builder, any *good* builder, to work with in the first place — particularly these days, when the number of suitors for joint-venturing builders is multiplying. One has to combat the myths and generalities of this business to get to the realities underlying them. Two of these myths are the "Corporate Investor" and the "Capital-Starved Builder." When people in real estate talk about the corporate investor, a warm glow sometimes comes over them and an awesome image of infallibility and superior sophistication is conjured. Every corporate investor is presumed to be a General Motors with the resources and prestige to command instant attention. The reality differs considerably. The average corporate investor — perhaps operating a successful tool and die company or electronics firm, or even a garment manufacturer — has the same problems, hesitancies and fallibilities of anyone else new to the real estate business. He may disguise ignorance by arrogance, but where that happens it only worsens his problems by making him afraid to ask the questions he must ask to learn the business. He's got the same problem of making the right contacts and selling himself — and then making the same right *judgment* as anybody else when the chips are down.

Now our de-mythified corporate investor runs into a second myth that generally falls into the "Gold in the Streets" category. He's heard all about those hordes of super-talented builders who need only his capital to create a world of profit, but when he actually goes out and starts looking for these builders he discovers that they may be pretty elusive. I have said much myself about the readiness of excellent builders with excellent packages to tie up with financial partners. But unless the corporate investor already knows the development business and its people inside out, he usually discovers on his first few discreet inquiries that the builders *he* has heard of and would feel safe working with are most likely already booked up years ahead by other corporate suitors who got there first. If one of these does go with him on a deal, the corporate investor is never sure that the builder is fully committed to the success of a program because he may be involved with others at the same time.

The problem of finding the right talent can be difficult because often such talent is not highly visible. Many of the most talented people are builders who never built much because they were genuinely undercapitalized and didn't understand financing or worked for other developers as highly paid employees. It's hard to generalize, but it can be truthfully said that a good many of these low-profile people have much more talent than their former bosses. Some of the bigger builders who look so talented are all surface and little substance. They've smooth-talked and PR'd and social-climbed their way into a position of visibility to attract financial partners. They create a polished impression with well-turned manners and polished diction and a modest flash of urbane wit, with an occasional obscure financial term absently thrown in during the conversation just to let the other guy know that they, of course, really know the game but are too cultured to discuss anything as crass as business openly. A lot of investors got into trouble on bad deals because they took the presence of the "right" personality in the "right" social circle as an infallible badge of actual ability; they could have done better by divining astrological tables, or the entrails of birds. Me, I'd rather joint-venture with a guy who wears blue or brown with white socks and who don't speak such good English, but who can do an excellent job of bringing in profits. To utter a profundity, the accent is on ability, not surfaces or social graces. I have also found that the quality of true gentlemanliness is genetically linked to competence.

The corporate suitor might be lucky and meet a good builder through a personal contact that can recommend the builder's quality, as in the case of Loew's introduction to Jerry Snyder. But I can appreciate the exasperation of one president of a sizable corporation who exclaimed to me: "Just where in hell *are* all these good builders who want my money?" For all his financial capability, plus the valid need for equity capital in the industry, the corporate investor can thus actually have a rough time entering the field advantageously. Money, after all, is only energy and it must be skillfully directed and employed by a development and marketing intelligence. Without such aware control it is only misdirected force, soon spent. It can be vexing to feel that you almost have to know the development business as well or better than the developer in order to select the right partner and the right venture. We hear a lot about the success of selected majors like Westinghouse or Chrysler or Alcoa Building Industries and perhaps a dozen other blue-chips who have tapped the joint-venture potentials of residential development extensively and, on the whole, profitably. This is because they possess marketing and development judgment in addition to financial skills.

successful in this field, perhaps a dozen others who have taken a flier without the benefit of such judgment have become embroiled in such problems

This is also why for every non-housing corporation that has been and remedies attending their ventures that break-even would be a blessing. It underscores the point that behind the facade of corporate infallibility there exist human beings who are just as confused and bewildered and occasionally overwhelmed as the scruffiest jackleg builder. The chief difference is, they give their mistakes fancier names. The other difference is, their financial resources give them a larger capability to multiply their errors.

I do not really intend to suggest that it is impossible or even very difficult to find a competent builder to work with, despite added numbers of competitors seeking builders. Once a corporation sets its cap for involvement in real estate it can, by working closely through one or more able consultants, monitoring the variety of builder/developer conferences and staying current on the trade publications in the field, usually come up with several talented candidates. I do suggest, however, that if a company is going to get involved in real estate at all it should retain at the outset not only a financially oriented professional but also one or more skilled *marketing-oriented* executives who through direct prior experience in the industry have the ability to accurately evaluate the marketing talent and the land acquisition abilities of potential builder-partners, as well as the suitability of their deals for a given market. It seems an obvious point to make, but all too often this has not been done. An independent marketing capability not only serves as a check on the validity of the financial projections but can enhance and improve the builder-partner's own marketing plans and strategies based on a strong awareness of workable principles and the creative ability to relate the product to a perceived need. This can save a lot of grief.

A MARKETING VIEWPOINT AS THE KEY

Every single joint-venture package analyzed must stand on its own as a sound deal. It is all too easy to have a couple of lemons neutralize many carefully wrought good ventures. The temptation to move fast and sacrifice close study of a program occurs as a dangerous aftermath to some mergers, when the builder is suddenly flush with corporate cash. As a private operator he has most likely been very careful about investing his own capital or that of private investors critical to his continued existence. But when acquired, or perhaps discovering a joint-venture source of capital with money to burn, he begins compromising on his usually careful screening and planning and can wind up in hot water. If the acquirer is in haste to see earnings out of the acquired builder, the latter may invest in or otherwise get into joint-venture or other projects at the expense of good judgment. It takes considerable economic maturity to realistically appraise what you are capable of doing financially, as contrasted with managerially. Many builders confuse money with talent and, moving too fast, soon become mired. The key is to peg profit goals to an orderly, *achievable* growth target. Crossed fingers are never the basis for a good relationship.

The cautioning words about moving at a measured pace apply perhaps even more particularly to non-housing corporations and institutional investors than to builders. Probably the truest, most basic point about the corporate investment community as a whole is that it has an extremely difficult time understanding the real estate business. This is as true in 1973 as it was in 1969, and it will be true in 1976, despite the obvious fact that many more outside investment sources are in realty today than formerly. What large industrial firm could possibly conceive of developing a different product line for every major and minor market and even neighborhood in the United States? This type of operation and the thinking that it calls for is often beyond the conventional manufacturing executives' imagination. Yet this is the housing business. So it must stand to reason that the amount of planning time per dollar of income *has to be multiplied* substantially beyond the planning requirements of any other business. It is not an industry in which to move precipitately, especially for newcomers.

Accurate judgment is the key, and this must be based on thorough and accurate marketing information. It is good thinking that separates the really first-rate companies from the others; financial strength is not by itself a distinguishing factor. Just because Levitt & Sons had ITT behind it doesn't mean it didn't make mistakes. But as a rule Levitt plans and thinks well. It has to. A refrigerator is a refrigerator is a refrigerator; the same product anywhere in the U.S. But a Levitt house may be a colonial, a Spanish, a rambler, a townhouse or any of a dozen other widely varying models. Each of these will have a completely different set of land-acquisition, zoning, design, financing, marketing, and construction and labor problems to boot, in every part of the U.S.

Most other manufacturers deal in products that are marketed on a national or international basis. But a builder in a new market has to respond to the specific tastes, prejudices and desires of people in a specific neighborhood and under certain economic, social and environmental criteria that may vary considerably from area to area. He caters to people, not to statistics. Until recently, in fact, he was almost entirely a local operator; only recently have the regional and national companies emerged. Even these operate independent divisions at the grass-roots level.

The builder must develop sensitivity to each new marketplace, starting without preconceptions. He must learn what type of housing product may be required and evolve the marketing program that will create the best response to that product. Marketing in itself is a large and complex function, ranging from determination of locations, square footages, and interior

and exterior amenities to subtleties of design, interior and exterior architectural treatments, and model furnishing. It also involves an ability to
recruit and train a skilled sales team that will be responsive to the local
customs and the coordination of a complete advertising and merchandising
program.

The response in each market is different. The sales approach in one
locale may differ entirely from another. The labor problems in each market
are different. (Boise Cascade at one time in Washington ran into difficulties
with subcontractors and had lots of sales but no units to deliver. Jerry
Snyder ran into subcontractor problems in Staten Island.) The builder must
also analyze and become sensitive to the political forces operative in each
community, as these have a large bearing on his program through every
step from zoning onwards. He must learn the attitude of the local HUD
office regarding acceptance and processing time on government-assisted and
government-subsidized units. He must determine the professionals — attorneys, engineers, sales and other people — that he can successfully work
with. He must learn the local population's attitude toward himself and/or
the company he represents. The list could be considerably longer but will
suffice as an impression.

A community doesn't get riled up about a shipment of refrigerators
coming into town. But it can get awfully upset about new housing, depending on a multitude of factors. These include who's building it; who's the
user; where it's located; what type of housing it is; and generally whose ox
is gored. The Planning Department of Santa Rosa, California, summarized
some of the tricky and contradictory human attitudes in a certain chart
published along with the housing element of the city's General Plan in
April 1971. For this contribution to the housing industry's understanding
Santa Rosa will always be remembered. The chart is reproduced below in
full. For the reader's information, Santa Rosa is a city of 50,000 population
located in Sonoma County, approximately one hour's drive north of San
Francisco.

CAST OF CHARACTERS

To understand housing (wrote the unknown Santa Rosa planner who
conceived this lineup), one must first understand the people who are in the
housing business. It is the attitudes and actions of these people that determine the machinations of the housing market. In order that the reader
may better understand how the local housing market operates, we are
presenting a list of the people — a cast of characters — who deal in housing. For the convenience of the reader and to eliminate any possible confusion, we are listing the good guys separately from the bad guys.

GOOD GUYS

BAD GUYS

Speculator
Sonoma County man risking his savings to buy land for needed housing

Speculator
Man from Los Angeles risking someone else's capital to buy back property he should have kept in the first place

Developer
Sensitive soul willing to dip into his own pocket to provide extra site amenities

Developer
Insensitive individual demanding a packet of concessions before his option expires tomorrow

Moneylender
Farsighted man willing to lend money at one-half percent above prime

Moneylender
Twelve-fingered man considering doing you the favor of lending money at ten percent plus ten percent of the gross

Planner
Cooperative man willing to work with developers to produce imaginative residential developments

Planner
Narrow man with rigid, preconceived notions unwilling to write anything but negative staff recommendations

Architect
Creative professional working hard to provide site amenities for each unit

Architect
Hack working hard to bring in five extra units per acre

Builder
Old man building houses with traditional care, like his father did

Builder
Man with ulcer building houses with abandon, like his competitors

Carpenter
Hardworking man asking for higher wages to carry him through the winter months

Carpenter
High-income person asking for higher income because he knows he can get it

Realtor
Ethical man unwilling to accept any unreasonable listing

Realtor
Man in iridescent suit willing to accept any listing from anybody

Homebuyer
Eager man waiting for interest rate to drop so he can qualify to buy

Homebuyer
Stubborn man refusing to buy because interest rate is too high

Seller
Smart man willing to provide financing so young family can afford to buy

Seller
Devious man asking $30,000 for a $20,000 house, actually masking the fact he really doesn't want to sell

GOOD GUYS	*BAD GUYS*
Renter	*Renter*
Poor man waiting in line to rent a 300-square-foot chicken coop for $200 a month	Drug-crazed freak refusing to pay rent and tearing Uncle George's old house apart
Landlord	*Landlord*
Softhearted man again refusing to raise the widow's rent	Hardhearted businessman raising the rent another $75 after a two-cent increase in the tax rate
Appraiser	*Appraiser*
Studious man doing careful independent study to determine true market value of property	Crafty man doing many independent studies until he gets one that satisfies his client
Neighbor	*Neighbor*
Liberal man willing to accept low-income housing for the good of the community	Little man willing to accept low-income housing as long as it is not in *his* neighborhood
Mobile-Home Owner	*Mobile-Home Owner*
Pensioner seeking to live within his income	Man with five children in public schools seeking to beat the property-tax game
Public Housing Tenant	*Public Housing Tenant*
Poor woman from Santa Rosa finally finding decent housing for her family	Deadbeat just in from out of town living in a better house than you do

I have been a marketing consultant to the development industry for quite a while, and I am always amazed at the lack of understanding that many head men of companies and their marketing chiefs display about the role of marketing. Most often they perceive marketing as a straightforward sales function. The marketing director usually rises through the sales ranks and may often be ill equipped to direct market research to come up with the panoply of answers he needs. Good research translates into judgments on land acquisition, product development, advertising and merchandising, sales management and training, public relations, after-sales service, and the creation of the overall marketing organization.

Marketing is the key to this business, and the key to an understanding of marketing is market research. With it you can understand this business and thus dominate it. Marketing makes possible that twenty-minute head start into new areas, geographic or product type. It can get you past the defeatist mold of the industry that locks most of its participants into solid imitation. Many pay lip service to good use of market research, to be sure, but do not understand it in any depth and therefore don't use it well. Thus they do not see the opportunities when they arise. I've often felt the frustration of a Billy Mitchell. You can warn builders about adapting to new product lines just so often; you can point to markets not being served or being served inadequately only so long. It is then frustrating to see the builder who ignored your advice shrinking when his organization had both the financial and managerial capability to take advantage of the new opportunities.

Lacking a full understanding of markets and marketing, many companies are first too slow to take advantage of the real opportunities, then often try to make up for it by moving too fast without the proper planning when the stampede toward some new area or product type has really started. It's an unhealthy flip-flop, from no action to hurried action. A true understanding of your markets and a refusal to be locked into the responses of the competition provides the cure. In 1972 and 1973, for example, many builders began getting involved in conversion of apartments to condominiums. We were involved in this activity long before it became fashionable — identifying markets and opportunities, expanding the builder's profit potential beyond what he could achieve merely through geographic diversification. Condo conversions, primarily an urban operation, enabled the builder to tap a new market right in his own backyard and diversify by product type instead of expanding in a linear fashion geographically. But for all the validity of this exciting new profit opportunity, it took another two to three years before the message got through. A few clearly observant builders have by now raked in a fortune from this activity, but most are only now awakening to the possibilities. They'll come stampeding in, falling all over each other, and settle for second best.

A real understanding of marketing enables new companies to grow, existing companies to get bigger, and gives troubled companies a new lease on life. It entails a full understanding of what is happening in the marketplace. On the basis of such understanding, imaginative brainstorming can find solutions to problems and thus create new opportunities for profit. That's how the condominium conversion business was born. Somebody perceived that if we as a nation were selling more resale than new homes each year, it was only logical we could sell apartments as homes, too — especially if by so doing we could satisfy a housing need that could not be satisfied by any other method for a comparable price.

Market research defines what the housing demand is by volume and by type of buyers and renters. It inventories the housing presently being offered to satisfy the perceived demand. It examines various alternatives that can be brought forth to satisfy demand. That was essentially the process that led to the condominium conversion boom: We know that many people are frozen out of single-family homes by rising prices; we know that the majority would rather own than rent; we know many attractive in-city apartments are available. Can we *do* something about the perceived unmet demand? The traditional homebuilder didn't see the answer first, being somewhat in the same position as the U.S. automobile industry, which did not respond to a demand for compact, low-priced automobiles first. In both cases the logical industry — already equipped to build and deliver the desired product — did not respond first. It was the outsiders. In the condo conversion field, a few clearheaded investors did it first. In the auto field it was Volkswagen, then Datsun and Toyota that perceived a need ignored by Detroit. It took both U.S. industries — building and automobile — some years to begin closing the communication lag.

Insufficient perception, incomplete communication. Marketing is essentially the faculty that perceives, analyzes, and draws conclusions relative to action. It is a pretty stinted faculty in the building industry. McKeon was selling fourplexes at moderate prices for an awful long time in a dead Sacramento market before anybody even thought of the possibility that he might be tapping an unmet demand for lower-priced ownership housing. The builders had to have it rammed down their throats before they moved. Suddenly, everybody was building fourplexes until they were coming out of every subdivision in the U.S. It was the same story with government-assisted housing programs. A very few guys were working them thoroughly for a long time; after a communication lag of three or so years, all hell broke loose on the Western Front. Why is it that so many of our industry's allegedly smart executives wait to see so much evidence before they act? This is not creativity but stimulus-response operation. In an amoeba it's fine; for a homebuilder it falls short of the ideal. The opportunities are as ample today as ever, with new ones cropping up continually. Any builder can assume the leadership position with regard to any of them by merely perceiving the market freshly and clearly and *trusting* himself to act on the basis of the data that he sees.

Building is a business in which people work with people. They must perceive, communicate, evaluate and draw accurate conclusions. To do this well takes a person skilled not only in the mechanics of construction, finance and reporting procedures but one who really lives in *present time* and actually is alive to what is going on out there in the big wide world and how it affects him personally as well as with regard to his business. This is the essence of good marketing. But at a time when we as an industry need this quality most because the stakes are bigger than ever, we are getting fewer such people. As the industry has moved into the orbit of Wall Street, we have begun to get the flow of young executives from prestigious business schools. They're financially oriented, sharp in the technology of management, and as a rule either awfully naïve or stupidly arrogant. Business schools are not too high on my list of favorite institutions. Their biggest failure is that they do not teach people how to communicate or work with people or how to observe events around them from the vantage point of present time and draw meaningful conclusions.

Too many of these folks are coming right out of schools into positions of substantial responsibility when they should still be learning. Their level of expectation is so high as to be unrealistic. Sometimes they get arrogant because they work with many people whose own educational credentials aren't so sexy. What would really be useful would be an extended apprenticeship period. Many of these talented newcomers have much to contribute, given a basis of realistic apprenticeship training. But in most cases such training is too short. The hazard is that they will never realize their innate ability because their learning has been primarily from books. You can only contribute when you truly understand the business from every practical viewpoint as well as from the people end. Consequently, it is often the people with the practical training and the broader human vision who rise faster. This criticism is not restricted to the young, by any means. Too many builders hire employees on the basis of their credentials or common social backround instead of the basis of experience and ability. The credentials look great on the letterhead but the business goes down the tube.

The corporation that would get involved in real estate via the joint-venture route has something to learn from all this. It all comes under the heading of marketing. I sometimes think that marketing — as defined in the homebuilding business — is the profession for a combination priest, philosopher and wise man.

A MARKET–ORIENTED APPROACH TO JOINT VENTURES

What I am stumping for is the creation of more corporate real estate departments with an active *marketing* intelligence, not just financial skills. Marketing is the perceiving and controlling faculty for the brawn of finance and construction. I define it broadly as the capability to identify and create the most salable project package in the best market at the right time with the most appropriate builder-partner based on a continually fresh and accurate perception and evaluation of:

1. National market dynamics and the potentials of strategic local markets
2. The constantly changing needs and desires of the consumer for whom the housing is built

3. The product and market strategies of successful competing builders
4. The availability and location of strategic parcels of land
5. The availability of the right builders for the right projects

With this type of capability a corporate venturer could also exploit the potentials of real estate far more fully and flexibly than by the conventional joint-venture method where he relies on one local builder to bring him the deals perceived only in one area. He can use the market talent to scan the national markets and identify and package the most profitable projects himself, then selecting the appropriate local builders to joint-venture the particular deal. A truly market-oriented capability would thus remove the corporate investor from a second-string, passive role and put him into the driver's seat when it comes to identifying and choosing the broadest range of potentially profitable projects and local builders. Instead of waiting for whatever might come his way, he goes out and creates the best joint-venture opportunities himself. I see it as inevitable that the successful corporations engaged in joint ventures will eventually go this route in order to secure a greater control over their future.

Where does a market-oriented approach to entering into a real estate joint venture begin? Let me suggest one format that operates in three stages:

Phase I — Analysis of Corporate Entry and Housing Market Trends

The first phase should provide a coordinated plan or strategy for real estate investment that is most appropriate for thé corporation in question and most responsive to its particular needs and capabilities.

1. A study program is conducted to develop an optimum structure for the corporation's involvement in the industry.
   The study should cover:
   a. A realistic definition of the company's proposed objectives in the field and the resources it is willing to commit to real estate involvement.
   b. An analysis of the short- and long-term benefits that may accrue to the company from this type of diversification weighed against alternative investments.
   c. A detailed study of comparable corporations' entry histories, isolating ill-conceived and advantageous entries and the reasons for them.
   d. A detailed study of the problems of entering the housing field and the strategies to overcome these problems.
   e. A definition of an appropriate corporate real estate format and program based on this and other elements of the Phase I program.

2. A detailed analysis of housing market trends is conducted to isolate present and future opportunities for development. The study should examine the potentials of the growing number of specialized housing markets (such as retirement and recreation-oriented housing; condominium and townhouse development for both the "price" market, competing with apartment rentals, and the luxury market; conversion of apartment buildings to condominium marketing programs; apartment potentials for singles, divorced persons, old people and families; etc.).

   a. Current product/market strategies of builders and developers should be examined to determine:

      i) What product lines and development concepts do successful bidders relate to different geographical markets?

      ii) How are other builder companies structuring themselves in relation to changes in competition? Are they engaged in market penetration, market development, product development or product diversification, and why?

   b. What are the viable trends that will shape market demand during the next five years?

   c. What will be the main thrust of competition during this period?

   d. Based on all data gathered in Phase I, what are the best product and market opportunities for the corporation to develop?

3. A national market analysis is conducted to evaluate in terms of strength and numbers the demand for residential units of all types in the top fifteen to twenty-five most active U.S. housing markets. This will be a preliminary analysis to assess the priority of markets to enter and the general product types that may be advantageously developed in such markets. During 1971, for example, one set of seventeen major markets that might have been studied was as follows:

> San Francisco-Oakland, California
> Anaheim-Orange County, California
> Denver, Colorado
> Los Angeles, California
> Phoenix, Arizona
> San Diego, California
> San Jose, California
> Atlanta, Georgia
> Dallas, Texas
> Ft. Lauderdale-Hollywood, Florida
> Houston, Texas
> Miami, Florida

Tampa-St. Petersburg, Florida
Chicago, Illinois
Detroit, Michigan
New York-Long Island
New Jersey-Philadelphia

The requirements for a broad analysis of housing development opportunities may vary. A corporation may confine its study to one national region closest to corporate headquarters, focusing on a number of smaller markets. Or it might expand its study well beyond the major markets outlined above. In arriving at an evaluation of the priority of markets to enter and the timing of such entry, the preliminary analysis of each market is based on the following factors tempered by marketing experience:

Population growth
Five-year population projections
Building activity by dwelling type
Employment base
Projected economic growth
Family size
Median family income
Total demand for residential units
Demand by price range for residential units
Total demand for rental units
Demand for rental units by rental range and type

Phase II — In-Depth Study of Selected Housing Markets and Land Acquisition

With its general objectives, capabilities and product/market strategies defined, the corporation is now ready to take further specific action. It should undertake a detailed on-site research program of the market areas it has preliminarily selected for potential entry to develop the exact data needed for a successful project program or programs. The research information and marketing analysis should define market size and absorption rates for up to five years for rental and ownership units in all rental and price categories. Specific market targets should be defined and product and amenities recommended having the greatest market appeal. The study should, in short, provide authoritative recommendations delineating specific housing programs, locations, and the *timing* of market entry. It should also serve as the guide for land acquisition with respect to the recommended project.

These specific recommendations are reached by synthesizing and interpreting data gathered by a four-tiered research approach. The corporation should:

1. Study in depth the economic and social foundations of the market,

taking a close reading of present and anticipated demand for housing.

2. Analyze in detail and evaluate all competitive housing activity.
3. Study people's tastes, preferences and prejudices not only for the metropolitan area but by geographic and housing submarkets to determine their desires and the existing and potential submarkets they form by housing type, price range, location and design preference. How well are the discerned wants and needs being met?
4. Develop a sensitive feeling for the unique characteristics of the overall market and its submarkets in terms of local customs, strategic locations and successful marketing strategies.

The importance of *qualitative* research in this type of study program cannot be overemphasized. Purely quantitative research has never conveyed much useful information about the potentials of a housing market. Demand statistics must be closely analyzed, and the correct interpretation is all-important. In some instances a reading of a high demand for a particular product type in a given price range can be a signal to abstain from developing it—when a close study of competitive activity also indicates that the specified product is being overbuilt. In another situation a statistical disclosure of overbuilding, warning other developers away from this sector, can be an indication of a new market opportunity. The best opportunity is indicated not by the greatest demand but by the *least satisfied* demand that is perceived by research. The statistical information alone can be so misleading that it serves no purpose or a detrimental purpose unless it is fully evaluated in the context of a four-tiered view of the market.

Getting Beyond the Statistics

For example, a comparison of a market area's annual population growth with the annual volume of, say, apartment building permits might show that apartment construction is outpacing the population growth and be taken as a signal of overbuilding. This kind of computation can be arrived at almost mechanically. In an area with a projected yearly population growth of 50,000 people where the average family size is computed to be 3.4 persons per household, the total housing demand is projected at 14,700 units. Assuming that the area's production ratio of homes to apartments has been running at about 50-50, this might be taken to mean the market couldn't absorb more than about 7,350 new apartments. If the rate of apartment starts approaches this figure, it could be interpreted as a danger signal for the market.

But it is impossible to draw this conclusion on the basis of the lump statistics themselves. They do not break down demand for different apartment types (singles, retirees, family-oriented units). They do not indicate demand for unit *sizes* (the market may be saturated with two-bedroom, two-bath units, for example, while demand for one-bedroom and studio units or two-bedroom one-bath units may continue strong). They do not indicate demand by *price range* (the demand for low- and medium-rent apartments can be far higher than for the luxury units and can be computed only by analyzing housing demand by income levels). They do not indicate demand by *location* (strategic location may rent well despite market saturation statistically).

An accurate evaluation of the apartment market will also take into account the present and projected impact of condominium and townhouse sales at price ranges whose monthly payments are competitive with rentals. This will alter the picture still further either positively or negatively. Specific features in certain apartment and housing types may also yield a higher absorption rate than indicated by demand, based on study of consumers' preferences. The final interpretation of the raw statistical data may thus differ considerably from the significance it conveys at first impression. The same sophisticated analytical approach to raw demand figures should be taken for every housing product type in a given market area.

The primary purpose of the Phase II research study should be to *delineate gaps in the market* and determine the local economic and social influences that will have a bearing on successful development. A qualitative four-tiered research program provides this information on a submarket basis. Vacancy figures and unsold inventory should be interpreted in the four-tiered context to evince the factual basis for 100% occupancy or excellent sales in some projects and poor rentals or for-sale communities dead in their "tracts" elsewhere. The study should forecast both demand and projected competitive activity by submarket, including single-family detached housing, single-family attached housing (planned-unit cluster projects and condominiums) and multifamily rental units. Demand figures should be projected by price and rental range and related to current and potential supply. Specific areas of opportunity should be examined by submarket for unmet and under-met housing needs of the so-called "empty nesters" and retired people; compact households composed of single people, divorced persons and widows; young "diaper set" families; and the general move-up market trading up from apartments to homes or older to newer homes. Of course, this should be done in the context of an intelligent study of the area's economy and socioeconomic characteristics, elucidating existing and probably future market conditions.

Include a Focus on Governmental and Social Concerns

It is important for the research study to focus on local governmental, social and development problems as these relate to successful housing development. In many areas of the nation, for example, conservationist and ecological groups now wield a significant influence in the field of planning and zoning and can block development that is not responsive to the stated priorities of the community. The research program should establish the community standard for acceptable residential development and define criteria that will meet zoning standards and community acceptance. Many locales also have ongoing problems with property taxation and school development and increasing difficulties in financing adequate municipal development of sewer, water and electric utilities. All of these factors have a great bearing on the feasibility of residential development and land prices.

Frequently, the extent of local zoning, utility or property-tax problems — and the attitudes of local political and civic groups — has not been evident to a developer moving into a new area until after he has made a substantial investment. The corporate Phase II research program should thus develop a sensitive awareness of these factors as they may have a bearing on its subsequent activity in a given market. Planning, municipal works and other governmental bodies should be consulted; key civic, conservationist or ecological groups should be identified and evaluted for an exact reading of their present and future plans and activities. This sensitivity to potential problems of local development not only enables the corporation to avoid difficult situations but also makes refined marketing strategy possible: knowing, for example, that a certain land area will be unavailable for development or that another may become available — or what zoning will be approved and disapproved — could significantly alter marketing and competitive strategy. This information is an indispensable input to any land acquisition and marketing program based on a four-tier research program.

The Detailed Elements of the Research Program

1. *Analysis of Economic and Demographic Market Conditions.* The first stage of the study should deal with a thorough analysis of the economic bases of the marketplace first evaluated in a preliminary way in the Phase I Program. This stage provides the necessary economic data base around which the rest of the study is developed. It covers the following factors for primary and secondary markets:

Population trends and projections
Age composition
Family composition
Household formations
Local customs
Income levels — past, present and projected
Work-force characteristics
Employment — past, present and projected
Industrial development — past, present and projected
Circulation — present and projected

Land-use patterns

Building activity by single and multiple additions

Demand by type for the study area and its submarkets, including close-up analysis of residential and multiple-housing unit demand in the market during the period of time in which the project is being developed. Projections beyond a three-year period get too theoretical, but some type of five-year outline is achievable.

Demand by price range and rental range for residential and rental housing over a ten-year period.

2. *Competitive Evaluation.* The second stage of the research program should discover and analyze the achievements and shortcomings of all competitors by resorting to extensive field investigation and analysis of significant items of comparison. The research will thus arrive at standards for the production and marketing of a specified product with the highest probability of success.

a. The intensive field investigation should determine:

Housing and apartment types offered, the number of bedrooms and baths

Price and rental ranges

Square footages

Value ratios and rent/square foot

Lot and density characteristics

Financing

Project sizes

Product feature packages

Product option packages

Community amenities and environmental factors

Market conditions in each project

Sales and vacancy rates

Land planning

Merchandising and sales efforts

b. The competitive analysis enables the corporate investor to do the following:

i. *Look for gaps in the market* — the sizes, styles, price ranges for which there is an indicated demand, yet which through some combination of circumstances are not being offered.

ii. *Establish a profile of successful and unsuccessful operators* and isolate the exact factors for their success and failure. The idea is to improve on the successful factors and to avoid the unsuccessful ones.

iii. *Pay special attention to comparative values* being offered by the competition — price per square foot of living area, design and interior features, advantages of location and community amenities.

3. *Consumer research.* The third stage of the research program enables the corporate investor to determine who the potential buyers and renters are and the potential submarkets they form by location, housing type, design amenities and price range. This is qualitative research conducted through direct interviews and close inspection of market characteristics to determine wants and preferences and discover if they are being met or how they may be met.

This facet of the study should establish:
> Where purchasers and renters live
> Their places of work
> Their incomes
> What their customs, desires and aspirations are
> What their housing needs, preferences and desires are
> How much they are able and willing to pay
> How large their families are

The third aspect of the research should thus tie together the two preceding stages and allow the corporation to zero in with great detail on exactly *who* will occupy its product, in what quantity, at what price range and with what amenities.

Conclusions and Recommendations. This three-tiered research approach should be evaluated in the context of a fourth tier — a strong and sensitive feeling for the unique characteristics of the market in terms of locations, customs and marketing strategies. The cumulative qualitative and quantitative findings and research-based perceptions should then be translated into *specific* recommendations and actions that include the following:

a. The specific markets and submarkets the corporate investor should enter
b. The timing of market entry
c. Housing product types to build
d. Price (or rental) ranges to build in
e. Projected absorption rates
f. Specific locations to build in
g. Guidance on land acquisition
h. Specific interior and design features to incorporate into products
i. Recommended marketing methods

Market-oriented land acquisition. The intensive study of a specific market not only enables the corporate investor to translate his research into specific lines and building programs but also makes him thoroughly familiar with the unique locational characteristics of the market. Once he knows exactly what type of product in what price range and with what design characteristics will experience a strong demand in the market; once he has translated his findings into a specific concept of a successful development package; he is then also in the best position to determine the *location* that is best for this product. He can exploit his strategic knowledge of the market to select the most advantageously located parcels of land for the product concept for which he has perceived the highest probability of success.

This becomes a direct translation of research findings into land acquisition criteria, giving the corporate investor the flexibility to incorporate the value of *specific location* into the design of a successful housing-marketing program he has perceived. The location of a land parcel for a specific housing product may often control the feasibility of the product; by relating land acquisition to research on product demand and marketing design, the optimal relationship between the product and the best location for it is achieved.

As a direct result of the research program, the corporate investor is now advantageously situated to acquire strategic parcels of land for development. He can also make these acquisitions based on a full awareness of planning and zoning attitudes in the local market. His marketing-oriented staff should be skilled in successfully relating the proposed development concept to the best interests of the community in order to achieve rezoning where this is required.

Phase III — Marketing Program Design and Execution

We have now brought the corporate investor to the implementation stage of the project in this marketing-oriented approach to joint-venture development. Having identified and created a specific, highly marketable development opportunity, incorporating the best architectural design, the corporation's marketing-oriented real estate department is now in a strong position to bring in a competent local builder to execute the program on a joint-venture basis. Many excellent builders and developers will jump at the opportunity to take part in a venture packaged in this manner. The company has thus gained control over its own future by creating the best deal possible in the best market area instead of passively waiting for whatever a builder who operates over a limited area might bring in. It now takes the builders' bids to participate with it in a venture, instead of bidding with other corporations for the attention of a choosy builder with a good deal. Having selected a builder it considers most appropriate for the venture, the company's market-oriented real estate department is also in a position to provide the joint venturer with such marketing assistance as might be necessary to assure the success of the venture. The steps encompassed by Phase III include the following:

1. Selection of a local builder to joint-venture with.
2. Design of a marketing program. The recommended package is analyzed for maximum impact on the local market and a complete program is developed to communicate the project most effectively to potential buyers. An overall marketing budget is prepared. A unique and imaginative merchandising/marketing theme is developed. Appropriate merchandising and advertising media are selected and cordinated in an effective program. The interior designers, model-compound, and landscape architects and advertising and public relations agencies who have the talent to perform outstandingly in the venture's behalf are selected and their activities are coordinated.
3. Selection and recruitment of a skilled marketing manager. The local builder may have a competent marketer, but if he does not the marketing-oriented corporate real estate department can help him select one. Or it may run the marketing and sales function itself.
4. Recruitment and Training of Sales Personnel. A key aspect in the success of any merchandising program is the selection — and *proper training* — of sales people who will be the actual point of contact with the buying public. A marketing-oriented corporate real estate department can undertake this role in behalf of the joint venture. It may also conduct further training and educational seminars for sales and marketing personnel as a useful adjunct to its initial recruitment and training program.
5. Consumer Research: Monthly Traffic Interviews. The corporate marketing staff should be able to monitor the project's sales program through monthly traffic interviews conducted at the site. The interviews should elicit specific information about shopper traffic by getting answers to the following questions:
   a. What specific medium attracted the shoppers' attention to the development?
   b. What reasons did they have for visiting the project?
   c. What were their specific feelings regarding the product and the development?
   d. What other residential/rental developments have they visited that they like better than this project, and why?
   e. In what specific price range are shoppers interested in purchasing or renting their next home or apartment?
   f. What specific monthly payments would they consider making?
   g. How many bedrooms and baths would suit the needs of the family?
   h. How do they regard the reputation of the builder?

    i. What do they consider the most desirable recreation facilities
and how much would they be willing to pay for them?

    j. In what types of housing units do shoppers presently live?

    k. What are the price range/monthly mortgage payment or rental
ranges of their present dwelling units?

    l. What is the length of residency?

    m. In what city does each shopper now live?

    n. What is his occupation and location of employment?

    o. What is the age of head of household?

    p. What is the total family income?

This information is compared with profiles of buyers/renters to determine
the market segment responding to the product and to the merchandising, as
well as the segments that are not being reached and why. The monthly
shopper research reports thus form an important basis for the marketing-
oriented corporate real estate department's recommendations regarding
product and merchandising techniques to increase the project's market
share.

6. Sales Evaluation Reports. The department should also conduct
monthly sales evaluations to determine or answer the following:

    a. Sales office appearance.

    b. Salesman's approach.

    c. General appearance of salesman.

    d. Salesman's opening.

    e. Does he try to make the product distinctive and interesting?

    f. Does the salesman have pride in the product?

    g. Did he ask qualifying questions?

    h. On what subjects did his sales presentation include information?

    i. What was salesman informed about down payment, taxes and in-
surance, monthly payment, interest rates on loan, cost of extras?

    j. Does salesman really try to answer or does he evade questions?

    k. The sales demonstration: Did salesman accompany prospect to
apartment or site? In salesman's car or prospect's car (where
applicable)? What sales aids were used?

    l. Does salesman try to close and what are his closing points?

7. Overall marketing consultation. In the course of project development, the properly staffed department will provide continuing
qualitative insight and control on merchandising/advertising programs and techniques that will enhance the image of the project
and its unit sales and otherwise assist the joint-venturing builder as
may be necessary. Operating in close coordination with the real
estate department's financial control functions, the in-house marketing approach is thus unbeatable when it comes to creating the

corporation's future profits by such flexible selection of the best projects in the best markets with the right timing.

NOTE: When a corporate investor considers the development of a large planned community with diversified land uses, additional factors enter into the preparation of a marketing program and should be incorporated into preliminary economic and marketing research studies preparing a viable basis for the program. These factors are introduced in the following outline of community design specifications.

RESEARCH, ARCHITECTURAL AND PLANNING FACTORS FOR DEVELOPMENT OF A VIABLE COMMUNITY DESIGN

"Community Design Specifications" is a description of the life-style of the proposed community, supported by a rational analysis of its social and economic characteristics, a detailed description of proposed population, the required amenities, and the infrastructure as it will exist when the community is fully developed.

The rationale of the analytical methods employed is of the utmost importance and should include consideration of the following factors:

1. Basic criteria
   A. Average family size
   B. Densities per acre
   C. Building heights
   D. Community character and quality
2. Population profile
   A. Age distribution
      1. Preschool
      2. Kindergarten
      3. Elementary school
      4. Junior High
      5. Senior High
      6. College
      7. Working age
      8. Retired
   B. Source distribution
      1. Seasonal residents
      2. Permanent residents
      3. Tourist and/or sales prospect impact and requirements based on average visit
      4. Work force, service personnel
      5. Population migration
   C. Economic Distribution
      1. Income distribution
      2. Product price/rental range demand
      3. Product type demand
3. Definitions
   A. Neighborhood
   B. Village
   C. Community

4. Living Units
    A. Single-family detached, occupant-owned —
       location, type, approximate size, densities
    B. Single-family attached, occupant-owned —
       location, type, approximate size, densities
    C. Multifamily rental —
       location, type, approximate size, densities
    D. Condominiums —
       location, type, approximate size, densities
    E. Hotels, motels, etc. —
       location, type, approximate size, densities

5. Schools
    A. Number of schools
    B. Type
    C. With or without adjacent park facilities
    D. Size of school
    E. Site size required and location
    F. Radius of area served

6. Recreational Activities
    A. Types of activities
        1. Active recreation:
           Boating, swimming, fishing, canoeing, other water sports;
           hiking, horseback riding, tennis, golf, etc.
        2. Passive recreation:
           Indoor recreation
           Outdoor theaters, parks, botanical gardens, etc.
    B. Space required for activities based on population demand
    C. Location
    D. Existing attractions in adjacent metropolitan area

7. Standards for Recreational Areas
    A. Type of area
    B. Acres per population
    C. Size of site required
    D. Radius served

8. Commercial Facilities — Shopping Centers — Neighborhood, Village
   Community, Resort Specialty Center
    A. Function
    B. Leading tenants
    C. Location
    D. Radius of area served
    E. Minimum population for support
    F. Gross site area required
    G. Desirable size of center as percent of area served
    H. Gross floor area required
    I. Number and type of stores and shops
    J. Parking requirements

9. Medical and Health Facilities
    A. Number and type
    B. Beds required

    C. Size
    D. Population served
    E. Land required
    F. Location
    G. Parking requirements

10. Library Facilities
    A. Service radius
    B. Population required for support
    C. Book stock
    D. Land required
    E. Location
    F. Parking requirements

11. Social Facilities
    A. Type: churches, bowling alleys, theaters, golf courses with clubhouse, riding academy and bridle trails, lake marinas with clubhouse and community center
    B. Population required for support
    C. Land area required
    D. Location
    E. Parking requirements

12. Transportation — highway, street, walkways and carriageway standards
    A. Type
    B. Function and traffic flow
    C. Spacing
    D. Required widths of right-of-way and pavement
    E. Speed control
    F. Bridge considerations
    G. Access way to amenities

13. Public Water Supply
    A. Volumetric requirements for estimated population
    B. Plant location

14. Sewage Disposal
    A. General requirements, including treatment criteria
    B. Expected quantities
    C. Plant location(s)

15. Drainage
    General requirements and recommendations

16. Electricity, gas and telephone
    A. General requirements
    B. Standards

17. Protection facilities
    A. Police requirements (public and/or private)
    B. Fire requirements
    C. Standards

18. Industrial requirements, if any
    A. Temporary facilities for construction—type, location and area re-required

  B. Permanent facilities—general requirements, location and area required

19. Other land use potential
  A. Agricultural leases
  B. Ranchette or farmette demand

20. Other considerations
  A. Architectural character; general considerations
  B. Landscaping—general considerations
  C. Vista points, towers, etc.
  D. Natural amenities preservation and accessibility
    1. Inland lakes
    2. Topography
    3. Open space
    4. Ecology, conservation, possible sources of air and water pollution
  E. Recommendations for land-use controls
  F. Airport requirements, if any, etc.
  G. Recognition and preservation of historical monuments

Epilogue

What's it all *for?*

—Caddles, in H. G. Wells's
novel, *The Food of the Gods*

People

The cosmos exploded, actualizing its potentiality of space and time. The Centers of power, like fragments of a bursting bomb, were hurled apart. But each one retained in itself, as a memory and a longing, the single spirit of the whole; and each mirrored in itself aspects of all others throughout all cosmical space and time.

—Olaf Stapledon, *Star Maker*

The people who get on in this world are the people who get up and look for the circumstances they want, and, if they can't find them, make them.

—George Bernard Shaw

The unhurried observer will occasionally perceive that successful organization for the development and marketing of homes, and then the actual successful production and sale of these homes, depends on an irritatingly recurrent factor: people. You can't get away from 'em. People are the essential element of both the organization and the marketplace. Particular people. Particular people organize, merge and run companies successfully — or run them down. Particular people living in our land have particular needs and desires for housing and aesthetic environment; the housing business will in the long run prosper or fail depending on whether it gives them what *they* really want, not what they are told they want or are forced to accept. Housing is a people business. Its successful operation accordingly depends on something called *awareness* — an awareness that can perceive conditions and events and people as they really are (and not as they are imagined or wished to be), and which can then make things go right on a basis of accurate data. We live in the world's most powerful economic system and our technologies of finance, economic analysis and management have taken us a long way. But all our sophisticated technical tools are only as effective as the awareness controlling them. Awareness, of course, begins with awareness of self; the more clearly you know yourself and your motives, the better you will be able to perceive others and the more effectively you will be able to use your tools. Clearly, as we look around at the economic and social disorder that surrounds us today, it must dawn on us that somehow our knowledge is incomplete.

One of the first things that might be apparent is that nothing effective ever truly gets done without ultimately *one* specific awareness consulting *another* specific awareness, working out unresolved or misunderstood areas, and coming to some agreement. We function in organizations, but life, like a football game, is also a one-on-one situation if it's going to be effective. This gives rise to the novel theory of human relations that individual people are very important, and that it is in our own interest to respect and reward them for ability: no matter how big our organization, we are ultimately dependent on the ability and performance of individuals for its well-being. Everybody knows the old joke about the camel being a horse designed by a committee. It is individual people who get things done, and get them done right. Ideally, the organization returns the obligation by setting and implementing policies that will enhance the individual's ability to play a better one-on-one game. The individual enhances the survival of the group, the group rewards and enhances the survival of the individual.

It is the individual's well-being that is supremely important to the organization's well-being, because an organization is only the sum of individuals. This begins by honoring the rights and rewarding the abilities of the individual, but it also entails the individual's assumption of responsibility for his acts. Organizations and events are moved by specific individuals. This gets us past the welter of fallacies that attribute events to generalities ("the masses" — "the organization" — "the Establishment" — "the recession" — "the energy shortage" — "rampant inflation" — "the overbuilt market"), for if we look deep enough we find that specific individuals and their actions cause both positive and negative effects which can be easily enough masked in the broadest generalities. Organizations that mask the actions of the individual in generality, or disperse among a "mass" individual responsibility and credit or which take specific action in response to an unexamined generality, do not strike me as oriented in the direction of survival. It is the individual who is important, and his acts — helpful or damaging in the context of his group's awareness and its aims — must be specifically recognized. Events proceed from specific individuals taking specific actions, not from generalities and theories. Let us avoid the lie of averages and the lie of generalities. Life is always very specific, even if people are often not.

Running things on a one-on-one basis, and not on a generality, requires one to observe what is actually happening and to respond to it. It takes caring. The housing entrepreneur, for example, typically runs his business on a one-on-one basis. But Lee Andre Davis, president of Goodkin Executives, an executive search firm based in Westlake Village, California, has taken a close look at what happens when, in effect, generality replaces one-on-one operation and, in his own way, he comes up with the same emphasis on the importance to the organization of the individual who knows himself. The following is excerpted from an article of his titled "Goal-Oriented Profit Centers — Requisite For Survival."

THE PROBLEM — EXIT ENTREPRENEURIAL INCENTIVE. Within the last five years, significant changes have taken place in the ownership and size of builder/developer companies. Giant financial firms have acquired the builders and have immediately striven for expansion and for earnings-per-share. Entrepreneurs, who had previously provided immediate personal supervision of every phase of their operations, were now called on to redirect their individual efforts to the financial needs and demands of their parent firms — firms which did not comprehend the business of land conversion. As these once tightly controlled companies were forced to grow fast, the entrepreneurial directive lessened, and a vacuum developed between the immediate supervision of the owners and their middle-management operational group. Into this vacuum slipped numerous men of image, but not of performance.

RESULT — MUSICAL CHAIRS. Some were cronies and unknowledgeable friends who held the industry in low regard; all, however, were cloaked with substantial financial authority which they proceeded to abuse with alacrity. Also drawn into this vacuum were men promoted from within and suitable for small operations, but incapable of comprehending or controlling the larger scale of development necessary to return large profits. If they had had any goals, they were operating destructively beyond them. Their credibility as trusted employes did not offset the needs of the larger corporate goals; their promotion to greater authority, in some cases, proved fatal. Had the builders qualified many of these men by analyzing their professional goals — or lack of them — no haven would have been provided to those mediocrities that sought to and did infiltrate the industry. In these years that they have been with us, they have made "musical chairs" synonymous with construction management.

SOLUTION — CRITERIA FOR CORPORATE "PROFIT CENTERS". Under the compression of economics and the exposure of time, the entrepreneurial directive is now being returned to all aspects of the construction industry — even though the companies are of much greater capacity and size. Top management has concluded that one man at $35,000 is more economical than three at $20,000 each—but you must be certain of that one-man replacement! More than simply trimming staffs, the current requisite for survival is that each person remaining must be a "profit center" for your company.

HE MUST BE A HEAVYWEIGHT. A "heavyweight" justifies his employment through the profits he creates. In goal-setting, he stretches to the point of hernia, but not rupture. He hires only strong men and is aware that the only person whom he can control is himself. He is a problem-solver and policy-maker. He is professionally competent and an innovator. He has an instinctive sense of timing, is accessible, is a giver, not a taker. He recognizes that his self-respect is reflected in his respect for others, and he expresses gratitude for every favor, no matter how small. He understands that success is where one is going, not where one has been, and constantly exposes himself to new ideas, incorporating those that he can utilize to improve himself.

HE MUST BE GOAL-ORIENTED. Among other things, this person is one who has made five decisions — which he has reduced to writing: (1) He has established his professional, civic and personal goals for specified time periods. (2) He knows his strengths. (3) He has quantified his significant accomplishments and noted his salable features. (4) He has selected immediate job objectives. (5) He has profiled the firms for which he will work. In essence, he knows himself, and what he wants. He defines employment as "mutual satisfactory exploitation" and fully utilizes his employer as the vehicle for his own professional and personal growth. Conversely, the man without goals, who believes that longevity without progress is a virtue, makes the mistake of believing that business buys experience. Progress and promotion are not his, for business buys accomplishment.

A "profit center," in short, is a heavyweight who is goal-oriented. He in no way allows himself to be considered a justifiable expense. When and where necessary, he will remove himself from employment — within the department or the company — when he himself discerns that his presence is no longer required or justified. Each position he assumes is one in which he tries to work himself out of a job — transferring functions to others, or eliminating them entirely. Profit centers are strong men who hire only strong men. They have no fear that their subordinates will take their jobs — for they are fully aware that to be irreplaceable is to be unpromotable. Without promotion and greater problem-solving and policy-making areas, there is no growth for them towards their individual goals.

CORPORATE DIRECTION. Within the company, individual "profit centers" are, of course, part of the staff team. Realistic and attainable goals for each person must be established and

monitored at intervals. Corporate goals should be compared to those of the employees (in general and in particular) to ascertain the most effective means by which there may be mutual satisfactory exploitation throughout the years. Staffs can be trimmed, but those remaining must be goal-oriented heavyweights. They are the profit centers of our industry. They are an absolute requisite for survival. Anything less is corporate suicide.

THE MAN WHO CARED

It is not a coincidence, by the way, that Lee Davis closely resembles the type of person he envisions as the competent corporate executive. The Goodkin Executives is a direct outgrowth of his own experience as a job-seeker, to the regret of executive placement agencies that treated him offhandedly once. When Lee went knocking on executive-agency doors some years ago, what he expected to get was a thorough evaluation of his strengths, sound counseling on career goals and, thereafter, an intelligent effort to align him with a corporation based on compatible "people chemistry." What he got was a common denominator of low regard for the executive job-hunter and a lack of sensitivity to the particular needs of the corporate client: in short, volume dealing, with little or no element of personal care.

Lee Davis weathered the round-robin routine; though, as he says, it was the loneliest time of his life. He found his own job, as project manager of a $50 million construction project. But he also vowed to set up his own executive placement firm to take advantage of his long background in construction management and to live up to his private vision of the type and quality of service that such an organization should provide. Today, he has two other strong men implementing that vision with him, and the roster of his major corporate clients at Goodkin Executives indicates the extent to which he has translated it into reality. The operative words for the company are those of its homely but very sincere motto: "We Care." As Lee says, "You might say that I'm a product of bad, inadequate and nonexistent counseling." Accordingly, he has also developed a twofold approach designed to bring out the best in both job-seeker and corporate client in his own placement activities.

First, he has developed and uniformly applies an almost ministerially thorough method of intensive personal ("know thyself") counseling and goal orientation, which clients say increases their prospective employees' productivity by 20% to 50% and their salaries by 10% to 25%. Every serious candidate goes through at least two evening group sessions, called the "Thursday Counsel," plus review sessions. Interestingly, Lee does not

charge a fee for this personnel work, other than asking candidates to send
$35 checks to a local nonprofit youth organization, "Adventures Unlimited
of Ventura County." "By this method," he explains, "I get to establish an
elite corps of the top 2% of the men in our industries. I find out who
the top 10% are overall—the heavyweights, each of whom is a profit
center. Among this group, which has in common a continuing search
for new and better ideas, I find those with goals large enough to motivate
them continually. My overall success is in the number of people I've helped;
so I achieve success twenty or more times a day." As the second aspect of
his operation, Lee evaluates thoroughly not just job candidates but every
client corporation, as a prerequisite to a search for an executive to meet
their need. The close familiarity with the personality of the client firm helps
him greatly in matching up the right man with the right job.

Because of this detailed individual approach, and because he charges
his clients a fee only if he delivers, many industry observers feel that Lee
is setting a performance standard for the entire executive-recruitment industry. Says Peter C. Kremer, senior vice president of Newhall Land &
Farming Company: "An extra value of Lee's service is his extraordinary
personal interest in the well-being of both candidate and company. Although he represents the employer, he concurrently can get on the same
side of the table as the candidate." Lee continues to expand his stable of,
as he terms them, loyal goal-oriented profit centers — the heavyweights who
become, in their turn, corporate clients for still other heavyweights. And
his own goals are by no means modest: to have 50% of the construction
and real estate industry management as "profit centers" he has processed
by 1980. I wouldn't bet against a one-on-one man like him.

ONE–ON–ONE IN THE MARKETPLACE

Our obligation to operate with awareness doesn't stop at the door of
our organization, of course. It's also a one-on-one life in the society that
forms the market for the housing we produce. To perceive the millions of
people out there as individuals, to recognize ourselves in them, is also to
confront the responsibility of meeting their needs and aspirations and re-
quiting their trust. Perhaps this would cause irreparable shock to some of
our game-players and rule-makers who see the whole process as a mere
statistical abstraction.

What, for example, is behind the sudden rise in popular awareness
during the past few years of concern about the quality of the nation's
environment? The way words such as "ecology" are used today, they mean
something different to everybody. Uttered as a battle slogan or an advertising jingle, they can also be misused in campaigns that would stop

all growth and development or perpetuate old perfidies under the banner of "reform." Basically, "ecology" can be defined as the science or study of the optimal interrelationship of all living things. We used to think of "ecology" as the study of the life cycle in a frog pond, but now it's been extended to the interaction of continental and planetary *society* (and its economic systems) as well as the entire physical environment. In the field of real estate development it includes, or should include, planning for the optimal interrelationship of people with a created environment that enhances and modifies existent features of water, land, animal and plant life. To the extent that developers have lagged in their own awareness of the growth of ecological concerns, and to the extent that they have not been in communication with the environment that they develop, they've increasingly run into protests from a community of homebuyers that outstrips them in awareness. To the extent that the economics of residential development, particularly inflationary economics, prices optimal development beyond the ability of people to pay for it, it is counterproductive to the enhanced survival of everyone. Let us opt for less abstract statistics and more perception of what *quality* is desired and produced.

Ecological planning for development is something the real estate industry will be seeing much more of in the coming years, as pressures for it increase. And there is a new type of planner arising to relate — sensibly and without wild-eyed theory — ecology and aesthetics to land development and housing construction. He serves as a *prior* link of intelligent information input to marketing research and to architectural and land planning, and works hand in hand with the architectural and marketing people. The best of these prove that there is no conflict between enlightened ecological planning and project profitability; that, in fact, the latter is often enhanced by the former.

Take, for example, California's Richard Reynolds, the Santa Monica-based consultant on ecological research, planning and design. His credits include the outstanding Sea Ranch second-home development on Northern California's Sonoma Coast; planning for the development of Flower Mound, a new town in Minnesota; and the handling of a difficult ecological problem in wind erosion at a luxury residential and resort development, False Bay Marina, in South Africa. Dick also works as consultant with such firms as GAC Properties and Irvine Ranch and served as prime design consultant for Center City Mall at Huron Park in Kansas City. The latter is a unique urban structure that is actually almost a sculpture as well as functionally serving the city's needs as a shopping center. Listen to Reynolds talk: "If you learn the history of the land over a hundred years, the knowledge can tell you what processes are at work in the region — both constructive and destructive. From these you can learn how to use the land, how to plan a development, where to locate buildings. You do not necessarily have to conform to the processes at work, but at least if you choose to go against them, you are in a better position to estimate the consequences and the costs."

Underlying Reynolds's success as an ecological planner are some highly developed philosophical viewpoints which should be food for thought for most people involved in the development field. "Our own purpose," he says, "is to bring about an ethically sound agreement between mankind and his environment. Ethics are usually addressed only between man and man. Heretofore, the only concern has been to establish relationships between individuals, groups and mankind as a whole only for human optimal survival. It is our position that mankind's survival requires that a similar ethical agreement be extended to plants and animals, and to air, water, earth, and energy relationships that make up local, regional and global environments. In the same way that a successful government repays its supporters by protection, service and making arrangements for the growth of the society concerned, man as an ecological dominant on earth must repay the environment for his use of its constituents and the support these constituents provide him. Self-sufficiency almost as an aesthetic principle is a very high-level principle; it ties in with a lot of other principles. You put something out and you get something back. The quality of what you get back is the same as the quality of what you put in."

A NOTE ON MARKET RESEARCH: ONE–ON–ONE

The responsibility of the housing industry is a large one because it is effectively responsible for the quality of the nation's physical environment and thus, at least in part, determines the quality of life for everyone. It could do with a broader perception of its function along the lines Reynolds indicates. Here the question of the proper role for market research enters. Too often, in the name of "marketing" and "sensitivity," we take refuge in the lie of generality and the lie of averages because we are too scared to run the moderate economic risk of producing a distinctive, aesthetic product. I am a great believer in market research, as I've made clear. But, honestly, even market research has limitations: unless modified by a strongly original viewpoint, it usually produces development recommendations that are only the safe average of existing patterns of development. This produces an inevitable downward spiral of averages over a period of time and degrades both the environment and us.

For a given project, the criteria for development become the safe average of similar existing projects. New features and design elements are often randomly agglomerated, not in response to any unified aesthetic view of the product but as a craven effort to appease an abstract, arbitrarily selected and crudely interpreted statistical sample. A new round of construction then takes for its criteria the average of existing, already averaged projects. A subsequent round of development takes as its guidelines the twice-averaged housing. The result is an inevitable bland hodgepodge of "safe" housing which is a monument to the lie of generality and incomplete perception, bespeaking not a care for people but an excessive fear for the safety of development capital. Prudence is advisable, to be sure, but you can get so prudent you've got rigor mortis, too. Oddly, excessive fear for the safety of capital ultimately defeats its own purpose in the long run and the investment is lost because people won't buy a surfeit of averaged blandness; they respond to the exciting, the new, the *uncompromised* product that is *also* useful and needful and whose form has some relation to its function. Henry Ford never compromised his viewpoint; he acted instead of reacting to averages. He made a fortune and gave the nation a better life through broad transportation. But look at the colossal, costly failure of the Edsel, a car designed completely by averaged opinion. It stands as a monument to the lie of averages. One sees old Henry Ford, always a one-on-one operator, ruefully tongue-lashing his posterity.

Marketing and market research are not "bad," but they are often practiced badly. It's our fault if we don't get the right answers; we haven't been asking the right questions. We have by and large not communicated with our public clearly or well, but have used them as an echoing board for our preconceptions. We have to get past the lie of superficial averages so that the importance of the individual and his individual creativity assert themselves. Research cannot be purely of a *reactive* nature. It must perceive not only the reactions but also the aspirations. It is at its best serving as a point of departure for new initiatives and the uncompromised concept, not as a corroboration for entrenched group-think. Unless we are a little braver about acknowledging our creative impulses and those of the people who buy our product, it may be that our housing and our environment may yet come to look like the committee's camel. No wonder people are revolting all over the place; they're revolted with the overextension of the law of averages—and not only in the housing field.

There are many builders and many architects and planning firms that can and do produce exciting and innovative work that is also economically feasible. But too often such concepts are diluted or perverted by the reluctance of sponsoring financial sources to innovate on development. Let market research *really* look. We can always research a market well enough to sell a product like gangbusters. But by looking more deeply, we can come up with an exciting product that actually gives people what they want instead of being something to settle for. The financial sponsors are always prating about the importance of market research. Let them trust the consequences of really perceptive research and finance something better than average. If they took the lead in this regard, instead of always being dragged kicking and screaming into innovation, the whole nation would profit.

DOES ECONOMICS REALLY TALK PEOPLE?

Perhaps our occlusions of personal vision stem from an inability to confront as individuals such large numbers of people that we in the building industry must of necessity deal with. We take refuge in the comfortable abstraction. We buy unquestioningly the language of economics and think that those technical abstractions are our market. We get so wrapped up with the gross generality of "The Consumer," whose sole function in life is to *consume*, that we forget to see him as a living person.

Those labels get pretty misleading and cover up a whole other reality. What can one say about the builders' anxious desire to please the allegedly hedonistic and hypersexed "swinger" who is now supposed to form such a large segment of our society? Most swingers that I've seen in apartments tailored for them are lonely and disappointed people on the run from themselves. Or take the abstract but haughty-sounding "affluent elite" and its cousin of a generality the "affluent youth market." From their alleged propensity to spend money for services and recreation, from their shift to apartment living, and from their increased mobility, a whole new lifestyle has been postulated by the marketeers.

It is not perceived (or if perceived, not admitted) that all the claptrap about affluence and mobility and a changed lifestyle is partly a public relations campaign to obscure the real source of the change. The real source is not just a spontaneous shift to a freer lifestyle but also a response to a constrictive downward spiral of inflationary economics which has displaced more and more people from the ability to own a home and bumped them into urban apartments. They spend more on services and recreation because they're not putting money into a home but attempting to escape. Increased mobility is too often a cover-up phrase for increased insecurity. What we glibly take as signs of affluence and increased freedom are too often the outward signs of lessened freedom and of chafing resistance to economic and other constrictions on personal freedom. These are not pleasant facts to face and it is much nicer to give all these symptoms nice, abstract, flashy labels so we can go on feeling good.

I will be the first to confess that I use all the jargon of "swingers," "youth market," etc., myself. But it should be recognized that its effect on perception and thought is dulling as well as lulling. It dehumanizes humanity and relieves us of our responsibilities to it. When mankind is perceived solely as a vast sea of gaping, unsated mouths, it gets easier to deal with it as a disposable generality. If people are not contentedly "consuming" out in the lush pastures of the Economy, they are (like Pavlov's dog) "stimulated" to "consume" by sex-based advertising. Now, I happen to think that sex is a lot of fun, but really now! I somehow cannot divest myself of the archaic notion that people are *more* than economically determined units of consumption and copulation. The evidence of my own experience tells me they're motivated by other aspirations also. I do not see much of such ordinary awareness built into our marketing practices and our economic planning.

Giving formal recognition only to the glandular qualities of people, it becomes a not very complicated ethical decision in economic planning to treat them as something less than people, or to take ethics out of consideration altogether. This is in part why it has been more expedient to devise jerry-built solutions that permit inflation to continue in real estate and housing than to do the hard, right things to stop it. It just doesn't seem important enough at this time, and the profits are still good. But to say that inflationary real estate economics no longer fully permits the creation of an aesthetic and wholesome environment and a decent home for every working person is to say that economics has stopped serving people and people have begun to serve economics — surely a curious inversion. In real estate, particularly, it has been a badly losing fight to inflation since the start of the Sixties. And it's a no-win game, indeed, that could result in the extinction of an entrepreneurially motivated housing industry at the same time as it ran down the environment and put private housing beyond the reach of all but the richest people. It could only happen if people and their wants and purposes are imperfectly perceived and their rights are regarded with contempt. It could only happen if it appears insignificant that the "consumer" is being outright blanketly *robbed,* through the erosion of his hard-earned material and nonmaterial values. It could happen if economic theorists do not recognize themselves in others and the plight of others in themselves, and play at economics as a denatured game without reference to the well-being of the people it is supposed to serve.

People are important. They are not a drove of insensate "consumers." They are not, and resent being thought of as, completely economically determined beings. They yearn for a recognition of what is essentially a spiritual integrity, for an economic and social stability that will permit them to afford a home for their honest work, for a clear program of some national and local priorities and incentives within the framework of which it would be possible to raise a family safely and to build a beautiful environment. They are looking for a statement of *purpose* that will be based upon an acknowledgment of their essential ethical nature. They require little — a recognition of their basic dignity, a rewarding of individual initiative and production, and the right to use their abilities to produce. They want to pitch in and be part of the game and contribute meaningfully to the survival of the national group, not to be set apart as the "working class" which is the earlier version of the "consumer." They intuitively understand that the entrepreneurial game can be set up more soundly in a framework of rules that acknowledge who people really are and what they want out of life.

The Declaration of Independence and the Bill of Rights recognized the essentially spiritual striving of people and their right to self-determination. We must question whether the basic assumptions underlying economic and social policy still reflect such a recognition. Between the goad of inflation and the harsh bite of the Internal Revenue Service, we have come close to achieving a perfect system of subtle enslavement. Wages rise to offset inflation while real earning power stays the same; but with the graduated tax on income, the individual is also bumped into a higher tax bracket and actually ends up earning less. This is enhancement of incentives? No wonder the country's in a productivity crisis, people are dispersed into fractious camps and an "everybody fend for himself" attitude prevails. Meanwhile, as inflation continues, the competitive conditions in the economy become harsher, more choices are eliminated, and more of the remaining sources of production are displaced toward today's locus of government — the major financial institutions. When economic considerations rule social policy, is it any wonder that we begin talking of the nation's battered people in such comfortable technical abstractions as "consumers"? It would be far too painful for anybody of ethical sensibility to view them as essentially spiritual beings, for then the cynicism of the various manipulations is too obvious.

Lincoln's great punishment was not to die by an assassin's bullet but to live while fully perceiving and feeling the magnitude of the chaos over which he was somehow fated to preside. Not only did he feel every death of the Civil War, he also recognized the destruction of the great inflation that he set loose upon the North in order to pay for the war. (It was a greater inflation than even the one we so far face today.) Lincoln understood the essential goodness of the individual and his right to be the master of his own life as well as of his production. And he knew that no matter how holy the cause, you can never injure another without injuring yourself. If he was unusual in any respect, it was that he could live through such carnage and not lie to others or to himself. He stayed in touch.

People will talk of the credibility gap of Watergate for years. But as far as I am concerned, the real lying in our own century has long been in the area of economics. How, for example, can a theory of national economic management be based on *consumption* rather than *production*? "Stimulate the consumer" in a recession, "curb the consumer through taxation" in a boom, "the real cause of inflation is excess demand," etc. If the nation were only to focus on production and stop both repressive graduated taxation and the creation of currency in excess of the growth rate of products and services, we could all be assured of affluence while consumption would surely take care of itself.

The whole clap-trap of *consumption*-based economics is generated to justify and manipulate *inflation*. The theory that "excess demand" creates inflation is the exact inversion of the truth. It is inflation — currency cranked out without corresponding production — that raises consumer demand in the short term (and prices in the longer term). Once inflation is initiated, the only way to keep creating "excess demand" is to accelerate the rate of inflation. Whole industries develop based on such easy money, and then they, too, must be supported by maintaining inflationary economics. The inevitable, ultimate end-product of *consumption*-based economics is *no consumption at all*, for spiraling inflation ultimately wipes out economic values, and the whole crazy pyramid built on its basis topples. In the short term, it is inflationary management that is responsible for both recessions and arbitrary manipulation of tax levels. And, as somebody said, "The power to tax is the power to destroy."

Inflation is the cheap-jack art of getting something for nothing. Print a counterfeit buck and buy a genuine product. When individuals do this they're put in jail; when governments do this, they call it "excess consumer demand" and tax the poor constituents out of existence. How long can you fool all of the people all of the time? The real benefits of "excess consumer demand" meanwhile accrue to a few loci of economic power which acquire monopoly positions through the displacement of competition by continued inflation and are then also subsidized by the "consumer's" taxes to deliver the product that the "consumer" can no longer afford on his own. We are grateful to Maynard Lord Keynes for his trailblazing contribution to this end by first suggesting the fully novel principle which essentially states that the more you spend the more you will produce. While I have not yet been able to perfect the principle in my own personal life, I am pleased to see that this inversion of reality appears to work handsomely at the level of nations. Can you wonder why Wright Patman is frustrated in his efforts to get the Federal Reserve open to congressional review?

People will not passively surrender to this destructive game, no matter how many theories of social management may be employed to justify and perpetuate the game by demonstrating that man is a mere animal who can always be gulled and molded by his social and physical environment. When an individual can no longer create his life freely and when he loses the right to his creations (as, for example, through inflation or arbitrary and repressive taxation), sooner or later he just does not go along with the "environment" any more but proceeds to change it, rather than become enslaved by it. He will change that environment until it is set up to enhance his condition.

This idea is corroborated in fields quite unrelated to economics per se. *Forbes*, for example, on two or three occasions quoted philosopher L. Ron Hubbard, founder of the Church of Scientology and author of the books *Problems of Work*, *Fundamentals of Thought*, and *Science of Survival*. Writing on the question of environment versus man, Hubbard observes: "Man does *not* adapt to an environment. He adapts the environment to himself. And in that lies his success. When he fails to adapt the environment, when he lags in his complete control of that environment, he has altered himself or his ideas until he could again change the environment. . . . Amongst the many things Man has done in his worries about his mind and his state of being, in his effort to control others, is the adoption of slave philosophies. Each person who invents or uses such a philosophy more or less tends to be, himself, exempt from the slavery thus imposed and to hold, by this invention, the forces of others nullified. This is a trick of very limited workability for it leads eventually into the entrapment of the user himself. It is a demonstrable law, not an opinion, that he who would enslave his fellows becomes himself enslaved. A 'therapy' which teaches that Man should adapt himself to his environment rather than adapt the environment to him is such a slave philosophy and is not workable only because it is quite the reverse from truth."

Let us remember that a lie is the weakest thing in the world; it cannot withstand the power of truth. So while a destructive economic game will succeed only in destroying those who play it, we can get on with our own purposes by communicating better and by taking more responsibility for our scene. It is only to incomplete communication that we owe the existense of personal, social, and economic conflict which is maintained by the skein of generalities, by a net of lying. And so, communication becomes very important. There are never any indissoluble conflicts or problems between people or groups of goodwill if they just sit down and talk long enough and really get down to sources. The secret of *real* communication and not just verbiage is, of course, that it always leads to some enlightenment and corresponding change of condition. People *are* basically good and they want to better themselves and to know the sources of their travail, and they always communicate about it. They want to *get on* with the business of saner and better living. We can all, indeed, get on with it while we, each of us, in the innermost recesses of our hearts, remember who we really are, and while we really communicate, and remain willing to communicate and keep our minds open, until we get at the truth.

ONE–ON–ONE ALSO MEANS PERSEVERANCE

It will take some perserverance to get on with it because we will have to get through a few curious ideas that are floating around. The national air is sometimes beclouded by advocates urging the greatest generality of all, typically classified as "freedom for the masses," by strenuously attacking such incompatible elements of their ideal as *individual* freedoms and values. Some of these folks cannot reconcile humanity with civilization and therefore advocate the elimination of the latter for the sake of the former. Let me select as an example only one candidate from my long list of favorites. This is the misbehaving Harvard behaviorist B. F. Skinner, who wrote *Beyond Freedom and Dignity* to propound his conviction that individual freedom and dignity are obstructive to the rehabilitation of people's well-being.

As the inheritor of Pavlov's mantle, Skinner suggests that people must be totally controlled by stimulus-response conditioning to keep them from reverting to the foolish and dangerous notions of free communication and responsibility for their own actions. Dr. Skinner of course speaks from long and successful experience as a modifier of behavior in pigeons. He denies that people possess the capacities of attention, intention, awareness, or ethical sensibility; to him we are only "sophisticated" animals. His contempt for the rights and values of the ordinary person and that person's ability and responsibility in solving his own problems does not bode well. The almost casual contempt, only lightly veiled, in his writings for the U.S. Constitution and the Bill of Rights surpasses comment. When ideas such as these receive wide currency, it is not surprising that elements of them start seeping over into economic and social planning. Such planning later becomes the subject of bitter conflicts among different segments of our society. It puts builders and people at each others' throats, and they don't know why they're fighting one another except that something is wrong somewhere.

In such a confused climate some proposals for housing "reform" get to be, like Alice's experiences in Wonderland, "curioser and curioser" inversions of survival-oriented realities. Take, for example, a study of America's housing problems titled "Shelter and Subsidies," published in August 1972 by the influential, tax-exempt Brookings Institution. It should be apparent that one of the basic conditions of individual freedom is the right of ownership, and this of course very basically includes homeownership. One would imagine that a nation concerned with enhancing people's freedom and sense of dignity — not to mention a homebuilding industry concerned with enhancing its own survival — would encourage such ownership through the preservation of incentives for it. But an important portion of the Brookings study advocates the elimination of such pitiful tax incentives as remain, and the imposition of tax penalties, for homeowners.

The Brookings study is authored by a senior fellow of that institution, Henry J. Aaron, who surveys the abuses in the directly subsidized Sec. 235 Federal homeownership program, and who is concerned about adequate housing for the poor. A key point in his proposal is the finding that the overall private housing market in the U.S. operates on a "filtering" basis, whereby "the homes of the rich often become homes for the middle class or for the poor as incomes change and job patterns shift." It is in connection with the purchase of older homes by poor families that some abuses of the Sec. 235 subsidy program have occurred, as homes were overpriced, etc. To stop such abuses, Mr. Aaron suggests a massive dose of overkill. He would in effect abolish the entire system of "filtering" on the grounds that, anyway, it is a very "inefficient" way of providing housing for the poor.

Mr. Aaron says that homeownership tax write-offs encourage the continuation of the "filtering" system, encouraging a homeowner to buy a newer or costlier house, thus freeing older homes for people with lower incomes. He would abolish the usual tax features associated with private homeownership to make ownership of a home less appetizing and thus end the "filtering" system. He would replace it and most of the existing federal housing programs with a "housing assistance plan" that would pay cash allowances as a *direct* subsidy to poor families according to their incomes, net worth, and local housing costs. The focus of housing development would shift even more strongly to rental housing which would be subsidized as necessary. While the poor *appear* to be well provided for in this plan, there is no provision for those who would become *ex*-homeowners because of the punitive housing taxation also proposed in the plan to end "filtering" — unless they also become eligible for the "housing assistance plan." On analysis, Mr. Aaron's dislike of conventional homeownership tax incentives seems to derive from the fact that only those who are able to afford private housing can afford to take advantage of such incentives. Mr. Aaron appears to regard this as discriminatory.

The incentives that Mr. Aaron favors eliminating are the IRS provisions for income-tax deductions for property taxes and mortgage interest costs which produce a modest "tax shelter" of sorts for the American homeowner. He would have the IRS treat the homeowner just like a renter who rents his own home to himself, taxing him on the "imputed" rental income of the owner-occupied building. Arousing us to a storm of indignation over the tax dodge that these greedy homeowners have enjoyed, Mr. Aaron points out that in 1966 they paid $7 billion less in taxes than they otherwise would have because of the existing "discriminatory" tax treatment. By 1970, he says, they had the temerity to skin the federal tax collectors out of nearly $10 billion by virtue of the "tax shelter" they enjoyed.

Mr. Aaron proposes to plug this loophole with his ingenious plan, which he summarizes for us:

"If the homeowner were taxed like other investors, he would have to report as gross income the rent he could have obtained on his house. He would be allowed deductions for maintenance, depreciation, mortgage interest, and property taxes as expenses incurred in earning income. In fact, rather than paying a tax on his imputed net rent he is allowed to deduct mortgage interest and property taxes from his gross income. . . . The direct benefits accrue primarily to upper-income homeowners. *With respect to any conceivable policy objective,* the pattern of tax benefits seems to be capricious and without rationale. *Apart from the alleged, but unsubstantiated, benefits accruing to the community when households come to own their own homes,* there appears to be no reason for subsidizing homeownership rather than other investments or subsidizing homeownership rather than renting or the consumption of other commodities." (My italics.)

Let us examine the elements of Mr. Aaron's proposal. The senior fellow attempts to enlist the reader's emotions to agreement with the plan by consistently suggesting a misleading generality: that it is aimed at eliminating an inequity perpetrated by the rich against the poor. The language is subtly colored by general words and phrases like "upper-income homeowners," "the homes of the rich," etc. He also hops on the bandwagon of the tax loophole, always a popular way of getting attention with the overtaxed citizen. But in fact, as the forgoing quotation makes clear, Mr. Aaron's proposal aims at the eventual elimination of *all* homeownership through increased taxes: as he says, he can see no reason for "subsidizing" homeownership rather than renting. Period. In the last analysis I suppose it's a good thing that he didn't stick solely to the generality of "the upper-income homeowners" as his villains. I would have liked to ask him who they are. For it is evident that he is actually talking about the great majority of homebuyers in the middle-income ranges, since it is well known that they are the ones through whom the "filtering" system primarily operates. Surely, he could not have meant solely the slow turnover of the few *mansions* of the *very* rich. In fact, given the adoption of Mr. Aaron's plan, it will *only* be the very rich who will ultimately have the means to continue buying their own housing. The great unwashed — the "upper-income homeowners" and the many gradations of lower-income people who "filter up" behind them — will filter into private ownership no more because of the backbreaking tax burden Mr. Aaron would have engineered for them.

This is not an exaggeration. Mr. Aaron must surely know that the inflationary spiral in housing has already driven more than half the nation's people out of the market for private housing. The rental market has grown not from any imagined changes in taste or increased mobility but out of sheer economic necessity. Many who remain owners do so by the skin of their teeth because of rising property taxes; those who buy new homes increasingly *must* be "upper-income homeowners" merely in order to afford a moderate home. In such a continuing inflationary scenario, the implementation of Mr. Aaron's punitive tax program would be the straw breaking the overstrained backs of a large proportion of the remaining active and potential homebuyers. The poor would also be betrayed, for the added tax on homeownership would make it more difficult than ever for them to attain the desired status of self-sufficiency and actual ownership of their own homes. As a program to kill personal incentive and to entrap welfare recipients in a lifelong cycle of dependency, Mr. Aaron's program is without equal. One also speculates that the $7 billion to $10 billion or more collected annually by driving people out of their homes with punitive taxation will not come remotely close to the annual amount required to pay for "housing assistance allowances" for the poor *and* the dispossessed. A necessary result of Mr. Aaron's program would also be a further rise in taxation. This would in turn dispossess more people from private housing, etc. The cycle of events would repeat itself in a dwindling spiral until it ground to a halt with everything and everyone dead stopped.

The reader will observe that Mr. Aaron's logic appears to proceed from his feeling that ownership of housing is an "alleged, but unsubstantiated" benefit. Mr. Aaron just seems to hate the idea of anybody (or almost anybody) just plain *owning* his own home. He seems oblivious to a fact commonly known in the development business: that when presented with a choice between ownership and renting, nine times out of ten those who can afford it will choose ownership.

He finds it "capricious and without rationale" that present tax laws still manage to preserve the distinction between owning *one's own home* and owning *income-producing property*. This is clever. By denying this distinction he effectively denies the right of plain ownership altogether, forcing even the homeowner to regard himself as *a renter to himself*. The homeowner is thus made his own serf, a self-destroyer. He pays a *real* tax on "imputed," i.e., nonexistent, income. In all sincerity, Mr. Aaron's program would have more merit if the homeowner paid an imputed tax on that imputed income. Or perhaps a homeowner "renting" his home from himself can be eligible for the suggested rent subsidies when he must begin charging higher rents of himself to pay higher taxes.

In sum, Mr. Aaron and the Brookings Institution talk help but they offer betrayal. What they have to offer is a disingenuous program that appears to broaden housing supply but which hazards personal incentive and private ownership for both the well-to-do *and* the poor, increases the level of taxation, and creates further dependency and uprootedness. People are simply not perceived as real people with real aspirations and concerns but as a vague, abstract, malleable generality. (Indicative of this is Mr. Aaron's dry phraseology: not people but "households come to own their own homes"; housing is a "commodity" that is "consumed." The technical language itself is bereft of common-sense valuation.) Effectively suggested is an eventual displacement of the entire population from private-home or condominium ownership to a condition of subsidized and unsubsidized renters living in rental complexes owned by — others. The actual effect of the Brookings plan is to consolidate ownership in the hands of a very few. The prime beneficiaries would be the emerging institutionally sponsored sources for the development and ownership of income-producing, i.e., rental, properties. (Even they do not gain in the *long* run as higher taxation and necessarily lowered production yield lower employment levels and poorer incomes for all.) Is it too much to hope that they and their clients will not permit the prospect of short-term gain blind them to the certainty of long-term loss?

The timing of Mr. Aaron's attack on home ownership was astonishingly prescient. It appeared just at a time when planning for federal subsidy programs began moving in the direction of direct housing allowances favoring urban renters rather than suburban homebuyers. Within a year, inflation had also accelerated to at least an 8.8% annual rate, thus displacing even more people from ownership to rental housing candidacy. And, if all this were not sufficient, the fuel scare and the rapid rise in gasoline prices also dictated a push toward compact, higher-density development closer to urban job centers, most of it of necessity to be rental units. It almost seemed as if Mr. Aaron was softening up the ground preparatory for a major push by the institutional investors into urban rental real estate — the direction of the housing industry in the latter part of the Seventies.

And here it looks as if he had some help. For, in an apparently unrelated move in mid-1973, U.S. Secretary of the Treasury George Schultz introduced a proposed tax "reform" package for real estate investment that would — very incidentally — enable the institutional investors to gain a greater measure of control over apartment ownership than they already had. Just as a tremendously larger long-term market for apartments was beginning to surface through a combination of governmental planning and economic crises, along came a proposal that could effectively reserve this market only to the major wielders of investment capital.

The pertinent portion of Schultz' tax-reform package was the section titled "Limitation on Artificial Accounting Losses," which would prohibit individual apartment investors from receiving major tax deductions for certain losses incurred by their investments. The problem is that the deductions have been the sole reason for investor participation in the first place.

While the apparent motive of the reform proposal was to eliminate tax loopholes for rich individuals, the actual effect would be to drive individual investors from this field altogether or result in sharply increased rents, or both. As individual investors presently account for a major share of equity capital in apartment development, their departure is likely to leave the field wide open for the only remaining major investors — the major financial and insurance institutions (although private builders, who are usually small potatoes, would also benefit). To the institutional investors, the apartment sector would remain feasible because they look more to a stable, long-term income than to tax shelter and have large, recurring cash flows to invest. It would be an especially profitable field, even though it would contribute more to inflation and taxation, if rents come to be subsidized through direct housing allowances. The publicly-owned building companies do not benefit, as the only way they can report high earnings is by selling new apartment properties to investors, and the latter's incentives would be eliminated. So the big builders have been getting out of the apartment field altogether. A "tax reform" that promotes such a consolidation of ownership while also raising rents sharply, encouraging further taxation and subsidies, and creating a greater scarcity of available housing (through the departure of the competition) scarcely strikes one as judicious. It is more in the category of applying the screws than broadening opportunity.

Here is how Secretary Schultz' proposal went. Under 1973 tax laws various accounting losses — accelerated depreciation, loan interest, real estate taxes and other fees occurring in the construction period — may be deducted from an investor's total income in the year his money is invested. Under Schultz' reform plan these losses were to be offset only against income earned specifically from real estate investments and only as that income is received in amounts sufficient enough to justify the deduction. The net effect is that these losses might never be deductible for part-time real estate investors like lawyers or doctors. Only full-time developer-owners and major long-term investors like insurance companies would find it worthwhile to take the permitted long-term deductions.

If the proposed tax package is enacted, the only way to offer the individual investor a fair return on his capital would be to increase rents to offset the lost tax benefits. The Council of Housing Producers worked out an example illustrating how much rents would have to rise to offset the tax incentives that would be eliminated.

The example was a theoretical 144-unit garden apartment complex with a conventional 30-year mortgage at 8%. It was assumed that the occupancy level would reach 95% one year after completion. Total land and building cost is $2.4 million, of which $2.1 million would come from the mortgage and $300,000 from one or more investors in the 50% tax bracket. The funds would be used as follows:

Land cost	$ 180,000
Interest during construction, loan commitment fee, etc.	193,500
Depreciable buildings	2,026,500
	$2,400,000

Under the 1973 tax rules the projected rents required to attract investors' dollars to this project averaged $236 per month. If only accelerated depreciation were to be eliminated, rents would rise by 12.9% to $297 per month. If only straightline depreciation is allowed, and interest, taxes and other fees occurring during construction have to be capitalized, the rents would have to rise by 27% to $334 per month. Over the 30-year mortgage period the amount of additional rents needed to compensate for the complete loss of tax benefits would amount to $2,905,000. If accelerated depreciation alone were eliminated, the compensating increase in rents would total $1,398,720 for the 30-year period.

The year 1974 would see whether Secretary Schultz' reform package would find acceptance on the floor of Congress. But the major builders, many of whom had built up large divisions for the construction and sale of apartments to investors, did not wait to find out. They began closing out their apartment and syndication activity rapidly, taking a write-off and moving on to other areas. Most apartment projects take two to three years to plan and develop, and no one wanted to be caught in mid-stream with a change of the game rules. Many syndication funds also folded their tents and stole away or went belly-up. It's true that many of the developers had previously pushed their luck on apartment development by hastily throwing up projects and showing paper profit by taking back heavy seconds on sales. The advent of percentage-of-competition reporting nipped this in the bud, and rightly so. But to drive the major builders and syndications from the field entirely is a disservice whose effects we will be feeling by early 1975 when apartment properties may be so scarce they'll be both an investor's goldmine and a renter's inflationary headache. In my view, the institutional investors are the only real beneficiaries of the proposed investor "tax reform."

Not only the homeowner and the apartment investor but American industry itself has much to lose if Mr. Aaron's plan to eliminate home-ownership incentives and Mr. Schultz' plan to eliminate investment incentives were ever to become reality. With ownership units being built, housing materials suppliers would find themselves racing to maintain earlier sales levels even in periods of rapidly rising housing starts. Apartment units, more compact than single-family homes, require less material for construction. The trend to apartments that has been in evidence from the late Sixties has already affected the sales of materials suppliers severely as it is.

With a broader shift to apartments a much larger cross-section of American business would also feel the pinch. Only homebuyers make permanent and relatively frequent improvements, not renters. And these home-improvers support by their frequent purchases a broad shelter-based industry that includes everything from appliance manufacturers of every type to furniture makers, drapery and carpet mills, tile and garden supply manufacturers. Add the gigantic home improvement industry that thrives on sales of wallpaper, lumber, paints, glass, cabinetry, tools as well as skilled services. In apartment units big-ticket items are scarcely if ever replaced once emplaced. Among homeowners the changes are frequent because personal pride of ownership and appearance is involved, plus the satisfaction of "building up" a secure investment.

Our research has amply shown us that among homeowners much of the pleasure of living is oriented around life in the home. But for renters, who have no identification with or emotional involvement in their apartment, the search for satisfaction or pleasure turns them to various substitutes. This is one reason why the so-called "swinger" apartment complexes have turned so intensively to recreational and social facilities. But as a rule these are poor substitutes indeed. It has long been an open secret among builders that many of the "swinger" apartment complexes are called "loser's clubs." It is as if by their presence there the renters admit they could not create a social or home life for themselves in any other way. It's a sad situation. Some percentage of such apartments is of course necessary but too often in recent years they have become enforced substitutes for a privately owned home.

In such instances apartments are poor substitutes because they subtly erode an individual's sense of security and freedom. The large number of rules and regulations enforced in so-called "managed apartments" turn life into an overcontrolled and irritating existence. One has only to experience the phalanx of warning signs posted in apartment buildings — "Park Front End In" — "No Barbecue on Patio" — "No Hanging of Clothes" — to get the sense of it. Good managers may be able to manage people well, but these are all too few in number. Thus a resentment sets in among apartment dwellers when they don't own. They do not take care of the property as well as homeowners look after theirs on the principle that "I'm driving a rented car." Our research shows us that they usually view renting as an interim step toward something better — ownership of one form or another.

Apartment dwellers also never get involved in the affairs of their community, having no roots, no vested interest in it. Of the hundreds of planning and council meetings that I've attended on zoning matters, I have never seen *renters* protesting or exhorting. It's always only the homeowners who pitch in even when their own homes are not directly involved, speaking on the issues of parks, corner gas stations and generally having a strong interest in the upkeep of their community. This uninvolvement also creates a further breach between homeowners and renters. The latter resent the former's aloofness or indifference to affairs vital to the community; they also resent the added tax burden that high-density rental projects impose on community schools.

It seems clear that ownership housing is a strongly positive and cohesive force in our urban environment, eliciting the qualities of civic pride, concern, involvement and responsibility. The privately owned home is perhaps the only product in America that has a connotation of permanency in the mind of the typical individual. The boom in low-priced and moderately priced condominiums converted from rental units is indicative of the American's great insatiable hunger for a privately owned home. By the way, it is interesting how this phenomenon corroborates our extensive research about how a buyer perceives privacy. Builders know that apartment dwellers are chronic complainers about the lack of privacy. Yet *owners* of apartment-type condominiums (converted from apartments and essentially the same structures) never complain. Typically, among builders the tendency has been to relate privacy to wall sounds and sound carried by plumbing. But when our research dug into the deeper aspects of the matter, we found that *ownership itself* is the real privacy that is perceived by people, and it is the insecurity caused by absence of personal ownership that often really bothers them when they complain. Ownership restores to them a sense of control over a "managed" environment that overcontrols them as renters.

The success of the condominium conversion trend certainly shows that further subsidized housing programs such as Mr. Aaron proposes are not the only answer to housing shortages. If we can sell non-subsidized condominium housing in the core cities in price ranges of $10,000 to $15,000, perhaps we should be seriously reexamining our concept of subsidies and their usefulness. The suggestion is that there may be a way for private enterprise to do the job without any increase in governmental housing programs. In fact, programs such as condominium conversion might even offer the prospect of *decreasing* the necessary levels of federal subsidy.

I've been temperamentally inclined to favor the Hamiltonian concept of a strong centralized governmental and banking system that would operate to enhance and reward personal incentive and competence. But in the absence of ethical criteria monitoring such a system to create an environment of optimal survival potential for every individual, every family, every group and mankind, such consolidation becomes potentially destructive. You cannot have finance controlling ethics. I then find myself turning to Jefferson's observation that "banks are more dangerous than standing armies." Each of these founding fathers had half a truth: there is strength in unity; there is repression in unity skewed by selfish interest or economic mismanagement. Which is to say that the *idea* of centralization, in itself neither good nor bad, cannot be viewed in an ethical vacuum; it can only be evaluated in practical terms by the measure of real survival potential it produces (or does not produce) in the above-mentioned categories. To be successful, and to be most profitable to everyone in the long run, a centralized system must be governed and shaped by ethical criteria based on the awareness of man as a spiritual being instead of by the sole criterion of short-term profit without reference to long-term survival goals. The banking system is a clearinghouse and control point for the productive energies of the nation quantified as money. Through its access to capital it winds up as beneficiary of nearly every economic and social crisis, broadening its own investment in areas such as real estate. In so doing it tends to reinforce the conditions that give it strength. We must ask ourselves if such a pattern is compatible with our own goals and purposes.

The reduction of personal security by the denial of *owning* to the many may appear to some as a twentieth-century version of a serfdom, albeit a hierarchic one, in which people are bumped down into various strata of rental and tax brackets, but where all are equalized by the denial of outright ownership. Given the continuation of inflation in housing and real estate, an unpleasant scenario may be foreshadowed: an environment in which the main operators are (1) the tax-collecting, mortgage-guaranteeing and subsidy-disbursing bureaucracy of the federal government; (2) the major financial institutions and their large, captive building companies which would construct and manage rental properties, collecting the large subsidies as rent because they own the properties *and* hold the mortgages; and (3) a large, behaviorally trained police force to keep the repressed population under control. I do not suggest that this will actually happen, for I do not believe that the American people will ultimately accept Mr. Aaron's proposals. But this picture *is* the ultimate consequence of both the housing "reform" plan he would implement and the clutter of compatible proposals.

The Brookings plan is a pernicious "solution" to the present problem of inflation in real estate and housing that takes the path of least resistance: downward. This is why Mr. Aaron's only "conceivable policy objective" finally sees the present pattern of tax benefits to homeowners as "capricious and without rationale." Individual freedom and dignity, and the rewarding of ability by the right of ownership, are always "capricious and without rationale" when it is not understood that even one's own well-being depends in the long run on the preservation of such values. Not everyone *wants* to own his own home, to be sure, but everyone wants to retain the *right* to do so and the conditions that permit him to do so at his option. Mr. Aaron's proposed cure would kill the patient by abolishing that right and that option.

GETTING ON WITH IT

Let us keep these things in mind as we attend to our specific work and as, avoiding the lies of generality, we shape our own purposes. Change and the choices it brings us are only unsettling if, adopting Dr. Skinner's view, we see ourselves as wholly controlled by, and solely the product of, our natural and created environment. That would be the ultimate in helpless passivity and the ultimate lie of generality. For who *created* the whole structure of our nation's present greatness, and who *created* our problems as well, by acts of omission and commission, if not we? Every situation is created by specific people. And specific people working together with high awareness can create it well instead of badly by restoring the importance of the individual being and the specific act to their perspective. It used to be called common sense. We are *Creators* of our environment — all of it. Knowing who we really are, we can be exterior to change; we can control it for our enhanced survival, instead of letting it control us. For as creators we are, of course, larger than all our creations. Perhaps we are even larger than time.

Index